LEARNING TO TEACH

This book was developed for Random House by Lane Akers, Inc.

LEARNING TO TEACH

RICHARD I. ARENDS

Random House   New York

First Edition
987654321
Copyright © 1988 by Random House, Inc.

All rights reserved under International and Pan-American Copyright Conventions.
No part of this book may be reproduced in any form or by any means, electronic
or mechanical, including photocopying, without permission in writing from
the publisher. All inquiries should be addressed to Random House, Inc.,
201 East 50th Street, New York, N.Y. 10022. Published in the United States by
Random House, Inc., and simultaneously in Canada by Random House of Canada
Limited, Toronto.

Library of Congress Cataloging-in-Publication Data

Arends, Richard.
    Learning to teach / Richard I. Arends.
       p.   cm.
    Includes bibliographies and index.
    ISBN 0-394-36465-1
    1. Teaching.   I. Title.
  LB1025.2.A773 1988
  371.1′02—dc19   87-21464
                                                CIP

Manufactured in the United States of America

Typographic Design: SUSAN PHILLIPS

Cover Design: SANDRA JOSEPHSON

Preface

Learning to be a teacher is a long and complex process full of excitement and challenge. It starts with the many early experiences we have with our parents and siblings; it continues as we observe teacher after teacher through sixteen to twenty years of formal classroom instruction. It culminates with professional training and teaching experiences that last a lifetime for those who choose teaching as a career.

Learning to Teach was written to help preservice and beginning teachers learn and use effective teaching practices. It was written from the point of view that there is important knowledge in the form of concepts and research findings that can inform classroom teaching. It highlights the knowledge produced over the past two decades that has provided strong evidence that what teachers do in their classrooms, and in their schools, affects in significant ways the achievement and self-esteem of their students.

Although knowledge about effective practice gives teachers control over what they do, much of teaching remains an art requiring individual judgements based on personal experience. This aspect of teaching is also explored in *Learning to Teach*, although by its very nature it is more difficult to convey in written words the art of teaching than it is the codified knowledge base on teaching.

To assist you with using this book and in learning to teach, several kinds of aids have been included:

1. *Main Ideas* Each chapter begins with a main ideas section that directs you to the most important information in the chapter and serves as an advance organizer for what is to be learned.

2. *Research Summaries* Each chapter contains two to four summaries of important research studies. These have been included to highlight the knowledge base on teaching and to give you a feel for how this knowledge is produced by the educational research community.

3. *Books for the Professional* At the end of each chapter several books are cited, and brief annotations are included. These are important books in the field of teaching and can assist you in your independent study.

4. *Learning Aids* By itself, reading about teaching is insufficient for learning to teach. The process also requires active involvement in and reflection about classroom teaching. Each chapter concludes with several learning aids aimed at helping you use what you have learned by observing and practicing in real classrooms and reflecting about your experiences.

I want to express my appreciation to many who supported my efforts during the past two years as *Learning to Teach* was being written. Timely and outstanding contributions were made by chapter authors Dr. Richard Jantz and Dr. Virginia Richardson-Koehler and by special topics chapter authors Ms. Sharon Castle, Dr. Linda Gambrell, and Dr. Nancy Winitzky. The book is much stronger as a result of their good work and of the painstaking reviews supplied by Carolyn Evertson (Vanderbilt U.), Don Cruickshank (Ohio St. U.), O. L. Davis, (U. of Texas), and Virginia Richardson-Koehler (U. of Arizona).

A very special thanks goes to Dr. Nancy Winitzky who helped in so many ways, ranging from tracking down citations in the library to providing substantive and valuable advice and in the end assuming a major role in the development of the *Instructor's Manual* and many of the learning aids.

A special thanks also goes to Lane Akers who had faith in the book from the beginning, who provided so much valuable editorial assistance and was a constant source of support and advice, and to Jean Akers, whose able and friendly assistance made the final tasks of completing the book much more enjoyable than anticipated.

I want to acknowledge and thank students in my principles of teaching class at the University of Maryland and my co-teachers Shelley Clemson, Lenore Cohen, Neil Davidson, and Suzanne Perry, who provided important critique and input on early versions of the manuscript. Special acknowledgment also goes to Dean Dale Scannell, who granted me a three-month leave to work on the book, and to Dr. Linda Gambrell, who did my other work while I was home writing.

Special thanks is extended to Mary and William who spent many weekends playing alone while Daddy "worked at the computer" and to Kevin and Krista, whose received fewer visits and long-distance phone calls than they deserved. I dedicate *Learning to Teach* to the hundreds of classroom teachers who helped me learn and to my three favorites—Bill Harris, Phil Runkel, and Dick Schmuck.

Richard Arends

Contents

SKILL LOCATOR GUIDE

(cont'd)

LIST OF RESEARCH SUMMARIES

PART 1

Part 1 is an overview of the processes involved in learning to teach. Naming the section with a phrase coined by N. L. Gage, one of America's foremost educational researchers, is intended to capture a major premise of the book, which is that teaching offers a rewarding career for those who can execute its scientific and artistic requirements.

The complexity of the teacher's role is described in Chapter 1, along with the historical and contemporary forces that have shaped the profession we call teaching. This chapter also explains the plan of the book and the major concepts that have guided its planning and writing.

How one goes about learning to teach is the subject of Chapter 2. This chapters explains how learning to teach is a developmental process that is nurtured by both research and personal experience. Research provides teaching with its scientific basis, but personal experience provides an equally valuable artistic one.

The Scientific Basis for the Art of Teaching

CHAPTER 1

MAIN IDEAS

- Teaching offers a rewarding career for those who can combine the scientific and artistic aspects of the job.
- The role of teacher is a complex one that has been shaped by both historical and contemporary circumstances.
- Nineteenth-century society emphasized teachers' moral character and conduct, whereas the late twentieth century has emphasized teachers' accountability and their use of appropriate pedagogical practices.
- Teaching in the twenty-first century will probably be characterized by a demand for quality education, increasing racial and ethnic diversity among students, and more accountability.
- Effective teaching is characterized by teachers who have control of the knowledge base on teaching, can execute a repertoire of best practices, have attitudes and skills necessary for reflection and problem solving, and consider learning to teach a lifelong process.
- This book is organized around what teachers do, particularly behaviors associated with the executive, the interactive, and the organizational functions of teaching.
- The unique features of this book include selected research summaries that highlight the knowledge base on teaching, learning aids that facilitate study, observation, and reflection, and five sections on special topics deemed important to beginning teachers.

Teaching

Teaching offers a bright and rewarding career for those who can meet the intellectual and social challenges of the job. Despite the recent spate of reports critical of schools and teachers, most citizens continue to support our schools and express their faith in education. The task of teaching the young is simply too important and complex to be handled entirely by parents or through the informal structures of earlier eras. Modern society needs schools staffed with expert teachers to provide instruction and to care for children while adults work.

In our society teachers are given professional status. As experts and professionals, they are expected to use "best practice" to help students learn essential skills and attitudes. It is no longer sufficient for teachers to be warm and loving toward children, nor is it sufficient for them to employ teaching practices based solely on intuition, personal preference, or conventional wisdom. Contemporary teachers are held accountable for using teaching practices that have been shown to be effective, just as members of other professions, such as medicine, law, and architecture, are held to acceptable standards of practice. This book is about how to learn and to use best practice—practice that has a scientific basis. It is aimed at helping beginning teachers master the knowledge base and the skills required of a professional teacher.

This book also explores another side of teaching: the art of teaching. Like most human endeavors, teaching has aspects that cannot be codified or guided by scientific knowledge alone but instead depend on a complex set of individual judgments based on personal experiences. Nathaniel Gage (1984) of Stanford University, one of America's foremost educational researchers, describes the art of teaching as:

> an instrumental or practical art, not a fine art aimed at creating beauty for its own sake. As an instrumental art, teaching is something that departs from recipes, formulas, or algorithms. It requires improvisation, spontaneity, the handling of hosts of considerations of form, style, pace, rhythm, and appropriateness in ways so complex that even computers must, in principle, fall behind, just as they cannot achieve what a mother does with her five-year old or what a lover says at any given moment to his or her beloved. (p. 6)

Notice some of the words chosen by Gage to describe the art of teaching—*spontaneity, pace, rhythm*. These words describe aspects of teaching that research cannot measure very well but that are nonetheless important characteristics of best practice used by experienced and expert teachers. This book strives to show the complexity of teaching—the dilemmas faced by teachers and the artistic choices that effective teachers make as they perform their daily work. It also presents an integrated view of teaching as a science and as an art.

HISTORICAL PERSPECTIVE ON TEACHING AND SCHOOLING ▬▬▬

Teaching has always been a complex role, and it has become more so as schools have taken on increased social responsibility. To understand the role of the teacher as it exists today requires a brief historical review of some of the more important changes that have taken place in teaching and schooling over the past two centuries.

Nineteenth-Century Role Expectations

During most of the nineteenth century the purposes of schooling were rather straightforward, and a teacher's role rather simple compared to later eras. Basic literacy and number skills were the primary goals of nineteenth-century education, with the curriculum dominated by what later came to be called the three Rs, reading, writing, and arithmetic. Most young people were not required (or expected) to attend school, and those who did so remained for relatively brief periods of time. Other institutions in society—family, church, and work organizations—held the major responsibility for child rearing and helping youth make the transition from family to work.

Teachers were recruited mostly from their local communities. Professional training of teachers was not deemed important nor was teaching necessarily considered a career. Teachers during this era were likely to be young men or women who had obtained a measure of literacy themselves and were willing to "keep" school until something else came along. Standards governing teaching practice were nonexistent, although rules and regulations governing teachers' personal lives and moral conduct could, in some communities, be quite strict. Take, for example, this set of promises women teachers were required to sign in one community in North Carolina even as late as the 1920s:

> I promise to take a vital interest in all phases of Sunday-school work, donating of my time, service and money without stint for the benefit and uplift of the community.
>
> I promise to abstain from dancing, immodest dressing, and any other conduct unbecoming a teacher and a lady.
>
> I promise not to go out with any young man except as it may be necessary to stimulate Sunday-school work.
>
> I promise not to fall in love, to become engaged or secretly married.

I promise to remain in the dormitory or on the school grounds when not
actively engaged in school or church work elsewhere.
I promise not to encourage or tolerate the least familiarity on the part of
any of my boy pupils.
I promise to sleep eight hours a night, eat carefully. . . . (Brenton, 1970,
p. 74).

This list of promises may be more stringent than many others in use at the
time, but it gives a clear indication of nineteenth-century concern for teachers'
moral character and conduct and apparent lack of concern for teachers' pedagogical
abilities.

Twentieth-Century Role Expectations

By the late nineteenth and early twentieth centuries the purposes of education
were expanding rapidly, and teachers' roles took on added dimensions. Comprehensive high schools were created, most states passed compulsory attendance laws
that required all students to be in school until age sixteen, and the goals of
education moved beyond the narrow purposes of basic literacy. Vast economic
changes during these years outmoded the apprentice system that had formerly
existed in the workplace, and much of the responsibility for helping youth to
make the transition from family to work fell to the schools. Also, the arrival of
immigrants from other countries, plus new migration patterns from rural areas
into the cities, created large, diverse student populations with more extensive
needs than simple literacy instruction. Look, for example, at the seven goals* for
high school education issued by the National Education Association in 1918, and
notice how much these goals exceed the focus on the three Rs of earlier eras:

1. Health
2. Command of fundamental processes
3. Worthy home membership
4. Vocational preparation
5. Citizenship
6. Worthy use of leisure time
7. Ethical character

Such broad and diverse goals made twentieth-century schools much more
comprehensive institutions and also places for addressing some of the societal
reforms that have characterized this century. Schools increasingly became instruments of opportunity, first for immigrants and later for blacks and other minority
groups who had been denied equal access to education. Expanding their functions

* These goals were named the Seven Cardinal Principles. Some historians believe that they were
symbolic statements of hope that reveal what schools in the new industrial society aspired to do rather
than descriptions of reality.

beyond academic learning, schools included such services as health care, transportation, extended day care, and the provision of breakfasts and lunches. Schools also took on various counseling and mental health functions—duties that in earlier eras belonged to the family or the church—to help ensure the psychological and emotional well-being of youth.

Obviously, expanded purposes for schooling had an impact on the role expectations for teachers. Most states and localities began setting standards for teachers that later became requirements for certification. Special schools were created to train teachers in the subject matter they were expected to teach and to ensure that they knew something about pedagogy. By the early twentieth century teachers were expected to have two years of college preparation; by the middle of the century most would hold bachelor's degrees. Teaching gradually came to be viewed as a career, and professional organizations for teachers took on growing importance both for defining the profession and for influencing educational policy. Teaching practices during this era, however, were rarely supported by research, and teachers, although expected to teach well, were judged by such global criteria as "knows subject matter," "acts in a professional manner," "has good rapport," "dresses appropriately." However, progress was made during this era, particularly in curriculum development for all the major subject areas, such as reading, mathematics, social studies, and science; also, major work was accomplished in helping to understand human intelligence and potential.

Twenty-First Century Role Expectations

No crystal ball can let us look into the next decade, the decade that leads into the twenty-first century. Certain trends, however, are likely to continue. For example, the first part of the twenty-first century will probably not see significant changes in the institution of education. Although many of the basic educational ideas of this century will probably be refined, the basic structures will remain. Society will continue to require young people to go to school, although they may be provided with more alternative types of schools. Education will remain committed to a variety of goals and some new ones may be added, but academic learning will remain the most important. It is not likely that the physical place called *school* will change drastically; neither will the ways of organizing and accounting for instruction. Schools will still be based in communities, and teachers will continue to provide instruction to groups of children in rectangularly shaped rooms. The nature of the student population and the expectations for teachers will, in all probability, be the elements that will change most drastically.

THE DEMOGRAPHY OF SCHOOLING

Harold Hodgkinson (1983) has written that "every society is constructed on a foundation of demographic assumptions. When these assumptions shift, as they do from time to time, the result is a major shock throughout the society" (p. 281).

Schools are experiencing such a demographic shock at the present time; this shock will continue, and it will cause a significant impact on teaching. The most important demographic shift involves the increasing number of students from minority backgrounds, particularly in the large urban areas. The trends in minority public school enrollments between 1970 and 1982 are displayed in Figure 1.1.

Another trend over the past decade has been the extension of educational opportunities to children and youth with various handicaps. Figure 1.2 shows the changes in the number of persons served by special education between 1977 and 1984.

These enrollment trends have significance for teaching and for those preparing to teach in at least two important ways.

First, for both social and economic reasons, society will remain committed to providing educational opportunities to all children. Society will also demand that minority and handicapped students do well in school. Some of these students will come from homes of poverty; others will come from homes in which parents do not speak English; some will be emotionally or physically different from their classmates. These students will experience school differently from those whose parents were themselves educated in our schools and who have prepared their

Figure 1.1   Minority Enrollment as Percentage of Total Enrollment in Selected Large Cities

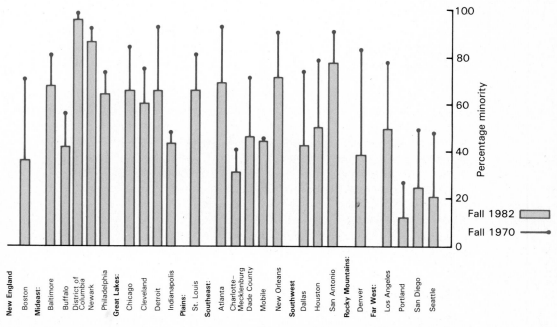

SOURCE: From Y. W. Plisko and J. D. Stern (Eds.) (1985), *The condition of education.* Washington, D.C.: National Center for Education Statistics, p. 27.

Figure 1.2 Persons 3 to 21 Years Old Served in Special Education Programs for the Handicapped

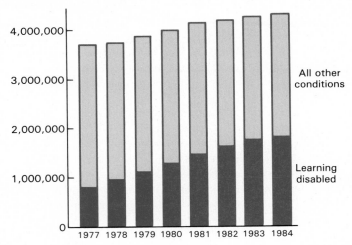

SOURCE: From Y. W. Plisko and J. D. Stern (Eds.) (1985), *The condition of education*. Washington, D.C.: National Center for Education Statistics, p. 183.

children for them. Working with youth from diverse cultural backgrounds and with various handicapping conditions will necessitate that beginning teachers have a repertoire of effective strategies and methods far beyond those required previously. Beginning teachers will also have to be able to adapt curriculum to make it more suitable for those students who may find school devastatingly difficult or irrelevant to their lives.

Second, it is likely that schools will continue to be scrutinized for racial and ethnic balance in their student and teacher populations. This will mean that during the next several decades teachers can expect to experience complex social and organizational arrangements in which school enrollment boundaries will be changed often, efforts will be made to diversify student populations through open enrollment and magnet school programs, and teachers themselves may be moved from school to school more often than in the past.

TEACHER DIFFERENTIATION AND ACCOUNTABILITY

Until very recently teachers were subjected to minimal preparation and few expectations as to performance. However, standards for teachers introduced during this century began to emphasize liberal arts preparation and some exposure to pedagogy. During the next few decades this trend will accelerate rather dramatically. Beginning teachers will increasingly be required to demonstrate their knowledge of pedagogy and subject matter prior to certification, and they will be held accountable for using best practice throughout their careers. Figure 1.3, for

Figure 1.3 State-Required Testing for Initial Certification for Teachers Testing Enacted Before 1984 and in 1984

Testing Enacted Before 1984 and in 1984

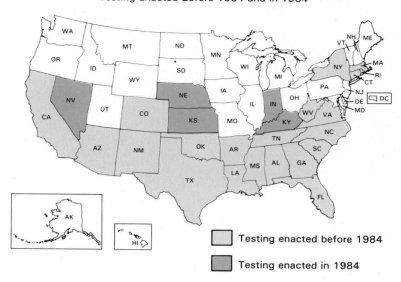

Testing in Effect, Planned in Next 3 Years, and Under Consideration

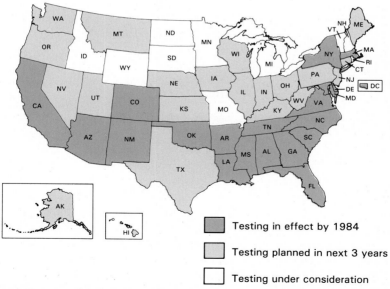

SOURCE: From Y. W. Plisko and J. D. Stern (Eds.) (1985), *The condition of education*. Washington, D.C.: National Center for Education Statistics, p. 163.

instance, shows the number of states where testing for initial certification was in effect or under consideration in 1984.

Current trends in teacher testing are likely to continue and to lead to extended training programs for teachers. In fact, many of you using this book may be in extended programs now. Before getting a license to teach you may be required to demonstrate through examination your knowledge and skill in teaching. Competency in academic subject matter will no longer be sufficient, particularly for teaching in classrooms that are culturally diverse and contain students with various handicapping conditions. Neither will liking children, in and of itself, be enough for tomorrow's teachers. Twenty-first century teachers will be required to have a command of various knowledge bases (academic, pedagogical, social, and cultural) and to be reflective, problem-solving professionals. The following description of teachers appeared in a recent report *A Nation Prepared: Teachers for the Twenty-First Century* sponsored by The Carnegie Forum on Education and the Economy (1986):

> Teachers should have a good grasp of the ways in which all kinds of physical and social systems work; a feeling for what data are and the uses to which they can be put; an ability to help students see patterns of meaning where others see only confusion; an ability to foster genuine creativity in students; and the ability to work with other people in work groups that decide for themselves how to get the job done. They must be able to learn all the time, as the knowledge required to do their work twists and turns with new challenges and the progress of science and technology. Teachers will not come to the school knowing all they have to know, but knowing how to figure out what they need to know, where to get it, and how to help others make meaning out of it.
>
> Teachers must think for themselves if they are to help others think for themselves, be able to act independently and collaborate with others, and render critical judgment. They must be people whose knowledge is wide ranging and whose understanding runs deep. (p. 25)

The Carnegie Forum on Education and the Economy has helped organize the National Board for Professional Teaching Standards. This board, formally created in May 1987, has the support of many important education groups including the two major teachers' unions—the American Federation of Teachers and the National Educational Association. The board's aim is to set standards for the teaching profession and to issue a national teaching certificate. Although it will take several years for the board's activities to be fully implemented, the following proposals are currently being considered as requirements for teacher certification: (1) an undergraduate degree in liberal arts, (2) a master's degree in education, (3) a one- to two-year postgraduate internship, and (4) successfully passing a set of oral, written, and performance exams.

A VIEW OF TEACHING AND THE PLAN OF THIS BOOK

Central to the process of learning to teach are concepts and definitions of the "good" and the "effective" teacher. Trying to define an effective teacher has long occupied the thoughts of many citizens, teachers, and professional researchers. For example, Gary Griffin (1986) summarizes some of the concepts of teaching that come from literature and the media as: "the strict but kindly teacher (remember Miss Dove?) . . . the bumbling but eventually effective academician (Mr. Chips?) . . . the slightly acerbic and mishap-prone post-teenager (Miss Brooks?)" (p. 5).

Within the educational community there has been a remarkable diversity in the definition of effective teaching. Some have argued that an effective teacher is one who can establish rapport with students and who can establish a nurturing, caring environment for personal development. Others have defined an effective teacher as a person who has a love for learning and a superior command of a particular academic subject. Still others argue that an effective teacher is one who can activate student energy to work toward a more just and humane social order.

The content of a teacher education curriculum is itself a statement about what effective teachers need to know. Clinical experiences and tests for certification, such as the National Teacher's Exam, make similar statements, as do the assessment systems used in schools to evaluate and counsel beginning teachers.

A concept of an effective teacher is also central to writing a book about learning to teach and influences its plan, its organization and unifying themes, and the choice of topics to include and exclude. The following section describes the point of view of the book and its plan of organization.

A View of Teaching

The concept of effective teaching that has guided the planning and writing of *Learning to Teach* does not include any of the stereotypes embodied in Mr. Chips or Miss Brooks; neither does it include an argument about whether academic competence is more important than nurturance or vice versa. Effective teaching requires as its base line individuals who are academically able and who care about the well-being of children and youth. It also requires individuals who can produce results, mainly those of student academic achievement and social learning. These characteristics are prerequisites for teaching, but they are insufficient without four higher-level sets of attributes:

- Effective teachers have control of a *knowledge base* that guides the art of teaching.
- Effective teachers have a *repertoire* of best practices.
- Effective teachers have the attitudes and skills necessary for *reflection* and *problem solving*.
- Effective teachers consider learning to teach a *lifelong process*.

In *Learning to Teach* these four attributes of an effective teacher are crucial themes and have been woven into each of the chapters in the book. The word *theme* is used here as it is used to describe a theme song in a Broadway musical—a song that recurs often throughout the production and becomes associated with the main ideas and characters in the play. Readers will find the four themes summarized here referred to again and again throughout the book.

CONTROL OF A KNOWLEDGE BASE TO GUIDE THE ART OF PRACTICE

Effective teachers have control over a knowledge base that guides what they do as teachers, both in and out of the classroom. In fact, professionals by definition have control over information (the knowledge base) that allows them to deal with certain matters more effectively than the average person. At the same time, no professionals, including doctors, engineers, and lawyers, have a complete knowledge base from which to find answers to every question or problem. Furthermore, not every problem can be solved by the use of best practice—patients die, design ideas fail, and legal cases are lost. The same is true in teaching. Despite the use of best practice, some students do not learn and others drop out of school.

Chapter 2 describes using scientific knowledge to guide teaching in more detail; this theme also reappears in subsequent chapters. Although most of this book concerns itself with the relationships between teacher behavior and student learning, readers will be reminded frequently that research-based knowledge about teaching only describes how things work in general; it does not describe the uniqueness of each learner or each classroom. Whereas the scientific basis for teaching can guide practice, it cannot provide recipes and formulas guaranteed to work in every instance.

REFLECTION AND PROBLEM SOLVING

One message presented throughout this book, then, is that there is a knowledge base for teaching. A second message is that this knowledge base alone is insufficient for skilled and effective practice. To become skilled professionals, teachers must adopt a reflective, problem-solving orientation.

This second message is important for two reasons. First, scientific knowledge only provides information about central tendencies or about how things work in general. It does not provide information about the many unique cases faced by teachers. Second, the knowledge base for effective practice will always have gaps and unknowns. Examples of gaps in medicine are the current lack of knowledge about many forms of cancer and about the common cold. A gap in air traffic control is the lack of foolproof procedures for preventing collisions at busy airports. Examples in teaching would include much that is not known about how to motivate reluctant learners and much yet to be learned about teaching those with learning disabilities and with different cultural backgrounds.

Much of the frustration for beginning teachers stems from having to teach groups of students who are unique and about whom they know very little. The effective teacher is one who learns to approach these situations with a problem-solving orientation and who learns the art of teaching through reflection about his or her own practice. Chapter 2 goes into some detail about how beginning teachers can learn the art of their profession, and subsequent chapters point out areas in which the knowledge base is incomplete and where teachers will need to adopt a reflective, problem-solving orientation.

REPERTOIRE OF EFFECTIVE PRACTICES

The third theme about effective teaching is that effective teachers have a repertoire of best practices. *Repertoire* is a word used mainly by people in the theater and in music that refers to the number of pieces (such as readings, operas, musical numbers) a person is prepared to perform. Obviously, more experienced and expert performers have larger, more diverse repertoires than do novices. This is also true for teachers.

The teaching practices described in this book comprise a minimum number of models, strategies, and procedures that should be in the beginning teacher's repertoire. Some are large and complex models of teaching; others are rather simple procedures and techniques. The practices described are obviously not all that exist; effective teachers add to their repertoires throughout their careers, and the process of expanding one's repertoire gets considerable attention in Chapters 2 and Chapter 13.

The book emphasizes that effective teachers have diverse repertoires and are not restricted to a few "pet" practices. This is in contrast to some arguments from earlier eras intended to prove the superiority of one approach over another, for example, inductive versus deductive teaching or the lecture versus discussion method. The result of all this debate was futile and misdirected because no one approach was found to be consistently superior to any other. Instead, many teaching approaches were found to be appropriate and the selection of a particular model depended on the teacher's goals for a specific group of learners.

This idea is developed throughout the book, particularly in Chapters 7, 8, 9, and 10, which describe four different teaching models in some detail and illustrate how each is intended to promote a different type of student interaction and learning.

LIFELONG LEARNING PROCESSES

The final theme developed in *Learning to Teach*, perhaps the most important in the long run, is that learning to teach is a lifelong process. This book describes much of the research on teaching as well as specific skills and procedures that can be used by beginning teachers. You will be able to understand this research and, with practice, will learn to execute the various models and procedures. Command of the knowledge base and a sufficient repertoire of practice, however, will not make any beginner an accomplished teacher. Becoming accomplished is a complex process and takes a long time. Chapter 2 describes the developmental processes of learning to teach and provides specific information about how you can begin. Chapter 13 comes back to this theme and provides information about how to establish attitudes for continuous learning during the first year of teaching. The learning aids (explained later) at the end of each chapter can be revisited several times while learning to teach—during college course work, during student teaching or internships, and during the first years on the job.

The Plan of This Book

Learning to Teach is divided into four parts. Part 1, "The Scientific Basis for the Art of Teaching," explores effective teaching and considers the processes and stages a novice goes through on the way to becoming an effective teacher. Part 1 also lays out for the reader the major themes of effective teaching.

Parts 2, 3, and 4 are constructed around concepts of what teachers do. These sections assume that teachers, regardless of their grade levels, their subject areas, or the types of schools in which they teach, are asked to perform three important functions. They are asked to provide leadership to a group of students, the *executive* functions of teaching; they are asked to provide direct, face-to-face instruction to students, the *interactive* functions of teaching; and they are expected to work with colleagues and others to perform the *organizational* functions of teaching. Obviously, these functions are not always discrete nor does the teacher always perform one independently of the others. These functions, however, are convenient organizers for helping beginning teachers make sense out of the bewildering array of events associated with teaching in a complex school setting.

THE EXECUTIVE FUNCTIONS OF TEACHING

In many ways the contemporary teacher's roles are similar to those of executives and managers who work in other types of organizations. Executives are expected to provide leadership, to establish procedures for effective motivation, and to coordinate and control the activities of various people working interdependently to accomplish organizational goals. Berliner (1982b) has called this aspect of teachers' work the executive functions of teaching and tells a story about what prompted him to start considering teaching from this perspective:

> During a break while attending a meeting on reading instruction at a prominent hotel, it was discovered that a business management seminar was underway in an adjoining room. The seminar was conducted under the auspices of the American Management Association. . . . The seminar leader was overheard saying: "One of the most crucial skills in management is to state your objectives— you have to have clearly stated objectives to know where you are going, to tell if you are on track, and to evaluate your performance and that of others." That

sounded very familiar to an educational psychologist. I stayed to listen, eventually spending the day as a free-loader and spy at their meeting and abandoning my own.

This group of managers, receiving in-service training, spent an hour on the topic of management by objectives. The instructors quoted Mager and Popham, names familiar to almost everyone in education. Their second topic was the use of time. They called this the greatest single management problem. Again, the relevance of their concerns and the concerns of educators seemed clear. The third topic they dealt with was motivation. They had two subtopics: First was a presentation consisting of lecture and case history on the benefits of positive reinforcement, the negative effects of criticism and punishment, the use of graphing and the beneficial effects of contracts; the second part of the motivational program was introduced by a film featuring a person well known to educators and psychologists—Robert Rosenthal. Rosenthal told these executives about the positive effects of high expectations. The last topic of the day was evaluation. The parallels between the training provided to business and public executives and some of the knowledge and skills needed to run a classroom . . . seemed obvious. (p. 2–3)

Berliner (1982b) also reminds his readers of the historical link between the concepts of teacher and manager that grew out of the industrialization process in Western societies. Although this image has been embraced by some educators, it has also been criticized for its tendency to make people think about schools the same way they think about factories; for its overemphasis on the technical and skill sides of teaching; and for its excessive attention to control, orderliness, and efficiency at the expense of creativity and spontaneity.

Regardless of past misuse of the teacher-as-manager metaphor, there are indeed many parallels between the work they perform. Part 2 of *Learning to Teach* presents these executive skills in a manner that does not violate the artistic side of teaching, that is, teacher creativity and spontaneity.

One important executive skill is planning. Chapter 3 is on teacher planning and draws from the literature of both management and education. Traditional linear approaches to planning, such as the use of objectives and lesson plans, are described, as are alternative concepts of planning.

A second important executive skill is allocating resources, particularly the scarcest resources in any situation: time and space. This executive function is discussed in Chapter 4 and revisited in several later chapters.

A third major executive task is organizing the work environment in such a way that goals and expectations are communicated clearly and people are motivated to work toward the goals deemed most important. These topics are the content of Chapter 5. As in the previous chapters, content is drawn from both the management literature and the literature of education.

Controlling and managing behavior and organizational reward systems comprise the final set of executive skills. Classroom management is typically the most troublesome problem for the beginning teacher, and Chapter 6 describes how teachers establish orderly and safe environments while simultaneously focusing on high expectations for academic achievement.

THE INTERACTIVE FUNCTIONS OF TEACHING

Whereas Part 2 describes the knowledge and skills needed to plan for instruction and to lead and manage the classroom, Part 3 focuses more specifically on what most people think of when they think of teaching—the day-by-day instruction of students. This aspect of teachers' work is labeled the *interactive function* of teaching. The overall framework for this section comes mainly from two sources: (1) the "models of teaching" concept developed by Bruce Joyce and Marsha Weil (1972) and (2) the principles of teaching that have resulted from teacher effectiveness research of the past two decades.

Over the years many different teaching approaches have been created. Some have been developed by educational researchers investigating how children learn and how teaching behavior affects student learning. Others have been developed by classroom teachers experimenting with their own teaching in order to solve specific classroom problems. Still others have been invented by psychologists, industrial trainers, and even philosophers such as Socrates. In the late 1960s, Bruce Joyce and Marsha Weil began tracking down the various teaching approaches available. In the process of recording and describing each approach, they developed a taxonomy, or classification system, to analyze the basic characteristics of a particular approach in terms of its theoretical base, its educational purposes, and the teacher and student behaviors required to successfully execute the approach.

Joyce and Weil (1986) labeled each of these approaches a *teaching model*. A model as defined by Joyce and Weil, and as used here, is more than a specific method or strategy. It is an overall plan, or pattern, for helping students to learn specific kinds of knowledge, attitudes, or skills. A teaching model, as you will learn later, has a theoretical basis or philosophy behind it, and also encompasses a set of specific teaching steps designed to accomplish desired educational outcomes.

You can think of teaching models as similar to forms of government. In the modern world there are several dominant forms, or models, of government— monarchies, dictatorships, theocracies, and democracies. Each of these forms has been created to accomplish certain values and goals various societies deem important. The specific procedures for each form of government, like each teaching model, differ in important ways. There is great variety in the basic ideologies behind forms of government, the goals considered most important, who becomes leader, who gets to vote. Each form of government, however, has some similarities with other forms. For example, all have systems for defining power relationships, for defining the role of citizen, or for making judgments about the innocence or guilt of those who break laws. The same is true for the various teaching models. Each model differs in its basic rationale or philosophical base and in the goals it has been created to achieve. Each model, however, shares many specific procedures and strategies, such as the need to motivate students, define expectations, or talk about things.

The Joyce and Weil (1986) classification system groups various approaches to teaching into four categories that they label "families of models." Their book,

Models of Teaching, identifies 20 major models and groups them into four major families: (1) information processing models, (2) behavioral models, (3) social models, and (4) personal models.

Information Processing Models A major purpose of schooling is to help students acquire and process information. This purpose includes both the acquisition of new information from the various academic disciplines and the use of existing information to organize, categorize, and think critically. The information processing models of teaching have been invented and designed to help teachers accomplish these goals. Examples of specific models from this family are: presentation using advance organizers, concept teaching, and inquiry training. Some of these models are quite simple, but others are very complex. However, they are similar in their aim, and each rests on a research base drawn from the fields of information science and cognitive psychology.

Behavioral Models A second family of models identified by Joyce and Weil are labeled behavioral models. They grew out of behavioral theory in psychology and its familiar stimulus-response, reinforcement, and behavior modification concepts. In contrast to the information processing models, which strive to affect the learners' cognitive processes (processes that cannot be observed), behavioral models concentrate on the observable actions of learners. Behavioral models break learning tasks into small components that can be learned sequentially and with some degree of specification. Examples from this family are use of feedback to modify behavior, direct instruction, and simulation models.

Social Models In addition to enhancing students' academic skills, teachers also have the responsibility to help students relate to all groups within our multicultural society. The social interaction models emphasize social understandings and skills. The models in this family vary widely in complexity and in their specific goals. Nonetheless, when used appropriately by teachers, they all help students to learn social skills and to think and inquire about important social and public issues. The philosophical basis for social interaction models rests firmly on the body of thought that has shaped democratic processes. The research base grows mainly out of social psychology and group dynamics. Examples from the social family include cooperative learning, role playing, and models that help students inquire into social policy and the values behind human behavior.

Personal Models The final family of models identified by Joyce and Weil they label personal models. Teachers use the models in this family to develop students' personal characteristics—those traits that will help them lead productive lives. Skills associated with positive self-concept, self-awareness, creativity, and meta-cognition are appropriate goals for teachers using the personal models of teaching. These models make use of techniques, such as nondirective teaching and the classroom meeting, that were, for the most part, created by clinical psychologists and persons associated with the human potential movement over the past quarter of a century.

Which Models for Beginning Teachers? Teachers need many approaches to meet their goals with a diverse population of students. A single approach or method is no longer sufficient. With sufficient choices, teachers can select the model that best achieves a particular objective, the one that best suits a particular class of students, or the models that can be used in tandem to promote student motivation, involvement, and achievement.

How many models should there be in a beginning teacher's repertoire? Obviously, it would be unrealistic to ask a beginner to master all the models created over many years—that is a lifelong process. Only to require command of a single model would be equally unrealistic. It seems fair and practical to ask you, as a beginning teacher, to acquire a modest repertoire to use during the initial stages of your career. Therefore, five models have been selected that, if learned well, can meet the needs of most teachers in their early years of teaching.

Two models have been chosen from the information processing family: (1) presentation using advance organizers and (2) concept teaching. The rationale for selecting the presentation using the advance organizers model is that a major goal of teaching is to help students acquire new information, for which presenting and lecturing is most appropriate. Also, teachers use this model more than any other, so it seems reasonable to expect teachers to be skilled in its use.

Concept teaching was chosen because it is probably the most effective approach for helping students to think critically and to process the information already in their memory banks. Both the presentation and concept teaching models have well-developed research literatures, and both are so straightforward that you can learn them reasonably well after instruction and practice.

From the behavioral family, the direct instruction model has been chosen. This model is important because much of a teacher's work is aimed at helping students acquire procedural knowledge and specific skills—how to write a sentence, perform a mathematical operation, or read a map. Teachers also want their students to develop study skills such as underlining, taking notes, or test taking. Acquiring procedural knowledge and skills consists in most instances of mastering a set of specific and often sequential tasks. The direct instruction model has a rather extensive research base, and its straightforward explication makes it very learnable.

The cooperative learning model has been chosen from the social family. This model, which is among the youngest, has been effective in improving race and ethnic relations within multicultural classrooms and relationships among regular and handicapped students. In addition, it has been effective in increasing students' academic learning. As you will find, there are several variations of cooperative learning, some of which are rather simple and can be readily learned. Other variations are more complex and not easily mastered at first.

Each of the selected models—presentation using advance organizers, concept teaching, direct instruction, and cooperative learning—is given its own chapter in Part 3 of *Learning to Teach*. The fifth model, taken from the personal family, has been tucked into the chapter on classroom management in Part 2. William Glasser's (1969) classroom meeting model, which aims at developing student self-understanding in terms of how the individual relates to the classroom group, has been well-developed and thoroughly tested. Properly used, it can serve as the basis for a positive and productive approach to classroom management and can help students develop important personal understandings and skills. Glasser's model can be learned quite easily, given a moderate amount of instruction and practice.

THE ORGANIZATIONAL FUNCTIONS OF TEACHING

Part 4 of *Learning to Teach* is devoted to the organizational functions of teaching. The common view of teaching, which focuses mostly on classroom interactions between teachers and students, is insufficient for understanding the reality of teaching in contemporary schools. Teachers not only plan and deliver instruction to their students, they also serve as organizational members in a complex work environment. This section of the book describes the work environment of schools and provides guidelines for beginning teachers as they become full members of a school staff in their first jobs.

Concepts regarding the organizational functions of teaching are drawn primarily from the fields of organizational theory and social psychology and are discussed in the last three chapters.

Chapter 11 describes the school as a place where adults carry out a variety of educational roles—principal, teacher, resource specialist, aide, and so forth. Schools are both similar to and different from other workplaces. Similarities include the ways coordination systems (for example, hierarchical authority and division of labor) are designed to get the work of the school accomplished. Beginning teachers will find that adults who work in schools are pretty much like adults who work in any other organization. They strive to satisfy their own personal needs and motives in addition to achieving the mission of the school. At the same time, those of you who have worked in other organizations (perhaps during the summer or in a previous career) will find some unique aspects to the school workplace. These include norms that give teachers a great deal of autonomy in their work but isolate them from their colleagues; clients (students) who do not voluntarily participate in the organization; and because the school is highly visible politically, diverse and unclear goals that reflect the multiple values and beliefs of contemporary, multicultural society.

Chapter 12 deals with working toward change and improvement in classrooms and schools. Many people preparing to teach have strong idealistic drives to make education and schools better. This idealism, however, is not always supported with sound strategies for putting good ideas into practice, even though the knowledge base on educational change and school improvement has increased substantially over the past decade. A knowledge base now exists to explain why many earlier reform efforts in education failed, and this knowledge can be applied to school improvement ideas you may want to implement.

Recent research has shown the importance of the first few weeks of school and the first year of teaching in determining later success in teaching. Chapter 13 provides a perspective about what happens to individuals as they make the transition from being a student to being a teacher. It describes the problems and anxieties faced by beginning teachers and explains how beginners can survive and flourish in their new jobs.

Information and guidelines found in Part 4 are important for two major reasons. First, your ability to perform organizational functions and to provide leadership within the school as well as the classroom will greatly influence your career. It is through performing organizational functions well that beginning teachers become known to other teachers, to their principals, and to parents. It is also how they become influential professionally with their colleagues and even beyond the confines of their schools. Conversely, a beginning teacher's inability to perform organizational functions effectively is the most likely reason for dismissal. Many teachers who are terminated in their early years are dismissed not for instructional incompetence but for their inability to relate to others or to attend to their own personal growth and psychological well-being within a complex organizational setting.

A final reason for focusing on organizational functions is because researchers and educators are starting to understand that student learning is not only related to what a particular teacher does but also to what teaching staffs within a school do in concert. The attributes of effective schools, described in Chapter 11, include such organizational skills as good relationships between colleagues, cooperative planning, and agreeing on common goals and common means for achieving those goals. The effective beginning teacher is one who can enter into school-wide dialogue about these important issues.

You can learn organizational skills just as readily as skills associated with the executive and interactive functions of teaching. Part 4 describes the most important organizational skills, those that can be learned with sufficient instruction and practice, and those that are most likely to be used by beginning teachers.

UNIQUE FEATURES OF *LEARNING TO TEACH*

This text has several unique features designed to make the process of learning to teach a bit less complex and puzzling.

Modeling and Theory-Practice Connections

To the extent that basic principles of teaching can be modeled using written text, that aim has been important in writing *Learning to Teach*. However, the written word works best when presenting information and describing things. It does not allow easy exploration of the many subtleties of teaching nor does it allow the live demonstrations and practice so critical to mastery of teaching principles and practices.

Making helpful connections between theory and practice is always a difficult task. Beginning teachers, for example, may understand a young person's stage of cognitive or moral development quite well. However, they can do nothing with that theory in a classroom of students at various stages of development unless they have been taught specific strategies and behaviors. On the other hand, technique without understanding leads to teaching by the numbers and following cookbooklike recipes.

Learning to Teach provides readers with the theory and rationale behind the specific principles and practices described. It explains why a recommended teaching principle or procedure works the way it does, not just how to execute it effectively. Because models, principles, and procedures of teaching were not invented yesterday, sometimes a short history lesson is provided. An example of this can be found in the chapter on cooperative learning. Even though significant developments have refined cooperative learning during the past decade, readers will discover that the basic model, including its theory and rationale, is lodged firmly in the mainstream of democratic thought and reaches back to Thomas Jefferson and John Dewey.

Research Summaries

Because *Learning to Teach* develops the point of view that there is a scientific knowledge base that can and should guide practice, it highlights this knowledge base for you. Each chapter includes a sampling of actual research studies, reduced in length but truthful to the investigators' methods and conclusions.

Several criteria guided the selection of research studies. First, the studies selected are representative of the main body of research done on a particular topic. This choice often was difficult because many fine studies have been conducted on almost every topic the book covers.

Second, in most of the studies selected the research was conducted with real teachers in real, not simulated, settings. Of course, this was not always possible because some aspects of teaching and learning do not lend themselves to direct observation or classroom investigation.

Third, the studies chosen were interesting, used straightforward methods, and found results that have direct implications for the practice of teaching.

Finally, the studies selected, when taken together, reflect the variety and richness of methods used by educational researchers over time and around the world.

Readers will find that most of the studies in the early chapters are rather straightforward and easy to understand, but those in later chapters are more complex. Some of the studies were conducted over 50 years ago, and some were conducted in other countries; these show the long research histories behind some of the principles and practices of teaching and the universality both of teaching practices and of the intellectual trends that guide educational research worldwide.

Presenting these research summaries to highlight the knowledge base on teaching has its pitfalls. Highlighting a single study might seem to imply that an extensive knowledge base exists when that simply is not true. A knowledge base exists in any profession only if many studies, conducted over time and in many settings, obtain results that converge. Similarly, presenting a single study to support a teaching principle or practice can lead the reader to the mistaken conclusion that most other studies have had similar results. To avoid these pitfalls, if contradictory results have been found this is pointed out to the reader. Do not overlook the warnings and contradictory or limited evidence that are given here.

Aids for Study, Observation, and Reflection

Some aspects of teaching cannot be learned by the mere acquisition of theory- or research-based knowledge. Instead, they require active involvement by the beginning teacher in seeking out experiences, observing other teachers, and reflecting upon these experiences and observations. At the end of each chapter, a set of aids intended to help you observe, study, and reflect upon your experiences has been included. Over 90 percent of the aids in *Learning to Teach* have been field-tested and found to work. Their use may, of course, be part of a course you are taking. But if not, enough instruction has been provided so you can launch a self-study program for yourself independently.

Special Topic Sections

Finally, *Learning to Teach* has five special topic sections, the content of which is important to beginning teachers but falls outside the main themes and functions developed in the chapters. These include (1) understanding research, (2) developing multicultural and mainstreamed classrooms, (3) testing and evaluation, (4) teaching comprehension and composition strategies, and (5) using computers in classrooms. These brief special topic sections are intended as introductions to motivate you to learn more about these important aspects of teaching.

Summary

This book was written for those in the process of learning to teach. Effective teachers promote academic knowledge and social learning in their pupils. To get these results requires considerable understanding of the scientific basis of teaching and the ability to master its art as well. The challenge is to gain control over the knowledge base on teaching, develop a repertoire of best practice, acquire attitudes and skills for reflection and problem solving, and approach this whole process as a lifelong quest.

▬▬▬▬▬▬▬▬▬▬ Books for the Professional ▬▬▬▬▬

Fenstermacher, G. D., and Soltis, J. F. (1986). *Approaches to teaching*. New York: Columbia Univ., Teachers College, Teachers College Press. Drawn from classical conceptions of teaching, this book can help beginning teachers analyze alternative approaches to teaching.

Gage, N. L. (1978). *The scientific basis of the art of teaching*. New York: Columbia Univ., Teachers College, Teachers College Press. This book discusses the value of educational research and how it has produced useful knowledge that supports practice.

Joyce, B., and Weil, M. (1986). *Models of teaching*. (Third edition). Englewood Cliffs, N.J.: Prentice-Hall. This book is a must. It provides more information on the models of teaching described here, plus fifteen others. This new edition has good chapters on how to acquire a teaching repertoire.

Lieberman, A., and Miller, L. (1984). *Teachers, their world, and their work*. Alexandria, Va.: Association of Supervision and Curriculum Development. This little book gives insightful descriptions of the day-to-day work of classroom teachers.

Richardson-Koehler, V. (Ed.). (1987). *Educators' handbook: A research perspective*. New York: Longman. This book provides an excellent review of the research on classroom teaching and effective schooling. It was written for teachers and administrators and includes such topics as classroom management, teacher planning, school effectiveness, and computers and education.

Wittrock, M. C. (Ed). (1986). *Handbook of research and teaching*. (Third edition). New York: Macmillan Publishing Co. This book is the most authoritative review of the mountain of research on teaching. Beginning teachers will find many of the chapters tough going; however, it is an invaluable reference work.

━━━━━━━━━━━━━ **CHAPTER 1** ━━━━━━━━━━━━━
LEARNING AIDS FOR PLANNING, OBSERVATION, AND REFLECTION

- Assessing My Efforts in Professional Development
- Interviewing Teachers About the Scientific Basis for the Art of Teaching
- Observing the Three Teaching Functions

The aids in Part 1 are designed to help you take stock of your own knowledge, to gauge your strengths and weaknesses, and to reflect on your growth as a teacher.

ASSESSING MY EFFORTS IN PROFESSIONAL DEVELOPMENT

PURPOSE: One of the most important goals of this text is to inspire your continuing efforts at professional development. This aid will help you to gain an overall impression of your efforts in pursuing the four attributes of effective teaching described in this chapter and to reflect on and plan for the next steps in your own professional growth.

DIRECTIONS: Circle the response that best corresponds to your level of agreement with the statement, then list the relevant activities under each category. Use the information to pinpoint gaps in your professional development activities.

1. I am actively engaged in developing my control over the knowledge base for teaching. (Circle one.)

Agree strongly   Agree   Neither agree nor disagree   Disagree   Disagree strongly

Topics I feel comfortable with	Topics I'm currently working on	Topics I will work on next
_____	_____	_____
_____	_____	_____
_____	_____	_____
_____	_____	_____

2. I am actively engaged in reflecting on myself as a teacher and in problem solving around educational issues. (Circle one.)

Agree strongly   Agree   Neither agree nor disagree   Disagree   Disagree strongly

Ways I currently reflect on and solve problems about teaching:

_____

_____

_____

_____

New ways I want to learn to help me reflect on and solve problems about teaching:

_____

_____

_____

_____

3. I am actively engaged in expanding my repertoire of teaching practices. (Circle one.)

Agree strongly   Agree   Neither agree nor disagree   Disagree   Disagree strongly

Practices I know   Practices I'm currently   Practices I will study next
                                 learning

_____   _____   _____

_____   _____   _____

_____   _____   _____

_____   _____   _____

4. I am actively engaged in the lifelong process of learning to teach. (Circle one.)

Agree strongly   Agree   Neither agree nor disagree   Disagree   Disagree strongly

Past actions I have taken to help me learn about teaching:

_____

_____

Actions I am currently taking to help me learn about teaching:

_____

_____

Actions I plan to take in the future to help me continue to learn about teaching:

_____

_____

INTERVIEWING TEACHERS ABOUT THE SCIENTIFIC BASIS
FOR THE ART OF TEACHING

PURPOSE: Teaching is both science and art. This aid will help you to uncover an experienced teacher's perceptions about the scientific basis for the art of teaching and to develop your own appreciation of teaching as art and science.

DIRECTIONS: Use the following questions to guide you as you interview a teacher about his or her understanding and application of the scientific basis for the art of teaching. (Note: Many experienced teachers may not be aware of the research base and yet may be using best practice. Some effective teaching research is based on what excellent experienced teachers do.)

1. To what extent has the way you plan your teaching been influenced by: (Estimate the percentage contribution of each.)

   _____ research on planning

   _____ your own experience and intuition

   _____ other (please specify) _____

2. Can you give an example of a planning principle you have learned from each source?

   Research: _____

   Experience: _____

   Other: _____

3. Do you find you sometimes need to modify these principles in practice? If so, in what way(s)?

   _____

   _____

4. To what extent has the way you allocate resources like time and space in your classroom been influenced by: (Estimate the percentage contribution of each.)

   _____ research on allocating time and space

   _____ your own experience and intuition

   _____ other (please specify) _____

5. Can you give an example of a principle of allocating resources that you have learned from each source?

   Research: _____

   Experience: _____

   Other: _____

6. Do you find you sometimes need to modify these principles in practice? If so, in what way(s)?

    _____

    _____

    _____

7. To what extent has the way you organize your classroom to create a productive learning environment been influenced by: (Estimate the percentage contribution of each.)

    _____ research

    _____ your own experience and intuition

    _____ other (please specify) _____

8. Can you give an example of a principle underlying the creation of productive learning environments you have learned from each source?

    Research: _____

    Experience: _____

    Other: _____

9. Do you find you sometimes need to modify these principles in practice? If so, in what way(s)?

    _____

    _____

    _____

10. To what extent has the way you manage your classroom been influenced by: (Estimate the percentage contribution of each.)

    _____ research

    _____ your own experience and intuition

    _____ other (please specify) _____

11. Can you give an example of a classroom management principle that you have learned from each source?

    Research: _____

    Experience: _____

    Other: _____

12. Do you find you sometimes need to modify these principles in practice? If so, in what way(s)?

_____

_____

_____

13. To what extent are the teaching strategies you use influenced by: (Estimate the percentage contribution of each.)

_____ research

_____ your own experience and intuition

_____ other (please specify) _____

14. Can you give an example of a teaching strategy that you have learned from each source?

Research: _____

Experience: _____

Other: _____

15. Do you find you sometimes need to modify these strategies in practice? If so, in what way(s)?

_____

_____

_____

16. To what extent is the way you work with other adults in the school influenced by: (Estimate the percentage contribution of each.)

_____ research

_____ your own experience and intuition

_____ other (please specify) _____

17. Can you give an example of a principle underlying adult interaction in the workplace that you have learned from each source?

Research: _____

Experience: _____

Other: _____

18. Do you find you sometimes need to modify these principles in practice? If so, in what way(s)?

   _____

   _____

   _____

19. To what extent is the way you work toward school improvement influenced by: (Estimate the percentage contribution of each.)

   _____ research

   _____ your own experience and intuition

   _____ other (please specify) _____

20. Can you give an example of a school improvement principle that you have learned from each source?

   Research: _____

   Experience: _____

   Other: _____

21. Do you find you sometimes need to modify these principles in practice? If so, in what way(s)?

   _____

   _____

   _____

Analysis and Reflection: Are there any patterns to where this teacher obtains ideas or principles for teaching? Are there any patterns to how this teacher modifies these ideas or principles in practice? Write a paragraph about any patterns you perceive and their relevance to your own teaching.

OBSERVING THE THREE TEACHING FUNCTIONS

PURPOSE: Teaching is a complex, multifaceted activity. This aid will help sensitize you to the multiple functions of teaching.

DIRECTIONS: Shadow a teacher for at least half a day. Make sure you have a chance to observe him or her either before school starts or after class is let out. Make a "tick" whenever you see the teacher perform one of the listed activities. At the same time, estimate the amount of time the teacher spends on that activity, and jot down any other observations you make. Perhaps certain activities tend to occur at certain times, or a particular emotional tone is evident, or several activities occur simultaneously. Make note of anything you think will help you refine your understanding of the three teaching functions.

Function	Observed	Time	Comments
Executive			
Planning	———	——	———
Allocating time and space	———	——	———
Organizing for a productive learning environment	———	——	———
Managing the classroom	———	——	———
Interaction			
Using an information processing model	———	——	———
Using a behavioral model	———	——	———
Using a social model	———	——	———
Using a personal model	———	——	———
Using other strategies (specify)			
_____	———	——	———
_____	———	——	———
Organizational			
Interacting with other adults to carry out the work of the school	———	——	———
Working alone on nonclassroom task	———	——	———
Working toward school improvement	———	——	———

Analysis and Reflection: Tally up the number of ticks for each category, and add the amount of time spent on each category. What did this teacher spend the most time doing? What did he or she do most often? How much time is spent on average on any one episode within a category? (Divide time spent by number of ticks.) Does this seem to be the most productive allocation of the teacher's time? Why or why not?

CHAPTER 2

MAIN IDEAS

- Popular notions of great teachers emphasize charismatic qualities, but this type of teacher may not be the most effective.
- Learning to teach is a lifelong process.
- Parents and teachers influence decisions to enter teaching and affect a beginning teacher's concept of teaching.
- Learning to teach is developmental, and teachers go through rather predictable stages of development and concerns.
- Teaching has a scientific basis that beginning teachers learn through studying the research themselves or learning about it from colleagues and at professional meetings.
- Research can support classroom practice, but it cannot be translated directly into fixed recipes and formulas.
- A vast network exists to help beginning teachers translate research into practice.
- Beginning teachers also learn to teach through experience, reflection, and observing in other teachers' classrooms.
- Listening, observing, and habits of reflection are critical skills to develop if experience is to be valuable.
- Personal theories of teaching are built through reflection about research and experience.

Learning to Teach

Some teachers, like fine wines, keep getting better with age. Others do not improve their skills after years of practice and remain about the same as the day they walked into their first classrooms. Why is it that some teachers approach the act of teaching critically and reflectively; are innovative, open, and altruistic; are willing to take risks with themselves and their students; and are capable of critical judgment about their own work? Conversely, why do others exhibit exactly the opposite traits?

Becoming truly accomplished in almost any human endeavor takes a long time. Many professional athletes, for example, display raw talent at a very early age, but they do not reach their athletic prime until their late twenties and early thirties and then only after many years of dedicated learning and practice. Many great novelists have written their best pieces in their later years only after producing several inferior and amateurish works. The biographies of talented musicians and artists often describe years of pain and dedication before the subjects reached artistic maturity. Becoming a truly accomplished teacher is no different. It takes purposeful actions fueled by the desire for excellence; it takes an attitude that learning to teach is a lifelong developmental process in which one gradually discovers one's own best style through reflection and critical inquiry. This chapter presents information about how you can approach this lifelong process of learning to teach.

The chapter describes a portion of what is known about learning to teach. It tells how beginning teachers can start the process of becoming effective teachers by learning how to access the knowledge base on teaching and how to reflect on their experiences. At the end of the chapter several aids are provided to assist you with your planning, observation, and reflection.

PERSPECTIVE AND RATIONALE

This chapter starts with the three basic premises. The first is that learning to teach is a lifelong process, not one limited to the period of time between the first methods class and the date a teaching license is acquired. The second is that few effective teachers are born that way. Rather, they become increasingly effective through attention to their own learning and development of their own particular attributes, skills, and unique styles. And third, memories beginning teachers may have of favorite teachers they hope to model themselves after may not be the route to effective teaching. Take, for instance, the four teachers profiled below.

Jack Ramsey In a small rural town in northeastern Kansas, Jack Ramsey walks into his twelfth-grade social studies class promptly at 8:45 A.M. Ramsey is a stout, robust man. His ex-marine bearing and reputation for toughness bring every eye in class to the front as he makes his predicted entrance. With the flair of the drill sergeant, he calls roll. Each student responds with a crisp "Here" to his or her name as it is precisely pronounced, always preceeded by the formal title of Mr. or Miss. Ms. is a modern invention Ramsey refuses to recognize.

Instruction for the day starts with current events. Calling students at random, Ramsey asks what they read in newspapers or news magazines during the past 24 hours. TV news is not allowed. Ramsey usually comments on each report; sometimes he "kids" a bit; sometimes he responds with slight ridicule or cynicism to a particular student's comments before moving on suddenly to someone else.

The formal lesson for the day grows from the text the class is using, and Ramsey's favorite teaching strategy consists of a brief lecture on some issue discussed in the text, followed by pointed questions to members of the class. On a normal day after several questions, a controversial issue is defined by Ramsey and for the remainder of the class Ramsey and three or four of the brighter students carry on an extended and spirited debate. Class ends with the next day's assignment and a reminder from Ramsey of the upcoming test for Friday.

Ramsey is a legend in the school. Bright students look forward to the challenge of twelfth-grade social studies, and the less able worry and fret but still like him. Ramsey is tough and hard-nosed, but is considered fair, interesting, and provocative. His debates with students are notorious for the entertainment they provide. His Friday tests cover every imaginable detail and are reason, in a school where homework normally is accomplished in class or study halls, for every student to burn the late-night oil. Parents love him.

Jane Middleton Urbane and sophisticated, Jane Middleton is an English teacher in Roosevelt Middle School. Her trademarks—bright scarves and chic designer clothes, outspoken criticism of bureaucratic rules, and unorthodox ideas—make her eighth-grade humanities class a "must" for every bright student at Roosevelt. Ms. Middleton's room is colorfully decorated with a wall-size map of the world and many prints of works by the old masters. An expensive Oriental rug (purchased by Middleton) provides a setting for intimate discussions and readings. Each day is a new and stimulating experience for students. It might bring a Shakespeare reading by Middleton herself, or an opportunity to listen attentively to classical music, or a provocative guest speaker—normally an artist who is a personal friend of Middleton's. Tests are not given in Middleton's class, but students are motivated to work hard, primarily by Middleton's own love of the humanities and her compelling, charismatic personality.

Donald Chavez Dr. Chavez teaches a sophomore class in United States history in a large university on the East Coast. Each class period is a delightful experience for his students. An eloquent speaker, Dr. Chavez has prepared over the years a series of lectures that fill the time to the minute and are sprinkled with jokes that have become notorious around campus and are familiar to students long before they set foot in his class. Chavez's lectures center for the most part on great men (more recently, women, too) in American history. His own research has produced a vast knowledge about many American leaders, particularly information about their vanities and personal lives. The high and mighty, both living and dead, seldom escape Chavez's biting tongue nor do their illicit dealings and love affairs, a Chavez speciality. Tests on the lectures are the primary means of grading in a Chavez class, and these tests are considered very difficult because Chavez expects students to remember every detail he covers, including his jokes.

Chavez's sections of United States history are always overenrolled. Twice during the past 15 years he has been given the university's award for excellence in teaching.

Mr. Chase Mr. Chase is a fifth-grade teacher at Elmwood Elementary School. Slightly overweight and with a bit of tummy always showing through the gap in the bottom of his shirts, Chase is a favorite among students and parents of Elmwood. He knows all the students in his class and their families and, in fact, knew several parents of current students when they were in his class years ago. Chase plays ball with the boys at recess and loves to stand in the hall before and after school saying "Hi" to students and teasing them (in playful ways) about their boyfriends and girlfriends. Chase prides himself on how he has individualized instruction for his students, relying heavily upon commercial texts and workbooks. Students love to hang around his desk asking for help and kidding with him. He never refuses to stay after school to help students.

Mr. Chase befriends every new student (and new teacher) in the school and helps him or her adjust to their new environment. The principal relies on Chase and seeks his advice often. She even appoints him acting principal when she has to be away from Elmwood.

No doubt you can conjure up from your own school experiences images of teachers like Ramsey, Middleton, Chavez, and Chase. They represent the popular concepts of great teachers—persons characterized by charismatic qualities and the ability to motivate or to befriend students. Oftentimes memories of such teachers become a kind of vague model for people learning to teach. But is it possible for all teachers to become like these teachers? In fact, are Ramsey, Middleton, Chase, and Chavez really effective teachers?

In truth, most individuals cannot learn to teach in these charismatic styles. For example, how many people can have the bearing and the commitment to discipline and command of Ramsey? How many have a knack for the dramatic and the stage presence of Middleton and Chavez? How many can know their students' personal lives as well as Chase, who also had some of his students' parents in his classes?

Most people preparing to teach have less colorful personalities that lead to subtler, less pronounced teaching styles. Does that mean that they cannot become great teachers? The answer is no, not at all. Those of you with normal talents, but perhaps without charismatic personalities, can become effective teachers if you have a strong grasp of your subject field, a knowledge of pedagogy, and a reflective mind.

In truth, some of the teachers remembered most vividly because of their charismatic qualities may not have been as effective as they seemed. Many times a very charismatic teacher like Middleton works best with the most talented and academically able students—students who already possess strong verbal and information processing skills. But what about the less able and less motivated students who populate the classrooms of most schools? They are the students most in need of good teachers. Similarly, some of the friendly and popular teachers you remember befriended the lonely and were fun to be around, but did they challenge the able? Did less able students learn those basic skills so vital to later success in school from them? These are questions that must be pondered in the process of developing teaching skills and styles.

SAMPLING THE RESEARCH BASE

Although quite a bit is known about how people learn to teach and why some reach a higher level of excellence than others, this knowledge base is not as fully developed as some others discussed in this book. Nonetheless, much is known, and in the next few pages three lines of inquiry will be described: the influence of early experiences on teaching, the developmental view of learning to teach, and an exciting new field of research that explores how the thought processes of beginning teachers differ from those of teachers with more experience.

Early Influences on Teaching

It appears that some aspects of learning to teach are influenced by the experiences that people have with important adult figures, particularly teachers, as they grow up and go through school. In the early 1970s Dan Lortie, a sociologist at the University of Chicago, spent several years studying why people become teachers, what kind of a profession teaching is, and what experiences affect learning to teach. As part of his study, he interviewed a rather large sample of teachers and asked them what experiences most influenced their teaching. Many experienced teachers told Lortie that early authority figures, such as parents and teachers, greatly influenced their concepts of teaching and their subsequent decision to enter the field. On the pages that follow portions of Lortie's study and his results are summarized.

The format used to present Lortie's research is one that will be followed throughout the book when research reports are summarized. The problem the researcher was addressing is presented first, followed by brief descriptions about who was studied and the types of procedures used. When needed, pointers are provided to help you read the research. Each research summary concludes with a description of important findings and statements about the implications of the research for practice.

This format is used because it is important that you become knowledgeable about the research base on teaching and learning, and it is equally important that you learn how to read and use research. At the end of this chapter there is a special topic section, Understanding Research, that provides further insight into the nature of research on teaching and a practice exercise for reading research. You may want to read the special topic section before going on.

Models of Teacher Development

Another area of research about how people learn to teach comes from the field of developmental psychology. There is a growing consensus among leading theorists and researchers that humans develop cognitively and affectively through stages. Sprinthall and Thies-Sprinthall (1983) summarized this perspective and listed the following assumptions of developmental theory:

1. All humans process experience through cognitive structures called stages—Piaget's concept of schemata.

2. Such cognitive structures are progressively organized . . . into stages from the less complex to the more complex.

3. Growth occurs first within a particular stage and then progresses to the next stage in sequence. This latter change is a qualitative shift—a major leap to a significantly more complex system of processing experience.

4. Growth is neither automatic nor unilateral but occurs only with appropriate interactions between the human and the environment;

5. Behavior can be determined and predicted by an individual's particular stage of development. Predictions, however, are not exact. (p. 16)

What this means is that becoming a teacher, like becoming anything else, is a process in which development progresses rather systematically through stages with a chance of growth remaining static unless appropriate experiences occur. The following are specific developmental theories about how people learn to teach.

================= **RESEARCH SUMMARY** =================
2.1

Lortie, D. (1975). *School-teacher: A sociological study.* Chicago: The University of Chicago Press.

PROBLEM: Lortie was interested in a variety of issues about teaching as an occupation, particularly the organization of the teacher's work, the sentiments teachers hold toward their work, and the "ethos" of the teacher's occupation as contrasted to other occupations.

SAMPLE AND SETTING: Lortie collected information from a number of sources. The focus here is on the data he collected through extensive interviews with 94 teachers from five towns in the Boston metropolitan area and from a national survey conducted by the National Education Association in the late 1960s.

PROCEDURES: By Lortie's own account his methods included: "historical review, national and local surveys, findings from observational studies by other research- ers, and content analysis of intensive interviews" (p. ix). His sample from the five towns around Boston included selecting school systems that were broadly representative of American education; he then randomly selected teachers from within the five systems. He interviewed the teachers about the attractions of teaching and various other features of their careers using techniques he had developed in earlier studies on the legal profession.

POINTERS FOR READING RESEARCH: The researchers who carried out many of the studies used in this book reported their results in numeric form and summarized them in data tables. Lortie's data are presented not in tabular format but, instead, as direct quotes from the people he interviewed. Information quoted directly from interviews is quite easy to read and to understand. However, readers of this type of research information always need to ask themselves questions about the data, such as: Did the researcher conduct the interviews in such a way that respondents provided honest and accurate information? From many possibilities, did the researcher select quotes that were representative of what the total sample reported, or did he or she select quotes to represent a particular point of view or bias? Are the conclusions reached by researchers using interview data consistent with the information the data contain?

RESULTS: Lortie's study is large and complex and has many insights into teaching and teachers. Here are some of his findings about why people go into teaching and the influence of early experiences on their teaching.

Interview Data: One teacher interviewed shows the influence of early adult figures on her decision to teach:

My mother was a teacher, her sisters were teachers—it's a family occupation. I always wanted to go into teaching. I can't remember when I didn't want to . . . . I remember as a little girl sometimes seeing teachers have a hard time. I thought, well, I will be careful because some day I'll be on the other side of the desk.   (p. 61)

Lortie also found that teaching is one of the few professions where the practitioner has been in the client (student) role for an extended period (several hours each day for 16 years) before switching to the professional role. It comes as no surprise that teachers told Lortie that their own teaching was greatly influenced by the teaching they had received as students. The following excerpts from Lortie's interviews illustrate this influence.

The teacher I had in sixth grade was good, interesting. There are a few things I used this year that I remember having done in her room.   (p. 63)

There was one particular teacher in my eighth and ninth grades. She was very hard, very strict, and used to say, "I know some of you don't like me since I'm so strict; but when you get out of school and think back, a lot of you will probably think of me as being the best teacher." She really was. She probably taught me how important classroom discipline was.   (p. 64)

My second-grade teacher was kind. She knew it was a terrific change for me to come all the way from Iowa and she'd take the time to talk to me, to take away some of the fright. I never forgot that and when new youngsters come into my room I always try to team them up with someone. I have a special word for them.   (p. 64)

I had a college professor . . . . This is the man who had more to do with my techniques than any other person.   (p. 64)

I had her in United States history and she whetted my appetite for history . . . . I may be one of her products. I think I am.   (p. 64)

DISCUSSION AND IMPLICATIONS: It is obvious that prior experiences with their own teachers have affected and will continue to influence the ways teachers think and act about teaching. In some ways this is positive, since it provides beginners with many models over the years. However, relying too completely upon these early experiences may make teachers rather conservative in trying new approaches. Many of the standard practices used by former teachers may not represent best practices, given current knowledge about teaching and learning. Also, if beginning teachers rely too heavily on their prior experiences, that may prevent them from being sufficiently reflective and analytical toward their work. This latter point will be discussed later in the chapter.

FULLER'S STAGES OF CONCERN

The late Frances Fuller studied student teachers, beginning teachers, and more experienced teachers at the University of Texas in the late 1960s and early 1970s. Through her research (1969) she developed a theory that describes three stages of concern teachers go through as they learn to teach.

1. Survival Concerns When people first begin thinking about teaching and when they have their first classroom encounters with children from in front of rather than behind the desk, Fuller's research suggests, they are most concerned about their own personal survival. They wonder and worry about their interpersonal adequacy and whether or not their students and their supervisors are going to like them. Also, they are very concerned about classroom control and worry about things getting out of hand. In fact, many beginning teachers in this initial stage have dreams about students getting out of control.

2. Teaching Situation Concerns At some point, however, and this varies for different individuals, beginning teachers start feeling more adequate. Various aspects of controlling and interacting with students become somewhat routinized. Teachers begin shifting attention and energy to the teaching situation itself. They start dealing with the time pressures of teaching and with some of the stark realities of the classroom, such as too many students, inappropriate instructional materials, and perhaps their own meager repertoire of teaching strategies.

3. Pupil Concerns Eventually, individuals mature as teachers and find ways of coping or dealing with survival and situation concerns. It is only then, according to Fuller, that teachers reach for higher-level issues and start asking questions about the social and emotional needs of students, being fair, and the match between teaching strategies and materials and pupil needs and learning.

The Fuller model is useful for thinking about the process of learning to teach. It helps to put present concerns in perspective and to prepare beginners to move on to the next and higher level of concern. For example, a beginning teacher who is overly worried about personal concerns might seek out experiences and training that build confidence and independence. If class control takes too much mental and emotional energy, ways to modify that situation can be sought. An aid that can help you to measure your concerns at this point in your career is included at the end of the chapter.

FEIMAN-NEMSER'S STAGES OF DEVELOPMENT

Sharon Feiman-Nemser (1983), a researcher at Michigan State University, has also identified several stages that teachers go through in the process of becoming teachers. These are similar to those described by Fuller, but are included here nonetheless to provide another set of lenses through which to view the development process.

1. Beginning Survival Stage This is the stage that beginners are in when they start their teaching careers. A beginner's knowledge of teaching and schools is limited to what he or she has picked up over the years as a student.

2. Consolidation Stage According to Feiman-Nemser, beginners eventually pass beyond the survival stage and become more confident in their ability to teach and to deal with students. Their personal and teaching goals become clearer and more concise, and many of the routines required for effective classroom management and instruction became habitual.

3. Mastery Stage During this stage of development, teachers master the fundamentals of teaching and of classroom management. These become effective and routine. As in Fuller's pupil concern stage, teachers now focus their energy and talent on pupil needs and strive to provide improved instruction from an ever-broadening repertoire of methods and strategies and an ever-deepening understanding of the subjects taught.

IMPLICATIONS OF DEVELOPMENTAL MODELS FOR LEARNING TO TEACH

As beginning teachers go through the process of learning to teach, the developmental models conceptualized by Sprinthall and Theis-Sprinthall, Fuller, and Feiman-Nemser have numerous implications. First, these models suggest that learning to teach is a developmental process in which each individual moves through stages that are simple and concrete at first and later, more complex and abstract. Developmental models thus provide a framework for viewing your own growth.

Second, you can use the models to diagnose your own level of concern and development. This knowledge can help teachers to accept the anxiety and concerns of the beginning years and, most important, to plan learning experiences that will facilitate growth to more mature and complex levels of functioning. For example some developmental theorists, such as Hunt (1970; 1974), argue that growth is a result of interaction between a person's level of development and environmental conditions. Optimal development occurs only when environmental conditions provide a stimulus to a person's cognitive and emotional growth. When environmental conditions are not optimal, are either too simple or too complex, then learning is retarded. In other words, as people learning to teach become more complex themselves, their environments must also become correspondingly more complex if they are to continue developing at an optimal rate. Although it is not possible to readily change many of the environments you will experience as you learn to teach, you can, nonetheless, try to seek out environments and experiences that will match your level of concern and development as a teacher.

Cognitive Processes of Expert and Novice Teachers

There are many approaches to thinking about teaching and about learning to teach. One is to focus on the specific things teachers do and how these affect student performance. The emphasis here is on trying to figure out how teachers learn to execute particularly effective techniques or procedures. Another approach is to examine the complex cognitive processes (thinking) engaged in by teachers as they plan and make decisions about what they are going to do. Some of this research (Borko and Niles, 1987; Peterson, Marx, and Clark, 1978; Shavelson, 1976) will be discussed in Chapter 3 because it shows how teachers think as they plan for instruction. The emphasis in this chapter, however, is on an interesting line of inquiry that has emerged in the past few years about the differences between the cognitive performances of expert teachers and those of novice teachers.

This line of inquiry has been influenced substantially by cognitive psychology and schema theory. Cognitive psychologists use the word *schemata* to describe an individual's knowledge structure and how information is stored and processed in memory. Four important principles from schema theory have major implications for learning how to teach:

1. Individuals store and organize knowledge in memory through knowledge structures or schemata.
2. A person's schemata and prior knowledge about any topic greatly influence what can be learned.
3. To be meaningful, new information must be structured in such a way as to hook into and activate existing schemata.
4. Differences in schemata account, in part, for performance differences in complex tasks such as teaching.

These principles will be elaborated on in later chapters, and their implications for how new information should be presented to students will be described. Here the implications for learning to teach are explored.

Reseachers such as Borko and her colleagues (1987), Calderhead (1981), and Leinhardt, and Greeno (1986) have investigated how a teacher's knowledge structure (schemata) works and how schema may differ among beginning novice and experienced expert teachers. Their research points out how expert and novice teachers think differently about problems and how they use different problem-solution strategies. Their research also suggests that information found to be useful for an experienced teacher may not take on the same meaning for a beginning teacher. This research is important and has value for beginning teachers because if beginners can gain insights into the knowledge structures and thinking processes of experienced teachers, these insights can advance their own efforts.

Gaea Leinhardt is one of the researchers interested in this topic. In one of her recently completed studies, summarized in Research Summary 2.2, Leinhardt used somewhat different terminology—"agenda" instead of schemata or knowledge structure—but the concept is the same. Agenda is simply a narrower term used by Leinhardt to express how teachers structure their knowledge about a specific lesson.

■■■■■■■■■■ LEARNING ABOUT TEACHING THROUGH RESEARCH

Chapter 1 presented the idea that there is a scientific basis for teaching; this is developed here along with a description of ways beginning teachers can use research to learn and to keep abreast of best practice. Three important questions are posed and then discussed: (1) What is meant by the scientific basis of teaching? (2) What are the limits of research? (3) How can a beginning teacher become knowledgeable about research?

The Scientific Basis of Teaching

The claim that there is a scientific basis for many of the things teachers do is made with some modesty, knowing that many of the practices of effective teaching have grown out of the experiences of teachers themselves, not research. The knowledge base for teaching, as has been pointed out, is still young and not yet very complete. Nonetheless, in contrast to the fragmentary and inconsistent knowledge base of two decades ago, the situation today is vastly improved. But what does it mean to have a knowledge base about teaching?

Scientific knowledge is essentially knowledge about relationships between variables. In the social sciences or applied sciences (such as education) this means that knowledge exists about how one variable is related to another and, in some instances, how one set of variables under certain conditions affects others. In education, the variables that have been most studied during the past decade, and also the ones most relevant to learning to teach, are those associated with student achievement and teacher behavior. In other words, the scientific knowledge available to guide teachers relates certain *teaching practices* to *student achievement* or other important outcomes.

From this knowledge teaching principles and in some instances guidelines for best practice have been derived. The beginning teacher, however, should not jump to the conclusion that principles based on research will work all of the time, for all students, in all settings. That simply is not true. Research knowledge explains what happens most of the time and under particular conditions. An example from medical research can help illustrate this point.

During the past decade, many studies have shown strong relationships between cigarette smoking and various diseases—particularly heart disease and cancer. However, you all know people who have smoked all their lives and have not had heart attacks. You also know people who did not smoke but who died of cancer. Similarly, it has been shown that hypothetical drug X is strongly related to the cure of disease Y, and medical researchers can cite many instances when patients using drug X were cured. However, doctors can also cite known instances where drug X has been administered, and the patient has died.

Another way of thinking about scientific knowledge and educational research is to contrast it to folklore and mythology. It could be said that educational research produces information that helps describe relationships in education more accurately than folklore and popular impressions. Through careful observation of

═══════════════ **RESEARCH SUMMARY** ═══════════════
2.2

Leinhardt, G. (in press). Math lessons: A contrast of novice and expert competence. *Journal for Research in Mathematics Education.* Used with permission of the author.

PROBLEM: Leinhardt was interested in the differences in the cognitive performances of novice and expert teachers. She was particularly interested in how experienced and novice elementary school teachers displayed competence in planning and conducting lessons in mathematics.

SAMPLE AND SETTING: Leinhardt studied four expert teachers and two novice teachers. The expert teachers were selected from a group of teachers who had consistently produced high student achievement in mathematics in self-contained elementary classrooms. Two of the expert teachers taught in integrated classrooms; two taught in classrooms with only black students. The two novice teachers were chosen from a pool of 20 student teachers. The student teachers taught in integrated fourth-grade classrooms.

PROCEDURES: Expert and novice teachers were observed over a 3½-month period. Over 25 hours of lessons were videotaped. The subjects were interviewed before and after each videotaped lesson on several aspects of their teaching including their knowledge of mathematics. Only one aspect of Leinhardt's study, the "teacher's agenda," will be considered here. Leinhardt defined the agenda teachers had for a particular lesson as the "unique operational plan a teacher used to teach a mathematics lesson. . . . (It was) the teacher's own mental note pad for a lesson" (p. 7). The researcher found out about the teachers' agendas by asking them just prior to the lesson what they were going to do and what they expected to happen during the lesson.

POINTERS FOR READING RESEARCH: Leinhardt's study is the first to be used in this book in which data are summarized with numbers and are reported in tabular format. Some readers will be familiar with the symbols and conventions of reporting educational research; others will not. If these are unfamilar to you, read the special topic section at the end of this chapter before going on. Also, Leinhardt's research uses several statistical concepts that the reader must understand. These are explained in the special topic section, but they are repeated here for the reader's convenience.

- $\bar{X}$ is the symbol used to designate the *mean score,* or what many would call the average score. These terms are interchangeable. Most know that averages are calculated by adding all scores and dividing by the number, or *N*.
- The symbol *SD* observed in Table 1 stands for *standard deviation.* This statistic is found in many data tables and is a measure indicating the spread of a particular set of scores from the mean. Differences in means, as well as differences in standard deviation, are used to compute statistical significance.
- When researchers come up with mean scores of two different groups (as Leinhardt did) they want to know whether the means are in fact different because

of the *relationships* they are studying or whether the difference is one that occurred by *chance*. Statistical tests are used for this purpose, which is referred to as testing for significance.

- In the table, the reader will find a column marked *t*. Leinhardt is referring to a particular statistic that tells the researcher the probability that the differences are due to chance.
- Below Leinhardt's table are the symbols $p<.10$ and $p<.005$. This communicates to the reader that for the particular *t* scores one can be confident, with .5 percent or 10 percent chance of error, that the differences between means are real and did not occur because of bias or chance.

RESULTS: Table 1 displays the results of one part of Leinhardt's study. It compares the agendas of novice and expert teachers on five dimensions: (1) the length of the teachers' descriptions (number of lines in the interview), (2) the number of times teachers referred to possible student actions, (3) the number of times teachers mentioned "check points" to see if students were understanding the lesson, (4) the number of times reference was made to specific actions the teacher planned to make, and (5) the logical applications of these actions to the total lesson.

TABLE 1 Comparison of Features of Novice and Expert Agendas

Feature	Novice		Expert		
	$\bar{X}$	SD	$\bar{X}$	SD	t
No. of lines of response	13.6	5.2	26.4	8.1	3.76*
No. of student actions	0.9	0.8	1.8	1.5	1.45**
No. of check points	0.0	0.0	0.8	0.7	***
No. of instructional actions	2.9	1.2	6.5	1.2	5.90*
No. of logic elements	0.1	0.4	1.4	0.9	3.54*

* significant at $p<.005$ ** significant at $p<.10$ *** When there is no variation in the data (SD
SOURCE: G. Leinhardt (1986), p. 14.   = 0), the *t* value cannot be calculated.

Inspection of the mean scores in Table 1 illustrates the amount of detail and the richness provided by the expert teachers as contrasted to the novice teachers. Note that expert teachers used twice as many lines to describe their lessons as novice teachers and were much more likely to describe student actions. No novice teacher mentioned a way to "check" to see if students were understanding the lesson. Expert teachers also had clearer and more detailed descriptions about their instructional actions and the internal logic of their proposed lessons.

DISCUSSION AND IMPLICATIONS: Leinhardt also studied how teachers explain new information to students and how they structure their lessons into meaningful segments. The data summarized in Table 1 and other aspects of the study led Leinhardt to the following conclusions:

Expert math teachers weave a series of lessons together to form an instructional topic in ways that consistently build upon and advance

(*cont'd*)

─────────────────── **RESEARCH SUMMARY** ───────────────────
2.2 (continued)

material introduced in prior lessons. Experts also display a highly efficient within-lesson structure, one that is characterized by fluid movement from one type of activity to another, by minimal student confusion during instruction, and by a transparent system of goals. These goals are consistently met by the application of cohesive well-rehearsed action systems. . . . Not all of these skills are explicitly recognized by the expert; and their existence, therefore, has been inferred.

Novice teachers' lessons, on the other hand, are characterized by fragmented lesson structures with long transitions between lesson segments, by frequent confusion caused by missent signals, and by an ambiguous system of goals which often appear to be abandoned rather than achieved. In our interviews of novices, they show significant subject matter competence but do not seem to access that knowledge while teaching. Their lessons do not fit well together within or across topic boundaries. . . . novices are aware of these problems while teaching, at least to some extent. However, novices lack the analytic skills to understand where failures occurred or when goals that were implicit in certain actions were not achieved. (pp. 28–29)

One implication of Leinhardt's research for those learning how to teach is that beginners at first will not have clear pictures about how lessons should proceed or have ways to modify lessons as they go along. Their mental agenda will not be as rich as more experienced teachers. Also it is likely that many beginning lessons will be fragmented and explanations will not be as rich or as complete as they will be after considerable practice.

This study also implies that beginners can learn from more experienced teachers by observing and studying the way they plan and execute lessons so, in Leinhart's words, "novices can see how to weave pieces of their actions . . . together" (p. 30).

Finally, this study highlights the complex and subtle nature of effective teaching and suggests why experienced and beginning teachers may miscommunicate with one another. Expert experienced teachers are likely to have more complex schemata for thinking about and doing teaching. As they try to explain what they know and do, beginners may or may not have the necessary prior knowledge and experience to find meaning in what they are saying. On the other hand, it may be that beginners will have information about new research and new teaching approaches that experienced teachers may have difficulty understanding and accepting because of their own lack of prior knowledge.

───

teaching practices, researchers have shown that some of the things teachers do seem to work, but others do not. Research on teaching, then, can dispel old wives' tales about teaching, just as other research can dispel myths about the physical and social world. For this reason, it is important for teachers to have a firm grasp of the knowledge base on teaching, including its application in various settings.

Everyone, however, should be cautious and remember that teaching is a tremendously complex set of processes that continually departs from fixed recipes and formulas.

What Are the Limits of Research?

There are several reasons why research can inform classroom practice in some instances but not in others.

EXPLANATION VERSUS RECOMMENDATION

Practicing teachers often ask researchers to make practical recommendations based on their research. Some examples of the types of questions they ask include: "Should we use ability groupings in third-grade classrooms?" "What are the best concepts to teach in tenth-grade social studies?" Or, "How can I motivate John, who comes to school tired every morning?" The reply to these types of questions has to be that research alone cannot provide answers to such specific practical problems. For example, take the question about what to teach in tenth-grade social studies. Even though a researcher might provide empirical information about what other school districts teach in the tenth grade, or about the abilities of most 15 year olds to understand certain concepts, this would not help a teacher decide what concepts to teach, given a particular group of students, the goals of a particular social studies curriculum or teacher, and the community values—all crucial factors to consider.

EXPLANATION VERSUS RECIPES

Research on teaching is very young. Many questions of interest have not been studied and many that have been studied still lack complete or adequate answers. The explanations provided by research do not normally translate directly into recipes that can be safely followed. Instead, research explanations help explain relationships between variables in a model of classroom teaching. These explanations can provide guidelines for teachers who are knowledgeable about their own abilities and skills, those of their students, and the contextual features of a particular classroom, school, and community.

Learning About Research

How can beginning teachers learn about research? Many educational researchers search for relationships among variables, but they do not necessarily attempt to translate their findings into practices for teachers. That is perhaps why research reports often leave teachers confused and with a negative attitude. There are, however, many things beginning and experienced teachers can do to learn from research. Two of these—where teachers can look for relevant research information and how to use professional meetings and colleagues for learning about research—are discussed below.

RESEARCH SERVICES AVAILABLE TO TEACHERS

Beginning in the mid-1960s, the federal government became more interested in educational research and created several services to encourage the dissemination of educational research to classroom teachers. Three of these services can be useful to the beginning teacher.

Regional Educational Laboratories Knowing that most research was not directly applicable to classroom teachers, regional educational laboratories were created in 1964 to translate research into classroom materials and strategies and to disseminate the results to teachers. Even though their budgets do not allow direct assistance in every classroom in their region, laboratory staffs hold many useful workshops and are eager to have classroom teachers visit their labs and learn about the work they are doing. These laboratories also provide opportunities for the more energetic teachers to participate in ongoing research and development projects. Appendix A at the end of the book provides the address and phone number of the laboratory in each region.

Educational Research Information Centers Also in the mid-1960s, the federal government started to put together a network of educational research information centers called ERIC. Today there are 16 of these centers. ERIC centers are charged with three major tasks: (1) collecting the available knowledge on topics associated with various specialized areas of education, (2) organizing this information so it can be retrieved via computers from any place in the United States, and (3) summarizing these data in short bulletins and papers on topics of particular interest to teachers and other educators.

Today, all libraries in major universities and many large school districts or intermediate educational agencies have direct computer connections to the ERIC centers. To access these centers you need only contact the person in charge of ERIC searches in your library or school. That person will set up an appointment and discuss the type of problem about which you would like research information. The contact person can then perform on-line searches to give you an example of the types of articles and reports that are available. You can then order abstracts of the most relevant articles. These come to you on computer printouts and are useful for making decisions about the complete reports you may want to read. Since most university libraries and major school districts have the complete ERIC collection on microfiche, all of this can be done with minimal charge, and in many instances, for free. Additional information is provided about the ERIC system in Appendix B.

The National Diffusion Network A third service available to teachers is the National Diffusion Network (NDN). Created in 1974, NDN now exists in every state for the purpose of disseminating information on classroom practices and curriculum materials that have been shown through research to work. Akin to the farm extension system that takes the results of research to farmers, NDN works through the following two procedures:

1. Programs that work. Each year many educational programs are developed by educational researchers and by practicing classroom teachers. If they wish, and if they have evidence that their program produces the results they claim for it, they can submit it to a national review board for consideration. If approved by the national review board, the program is then described and appears in a yearly publication called *Programs That Work*. This publication is readily available to classroom teachers and other interested educators.

2. State facilitators. More important for the classroom teacher, however, is the availability of a person or team in each state who will respond to requests by teachers for information about various programs that might be available to assist with a particular classroom or school problem. For example, suppose you are in your first year of teaching and you discover during your first open house that few parents show up. This confirms your previous hunch that your students are receiving little support and encouragement from home. Consequently, you call the NDN state facilitator and find that indeed there are programs that have been shown to be successful in increasing parental involvement. The facilitator may come to your school or invite you to his or her office and go over the programs that have received national endorsement. You can then order these programs and obtain materials explaining their use. You may also decide to involve other teachers in the school and together establish a school-wide program to increase parental support. When this happens, the state facilitator can often provide assistance to get you and the faculty started, sometimes even to the point of bringing the original developer of the program to your school.

LEARNING ABOUT RESEARCH FROM COLLEAGUES AND AT MEETINGS

Even though teachers should understand research procedures and be able to seek out research, the reality of the pressures of teaching leaves little time for reading the research literature and using that information to guide teaching practice. It is more likely that beginning teachers will learn about research either by attending workshops and professional meetings or by using their colleagues. Unfortunately, many teachers do not seem to have good professional networks and do not regularly attend meetings where research is presented and interpreted.

It is important for beginning teachers to set goals for themselves early in their careers which will help guide professional growth and establish professional networks. See Appendix C at the end of this book for lists of the names and addresses of several organizations that have meetings both nationally and locally where teachers and researchers present research on topics of interest to classroom teachers. An example of such a professional organization is the Association for Supervision and Curriculum Development (ASCD). This organization publishes a monthly journal, *Educational Leadership*, that contains many interpretive articles on research. The organization also has local units in every state that produce newsletters and hold regular meetings of interest to teachers. Phi Delta Kappa also provides similar services to teachers, as do the National Education Association, the American Federation of Teachers, and many subject-speciality associations. The beginning teacher who wants to grow will become a member of some of these associations and will build a network of colleagues interested in improving their teaching by keeping abreast of the latest research and practices.

LEARNING ABOUT TEACHING THROUGH EXPERIENCE

A firm grasp of educational research alone will not make someone a skilled and reflective teacher. This is true for two reasons. First, the knowledge produced by educational researchers relates to the way things work in general and not specific cases; whereas the problems faced by teachers in real classrooms are characterized by their uniqueness. The same is true for other professionals, such as doctors, lawyers, and architects, as this observation made by Donald Schön (1983) illustrates:

> The situation of practice is characterized by unique events. Erik Erikson, the psychiatrist, has described each patient as a "universe of one," and an eminent physician has claimed that "85 percent of the problems a doctor sees in his office are not in the book." The unique case calls for an *art of practice* which "might be taught," if it were constant and known, but it is not constant.   (pp. 16–17)

A second reason that research alone cannot guide effective teaching practice is that research knowledge takes many years to produce and, consequently, tends to focus on traditional patterns of practice. The world of teaching, however, calls for new patterns of practice that reflect the complexity, instability, and value conflicts of the present.

Finally, as described earlier, many of the problems facing teachers become problems of values and priorities that scientific knowledge can help explain but cannot help decide. A second observation from Schön (1983) underscores the value-laden world of practicing teachers.

> Practitioners are frequently embroiled in conflicts of values, goals, purposes and interests. Teachers are faced with pressure for increased efficiency in the context of contracting budgets, demands that they rigorously "teach the basics," exhortation to encourage creativity, build citizenship, and help students to examine their values.   (p. 17)

If scientific knowledge cannot provide a complete guide for effective practice, how do practitioners become skilled and competent in what they do? Again Schön (1983) provides valuable insights:

If it is true that there is an irreducible element of art in professional practice, it is also true that gifted engineers, teachers, scientists, architects, and managers sometimes display artistry in their day-to-day practice. If the art is not invariant, known and teachable, it appears nonetheless, at least for some individuals, to be *learnable*.   (p. 18)

Thus, Schön (1983; 1986) takes the position that the art of professional practice is *learnable* and that it is experience, coupled with careful analysis and reflection, that produces this learning. The remainder of this chapter attempts to describe how you can learn from your experiences, whether they are part of your teacher preparation program or a learning agenda you establish for yourself. Three facets of learning from experiences include (1) the nature of experiental learning, (2) developing the receptive skills—listening and observing—that promote learning from experience, and (3) critical review and reflection.

Nature of Experiential Learning

Everyone learns from experience and knows that experience is a basis for new ideas and behavior. For example, you probably learned to ride your first bicycle by riding one, and you learned about being a sister or brother by being one. Similarly, most people have learned a great deal about teaching by the informal teaching they have done in their day-to-day lives. Conversely, even though everyone can read books about marriage and child rearing, those who have married and raised children know that it is never the same as described in the books. Experience provides insights, understandings, and techniques that are difficult to describe to anyone who has not had similar experiences. The same is true for teaching.

Experiential learning differs from much of the learning people are exposed to as students. Instead of starting with a set of academic principles or rules, in experiential learning learners start with concrete experiences, or activities, and then, by observing their own behavior and that of others, formulate concepts and principles that can be applied to new situations. Johnson and Johnson (1975) have conceived experiential learning as a four-stage cycle.

(1) concrete, personal experiences followed by (2) observation of, reflection upon, and examination of one's experiences, which leads to (3) the formulation of abstract concepts and generalizations, which leads to (4) hypotheses to be tested in future action and experience.   (p. 7)

These four stages are portrayed in Figure 2.1.

Dewey (1938) suggested that to learn from experience is to make a backward-forward connection between what we do to things and what we learn from these things and experiences. Johnson and Johnson (1975) have provided a more detailed explanation:

Figure 2.1 Experiential Learning Cycle

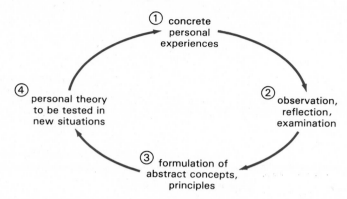

SOURCE: From D. W. Johnson and F. P. Johnson (1975), *Joining together: Group theory and group skills.* 1/e, © 1975, p. 7. Adapted by permission of Prentice-Hall, Inc., Englewood Cliffs, New Jersey.

> Experiential learning is based upon three assumptions: that you learn best when you are personally involved in the learning experience, that knowledge has to be discovered by yourself if it is to mean anything to you or make a difference in your behavior, and that a commitment to learning is highest when you are free to set your own learning goals and actively pursue them within a given framework. Experiential learning is a process of making generalizations and conclusions about your own direct experiences. It emphasizes directly experiencing what you are studying, building your own commitment to learn, and your being partly responsible for organizing the conclusions drawn from your experiences. (p. 7)

Experiential learning is especially useful in complex learning situations such as teaching, which can never be completely described to the beginner. It is also useful for applying many of the skills and guidelines described later in this book.

Experience alone, however, is not sufficient. For best results, the learner must be willing to depend less upon the teacher than in other types of learning. The learner must have a set of "learning skills," that is, must be able to observe and reflect on experiences in order to conceptualize from them. The following sections describe some of these skills in more detail.

Training the Senses for Experiential Learning

People learn from experience primarily through their senses. Two are of particular importance for learning to teach—listening critically and observing keenly. These come together through reflective thinking and analysis.

LISTENING

Learning to listen carefully and pick up subtle cues from experienced, expert teachers is one important skill for those learning to teach. On the surface, listening appears simple but, in fact, it is a rather complex, sophisticated process. Jung (1972) has written that most people strike one of three listening postures when they hear new information or are experiencing a new environment for the first time:

1. **Listening to Confirm** The first listening posture, and by far the most common, is to listen for information that confirms what you already know. Although such information can be important, such a posture is obviously limiting. You may think that a person who says things you already believe is pretty smart, but you don't really learn much from what you hear. If your posture is only to listen for supporting comments, you may actively distort the meanings of what others say.

2. **Listening to Answer Questions** The second listening posture, one which seems fairly rare, is to seek answers to honest questions. When you recognize a discrepancy or dilemma for which you personally need an answer, you can formulate honest questions about it. Often the need for certainty in our lives makes us uncomfortable with honest questions, so we either discredit the questions or seek only superficial answers. If, however, you seek answers to honest questions, you are likely to hear more and differently than those who do not. Honest questions that are not simply critical doubting give direction to listening and new meanings to information. However, questions also have a limiting effect. They tend to limit your attention to information that seems relevant to your questions, a process referred to as selective perception. Also questions invite certain interpretations of information to the exclusion of other possibilities. They tend to create a "set" for understanding.

3. **Listening to Confront** The third listening posture, which is very rare, involves being open to information as a means of creating new insights and perspectives. How many people saw apples fall before Newton conceived the laws of gravity? In a world of continuous, accelerating change and awesome technologies, it is essential that we listen for new understandings and new ways to comprehend our experience. Paradoxically, we simultaneously sense that our ways of experiencing are limited yet believe that the basis for all human understanding already lies within our experiences.

OBSERVING

Although classroom observation is one of the most frequently used ways to learn about teaching, observation alone is insufficient and can, in fact, lead to incorrect conclusions. This is true for several reasons, two of which are most important. First, when you go into a classroom to observe you take with you a whole set of anxieties and biases from past experiences, and, second, life in classrooms is a series of rapidly moving, complex events. Each of these problems is described in more detail in the sections that follow.

Bias and Anxiety You are all aware of many instances in everyday life in which bias and anxiety distort people's perceptions. Note the number of times that victims or eyewitnesses of criminal acts are unable to give investigators a detailed or complete description of the event, even moments after it occurred. Or think of the times that the wrong person is picked out of a police lineup. Think also of the times that you have heard two friends tell you about what they saw on their vacation, and the wide discrepancies in their reports.

Being an eyewitness of classroom events is no different from witnessing other events, except it may be a bit more complicated. Every person in the process of learning to teach has biases that influence what he or she attends to while observing classrooms. These may concern concepts of good teaching or, perhaps, values about what is appropriate behavior for children and young adults. They may be attitudes about classroom life carried over from early experiences as a student—a sense of boredom and withdrawal associated with a grammar lesson or antipathy to a teacher with a gruff voice. The important point is that these concepts, values, attitudes, and past experiences inevitably influence what an observer perceives and learns from classroom observation.

Anxiety is another important influence, particularly for beginning teachers. When people are nervous and anxious in a situation, their vision and perceptual fields tend to narrow, and they miss much that they normally would attend to. When beginning teachers are observers in someone else's classroom, it is natural for them to be unsure and to worry, "Are we intruding on the teacher's lesson? Why are the children looking at us?" Similarly, initial teaching situations are stressful, anxiety producing, uncomfortable. A normal reaction is to distort what is observed and, many times, to ignore threatening information.

Classroom Complexity Finally, it is difficult to observe accurately in classrooms because events move rapidly and the total classroom environment is complex. Philip Jackson (1968) has observed that teachers have literally thousands of independent interactions daily with students—more interactions with clients than occur in any other occupation except perhaps air traffic controlling. Classrooms with teacher aides and ones where teachers have several small groups working simultaneously present even more rapid movement and complexity.

Guidelines for Observing in Classrooms Several things can be done to overcome bias in observation and to reduce the complexity of classroom life. If followed, they can make observations more accurate and more valuable as learning experiences. Several guidelines are offered below that have been found useful by beginning teachers as well as researchers (see, for example, Good and Brophy, 1984).

GUIDELINE 1 Become aware of one's own values, attitudes, and conceptual blinders.

People never become completely aware of the attitudes and prejudices they hold, just as they are never completely aware of the sources of daily fears and anxieties. However, setting aside time now and then for self-reflection and introspection heightens awareness. A learning aid at the end of this chapter poses some questions that foster reflection and introspection.

GUIDELINE 2 Make careful arrangements with teachers prior to observations.

Careful arrangements prior to a visit will relieve some of the anxiety associated with observations in a strange classroom. A talk with the teacher, either in person or over the phone, a few days prior to a visit will help clarify expectations about what you want to accomplish as an observer and about how the teacher wants you to behave during the visit. Arrangements can be made about where you should sit, how you are to be introduced to the class, and so on. A learning aid at the end of this chapter provides a checklist of things to do prior to and following a classroom visit.

GUIDELINE 3 Reduce complexity by focusing observations.

Even the most experienced observers cannot see everything going on in a classroom, so they focus on particular events or behaviors. This is particularly important for the beginner. One does this either by observing a *few of the actors* in the classroom—four or five students rather than the whole class—or watching for a *few behaviors* at a time, such as the way students respond to a teacher's questions or praise. In the learning aid section of this and other chapters several recommendations are provided for focusing classroom observations by reducing complexity.

GUIDELINE 4 Attend only to observable behaviors.

A very common cause of distortion in what a person sees is that too often the observer tries to interpret motives from behavior instead of just observing it. Take, for example, the following written notes from an observation.

The teacher spoke in a loud voice and frowned.

The teacher was angry with the children.

The first is an example of what the observer actually saw. The second is an interpretation of the teacher's feelings. Observers should concentrate on observable behavior, as in the first example.

GUIDELINE 5 Remain unobtrusive during observations.

Harry Walcott, a noted educational anthropologist, says that when he is observing people in any social setting he keeps his eyes on his paper and his pencil going all the time. This is important advice for classroom observers. A note taken once in a while cues teachers and students about what the observer is looking for. Making eye contact with students in class increases the chances of their wanting to interact with the observer, thus interrupting the observer's concentration and perhaps the teacher's lesson.

GUIDELINE 6 Extend a thank you to the teacher and to the students (if appropriate) after your observation.

Observers are guests in classrooms. A thank you is required just as it would be to a friend at whose home you spent a weekend.

Reflecting About Experience

Through reflection experiences become more valuable. It is when teachers start to conceptualize and formulate their own rules and principles that they start to build personal theories that can guide teaching practice and serve as springboards for new discoveries. But how does one begin reflecting? Although reflective thinking is not a haphazard trial-and-error process, neither can it be scheduled to happen every morning at 9:15 A.M., as jogging can be.

One of the most productive ways to foster reflective thinking is by using a journal. Here is advice to beginning teachers provided by Frank Lyman (1983), a teacher educator at the University of Maryland, about how to approach the process of reflection:

> A person learns by experience. However, for the fastest, most advanced learning to take place, disciplined reflection is necessary. Experience is not the best teacher; reflection, or analysis, is. There are many ways to reflect on experience and it is helpful to try out several. During student teaching, you will master one way and be invited to invent others. The journalling strategy is the prescribed way. Use it four times a week. For the fifth entry use any format to probe an issue related to curriculum/instruction/school climate. (If you can invent an effective strategy for analyzing a teaching/learning event, show me.)   (p. 1)

More information about Lyman's reflective journalling strategy is provided in a learning aid at the end of this chapter.

Summary

This chapter stressed that learning to teach is a lifelong process that requires a teacher's active commitment to the role of learner. Many aspects of teaching are knowledge based and can be learned from reading research and networking with colleagues in professional meetings and activities. Other aspects of teaching can be learned only from experience, a difficult task since experience can lead to bad as well as best practice. Beginning teachers can maximize their opportunities to learn from experience by sharpening their listening and observation skills and by learning to be reflective about their own and others' teaching practices.

Books for the Professional

Combs, A. W. (1982). *A personal approach to teaching: Beliefs that make a difference*. Boston: Allyn and Bacon. A very important book discussing why personal beliefs in teaching are important and how beginning teachers can fashion personal approaches to teaching.

Good, T. L., and Brophy, J. E. (1987). *Looking in classrooms*. (Fourth edition). New York: Harper and Row. This book is packed with ideas about teaching and it has numerous observation guides to help teachers see classroom life more clearly.

Lortie, D. C. (1975). *School-teacher: A sociological study*. Chicago: University of Chicago Press. A definitive and provocative book on the nature of teaching and the teaching profession. Although a complicated sociological study, Lortie's book is written so as to be understood by beginning teachers.

Ryan, K., and Cooper, J. M. (1983). *Those who can, teach*. (Fourth edition). Boston: Houghton Mifflin. This text for beginning teachers explores many important topics such as the nature of schools and their place in society. It contains an interesting chapter on the process people go through in becoming teachers.

Schön, D. A. (1983). *The reflective practitioner*. San Francisco: Jossey-Bass. This book explores the complexity of learning to become a professional and emphasizes the importance of developing skills for "reflection in action." Many examples are provided from the professions of teaching, law, medicine, engineering, and business.

───────────────────────────── **CHAPTER 2** ─────────────────────────────
LEARNING AIDS FOR PLANNING, OBSERVATION, AND REFLECTION

- ▪ My Teaching Concerns
- ▪ Teacher Concerns Questionnaire
- ▪ Guidelines for Arranging and Reflecting on Classroom Observations
- ▪ Assessing Your Biases About Students
- ▪ Interviewing Expert and Novice Teachers About Their Agendas
- ▪ Journal Guide and Worksheet

MY TEACHING CONCERNS

PURPOSE: Experience coupled with reflection is a powerful combination for learning. This aid will help you to begin to systematically observe and reflect on teaching.

DIRECTIONS: In the space below keep a log for five days, each day writing a brief paragraph about the concerns you have experienced about teaching or your anticipation of teaching.

Day 1 _____

_____

_____

Day 2 _____

_____

_____

Day 3 _____

_____

_____

Day 4 _____

_____

_____

Day 5 _____

_____

_____

_____

Analysis and Reflection: In the space below write about the common patterns you find in your concerns. Write a paragraph about what your concerns mean to you.

TEACHER CONCERNS QUESTIONNAIRE
BY FRANCES FULLER AND ARCHIE GEORGE

PURPOSE: Learning to teach is a developmental process—people progress through stages, and awareness of the stage you're in can facilitate this process. This aid will help you develop awareness of your level of concern about teaching.

DIRECTIONS: Read each statement, then ask yourself: When I think about my teaching, how much am I concerned about this?

$$1 = \text{Not concerned}$$
$$2 = \text{A little concerned}$$
$$3 = \text{Moderately concerned}$$
$$4 = \text{Very concerned}$$
$$5 = \text{Extremely concerned}$$

Being concerned about something is not the same as thinking it is important. Being concerned means you think about it frequently and would like to do something about it personally. Thus you can be concerned about problems or opportunities, current or anticipated issues, and so on. For each statement mark the number that best corresponds to your level of concern.

1. Lack of instructional materials	1	2	3	4	5
2. Feeling under pressure too much of the time	1	2	3	4	5
3. Doing well when a supervisor is present	1	2	3	4	5
4. Meeting the needs of different kinds of students	1	2	3	4	5
5. Too many noninstructional duties	1	2	3	4	5
6. Diagnosing student learning problems	1	2	3	4	5
7. Feeling more adequate as a teacher	1	2	3	4	5
8. Challenging unmotivated students	1	2	3	4	5
9. Being accepted and respected by professional persons	1	2	3	4	5
10. Working with too many students each day	1	2	3	4	5
11. Guiding students toward intellectual and emotional growth	1	2	3	4	5
12. Whether each student is getting what he needs	1	2	3	4	5
13. Getting a favorable evaluation of my teaching	1	2	3	4	5
14. The routine and inflexibility of the teaching situation	1	2	3	4	5
15. Maintaining the appropriate degree of class control	1	2	3	4	5

Analysis and Reflection: One way to reflect would be to arrange your concerns in order of importance and compare them with those of others. You may think of other ways to help you reflect on your teaching concerns.

SOURCE: Adapted from H. J. Freiberg, J. M. Cooper, and K. Ryan (1980), *Those who can, teach: Learning guide,* 3rd ed., pp. 21–22. Copyright © by Houghton Mifflin Company. Adapted by permission.

GUIDELINES FOR ARRANGING AND REFLECTING ON CLASSROOM OBSERVATIONS

PURPOSE: Making systematic observations in classrooms is a frequently recommended activity in this text. This aid is to help you plan, organize, and carry out classroom observations.

DIRECTIONS: Check off each activity after it is accomplished.

Arranging for Classroom Visit

_____ Called teacher or appropriate person prior to visit

_____ Checked map to ensure timely arrival

_____ Found out time class begins and topic of lesson to view

_____ Decided on classroom actors to observe (teacher, students, few students, aides, etc.)

_____ Decided on behaviors to observe

_____ Collected observational schedule if appropriate

_____ Planned strategy to remain unobtrusive (note taking, seating, avoiding eye contact with students)

_____ Prepared a note to the teacher and class thanking them for the visit

Summary of Observation (brief summary of behaviors, not motives)

_____

_____

_____

_____

Analysis and Reflection: What questions have been answered? What questions have been raised?

ASSESSING YOUR BIASES ABOUT STUDENTS

PURPOSE: All of us hold conscious and unconscious biases about other people. Critical to your success as a teacher is your ability to become conscious of these biases, to understand how they influence your perception and learning, and to modify them if necessary. This aid will help you uncover your biases about students.

DIRECTIONS:

1. Spend several minutes getting oriented to the classroom and the students; get a "feel" for the students. (Or observe in a room where you already know the students.)
2. Select two contrasting groups, from the list below, for study (e.g., group (a) and group (b), or group (a) and group (c), etc.).
   a. Two students with whom you most enjoy working (positive feelings).
   b. Two students whom you dislike the most (negative feelings).
   c. Two students for whom you have no strong feeling whatsoever (indifferent feelings).
   d. Two students (one boy, one girl) who best represent the child you would want your son or daughter to be like at this age (identification). Note: Do not select this group with group (a), as both deal with positive feelings; pick contrasting pairs.
3. Observe the four students you have selected closely during class activities. It is a good idea to keep notes, and if you do, be sure to mask the identities of the students. Keep in mind the following questions as you observe:
   a. What are the students like physically? Do they have nice clothes? Are they attractive? What makes them so? Are they clean? Are they large or small for their age? Male or female?
   b. What are their favorite subjects? What lessons bore them? What are their strong and weak points as students? As persons?
   c. What are their most prominent behavior characteristics? Do they smile a lot? Do they thank you for your attention? Do they seek you out in the classroom—more or less than the average student? Do they raise their hands to answer often? Can they be depended upon to do their own work? How mature are they? Are they awkward or clumsy?
   d. What are their social characteristics and what socioeconomic level do they come from? What is their ethnic background?
4. Pinpoint the similarities and differences among the four students. It's often helpful in doing this sort of analysis to construct a grid or a table, with the students' characteristics along one dimension and the students' names along the other dimension. Here is an example:

Name	M/F	Characteristics		
		Shy/Outspoken	Cute/Plain	Self-Starter/Needs Help
Amy	F	S	P	NH
Irv	M	O	P	NH
Jim	M	O	C	SS
Dot	F	S	C	SS

It is easy to see patterns when information is laid out this way. In this example, it is clear that neither the sex nor the shyness of the child matters to the teacher. What does matter is how cute the child is and whether or not the child needs the teacher's help.

Analysis and Reflection: Construct your own grid, as in the example above, to analyze your own biases. This analysis should provide you with clues regarding the types of student behavior that are likely to touch off positive and negative responses in you. You will then be in a better position to understand why you behave as you do, and be better equipped to change your behavior in order to facilitate more positive interaction with students who irritate you. Write a paragraph about what your biases are and how you will guard against their interfering with your teaching.

SOURCE: Adapted from T. L. Good and J. E. Brophy (1984), *Looking in classrooms.* New York: Harper and Row, pp. 53–54.

INTERVIEWING EXPERT AND NOVICE TEACHERS
ABOUT THEIR AGENDAS

PURPOSE: Expert and novice teachers differ. Understanding these differences can help the novice develop expertise. This aid will help you to gain insight into the nature of the differences between expert and novice teachers' agendas.

DIRECTIONS: Following Leinhardt's procedure as discussed in the chapter, interview one expert experienced teacher and one student teacher just before each begins a lesson. Then observe the lesson.

For the expert experienced teacher:

What are you going to do today? _____

_____

_____

_____

What do you expect will happen in the lesson? _____

_____

_____

_____

For the novice student teacher:

What are you going to do today? _____

_____

_____

_____

What do you expect will happen in the lesson? _____

_____

_____

_____

Analysis and Reflection: For each teacher, record the following information about each feature of his or her agenda:

Feature	Expert	Novice
Number of lines of response	_____	_____
Number of references to student actions	_____	_____
Number of check points for understanding	_____	_____
Number of references to instructional actions	_____	_____
Number of references to the logical connections between instructional actions and the lesson as a whole	_____	_____

What differences did you observe between the expert and the novice in the actual

performance of the lesson? _____

_____

_____

What differences in student behavior or learning did you observe? _____

_____

_____

What connection do you see between how these teachers were thinking prior to

their lessons and the success of their lessons? _____

_____

_____

SOURCE: Adapted from G. Leinhardt (in press), Math lessons: A contrast of novice and expert competence. Journal for Research in Mathematics Education. Used with permission of the author.

JOURNAL GUIDE AND WORKSHEET

PURPOSE: To facilitate reflection on and learning from experience.

DIRECTIONS: A person learns by experience. However, for the fastest, most advanced learning to take place, disciplined reflection is necessary. Experience is not the best teacher; reflection or analysis is. There are many ways to reflect on experience. It is helpful to try out several. Start with the following strategy and use it for one week. When you make a journal entry, try to include content from each category.

Model for Journal Strategy

Content	Example
Brief description of teaching/learning event	A small group discussion on . . . in which I . . . the children . . . connected to literature.
Some consequences (effects, outcomes) of the event	Very few listened to directions . . . Most were on task in the pair talk . . . About 60% got the concept.
Value (worthiness of outcomes and projected outcomes)	It is important for children to consider connections between themselves and book characters, because . . .
Some causes of success and/or failure	Interaction pattern Relevance (stories they like) Zoning (seating arrangements) Social considerations (pairing) Abstract/concrete
Some next steps	Allow free pattern of talk Maintain relevant examples Change seating Reduce potential friction in pairing Connect examples to ideas
Some hypothetical principles	If pairs are allowed to speak freely, both individuals will talk more in pairs. People learn those things they can connect to their own experience. Extreme extroverts will show off less when seated in less central positions. The more that pairing in a group is made of friends, the easier it is to manage the pair mode. Learning of concepts proceeds best when sufficient concrete examples are connected to an abstract idea.
Analogs, if any	This event reminds me of what happened in a Sunday School class . . .

Questions for inquiry

What is the difference in involvement when pairs talk freely as opposed to when they follow a certain interaction pattern?

What happens during directions when children have eye contact with each other?

SOURCE: Adapted from F. Lyman (1983), Journalling procedures, Mimeographed. College Park, Md., University of Maryland.

Understanding Research

Chapters 1 and 2 described how educational research supports the practice of teaching and frees teachers from an overreliance on the "common sense" and "rules of thumb" approaches of earlier eras. Like other complex human activities, research has its own set of rules and a specialized language that can be very confusing to the novice. Learning to learn from research requires some understanding of the methods and language used by researchers. Whereas a broad understanding of educational research is obviously beyond the scope of this book, certain key concepts that are important for reading and understanding research studies are presented here.

KEY CONCEPTS

Research Problems and Questions

Researchers strive to find answers to *problems* by posing particular types of *questions*. Their definition of a problem, however, differs from the common usage of that term. A researchable problem, according to one educational researcher (Kerlinger, 1964), has three ingredients: (1) it is clearly stated in question form; (2) it focuses on relationships between two or more variables; and (3) it implies the possibility of testing (pp. 19–20). Practical problems, on the other hand, although sometimes stated in question form, rarely focus on relationships that can be tested. Instead, they normally strive to state a descrepancy between the "way things are" and the way the problem solver would like them to be. To show the difference between a practical problem faced by teachers and a researchable problem posed by researchers, consider two types of questions that might be asked about student motivation. A teacher might ask a practical question, such as "How can I get my unmotivated students to do their homework each night?" A researcher might ask a researchable question, such as "What are the effects of two different reward systems (free time in school versus parental praise) on time devoted to homework by unmotivated students?" Both problems are clearly stated in question form, but only the latter focuses on relationships among variables and has a built-in procedure for empirical testing.

Figure S1.1 Dunkin and Biddle Model for the Study of Classroom Teaching

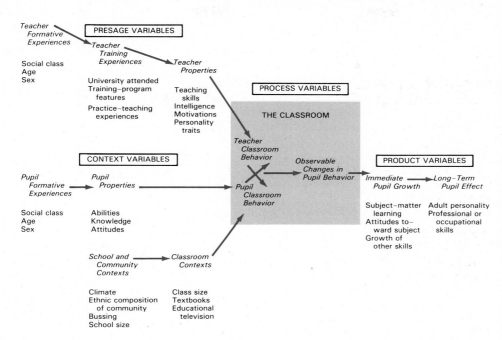

SOURCE: From M. J. Duncan and B. J. Biddle (1974), *The study of teaching*. New York: Holt, Rinehart and Winston, p. 38. Used with permission of the publisher.

Research Variables

When educational researchers study problems they normally do so by thinking about variables within a particular situation that can help explain relationships and causation. A research *variable* is a characteristic of a person (teacher, student, parent) or of some aspect of the environment (classroom, home, school) than can vary. Essentially, researchers try to sort out what goes with and influences what in the very complex environment of teaching and learning. They are also interested in arranging these variables into models that can explain teaching more fully. Much of the research during the last few decades has come from researchers who think about variables in a way similar to that shown in the model provided by Dunkin and Biddle (1974), displayed in Figure S1.1.

As can be observed, this model organizes 12 sets of variables into four larger classes that were first named by Mitzel (1960):

1. *Presage variables* These variables refer to the characteristics of teachers, namely their experiences, their training, and special properties they have such as skills and motivations.
2. *Context variables* These variables refer to the environment to which teachers must adjust, such as students' formative experiences, prior knowledge, students' abilities, and school, community, and classroom characteristics.
3. *Process variables* These variables refer to the activities and procedures that occur in classrooms. They are variables associated with what teachers and students do. Process variables are those of most concern in this book.
4. *Product variables* These variables refer to the outcomes of teaching and classroom interaction. They have been divided into two subsets by Dunkin and Biddle—immediate pupil growth and long-term effects. Two very important outcomes most teachers are concerned with are academic achievement and self-esteem.

Other researchers have developed models that differ from Dunkin and Biddle's, but the essential variables and their arrangement are the same. Notice the arrows in the model. These are provided to show the presumed causative relationships among the variables. It is important to point out, however, as do Dunkin and Biddle (1974), that "each arrow is but a source of hypotheses and not a symbol of invariant truth." As they explain:

> For example, let us assume that teachers who come from middle-class backgrounds are known to approach pupils somewhat differently than those with lower-class backgrounds. Does this mean that social class "causes" differential classroom behavior? Indeed this interpretation might be correct. But it might also be true that teachers who come from middle and lower-class backgrounds are more likely to attend different colleges and thus to have had different experiences in teacher training; this latter factor, then, would be the actual cause of their different behaviors in the classroom. (p. 37)

INDEPENDENT AND DEPENDENT VARIABLES

When you read the research on teaching summarized in this book and elsewhere, you will often come across words independent and dependent variable. These are words used by researchers to describe a particular aspect of the variables they are studying. Strictly speaking, *independent variable* refers to a property that is the presumed *cause* of something, whereas *dependent variable* is the *consequence*. In the study of teaching, variables associated with teacher behavior (causes) are normally important independent variables and student self-esteem or achievement (consequences) are important dependent variables.

You will read in subsequent chapters how knowledge about teaching is really knowledge about the relationships among the many independent and dependent variables in the model displayed in Figure S1.1, and that many of the relationships that appear to exist are only tentative and are always open to alternative interpretations. Subsequent chapters will also point out that an enterprise as complex as teaching does not always fall neatly into the models devised by researchers.

APPROACHES TO EDUCATIONAL RESEARCH

Educational researchers use several methods to study problems related to teaching and learning. The critical differences between the various approaches include: (1) the ways researchers design their studies, (2) the ways they collect information, and (3) the means they use to interpret their results. Three of the most common approaches are described briefly in the following section.

Descriptive Research

Most of you can readily cite examples of descriptive research, not only in the field of education but also in noneducational fields. Hardly a day goes by that one cannot pick up a newspaper and read the results of a survey someone has done. A survey is one type of descriptive research. Researchers using this approach commonly use questionnaires or interviews to gather information about the characteristics of some phenomenon or they measure people's opinions or attitudes on some subject.

Although it is difficult to do "good" survey research, the results of such research are easily understood. In most cases the results are presented numerically and describe the number and percentage of people who have a specific characteristic or who believe in a particular way. The part of Lortie's study summarized in Chapter 2 is an example of one type of survey research. In this instance, information was collected by interview on why people chose to go into teaching. The well-known yearly survey conducted by Gallup to get citizens' opinion about the schools is another example of survey research.

Sometimes researchers using the descriptive approach are interested in a type of problem that can best be studied through direct observation of a single case or a small number of cases. These approaches take the form of case studies or, in some instances, ethnographies. *Ethnography* is a word that comes from the field of anthropology and means an extensive study of an intact group of people, such as a culture, a society, or a particular role group. Normally what the researcher does when conducting this type of research is to select from many possibilities what might be called a typical case, and then to conduct in-depth observations of that single case. The aim of a case study, or an ethnography, is to collect extensive information so that a rich description and an in-depth understanding of the research problem will result. Examples of this type of research would include the work of anthropologists such as Margaret Mead, who lived with and studied the people in Samoa to discover some of the important underlying patterns of that culture; or the work of Jean Piaget, who conducted in-depth case studies of children to discover how a young child's mind develops and grows.

Normally researchers using observational techniques must get quite close to the subjects they are studying. In fact, some become participants themselves and try to influence the problems they are studying. Seymour Sarason's work (summarized in Chapter 12) is an example of a researcher who studied the implementation of the "new math" while he was also helping teachers improve their schools.

As contrasted to collecting information using questionnaires or interviews, observation allows the researcher to study the point of view of a group or person and, in turn, to construct a more complete picture of the situation. A weakness of this type of research, however, is that the researcher is only studying a single or small number of cases. Readers or users of this research must always ask how typical or representative the researcher's case was and whether the researcher's conclusions would hold up in other cases or in other settings.

Experimental Research

A second approach to research in education is the *experiment*. Most readers are already familiar with the basic logic and procedures of this approach through their high school and college science and social science classes. The results of this type of research are also frequently reported in the mass media.

The experimental study of teaching involves procedures in which the researcher, instead of describing or studying variables as they exist naturally in the world, sets up conditions so specified variables can be manipulated. Although there are over a dozen variations of educational experiments, the classical approach is for the researcher to perform three important acts: (1) to establish two groups believed to be the same; (2) to give one group (the experimental group) a special treatment and withhold the treatment from the other (the control group); and (3) to compare some measurable feature of the two groups to see if the treatment made any difference.

True experiments are difficult to do in education because many of the problems teachers and researchers are interested in are not amenable to experiments for either logistical or ethical reasons. When they can be done, however, experiments produce powerful results because they allow the researcher to draw conclusions about cause-and-effect relationships among variables. The educational problems most amenable to experimental manipulations are those associated with particular models and methods of teaching. This can be seen in the number of studies using experimental approaches summarized in Part 3.

Correlational Research

Because so many aspects of teaching and learning cannot be studied experimentally, a third major research approach is often employed. *Correlational research* is used when the researcher explores the relationships between two or more variables that exist naturally and trys to sort out what goes with what. This approach is also familiar to most of you. Take, for example, the now well-known correlational studies showing strong relationships between cigarette smoking and certain diseases. Over many years, medical researchers have shown that people who smoke have a higher incidence of lung cancer and heart attacks than nonsmokers have. Nonetheless, the cause-and-effect relationship remains experimentally unproven because of the ethics of setting up a true experiment in which members of one group would be given a treatment that might lead to their deaths. Much of the research on effective teaching is also correlational research. For example, the many studies that show strong relationships between certain features of classroom management and student learning are nearly all correlational.

In the study of teaching, the researcher is normally interested in finding relationships between some type of teacher behavior and student learning. Although very useful in education, it is important to keep in mind that correlational research does not establish cause and effect among variables, only relationships. More will be said about this later.

STATISTICAL CONCEPTS AND RESEARCH CONVENTIONS

The vast majority of educational research involves measuring individual or group traits that produce quantitative data. Over the years researchers have developed statistical procedures to help organize, analyze, and interpret their data. To read and to use research requires an understanding of some of the basic procedures and agreed-upon conventions used by researchers. There is nothing magic about statistics or about symbols used by researchers. They are merely a means to communicate clearly and objectively. They may, however, appear mysterious to the novice. Brief descriptions of several key ideas can help beginning teachers understand research and perhaps motivate further study.

Sampling

Since it is obviously impossible to study all teachers or all students, educational researchers must, out of necessity, confine their studies to a small portion, or *sample*, of a total population. An example of this technique is the sampling done by Nielsen to find out which TV shows people watch. From the millions of viewers at a given programming hour, Nielsen polls 1,500 to 2,000 persons selected from known segments of the viewing population. Users of the Nielsen ratings accept the results because they know that what the sample is watching represents (more or less) the habits of the total viewing audience.

The way a sample is selected is very important because, if it does not accurately represent the intended larger population, the results will obviously be biased. A famous mistake in sampling occurred in the 1948 presidential election when a sample of citizens drawn from telephone directories across the country the night before the election indicated that Thomas Dewey, the Republican candidate, would be elected. The next day, however, Harry Truman, the Democratic candidate, was elected. Upon analysis the polling firm discovered that in 1948 many voters still did not have telephones and those without phones, who could not be included in the sample, were more prone to vote Democratic. Drawing a sample from the telephone directory was not appropriate if the pollsters wanted to know what the total population of voters was going to do. When reading reports of educational research, it is important to study carefully the sampling techniques used by the researcher.

Randomness

The concept *randomness* is also very important in educational research. Normally random sampling or random assignment to groups means that individuals in any population have an equal chance of being selected for study. In survey research, this means that the researcher strives to define the total population of people he or she is going to study and then decides by chance which ones will be chosen for study. In experiments where one group is to receive a special treatment and the other to serve as a control, the researcher is careful that subjects are assigned to one of the two groups on a random basis. The logic behind random sampling or random assignment to groups is that by using this procedure the sample or the groups under investigation will have the same characteristics. This, however, is not always the case. For example, just as there is a chance, although very small, of flipping heads in a coin toss 100 times in a row, there is also always a chance that a random sample will indeed not represent the total population or that two groups assigned at random will differ from one another in important ways.

Numbers and Conventions

Researchers also use certain conventions to organize and report the results of their work to others.

MEAN SCORES

In many of the research studies summarized in this book as well as elsewhere, researchers report mean scores that allow comparison of one group with another. A *mean score* is nothing more than an average score and is calculated by adding all scores and dividing by the number of cases. The reporting convention of researchers is to use the symbol $\bar{X}$ or M to designate the mean score and the symbol N to communicate to readers the number of cases used to compute a particular mean. Mean scores are used to perform many of the statistical tests used in educational research.

STANDARD DEVIATION

Standard deviation is another statistic that provides information about a set of scores. This statistic, found in many data tables, indicates the spread of a particular set of scores from the mean. Differences in means as well as differences in standard deviation are used to compute tests of statistical significance.

CORRELATION AND CORRELATION COEFFICIENTS

Correlation expresses the degree to which a relationship exists between two or more variables. Familiar examples would be the relationship between student I.Q. and student achievement, or the relationship between particular teaching behaviors (keeping students on task) and student achievement. Another might be the relationship between a person's height and his or her performance on the basketball court.

To express these relationships in mathematical terms, researchers use a statistic called the *correlation coefficient*. A correlation coefficient can range from $+1.00$ through $.00$ to -1.00. The sign does not have the traditional mathematical meaning. Instead, a plus sign represents a positive relationship, a minus sign a negative relationship. Thus, *.00* means no relationship exists, *+1.00* means a perfect relationship exists, and *−1.00* means a perfect reverse relationship exists. As will be observed in many of the studies summarized in this book, few instances are found in education (or any other aspect of human behavior) where perfect positive or reverse relationships exist.

As described earlier, an important thing to remember about correlational studies and correlational coefficients is that even though they may show relationships among variables, they do not explain cause and effect. As an example, many studies show a positive relationship between students' time on task and academic achievement. Consequently, it is assumed that teachers who can keep students on task more will produce superior scores on achievement tests. Although this may be true, the time-on-task principle could be turned around. It could be logically argued that it is not time on task that produces achievement, but instead it is high-achieving students who produce high time-on-task ratios.

TESTS OF SIGNIFICANCE

In any research on human behavior there is always the possibility that a specific outcome is the result of chance instead of some presumed relationship that is being studied. Researchers have developed a procedure called the *test of statistical significance* to help decide whether research results are indeed true or perhaps a matter of chance. Several different tests of significance occur in the research reports found in subsequent chapters. The main idea to remember is that when researchers use the word *significance* they are using it differently than in common usage, where it normally means *important*. In the language of researchers, *significance* means the degree of truth rather than chance that they assign to their results. In general, researchers agree that differences between two sets of scores are statistically significant if they could occur by chance only 1 to 5 times out of 100. When you read the research reports in this text you will often see the notation $p<.01$ or $p<.05$. This means that the probability (p) of such results could occur by chance less than ($<$) 1 time out of 100 (.01) or 5 times out of 100 (.05).

READING A RESEARCH REPORT: AN EXAMPLE

It is time now to see if you can apply these research concepts to an actual research report. The following pages summarize research done by Wayne Hoy. Hoy was studying the general problem of how people learn to be teachers and what influence prior experience has on that learning. Read the summary of Hoy's study carefully and see if you can answer the following questions:

1. Is Hoy's study an example of descriptive, experimental, or correlational research?
2. What two variables were studied? Which variable is the independent variable? Which is the dependent variable?
3. Where would Hoy's variables fit in the Dunkin and Biddle research model?
4. What is the nature of Hoy's sample?
5. How did Hoy use the mean statistic? From studying the mean scores and tests of statistical significance, what conclusions would you draw?
6. Based on your conclusion, what might you say about the impact of experience on teaching and how might this influence your own experiences?
7. What are the limitations of Hoy's study?

Summary

This special topic section on understanding research has highlighted the importance of educational research and provided very brief descriptions of three main approaches to research on teaching: descriptive study, experimental study, and correlational research. Key concepts and research conventions were also described. Although educational research is a complex subject, the introduction provided here will help you read and understand the research summaries presented throughout this text. Hopefully, you will also use it as a springboard for further study of this important topic.

Books for the Professional

Borg, W. R., and Gall, M. D. (1983). *Educational research: An introduction.* (Fourth edition). New York: Longman. Although this book was intended for more advanced students, the clarity of the authors' style makes many chapters understandable and useful to the beginning teacher who is just learning how to read research.

Katzer, J., Cook, K. H., and Crouch, W. W. (1982). *Evaluating information: A guide for users of social science research.* (Second edition). Reading, Mass.: Addison-Wesley. A good nontechnical presentation of how to evaluate research, including an evaluation guide and set of questions to ask when reading a research article.

━━━━━━━━━━ RESEARCH SUMMARY ━━━━━━━━━━
S1.1

Hoy, W. K. (1968). The influence of experience on the beginning teacher. *School Review, 76,* 312–323.

PROBLEM: Hoy was interested in the degree to which teaching experience influenced beginning teachers, particularly the way beginners control students. The specific question he posed for his research was: What is the relationship between teaching experience and the pupil control ideology (PCI) of beginning teachers?

SAMPLE AND SETTING: Hoy studied 82 elementary and 93 secondary student teachers at Oklahoma State University. This sample was essentially all the student teachers at the university during the term in which Hoy started his study.

PROCEDURES: Hoy developed a 20-item instrument to measure how humanitarian versus custodial (authoritarian) beginning teachers were in their pupil control ideology. Examples of items included: "A few pupils are just young hoodlums and should be treated accordingly"; "It is often necessary to remind pupils that their status in schools differs from that of the teachers"; and "Pupils can be trusted to work together without supervision." This instrument produced a mean score. High mean scores meant the teacher was more custodial or authoritarian; more humanitarian teachers had lower mean scores. All subjects completed Hoy's questionnaire three times—just prior to student teaching, again after the completion of student teaching, and one year later. One year later found some subjects teaching in public schools, some in graduate school serving as graduate teaching assistants, and others who had decided not to go into teaching.

RESULTS: Table 1 shows the results of Hoy's study. Note that Hoy reports his results using mean scores. The symbol *t* and the number found in the last column stand for the test of significance used by Hoy.

TABLE 1 A Comparison of the Pupil Control Ideology of Teachers Before and After Student Teaching and After the First Year of Teaching

Position	N	Experience	PCI Mean Score	t
Public school teachers	116	Before student teaching	44.56	—
		After student teaching	48.93	6.569*
		After first year teaching	51.48	3.783*
Graduate assistants	7	Before student teaching	43.86	—
		After student teaching	48.00	2.008
		After first year teaching	43.14	2.303
Not teaching	39	Before student teaching	44.80	—
		After student teaching	47.31	2.404*
		One year later	47.05	.270

* Significant at the .01 level of confidence ($p < .01$).
SOURCE: W. K. Hoy (1968), p. 317.

(cont'd)

━━━━━━━━━━━━━━━ **RESEARCH SUMMARY** ━━━━━━━━━━━━━━━
S1.1 (continued)

DISCUSSION AND IMPLICATIONS:

  1. Hoy's study is an example of descriptive research. Even though he measures attitudes at three points in time, he does not manipulate the independent variables (experimental research) nor does he use correlation coefficients to look at the relationships under investigation.

  2. The independent variable in Hoy's study was experience; the dependent variable was attitude toward pupil control.

  3. Hoy was studying the relationships between a particular presage variable ˙ (teacher experience) and a process variable (teacher classroom behavior).

  4. Hoy's sample was confined to the total population of student teachers at one university at one point in time.

  5. A study of the mean scores of the beginning teachers at three points in time provides a fairly convincing argument that experience does influence beginning teachers' attitudes toward student control and in a significant way. However, experience does not always teach what is desired. For example, beginning teachers in Hoy's study became more custodial (authoritarian) toward their students as they gained more experience and lost some of the humanistic qualities and idealism that most people would desire in teachers.

  6. For the people who did not go into teaching, their PCI stayed the same after student teaching. The lesson from this research drawn by Hoy is that the culture of schools is very powerful and moves beginning teachers toward more custodial and authoritarian attitudes. If a beginning teacher wants to embrace humanistic norms regarding pupil control, it is probably important that during student teaching and the first year that beginners seek out experienced teachers who value and demonstrate these qualities.

  7. One has to be careful about the results of Hoy's study. Hoy himself stated in his report that the results of this study should be interpreted with some care because the sample came from only one university and had a high proportion of female teachers in the group of teachers completing their first year of teaching. In other words, Hoy is warning readers that what he found may be true for female teachers in Oklahoma and not in other places.

  You may be interested to know that since this study Hoy, and others, have found similar results in other parts of the country and with different samples.

PART 2

This section of *Learning to Teach* is about the executive functions of teaching. Teachers, like executives in other settings, are expected to provide leadership to students and to coordinate a variety of activities as they and students work interdependently to accomplish the academic and social goals of schooling. The executive functions of teachers are critical because if students are not motivated to participate in and persist with academic learning tasks, or if they are not managed effectively, all the rest of teaching can be lost. Yet these complex functions must be performed in classrooms characterized by fast-moving events and a large degree of unpredictability, and unlike many of the instructional functions of teaching that can be planned ahead of time, most of the executive functions require on-the-spot judgments.

This section focuses on four important executive functions: planning, allocating scarce resources, building productive learning environments, and managing classroom groups. Even though each function is described and discussed separately, in the real day-to-day life of teaching the distinctions are not nearly so tidy. When teachers plan, as described in Chapter 3, they are also setting conditions for allocating time and building productive learning environments, the subjects of Chapters 4 and 5. The way students behave and how they are managed on any particular day, the focus of Chapter 6, cycles back to influence future plans and resource allocation decisions.

There is a substantial knowledge base on each of the executive functions that can provide a guide for effective practice. There is also considerable wisdom that has been accumulated by teachers over the years to help beginning teachers get started with learning to plan, to allocate resources, and to deal with students in group settings. Information from both of these sources is presented and discussed.

You will discover as you read and reflect on the executive functions of teaching that providing leadership in classrooms is no easy matter and cannot be reduced to simple recipes. Instead, leadership is tightly connected to specific classrooms and schools, and what works in general may not work in any specific case. Learning to read specific situations and to act on them effectively in real classrooms is one of the most important challenges facing beginning teachers. When mastered, this is a most rewarding ability.

The Executive Functions of Teaching

CHAPTER 3

MAIN IDEAS

- Planning for teaching is one of the most important functions of teaching and one that is hidden from public view.
- The traditional view of planning is based on rational-linear models characterized by setting goals and taking specific actions to accomplish desired outcomes.
- New perspectives on planning put more emphasis on planners' actions.
- Research shows that planning can enhance student motivation, help focus student learning, and decrease classroom management problems. It shows, too, that experienced and beginning teachers plan differently.
- Teachers must attend to planning cycles and in addition to daily planning must plan for weeks, months, and a full year.
- Critical aspects of planning include choosing content, selecting activity structures, establishing routine procedures, and building group morale and cohesion.

Planning for Instruction

Even though planning and making decisions about instruction are demanding processes that call for rather sophisticated understanding and skills, a beginning teacher does not have to feel overwhelmed. Most of you have planned trips that required complicated travel arrangements. You have planned college schedules, made to-do lists, and survived externally imposed deadlines for term papers and final examinations. Graduation celebrations and weddings are other events most people have experienced that require planning skills of a high caliber. Planning for teaching may be a bit more complex, but the skills you already have can serve as a foundation on which to build.

This chapter describes some of what is known about the processes of teacher planning and decision making. The rationale and knowledge base on planning, particularly the impact of planning on student learning and on the overall flow of classroom life, are described, as are the processes experienced teachers use to plan and make decisions. Also included is a rather detailed explanation of specific planning procedures and a number of aids and techniques used for planning in education and other fields. The discussion that follows strives to capture the complexity of teacher planning and decision making and to show how these function are performed by teachers under conditions of uncertainty. Although the chapter's emphasis is on the planning tasks carried out by teachers in solitude prior to instruction, attention is also given to the varied in-flight decisions teachers make in the midst of lessons.

PERSPECTIVE AND RATIONALE

People today express great confidence in their ability to control events through sophisticated planning. The importance given to planning is illustrated by the many special occupational rules that have been created for just this purpose. For example, a professional cadre of land-use planners, marketing specialists, systems analysts, and strategic planners, to name a few, work full time putting together detailed, long-range plans to influence and direct the economy, control industrial output, stimulate manpower production, and assure appropriate military offensive and defensive initiatives. Family planning, financial planning, and career planning are topics taught to students in high schools and universities and to adults in many settings. The skills associated with these topics are deemed important and become commonplace to many adults.

Thinking about and conducting research on the teacher's role as a planner has recently gained attention in education. It is motivated by the same assumptions that inspire a wish to understand planning in other areas of life—namely, the drive to control what happens through purposeful, organized activities that lead to targeted outcomes. Planning and decision making are vital to teaching and interact with all the other executive functions of teachers. One measure of the importance of planning is illustrated when you consider the amount of time teachers spend on this activity. Clark and Yinger (1979), for example, report that teachers estimate they spend between 10 percent and 20 percent of their working time each week on planning activities. The importance of planning is illustrated in another way when you consider the wide variety of educational activities affected by the plans and decisions made by teachers as described by Clark and Lampert (1986):

> Teacher planning is a major determinate of what is taught in schools. The curriculum as published is transformed and adapted in the planning process by additions, deletions, interpretations, and by teacher decisions about pace, sequence, and emphasis. And in elementary classrooms, where a teacher is responsible for all subject matter areas, planning decisions about what to teach, how long to devote to each topic, and how much practice to provide takes on additional significance and complexity. Other functions of teacher planning include allocating instructional time for individuals and groups of students, composing student groupings, organizing daily, weekly, and term schedules, compensating for interruptions from outside the classroom and communicating with substitute teachers. (p. 28)

Planning—The Traditional View

The planning process in all fields, including education, has been described and studied by many researchers and theorists. The dominant perspective that guides most of the thinking and action on this topic has been referred to as the *rational-linear model*. This perspective puts the focus on goals and objectives as the first step in a sequential process. Modes of action and specific activities are then selected from available alternatives to accomplish prespecified ends. The model assumes a close connection between those who set goals and objectives and those charged with carrying them out. It also assumes that the social environments for which plans are made are somewhat static over time and that an information base can be established to show the degree to which goals and objectives have been accomplished. Figure 3.1 illustrates the basic linear planning model.

This model owes its theoretical base to planners and thinkers in many fields. In education the basic concepts are normally associated with early curriculum

Figure 3.1   Linear Planning Model

GOALS ─────────────→ ACTIONS ─────────────→ OUTCOMES

planners and theorists, such as Ralph Tyler (1950), and with later instructional designers, such as Mager (1962), Popham and Baker (1970), and Gagné and Briggs (1979). For both groups, good educational planning is characterized by carefully specified instructional objectives (normally stated in behavioral terms), teaching actions and strategies designed to promote prescribed objectives, and careful measurement of outcomes, particularly student achievement.

Planning—An Alternative Perspective

During the last decade many observers (Clark et al. 1981, for example) have questioned whether the rational-linear model accurately describes planning in the real world. Its view that organizations and classrooms are goal driven has been challenged, as has its view that actions can be carried out with great precision in a world characterized by complexity, change, and uncertainty. For example, Weick (1979) observed the following about organizational goals and goal-based planning:

> Organizational actions at best seem to be goal-interpreted. Goals are sufficiently diverse, the future is sufficiently uncertain, and the actions on which goal statements should center are sufficiently unclear that goal statements explain a relatively small portion of the variance in action. It is probable that goals are tied more closely to actual activities than is commonly recognized and that they are more productively understood as *summaries of previous actions*. (p. 239)

Weick's model for planning and the relationship of goals to actions could be illustrated as in Figure 3.2.

Note that Weick turns the rational-linear model found in Figure 3.1 upside down. He argues that what planners really do is to start with actions that in turn produce outcomes (some anticipated, some not), and finally they summarize and explain their actions by assigning goals to them. Proponents of this model of planning argue that plans do not necessarily serve as guides for actions, but instead become symbols, advertisements, and justifications for what people have already done. As will be shown later, this model probably describes the way many experienced teachers actually approach some aspects of planning. Although they set goals and strive to get a sense of direction for themselves and their students, teachers' planning proceeds in a cyclical, not a straight linear fashion with a great

Figure 3.2   Nonlinear Planning Model

ACTIONS ─────────────→ OUTCOMES ─────────────→ GOALS

deal of trial and error built into the process. Indeed, experienced teachers pay attention to features of both the linear and nonlinear aspects of planning and accommodate both.

SAMPLING THE RESEARCH BASE

The research on teacher planning and decision making is substantial and has grown significantly in the past two decades. It provides teachers with insights about the effects of planning on students. It also provides critical information about how experienced teachers approach planning and how environmental cues influence their in-flight decisions. The studies summarized in this section have been selected to represent the work of several major researchers in the field of teacher planning and decision making. They also illustrate the complexity of teacher planning and how certain kinds of planning can produce unanticipated and surprising results.

Consequences of Planning

Both theory and common sense suggest that planning for any kind of activity improves results. Research also favors instructional planning over undirected events and activities, but as you will see, some types of planning may lead to unexpected results.

The literature in the fields of both management and education suggests that planning that leads to shared understanding and acceptance of clear and attainable goals enhances employee or student performance. David McClelland and his colleagues (1958;1961;1965), who have studied motivation for many years, take the position that all people, including children, are motivated toward action in the quest to fill three basic needs: the need to have influence, to experience affiliation with others, and to achieve. Achievement appears to be the dominant motivation, particularly in our society, and the one that has been most studied. It is also the one most important to discussions of teacher planning because the need for achievement is satisfied in students when they work toward and reach challenging, but attainable, goals.

Planning processes initiated by teachers can give both students and teachers a sense of direction and help students become aware of the goals that are implicit in the learning tasks they are asked to perform. Two important studies done at about at the same time highlight the effects of planning on teacher behavior and its consequence for students. The first study, conducted by Duchastel and Brown, shows how instructional objectives help focus student learning and lead to better achievement. This study is described in Research Summary 3.1.

John Zahorik (1970), working about the same time as Duchastel and Brown, was interested in the effects of planning on *teacher behavior*, particularly planning behaviors associated with identifying objectives, diagnosing student learning, and choosing instruction strategies. He wanted to find out if teachers who planned lessons were less sensitive to pupils in the classroom than teachers who did not plan.

Zahorik studied 12 fourth-grade teachers from four suburban schools near Milwaukee, Wisconsin. The 12 teachers in the study were randomly divided into two groups designated "teachers who planned" and "teachers who did not plan." Teachers in the planning group were given a lesson plan with objectives and a detailed outline on the topic *credit cards*. They were asked to use it with their classes. Teachers in the nonplanning group were asked to reserve an hour of classroom time to carry out some unknown task—the task later to be announced as teaching about credit cards. All lessons were tape-recorded and teacher behaviors were coded using a system designed to categorize the teachers' sensitivity to students.

Zahorik found *significant* differences between the teachers who had planned and those who had not planned. Teachers who planned were less sensitive to student ideas and appeared to pursue their own goals regardless of what students were thinking or saying. Conversely, teachers who had not planned displayed a higher number of verbal behaviors that encouraged and developed student ideas. Zahorik concluded that goal-based planning may inhibit teachers from being as sensitive to students as they could be.

The question that immediately arises from this study is, If goal-based planning makes teachers less sensitive to students, should teachers eliminate planning? Zahorik concluded that the answer is obviously no. Elimination of planning might "also bring about completely random and unproductive learning. If a lesson is to be effective, it would seem that some direction in the form of goals and experiences, no matter how general or vague, is needed" (p. 150).

Both the Duchastel and Brown and the Zahorik studies are interesting because together they show the importance of goal-based planning; but they also warn that this type of planning can lead to unanticipated consequences that are not always desirable. To resolve this dilemma, Zahorik recommends that teachers establish goals that focus on their own behavior. He states: "Along with the typical plan, which can be described as a plan for pupil learning, develop a teaching plan that identifies types and patterns of teacher behaviors to be used during the lesson" (p. 150).

Another consequence of teacher planning is that it produces a smoothly running classroom with fewer discipline problems and fewer interruptions. A full chapter is devoted to classroom management later, so the research on this topic will not be highlighted here. It is important to note, however, that educational research for the past three decades has consistently found that planning is the key to eliminating management problems. Beginning teachers who plan well find they do not have to be police officers because their classrooms and lessons are characterized by a smooth flow of ideas, activities, and interactions. Such planning encompasses the "rules" and "goals" teachers establish for their classrooms and emphasizes how responsible and businesslike classroom behavior is an integral part of learning.

RESEARCH SUMMARY
3.1

Duchastel, P. C., and Brown, B. R. (1974). Incidental and relevant learning with instructional objectives. *Journal of Educational Psychology, 66,* 481–485.

PROBLEM: Duchastel and Brown were interested in the effects of instructional objectives on student learning. At the time of their study, previous research results were contradictory and some had failed to support the contention that clear objectives led to higher student achievement. Duchastel and Brown decided to study one specific aspect of this problem, namely , do objectives facilitate student learning by providing focus for learning?

SAMPLE AND SETTING: Fifty-eight volunteer college-age students from a communication's course at Florida State University participated in the study.

PROCEDURES: Students were randomly assigned to two groups and asked to study several units on the topic of mushrooms. Twenty-four objectives existed for each unit and a specific test item had been written to correspond to each objective.

Group 1: Students in this group were given 12 of the 24 objectives to use as a study guide and were taught how to use the objectives to focus their learning.

Group 2: Students in this group were *not* given any of the objectives and were told to learn as much as they could from the assigned mushroom materials.

During the experimental period both groups were given 30 minutes to prepare for a test—group 1 with objectives, group 2 without objectives. The researchers defined learning associated with the 12 objectives given to group 1 as *relevant learning* and the learning associated with the other 12 objectives as *incidental learning.*

POINTERS FOR READING RESEARCH:

- The meaning of a mean score was described previously, and it was explained that the symbol for the mean score often is $\bar{X}$. In the data table that follows, the researcher chose to use the symbol M for mean score instead of $\bar{X}$. This is also an acceptable convention.
- The symbol SD in Table 1 stands for standard deviation. Remember that SD is a measure indicating the spread of a particular set of scores from a mean.
- Random assignment means that the researcher has assigned subjects to experimental conditions on the basis of chance. The logic behind this procedure is that if subjects are assigned randomly, the chance that the groups will be

---

Planning for the Experienced and Beginning Teacher

A new body of research that has flourished over the past few years focuses on the planning and decision-making processes used by experienced teachers and by beginners. Although this research does not provide clear-cut guidelines for teacher

different on important variables that may affect the results of the study is reduced.

RESULTS: Table 1 displays the results of the Duchastel and Brown study. Note the two subscores and the footnotes explaining these subscores.

▪ Subscore 1 shows the scores achieved by students on questions associated with the 12 objectives given to the experimental group to focus learning and defined as *relevant learning.*
▪ Subscore 2 shows the scores achieved by students on questions associated with the 12 objectives not given to the experimental group of students and defined as *incidental learning.*

TABLE 1   Student Mean Scores and Standard Deviations on the Posttest

No. Objectives Per Group	Subscore 1[a]		Subscore 2[b]		Total Score	
	M	*SD*	*M*	*SD*	*M*	*SD*
Half	7.4	2.7	3.2	1.9	10.6	3.2
None	5.1	2.1	5.6	1.9	10.8	3.3

[a] Relevant learning for the group receiving half of the objectives.
[b] Incidental learning for the group receiving half of the objectives.
SOURCE: P. C. Duchastel, and B. R. Brown (1974), p. 483.

DISCUSSION AND IMPLICATIONS: Table 1 shows that both groups scored the same on the total test. What is interesting and important, however, is the fact that the students who were given 12 objectives to focus learning outscored other students by 7.4 to 5.1 on *relevant learning* (test items associated with the objectives). In other words, objectives did help provide direction to student learning as the researcher predicted. This difference was statistically significant according to the researchers. Of equal interest is the fact that for *incidental learning* (test items not associated with the objectives) the students without any objectives outscored their counterparts with mean scores of 5.6 to 3.2.

The results of this study indicate that objectives have a focusing effect on students, which leads to the recommendation that teachers make students aware of objectives for lessons and units of instruction and help them learn how to use objectives to focus their studying. On the other hand, teachers should be careful because, as the Duchastel and Brown study also illustrates, focusing too much on objectives may limit other important student learning.

planning, it does provide many insights and provocative issues for study and reflection.

For a number of years researchers (Joyce and Hartoonian, 1964, for example) have tried to understand teacher planning and decision-making behavior and have been particularly interested in whether or not the real-life behavior of experienced teachers actually corresponds to the planning processes prescribed in the rational-linear model. In general, this research shows only a limited adherence to the model and indicates that, instead of focusing on objectives, teachers focus on the content to be taught and specific instructional activities. Only rarely are objectives formally considered by experienced teachers. In 1978, Peterson, Marx, and Clark studied the planning processes of experienced teachers in a controlled laboratory setting, and their study has become widely accepted as confirmation of earlier speculations and findings. A portion of this study is described in Research Summary 3.2.

Researchers and educators have puzzled for a number of years about why it seems so difficult for beginning teachers to learn some of the important planning skills. One insight gleaned over the past few years is that it is difficult to learn planning from experienced teachers not only because they think differently about teaching (as illustrated by Leinhardt's study in Chapter 2) but also because they approach planning and interactive decision making differently than do beginning teachers. A unique and interesting study on this topic, conducted by Housner and Griffey a few years ago, is highlighted in Research Summary 3.3.

The fact that experienced teachers do not always follow the planning procedures emphasized in most linear models and that they attend to different planning tasks and cues from those attended to by inexperienced teachers presents some challenging problems for the beginning teacher. Unlike other acts of teaching, most teacher planning occurs in private places like the teacher's home or office. Also, by their very nature planning and decision making are mental, nonobservable activities. Only the resulting actions are observable by others. Even when written plans are produced, they represent only a very small portion of the actual planning that has gone on in the teacher's head. The private nature of planning makes it difficult for beginning teachers to learn from experienced teachers. Beginning teachers may ask to look at lesson plans or they might talk to experienced teachers about planning and decision-making processes. However, many experienced teachers cannot describe in words the novice can understand the thinking that went into specific plans and decisions. This is particularly true of moment-to-moment planning decisions that characterize the rapid flow of classroom life. Teacher planning and decision making may be one of the teaching skills where research can be of most assistance in helping beginning teachers learn about the hidden mental processes of the experienced expert.

PLANNING DOMAINS AND PROCEDURES

This section explores several domains, or areas of teaching, for which teachers need to plan and also describes specific planning procedures for beginning teachers. Each of these topics must be mastered if positive classroom life and student learning are to be achieved.

The Phases of Teaching

Those who study teacher planning and decision making normally consider these functions as they relate to the periods before instruction, during instruction, and after instruction. These three phases of teacher planning and the types of decisions associated with each were summarized by Berliner (1982a) as shown in Table 3.1.

The meanings of some of the variables listed in Berliner's table are defined more precisely later. The important point to understand here is that teacher planning is multifaceted and many aspects of teaching in addition to those associated with deciding on the purposes and content of a lesson require planning. It is also important to note that the mental processes involved vary from one phase of teaching to the next. For example, choosing content can be done after careful analysis and inquiry about students' prior knowledge, the teacher's understanding of the subject, and the nature of the subject matter itself. Many postinstructional decisions, such as the type of test to give or how to assign grades, can also be made after careful consideration. Planning and decision making during instruction itself, on the other hand, must be done spontaneously and on the spur of the moment.

The remainder of this chapter focuses mainly on those planning tasks and decisions associated with the preinstructional phase. Interactive and postinstructional planning and decision making will be highlighted later in relation to each of the particular teaching models described in Chapters 7 through 10. A special topic section also gives information about a most important postinstructional planning task: testing and evaluating student performance.

Table 3.1 Phases of Teacher Planning and Decisions to Consider in Classroom Instruction

PREINSTRUCTIONAL DECISIONS	DECISIONS DURING INSTRUCTION	POSTINSTRUCTIONAL DECISIONS
Content choice/opportunity to learn	Engaged time	Feedback
	Transition time	Praise
	Wait time	Use of ideas
Pacing of instruction	Success rate	Criticism
	High success	Corrective feedback
	Low success	Tests
Allocation of time	Academic learning time	Grades
Activity structures	Structuring	
	Monitoring	
	Questioning	
	Academic orientation	

SOURCE: Adapted from D. C. Berliner (1982a), Recognizing instructional variables. In D. E. Orlosky (Ed.), *Introduction to Education*. Columbus, Ohio: Charles E. Merrill, p. 200. Used with permission of the publisher.

========= **RESEARCH SUMMARY** =========
3.2

Peterson, P. L., Marx, R. W., and Clark, C. M. (1978). Teacher planning, teacher behavior and student achievement. *American Educational Research Journal, 15,* 417–432.

PROBLEM: Peterson, Marx, and Clark were interested in how experienced teachers approach the planning process and how teacher planning is related to student achievement and attitudes. The part of their study that investigated the extent to which teachers attend to various planning categories, such as clarifying objectives, attending to learners' abilities, selecting instructional strategies, and other planning tasks, is summarized here.

SAMPLE AND SETTING: The researchers studied 12 elementary teachers (8.3 years average experience) and 288 junior high students, who were paid to participate in the study. The teachers included 6 women and 6 men.

PROCEDURES: The teachers were given materials (text and slides) and asked to plan for and teach (any way they wanted) three lessons on the topic of a town in France to students randomly assigned to groups of eight. The teachers were also given 11 cognitive and affective student objectives. Each day before class, teachers were given 90 minutes to plan and were asked to "think aloud" as they planned. Statements made in the "think alouds" were taped-recorded and later coded using the category system described in Table 1.

TABLE 1 Definitions of Teacher Planning Categories

Category	Definition
Productivity	Total number of statements coded
Objectives	Statements about the end products or intended student outcomes toward which the teacher is working
Subject matter	Statements dealing with information found in the text, or concepts, principles, etc., that are clearly derived from material found in the text
Instructional process	Statements describing an activity or move that the teacher intends to use during instruction, including parts of large, complex strategies
Materials	Statements about instructional or noninstructional materials and their use, or about other aspects of the physical environment
Learner outcomes	Statements that account for one or more specific aspects of students' cognitive development, cognitive ability, ability to respond to a cognitive task, or their equivalents in the affective domain
Miscellaneous	Statements that do not fit into any of the above categories

SOURCE: From P. L. Peterson, R. W. Marx, and C. M. Clark (1978), p. 419.

RESULTS: Table 2, in which the results of the study are given, shows the mean and percentages of teacher planning statements coded into each of the categories. The table also shows means and percentages for teacher productivity of statements.

TABLE 2   Total Planning Productivity and Mean Proportions of Planning Time Devoted to Various Planning Categories for the Three Experimental Days

	Day		
Planning Category	1	2	3
Productivity (mean)	199.75	124.25	112.08
Objectives	.039	.039	.044
Subject matter	.399	.334	.210
Instructional processes	.244	.316	.309
Materials	.064	.050	.101
Learner outcomes	.052	.071	.084
Miscellaneous	.202	.189	.259

SOURCE: Adapted from P. L. Peterson, R. W. Marx, and C. M. Clark (1978), p. 423.

DISCUSSION AND IMPLICATIONS: As can be observed in Table 2, teachers in the study made more planning statements during the first day and fewer on each subsequent day. The largest number and proportion of planning statements focused on subject matter content, followed by instructional processes. Very small numbers of planning statements fell into the categories of materials and learner outcomes, and the smallest planning category was statements associated with objectives.

Although the results of this study do not translate into specific guidelines for beginning teachers, they do have some serious and important implications for the beginning teacher to think about.

- Starting With Objectives: Even though beginning teachers may be required to write lesson plans that begin with objectives, they should not feel guilty if their innate sense tells them to plan for content and instructional activities first and then come back to objectives. That is what experienced teachers appear to do. As the researchers concluded: "Even though the teachers were provided with a list of desired cognitive and affective student objectives, they did not refer to them in their planning, nor did they relate their choices of instructional processes to learning objectives" (p. 424).

- Experienced Teachers as Models: The beginning teacher should also consider whether the experienced teachers in this study are, in fact, good models to follow. It may be that the planning patterns of experienced teachers do not represent best planning practice.

- Planning Time: The beginning teacher who is spending many hours planning for the next day's lesson can take heart from the results of this study, which seem to suggest that as teachers become more familiar with a topic and with its materials they feel more comfortable and do less planning.

━━━━━━━━━━━━ **RESEARCH SUMMARY** ━━━━━━━━━━━━
3.3

Housner, L. D., and Griffey, D. C. (1985). Teacher cognition. Differences in planning and interactive decision making between experienced and inexperienced teachers. *Research Quarterly for Exercise and Sport, 56,* 45–53.

PROBLEM: Housner and Griffey were interested in the differences in planning and decision making of experienced and inexperienced teachers.

SAMPLE AND SETTING: The researchers studied 16 physical education teachers. Eight of the subjects had more than five years of teaching experience; the other eight were preservice teachers training to be physical education teachers.

PROCEDURES: The teachers were given 60 minutes to plan a lesson on how to teach soccer and basketball dribbling skills to eight-year-old children. They were to teach two lessons, one for each of the skills. Subjects were told they could ask for more information if they needed it and to think aloud while planning so their thought processes could be recorded. Teachers then taught their lessons to students in groups of four. Lessons were video-taped and teachers viewed their lessons with the researchers and told them what they were thinking and the decisions they made while teaching.

POINTS FOR READING RESEARCH: Often researchers are interested mainly in presenting descriptive information about their study. In the data tables from the Housner and Griffey study you will find this situation. The researchers counted teacher behaviors in various categories and described these for the reader using straight percentage figures.

RESULTS: In Table 1 are data about the kinds of decisions experienced and inexperienced teachers made during the planning period. The researchers divided these into two broad sets—activity decisions and instructional decisions; each set has several subsets.

TABLE 1 Comparison of Types of Activity and Instructional Strategy Decisions Made by Experienced and Inexperienced Teachers

Activity Decisions	Exp.	Inexp.	Instructional Strategy Decisions	Exp.	Inexp.
Structure	42.6%	54.5%	Management	13.4%	4.8%
Procedures	24.6	28.0	Assess/feedback	22.8	15.9
Formations	4.9	1.5	Demonstrate	7.9	7.9
Time	9.0	6.8	Transitions	5.5	6.4
Adaptations	18.9	9.1	Focus attention	18.9	19.1
			Equipment use	7.9	7.9
			Verbal instruction	19.7	34.9
			Time	3.9	3.2

SOURCE: Adapted from L. D. Housner and D. G. Griffey (1985), p. 48.

Table 2 shows the types of cues that experienced and inexperienced teachers attended to as they taught the lesson and made in-flight decisions.

TABLE 2 Types of Cues Heeded by Experienced and Inexperienced Teachers During Interactive Teaching

Cues	Experienced	Inexperienced
Student performance	30.1%	19.0%
Student involvement	27.4	22.6
Student interest	11.8	27.3
Student requests	3.2	7.7
Student mood/feelings	3.2	6.5
Teacher's mood/feelings	5.3	1.7
Other	19.0	15.2

SOURCE: Adapted from L. D. Housner and D. G. Griffey (1985), p. 49

DISCUSSION AND IMPLICATIONS: Table 1 shows that experienced and inexperienced teachers differed in the percentage of their thinking that went into four categories: adaptations, management, verbal instructions, and assess/feedback. Experienced teachers planned ahead for more adaptations that might be needed in a lesson as it got underway and were more concerned than inexperienced teachers with establishing rules for activities and means for giving students feedback. Inexperienced teachers devoted a larger percentage of their planning to verbal instructions.

Table 2 shows that experienced and inexperienced teachers varied in the types of cues they attended to while teaching the lesson. The experienced teachers were most attentive to student performance, whereas inexperienced teachers attended most often to student interest and were more interested in keeping the class on task.

If beginning teachers want to model their planning and decision making after experienced teachers they would do well to consider the following:

- When planning, submerge a natural tendency to think about verbal instructions and think more about ways to structure rules and routines, give feedback to students, and plan for contingencies.
- When teaching, pay attention to student performance as a basis for making in-flight decisions rather than the stated interests of students or their requests for changes in the lesson.

Attending to Planning Cycles

Teachers must plan for different time spans, ranging from the next minute or hour to the next week, month, or year. If school-wide planning or one's own career planning is involved, time spans may even cover several years. Obviously, planning what to do or to accomplish tomorrow is much different from planning for a whole year. However, both are important. Also, plans carried out on a particular day are influenced by what has happened before and will in turn influence plans for the days and weeks ahead.

Robert Yinger (1980) of the University of Cincinnati conducted an interesting and important study a few years ago that can provide beginning teachers with a model for thinking about the time dimensions of teacher planning. Yinger made a detailed study of one first–second-grade elementary school teacher in Michigan. Using participant-observation methods, he spent 40 full days over a five-month period observing and recording the teacher's activities. From this work, Yinger was able to identify the following time spans that characterized this teacher's planning: daily planning, weekly planning, unit planning, term planning, and yearly planning. Figure 3.3 illustrates these five basic levels of planning and plots their occurrence across the school year.

Figure 3.3 Levels of Preactive Planning

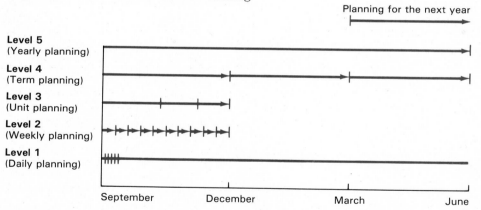

SOURCE: From R. J. Yinger (1980), Study of teacher planning. *The Elementary School Journal, 80,* 113. Copyright 1980 The University of Chicago Press. Used with permission.

Yinger also found that for each level of planning the teacher attended to the following four items: goals of planning, sources of information, form of the plan, and criteria for judging the effectiveness of planning. Table 3.2 summarizes these four aspects of planning for each of the five levels.

In the sections that follow, Yinger's model is elaborated and specific information about the tasks and purposes associated with the various time dimensions of planning are provided in some detail.

Table 3.2   Planning at Each Level of the Model

	GOALS OF PLANNING	SOURCES OF INFORMATION	FORM OF THE PLAN	CRITERIA FOR JUDGING THE EFFECTIVENESS OF PLANNING
Yearly Planning	1. Establishing general content (fairly general and framed by district curriculum objectives) 2. Establishing basic curriculum sequence 3. Ordering and reserving materials	1. Students (general information about numbers and returning students) 2. Resources available 3. Curriculum guidelines (district objectives) 4. Experience with specific curricula and materials	General outlines listing basic content and possible ideas in each subject matter area (spiral notebook used for each subject)	1. Comprehensiveness of plans 2. Fit with own goals and district objectives
Term Planning	1. Detailing of content to be covered in next three months 2. Establishing a weekly schedule for term that conforms to her goals and emphases for the term	1. Direct contact with students 2. Time constraints set by school schedule 3. Resources available	1. Elaboration of outlines constructed for yearly planning 2. A weekly schedule outline specifying activities and times	1. Outlines—comprehensiveness, completeness, and specificity of elaborations 2. Schedule—comprehensiveness and fit with goals for term, balance 3. Fit with goals for term
Unit Planning	1. Developing a sequence of well-organized learning experiences 2. Presenting comprehensive, integrated and meaningful content at an appropriate level	1. Students' abilities, interests, etc. 2. Materials, length of lessons, set-up time, demand, format 3. District objectives 4. Facilities available for activities	1. Lists of outlines of activities and content 2. Lists of sequenced activities 3. Notes in planbook	1. Organization, sequence balance, and flow of outlines 2. Fit with yearly and term goals 3. Fit with anticipated student interest and involvement
Weekly Planning	1. Laying out the week's activities within the framework of the weekly schedule 2. Adjusting schedule for interruptions and special needs 3. Maintaining continuity and regularity of activities	1. Students' performance in preceding days and weeks 2. Scheduled school interruptions (for example, assemblies, holidays) 3. Materials, aides, and other resources	1. Names and times of activities in plan book 2. Day divided into four instructional blocks punctuated by A.M. recess, lunch, and P.M. recess	1. Completeness of plans 2. Degree to which weekly schedule has been followed 3. Flexibility of plans to allow for special time constraints or interruptions 4. Fit with goals

(Cont'd)

Table 3.2   Planning at Each Level of the Model (*continued*)

	GOALS OF PLANNING	SOURCES OF INFORMATION	FORM OF THE PLAN	CRITERIA FOR JUDGING THE EFFECTIVENESS OF PLANNING
Daily Planning	1. Setting up and arranging classroom for next day 2. Specifying activity components not yet decided upon 3. Fitting daily schedule to last-minute intrusions 4. Preparing students for day's activities	1. Instructions in materials to be used 2. Set-up time required for activities 3. Assessment of class "disposition" at start of day 4. Continued interest, involvement, and enthusiasm	1. Schedule for day written on the chalkboard and discussed with students 2. Preparation and arrangement of materials and facilities in the room	1. Completion of last-minute preparations and decisions about content, materials, etc. 2. Involvement, enthusiasm, and interest communicated by students

SOURCE: R. J. Yinger (1980), A study of teacher planning. *The Elementary School Journal, 80,* 114–115. Copyright 1980 The University of Chicago Press. Used with permission.

DAILY PLANNING

The teacher's daily plan is the one that receives most attention. In some schools it is required. In other schools even the format for daily plans is prescribed. Normally, daily plans outline what content is to be taught, motivational techniques to be used, specific steps and activities for students, needed materials, and evaluation processes. The amount of detail can vary. During student teaching cooperating teachers may require the beginning teacher to write very detailed daily plans, even though their own plans may be more brief.

Most beginning teachers can understand the logic of requiring rather detailed daily plans at first. Think of the daily lesson plan as similar to the text of a speech to be delivered to a large audience. Speakers giving a speech for the first time need to follow a set of detailed notes or perhaps even a word-for-word text. As they gain experience or as their speeches are gradually committed to memory from repeated presentations, they find less and less need for notes and can proceed more extemporaneously.

Daily plans can take many formats. The features of a particular lesson often determine lesson plan format. For example, each of the teaching models described in Chapters 7 through 10 requires a somewhat different lesson format. The beginning teacher will find, however, that some schools have a preferred format that they require of all their teachers. One format that has been accepted by people in many schools was developed by Madeline Hunter, an educator from the University of California at Los Angeles. Her lesson format includes all the important ingredients of a lesson plan, and it has been widely disseminated and used by schools throughout the United States and in other countries as well. It

Figure 3.4   Elements of an Effective Lesson

1. Objective	Anticipated outcome of lesson
2. Anticipatory set	Establishing lesson's rationale and motivation
3. Input	Concepts and skills to be explained
4. Modeling	Demonstration of concepts or skills
5. Guided practice	In-class practice of concepts or skills
6. Checking for understanding	Way to see if students understand lesson
7. Independent practice	Homework to continue practice

appears in Figure 3.4 as it has been prescribed for teachers in the Prince Georges County, Maryland, public schools.

Observe that the Hunter lesson format includes a clear statement of the objectives or outcomes of a lesson, a means for motivating students, and a sequence of instructional activities starting with input of new materials and concluding with practice, checking for understanding (to see if students understand the lesson), and homework.

A common ingredient of daily lesson plans is a statement of objectives. In college methods classes, during student teaching, or in the first year of teaching, beginning teachers will be encouraged (often required) to provide supervisors with daily lesson plans that have specific objectives. You can become effective in writing objectives quite readily if you understand the logic and content of good objectives. Figure 3.5 summarizes important information about instructional objectives. Aids at the end of this chapter have also been designed to give you additional practice.

WEEKLY AND UNIT PLANNING

Most schools and teachers organize instruction around weeks and units. A unit is essentially a chunk of content and associated skills that are perceived as fitting together in a logical way. Normally more than one lesson is required to accomplish a unit of instruction. The content for instructional units might come from chapters in books or from major sections of curriculum guides. Examples of units could include such topics as: sentences, the Civil War, fractions, thermodynamics, the heart, or the short stories of Hemingway.

Unit planning is, in many ways, more critical than daily planning. The unit plan links together a variety of goals, content, and activities the teacher has in mind. It determines the overall flow for a series of lessons over several days, weeks, or perhaps even months, and often reflects the teacher's understanding of both the content and processes of instruction.

Most people can memorize plans for an hour or a day, but they cannot remember the logistics and sequencing of activity over several days or weeks. For this reason teachers' unit plans are generally written in a fair amount of detail. When unit plans are put into writing they also serve as a reminder later that some

Figure 3.5   Instructional Objectives

The Three Basic Ingredients of a Good Objective

1. **Student Based and Specific**   The objective should identify what the student is supposed to learn as a result of instruction (as contrasted to what the teacher is going to do). For example:
   - The student will be able to identify the capitals of the states in the Pacific Northwest, instead of . . .
   - Students will be introduced to the capitals of the PNW states.

   The objective should also be as specified as possible about what the student is supposed to learn. This is normally done by using words that are precise in identifying learning outcomes. For example:
   - The student can solve for one unknown in a linear algebraic equation, instead of . . .
   - The student will understand linear algebraic equations

2. **Testing Situation**   The objective should define the testing situation, such as:
   - On a written essay test
   - Given a map
   - A test with the use of notes

3. **Performance Level**   The objective should describe the performance level that the teacher will find acceptable. For example:
   - The student can solve five linear equation problems within 40 minutes, instead of . . .
   - The student can solve linear equation problems

The Ingredients Applied

The following is an all-purpose guide that can be used over and over by beginning teachers faced with the task of writing objectives:

Testing Situation	Student Based	Performance Level
Given a map . . .	The student will be able to:	at least 85 percent
Without notes . . .	identify	four of five reasons
With the text . . .	solve	correct to nearest percentage
	compare	
	contrast	
	recite	

lessons require supporting materials, equipment, motivational devices, or evaluation tools that cannot normally be obtained on a moment's notice. If teachers are working together in teams, unit planning and assignment of responsibilities for various unit activities are most important.

Unit plans can also be shared with students because they provide the overall road map that explains where the teacher or a particular lesson is going. Through the communication of unit goals and activities students can recognize what they are expected to learn. Knowledge of unit plans can help older students allocate their study time and monitor their own progress.

Over time, experienced teachers develop unit plans and supporting materials that can be reused. However, most beginning teachers will have to rely on textbooks and curriculum guides. There is nothing wrong with doing this, and the beginning teacher should not feel guilty about it. Most curriculum guides have been developed by experienced teachers and, even though their approach to subjects cannot be expected to fit the preferences of an individual teacher, they do provide a helpful overall design to follow.

Two notes of caution are worth mentioning, however. First, some beginning teachers, particularly in middle schools and high schools, rely heavily on their college textbooks or the course and unit plans of their college instructors. These plans and materials are always inappropriate for younger learners, who are not ready for the advanced content found in college courses. Second, there are teachers who, after several years of experience, still rely on textbooks for planning and sequencing their instruction. Teaching and learning are creative, evolutionary processes that should be keyed to a particular group of students at a particular point in time. Only when this is done can lessons rise above the humdrum and provide intellectual excitement to students.

YEARLY PLANS

Yearly plans are also critical but, because of the uncertainty and complexity in most schools, cannot be done with as much precision as daily or unit plans. The effectiveness of yearly plans generally revolves around how well they deal with the following three features:

1. Overall Themes and Attitudes Most teachers have some global attitudes, goals, and themes they would like to leave with their students. Perhaps a teacher in a mixed-race elementary classroom would like his or her students to end the term with a bit less bias or misunderstanding and a bit more tolerance of people who are racially different. No specific lesson or unit can teach this attitude, but many carefully planned and coordinated experiences throughout the year can. Or perhaps a high school biology teacher would like students to understand and embrace a set of attitudes associated with scientific methods. A single lesson on the scientific method will not accomplish this goal. However, personal modeling and formal demonstrations showing respect for data, the relationships between theory and reality, or the process of making inferences from information can eventually influence students to think more scientifically. As a last example, a history teacher may want students to leave her or his class with an appreciation of the very long time frame associated with the development of democratic traditions. Again, a single lesson on the Magna Carta, the Constitution, or the Fourteenth Amendment will not develop this appreciation. However, building a succession of lessons that come back to a common theme on the "cornerstones of democracy" can achieve this end.

2. Coverage There are few teachers who run out of things to do. Instead, the common lament is that time runs out with many important lessons still to be taught. Experienced teachers carry many of their yearlong plans in their heads. Beginning teachers, however, will have to take care to develop yearlong plans if they want to get past the Civil War by March. Planning to cover desired topics requires asking what is really important to teach, deciding on priorities, and attending carefully to the instructional hours actually available over a year's time. In most instances teachers strive to teach too much, too lightly. Students may be better served if a reduced menu is planned. In short, most beginning teachers overestimate how much time is actually available for instruction and underestimate the amount of time it takes to teach something well. Careful planning can help minimize this error in judgment.

3. Cycles of the School Year Experienced teachers know that the school year is cyclical, and that some topics are better taught at one time than another. School cycles and corresponding emotional or psychological states revolve around the opening and closing of school, the days of the week, vacation periods, the changes of season, holidays, and important school events. Some of these can be anticipated; some cannot. Nonetheless, it is important to plan for school cycles as much as possible. Experienced teachers know that new units or important topics are not introduced on Friday or the day before Christmas vacation. They know that the opening of school should emphasize processes and structures to facilitate student learning later in the year. They know that the end of the school year will be filled with interruptions and decreasing motivation as students anticipate summer vacation. They also know that it is unwise to plan for a unit examination the night after a big game or the hour following the Halloween party.

As beginning teachers you know something about these cycles and corresponding psychological states from your own student days. You can use this information, along with information provided by experienced teachers in a school, as you proceed with making long-range, yearly plans.

TIMETABLING TECHNIQUES TO ASSIST
UNIT AND YEARLY PLANNING

There are several techniques for assisting beginning teachers in making clear and "doable" instructional plans that go over several days or weeks or where many specific, independent tasks must be completed prior to moving on. One such technique is called *timetabling*. A timetable is a chronological map of a series of instructional activities, or of some special project, the teacher may want to carry out. It describes the overall direction of activities and any special products which may be produced within a time frame. The most straightforward timetabling technique consists of constructing a special chart called a Gantt Chart. A Gantt Chart allows you to see the work pieces in relation to each other—when each starts and finishes. Two Gantt Charts, one devised by a social studies teacher to plan a semester's study in American government and the second constructed by an elementary teacher for planning the logistics of a field trip to a local museum are shown in Tables 3.3 and 3.4.

There are many formats for making timetables. Some teachers believe in evolving processes and prefer a more open and nonspecific approach. Others prefer just the opposite and write everything down in great detail. One's own personal philosophy and work style influence the exact approach and level of detail required. Regardless of the extent to which you choose to make timetables a part of your planning, it is at least important to consider their use because they help planners recognize the limits of a very important and scarce resource—time. Aids at the end of the chapter are provided to help you to practice timetabling techniques and to consider them in more detail. Chapter 4 returns to the topic of time and the importance of using it effectively.

Choosing Content

Another important domain of teacher planning is the way decisions are made about the content of instruction. The curriculum in most elementary and secondary schools is currently organized around the academic disciplines (history, biology, mathematics, and so forth) used by scholars to organize information about the social and physical world. And even though some curriculum reformers have repeatedly argued that this is an inappropriate way to organize content for young people, the current structures are likely to remain for some time. Consequently, an important planning task for teachers will continue to be choosing the most

Table 3.3   Gantt Chart, Social Studies

	TIME								
TASK	SEPT	OCT	NOV	DEC	JAN	FEB	MAR	APRIL	MAY
Background to Settlement	xx●								
The Colonial Era	xxxx●								
The Revolutionary War	xxxx●								
Constitutional Deliberations	xxxxxxxx●●								
The Early Republic	xxxxx●								
The Civil War	xxxxxxxx●								
●Unit exams									
●●Midterm exams									

Table 3.4   Gantt Chart, Museum Trip

TASK	TIME			
	MAR 10–15	MAR 18–23	MAR 26–31	APRIL 3–7
Call museum director	xx			
Talk to principal	xx			
Request bus for field trip	xx			
Introduce unit on art history	xxxxxxxx			
Prepare field trip permission slips	xx			
Send permission slips home		xx		
Require slips to be returned		xx		
Teach unit on art history		xxxxxxxxxxxxxxxxxxxxxxxx		
Go over logistics of field trip			xxxxxxxx	
Discuss what to look for on trip				xxxx
Take trip				x
Follow-up trip in class				xxxx
Write thank-you letters				xxx

appropriate content from the various subject matter areas for a particular group of students. This is no small feat because there is already much more to teach on any topic than time allows, and new knowledge is being produced every day. Consequently, most schools do not assume that beginning teachers, by themselves, can make major content decisions but that they should be guided by textbooks and curriculum guides. Thus content decisions are normally made by experienced teachers and curriculum specialists long before the student teacher, or first-year teacher, steps into a classroom. When textbooks have been carefully selected and curriculum guides planned and prepared with wisdom, they provide excellent tools for the beginning teacher to use. The experts who prepare these materials have taken considerable time to ask what should be taught and how various topics should be sequenced over time—both over the course of a year and over several years. The job of beginning teachers becomes mainly that of making sure they understand the scope and sequence of this content and finding ways to interpret and teach it effectively to a particular group of students, adding and deleting material as needed.

However, some beginning teachers may find themselves facing the time-consuming task of having to select content. For instance, textbooks in some schools may be out of date in terms of the new knowledge that beginning teachers have learned in college. If this is true, then it is beginning teachers' responsibility to plan ways to incorporate that knowledge into their lessons. Adding new knowledge normally requires taking something else out of the already crowded curriculum.

A beginning teacher may also find instances where curriculum guides do not exist, or if they do, consist only of a brief list of topics. Again, when a beginning teacher faces this situation, content decisions will have to be made without much assistance and will require considerable understanding of the subject matter and of how students at a particular age level learn.

Two general guidelines can provide assistance in making content decisions. First, in every field there is much more to learn than it is possible to master in a single year, or even a lifetime. Teachers must choose content based on the basic ideas and structures of knowledge for a particular field, taking into account, of course, their students' prior knowledge and abilities. In all fields of knowledge advanced concepts and understandings are built pyramid fashion on simpler ones, as described in Figures 3.6 and 3.7.

Notice in both figures that information is divided into more complex and abstract ideas and into simpler, less complex concepts and skills. Notice also that information is structured to show relationships between various subsets of ideas and understandings.

A second guide for choosing content is to base that choice on the type of test students will be expected to perform well on. Berliner (1982a) notes that "students may learn what they are given to learn, and *rarely* learn what they are not given to learn" (p. 202). The point here is obvious. If a teacher or school system plans to test students on certain information, it is only logical that content decisions be based on the body of knowledge to be covered on the tests. Sometimes this is not done, however. To illustrate this problem of matching content with tests, look at the information in Figure 3.8 adapted by Berliner (1982a) from research done by Freeman et al. (1980) at Michigan State University. Note a lack of congruence between the content of selected achievement tests and that of the textbooks being used by teachers in this particular instance.

Choosing Activity Structures

Activity structures are those patterns of behavior that characterize what teachers do as they teach and what students do as they engage in learning tasks. These patterns of behavior can range from specific steps or phases associated with a particular lesson (described in some detail in each of the Part 3 chapters) to the overall patterns that characterize a particular classroom, teacher, or group of

Figure 3.6

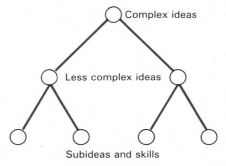

Figure 3.7

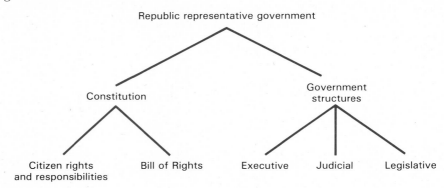

students. Activity structures also consist of planning decisions associated with large or small group instruction, use of films or microcomputers, reading circles, cooperative learning groups, individual seatwork, or silent reading.

Yinger (1980) observed from his research that activities are "the basic structural units of planning and action in the classroom" and that nearly "all classroom action and interaction occurred during activities; the remaining time was used for

Figure 3.8   Congruence Between What Is Tested and What Is Taught

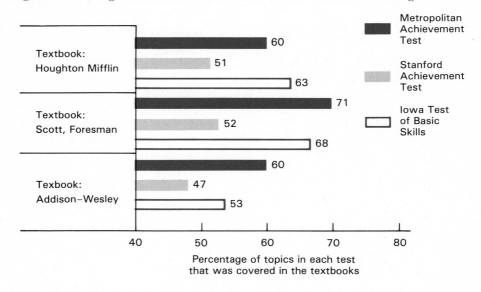

SOURCE: From D. C. Berliner (1982a), Recognizing instructional variables. In D. E. Orlosky (Ed.), Introduction to Education. Columbus, Ohio: Charles E. Merrill. Used with permission.

preparing for activities or making transitions between activities" (p. 111). The research described previously showed how experienced teachers spend considerable time planning for this domain of instruction. It is likely that these planning tasks do more than anything else to establish the climate in a particular classroom. Important activity structures for beginning teachers to think about include activities that accomplish routines, build group cohesion and morale, and provide appropriate sequence and variety for accomplishing instructional tasks. Each of these is described briefly here and revisited later in a different context and in more detail.

ACTIVITIES TO ESTABLISH ROUTINES

In both elementary and secondary classrooms teachers and students are expected to perform certain housekeeping activities such as taking attendance; keeping the classroom space safe and livable; making assignments; collecting papers; and distributing or storing books, equipment, and the like. Even if teacher aides have been employed to assist with many of these tasks, they still require careful planning by the teacher. Experienced teachers plan housekeeping tasks so thoroughly and efficiently that the naive observer may not even notice they are occurring. A beginning teacher who has not planned efficient ways to accomplish housekeeping routines will suffer from ongoing confusion and wasted instructional time. From experience and from observing effective teachers, the following planning guidelines for routines are provided for beginning teachers:

GUIDELINE 1 Make sure detailed written plans exist for taking roll, giving assignments, collecting and distributing papers, and storing books and equipment.

GUIDELINE 2 Distribute these written plans and procedures to students the first time a housekeeping activity occurs in a particular year or with a particular class.

GUIDELINE 3 Post copies of the housekeeping plans on the bulletin board or on chart paper to serve as public reminders about how particular activities are to be carried out.

GUIDELINE 4 Train student helpers immediately to provide leadership and assistance in carrying out routines. Students at all ages can and like to be in charge of taking roll, picking up books, getting and setting up the movie projector, and the like.

GUIDELINE 5 Follow the plan that has been developed consistently, and make sure that plenty of time exists to carry out each activity, particularly early in the year.

GUIDELINE 6 Be alert to ways housekeeping activities can become more efficient and seek feedback about how students think the housekeeping activities are going.

ACTIVITIES TO ESTABLISH GROUP MORALE AND COHESION

Good teachers who work with classes of students at any age (three-year-olds to adults) recognize the need to plan some classroom activities whose objectives are not to increase student learning but to build the morale and cohesion of the classroom group itself. In elementary schools favorite activities consist of weekly or daily meetings in which students share their reactions about what is going on in the class, reading parts of a favorite story after lunch each day, or taking a morning break to talk informally with friends. Parties in celebration of holidays and birthdays are also used to build group cohesion.

In high schools and with older students, this task becomes a bit more difficult, but it is just as important. Taking a break to tell a joke or to recognize a particular student's accomplishment outside of class is one technique effective high school teachers use. Devoting periods of time for students to get to know one another or to plan for the next unit of instruction is another. Regardless of the activity, group morale and cohesion affect classroom behavior, attitudes, and achievement. Developing a cohesive group requires every bit as much planning as any other classroom activity. In fact, these kinds of activities are known to get out of hand rather quickly in beginning teachers' classrooms if appropriate planning has not taken place. Some beginning teachers, for instance, report that they were ready to quit teaching after their first Halloween party.

ACTIVITIES TO SEQUENCE INSTRUCTION
AND TO PROVIDE VARIETY

Other activity structures teachers must attend to are those that provide overall sequence and choreography to instructional events. These activities often present beginning teachers with the most trouble. Planning for sequence deals with how instructional activities begin, develop, and end. When planning is done well, events flow smoothly from one phase or step to another. To the novice observer and to students themselves, the transitions are hardly noticeable. Experience gradually provides teachers with a sense of how much to cover and how quickly, how to start a lesson and end it, and how to modify it if things are not going as planned. In the beginning, however, there is no substitute for careful planning.

Maintaining variety in instruction, as in life, is the spice that makes things interesting. The effective teacher is one who plans for variety. Instructional models are varied from day to day, just as are the activities associated with homework and group work. Daily and unit plans are designed to include a mixture of teacher talk, student talk, large and small group work, reading, working with computers, and using games and simulations. The variety that can be provided by beginning teachers depends upon their repertoire of teaching models and techniques.

Summary

This chapter presented information about the types and processes of teacher planning. It showed that even though teacher planning and decision making do not always conform to rational-linear planning models or to popular models for goal-based instruction, they are nonetheless among the most important executive functions. Beginning teachers need more detailed plans than do veteran teachers, and must make sure their personal schedules allow for sufficient planning time. Planning has consequences for both student learning and teaching behavior. Effective teachers are those who have learned how to plan for and to make appropriate decisions about the content of instruction and the activity structures that guide classroom life. They have also learned how to make adjustments when plans prove to be inappropriate or ineffective. They know that planning extends beyond simply deciding what kinds of verbal messages and instructions to give students.

Books for the Professional

Lerup, L. (1977). *Building the unfinished: Architecture and human action*. Beverly Hills, Calif.: Sage Publications. Written by an architect, this book is not about teaching. It does, however, explore clearly and precisely the interaction between people and their environments and the impact of planning on this process. With examples from studies of fishing villages in Scandinavia and student housing at Berkeley, Lerup shows how planning processes, if they are to serve people, must be conceived as cyclical and interactive and remain open with a touch of the unfinished.

Mager, R. F. (1984). *Preparing instructional objectives*. (Second revised edition). Palo Alto, Calif.: D. S. Lake Publishers. This book, now a classic, makes a strong case for instructional objectives and tells why they should be stated clearly and precisely. It provides detailed instructions on how to become proficient in writing objectives.

Posner, G. J., and Rudnitsky, A. N. (1986). *Course design: A guide to curriculum development for teachers*. (Third edition). New York: Longman. Provides many excellent examples and step-by-step instructions for course design and unit planning.

Taylor B. L., Sullivan. E. W., and Dollar, B. (1978). *Mapping teacher corps projects: A planning resource book*. New York: Center for Policy Research. This manual provides excellent discussions about how to plan and it is packed with specific planning techniques and procedures. It is particularly useful for understanding the relationships between planning processes and the social system (such as the classroom) for which planning occurs.

═══════════════ **CHAPTER 3** ═══════════════
LEARNING AIDS FOR PLANNING, OBSERVATION, AND REFLECTION

- Assessing My Planning Skills
- Writing Objectives
- Format for Daily Lesson Plans
- Timetabling Techniques
- Interviewing Teachers About In-Flight Decision Making
- Observing Lesson Activities and Segments

Included in Part 2 are aids to assist you in thinking about and developing your skill in exercising the executive functions of teaching—planning, allocating time and space resources, building productive learning environments, and managing classroom groups. Each set of aids begins with an overall assessment of your current level of knowledge and skill. The assumption is that everyone has some teaching skill from prior experience with younger siblings, as camp counselors, and so on. These assessments will help you take stock of yourself and pinpoint areas where improvement is needed. Other aids, such as Interviewing Teachers About In-Flight Decision Making, will help you refine your understanding of teaching.

ASSESSING MY PLANNING SKILLS

PURPOSE: To assess your skill level in various aspects of planning.

DIRECTIONS: Check the level of skill you think you have for the preinstructional planning domains listed below.

Skill or Competency	My Level of Effectiveness		
	High	Medium	Low
Cycles of planning			
Daily planning	_____	_____	_____
Weekly and unit planning	_____	_____	_____
Yearly planning	_____	_____	_____
Choosing content	_____	_____	_____
Choosing activity structures			
Establishing routines	_____	_____	_____
Establishing group morale and cohesion	_____	_____	_____
Sequencing instruction and providing variety	_____	_____	_____

WRITING OBJECTIVES

PURPOSE: Even though objectives are not always written by experienced teachers, they are still an important aspect of teaching practice. Beginners may need to focus their lessons more carefully than experts. For this reason, you must gain facility in writing objectives. This aid will give you practice in writing and evaluating objectives.

DIRECTIONS: Write ten objectives for your grade level or subject area. Evaluate them using the guide below.

1. _____

2. _____

3. _____

4. _____

5. _____

6. _____

7. _____

8. _____

9. _____

10. _____

Rate each objective good, fair, or poor according to whether it is student based, how specific it is, and whether it defines the testing situation and performance level well.

	Objective Number									
	1	2	3	4	5	6	7	8	9	10
Student based										
Specific										
Testing situation										
Performance level										

Analysis and Reflection: Now revise each objective as needed. Was there any aspect of objective writing that was especially difficult? What was it? How could you make it easier?

FORMAT FOR DAILY LESSON PLANS

PURPOSE: This aid provides a basic guide for planning lessons. There is no magic, or right, format for lesson plans. Much depends upon a particular teacher's preference and taste. Each of the chapters on the instructional functions of teachers provides sample plans to fit specific models being described. The following is a generic lesson plan format some teachers have found useful.

DIRECTIONS: Using this format as a starting point, develop two other formats for constructing lesson plans you think would be appropriate for the subjects and ages you will be teaching. As opportunities for teaching arise, experiment with these different formats. Are they all equally useful? Is one more appropriate for certain situations than others? Is there one that is most comfortable in all cases?

Date _____ Topic _____

Objective(s): _____

_____

_____

Motivation and set: _____

_____

_____

Instructional activities: _____

_____

_____

Checks for understanding: _____

_____

_____

Classroom practice: _____

_____

_____

Homework and independent practice: _____

_____

_____

Pitfalls to avoid next time: _____

TIMETABLING TECHNIQUES

PURPOSE: Gantt Charts can be very helpful time management devices. This aid is to assist you in gaining facility in using Gantt Charts.

DIRECTIONS: Use the guidelines below to plan the following three different kinds of activities: getting ready for school, writing a paper, and arranging a field trip.

1. Think about each activity you must do to get ready for school or work each day. List each activity along the left side of the chart below. Then draw a line horizontally from the beginning to ending time of each activity.

Activity	6:00	6:15	6:30	6:45	7:00	7:15	7:30	7:45	8:00	8:15	8:30

2. Think about all the tasks that need to be done when you are writing a paper for a class. This time, make your own chart. Again, list the activities on the left. Then decide if your time demarcations should be days, weeks, or months and draw a line between the beginning and ending times for each activity.
3. Finally, think about all the things that would need to be done if you were planning a field trip for a class you were teaching. Make your own chart, list the activities, and mark the beginning and ending times for each activity.

Analysis and Reflection: Do you notice any patterns in the way you plan? Are there ways you can facilitate your own planning? For example, are you able to plan efficiently in snatches of time on the subway, waiting in the doctor's office, or waiting for the kettle to boil? Or do you need to set aside a quantity of time and arrange for peace and quiet in order to get your planning done? Write a paragraph on your planning style.

INTERVIEWING TEACHERS ABOUT IN-FLIGHT DECISION MAKING

PURPOSE: Not all planning and decision making can be slow and deliberate. Some must happen on the spur of the moment, in the midst of a lesson. This aid is to assist you in understanding this type of decision making.

DIRECTIONS: Observe a lesson and interview the teacher as soon as possible about it. Ask the questions in the order shown on the flow chart. You will need another piece of paper to note the teacher's answers.

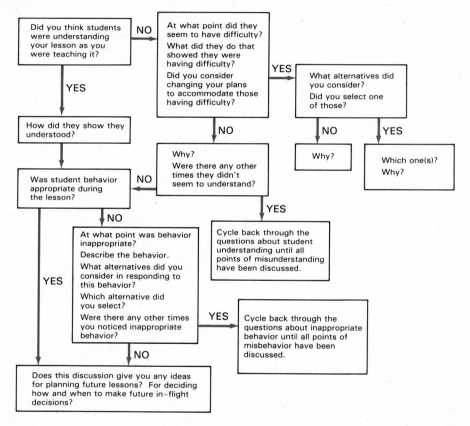

SOURCE: Adapted from P. H. Winne and R. W. Marx (1982). Students' and teachers' views of thinking processes for classroom learning. *Elementary School Journal, 82,* 499. Copyright 1982 The University of Chicago Press. Used with permission.

assignment 7

OBSERVING LESSON ACTIVITIES AND SEGMENTS

PURPOSE: Activity structures, or lesson segments, form the basic structural units of a lesson. Becoming sensitive to these structures will assist you in your own planning. The purpose of this aid is to help you uncover the internal structure of an experienced teacher's lesson.

DIRECTIONS: Each time the teacher begins a new lesson segment, record the time the segment begins and the type of activity that occurs during that segment. You may see activities like "lecturing," "checking for understanding," "conducting a discussion," "giving an exam," "demonstrating"; you may see other activities. Also note the teacher's transition statements and/or actions.

Time	Activity	Transition Statement/Action
____	____	____
____	____	____
____	____	____
____	____	____
____	____	____
____	____	____
____	____	____
____	____	____
____	____	____
____	____	____

Analysis and Reflection: Figure the amount of time the teacher spent on each segment and each type of activity. Which activities took more time? Which less? Which transition statements and actions were the most common? Which seemed to work the best?

CHAPTER 4

MAIN IDEAS

- Time is a scarce commodity in teaching and its use should be planned carefully.
- There are several different types of time that should be attended to by teachers.
- The amount of time students spend on a task is related to how much they learn.
- Homework is one way of extending time on task.
- The way space is used affects the learning atmosphere of the classroom and influences communication patterns within classrooms and power relationships among teachers and students.
- Since little is known about the effects of different uses of space, teachers need to experiment with space and reflect upon the results.

Allocating Time and Space Resources

VIRGINIA RICHARDSON-KOEHLER

One aspect of the executive function of teaching is the allocation and management of scarce resources to create productive learning environments. But what resources does a teacher have control over? States and school districts are mandating objectives and curricula, principals make decisions about which students should be in which classes, and textbook decisions are made by school district or state-level textbook committees. The furniture is already in the classroom, and unless the teacher is in an open-space school, the size of the classroom is fixed.

It turns out that the most important resource a teacher controls is *time:* not only how much time to spend on a particular subject, but how to manage and focus students' time on academic issues in general. Another important resource is the classroom *space:* how to move around in it, where to place students, materials, and desks, and how to create an ambience for learning.

The management of classroom time is extremely complex. It requires knowledge of the curriculum, of learning principles, of individual students in the classroom, and of good management practices. Above all, it requires a commitment to cover specific academic topics and a belief that students can learn.

Whereas the research base on the management of time is quite well developed, much less is known about the management of space. Consequently, when considering the use of classroom space it is important to remain flexible regarding the placement of desks and tables and the grouping of students. However, it is difficult, given the research base, to predict how decisions regarding these matters will affect student behavior and learning. Although some principles emerge, it is also the case that effective teachers often experiment with desk placement and space arrangements. Management of these important resources is the focus of this chapter.

PERSPECTIVE AND RATIONALE

Time is clearly important to classroom teachers, just as it is to all workers. Some workers look upon time as something to get through: "I can't wait till quitting time." For most professionals, however, it is a commodity that is scarce and in high demand: "If only I had more time."

In teaching, time can be seen as a critical resource that, in combination with other resources, produces student learning. There are more and less efficient ways of using time, and more and less effective ways as well. It is one thing to efficiently race through a topic in as little time as possible, but if students do not learn, this coverage is not effective. Therefore, the concept of optimization suggests that some particular *amount* of time spent on a topic, when combined with some optimal amount and kind of other resources, will maximize student learning.

A second view of time is psychological in nature and closely related to the first. In this view, learning is seen as a process (rather than a product, as in the approach just described), and time is seen as a determinant of that learning process. Time has been a major variable in animal studies and laboratory studies of human learning for some time. Only recently has it been used in studies of classrooms.

Current interest in the nature of time began with the publication of an article by John B. Carroll (1963) called "A Model of School Learning." In his model, Carroll posited that student learning, or "degree of learning," is a function of five factors. Three of the factors are related to the student:

1. *Aptitude,* or the amount of time it takes a student to learn a task under optimal conditions
2. *Ability* to understand instruction
3. *Perseverance,* or the amount of time the student is willing to remain actively engaged in learning

In addition, two elements are external to the student:

4. *Quality of instruction*
5. *Opportunity time* allowed for learning

Note that Carroll mentioned three types of time in his model: time needed, time allowed, and time spent. Carroll later elaborated on his model to provide a fuller picture of time and the learning process. His complete model is shown in Figure 4.1.

Carroll explained that in his model quality of instruction depends on the clarity with which task demands are communicated, how adequately tasks are presented, how adequately the subtasks are sequenced and paced, and how well student needs and characteristics are accounted for. Further, his model suggests that perseverance is not just an individual trait, but can be altered by the teacher and instructional quality. In other words, students can be motivated to persevere longer.

One of the most difficult problems faced by teachers is how much time is "needed." As Figure 4.1 shows, this depends upon knowledge of students' abilities and aptitudes as well as the particular learning task. As Carroll's model makes obvious, a teacher's use of time is not the simplistic matter that some might think it is.

Figure 4.1 Model of School Learning

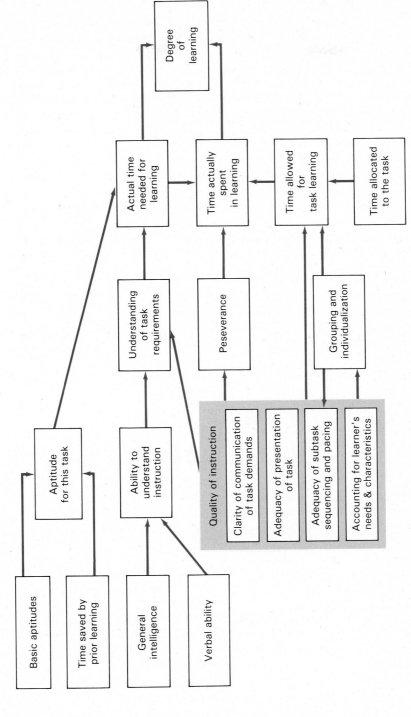

SOURCE: From A. Harnischseger and D. Wiley (1978), Model of school learning, *Journal of Curriculum Studies*, p. 216.

The arrangement of space and other resources is not a simple matter either. Consider, for example, how a teacher might conduct a discussion with students. The teacher and students could be arranged in a circle that permits equal communication between all parties or, as is more usual, the students could be arranged in straight rows with all information directed to and from a central figure (the teacher). The way space is designed influences both communication patterns and power relationships among teachers and students.

Social psychologists have investigated how different communication patterns work and influence group members. Examples of several different networks are shown in Figure 4.2. The circle, at the bottom, was described above. In the top three patterns the teacher has all the power. The horseshoe pattern occurs in a hierarchical situation: individuals in a small group report to their team leader, and the team leader then reports to the teacher. The Y pattern occurs when teachers listen to two different views and then synthesize them into a third view for another student. The circle describes situations in which communication is open, and no one person has control over the information or communication pattern.

Figure 4.2 Four Types of Communication Networks

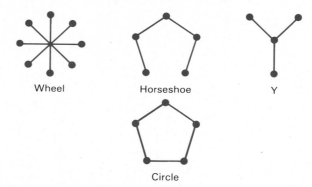

Wheel   Horseshoe   Y

Circle

These and other arrangements of students, desks, and chairs not only help determine classroom communication patterns and interpersonal relationships, but also influence a variety of daily decisions teachers must make concerning how scarce resources are managed and used. These are not easy choices. Fortunately, a substantial body of research can provide guidelines for beginning teachers as they think about these decisions.

SAMPLING THE RESEARCH BASE

Research on Time

Research has been conducted on the way teachers manage their students' use of classroom time and also their own personal time across many different professional activities. This chapter focuses specifically on teachers' use of classroom learning time. Other aspects of teachers' use of time are described in Chapters 11 and 13.

DIFFERENT TYPES OF TIME

The Carroll model described above is a compelling way of thinking about effective instruction. However, his model was just that: a manageable way of organizing his thinking after years of scholarly involvement in educational psychology. During the 1970s several researchers began to test Carroll's model using a number of different concepts of time. These are:

- *Planned time* When teachers fill in plan books, they set aside a certain amount of time for the different subjects and activities. This is called planned time.
- *Allocated time* The amount of time the teacher actually spends on a particular subject, task, or activity is called allocated time. This is also called *opportunity to learn* and is measured in terms of the amount of time teachers have their students spend on a given academic task.
- *Engaged time* (also called *time on task*) The amount of time *students* actually spend on an activity or task is called engaged time. This type of time is measured in terms of on-task or off-task behavior. If a teacher has allocated time to seatwork on math problems, and the student is working on these problems, the student's behavior is on task. Conversely, if the student is doodling, or talking about football with another student, the behavior is counted as off task.
- *Academic learning time* The amount of time a student spends engaged in a task at which he or she is successful is called academic learning time. As described below, this concept is the one most closely related to student learning (Fisher et al., 1980).
- *Time needed* The time an individual student actually needs to master a task is called time needed. This feature of time is usually determined on the basis of ability and aptitude.

These concepts of time are all different and yield different results in their measurement. For example, suppose a teacher plans 40 minutes for a math lesson, but an observer notes that the transition from reading to math takes 5 minutes. Further, suppose several discipline problems reduce the amount of time another 5 minutes, while loudspeaker announcements and lunch money collection account for another 8 minutes. Allocated time is, therefore, 23 minutes as contrasted to the 40 minutes of planned time. Further, assume the observer notes that the students are quite restless. During their seatwork assignments they talk and giggle with their fellow students while the teacher is working with individual students. In addition a number of students are not paying attention when the teacher is explaining new material on the board. The average engaged time for the students thus becomes only 12 minutes. Further, a number of students really need one full hour for this particular task in order to master it. One could predict, then, that a large number of students will not master the task.

RELATIONSHIP BETWEEN TIME AND ACHIEVEMENT

Several important studies in the 1970s investigated the relationships between various aspects of time and student learning. Is student learning related to the amount of time allocated to a task, or the amount of time students are engaged on task, or both? The answer in most studies of regular classroom teaching was both. The more time teachers allocate to an academic topic and the more students are engaged in that topic, the more they will learn about it.

Researchers also learned from the various time studies that there was considerable variation from teacher to teacher in the amount of allocated time given to different subject areas. Even in those school districts where the amounts of time teachers were supposed to devote to math and reading were prescribed, the variation was extreme. In addition, the time studies discovered that the engaged time varied from classroom to classroom. Some of this variation was related to the teachers' classroom management skills, and to the types of students found in the different classrooms.

In the late 1960s and early 1970s, a major program was initiated at the federal level. This program, called Project Headstart, supplied school districts with funds to develop early childhood programs for disadvantaged children. Despite the social and academic gains made in these Headstart classrooms, researchers soon found that the Headstart children lost many of their initial gains once they entered a regular classroom environment. Therefore, Project Follow Through was developed to supply funds for ongoing special services to the same group of disadvantaged students for whom Headstart had been designed. Project Follow Through consisted of a number of programs developed from theories of how children, particularly low-socioeconomic-status children, learn. These programs ranged from highly structured, basic-skills orientations to open classroom and independent learning approaches. An individual school could choose to implement one of several approaches offered.

Given the amount of federal money provided for these programs, legislators soon inquired as to whether they were working. If so, which of the programs was working best, and which aspects of the programs seemed to be the most effective in raising student achievement? The second of these two questions was tackled in a study by Stallings and Kaskowitz (1974).

The study involved 108 first-grade and 58 third-grade classrooms taught by teachers who were implementing one of seven approaches. Teachers were observed three times, and then selected students in those Follow Through classrooms were observed. Students were tested for learning gains in mathematics and reading. The analysis determined which of the seven approaches produced the strongest learning gains, and which aspects of teaching across the seven approaches seemed to contribute the most to learning gains.

The approaches that emphasized structured learning of the basic skills produced the strongest learning gains. However, attendance in these classrooms was below average, as were students' self-concepts.

Many findings emerged from this study, but the most pronounced was that *opportunity to learn* (or allocated time) on academic content was strongly related to student achievement. In other words, no matter what specific approach was used, in classrooms where teachers spent the most time on academic work, student gains in reading and mathematics were the highest. Students who spent a lot of time on nonacademic activities, or who were expected to learn by themselves, gained less.

This study was extremely important in the time-on-task literature. First, the variable of time was no longer a feature found only in laboratory studies about which one could speculate. It affected real classrooms across the United States. The sample was reasonably large, and the observation measure detailed and objective. It emphasized what many people felt they already knew: if you want to learn something, you have to spend time studying it.

This study was the first in a number of studies of this sort to suggest that student learning in mathematics and reading is dependent upon their being directly instructed in these subjects. A second study done a few years later by Barak Rosenshine pinpointed the need to think not only about the time teachers allocate for instruction but also about actual engaged time. This important study is highlighted in Research Summary 4.1.

MAINTAINING HIGH ENGAGEMENT RATES

The Beginning Teacher Evaluation Study in California showed that in classrooms where the teachers allocated more time to a particular content area, the students learned more in that area; that engagement rate (the percentage of allocated time that students are engaged) is also related to student learning: and that students who perform tasks at a high success rate learn more than those who perform at a low success rate. Finally, researchers determined that five teaching functions were important in promoting high academic learning time: diagnosis, prescription, presentation, monitoring, and feedback. These functions are displayed in Figure 4.3.

The researchers found that although each of these functions needed to be carried out well, they could be combined in various instructional approaches that were equally successful; no one method of instruction was found to be more effective than another. Effective teachers approached their tasks and functions in different ways, but they all approached them very well and managed to maintain their students' attention on the academic tasks at hand.

RESEARCH SUMMARY
4.1

Rosenshine, B. (1980). How time is spent in elementary classrooms. In Denham, C., and Lieberman, A. (Eds.), *Time to learn.* Washington, D.C.: U.S. Department of Education.

PROBLEM: Given the relationship of allocated and engaged time to student learning, how much time do elementary teachers spend in teaching the two basic skills that are of most interest to parents and others: reading and mathematics? And what do teachers do with the rest of their time? Barak Rosenshine analyzed a data base from an important study conducted in the state of California called the Beginning Teacher Evaluation Study. He looked specifically at the time variable from each of the classrooms in the study.

SAMPLE AND SETTING: One phase of the Beginning Teacher Evaluation Study involved 25 second-grade and 25 fifth-grade teachers in schools located in urban, suburban, and rural school districts. These teachers were identified as more or less effective on the basis of how much their students learned in reading and mathematics during the school year. In each classroom three male and three female students were selected for intensive observation.

PROCEDURES: The teachers were intensively observed for a period of weeks, as were their six students. In addition, the teachers kept logs of their time use, and they were interviewed by the researchers. Rosenshine analyzed information on the average amounts of time teachers allocated to reading, mathematics, and other subjects, and the amounts of time their students were engaged on these tasks.

FINDINGS: Table 1 gives the teachers' average allocated time per day in different activities in grades 2 and 5. The total allocated time on academic activities, including reading, mathematics, and such "other academic" subjects as science and social studies was 2 hours and 12 minutes in grade 2, and 2 hours and 51 minutes in grade 5. Time allocated to nonacademic pursuits that included art, music, physical education, flag salutes, sharing, and storytelling was 55 minutes in grade 2 and 1 hour and 5 minutes in grade 5. Noninstructional time took up 19 percent of the major in-class time in grade 2, and 17 percent in grade 5.

Teachers varied considerably on the amounts of time spent in reading and mathematics. Table 2 lists the allocated time, engaged minutes, and engagement rate of the three teachers in each grade who obtained the highest engaged time, the average for all teachers, and for the lowest three teachers. Note that there are considerable differences in engaged minutes between the highest and lowest three teachers. In the grade two sample, for example, some students were engaged 1 hour and 25 minutes in reading, and others, 43 minutes. There was more than an hour's difference in the combined engaged minutes in grade five.

DISCUSSION AND IMPLICATIONS: Since the publication of this and similar studies, a number of programs have been developed to help teachers increase time on task. It is possible that if such a study were conducted today, the time on task would be considerably higher than it was in this study. Nonetheless, there are undoubtedly

TABLE 1 Average Allocated Time per Day in Different Activities

Time Category	Grade 2			Grade 5		
	Minutes per Day	Combined Minutes	Combined Percentage	Minutes per Day	Combined Minutes	Combined Percentage
Academic activities		2'12"	57%	1'50"	2'51"	60%
Reading and language arts	1'28"			1'50"		
Mathematics	36"			44"		
Other academic	8"			47"		
Nonacademic activities	55"	55"	24%	1'05"	1'05"	23%
Noninstructional activities		44"	19%		47"	17%
Transition	34"			34"		
Wait	4"			4"		
Housekeeping	6"			9"		
Major in-class time	3'51"	3'51"		4'44"	4'44"	
Lunch, recess, breaks	1'15"	1'15"		1'17"	1'17"	
Length of school day	5'06"	5'06"		6'00"	6'00"	

SOURCE: B. Rosenshine (1980), p. 125.

TABLE 2 Highest, Average, and Lowest Teachers in Academic Engaged Minutes

	Reading			Mathematics			Total	
	Allocated	Engagement Ratio	Engaged Minutes	Allocated	Engagement Ratio	Engaged Minutes	Allocated Time	Engaged Minutes
				Grade 2				
High 3	1'45"	81%	1'25"	35"	82%	30"	2'20"	1'55"
Average	1'30"	73%	1'04"	36"	71%	26"	2'06"	1'30"
Low 3	1'00"	72%	43"	30"	75%	22"	1'30"	1'05"
				Grade 5				
High 3	2'10"	80%	1'45"	53"	86%	45"	3'03"	2'30"
Average	1'50"	74%	1'20"	44"	74%	35"	2'25"	1'55"
Low 3	1'25"	63%	1'05"	38"	63%	22"	2'03"	1'25"

SOURCE: B. Rosenshine (1980), p. 114.

differences among teachers in engaged time. Given the relationship between engaged time and student learning, these differences are important. Students receiving the lesser amount of instruction are still expected to do well on the standardized tests given at the end of the year and are compared with students whose teachers maintain high engagement time. It therefore behooves teachers to maximize allocated time on academic subjects and to manage their classrooms so that the engagement rate is also high.

Figure 4.3 Instructional Functions in the Academic Learning Time Model of Classroom Instruction

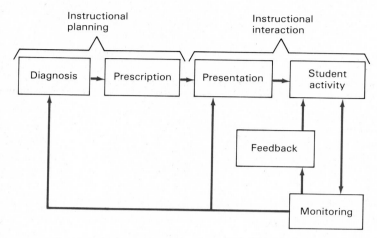

SOURCE: From Fisher et al. (1980), Teaching behavior, academic learning time, and student achievement: An overview. In C. Denham and A. Lieberman (Eds.), *Time to learn*. Washington, D.C.: National Institute of Education, Department of Education, p. 10.

Research on Space

The way space is managed has important cognitive and emotional effects on students. Although teachers do not control the amount of space provided, they have considerable leeway concerning its management.

PLACEMENT OF RESOURCES

In traditionally arranged classrooms (row upon row), teachers seem to interact mostly with a limited number of students: those located in the front row and the middle column. This phenomenon has been observed in elementary, secondary, and college classrooms. The students sitting in these positions participate more in discussion and initiate more comments than other students. Because of the heavy student activity in this part of the classroom, it has been named "the action zone."

One question asked by researchers was whether more motivated students choose action zone seats, or whether the action zone affects the participation rates of students regardless of who they are. Schwebel and Cherlin (1972) conducted several experiments and concluded that the action zone does affect the participation rates of students. Other researchers suggested that an important ingredient in this puzzle is teachers' eye contacts. Teachers establish better eye contact with those students in the action zone which, in turn, causes them to participate more in classroom activities and discussion. An interesting study conducted by Raymond Adams and Bruce Biddle almost two decades ago provides insight into the nature of the action zone. This study is described in Research Summary 4.2.

DESK AND STUDENT ARRANGEMENT

There is some evidence that teachers' personal needs affect their placement of desks and students. Feitler, Weiner, and Blumberg (1970) found that preservice teachers with a high need for control liked classroom arrangements in which the teacher was in an obvious position of control while preservice teachers with a low need for control selected settings in which the teacher was less visible and obvious.

Although the arrangement of desks, tables, and students appears to influence certain types of student behavior and attitudes, no study has yet demonstrated a relationship between desk and furniture placement and student achievement. For example, Horowitz and Otto (1973) found no differences in student achievement between those taking a course in a traditional classroom, and the same course in an alternative classroom with movable panels, flexible and comfortable seats. They did, however, find differences in student behavior. Attendance was higher, as was group cohesion and participation and visits to the instructor's office in the alternative room. The behaviors researchers have studied to date include attendance, attention, participation levels, student movement patterns, student-to-student interactions, and group cohesion.

Carol Weinstein was able to demonstrate how students' behavior in a primary classroom changed due to changes in physical space. This study is described in Research Summary 4.3.

Of interest to a number of researchers has been the placement of desks and students, for example, in a circle, traditional straight rows, or a horseshoe pattern. Circles appear to be extremely useful for some instructional functions. For example, one study found that when students crowd around a teacher during story-reading time they are less attentive than when they are sitting in a semicircle around the teacher (Krantz and Risley, 1972). Further, it would appear from a very recent study conducted by Peter Rosenfield and his colleagues that a circle formation enhances interaction in discussions. The study is described in Research Summary 4.4.

NOISE, DENSITY, AND THE PHYSICAL ENVIRONMENT

Many teachers and principals place a premium on maintaining a quiet atmosphere in the classrooms and halls. A quiet atmosphere is generally thought to contribute to effective learning. However, research has found that students seem to adjust to normal school noises, such as students pushing and yelling in the halls or power mowers outside windows. There appears to be no clear-cut relationship

RESEARCH SUMMARY
4.2

Adams, R. S., and Biddle, B. J. (1970). *Realities of teaching: Explorations with videotape.* New York: Holt, Rinehart and Winston.

PROBLEM: What do teachers do all day? What language can be used to describe what they do? Does one teacher act differently than another? Why? When parents, administrators, and journalists complain about what goes on in schools, can teaching be talked about in a way that illustrates the complexity of the task?

These questions propelled Adams and Biddle to look at samples of classroom behavior and attempt to develop a way of talking about what they saw. They believed that the best way to do so was to video-tape the activities of a few teachers, to view them together, and then attempt to describe what they saw. This, then, was one of the first major studies to systematically use videotaping to describe teaching, and it gives us valuable information about the action zone.

SAMPLE AND SETTING: The researchers video-taped and analyzed 32 lessons in 16 classrooms. Grades 1, 3, and 11 classrooms were used. Half of the lessons observed were in elementary and half in secondary schools. The subjects were social studies and mathematics. The researchers estimated that the quality of teachers, administrators, and equipment in these classrooms was above average.

PROCEDURES: Two cameras were used in each room: one had a wide-angle lens to pick up activity in the classroom; the second had a zoom lens to concentrate on the teacher. A number of microphones picked up the classroom sounds.

The videotapes were coded using a system developed by the researchers. The system was able to code the type of activity as well as the duration of the activity. For example, the researcher would code teacher talk, how long the teacher talked without interruption, where the teacher was standing during this time, and whom he or she was addressing.

RESULTS: Adams and Biddle found that classrooms are busy places. In one classroom, changes in activities occurred on the average of once every five seconds. But there were considerable differences among the teachers: some had as few as 157 episodes, others as many as 738.

---

between fairly common school noise, even at a high level, and student performance on tasks.

On the other hand, extremely high levels of noise outside of a school, such as a nearby train, or a low-flying airplane, do appear to affect achievement. Some hypothesize that such noise bothers teachers more than students, causing teachers to allocate less classroom time to academic content (Kyzar, 1977).

They also found that teachers move quite often but their movement is limited to three areas: front and center, up and down the central aisle, and around the edges of the room.

The researchers found that in most lessons and at all grade levels there was a central group of actively participating students. The teachers talked to them, asked them questions, and they responded and also asked questions and contributed to discussions. The others did not actively participate—they either withdrew, talked with neighbors, or worked.

It turned out that these active students were almost always located in one section of the classroom that was called the *action zone*. The action zone consisted of the front three middle students and the three down the middle aisle. These students received 64 percent of the questions. Part of this was due to the unusual position of the teacher—front and center.

DISCUSSION AND IMPLICATIONS: It is clear that the videotaping and the analysis of classroom behavior used in this study uncovered some little known aspects of classroom life. First, it is extremely complex, with many activities going on quickly, if not simultaneously. It also uncovered a relationship between where a teacher stands and a pupil sits, and the participation pattern in the classroom. Students sitting in the front row and center aisle receive more attention from the teacher, possibly because of eye contact. This presents an equity problem, particularly if a student who is naturally reticent sits out of the action zone.

Because this was an observation study, it is not clear whether or not students who wish to volunteer sit in the action zone. But it is clear that these are the students who are actively participating. What are the other students doing while the lesson is going on? And how can teachers involve pupils not in the action zone in their lessons?

Possibly if teachers stood in different places in the classroom, and made sure that they had eye contact with more students than those in the action zone, more students would participate.

Intuition about density is not always backed by research evidence. Many people would hypothesize that a crowded classroom would affect achievement, but this is not always true. There are two types of density: social density, in which the size of the group varies in a given space, and spatial density, in which the size of the group remains constant, but the size of the space varies. In terms of social density, the achievement of students in classes with 40 or more students

═══════════════════════ **RESEARCH SUMMARY** ═══════════════════════
4.3

Weinstein, C. S. (Summer 1977). Modifying student behavior in an open classroom through changes in the physical design. *American Educational Research Journal, 14,* 249–262.

PROBLEM: While many teachers go to great lengths to arrange the desks, work spaces, learning centers, and so forth, it has not been shown experimentally that these changes make a difference in student behaviors. While such studies have been done in other fields, few studies have been able to guide teachers in their arrangements of work spaces in open classrooms. The purpose of this study was to determine if changes in the arrangement of furniture would cause students to operate in a manner more closely aligned with the teachers' goals.

SAMPLE AND SETTING: Twenty-five second- and third-grade students in a self-contained, open classroom were the subjects in this study. The classroom had been divided into five areas: mathematics, reading, games, art, and science. Students were not confined to working on the specific subject matter in the areas: there were other places where the material could be located such as corners and files. The teacher worked with small groups and individuals during the day, introducing new material and checking on academic progress.

PROCEDURE: Students were observed through time sampling. The researcher coded a child's behavior and then went on to the next child. The researcher was interested in where the child was in the classroom, to whom she or he was talking, and the nature of the activities.

As the patterns of student behavior were discussed with the teacher, certain problems were identified. The researcher changed the design of the room in an attempt to alleviate these problems. For example, the science area was cleaned up, and more space was allocated to storage. Behaviors before and after these changes were statistically compared to determine whether the differences were significant.

The problems identified by the analysis prior to the change were:

1. Students were not distributed evenly across the room. This meant overcrowding in some areas and underutilization in others.
2. Girls avoided the games and science areas.
3. Not much variety in behavior was observed in the games and science areas.
4. The manipulatives in these two areas were underused.
5. Too much undesirable behavior was occurring in the reading area.

───

is negatively affected, but in classes with 18 or fewer students it is positively affected (Glass, Cahen, Smith, and Filby, 1982). However, varying classroom populations from between 20 to 30 students does not seem to affect achievement consistently. One explanation may be that teachers learn to compensate for

RESULTS: The prechange and postchange participation patterns are shown in Table 1. As can be observed, many adjustments were made. The math area became less crowded, and more students—both male and female—used the science and games areas. In the reading area, students exhibited less "looking at people" behavior.

TABLE 1   Area Populations by Sex

Area	Prechange Population		Postchange Population	
	Males (%)	Females (%)	Males (%)	Females (%)
Art	15.9	14.0	12.8	19.6
Corner	3.8	4.7	2.8	5.5
File	10.9	9.1	4.2	3.3
Games	14.9	3.0	21.9	13.5
Mathematics	12.8	29.0	15.6	15.9
Reading	26.6	30.1	24.3	29.7
Science	14.0	8.6	18.2	12.3
	98.9[a]	98.5	99.8	99.8

[a] The percentages unaccounted for represent the students observed in the hall.
SOURCE: C. S. Weinstein (1977), p. 256.

DISCUSSION AND IMPLICATIONS: This study was limited to second- and third-grade students and to an open classroom setting. Nonetheless, it is experimental, meaning that cause can be attributed to the changes in student behavior. It is clear from this study that the design of the classroom can increase positive student behavior and reduce negative student behavior.

It is not always possible to invite a researcher into the classroom to observe patterns of behavior and redesign the room, but it is possible to: (1) assess goals during the year with respect to classroom activities—e.g., are girls participating as much as you would like, or too much? (2) look carefully at the room arrangement to determine if there are barriers or space problems that could be adjusted; (3) make physical changes and look for behavior changes in the students. Furniture is probably one of the easier aspects of the classroom to adjust; teachers should find it quite easy to experiment with room arrangement.

moderate variations of density.

Finally, the atmosphere of a classroom itself can influence student attitudes and behaviors. Classroom atmosphere is not discussed here, however, since a complete chapter is devoted to this topic later.

RESEARCH SUMMARY
4.4

Rosenfield, P., Lambert, N., and Black, A. (1985). Desk arrangement effects on pupil classroom behavior. *Journal of Educational Psychology, 77,* 101–108.

PROBLEM: Desks in classrooms are no longer nailed to the floor. In most settings, they can be moved around with some ease. Are there better or worse arrangements for desks? Do some arrangements facilitate certain classroom tasks such as discussions? The purpose of this study was to compare student on- and off-task discussion behavior in rooms where the desks were arranged in a circle, in a row, or in clusters.

SAMPLE AND SETTING: Students in 2 fifth-, 2 fifth-sixth-, and 2 sixth-grade regular classrooms in several elementary schools in California participated in the study. In each of the 6 classrooms, eight students (four girls, four boys) were observed: two high ability, two low ability, two high interactors, and two low interactors. They were observed while brainstorming ideas for reading assignments. Brainstorming is a process used in a writing program called *Project Write.* All teachers had been trained in brainstorming techniques.

PROCEDURES: The classroom of each grade level was a control classroom, and was organized in a circle, row, or clusters. The three experimental classrooms were organized in all three structures at different times. The eight students in all classrooms were observed in on- and off-task behaviors, and the behaviors of the students in the different structures were compared.

RESULTS: Table 1 lists the frequency of observed behavior of the students in the three different structures in the experimental classrooms. As can be seen from the table, the arrangement least conducive to on-task and most related to off-task behavior during discussion is with the desks in rows. Desks in rows seem to be more related to student withdrawal than desks in clusters or circles. In addition, the circle arrangement was related to more on-task, out-of-order comments than rows and clusters.

USING TIME AND SPACE EFFECTIVELY

Time and space are two resources over which teachers have considerable control. Although they must still abide by the concept of a school period of fixed duration, at least in secondary schools, and cannot make their classrooms larger, teachers still have a wide variety of options available to them. There is, however, an interesting difference between time and space. Both are finite and limited, but time is the more crucial and coveted resource in terms of academic goals. Time pressures lead to considerations of efficiency, such as, "How can I maximize instruction to increase student time on task?" Space, although also finite, is in less demand for most teachers and is less likely, therefore, to produce considerations of efficiency. The primary concern with space is not to race with it as it is with

TABLE 1   **Average Frequency of Observed Behavior by Desk Arrangement**

Behavior	Rows	Cluster	Circle	Significant Contrasts[a]
	On-Task Behavior			
Hand-raising	2.82	3.40	2.35	cluster ⟩ circle
Listening	11.85	11.72	12.40	ns
Discussion comment	0.50	0.50	0.68	ns
On-task out-of-order comment	0.67	1.25	1.60	circle ⟩ rows
On-task oral response	1.18	1.76	2.28	circle ⟩ rows
Total	15.78	16.89	17.03	cluster ⟩ rows circle ⟩ rows
	Off-Task Behavior			
Disruptive behavior	0.62	0.68	0.69	ns
Withdrawal	3.54	2.43	2.28	rows ⟩ cluster rows ⟩ circle
Total	4.17	3.11	2.97	rows ⟩ circle

NOTE: Average frequency was based on number of observed behaviors during a total of 540 minutes of observation.
[a] Tukey's tests were used to calculate those significant contrasts $p < .05$.
SOURCE: P. Rosenfield, N. Lambert, and A. Black (1985), p. 105.

DISCUSSION AND IMPLICATIONS: Most of the past research on arrangement of desks or chairs took place in highly artificial, experimental situations. This experiment took place in regular classrooms in connection with the type of writing task often seen in elementary schools.

It appears that discussions, such as brainstorming, should take place with desks arranged in a circle. In clusters, students raise their hands more than in circles. In circles they also make on-task, out-of-order comments more often than in clusters or rows. This indicates more active participation in circles than in rows and clusters. In rows, more students withdraw.

time, but to experiment reflectively with rearranging the design of the classroom.

Effective, experienced teachers often make decisions about time and space almost automatically. They seem to know how to arrange a room for the most effective learning and management. They seem to know how much time is required for students to master a difficult idea or task. Beginning teachers, however, are less sure when performing these important executive functions. This section provides some ways to think about how to manage time and space.

Using Time

In planning, beginning teachers must consider how long to spend on each subject and activity. They must constantly ask themselves, "Is there enough time to cover another activity? Am I spending too much time on that task?"

The time research described in the previous section provides teachers with a method for determining whether students are learning. It is sometimes difficult to know this without using a test. But because studies have correlated student achievement with academic learning time, teachers can gauge whether their students are learning by quick scans to determine whether they are on task, and whether their success rates at the tasks are high. If academic learning time is high, the students are probably learning the material that is being presented to them. If it is low, changes should be made in the management of instruction or in the difficulty level of the content.

HOW TO INCREASE TIME ON TASK

Maximizing time on task requires, first and foremost, a teacher attitude that says student learning of the academic material is the goal of instruction, and that the responsibility of the teacher is to provide conditions conducive to learning. Time is not something to get through; it is a valuable resource that should be used to maximum advantage. The findings from the Beginning Teacher Evaluation Study (Fisher et al., 1980) provide some guidelines to use in maximizing academic learning time.

These guidelines are presented as research findings rather than as prescriptions (statements about what a teacher should do). Their purpose is to help beginning teachers keep their minds on the goal of maximizing time and to think about the use of time in relationship to their own classrooms. Such thinking should encourage the teacher to experiment with different management systems and evaluate them in order to increase academic learning time. The effective systems, however, will differ from classroom to classroom, which is why specific prescriptions for behavior are not always useful. The following research findings relate to the concept of academic learning time:

- *Allocated and engaged time* Students in classrooms in which the allocated time is high and the proportion of student engaged time is high learn more than in any other type of classroom.
- *Success level* If the tasks presented by the teachers are performed at a high level of success by the students, the students will learn more than if the tasks are performed at a low level of success.

The following management and interaction behaviors of teachers help to maximize academic learning time and thus student achievement:

Accurate *diagnosis* of student skill level
Prescription of appropriate tasks
Substantive interaction (as compared with social, disciplinary, or procedural interaction) with students

Provision of *academic feedback* to students, particularly when they make an
  error
Structuring the lesson and providing directions on task procedures
Creating a *learning environment* in which students take responsibility for
  their work and cooperate on academic tasks

The following teacher behaviors were negatively related to maximizing
academic learning time and student achievement:

Explanation in response to student need
Frequent reprimands for inappropriate behavior

The second-to-the-last finding is curious, is it not? Does it mean that a
teacher should not answer students' questions when they are having difficulty
completing a task? More likely, it means that if students need to ask many
questions in order to complete a task, the teacher either has not explained the
task well to the students, or the task is set at an inappropriate level. Remember,
it is important for students to be successful in their task performance. If it is too
difficult for them, they will ask many questions. These issues are discussed in
more detail in Chapters 5 and 6.

Another curious finding relates to the reprimands for inappropriate behavior.
What does one do if a student behaves inappropriately? In well-managed
classrooms, teachers catch problem behavior before it disrupts the classroom.
Therefore, a significant number of reprimands in a classroom indicates that the
classroom is not well managed.

This picture of the well-managed classroom indicates that teachers require
skills in diagnosis and prescription; they must be sensitive to individual differences
and be able to present material at an appropriate level. Above all, effective teachers
must value student achievement and emphasize academic goals.

HOW TO USE HOMEWORK TO EXTEND LEARNING TIME

One way to extend academic learning time is to give students homework. If
students practice their skills at home, more time will be available during the
school day for academic instruction. But homework cannot be given out carelessly
or frivolously. If the teacher doesn't value it, the students won't. Here are three
general guidelines for homework:

1. Students should be given homework that they can perform successfully.
   Homework should not involve the continuation of instruction, but the
   continuation of practice.
2. Parents should be informed of the level of involvement with their children's
   homework expected of them. Are they expected to help their sons or daughters

with answers to difficult questions or simply to provide a quiet atmosphere in which the students can complete their homework assignments? Are they supposed to check it over? Do they know the approximate frequency and duration of homework assignments?

3. Feedback should be provided on the homework. Many teachers simply check to determine whether the homework was performed. What this says to the students is that it doesn't matter how it is done, as long as it is done. Students soon figure out that the task is to get something—anything—on paper. One method for providing feedback is to involve other students in correcting the homework.

What if the students do not perform their homework? This is a difficult problem in schools that have not communicated the importance of completing homework assignments or in schools where parents do not value homework. The rules for doing homework must be fair and clear and the consequences for not doing it should be laid out during the first week of class. One consequence, for example, might be a lower grade for a certain number of assignments missed, and if the student goes beyond that level, the teacher might involve the parents.

The consequences must also be fairly and consistently applied in cases in which students do not perform their assignments. Consistency is important, but so is compassion. A truly reasonable excuse should be accepted, although it is also helpful to demand some evidence, such as a note from a parent.

In summary, time is an important and scarce commodity that has sparked a continuing research effort over the past two decades. The importance of this body of research is that it focuses teachers' goals on maximizing academic learning time and provides a rationale for insisting on a task-oriented classroom. Above all, it provides teachers with a way of thinking about their classrooms. One teacher (Muir, 1980) who had been involved in a research study around academic learning time (ALT) put it this way:

> ALT is a powerful tool, not a prescription for how and when to use the tool. ALT as a concept is dynamic and ever-changing in each classroom because it focuses on ever-changing and growing human beings. A teacher must make constant adjustments in practices within the year as well as from year to year. Teachers do make a difference through their sensitivities and perceptions of their students, as well as with their academic knowledge. Only a teacher, a growing human being, can use tools such as ALT and utilize the skills mentioned in the study to synthesize a program and environment that are flexible, personalized, and appropriate for both teacher and student. . . .
>
> I suggest that teachers "play" with the issues and concepts presented in BTES [Beginning Teacher Evaluation Study]. Experiment with the ideas and the variables that appear relevant for your grade level and classroom. Primary and upper elementary classrooms are very different. Measure your ALT and transition time. Challenge yourself to increase ALT and decrease transition time regardless of your basic educational philosophy. Interesting changes may occur for you. (p. 212)

Using Space

FURNITURE ARRANGEMENT

A major decision that most teachers make at the beginning of the school year relates to the configuration of furniture in a room. (In secondary schools, this is not always the case, as some teachers move from classroom to classroom.) The way in which the furniture is arranged can influence academic learning time and, thus, student learning.

The first step in this decision-making process is to assess the quantity and type of furniture that is available. Are there chairs with desks attached? This is often the case in secondary schools. Are there tables and chairs? Are there larger tables available for activity centers? Are there more tables and chairs than students? Are there bookcases? Bulletin boards? It may be useful to talk to the person in the school responsible for furniture to determine if there is a storage room with extra furniture.

The second step is to assess your own style of teaching. Will you like to see all the students at once? Will you use small group activities? Centers? Will you lecture with recitation most of the time?

The form of the classroom should match its functions with different formations being used for different functions. Here are the three most used formations:

- *Row and column* This is the most traditional formation. In fact, not too long ago (and perhaps in some schools today), the desks were attached to the floor in rows. This formation is best suited to situations where the teacher wants attention focused in one direction, for example, on him or her during lecture or recitation, or during independent seatwork. A variant on the row and column arrangement is the horizontal row formation in which students sit quite close to each other in a fewer number of rows. This arrangement is useful for demonstration because the students are sitting quite close to the teacher. Neither of these arrangements is conducive to class discussion, however, or to small group activities.

- *Circles* As described in the research section, circles are useful for class discussion and independent seatwork. They are not the best arrangement for presentations or demonstrations because some students would inevitably face the teacher's back. For early elementary situations in which the teacher is reading to the students, students should sit in a semicircle rather than randomly sitting on a rug.

- *Clusters* Seating clusters of four or six, such as those illustrated in Figure 4.4, are useful for group discussion, for cooperative learning, or other small group tasks. If this arrangement is used, students may have to be asked to move their chairs for lectures or demonstrations so that all students will be facing the teacher. Movement, however, as will be described in Chapter 6, can lead to disruption and cause management problems.

Figure 4.4   Four- and Six-Cluster Seating Arrangements

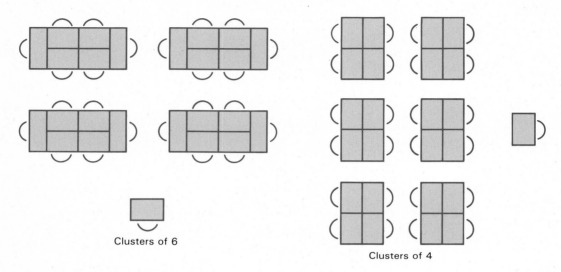

Clusters of 6

Clusters of 4

Beginning teachers who are organizing rooms so that a number of independent activities can take place simultaneously should keep the following six guidelines in mind:

1. If there are not enough clearly marked paths from one activity center to another, the students will push and pull in their attempts to move to another center. Research indicates that one-third to one-half of the classroom should be devoted to paths (Prescott, Jones, and Kritchevsky, 1967).
2. Play units should not be hidden from students' sight or they will fall into disuse.
3. Large, empty spaces encourage students to roughhouse.
4. At all centers, the number of students should be limited to the amount of material available.
5. Storage space for materials should be easily reached by the students and should be close to the surfaces on which they work.
6. In order to supervise all activities at once, the teacher should be able to see what is going on in the activity centers. Therefore, barriers should be low and centers should not be hidden from sight.

But what happens when a classroom is not big enough or there is not enough furniture to have different configurations at the same time? One way to handle this is to determine what teaching model is employed most frequently and then to match the basic configuration of the classroom to it. Does the teacher lecture, provide group activities, or conduct discussions with the students? For example, if the teacher provides a lot of group or individual seatwork tasks, the students can sit in clusters of four. When the teacher lectures to the whole group, one of the students in each cluster can shift his or her chair around so that it is facing the teacher. Further, students can be provided with hinged cardboard separators that they can place on their desks during tests or during individual seatwork when they do not want to be disturbed.

Above all, teachers should be flexible and experiment with different seating arrangements. It is important to highlight, however, that each configuration has its own rules of participation, and these need to be clearly spelled out to students. For example, during presentations, teachers generally ask students to raise their hands before they ask or answer questions; in a circle-discussion session, students may be encouraged to speak out without raising their hands. Therefore, too much experimentation can confuse students who have just learned the rules from a preceeding form. Rules and procedures for various classroom activities must be taught to students like any other topic. Procedures for moving from one arrangement to another must also be taught and practiced. All of this will be described in more detail in Chapters 5 and 6.

CLASSROOM AMBIENCE

Although evidence about the ambience of the classroom is not conclusive, experienced teachers know that it is important. Studies in later chapters illustrate how cheerful rooms affect students' concentration. You know from other experiences that some environments are warm and inviting places but others are cold and sterile places you try to avoid.

The teacher does not have to be an artist or interior designer to decorate a classroom and make it a pleasant place for students to be. Nor does it require large amounts of money. In fact, students can even help produce an interesting-looking, warm-feeling room. Many students feel good about seeing their work on the walls, and such displays can be used as an incentive system. For example, the teacher can institute a "drawing of the week" or an "essay of the week" to hang on a colorful bulletin board. Or groups of students can draw murals to illustrate a story they have read. This is just as important in secondary classrooms as it is in elementary classrooms.

SOUND

As explained previously, there is not a direct relationship between school and classroom noise and student learning. For example, a buzzing in the classroom could indicate that the students are working together on an academic task despite noise in the hall. In fact, it is important for students to talk to each other when learning new skills and concepts and to help each other with important classroom tasks. Classroom noise *per se* is not a problem. Only certain types of noise made at inappropriate times should be viewed as a classroom problem—that is, as a deterrent to the academic tasks at hand. What is important is what the students are talking about and when. If two students are having a social conversation, even if they are quiet about it, they are not maintaining high academic learning time. If a number of students are talking while the teacher is talking, other students' concentration may be disrupted. This issue will be explored more fully in Chapter 6 and also in the chapters on the interactive functions of teaching.

Summary

This chapter pointed out that the way in which teachers manage time and space affects what and how much their students learn. Time can be viewed as something to get through, or as a scarce resource to manage with care and foresight. The arrangement and the ambience of classroom space affects how classroom participants feel about school, how they communicate with each other, and how well they accomplish academic tasks. Time and space are related to each other around the learning task. If the arrangement of space produces management problems or inhibits task completion, time on task is reduced.

The effective management of time and space demands an attitude of flexibility and experimentation and a belief that students are there to learn. Flexibility is important because every classroom is different and therefore plans and activities must often be adjusted to particular circumstances. Experimentation involves trying various classroom configurations and seating arrangements and being reflective about the results. Flexibility and experimentation without careful reflection about results do not necessarily lead to the optimum arrangement and may actually confuse students.

Above all, teachers must adopt the attitude that they are there to enable students to learn, and that all students are able, with guidance, to learn the knowledge and skills that are set for them.

Books for the Professional

Denham, C., and Lieberman, A. (Eds.). (1980). *Time to learn*. Washington, D.C.: U.S. Department of Education. This book contains a description of the study that led to the concept of academic learning time and a set of responses to the concept by scholars and practitioners.

Time on task. (1982). Alexandria, Va.: American Association of School Administrators. This little booklet describes the time-on-task research and provides pointers for observing the different types of time in the classroom. While this booklet was prepared for administrators, it is also extremely useful for teachers.

CHAPTER 4
LEARNING AIDS FOR PLANNING, OBSERVATION, AND REFLECTION

- Assessing My Thinking About Using Time and Space Effectively
- Observing Off-Task Time in Classrooms
- Analysis of Cases of Classroom Space Arrangements
- Observing Space Arrangements in Different Classrooms
- Observing Differences Between Planned Time and Allocated Time
- Planning Guide for Homework Assignments

ASSESSING MY THINKING ABOUT USING TIME
AND SPACE EFFECTIVELY

PURPOSE: Time and space are scarce resources that can require complex management strategies. This aid is to help you clarify your thinking about managing time and space.

DIRECTIONS: Write a paragraph on how you think about time for teaching. You can project ahead and imagine how you will feel as a teacher, or you can think about actual teaching experiences in field work or microteaching. How many times did you feel that there was not enough time? How many times did you worry about filling in time? Did you sense that the time was filled with academic tasks? With management concerns?

Write a paragraph on your favorite activities in class; again, imagine yourself in your own classroom or think about actual teaching experiences you've had. Describe the space arrangements in the classroom. Do space arrangements mesh with the activities? What do you like to do most in the classroom: lecture, allow students to learn independently or do seatwork, allow students to work together in groups, and so on? Now consider the space arrangement in the classroom. Does that arrangement allow for the types of activities with which you feel most comfortable?

OBSERVING OFF-TASK TIME IN CLASSROOMS

PURPOSE: Time on task is one of the most important variables in student learning. It is vital that teachers learn how to spot off-task behavior. This aid will help sensitize you to the signs that students are off task. It has been designed around some of the ideas of Stallings, whose research was described earlier in the chapter.

DIRECTIONS: Fill in the first two lines of the form below. In the space, draw a map of the seating arrangement in the classroom. Draw a box for each student, leaving space below the line for four marks. At five-minute intervals, make marks below the names of students who are off task to describe their activities, using the codes below. Before each mark, write 1, 2, 3, 4, to record the observation number. Also, fill in the top of the form to describe the teacher activity.

Students Off-Task Seating Chart

Date _____   Teacher _____

Activity 1 _____ Time _____

Activity 2 _____ Time _____

Activity 3 _____ Time _____

Activity 4 _____ Time _____

front of classroom

CODES: S = Socializing
        U = Uninvolved
        W = Waiting for assistance

ANALYSIS OF CASES OF CLASSROOM SPACE ARRANGEMENTS

PURPOSE: As discussed in the chapter, space is not as scarce a resource as time, but it still can be managed effectively to produce desired effects on learning and student behavior. This aid will help you gain facility in planning for the use of space.

DIRECTIONS: Analyze the following cases of classroom space arrangements. Will the teachers experience management problems because of the arrangement? At what points? What changes would you suggest?

1. Having heard that students should sit in a circle during small reading groups, Ms. Green found two curved tables and placed them together in a corner of her first-grade classroom for her small reading groups. (Ms. Green does not have an aide in her 24-student classroom.)

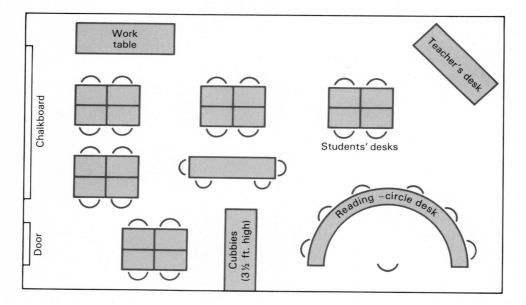

2. In an attempt to promote peer group teaching, Mr. Gold rearranged his ninth-grade algebra class to allow for more student-student interaction during seatwork. He spends 40 minutes of each period working on problems on the board.

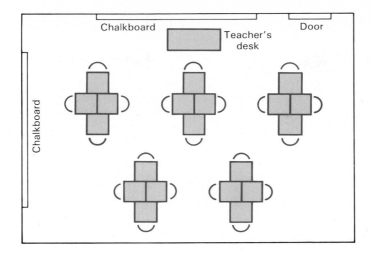

3. Ms. Scarlet has a small third-grade classroom with 26 children. She believes in learning centers and lots of independent reading in an inviting and comfortable area. She established three learning centers along one side of the classroom, a small group reading table, and a library with a rug on the floor.

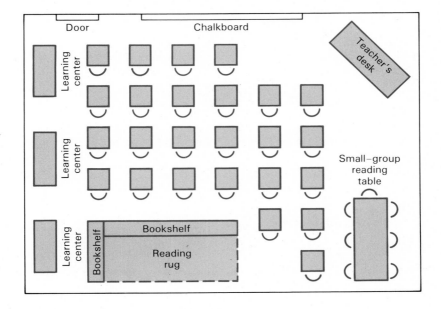

Analysis and Reflection: Reflect on what you consider to be your own emerging teaching style. What space arrangements will best suit it?

OBSERVING SPACE ARRANGMENTS IN DIFFERENT CLASSROOMS

PURPOSE: This aid will give you further practice in making the link between classroom activities and space arrangements.

DIRECTIONS: Observe the use of space in two different classrooms at the same grade level or, if in a secondary school, the same subject. Draw a diagram of the classroom. Observe students' movements in the space. Compare the two arrangements by answering the following questions for each:

1. What are the dominant modes of instruction in the classroom?

_____

_____

2. How much do students move around? During what periods of time?

_____

_____

3. Does there appear to be congestion in the classroom? At what points?

_____

4. How much is each classroom area used during the course of the day?

_____

5. How much decoration is there in the room? Does it relate to the subject? Is it student made? _____

_____

_____

Analysis and Reflection: Which room achieves a better use of space? Why?

OBSERVING DIFFERENCES BETWEEN PLANNED TIME AND ALLOCATED TIME

assignment 7

PURPOSE: An important element of time on task is how much time the teacher actually makes available for learning, or allocated time. This aid will help you highlight the difference between planned time and allocated time and show how planned time can become lost.

DIRECTIONS: Keep a running log of a teacher's classroom activities using a stopwatch. Record the time and nature of each transition from direct instruction to other activities, such as management or transition, disciplining, socializing, and back to direct instruction, that the teacher engaged in. An example is provided below.

Teacher _____ Date: _____ Time: _____

Time	Activity
12:00	Bell rings for beginning of period. Teacher asks students to take their seats and be quiet. (Management)
12:03	Teacher asks students to take out their homeworks and pass them to the students behind them. (Management)
12:05	Teacher starts going over each problem. (Direct instruction)
12:09	Teacher reprimands two students who are arguing over what one really wrote on page. Students continue to argue. (Discipline)
12:11	Teacher goes back to problems. (Direct instruction)
12:15	Teacher asks students to write the number correct on the papers and pass them to the front.
12:17	Teacher begins explaining the new work.

Total time elapsed: 17 minutes
Amount of direct instruction: 8 minutes
Percentage of direct instruction: 47 percent

Use the following form for recording your own observations.

Time	Activity
_____	_____
_____	_____
_____	_____
_____	_____
_____	_____
_____	_____
_____	_____

Total time elapsed: _____

Amount of direct instruction: _____

Percentage of direct instruction: _____

Analysis and Reflection: Did this teacher lose any planned time in management, discipline, or other ways? What could he or she have done to prevent this loss of instructional time?

PLANNING GUIDE FOR HOMEWORK ASSIGNMENTS

PURPOSE: Assigning homework is an important element in proper use of instructional time. Different homework policies have different impacts on the teacher. This aid will help you clarify your beliefs about homework, so that whatever policy you select can be implemented properly.

DIRECTIONS: Answer the following questions about homework to help you establish your own future homework policies.

1. Do you believe homework should be given every night? (This means that you are willing to correct it or have the other students correct it every day.) If not, how many times per week? _____

   _____

2. Should students be allowed to begin and possibly finish their homework in class?

   _____

3. How long should students spend on homework in class? _____

   _____

4. What type of homework do you think should be given students? Practice work? Creative work? Library work? Other work? _____

   _____

5. Would you plan any long-term assignments that require parents' help to make sure that students obtain information at libraries or other sources? _____

   _____

6. What incentives would you provide for doing homework? _____

   _____

7. Will you grade the homework or just make sure it is completed?

   _____

   _____

8. What happens if a student does not bring in his or her homework? Will you listen to excuses (for example, I left it at home; the dog ate it)? _____

   _____

9. What percentage of the grade should be homework? _____

_____

10. In what ways should parents be involved in helping students with their homework? (For example, will you want them to correct it or just ensure that it is completed?) _____

_____

Analysis and Reflection: Now that you have thought about and answered the above questions about homework, draft a sample letter to parents explaining your policies and indicating their responsibilities. This letter should not be overly prescriptive nor heavy-handed. Further, it should be written in such a way as to be understood by all parents. Finally, it should suggest a partnership between you and them to work on their children's homework. You may wish to include a survey to gauge parents' knowledge about their children's homework. Possible questions include: "How many nights per week does your son or daughter bring home homework from this class?" "On nights he or she does have homework, how much time does your son or daughter spend on it?"

CHAPTER 5

MAIN IDEAS

- Classrooms are social systems, and as such they influence both student and teacher behavior. The relevant forces include the needs and motives of individuals, institutional roles, and the interaction between members' needs and group norms.
- Classroom structures and processes in some cases can be altered by the teacher and in some cannot.
- Student motivation and learning are influenced by the types of processes and structures created in particular classrooms.
- Research on classroom environments has uncovered important relationships between leader and member behaviors and their influence on student learning.
- Teachers create productive learning environments by focusing on things that can be altered, such as: increasing student motivation, encouraging group development, and facilitating classroom communication and discourse.

Building Productive Learning Environments

Students and teachers spend roughly half of their waking hours in the social arrangement we call a classroom and, as in all social settings, they interact with each other. Teachers interact with students and students with teachers; students interact with each other and with various academic materials. As this collection of individuals works with one another, a group develops. Teachers report that each class takes on a "distinct personality." Students report that their class is "great" or "not so great," and they remember for years their third-grade class, their fifth-period English class, or their homeroom. What classroom participants remember is not necessarily what the teacher taught. Instead, they describe and remember the social-psychological dimensions of the classroom. Luft (1970) described this unique dimension in the following way:

> A (classroom) group may be thought of as a developing system with its own structure, organization and norms. Classes may look alike from a distance or on paper, but actually each class is as unique as a fingerprint. Each class develops its own internal procedures and patterns of interactions and its own limits. It is as if imaginary lines were guiding and controlling behavior within the group. In spite of day-to-day variation there is a certain constancy in each class which emerges from its individual history. (p. 81)

The processes and structures teachers choose to build in classrooms are very important factors influencing how a class develops and the norms it establishes for social and academic learning. Providing leadership for building productive classroom environments is a critical executive function performed by teachers and provides the focus for this chapter. The chapter first introduces you to a set of conceptual frameworks to help you understand classroom environments, then presents a sample of the research on this topic. The chapter concludes with specific procedures teachers use to build productive learning environments plus several learning aids.

PERSPECTIVE AND RATIONALE

A productive learning environment is characterized by (1) an overall climate where students feel positive about themselves, their peers, and the classroom as a group;

159

(2) structures and processes where students' needs are satisfied and where students persist with academic tasks and work in cooperative ways with the teacher and other students; and (3) a setting where students have acquired the necessary group and interpersonal skills to accomplish the academic and group demands of the classroom.

Many of the concepts needed to understand classroom environments cannot be readily observed. They are psychosocial processes that are carried around in the minds of classroom members (teachers and students) and in the "ethos" of their group life. So, to understand classroom structures and processes one must acquire conceptual "lenses" with which to interpret what is observed. Increasingly scholars have tried to describe and understand what happens in classrooms. The following descriptions of some of their work will help you to understand the complexity of classrooms and how to build more productive learning environments.

Classroom Climate

Classroom climate is a fairly abstract concept that nevertheless helps researchers and teachers comprehend the atmosphere or ethos of classrooms. The theoretical basis for the concept of classroom climate emanates mainly from the work of Kurt Lewin and his many colleagues, who showed how the interactions between individuals' needs and environmental conditions were key factors in explaining human behavior. Getzels and Thelen (1960) applied some of these ideas by developing a framework to clarify what goes in classrooms. They described, in broad terms, the following characteristics of classroom groups: (1) a group that comes together for the purpose of learning; (2) a group where the participants are, for the most part, randomly selected and required to be group members; and (3) a group where formal leadership is given by law to one group member, the teacher. It was Getzels and Thelen's premise that understanding the relationships within such settings requires an explicit conceptual framework.

Getzels and Thelen's model of classroom groups has two important dimensions. The first dimension of the model describes how, within a classroom, there are individuals with certain personalities and needs. This psychological perspective can be labeled the *personal dimension* of classroom life. From this perspective, behavior is determined as a result of individual needs, motives, and attitudes, regardless of institutional role. The personal dimension can be illustrated as in Figure 5.1.

The second dimension of the model describes how classrooms exist within the school and how certain roles and expectations develop within that setting to fulfill the goals of the system. This dimension can be labeled the *social dimension of the classroom*. From this perspective classroom behavior is determined by the

Figure 5.1

INDIVIDUAL ⟶ PERSONALITY ⟶ NEEDS ⟶ BEHAVIOR

shared expectations (norms) that are part of institutional roles. They graphically portray behavior in this social dimension as shown in Figure 5.2.

Figure 5.2

INSTITUTION ⟶ ROLE ⟶ EXPECTATIONS ⟶ BEHAVIOR

It is the interaction of both the social and personal dimensions that determines behavior within a classroom setting and shapes a particular classroom's climate. Or, to simplify matters a bit, classroom social interaction is a result of individually motivated people responding to each other in a social setting. It is out of this self-other interaction that classroom climate evolves, sustains itself, and produces certain student behaviors for social and academic learning. This concept of classroom climate and its relationship to behavior can be diagrammed as in Figure 5.3.

Figure 5.3   The Class As a Social System

INDIVIDUAL ⟶ PERSONALITY ⟶ NEEDS

ACADEMIC LEARNING

GROUP ⟶ CLIMATE ⟶ INTENTIONS ⟶ BEHAVIOR ⟶

SOCIAL LEARNING

INSTITUTIONS ⟶ ROLE ⟶ EXPECTATIONS

Individual Needs and Motivation

Figure 5.3 illustrates how student behavior results from an interaction of both personal and social dimensions of classroom life. The consideration of students' needs in the personal dimension leads to a discussion of motivation, a very important topic for teachers. Motivation, like classroom climate, is an abstract concept that is not easy to define. It is internal to the person and thus cannot be observed. Nonetheless, experienced teachers know the importance of motivation and know that it is one of the important forces that guides students' actions. Although there are several features of the personal dimension of classrooms that would be discussed, this section will focus on the concept of motivation, because it is most directly applicable to classroom teaching and most alterable by teacher behavior. Two major ideas guide contemporary thinking on motivation: need disposition theory and attribution theory.

NEED DISPOSITION THEORY

Developed in the 1950s and 1960s (McClelland, 1958; Atkinson, 1958; Atkinson and Feather, 1966; Alschuler et al., 1970), need disposition theory presents the point of view that people are motivated to take action and invest energy in pursuit of three outcomes: achievement, affiliation, and influence.* The desire for achievement is evident when students are trying hard to learn a particular subject or when they are striving to reach the objectives of a particular teacher. Achievement manifests itself in teachers as they strive to provide good instruction and act as competent professionals. Affiliative motives become important when students and teachers come to value the support and friendship of their peers. The motivation toward influence can be seen in those students who strive to have more control over their own learning and in those teachers who strive to have a larger say in the way schools are run. Students' feelings of self-esteem are related to feelings they have about their competence, affiliation, and influence. When these emotional states are frustrated by the activities in a classroom or a school, students may become less involved in the school. When these states are frustrated for teachers they are likely to feel incompetent, lonely, and powerless.

Achievement motivation or the student's "intent to learn" is the most important aspect of this theory of motivation for classroom teaching and has been the focus of other theorists and researchers as they have refined and extended some of McClelland's and his colleagues' original ideas.

ATTRIBUTION THEORY

Much of the early research on achievement motivation found strong relationships between the child-rearing practices of parents and a child's achievement motivation. Parents who encourage their children to try new things and who reward them for high performance establish in their children a need to achieve and a willingness to take risks. On the other hand, parents who overly protect their children and punish them for failure tend to raise children with low achievement motivation. The assumption that achievement motivation is an unalterable result of early childhood experiences means teachers have little hope of changing a child's aspiration to learn. This led Bernard Weiner and several of his colleagues in the 1970s to propose attribution theory as an alternative explanation of achievement motivation. Attribution theory is a rather major reinterpretation of need disposition theory and is based on the proposition that the way persons come to *perceive* and to *interpret* the causes of their successes or failures are the major determinants of their achievement motivation, rather than fixed early experiences. According to Weiner (1974; 1979), success or failure can be attributed to four causes: ability, effort, luck, and the difficulty of the learning task. Some people tend to associate their success with their abilities and their failures with their lack of effort. Conversely, other people attribute their success to luck and their failures to their lack of ability. People with high achievement motivation seem to fall mostly in the first category; people with low achievement motivation in the second.

* Part of this discussion is adapted from Arends et al. (1981).

Attribution theory offers hope for teachers because, as is described later, teachers can do things to change students' perceptions of themselves and the things around them, and this in turn can lead to a corresponding increase in student effort.

Classroom Properties

The *social dimension* of the model developed by Getzels and Thelen helps teachers think about some of the global aspects of classroom life. In particular, it shows teachers that classroom behavior is a result of human interaction within a social system where each part of the system affects what goes on in other parts. This framework alone does not provide much detail about specific properties and processes that teachers might find in classrooms, but recent scholars have developed more detailed and helpful insights.

Among others, Walter Doyle (1979; 1980; 1986) has studied and described the nature of classroom groups. His perspective is that classroom settings have distinctive *properties* that shape behavior regardless of how students are organized for learning or what approach a particular teacher is using. The important properties from Doyle's (1986) perspective include:

1. Multidimensionality . . . a classroom is a crowded place in which many people with different preferences and abilities must use a restricted supply of resources to accomplish a broad range of social and personal objectives. Many events must be planned and orchestrated to meet special interests of members and changing circumstances throughout the year. Records must be kept, schedules met, supplies organized and stored, and student work collected and evaluated. In addition, a single event can have multiple consequences: Waiting a few extra moments for a student to answer a question can affect that student's motivation to learn as well as the pace of the lesson and the attention of other students in the class. Choices, therefore, are never simple.

2. Simultaneity . . . many things happen at once in classrooms. While helping an individual student during seatwork, a teacher must monitor the rest of the class, acknowledge other requests for assistance, handle interruptions, and keep track of time. During a discussion, a teacher must listen to student answers, watch other students for signs of comprehension or confusion, formulate the next question, and scan the class for possible misbehavior. At the same time, the teacher must attend to the pace of the discussion, the sequence of selecting students to answer, the relevance and quality of answers, and the logical development of content. When the class is divided into small groups, the number of simultaneous events increases, and the teacher must monitor and regulate several different activities at once.

3. Immediacy . . . [there is a] rapid pace of classroom events. Gump (1967) and Jackson (1968) have estimated that an elementary teacher has over 500 exchanges with individual students in a single day, and, in a study of first and fifth grade classes, Sieber (1979) found that teachers publicly evaluated pupil conduct with either praise or reprimands on an average of 15.89 times per hour, or 87 times a day, or an estimated 16,000 times a year . . . therefore, teachers have little leisure time to reflect before acting.

4. Unpredictability . . . classroom events often take unexpected turns. Distractions and interruptions are frequent. In addition, events are jointly produced and thus it is often difficult to anticipate how an activity will go on a particular day with a particular group of students.

5. Publicness . . . classrooms are public places and . . . events, especially those involving the teacher, are often witnessed by a large portion of the students. . . .

6. History . . . classes meet 5 days a week for several months and thus accumulate a common set of experiences, routines, and norms which provide a foundation for conducting activities. Early meetings often shape events for the rest of the term or year (Emmer et al., 1980), and routines and norms are established for behavior. A class is also affected by seasonal variations, periodic absences, the addition of new members, and the broad cycle of the year. (pp. 394–395)

Doyle's six properties directly affect the classroom climate and shape the behaviors of both teachers and students. As will be discussed later, some classroom properties can be altered by teachers; others cannot, at least not very easily.

Classroom Processes

Working with concepts and research on interpersonal relations and group dynamics, Richard Schmuck and Patricia Schmuck (1975) developed a slightly different framework for looking at classrooms. Classroom climate is an important concept in the Schmucks' framework just as it was for Getzels and Thelen. The Schmucks' unique contribution, however, is the way they define climate and the way they view interpersonal and group *processes* as important factors contributing to positive climates. The Schmucks define a positive climate as follows:

> A positive climate is one in which the students expect one another to do their intellectual best and to support one another; where the students share high amounts of potential influence—both with one another and with the teacher; in which high levels of attraction exist for the group as a whole and between classmates; where norms are supportive for getting academic work done, as well as for maximizing individual differences; where communication is open and featured by dialogue; and where the processes of working and developing together as a group are considered relevant in themselves for study. (p. 24)

For the Schmucks, positive classroom climates are created by teachers when they teach students important interpersonal and group process skills and when they help the classroom develop as a group. The Schmucks identify six group processes that, when working in relation to one another, produce a positive classroom climate.

1. *Expectations* In classrooms, people have expectations for each other and for

themselves. The Schmucks are interested in how expectations become patterned over time and how they influence classroom climate and learning.

2. *Leadership* This refers to how power and influence are exerted in classrooms and their impact on group interaction and cohesiveness. The Schmucks view leadership as an interpersonal process rather than as a characteristic of a person, and they encourage leadership to be shared in classroom groups.

3. *Attraction* This refers to the degree to which people in a classroom have respect for one another and how friendship patterns within classrooms affect climate and learning. The Schmucks encourage teachers to help create classroom environments characterized by peer groups free from cliques and where no student is left out of the friendship structure.

4. *Norms* Norms are the shared expectations students and teachers have for classroom behavior. The Schmucks value classrooms with norms that support high student involvement in academic work but at the same time encourage positive interpersonal relationships and shared goals.

5. *Communication* Most classroom interaction is characterized by verbal and nonverbal communication. The Schmucks argue for communication processes that are open, lively, and have a high degree of participant involvement.

6. *Cohesiveness* The final process refers to the feelings and commitments students and teachers have to the classroom group as a whole. The Schmucks advocate peer group cohesiveness but point out that it is important for this cohesiveness to be in support of academic work and member well-being.

Unlike the *properties* described by Doyle, classroom *processes* are highly influenced by the teacher's actions and can be altered to build productive classroom environments.

Classroom Structures

A final framework for viewing classroom life is one associated with classroom structures. Unlike the classroom properties described by Doyle, which are mostly fixed, or the classroom processes described by the Schmucks, which are highly alterable, classroom structures are the basic *patterns* of classroom organization. Although in many instances these patterns are fixed by tradition, they can be altered. One might compare classroom structures to the designs of houses. The way space in a house is designed and partitioned could be called the house's structure. This structure influences how people in the house normally interact with one another. For example, if the all the rooms are small and closed off, it is difficult to have a party where lots of people can move around and interact easily. Conversely, if the house is wide open, it is difficult for individuals to find privacy. While structures influence certain types of behavior, they do not guarantee or prevent specific behaviors. For example, you know of instances where good parties have occurred in small spaces; you also know of instances where ideal structural conditions have not produced positive family relationships. Structures, however, can be changed. Using the house analogy again, walls can be removed to encourage wider interaction, or screens can be stationed to provide privacy.

Three particular classroom structures are important to understand: task structures, goal structures, and reward structures.

CLASSROOM TASK STRUCTURES

Walter Doyle (1986), who has given considerable attention to the task structures found in classrooms, wrote that "broadly speaking, classroom teaching has two major task structures organized around the problems of (a) learning and (b) order" (p. 395). *Learning* task structures are those associated with instructional functions, such as covering academic content and promoting skill development. They also include what teachers do to motivate students so they will persist in learning tasks.

Order task structures are those associated with the managerial functions of teaching, such as establishing rules and routines, using space, pacing classroom activities, and reacting to student misbehavior. The task structures associated with learning are the most important for the purposes of this chapter; those associated with order will be emphasized in Chapter 6.

Classroom learning tasks not only help shape the way teachers and students behave but also help determine what students learn. Some task structures, and the demands they place on teachers and students, for example, are embedded in the subjects themselves. A lesson aimed at teaching the multiplication tables in mathematics, for instance, makes a different set of demands on learners than does an inquiry lesson in social studies. A literature lesson on character development makes different demands than does a spelling lesson.

Task structures also differ according to the particular teaching strategy or model being used by the teacher. As described in later chapters, lessons organized around lectures place far different demands on teachers than do lessons organized around small group discussions. Similarly, the demands on students during discussion periods differ from those associated with seatwork.

The nature of classroom tasks, according to Doyle, influences the degree of student cooperation and involvement in a particular lesson as well as the type of information processing and learning that occurs. For example, during a lesson on cells students will not only acquire information about cells but will also gain practice in *memorizing* the different layers in a cell and *classifying* cells according to some taxonomy. The important thing to remember is that classroom task structures influence the environment of the classroom and the thoughts and actions of the classroom participants. In a later section you will see how students need to be taught learning strategies in order to satisfy the task demands being placed on them in classrooms.

CLASSROOM GOAL STRUCTURES

A second important structure is one David Johnson and Roger Johnson (1975) labeled classroom goal structures. In Chapter 3, the concept of instructional goals was introduced and a definition provided. The Johnsons provided a similar definition, describing an instructional goal "as a desired state of future affairs . . . such as ability to spell a list of words, the successful completion of a mathematics problem or . . . understanding a basic set of concepts within a subject area" (p. 5). The goal structure of the classroom, not to be confused with instructional goals, specifies the type of interdependence sought among students. It specifies the ways in which students will relate to each other and to the teacher while working toward instructional goals. The Johnsons (1975) defined three different types of goal structures:

> 1. *Cooperative goal structures* A cooperative goal structure exists when students perceive that they can obtain their goal if, and only if, the other students with whom they are linked can obtain their goals. . . . A cooperative goal structure requires the coordination of behavior necessary to achieve the mutual goal.
>
> 2. *Competitive goal structures* A competitive goal structure exists when students perceive that they can obtain their goal if, and only if, the other students with whom they are linked fail to obtain their goals.
>
> 3. *Individualistic goal structure* An individualistic goal structure exists when the achievement of the goal by one student is unrelated to the achievement of the goal by other students; whether or not a student achieves her goal has no bearing upon whether other students achieve their goals. . . . Usually there is no student interaction in an individualistic situation. (p. 7)

A later section of this chapter will discuss how classroom goal structures are related to student motivation. In Chapter 10, a model of teaching developed specifically around cooperative goal structures will be described.

CLASSROOM REWARD STRUCTURES

Finally, classroom environments and behaviors are influenced by classroom reward structures. Just as goal structures can be competitive, individualistic, or cooperative, so too can reward structures. Slavin (1983) has written that competitive reward structures are those that reward students for their own individual efforts in comparison with other students. Grading on a curve would be an example of a competitive reward structure, as is the way winners are defined in most track and field events. In contrast, cooperative reward structures are situations where individual effort helps others to be rewarded. Slavin (1983) gives the following examples: "If three people traveling in a car help push the car out of the mud, all of them benefit from each other's effort (by being able to continue the trip). A football team also is an example of a cooperative reward system, even though the team as a whole is in competition with other teams" (p. 4).

The important point about classroom goal and reward structures is that they are at the core of life in classrooms and influence greatly both the behavior and learning of students. Regardless of the teacher's personal philosophy toward the use of rewards, the current reality is that student motivation centers around the dispensation of grades. In fact, Doyle (1979) argued that the primary feature of classroom life is the way students engage in academic work and how they "exchange [their] performance for grades." The way teachers organize goal and reward structures determines which types of goals are accomplished and how the exchange occurs.

Key Features of a Classroom

This section has described key features of classroom life. The frameworks provided view classrooms as complex social systems where students and teachers' behaviors result from the interactions of individual needs and institutional roles. The climate created in classrooms from this two-way interaction influences participants' behavior and their academic learning. Some features of classroom life, such as the properties of *multidimensionality* or *immediacy* described by Doyle (1986), probably cannot be influenced very much by the teacher. Classrooms will remain crowded places and teachers will have to learn to deal with the rapid pace of classroom events, at least in the near future. Basic motivational patterns resulting from early childhood experiences may also be unalterable. Other features of classroom life, such as the *group processes* defined by the Schmucks, some aspects of *achievement motivation*, and the *task, goal, and reward structures* are strongly under the control of the teacher, and it is the way these processes are developed and maintained by teachers that determines whether or not a classroom environment is productive.

SAMPLING THE RESEARCH BASE

The research literature supporting the topic of productive classroom environments is extensive and represents scholarship from many fields: the social psychology of education, group dynamics, motivation, the social context of teaching, and organizational psychology. It is not the aim of this section to review all of this research. Instead, three interesting studies are provided to give beginning teachers insights into the way some of this research is carried out and to provide examples of some important findings. The three studies cover a span of a half century and focus on the effects of classroom environments on motivation, how teacher behaviors influence group life, and how students themselves can influence each other and their teachers.

Effects of Classroom Environments on Student Motivation

Researchers have been interested for a long time in how classroom environments influence student motivation and learning. In general, the findings from this research indicate that environments characterized by mutual respect, high standards, and a caring attitude enhance student motivation. Some of the research on this topic has been conducted on open-space classrooms and schools which, by design, emphasize structures to build environments that are warm and caring. A number of studies compare traditional and open-space schools in terms of student achievement and attitudes. It is difficult to compare such schools because certain types of teachers gravitate to open-space schools—those who wish to experiment, are tolerant of noise and confusion, and whose philosophies reflect a more child-oriented approach than those in traditional schools. Further, open-space schools vary considerably among themselves, and it is difficult to generalize from one study, since most studies take place within only one school.

Research Summary 5.1 is an interesting and unique study conducted by J. W. Santrock. It explored directly the relationships between some dimensions of the classroom environment—happy and sad moods—and students' motivation to persist on classroom tasks.

Effects of Teacher Behavior on Students

For many years teachers have known that what they do has an influence on the behaviors of their students. In fact, teaching by definition is an attempt to influence the behavior and learning of students. Also, from the beginning of formal schooling in Western societies many educators have held the belief that a teacher's behavior should be "democratic" in character, thus reflecting the larger societal value about the way people should interact with one another. Take, for example, these comments written by John Dewey almost 75 years ago:

> We can and do supply ready-made "ideas" by the thousand; we do not usually take much pains to see that the one learning engages in significant situations where his own activities generate, support, and clinch ideas—that is, perceived meanings or connections. This does not mean that the teacher is to stand off and look on; the alternative to furnishing ready-made subject matter and listening to the accuracy with which it is reproduced is not quiescence, but participation, sharing, in an activity. In such shared activity the teacher is a learner, and the learner is, without knowing it, a teacher—and upon the whole, the less consciousness there is, on either side, of either giving or receiving instruction, the better. (Dewey, 1916, p. 176)

But what effects do more democratic procedures or behaviors have on students? In what has become a set of classic studies, Lewin, Lippitt, and White asked that question a half century ago. Actually, Lewin, Lippitt, and White conducted a series of studies and the first results appeared under their names in 1939. The part of their work summarized in Research Summary 5.2 appeared later and was authored by Lippitt and White.

Effects of Student Behavior on Each Other and on Teachers

Studies such as the one you just read by Lewin, Lippitt, and White provide evidence that what teachers do influences what their students do. Influence in

─────────────── **RESEARCH SUMMARY** ───────────────
5.1*

Santrock, J. W. (1976). Affective and facilitative self-control: Influence of ecological setting, cognition, and social agent. *Journal of Educational Psychology, 68* (5), 529–535.

PROBLEM: It is difficult to motivate young children to persist at a task. Some students persist longer than others, and some tasks appear to be more interesting to some students than other tasks. It could also be that some environments are more conducive to student persistence than other environments. The purpose of this study was to determine whether the environment of the classroom (happy, neutral, sad) and the nature of the content of children's thoughts (happy, neutral, sad) affected their persistence of tasks.

SAMPLE AND SETTING: The subjects were 108 first- and second-grade students in a small town in Georgia. Half were boys, and half were girls.

PROCEDURES: The students were randomly divided into treatment groups. Each child was involved in various combinations of the following treatments. On the way to a classroom, students were told one of three stories: a happy one, a sad one, and no story at all. The experimenter acted happy in relating the happy story, sad in relating the sad story, and neutral for no story. The room was decorated in one of three ways: happy pictures, sad pictures, or neutral pictures. In the room, the children were asked to work at a task at which they were interrupted from time to time and asked to think either a happy, sad, or neutral thought. They could stop working on the task whenever they liked.

RESULTS: There were strong ecological effects on student persistence. As shown in Table 1, students with a happy experimenter, in a happy room, and thinking happy thoughts persisted longest at the task; those with a sad experimenter, in a sad room, and thinking sad thoughts persisted the least of all groups.

* This research report was summarized by Virginia Richardson-Koehler.

classrooms, however, does not always flow just from their teacher. Students influence each other and can even influence the behavior of the teachers. One particularly interesting line of inquiry over the years has been research that investigates how the student peer group, through both formal and informal interactions, affects attitudes and achievement. Peer group influences have been documented in studies of college dormitories and living houses (Newcomb, 1961, for example), and in many different public and private school settings. Much of the research shows that many students conform to peer group norms and that all too often these norms are in contradiction to those held by educators and teachers. James Coleman (1961) studied ten American high schools in the 1950s. He found many instances where the adolescent peer group supported norms for being popular and being athletic over the school's norms in support of academic

TABLE 1 Means and Standard Deviations of Persistence Scores for Children in Different Affectively Toned Situations

	Cognition					
	Happy		Sad		Neutral	
Ecological setting	*M*	*SD*	*M*	*SD*	*M*	*SD*
Happy						
Happy experimenter	796.2	310.6	100.5	30.4	357.2	126.4
Sad experimenter	309.7	140.2	180.2	70.9	426.0	186.5
Neutral experimenter	240.0	100.1	214.0	110.6	666.5	254.5
Sad						
Happy experimenter	252.5	106.8	49.5	26.5	95.7	48.6
Sad experimenter	83.5	49.3	52.0	29.0	72.5	45.7
Neutral experimenter	103.5	52.4	142.5	80.6	269.5	128.9
Neutral						
Happy experimenter	269.0	141.8	209.5	98.5	192.2	84.3
Sad experimenter	64.0	32.8	81.2	51.6	144.2	79.0
Neutral experimenter	90.0	51.4	65.5	38.4	154.5	81.0

SOURCE: J. W. Santrock (1976), p. 533.

DISCUSSION AND IMPLICATIONS: Although the sample was quite small and confined to a small town in one state, the experimental work was very carefully conducted, and the evidence quite compelling. It indicates that persistence at a task for a young child is not simply a function of the child's self-control but can be influenced by the environment.

It does not take a lot of time for a teacher to make a room brighter and happier. Further, a teacher can help to brighten the thoughts of students through interesting and happy stories. Thus, it may be possible to increase students' persistence at a task—particularly one that is repetitive—by brightening the environment that surrounds the students and making it a happy, caring place to be.

achievement. This finding has been replicated in American high schools in every decade since Coleman's original work.

Richard Schmuck (1963) also studied classroom peer groups, particularly friendship patterns in elementary schools. From a sample of 27 classrooms and over 700 students in rural, urban, and suburban Michigan, Schmuck found that the friendship patterns of students in elementary schools varied from classroom to classroom. In some classrooms many students liked one another and were highly involved with their classmates. In other classrooms students were very cliquish, with a few students identified as very popular and others rejected by their peers. In classrooms with broad peer-liking structures, Schmuck found that all students were more likely to have higher feelings of self-esteem and to make more use of their academic abilities as contrasted students in the cliquish classrooms.

RESEARCH SUMMARY
5.2

Lippitt, R., and White, R. (1958). An experimental study of leadership and group life. In E. E. Macoby, T. M. Newcomb, and F. L. Hartley *Readings in social psychology.* New York: Holt, Rinehart and Winston.

PROBLEM: The researchers were interested in the general problem of how different types of leadership behaviors would influence both individual and group behavior.

SAMPLE AND SETTING: The sample consisted of 11-year-old children who volunteered to form small boys' clubs and participate in a series of club projects and activities.

PROCEDURES: The researchers matched children according to their leadership and friendship patterns and placed them into four clubs: Sherlock Holmes Club, Dick Tracy Club, Secret Agents Club, and Charlie Chan Club. Adult club leaders (teachers) were taught to exhibit three different types of leadership behaviors.

1. *Authoritarian Leadership* When using this role, the club leader made all policies about activities and procedures and remained aloof from club members.
2. *Democratic Leadership* When using this role, the club leader made all policies and procedures a matter of group discussion and decision. The leader strived to be a part of the group in spirit and encourage club members.
3. *Laissez-Faire Leadership* When using this role, the club leader was passive and left complete freedom to the group.

The researchers carefully observed the boys' behavior on a number of different variables and collected a vast amount of information on both leadership and group member behavior. The researchers also arranged for the leader to be called away at a designated point in time and the boys' work behavior (without any adult in the room) was recorded by a hidden observer. This behavior was subsequently compared to behavior when the leader was present.

POINTERS FOR READING RESEARCH: Most researchers of previous research summaries in this book have reported their information in data tables. Sometimes researchers choose to show their results in graphs and charts. Graphs and charts are actually quite easy to read, and most of you are very familiar with them. However, when several variables have been included in a graph, as is the case in this study, readers must inspect each aspect of the graph carefully to make sure they accurately understand the relationships being illustrated.

RESULTS: Below are two graphs showing some of the effects of the three types of leader behavior on the climate of the boys' groups. Figure 1 shows how the three different types of leadership produced four patterns of reactions on member behavior. Figure 2 shows the activity patterns of the boys when their leader was present, when he was out of the room, and when he returned.

DISCUSSION AND IMPLICATIONS: The researchers found that the boys reacted to autocratic leadership in one of two ways: aggressive (being rebellious and critical) and apathetic, being turned off and noninvolved. Figure 1 indicates that in the clubs with autocratic leadership members were more dependent on the leaders' actions, showed more discontent, were less friendly to one another, made fewer

FIGURE 1 Four Patterns of Group Reaction to the Three Types of Leadership

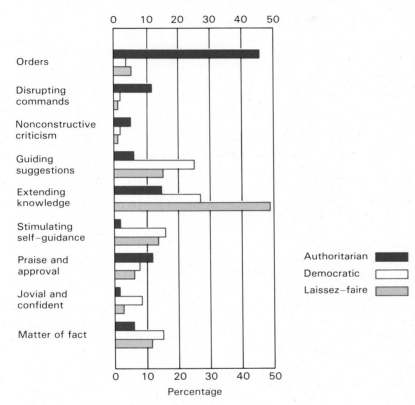

SOURCE: From Lippitt and White (1963), p. 146.

suggestions and fewer requests for information, and carried on less conversation with each other than did members in clubs with more democratic leaders.

Figure 2 shows the involvement pattern for the two types of autocratic groups, the democratic groups, and the laissez-faire groups when the leader was present, when the leader was absent, and immediately after the leader returned. Members of the group with the democratic leader used about the same proportion of their time when the leader was present as when the leader was absent. Laissez-faire group members were more involved when the leader was gone. The researchers concluded this was because certain boys were stepping in and providing leadership during this period. For the autocratic groups, it can be observed that the involvement dropped drastically when the leader left the room and then rose correspondingly upon the leader's return.

(Cont'd)

━━━━━━━━━━━━━━━━━━━━ **RESEARCH SUMMARY** ━━━━━━━━━━━━━━━━━━━━
5.2 (continued)

FIGURE 2 Percentage of Time Spent in High Activity Involvement

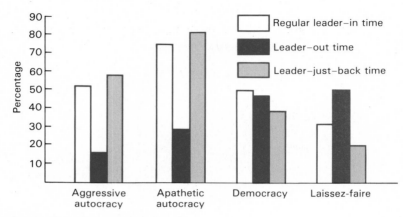

SOURCE: From Lippitt and White (1963), p. 147.

The Lewin, Lippitt, and White studies showed rather convincingly that leader (or teacher) behavior has important influences on children's willingness to cooperate and stick to learning tasks. Many have concluded from this study (and others like it) that teachers who are overly strict and autocratic may get a lot of work from their students if they are physically present, but that involvement will drop once close supervision is removed because of the dependency group members develop under autocratic leadership. The results from this study have also led to the conclusion that laizzez-faire teachers present problems to students in that leaderless groups or classrooms have difficulty persisting at tasks and defining expectations for accomplishment.

━━━

Finally, student and peer group norms can even influence the behavior of their teachers. This idea was illustrated in a unique and very interesting study conducted by Willis Copeland (1980) and is summarized in Research Summary 5.3.

BUILDING PRODUCTIVE LEARNING ENVIRONMENTS ━━━━━━━━━━━━━━

Building productive learning environments—places where students have positive attitudes toward themselves and their classroom group and where they display a high degree of achievement motivation and involvement in academic tasks—is a difficult and complex process for most beginning teachers. Experienced teachers who have skills in working with the alterable aspects of group and motivational processes are not always able to communicate these skills clearly to novice teachers. Experienced teachers, however, usually emphasize to beginning teachers that there is no one list of "things to do," nor a single, dramatic event that will produce a productive learning environment. Instead, as with so many of the executive functions of teaching, success depends on doing a lot of "little things" well. Using the frameworks and research summarized in the previous sections as a backdrop, this section is organized under the following topics: increasing student motivation, encouraging group development, and promoting positive classroom discourse.

Increasing Student Motivation

You saw in the Getzels-Thelen model that one major determinant of students' behavior was their personal needs and the individual attributes and interests they bring with them to the classroom. You also saw in the explanations of need disposition and attribution theories that there are some aspects influencing student motivation, such as early childhood experiences, on which teachers can have little influence. Unfortunately, many teachers attend only to these aspects of student motivation. Often the lunchroom conversations of teachers focus on the social backgrounds of students: "He comes from a broken home"; "she lives in poverty"; "his family has never been to college"; "her mother is a social climber and has unrealistic expectations for her." Psychological analysis is also a favorite topic of discussion: "John is insecure"; "Richard is overly dependent"; "Mary is anxious"; "Ben is afraid to risk failure." Even though these observations and diagnoses may be accurate, there really isn't very much teachers can do to alter or influence past events. There are, however, specific steps teachers can take in their classrooms that will increase their students' motivation to learn. In this section several concrete factors contributing to motivation that *can* be influenced by the beginning teacher are described. Several of these have been borrowed from the work of Madeline Hunter (1982) and her translation of Weiner's attribution theory. Others come from ideas discovered by teachers themselves.

ALTERABLE FACTORS AND MOTIVATION

Madeline Hunter (1982) concluded that there are several factors associated with motivation that teachers can modify and control. These factors are not discrete, nor is one more important than the other. Instead, they interact with one another and together can increase students' motivation to learn.

1. Level of Concern One aspect of motivation is the level of concern students have toward achieving some learning goal. Concern is also associated with stress. If students find a task too easy or the present level of performance satisfactory, they will feel little need to achieve and will put out little effort. On the other

Copeland, W. D. (1980). Teaching-learning behaviors and the demands of the classroom environment. *The Elementary School Journal, 80,* 163–177.

PROBLEM: Copeland, in a novel study, turned around the traditional research question, "What do teachers do to influence students?" and asked, "What do students do to influence the behaviors of their teachers?"

SAMPLE: Participants for the study were students in two middle-grade elementary school classrooms (Classrooms A and B) and two student teachers assigned to those classrooms. One student teacher in the study was a 22-year-old man (Al); the other a 24-year-old woman (Beth). Both were in the elementary education program at the University of California, Santa Barbara. According to the researcher:

> Classroom A, a fourth-grade class, was located in a racially and ethnically mixed school and had a large proportion of underachieving pupils. The resident teacher had 11 years' experience and was considered by her principal as exceptionally successful when working with this type of pupil. (pp. 164–165)
>
> Classroom B, a third-fourth combination class, was located in a school in an affluent, upper-middle- and upper-class neighborhood. . . . The teacher in this classroom had nine years' experience and was considered by her principal to be among the most capable and academically oriented teachers in the school. (p. 165)

PROCEDURES: This research was conducted in three phases:

Phase 1: Observations were made by the researcher of the behaviors of students and student teachers during a two-month period in both Classroom A and Classroom B.

Phase 2: The two student teachers exchanged assignments. The student teacher in Classroom A went to Classroom B, and the student teacher in Classroom B went to Classroom A.

Phase 3: The behaviors of students and student teachers (now in their new assignments) were again observed for a two-month period.

The researcher identified six sets of teaching-learning behaviors from his observations and divided these into two major categories:

1. Behaviors related to pupil conduct and teachers' control
   Pupils' attending behavior—how much students paid attention to lessons
   Pupils' nonparallel activity—inattention to lessons
   Teachers' pupil-control techniques—what teachers did to maintain attention
2. Behaviors related to questioning and responding
   Teachers' question-directing behavior—how teachers asked questions
   Pupils' response to teachers' questions—answering, raising hands
   Pupils' verbal initiating behavior—actions to interject ideas

POINTERS FOR READING RESEARCH: Copeland's study is an example of where the researcher spent intensive time making actual observations of his subjects. These types of data normally cannot be summarized in data tables with numbers. Instead it is reported with words in such a way as to convince the reader of its accurateness.

RESULTS: Remember Copeland collected information about both teacher control behaviors and questioning and responding behaviors. Space allows only a report of what Copeland found about teacher's questioning and responding behaviors. These data are displayed in Table 1.

TABLE 1 Three Sets of Behavior Related to Questioning and Responding as Observed in Classrooms A and B Before and After the Exchange of Student Teachers

Behavior Set	Behaviors Observed Before Student Teacher Exchange	Behaviors Observed After Student Teacher Exchange
	Classroom A	
Teacher's question-directing behavior	Al directed questions at class and waited for shouted-out responses	Beth directed questions at class and waited for shouted-out responses
Pupils' response to teacher's question	Shouted-out responses when inclined to participate	Behaviors observed before exchange continued
Pupils' verbal initiating behavior	Interjected without permission	Behaviors observed before exchange continued
	Classroom B	
Teacher's question-directing behavior	Beth directed questions at individuals and called on pupils with raised hands	Al directed questions at class and waited for shouted-out responses
Pupils' response to teacher's question	Raised hands and waited for permission to speak	Shouted-out responses when inclined to participate
Pupils' verbal initiating behavior	Raised hands and waited for permission to speak	Shouted-out responses when inclined to participate

SOURCE: W. D. Copeland (1980), p. 172.

DISCUSSION AND IMPLICATIONS: In Table 1 you can observe that the student teacher from Classroom B (Beth) had developed techniques of directing questions to individual pupils as they raised their hands. Within a few weeks she found that this approach would not work in Classroom A and she adopted a more forceful questioning and responding style. Similarly, the student teacher from Classroom A (Al), as he moved into Classroom B, soon adopted the more indirect questioning style previously exhibited by Beth.

Although not reported in this summary, Copeland said he observed the same pattern for behaviors associated with pupil control. Pupils' behavior, for example, in Classroom A was characterized by low pupil attending behavior and high off-task behavior. The student teacher from Classroom B (Beth), who had been accustomed to a different set of management techniques (more indirect), within a few weeks adopted more direct methods of pupil control when she moved to Classroom A. Similarly, the student teacher from Classroom A (Al) adopted more indirect methods of pupil control soon after he moved into Classroom B.

Copeland's study supports the idea that behavior in classrooms is *bidirectional*, that is, behaviors of the participants are influenced not only by what the teacher does but also by what the students do. In this situation, the students perhaps had been accustomed to a certain way of interacting by the cooperating teacher and continued to behave that way regardless of who the student teacher happened to be. At the same time, Copeland points out that the academic abilities and development of the students themselves serve to influence a teacher's behavior. In other words, certain teacher behaviors seemed to work with the less able and less motivated students found in Classroom A and a different set for the more able and motivated students in Classroom B. Teachers appear to experiment with a set of behaviors until they find some that work with a particular group. Thus, in essence, they are influenced by the nature and behaviors of their students.

hand, if a task is too difficult or if it causes too much stress, then the stress itself becomes dominant and little energy will be expended on learning. Figure 5.4 illustrates the balance needed for a learning task to be at the right level.

Figure 5.4

Difficulty	Stress
Not too easy, not too hard	Not too high, not too low

Hunter (1982) reported that a "moderate level of concern stimulates effort to learn" (p. 12) and offered the following examples of ways teachers can raise or lower students' levels of concern toward learning tasks:

a. Stand next to a student who is not participating to raise concern, or move away from an anxious student to lower concern.
b. Announce that, "This will probably be on the test," or reassure your class that, "Everyone has trouble with this at first but, as we work, it will become increasingly clear."
c. Give a test that you grade, or give a test followed by the answers so students can check their own learning.
d. Announce that, "This part is difficult and a high level of concentration and effort is required," or that, "This is difficult but we will work on it for several days before you are expected to know it." (p. 12)

2. Feeling Tone As observed in Santrock's study, students put forth more or less effort according to the pleasantness or unpleasantness of the learning environment and the particular learning situation. Hunter (1976) provided the following examples of things teachers can say to establish a positive, neutral, or negative feeling tone:

Positive "You write such interesting stories, I'm anxious to read this one."
Negative "That story must be finished before you're excused for lunch."
Neutral "If you aren't finished, don't worry, there'll be plenty of time later."
(p. 32)

An important point for teachers to consider, if they choose to use unpleasant feeling tones to motivate students to complete a difficult learning task, is to return as soon as possible to a positive one. Again Hunter (1982) provides some good examples: "I really put a lot of pressure on you and you've responded magnificently," or "I know you were angry about the demands being made, but you should be proud of the improvement in your performance" (p. 13).

Feeling tones in the classroom are not only the result of specific things teachers say at a particular moment, they are also the result of many other structures and processes created by teachers to produce productive learning environments. Some of these will be described in later sections of this chapter.

3. Success A third factor that can influence a student's achievement motivation, feelings of success, is associated with the degree of difficulty of a task and the amount of effort expended. Tasks that are too easy require too little effort and produce no feelings of success and, consequently, are unmotivational. At the same time, tasks that are too difficult for students, regardless of the effort they expend, will also be unmotivational. Effective teachers learn how to adjust the level of difficulty of learning tasks for particular students. Sometimes this means providing special challenges for the brightest in the class and providing more support and assistance for those who find a particular task too difficult.

4. Interest The interest level students have in a particular learning task is certainly associated with their motivation to achieve. The teacher can do a number of things to relate learning materials and activities to students' interests. Hunter (1982) provided the following examples:

> Relating materials to students' life and using the students' names: "Suppose John, here, were presenting an argument for electing his friend and Charles wished to challenge his position . . ." Or, "Mary, here, has the pigmentation most commonly associated with Nordic races while Sue's is more typical of the Latinos." (p. 19)
>
> Making materials vivid and novel: "When you order your favorite McDonald's milkshake, it won't melt even if you heat it in the oven. That's the result of an emulsifier made from the algae we're studying." Or, "Suppose you believed in reincarnation. In your next life what would you need to accomplish that you didn't accomplish satisfactorily in this life?" (pp. 19–20)

Two cautions need to be highlighted about using student interests for motivational purposes. Stressing the novel or vivid can sometimes distract students from learning, a topic that will be discussed in more detail in Chapter 7. Similarly, new interests are formed through learning about a new topic. Teachers who expose their students only to materials in which they are already interested prevent them from developing new interests.

5. Knowledge of Results Getting feedback about performance is a fifth motivational factor described by Hunter (1982). This includes feedback about areas in which students are doing well in addition to those that need improvement. Knowledge about performance needs to be more specific and immediate than the grades teachers put on report cards every six to nine weeks. In Chapter 9 specific guidelines for giving feedback are provided. This topic is also covered in a special topic section on testing and evaluation. It is enough to say here that feedback needs to be as immediate as possible (handing back tests the next day), as specific as possible (comments in addition to an overall grade on a paper), and nonjudgmental ("Your use of the word 'that' is incorrect—you should have used 'which' instead," rather than, "What's wrong with you? We have gone over the difference between 'that' and 'which' a dozen times").

Assignments can also be designed with built-in-feedback features. The use of videotaping and the microcomputer are particularly good for assignments and practice with built-in feedback.

6. Classroom Goal and Reward Structures Competitive goal and reward structures lead to comparisons and win-lose relationships among students and make a student's ability, rather than effort, the primary factor for success. Cooperative goal and reward structures lead to social interdependence, and shared activity makes student effort the primary factor for success. Chapter 10 will go into greater detail about how to set up cooperative goal and reward structures.

7. Attending to Influence and Affiliation Motives Most motivational research has focused on achievement motivation. Although less is known about influence and affiliation motives, they too play a role in determining the type of effort students will expend on learning tasks and how long they will persist. In general, students' influence needs are satisfied when they feel they have some power or say over their classroom environment and their learning tasks, as illustrated in the Lewin, Lippitt, and White (1939) studies. Here are a few specific examples of how teachers can use influence needs to motivate students:

▪ Hold weekly planning sessions with students, assessing how well the previous week has gone and what they would like to see included in next week's lessons. Some experienced teachers use a technique called "pluses and wishes." On large newsprint or butcher paper the teacher makes two columns and labels them as shown in Table 5.1. Together students and teachers list their suggestions for all to consider. The teacher can use information on this list in his or her own planning and can come back to it to show students that particular lessons and activities have been influenced by their input.

Table 5.1

PLUSES	WISHES
The lecture on cells was clear.	We wish we had had more time on the experiment.
The group work was interesting.	We wish more students would cooperate.
We enjoyed the principal's visit.	We wish the test had been fairer.

- Assign students to perform important tasks, such as distributing and collecting books and papers, taking care of the aquarium, taking roll, acting as tutors to other students, taking messages to the principal's office, and the like.

In most schools, it is the peer group that students look to for satisfying their affiliation needs. Unfortunately, norms for peer group affiliation often conflict with the strong achievement norms teachers would like to see. In some instances, very competitive cliques that exclude many students from both the academic and social life of the school are found. In other instances, peer group norms exist that apply negative sanctions to those students who try to do well in school work. Teachers can make needs for affiliation work in a positive way by following some of these procedures:

- Make sure that all the students in the class (even in high school) know one another's names and some personal information about each student.
- Initiate cooperative goal and reward structures as described in Chapter 10.
- Take time to help individuals in the classroom develop as a group, using procedures described in the following section.

This section concludes with Table 5.2, which shows a "menu" of motivational ideas put together by teachers from all over the county as part of special workshops sponsored by the Midcontinent Regional Educational Laboratory.

Facilitating Group Development

Chapter 2 described the developmental stages teachers go through in learning to teach. In Chapter 7 the stages of student intellectual development are explained. Groups, like individuals, also develop, grow, and pass through discernible stages in this process. The Schmucks (1975) have adapted general theories about group development and have created a four-stage developmental model for classroom groups. These four stages are summarized in Table 5.3.

The Schmuck's are quick to point out, and rightfully so, that the stages of classroom development are not always sequential. Instead, they are often cyclical in nature with many of the stages repeating themselves several times during the school year. When new students are placed in classrooms, membership issues again become important. Student growth in interpersonal skills keeps influence issues unstable and in constant flux. Larger societal issues cause change and a need to renegotiate norms associated with academic goals and performances.

The stages of classroom group development also have no *definite* time frames associated with them. The time it takes each group to work out issues associated with membership, influence, and task accomplishment will depend upon the skill of individual members within the class and the type of leadership the teacher

Table 5.2 Motivational Ideas Teacher Have Used With Students, Classes, and Schools

RECOGNITION/REWARDS/ STROKES	SPECIAL PROJECTS	SPECIAL EVENTS
Teaching others	Sing for elderly	Friendship day
Smiley faces	Making books	T-shirt day
Child input	Song fests	Family fun night
Knowledge of results	School store	Ethnic pride day
Happy-grams	Birthday charts	Wear-a-flower day
Peer tutoring	Make a movie	Appreciation day
Happy notes to parents	School carnival	Everyone-compliment day
Specific praise	School-wide breakfast	Cowboy day
Citizenship assembly	Canned food drive	Elizabethan festival
School stationery	Attendance charts	Secret pals day
Good citizenship pictures	Cookouts with parents	Field trips
Please/thank you	Student profiles	Security blanket day

SPECIAL EXPRESSION/ UNDERSTANDING	CONTESTS/COMPETITION/GOALS	EVERYBODY CAN PARTICIPATE
Role-playing	Math contest	Song fests
Planting a garden	Tournaments	Noncompetitive games
Speakers	Bingo	Board work
Open lunch for upperclass persons	Popcorn party for best class	Wall charts
Storytelling	Spelling bee	Review teams for tests
Music in lunchroom	Design school flag/mascot	Mini-courses

SHOW OFF WORK	SUSPEND THE RULES	ROOM ARRANGEMENTS
Harder tests	Free time	Pads
Bulletin board displays	Special privileges	Warm lighting
Talk with principal	Special excursion	Learning centers
Talent show	Sit-where-you-want	Subject area labs
Display of class work	Gum in class	Pleasant room

SOURCE: Adapted from *McRel Quality Education Folio* (1983), Kansas City, Mo.: Midcontinent Regional Educational Laboratory, p. 6–8.

provides. *General* time frames, however, can be inferred from the statements of experienced teachers. They report that membership issues consume students during the first month of school and that the most productive period for student learning and attention to academic tasks is between November and early May.

Teachers can assist the development of their classroom group in two important ways. They can teach students that groups grow and learn in some of the same ways individuals do. They can also explain and help students learn how to work in groups and provide leadership to group efforts.

Teachers can help students resolve membership and inclusion issues by having lessons that help students learn each others' names and find out information

Table 5.3 Schmucks' Stages of Classroom Development

STAGE	GROUP AND MEMBER NEEDS AND BEHAVIORS
Stage 1 Inclusion and Membership	Early in classroom life students seek to find a notch for themselves in the peer group. Students want to present a good image and are on their good behavior. Teachers have great influence during this period because of their assigned authority. Everyone is sizing up one another, and the issues of inclusion and membership must be resolved before the group can move along to the next stage.
Stage 2 Influence and Collaboration	Members of the class enter into two types of power struggles. One struggle tests the authority of the teacher; the other establishes the peer group pecking order. Tensions will exist between the students and the teacher and between the students themselves during this stage. If these tensions cannot be resolved and power relationships balanced, the group cannot move along very productively to the next stage.
Stage 3 Individual and Academic Goals	The classroom enters a stage of development for working productively on academic goals. Students during this stage can set and accomplish goals and work together on tasks. The classroom can also be pulled back into earlier stages during this stage.
Stage 4 Self-Renewal/Adaptive Change	This stage is one in which members can think about their continuous growth and about taking on new and more challenging tasks. This is also a stage that can produce conflict because change in tasks will perhaps upset earlier resolutions of issues around membership and power.

SOURCE: Based on material from pp. 178–187 in R. A. Schmuck and P. A. Schmuck, *Group processes in the classroom*, 2d ed. © 1975 Wm. C. Brown Publishers, Dubuque, Iowa. All rights reserved. By permission.

about one another. When new students enter the group special efforts can be made to assure their acceptance. Influence issues can be resolved by using many of the techniques described later in relation to classroom management. Communicating goals and expectations to students can help groups aspire to high individual and group achievement.

Promoting Positive Classroom Discourse

Communication is perhaps the single most important variable for building productive learning environments. It is through classroom discourse that norms are established and classroom life defined for each individual. Fortunately, the way discourse occurs in classrooms can be heavily influenced by the teacher's leadership.

PROCESSES OF INTERPERSONAL COMMUNICATION

Communication is essentially a process of sending and receiving messages. On the surface this process looks quite simple; in reality, it is very complicated.

THE COMMUNICATION GAP

Communication among people is complicated because it requires the sender of a message to express clearly what he or she intends to communicate, and for the receiver to interpret the message accurately.

Often the message a person intends to send is not the one the other person receives. Intentions, for example, are private and in the mind of the sender and may or may not be accurately received and encoded by the person receiving the message. Whenever there is a breakdown in this process a "communication gap" exists.

COMMUNICATION SKILLS

A number of years ago John Wallen (1972), then an organizational psychologist in a large electronics firm and a consultant to the Northwest Regional Educational Laboratory, described four skills people can use to make the process of sending and receiving messages more effective and to reduce the gap in communication. Two of these skills are intended to assist the sender; two assist the receiver. These skills are essential for positive classroom discourse and can be taught to students at all age levels quite readily.*

1. Paraphrasing Paraphrasing is a skill for checking with others to be sure you understand their ideas as they intended you to. Any means of revealing your understanding of a message constitutes a paraphrase. Paraphrasing is more than word-swapping or merely saying back what another person has said. Instead, it answers the question, "What exactly does the sender's statement mean to him or her?" and requests the sender to verify the correctness of your interpretation. The sender's statement may convey something specific, an example, or a more general idea to you, as in the following examples:

SENDER: I'd sure like to own this book.
YOU: (*Being more specific*) Does it have useful information in it?
SENDER: I don't know about that, but the binding is beautiful.

SENDER: This book is too hard to use.
YOU: (*Giving an example*) Do you mean, for example, that it fails to cite research?
SENDER: Yes, that's one example. It also lacks an adequate index.

SENDER: Do you have a book on teaching?
YOU: (*Being more general*) Do you just want information on that topic? I have several articles.
SENDER: No, I want to find out about cooperative learning.

* Some of this material is adapted from Arends and Arends (1977).

2. Behavior Description In a behavior description, one person reports specific observable behaviors of another person without evaluating them or making inferences about the other's motives. If you tell me that I am rude (a trait) or that I do not care about your opinion (my motivations), when I am not trying to be rude and do care about your opinion, I may not understand what you are trying to communicate. However, if you point out that I have interrupted you several times in the last ten minutes, I would receive a clearer picture of what actions of mine were affecting you. Sometimes it is helpful to preface a behavior description with "I noticed that" or "I hear you say" to remind yourself that you are trying to describe specific actions. Consider the following examples:

> "Jim, you've talked more than others on this topic."
> *instead of,*
> "Jim, you always have to be the center of attention."

> "Bob, I really felt good when you complimented me on my presentation before the class."
> *instead of,*
> "Bob, you sure go out of your way to say nice things to people."

3. Describing Feelings Although people often take pains to make sure that others understand their ideas, only rarely do they describe how they are feeling. Instead, they act on their feelings, sending messages that others draw inferences from. If you think that others are failing to take your feelings into account, it is helpful to put those feelings into words. Instead of blushing and saying nothing, try "I feel embarrassed," or "I feel pleased." Instead of, "Shut up!" try, "I hurt too much to hear any more," or, "I'm angry with you."

4. Checking Impressions This skill complements describing your own feelings and involves checking your sense of what is going on inside the other person. You transform the other's expression of feelings (the blush, the silence, the tone of voice) into a tentative description of feelings and check it out for accuracy. An impression check: (1) describes what you think the other's feelings may be, and (2) does not express disapproval or approval—it merely conveys, "This is how I understand your feelings. Am I accurate?" Examples include:

> "I get the impression you are angry with me. Are you?"
> "Am I right that you feel disappointed that nobody commented on your suggestions?"

Often an impression check can be coupled easily with a behavior description, as in these examples:

> "Ellen, you've said nothing so far and seem upset with the class. Are you?"
> "Jim, you've made that proposal a couple of times. Are you feeling put down because we haven't accepted it?"

USING COMMUNICATION SKILLS AND TEACHING THEM TO STUDENTS

Teachers can learn and practice these skills and find them useful in a variety of settings and relationships. In the classroom, teachers can model these skills whether or not they choose to explain them to students and teach students to label them.

It is recommended that teachers teach these skills directly to students just as they teach many other skills. The teaching model described in Chapter 9 provides an appropriate strategy for teaching communication skills. A typical lesson is outlined in Figure 5.5.

ENCOURAGING PARTICIPATION

Much of what goes on in classrooms is discourse among students and teachers. The effective teacher has in his or her repertoire strategies to facilitate student interactions with learning materials in small groups and also in whole-class settings. Effective teachers also use strategies such as the following to encourage participation by all students:

Small Group Strategies It is not uncommon in classroom discussions to find the teacher interacting with a very small group of students—sometimes as few as four or five out of a classroom of thirty. Remember the action zone described in Chapter 4. One means to allow more student interaction with important learning materials is to have students interact in pairs or trios. Here are two strategies that work.

1. *Think-Pair-Share* The think-pair-share strategy has grown out of cooperative learning research and is a way to extend student thinking and interaction with learning materials (see Lyman, 1985). Suppose a teacher has just completed a

---

Figure 5.5 Typical Lesson Plan for Teaching Communication Skills

Step 1: Introduce and explain the four communication skills and define a topic for students to talk about.

Step 2: Have students get into groups of three for practice purposes. Each person in the trio is assigned a role as sender, receiver, or observer. The sender begins a conversation and tries to describe his or her feelings or the receiver's behavior while discussing the topic. The receiver listens and either paraphrases or checks his or her impressions of the sender's feelings. The observer notes instances of communication skill use and instances where there are gaps in communication.

Step 3: Roles are exchanged so different persons become senders, receivers, and observers.

Step 4: Finally, the teacher holds a class discussion about which skills are easy and which are difficult to learn and about how these skills can be applied in other aspects of classroom and outside life. During the discussion the teacher should model use of the skills and encourage students to use them.

short presentation and now wants students to consider more fully what has been explained. She chooses to use the think-pair-share strategy as contrasted to whole-class recitation. She would employ the following stages.

> *Step 1—Thinking* The teacher would pose a question or issue associated with the lesson and ask students to spend a minute thinking alone about the answer or the issue. Students need to be taught that talking or walking about is not part of think time.

> *Step 2—Pairing* Next the teacher asks students to pair off and talk about what they have been thinking. Interaction during this period could be sharing answers if a question has been posed or sharing ideas if a specific issue was identified. Normally, teachers would allow no more than four or five minutes for pairing.

> *Step 3—Sharing* Finally, the teacher asks the pairs to share with the total class what they have been talking about. It is effective to simply go around the room from pair to pair until about a fourth or a half of the pairs have had a chance to report.

2. *Buzz Groups* Buzz groups are another effective means of increasing the number of students who can interact around important learning materials or classroom issues. In using buzz groups, the teacher asks students to form quickly into groups of three to six to discuss ideas they have about the lesson. Each group assigns a person to make a list of all the ideas group members have. After a few minutes, the teacher asks the recorders to summarize for the whole class the major ideas and opinions expressed in their groups.

Buzz groups and think-pair-share techniques allow for more student participation and make it difficult for one or a few class members to dominate discussions. Most beginning teachers can master these techniques quickly and can teach students to follow the procedures and rules that are required for successful implementation.

Listening to Students' Ideas A final aspect of promoting positive discourse in classrooms is for teachers to learn to listen to students and their ideas. A favorite discussion technique used by many professors at the college and university level is one referred to as "playing the devil's advocate." Teachers who use this technique purposely take the opposite point of view from that being expressed by students and enter into debate with individuals or groups of students. Even though this approach can create lively exchange between the teacher and a small group of students, normally it does not work well with younger students or with high school students, except perhaps for the very bright and verbal. Debate and argument arouse emotions, and (although in some instances great motivators) they may divert the students' attention from the lesson. They also cause many of the less verbal or shy students to shrink from participation. If the teacher's goal is to help students understand the lesson or to build discourse for a productive learning environment, carefully listening to each student's ideas and pointing out errors if they exist, but remaining nonjudgmental and inquiry oriented, is probably a better strategy than challenging and arguing with students.

TEACHING DISCOURSE SKILLS

Students, like teachers, need to learn and practice discourse behaviors. For successful classroom discourse to occur students need to be taught skills, and norms need to be established. Four skills and norms are critical: listening, taking turns, encouraging participation by all, and speaking clearly and briefly.

Most students do not have these skills, so they must be taught by the teacher just as other skills and ideas are taught. Below are some techniques found successful in teaching students how to participate in effective discussions and carry on classroom discourse:*

The Chance to Listen During many discussions, students are not listening to one another. Instead, they sit with their hands in the air waiting for their turn to speak. One way to promote listening skills is to insist that during some discussions (those where the main objective is to learn discussion skills) before a student can speak, he or she must first paraphrase what the student who just finished speaking said.

High-Talker Tap-Out It is not uncommon in whole-class discussions to find only a very small percentage of the students participating. One way to encourage more balanced participation is to assign one student to monitor student participation. If the monitor observes a particular student talking several times, he or she can pass a note asking that student to refrain from further comments until everyone has had a turn.

Time Tokens If the teacher has a class where a few people speak all the time and a few never say anything, time tokens can be used to help distribute participation more equitably. Each student is given several tokens that are worth 10 or 15 seconds of talk time. A student monitors interaction and asks talkers to give up a token whenever they have used up the designated time. Students who use up all of their tokens can say nothing more. This, of course, encourages those with tokens left to enter into the discussion.

Beach Ball A final technique (particularly effective with younger students) for broadening participation and limiting talking to one person at a time, is to use a beach ball. The teacher gives the ball to one student to start the discussion with the understanding that only the person with the ball is permitted to talk. Other students raise their hands and get the ball when they wish to talk.

* Some of these ideas follow the discussion in R. A. Schmuck, P. Runkel, J. Arends, and R. Arends (1977).

Final Thoughts

To ask beginning teachers to create productive learning environments in addition to teaching academic topics may at first glance appear to be an overwhelming demand. In some ways it is, but unless a productive learning environment is created, efforts to teach academic lessons will be frustrated. Here are some final guidelines about how to teach all the processes and strategies needed to create productive learning environments.

USE TEACHING MODELS KNOWN TO BE EFFECTIVE FOR SKILL ACQUISITION

Teaching process skills, such as interpersonal communication skills or active listening, is no different than teaching more content-specific skills, such as map reading or how to use a microscope. Chapter 9 describes a model of instruction for skill acquisition. Labeled the *direct instruction model*, it requires teachers to demonstrate and model the skill being taught and to provide time for students to practice the skill and receive feedback on how they are doing. In general this is the model that teachers should use when teaching important process skills or learning strategies to students.

LEARN TO TEACH TOWARD MULTIPLE OBJECTIVES

Until very recently, teachers were admonished to teach toward a single objective. This recommendation is now being reevaluated by many experienced teachers. Teaching toward a single objective would be similar to telling a doctor to pay attention only to the way incisions are made during an operation or an NFL quarterback to pay attention only to the behavior of the linebackers. Experts in any profession must learn how to read complex environmental cues and respond appropriately so that a number of objectives and activities can be accomplished simultaneously. Many interpersonal and group skills can be taught by skillful teachers right along with academic content with little additional time required. Here are several examples:

- A high school literature teacher who is discussing how the short stories of Ernest Hemingway reflect his life and times can use think-pair-share strategies to encourage broader participation by students. Also, by taking a few moments at the end of the lesson to answer the question, "How did our discussion go today?" he can focus student attention on important classroom discussion and discourse skills.

- A teacher who is helping elementary students plan an important field trip to the airport as part of a unit on transportation systems can form the class into two groups and arrange them in the fishbowl seating pattern displayed in Figure 5.6. The group in the inner circle does the planning for 20 minutes while the other group acts as observers. Observers are assigned to

Figure 5.6

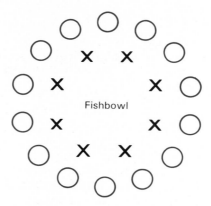

Fishbowl

watch the specific behaviors associated with the planning task and after 20 minutes they give a short report on what they saw. The original observers then become the planners, and the original planners, the observers.

▪ A high school Spanish teacher who wants students to work on their conversation skills and also on the interpersonal communication skill of paraphrasing can conduct a discussion on Spanish culture and ask each discussant to paraphrase what the previous student said, before making a new contribution. The teacher provides feedback to students on the content of their discussion (Spanish culture), their use of vocabulary, and their use of the paraphrase technique.

FIND TIME FOR PROCESS AND STRATEGY INSTRUCTION

Sometimes teachers will want to provide instruction aimed specifically at a process or learning strategy objective. This time can be found through using the various strategies proposed in Chapter 4. It can also be found by using the concepts of power and economy described in Chapter 7 for selecting academic content. In addition, the teacher does not have to apologize for taking time for direct instruction on process and learning skills. Students in a classroom that is running smoothly learn more with less effort. Students who are already proficient in learning on their own can increase their efficiency immensely in a productive environment as they pursue important academic goals independent of the teacher.

Summary

This chapter described some of the complexities of classroom life by providing conceptual frameworks and research on classroom climate and the processes and structures that characterize classrooms. It took the point of view that building positive learning environments is probably the most important and difficult challenge facing beginning teachers. The key to success for beginning teachers is to focus attention and energy on those aspects of the classroom that are alterable, such as student motivation, group development, classroom discourse, and important learning strategies needed by students to satisfy the academic demands of the classroom. Skills to help students become more effective classroom members and to become more effective learners must be taught just as directly as any other academic-related skill. Time allocated to building productive classroom environments will reduce many of the frustrations experienced by beginning teachers and it will extend their abilities to win student cooperation and involvement in academic tasks.

Books for the Professional

Egan, G. (1974). *The skilled helper: A model for systematic helping and interpersonal relationships.* Monterey, Calif.: Brooks/Cole Publishing. This is an excellent presentation of theory behind helping relationships and good specific examples that can be adapted by teachers.

Gordon, T. (1974). *Teacher effectiveness training.* New York: Peter H. Wyden. This book includes information on communication and conflict in classrooms and presents a model for effective teacher-student relationships. Features many case studies and ideas for teaching.

Johnson, D. W., and Johnson, F. P. (1987). *Joining together: Group theory and group skills.* (Third edition). Englewood Cliffs, N.J.: Prentice-Hall. This book is an excellent introduction to group theory with many practical exercises that can be used by teachers in the classroom.

Schmuck, R. A., and Schmuck, P. (1983). *Group processes in the classroom.* (Fourth edition). Dubuque, Iowa: William C. Brown Pubs. This book provides a thorough review of group dynamics literature as it applies to the classroom as a learning group. Includes many activities and ideas to help teachers build productive learning environments.

Wilkinson, L. C. (Ed.). (1982). *Communicating in the classroom.* New York: Academic Press. This book of readings reports theory and research on the use of language for communicating in classrooms. Many implications for practice can be teased from the work described.

CHAPTER 5
LEARNING AIDS FOR PLANNING, OBSERVATION, AND REFLECTION

- ▪ Assessing My Skills for Building Productive Learning Environments
- ▪ Surveying Students About Classroom Climate
- ▪ Interviewing Teachers About Classroom Goal and Reward Structures
- ▪ Motivation Questionnaire for Students
- ▪ Observing Student Participation in Discussions
- ▪ Reflecting on Teaching Toward Multiple Objectives

ASSESSING MY SKILLS FOR BUILDING PRODUCTIVE LEARNING ENVIRONMENTS

PURPOSE: To evaluate one's level of skill in building productive learning environments.

DIRECTIONS: Check the level of skill you think you have for the areas listed below.

Skill or Competency	My Level of Effectiveness		
	High	Medium	Low
Increasing student motivation by adjusting			
Level of concern	——	——	——
Feeling tone	——	——	——
Success	——	——	——
Interest	——	——	——
Knowledge of results	——	——	——
Goal and reward structures	——	——	——
Influence and affiliation motives	——	——	——
Facilitating group development by attending to			
Inclusion and membership issues	——	——	——
Influence and collaboration issues	——	——	——
Individual and academic goals	——	——	——
Self-renewal and adaptive change	——	——	——
Promoting positive classroom discourse through			
Using and teaching communication skills	——	——	——
Encouraging student participation	——	——	——
Teaching discourse skills	——	——	——
Teaching toward multiple objectives	——	——	——

SURVEYING STUDENTS ABOUT CLASSROOM CLIMATE

PURPOSE: A positive classroom climate can facilitate learning. This aid will give you a means of determining students' perceptions about classroom climate.

DIRECTIONS: Ask a teacher if you can conduct the survey in his or her class. Then distribute the survey to students for them to fill out in class. If you are working with younger children or those with reading difficulties, you may wish to read each item aloud and have students fill out answer sheets with happy, indifferent, or frowning faces. Add other questions that may be of special interest to you.

Classroom Life

Here is a list of some statements that describe life in the classroom. Circle the letter in front of the statement that best tells how you feel about this class. *There are no right or wrong answers.*

1. Life in this class with your regular teacher has:
   a. All good things
   b. Mostly good things
   c. More good things than bad
   d. About as many good things as bad
   e. More bad things than good
   f. Mostly bad things

2. How hard are you working these days on learning what is being taught at school?
   a. Very hard
   b. Quite hard
   c. Not very hard
   d. Not hard at all

3. When I'm in this class, I usually am:
   a. Wide awake and very interested
   b. Pretty interested, kind of bored part of the time
   c. Not very interested, bored quite a lot of the time
   d. Bored, don't like it.

4. How hard are you working on schoolwork compared with the others in the class?
   a. Harder than most
   b. A little harder than most
   c. About the same as most
   d. A little less than most
   e. Quite a bit less than most

5. How many of the pupils in this class do what the teacher suggests?
   a. Most of them do
   b. More than half do
   c. Less than half do
   d. Hardly anybody does

6. If we help each other with our work in this class, the teacher:
   a. Likes it a lot
   b. Likes it some
   c. Likes it a little
   d. Doesn't like it at all
7. How good is your schoolwork compared with the work of others in the class?
   a. Much better than most
   b. A little better than most
   c. About the same as most
   d. Not quite as good as most
   e. Much worse than most
8. How often do the pupils in this class help one another with their schoolwork?
   a. Most of the time
   b. Sometimes
   c. Hardly ever
   d. Never
9. How often do the pupils in this class act friendly toward one another?
   a. Always
   b. Most of the time
   c. Sometimes
   d. Hardly ever

Analysis and Reflection: Tabulate and examine the results of the survey to obtain a broad view of the classroom's feeling tone, of student motivation, and the norms and expectations of the group. Look for classroom trends and for individuals or subgroups that may deviate from the classroom. Write a paragraph about this classroom's climate and its strong and weak points; suggest ways it might be improved.

SOURCE: Adapted from R. Fox, M. B. Luszki, and R. Schmuck. (1966). *Diagnosing classroom learning environments*. Chicago: Science Research Associates, pp. 11–13.

INTERVIEWING TEACHERS ABOUT CLASSROOM GOAL
AND REWARD STRUCTURES

PURPOSE: Goal and reward structures can have a significant impact on the learning environment. This aid is to help you examine how goal and reward structures are exhibited in classrooms.

DIRECTIONS: Use these questions as a guide in interviewing teachers about how they use classroom goal and reward structures.

(Remember that goal structures can be individualistic, competitive, or cooperative; that is, students' attainment of a goal can be unrelated to others' attainment, dependent on the failure of others, or dependent on the success of others, respectively. Reward structures are distinct from goal structures in that they refer to the rewards students receive for attaining their goals. Reward structures can also be individualistic, competitive, or cooperative. As in goal structures, if rewards are given individually and independently of the rewards others receive, then the reward structure is individualistic; if one's reward is dependent on the failure of others to receive the reward, the reward structure is competitive; and a reward structure in which one's reward is dependent on the success of another is a cooperative reward structure. Think about a track meet as an example. If the goal is to win the race, then one person winning means others fail. This is a competitive goal structure. The ribbon or trophy is the reward. If only the winner receives the ribbon, then the reward structure is competitive. If everyone receives a ribbon, say for participation, then the reward structure is individualistic.)

1. What activities do you have students do in which their ability to complete the activity or attain the goal of the activity is unrelated to whether other students complete it?

   _____

   _____

   _____

2. What activities do you have students do in which their ability to complete the activity or attain the goal of the activity depends on other students not completing it or attaining the goal?

   _____

   _____

   _____

3. What activities do you have students do where they must work together, where one student's ability to complete the activity to attain the goal depends on other students also being able to complete it or attain the goal?

   _____

   _____

4. In what ways do you reward students so that one student's reward is unrelated to rewards for any other students?

_____

_____

_____

5. In what ways do you reward students so that one student's reward depends on another student not receiving the reward?

_____

_____

_____

6. In what ways do you reward students so that one student's reward hinges on whether other students also receive the reward?

_____

_____

_____

Analysis and Reflection: What are the predominant goal and reward structures in these teachers' classes? Are all three types of structures represented? Is the mix of structures appropriate? What would be a better mix?

assignment 6

MOTIVATION QUESTIONNAIRE FOR STUDENTS

PURPOSE: Motivation is a critical element in building productive learning environments. This student questionnaire can help uncover strengths and weaknesses around motivation.

DIRECTIONS: Ask a teacher if you can survey his or her students about motivation. Distribute the survey and have students rate each statement on a scale of 1 to 5, agree strongly to disagree strongly.

1 Agree strongly   2 Agree   3 Neither agree nor disagree
4 Disagree   5 Disagree strongly

1. Sometimes I get a little nervous about
   my work in this class.   1 2 3 4 5
2. I want to do really well in this class.   1 2 3 4 5
3. I usually have to do boring things in this class.   1 2 3 4 5
4. This is a very pleasant class.   1 2 3 4 5
5. If I try, I can usually manage the work in this class.   1 2 3 4 5
6. I really don't care about grades very much.   1 2 3 4 5
7. My teacher is the only one who decides what happens in
   this class.   1 2 3 4 5
8. My teacher takes a long time to grade my papers, and
   seldom writes comments on them.   1 2 3 4 5
9. This class is way too easy for me.   1 2 3 4 5
10. I worry a lot all the time about my work in this class.   1 2 3 4 5
11. We never work in groups in this class.   1 2 3 4 5
12. I feel like I have a say in what happens in this class.   1 2 3 4 5
13. Sometimes we work and get graded in groups in this class.   1 2 3 4 5
14. This class makes me feel unhappy.
15. Interesting things happen in this class.   1 2 3 4 5
16. This class is way too hard.   1 2 3 4 5
17. My teacher almost always tells me why I got the
    grade I got right away.   1 2 3 4 5

Find the mean score for the class for each item. Fill in the accompanying form with the mean score for each item. The items are sorted out according to the different domains, or elements of motivation. A high score on the positively worded items indicates a good job has been done in motivating students in that domain. A high score on the negatively worded items indicates a need for improvement.

Domain	Positively Worded	Negatively Worded
Level of concern	1 _____	10 _____
Feeling tone	4 _____	14 _____
Success	5 _____	9 _____
		16 _____
Interest	15 _____	3 _____
Knowledge of results	17 _____	8 _____
Goal and reward structures	13 _____	11 _____
Influence needs	12 _____	7 _____
Achievements	2 _____	6 _____

Analysis and Reflection: Write a paragraph detailing the ways students are motivated in this class and suggesting ways motivation could be improved.

Assignment 6

OBSERVING STUDENT PARTICIPATION IN DISCUSSIONS

PURPOSE: Broad student participation is an important goal in classroom discussions. This aid can be used to gather information about patterns of student participation in class discussions.

DIRECTIONS: Obtain a copy of the class seating chart, or if observing a small group, note everyone's name and location on your paper. You can use a format like the one pictured below. Whenever a student contributes to the discussion, make a "tick" on your chart by that student's name.

Front

☐ _____   ☐ _____   ☐ _____   ☐ _____

☐ _____   ☐ _____   ☐ _____   ☐ _____

☐ _____   ☐ _____   ☐ _____   ☐ _____

☐ _____   ☐ _____   ☐ _____   ☐ _____

Analysis and Reflection: Who talks the most? the least? Is there an action zone, that is, an area of the room that the teacher seems to favor during whole-class discussions? Are there any sex differences in participation? racial differences? Any other patterns observed? How might the quieter students be encouraged to participate?

REFLECTING ON TEACHING TOWARD MULTIPLE OBJECTIVES

PURPOSE: It is important to teach toward multiple objectives. This aid will help you analyze your own or another teacher's current level of skill in this area.

DIRECTIONS: If you are teaching, at the end of a week spend some time reviewing your plan book and that week's lessons. Make a "tick" on the chart any time one of the lesson's objectives fits one of the categories provided. Add new categories as you learn more about the kinds of objectives you wish to achieve. If you are a student, observe one of your own teachers and categorize the goals you note the same way. Keep track this way for two or three weeks.

Goals that relate to:

Content   _____

Learning strategies   _____

Classroom discourse   _____

Group development   _____

Motivation   _____

Analysis and Reflection: Examine the pattern of goals you have uncovered. Is the distribution of goals between the various categories appropriate? Compare this week's pattern with previous weeks. Are some categories underused? Are some overused? If you are a student teacher, use this information in planning for the upcoming week.

SPECIAL TOPIC   by NANCY WINITZKY

Developing Multicultural and Mainstreamed Classrooms

Multicultural education and mainstreaming are two recent and important ideas in American education. Both are concerned with equity and fair treatment for minority groups. Both have engendered some controversy. It is important for beginning teachers to incorporate into their philosophical and practical repertoire some basic ideas and practices from multicultural and mainstreaming education.

This special topic section will first treat multicultural education, tracing its roots and aims and showing how to apply it in the classroom. Next, mainstreaming will be discussed in similar fashion. The intent of this section is not to describe all that is known about multicultural education and mainstreaming, but instead to provide beginning teachers with an overview from which further study and work can proceed.

MULTICULTURAL EDUCATION

Rationale

The term *multicultural education* has come to signify the fostering of recognition, understanding, and appreciation for all cultural groups, and the development of skills in working with members of different groups. The term goes beyond race to include ethnic and religious groups, women, the disabled, the elderly, and all socioeconomic classes. It also conveys an international flavor: the desire to recognize cultures outside our own borders and to place ourselves within the context of the global community.

Some of the same forces that gave rise to the civil rights movement provided the impetus for the concept of multicultural education. The realization of injuries suffered by minority groups, the desire to right those wrongs, and the resurgence of pride in heritage all converged on the classroom in the late 1960s and early 1970s to increase concern for multicultural education. The realization, described in Chapter 1, that the United States is increasingly a multicultural society, that minority groups will soon become majority groups, and that it is increasingly important for all subcultures to understand and appreciate each other are factors sustaining educators' interest in multicultural education.

Promoting multicultural education is an important goal no matter what the cultural composition of any given classroom. In fact, providing a strong multicultural component is more important when only a single culture is represented. Students attending all-white or all-black schools, for example, have an even greater need to be exposed to the other cultures, since they do not have an opportunity to interact with persons different from themselves in other settings.

Philosophical Roots

The philosophy underlying multicultural education in cultural pluralism. Horace M. Kallen (1924), one of the major theorists, saw cultural pluralism as a step beyond two other competing ideologies—"Americanization" and the "melting pot." Americanization was strongly advocated by prominent educators and politicians at the turn of the century and well into the 1920s and 1930s. Advocates believed that there existed an American race, culture, and value system that was based on the mores of northern Europe, and that minority groups should forsake their own cultures and assimilate completely into the dominant American culture. Elwood P. Cubberley, a noted early-twentieth-century educator, succinctly described the Americanization position:

> The southern and eastern Europeans are a very different type from the north Europeans who preceded them. Illiterate, docile, lacking in self-reliance and initiative and possessing none of the Anglo-Teutonic conceptions of law, order and government, their coming has served to dilute tremendously our national stock, and to corrupt our civic life. . . .
>
> Our task is to break up their groups or settlements, to assimilate and to amalgamate these people as part of our American race, and to implant in their children, so far as can be done, the Anglo-Saxon conceptions of righteousness, law and order and popular government, and to awaken in them reverence for our democratic institutions and for those things in our national life which we as people hold to be of abiding worth. (Krug, 1976, pp. 7–8)

In contrast, the melting pot idea, although often confused with Americanization, was very different. Proponents of the melting pot believed that all ethnic groups had strengths and that in the "crucible" of America, these strengths would be merged into a new, superior culture. Rather than being contemptuous of cultural diversity, melting pot advocates welcomed diversity as a source of strength.

> They believed that the new emerging American culture must be built not on the destruction of the cultural values and mores of the various immigrant groups but on their *fusion* with the existing American civilization. . . . In the burning fires of the melting pot, all races were equal—all were reshaped, and molded into a new entity. (Krug, 1976, p. 12)

Cultural pluralism, as currently defined, rejects the racism of Americanization and also rejects the conception of a single culture emerging from the melting pot. Cultural pluralism instead, while acknowledging the existence of a dominant American culture, also recognizes the strength and permanence of its subcultures. In Kallen's (1924) conception, minority groups should accept the common elements of the dominant culture but should be constantly interacting with it and injecting into it new elements, to the benefit of all. The melting pot metaphor, with its implications of homogeneity, has now been replaced with the salad metaphor, in which each ingredient is distinct and valued by itself, while at the same time contributing to the whole, and bound together with a common "dressing," that is, the dominant culture.

Teaching That Is Multicultural

There are two main approaches a beginning teacher can take to facilitate multicultural education. One, sometimes called the *topical approach*, consists of recognizing and teaching about nondominant cultures. Teachers can devote special lessons to the heros of various cultures, celebrate special holidays, and design lessons to recognize the art, literature, and language of specified subcultures. Although these are important educational activities, this approach tends to emphasize differences between groups, not similarities. It may also be superficial and fragmented and not lead to real understanding and appreciation among groups.

The second approach is called the *conceptual approach*. When teachers use this approach, they incorporate a series of concepts associated with cultural pluralism into ongoing lessons. A set of key multicultural concepts were identified by the University of Maryland/Charles County Teacher Corps Project (1981) for teachers wishing to use the conceptual approach. These are outlined in Figure S2.1. These are not the only concepts that could be used; you may come up with other concepts that better suit your subject area or grade level.

Here are just a few examples of lessons using these concepts: (1) The concept of pluralism itself could be infused into an intermediate school lesson on bar graphs, in which students plot the proportions of various ethnic and other groups in their community. (2) The concept of interdependence could be infused into an elementary science unit on ecology. (3) A secondary social studies lesson on voting rights could infuse the concept of exploitation.

Teachers using the conceptual approach would first consider which of these concepts are complementary to material they are already teaching. Then, as opportunities arose, they would incorporate the appropriate concepts into their lessons. In planning for such lessons, teachers should couple the multicultural concept with the regular instructional objective, and should specify learning materials and activities that achieve both goals. Obviously, this means teaching toward multiple objectives, a topic covered in some detail in Chapter 5.

What else can beginning teachers do to build multicultural concepts and attitudes into their teaching? First, beginning teachers can become aware of their own biases, and become conscious of how these biases might influence their

Figure S2.1 Concepts to Guide Multicultural Education

- **Individuality**: Refers to the personal characteristics that are unique to an individual and distinguish him/her from others. Respect for individuality leads to positive concepts of self and others.

- **Cultural patterns**: Common elements such as values, norms, beliefs, customs, and rituals that unite members of a group and distinguish them from other groups.

- **Subsistence**: Refers to the essential needs common to all people—food, clothing, and shelter.

- **Social structure**: The organization of any society through the development of family and of educational, political, religious, and social institutions.

- **Interdependence**: The reliance of one or more individuals or groups upon one another for a successful, cooperative existence.

- **Communication**: The process by which individuals or groups transmit messages through the use of language, symbols, signs, or behavior.

- **Exploitation**: The taking advantage of one person or group for the benefit of another individual or group. There are different forms of exploitation within a society such as prejudice, discrimination, and stereotyping.

- **Pluralism**: A state of society in which members of diverse ethnic, racial, religious, or social groups maintain participation in their specific groups while functioning effectively within a common civilization.

---

teaching and their interaction with students, parents, and coworkers. This is particularly important because teachers are often significant role models for students. Self-awareness is important for another reason, and that is that people generally live up to what is expected of them. If a teacher, consciously or unconsciously, is biased against members of a certain group and expects stereotypically "bad" behavior from them, that is precisely the sort of behavior the teacher is likely to engender.

In addition to self-understanding, beginning teachers can also educate themselves about cultural differences and be alert to problems these differences might cause in the classroom. For example, many non-Western cultures have a very different sense of time than Americans do. For Americans, punctuality is an unquestioned virtue, and children in school are penalized for tardiness, turning work in late, and so on. But in many cultures people are much more relaxed about time, do not regard punctuality as particularly virtuous, and do not pay strict attention to deadlines. There are pros and cons to each set of values about time that cannot be discussed here. What is important is to see how easily teachers and students with different time values could come into conflict, to the detriment of the students.

Respecting the culture of such students does not mean abandoning the rules of the school. Punctuality and other aspects of American culture may not be regarded as important elsewhere, but they are important here, and in order to be successful here, all students must learn these values. Not enforcing such rules at school would be to perform a disservice to all students. However, the attitude and spirit with which these rules are enforced need not be demeaning nor punitive. Teachers can explain rules and consequences in a neutral way to students and parents and can offer suggestions on how they might cope with such rules. Teachers can also make clear that rules at school apply only at school and that students are certainly free and encouraged to express their own values within the context of their subcultures.

Teachers also need to apply multiculturalism to curricular materials. Textbooks, workbooks, dittos, bulletin boards, and other visual learning materials should portray a variety of racial, ethnic, class, age, and disability groups from both sexes. All curricular materials need to be free from stereotyping.

Finally, teachers have instructional, as well as curricular, tools at their disposal to help foster a multicultural classroom. As described in Chapter 10, cooperative learning models such as STAD, TGT, and Group Investigation all promote intergroup appreciation and understanding and help students develop skills in working cooperatively with people from different groups. These cooperative learning models should form an active part of the repertoire of every teacher who aspires to achieve multicultural goals.

MAINSTREAMING

Rationale

Legally the concept of mainstreaming came into existence in 1975 with the passage of Public Law 94–142, the Education for All Handicapped Children Act. This legislation was a response to perceived inequalities and discrimination in educational services provided to handicapped children. In some jurisdictions, for example, handicapped children were barred from attending school because of their special needs. The aim of the law was to ensure a free public education for all children, including those with handicaps.

Mainstreaming, however, would be important even if it weren't mandated by law. Other educational benefits accrue besides alleviating discrimination. For example, handicapped children have the opportunity to learn appropriate social and academic behavior from observing and modeling nonhandicapped children. The nonhandicapped children also benefit in that they are able to see firsthand the strengths and potential contributions, as well as the limitations, of their handicapped peers. The school environment and society at large are thereby enriched.

Public Law 94–142

The law has several provisions, among them the following:

Children are to be educated in the "least restrictive environment." This means that, to the extent possible, children with handicaps should be integrated into the regular classroom. Those with very mild physical, emotional, and learning disabilities are to spend their entire school day in the regular classroom. Those with slightly more serious problems are to receive extra assistance from a special educator, either in or out of class. As the disabilities grow more serious, the responsibility of the regular classroom teacher is reduced further, and the child is to receive a larger portion of his or her education in more specialized settings, culminating, if necessary, in a full-time residential school. In practice, the majority of handicapped children who attend regular classes are those who have historically been there for at least part of the day, and those who experience mild physical or learning disabilities.

Each handicapped child is to have an individualized educational plan. These plans, abbreviated IEPs, are to be developed by a committee composed of the regular classroom teacher, the child's parents, the special education teacher, and any other personnel that may be helpful, such as psychologists, speech therapists, or medical personnel. Contained in the IEP should be information about the child's current level of academic performance, a statement of both long- and short-term educational goals, a plan for how these goals will be achieved, the amount of time the child will spend in the regular class, and an evaluation plan. The IEP is to be revised annually.

Evaluation procedures are to be nondiscriminatory. In screening children for special services, school officials are required to use a variety of tests and to consider the child's cultural background and language. The involvement of parents in this process in mandated, and no major educational decisions may be made without their written consent. Parents must be informed of intended school actions in their own language.

Teachers' Responsibilities

Teachers have several responsibilities for mainstreaming, but many of these overlap with their regular duties. Teachers need to be able to identify potentially handicapped children and make referrals for them. They need to participate in IEP meetings and be able to work in a team with other professionals to serve the special student. They may also need to assist handicapped children with special equipment. As always, they must accommodate individual differences and maintain communication with parents. And they must help handicapped and nonhandicapped children work and play together. All in all, many of these responsibilities and skills are not much different from others described in this book.

Most beginning teachers worry about what can be done in the classroom to accommodate special students. As with multicultural education, one of the teacher's first actions should be to examine his or her own biases and to modify them, if necessary. Recall that students model teachers' intended and unintended behaviors and often live up to the teacher's expectations, whether positive or negative. Positive regard for handicapped students is a prerequisite to effective teaching. Teachers need to carefully think through the physical layout of their classrooms and make any changes that will facilitate easy movement for all students, particularly those who may require wheelchairs or special walking devices. Teachers also need to think through scheduling and time constraints and how these might affect special students. For example, transition time between lessons may need to be extended for a student who is physically hampered, and the downtime thus created for the nonhandicapped students managed appropriately. Routines and procedures for such contingencies must be planned and taught to the whole class. Teachers should develop learning materials and activities commensurate with handicapped childrens' abilities, much as they should attempt to adapt lessons to the individual differences of all students. In doing so, they should expect to work closely with resource teachers and other support personnel. Most schools have such support services readily available. Finally, cooperative learning strategies should be used regularly, both to facilitate achievement and to help handicapped and nonhandicapped children accept and appreciate each other.

The students most likely to be mainstreamed are those with mild physical handicaps, learning disabilities, or behavioral problems. The following tips for teaching these students have been adapted from recommendations offered by the National Information Center for Handicapped Children and Youth:

1. Use highly structured materials. Tell the student exactly what is expected. Avoid distractions, such as colorful bulletin boards, in work areas.
2. Allow alternatives to the use of written language, such as tape recorders or oral tests.
3. Expect improvement on a long-term basis.
4. Reinforce appropriate behavior. Model and explain what constitutes appropriate behavior.
5. Provide immediate feedback and ample opportunities for drill and practice.

Note that these actions are not very different from the behaviors consistent with effective teaching described throughout this book.

Resource Organizations

This brief treatment of the complexities of multicultural education and mainstreaming is clearly only the beginning. You will need to read further, take further training, and reflect on how to apply what you have learned. The following organizations can supply you with information about multicultural education and about working with mainstreamed children:

The Council of Interracial Books for Children, Inc., 1841 Broadway, New York, N.Y. 10023

National Information Center for Handicapped Children and Youth, P.O. Box 1492, Washington, D.C. 20013

Books for the Professional

Banks, James. (1979). *Teaching strategies for ethnic studies*. (Second edition). Boston, Mass.: Allyn and Bacon. This book gives a thorough and careful presentation of the issues surrounding multicultural education, along with numerous strategies for teachers to use.

Biklen, D. (1985). *Achieving the complete school*. New York: Teachers College Press. Through numerous case studies, this book describes principles and methods for teachers to achieve mainstreaming in their classrooms.

CHAPTER 6

MAIN IDEAS

- Classroom management is possibly the most important challenge facing beginning teachers.
- Classroom management is not an end itself but a part of the teacher's overall leadership role.
- Classroom management and effective teaching are closely related and cannot be separated.
- A well-developed research base on classroom management provides guidelines for successful group management and dealing with disruptive students.
- A large portion of disruptive student behavior can be eliminated by using preventive classroom management measures such as clear rules and procedures and careful orchestration of learning activities.
- The effective teacher reduces management and discipline problems by helping students learn self-management skills.

Managing Classroom Groups

When teachers talk about the most difficult problems they experienced in their first years of teaching, they mention classroom management and discipline consistently. Although a rich knowledge base on classroom management has been developed over the past two decades, as well as a spate of management training programs, beginning teachers continue to feel insecure about managing their first classrooms.

Many of these anxieties are, in fact, similar to the anxieties experienced by people in any field when they are asked to assume positions of leadership and to exert influence and authority for the first time. Nonetheless, gaining a set of basic management understandings and skills will do much to reduce the anxiety that naturally accompanies one's first classroom assignment. Describing the important concepts and skills associated with classroom management is the aim of this chapter. The first section of the chapter builds on the conceptual frameworks introduced in Chapter 5 and then presents a sampling of summaries of key research studies from the classroom management literature. In the final section of the chapter are specific and concrete procedures beginning teachers can use as they prepare for effective classroom management.

PERSPECTIVE AND RATIONALE

Many of the conceptual frameworks for understanding classroom management have been presented in previous chapters and do not need to be repeated here. There are, however, three ideas that can provide additional perspective.

1. *Classroom management is not an end itself; it is merely one part of a teacher's overall leadership role.* In this regard, classroom management cannot be separated from the other executive functions of teaching. For example, when teachers plan carefully for lessons, as described in Chapter 3, they are doing much to assure good classroom management. When teachers plan ways to allocate time to various learning activities or consider how space should be used in the classroom, they are again making important decisions that will affect classroom management. Similarly, all of the strategies for building productive environments described in

Chapter 5, such as helping the classroom develop as a group, attending to student motivation, or facilitating honest and open discourse, are also important components of classroom management.

2. *It is impossible to totally separate the managerial and instructional functions of teaching.* Each teaching model or strategy a teacher chooses to use has its own social system and its own task demands that influence the behaviors of both teachers and learners. The instructional tasks associated with giving a lecture, for example, call for behaviors on the part of students that are different from those needed for tasks associated with learning a new skill. Similarly, behavioral demands for students working together in groups are different from those required for working alone on a seatwork assignment. Instructional tasks are integrally related not only to the problem of instruction but also to the problems of order and management. An important theme stressed in this chapter is what Brophy and Putnam (1979) and Evertson and Emmer (1982) have called preventive management. Teachers who plan appropriate classroom activities and tasks, who make wise decisions about time and space allocation, and who have a sufficient repertoire of instructional strategies will be building a learning environment that minimizes management and discipline problems.

3. *Classroom management is possibly the most important challenge facing beginning teachers*, since their reputation among colleagues, school authorities, and even students will be strongly influenced by their ability to perform the managerial functions of teaching, particularly creating an orderly learning environment and dealing with student behavior. Sometimes, beginning teachers think this is unfair and argue that schools and principals put too much emphasis on order as contrasted to learning. Perhaps it is unfair. Nonetheless, teachers' leadership ability is tested in the arena of management and discipline, and when something goes wrong it is known more quickly than other aspects of teaching. More importantly, without adequate management little else can occur. Dunkin and Biddle (1974) pointed out this important fact over a decade ago when they wrote that "management of the classroom . . . forms a necessary condition for cognitive learning; and if the teacher cannot solve problems in this sphere, we can give the rest of teaching away" (p. 135).

SAMPLING THE RESEARCH BASE

The research on maintaining order in the classroom has been guided by at least three major orientations: focus on the individual, on classroom ecology and group processes, and on effective teaching.

Focus on the Individual

Research that focuses on the individual student seeks to understand the causes of behavioral problems and recommends specific interventions and discipline procedures for teachers to use. This tradition has been led mainly by clinical and counseling psychologists, such as Dreikurs (1968), Grey (Dreikurs and Grey, 1968), and Glasser (1969) and by behavioral psychologists and those who apply behavioral theory such and Canter and Canter (1976). Their research or practice has focused on such psychological causes as insecurity, need for attention, anxiety, and lack of self-discipline, as well as sociological causes such as parent overprotection, bad peer relationships, or disadvantaged backgrounds. Their recommendations to teachers normally emphasize ways to help individual students through counseling or behavior modification and show less concern for managing the classroom group. This tradition is mentioned only briefly for two reasons. First, many of the psychological and sociological causes of student behavior are beyond the influence of classroom teachers, and second, the management of classroom groups is a more pressing issue for the beginning teacher. The final section of this chapter does include a description of Glasser's approach to classroom management because it incorporates concrete procedures for helping students develop self-management skills within a group setting.

Classroom Ecology and Group Processes

In Chapter 5 several ideas were described that help explain the classroom as a social system and show how classrooms develop important group processes for accomplishing learning tasks. The ecological perspective is an extension and refinement of these ideas that addresses directly the problem of classroom control and group management procedures. Researchers such as Gump (1967), Barker (1968), and Kounin (1970), and more recently Walter Doyle have held to the idea that behavior in classrooms "including cognition, is . . . an adaptive response to the demands of the classroom environment" (Doyle, 1979, p. 43). Researchers working out of the ecological orientation pay close attention to the behavioral settings that exist within classrooms and the kind of *activities* and *tasks* students are asked to perform. According to Doyle (1979), the phrase *classroom activities:*

> designates bounded segments of classroom time, for example, seatwork, tests, small-group discussion, lecture, recitation, reading. Activities can be described in terms of the physical space in which they occur, the type and number of participants, the resources or props used, the format for behavior, and the concern of or focal content of the segment (for example art, mathematics, vocabulary). (p. 45)

The phrase *classroom tasks* on the other hand refers, according to Doyle (1979):

> to the way in which information-processing demands of an environment are structured and experienced. Such demands are affected not only by the flow of events in an activity but also by the point or end of the activity. A task is defined, therefore, in terms of (a) a goal and (b) a set of operations designed to achieve the goal. . . .

A study of activities might report, for example, that a student spent twelve minutes listening to a lecture. A study of tasks would attempt to identify the situationally defined purpose of this activity (that is, what was the student supposed to learn from the lecture). (pp. 45–46)

Classroom management researchers in this tradition study the way student cooperation and involvement is achieved so that important learning activities can be accomplished. The major function of the teacher from this point of view is to plan and orchestrate well-conceived group activities that flow smoothly. Misbehavior of students is conceived as actions that disrupt this activity flow. Examples of disruptions might include students talking when quiet is desired, students not working on a seatwork assignment the teacher has given, or students getting out of their seats at inappropriate times. Teacher interventions in regard to student misbehavior, as will be described later, should be quick, many times minor, and aimed at keeping the flow of learning activities and tasks on the right track. The classic piece of research in this tradition, done by Kounin and his colleagues, has greatly influenced the concept of classroom management and the ideas used to describe management processes. This work is described in Research Summary 6.1.

Other researchers of particular interest who have used the ecological framework to guide their research are Walter Doyle and Kathy Carter (1984) at the University of Arizona. They were interested in how specific academic tasks are connected to student involvement and to classroom management. To explore this topic, they observed one junior high school English teacher and the students in three of her classes in a middle-class suburban school for a period of almost three months. The teacher, Mrs. Dee, was selected for study because she was an experienced teacher and she was considered to have considerable expertise in teaching writing to students.

This work is informative to the topic of classroom management because the researcher found that students had considerable influence over the task demands of the classroom. For instance, over a period of time Mrs. Dee would assign students a variety of major and minor writing tasks. Examples included: writing an essay comparing Christmas in Truman Capote's story "A Christmas Memory" with Christmas today, writing a short story report, or writing descriptive paragraphs with illustrations. In some of the writing tasks, Mrs. Dee tried to encourage student creativity and self-direction and to do that she left the assignments somewhat open-ended. From detailed observations of Mrs. Dee's classroom, Doyle and Carter found, however, that students would press to reduce the amount of self-direction and independent judgment in some of the writing assignments. Students, even those considered very bright, would use tactics such as asking questions or feignng confusion to force Mrs. Dee to become more and more concise and explicit. In other words, the students influenced the teacher to do more and more of their thinking.

Doyle and Carter also found that by asking questions about content and about procedures students, in addition to changing the assignment, could also slow down the pace of classroom activities. This was done to get an assignment postponed or just to use up class time. When Mrs. Dee refused to answer some of the students' delaying questions things seemed only to get worse. Here is a direct quote from a report of what the researchers observed: "Some students became quite adamant in their demands. . . . On such occasions, order began to break down and the normal smoothness and momentum of the classes were reinstated only when the teacher provided the prompts and resources the students were requesting. The teacher was pushed, in other words, to choose between conditions for students' self-direction and preserving order in the classroom" (p. 146). Mrs. Dee was an experienced enough teacher to know that order had to come first or everything else was lost.

Classroom Management and Effective Teaching

The third research orientation to classroom management incorporates important ideas from the ecological orientation but also has been closely associated with the research on effective teaching. Researchers working with an effective teaching orientation emphasize the importance of student engagement with academic activities and tasks. They do this because, as you read in Chapter 4, strong relationships have been found between student engagement and student achievement.

Starting in the 1970s Edmund Emmer, Carolyn Evertson, Julie Sanford, and a number of their colleagues, all researchers then at the Research and Development Center for Teacher Education at the University of Texas, began to find that the classroom management practices of some teachers were markedly different from those of others. By watching and studying the effective teachers closely, recommendations for effective classroom management emerged. A study by Julie Sanford, while she was involved with the Texas group, is representative of this research orientation. Her work is described in Research Summary 6.2.

PREPARING FOR EFFECTIVE CLASSROOM MANAGEMENT

This section of Chapter 6, focused directly on procedures beginning teachers can use to assure effective classroom management, is organized around three major topics: preventive classroom management, managing inappropriate and disruptive behavior, and exhibiting confidence and exerting influence.

Preventive Classroom Management

Many of the problems associated with student misbehavior are dealt with by effective teachers though preventive approaches. Much of this section is based on

RESEARCH SUMMARY
6.1

Kounin, J. S. (1970). *Discipline and group management in classrooms.* New York: Holt, Rinehart and Winston.

PROBLEM: After several years of trying to understand discipline in classrooms, Kounin discovered that the key was not so much the way teachers controlled and disciplined individual students but, instead, the way they managed groups. In the late 1960s he decided to study group management directly.

SAMPLE: The sample of Kounin's study reported here consisted of 49 teachers and their students in upper elementary classrooms.

PROCEDURES: Kounin developed elaborate procedures for observing classrooms, including video-taping teacher and student interaction and doing transcript analysis. Many variables were measured in the complete study. Here, only a few of the most important variables are described.

Dependent Variables: For Kounin, managerial success consisted of classrooms where work involvement was high and student deviancy was low:

1. Work involvement could fall into three categories: (a) definitely doing the assigned work, (b) probably doing the assigned work, (c) definitely not doing the assigned work.
2. Deviancy consisted of a three-category scheme: (a) student not misbehaving, (b) student mildly misbehaving, and (c) student engaging in serious misbehavior.

Contextual Variables: Kounin observed two types of learning activities: recitations and seatwork.

Independent Variables: Kounin conceptualized eight different variables for describing the group management behavior of teachers.

1. Withitness: the ability to accurately spot deviant behavior, almost before it starts
2. Overlappingness: the ability to spot and deal with deviant behavior while going right on with the lesson
3. Smoothness: absence of behaviors that interrupt the flow of activities
4. Momentum: absence of behaviors that slow down lesson pacing
5. Group Alerting: techniques used by teachers to keep noninvolved students attending and forewarned of forthcoming events
6. Accountability: techniques used by teachers to keep students accountable for their performance
7. Challenge Arousal: techniques used by teachers to keep students involved and enthusiastic
8. Variety: the degree to which various aspects of lessons differed

POINTERS FOR READING RESEARCH: Up to this point in presenting statistics, the researchers have depended on mean scores and used *t* tests or analysis of variance (*f* tests) to see if mean scores between two groups were significant. To understand Kounin's study, a new statistic—the correlation coefficient described in the special topic section on understanding research—needs to be reviewed. Remember, correlation refers to the extent of a relationship that exists between pairs of measures. The coefficient can range from +1.00 through .00 to −1.00. The sign does not have the traditional mathematical meaning. Instead, a plus sign represents a positive relationship, a minus sign a negative relationship. A .00 means no relationship exists, +1.00 means a perfect relationship exists, and −1.00 means a reverse relationship exists. Correlations can be tested for significance just as mean scores can.

RESULTS: Table 1 shows the correlations Kounin found between various aspects of teacher managment behavior and children's behavior during recitation and seatwork.

TABLE 1 Correlations of Selected Teacher's Management Behaviors and Children's Behavior in Recitation and Seatwork Settings

N = 49 Classrooms (correlation of .276 is significant at .05 level)

Dependent Variable	Recitation		Seatwork	
	Work Involvement	Freedom from Deviancy	Work Involvement	Freedom from Deviancy
Momentum	.656	.641	.198	.490
Withitness	.615	.531	.307	.509
Smoothness	.601	.489	.382	.421
Group alerting	.603	.442	.234	.290
Accountability	.494	.385	.002	−.035
Overlappingness	.460	.362	.259	.379
Challenge arousal	.372	.325	.308	.371
Overall variety and challenge	.217	.099	.449	.194
Class size (*R* = 21–39)	−.279	−.258	−.152	−.249

SOURCE: Adapted from J. S. Kounin (1970), p. 169.

DISCUSSION AND IMPLICATIONS: Kounin's research provides a rich source of ideas for how teachers can approach the problem of classroom management. In Table 1, withitness, momentum, overlappingness, smoothness, and group alerting all appear to increase student work involvement, particularly during recitation lessons. Similarly, withitness and momentum decrease student deviancy. Withitness also decreases student deviancy in seatwork lessons, whereas variety appears to be the major behavior that helps promote work involvement in seatwork.

Note that all the relationships in the table, although not significant, are positive, except for the negative correlation coefficients for the relationships between accountability and freedom from deviancy during seatwork and those associated with class size. These negative correlations are small and what they mean essentially is that no relationships were found between those variables.

The implications for teacher behavior from Kounin's work are great, and these will be described in some detail in the next section of this chapter.

━━━━━━━━━━━━━━━ **RESEARCH SUMMARY** ━━━━━━━━━━━━━━━
6.2

Sanford, J. P. (1984). Management and organization in science classrooms. *Journal of Research in Science Teaching, 21,* 575–587.

PROBLEM: Sanford was interested in the relationships among teacher behaviors and the links between this behavior and student on-task behavior. In this particular study she explored two important questions: (1) Which classroom management practices are related to student on-task behavior and disruptive behavior? (2) What similarities and differences exist between the practices of more and less effective classroom managers?

SAMPLE: Thirteen teachers and their students in 26 middle school science classrooms comprised the sample in this study. Sanford reports that all classes were heterogeneous in ability and that the teachers were volunteers from two urban school districts. Most of the teachers could be classified as beginning teachers and had less than three years of experience. Three teachers were in their first year; one had seven years' experience.

PROCEDURES: The researchers observed each teacher 16 to 18 times in two different classes during the first eight weeks of school and eight times during January and February of that same school year. Observations were made by trained observers who kept a detailed narrative record of both teacher and student behavior. A special device, called the "Student Engagement Rate" instrument, was used to measure the amount of student on-task and off-task behavior.

POINTERS FOR READING RESEARCH: Sanford's study produces several types of information: (1) correlation coefficients similar to those found in the Kounin study, (2) means for various types of engagement behaviors found in effective and ineffective classrooms, and (3) her own descriptions based on observations. The reader has been introduced to all the concepts needed to read the data. However, since Sanford's study has so much information in it, full attention is required to understand each step of it.

RESULTS: Table 1 lists some independent variables and correlation coefficients relating to four areas of classroom management: classroom procedures and rules, student work procedures, management of student behavior, and organization and presentation of instruction, plus a miscellaneous category.

A second step in Sanford's research was to rank the management practices of the 13 teachers. Three groups of teachers were identified: (1) three teachers called best managers, (2) seven teachers called middle (average) managers, (3) three teachers called low (poor) managers. Table 2 compares the behaviors of these three groups of teachers on eight identified effectiveness variables.

DISCUSSION AND IMPLICATIONS: The data presented in Tables 1 and 2, plus other descriptive information that was collected, led Sanford to make several conclusions. Because so many of Sanford's conclusions were based not only on the data

TABLE 1 Correlation of Selected Classroom Management Variables With Student Behaviors

Variable Description	Based on 13 Teachers		
	Off task	On task	Disruptive
Class procedure/rules			
Efficient administrative routine	−.87	.81	−.85
Appropriate general procedures	−.95	.76	−.92
Efficient small group procedures	−.83	.46	−.64
Student work procedures			
Consistently enforces work standards	−.91	.73	−.89
Routines/assigning, checking work	−.88	.74	−.81
Managing student behavior			
Consistency in managing behavior	−.94	.73	−.89
Effective monitoring	−.92	.67	−.84
Stops inappropriate behavior	−.95	.73	−.94
Ignores inappropriate behavior	.82	−.62	.78
Allowing wandering not task related	.93	−.83	.86
Organizing and presenting instruction			
Describes objectives clearly	−.75	.67	−.76
Clear directions	−.81	.77	−.84
Appropriate pacing of lessons	−.82	.78	−.78
Efficiency of transitions	−.89	.72	−.84
Planning enough work	−.84	.61	−.80
Miscellaneous variables			
Teacher confidence	−.78	.68	−75
Teacher enthusiasm	−.36	.10	−.31

All correlations except those underlined were significant at least at the .05 level.
SOURCE: Adapted from J. P. Sanford (1984), p. 580.

presented in Tables 1 and 2 but also on her observations, some of her own words are used below to convey to readers what she found.

1. *General classroom procedures/rules* The more effective classroom managers "had procedures that effectively governed student talk, participation in oral lessons and discussions, getting out of seat, checking or turning in work, what to do when work was finished early, and ending class" (pp. 581–582). "The three best managers monitored student behaviors closely, circulating around the room to look at students' work" (p. 582).
2. *Class time use and activities* "Analysis of activity(ies) . . . failed to show differences between more and less effective managers' classes with regard to total instructional time" (p. 583).

(Cont'd)

━━━━━━━━━━━━━━━━ **RESEARCH SUMMARY** ━━━━━━━━━━
6.2 (continued)

TABLE 2 Comparison of Three Subgroups of Teachers

Variable	Best Group (n = 3)	Middle Group (n = 7)	Low Group (n = 3)
Students off task	2%	4%	13%
Students on task	94%	87%	80%
Disruptive behavior*	1.11	1.39	2.48
Good procedures	4.55	3.79	2.36
Good work standards	4.20	3.42	1.98
Consistency	4.36	3.44	1.96
Clear directions	4.36	3.90	3.00
Good pacing	4.33	3.62	2.54

* Means based on 16–18 fall observations. Ratings based on 1–5 scale, with 5 being most effective and 1 being least effective
SOURCE: Adapted from J. P. Sanford (1984), p. 582.

3. *Laboratory procedures* "Laboratory activities conducted by poor managers were often characterized as chaotic, with very little work accomplished by students. Students often did not appear to listen to or follow teachers' instructions. Classes were very noisy and many students were rowdy. Teachers ignored most off-task and inappropriate behavior, while trying to help individuals. In contrast, laboratory activities in classes taught by the three best managers usually ran smoothly and efficiently" (p. 583).
4. *Student work procedures* "In classes taught by more effective managers, there were very clear work requirements, good monitoring of student progress on assignments, and frequent checks of daily work and quizzes in class. . . . In classes taught by the other less effective managers . . . there were poor and inconsistent procedures for assigning, collecting; and checking work, and little monitoring of student progress or completion of assignments" (p. 584).
5. *Content presentations* "Good managers were different from less effective ones in that their presentations and explanations were clearer, their directions about note taking were explicit and firm, and they held students accountable for notes that were supposed to have been taken" (p. 585).

Implications from this study and from other studies by the Texas research group will be discussed in the next section.

━━

the research emanating from Kounin's work and from the research of the Texas project, summarized earlier. The ideas and procedures are introduced here and they are revisited in Chapter 13 in connection with starting the first year of teaching because one of the important findings from the work at the University of Texas is the importance of establishing routines for effective management at the start of the school year. In fact, there is evidence that later in the year, when teachers who are having problems try to create better management practices, student cooperation then is difficult to achieve (Evertson, Emmer, Sanford, and Clements, 1983).

ESTABLISHING RULES AND PROCEDURES

In classrooms, as with most other settings where groups of people interact, a large percentage of potential problems and disruptions can be prevented by planning rules and procedures beforehand. To understand the truth of this statement, think for a moment about the varied experiences you have had in nonschool settings where fairly large numbers of people come together. Examples most people think about include driving a car during rush hour in a large city, attending a football game, going to Disneyland, or buying tickets for a movie or play. In all of these instances established rules and procedures indicated by traffic lights and queuing stalls help people who do not even know each other to interact in regular, predictable ways. Rules, such as "the right of way" and "no cutting in line," help people negotiate rather complex processes safely and efficiently.

Think for a moment of what happens when procedures or rules suddenly break down or disappear. You can probably recall an instance when a power outage caused traffic lights to stop working or when a large crowd arrived to buy tickets for an important game before the ticket sellers set up their queuing stalls. Recently, a professor was in Detroit for a conference, and her return flight was booked on an airline that had merged with another airline on that particular day. When the two airlines combined their information systems, something went wrong with the computers. This computer malfunction made it impossible for the ticket agents to know who was on a particular flight and prevented them from issuing seat assignments. Disruptive behavior and bedlam resulted. People were shoving each other as individuals tried to assure a seat for themselves; passengers were yelling at each other and at the cabin crew. At one point members of a normally well-disciplined crew were even speaking sharply to each other. The story turned out okay, because a seat was found for everyone. The boarding process, however, had not proceeded in the usual orderly, calm manner because some well-known procedures were suddenly unavailable.

Classrooms are not too different from busy airports or busy intersections. They, too, require rules and procedures to govern such important activities as student movement, student talk, and what to do with downtime.

Student Movement In many secondary classrooms, such as a science laboratory, the art room, or the physical education facility, and in all elementary classrooms, students must move around to accomplish important learning activities. Materials have to be obtained or put back, pencils need sharpening, small groups are formed, and so on.

Effective classroom managers devise ways to make needed movements by students flow smoothly. They devise queuing and distribution procedures that are efficient; they establish rules that minimize disruptions and assure safety. Examples of rules might include those that limit the number of students moving at any one time, those that specify when to be seated, procedures for lining up and moving in the halls, and those that specify how to go unattended to the library or a special resource center.

Student Talk Students talking at inappropriate times or asking questions to slow down the pace of a lesson pose a classroom management problem that is among the most troublesome to beginning teachers. This problem can vary in severity from a loud, generalized classroom clamor that disturbs the teacher next door, to a single student talking to a neighbor when the teacher is explaining an important idea.

Effective classroom managers have a clear set of rules governing student talking. Most teachers prescribe when no talking is allowed (when the teacher is lecturing or explaining), when low talk is allowed and encouraged (during small group work or seatwork), and when anything goes (during recess and parties). Effective classroom managers also have procedures that make classroom discourse more satisfying and productive, such as talking one at a time during a discussion, listening to other people's ideas, raising hands, and taking turns.

Downtimes A third area of classroom life for which rules and procedures are required is during downtime. Sometimes, lessons are completed before a period is over, and it is inappropriate to start something new. Similarly, when students are doing seatwork some finish before others. Waiting for a film projector to arrive for a scheduled film is another example of downtime.

Effective classroom managers devise rules and procedures to govern student talk and movement during these times. Examples include: "If you finish your work, you can get a book and engage in silent reading until the others have finished." "While we wait for the film to start, you can talk quietly to your neighbors, but you cannot move around the room."

TEACHING RULES AND PROCEDURES

Rules and procedures are of little value unless participants learn and accept them. This requires active teaching. Effective classroom managers generally establish only a few rules and procedures, then teach them carefully to students and make them routine through their consistent use. In most classrooms only a few rules are needed, but it is important for the teacher to make sure students understand the purpose for the rule and its moral or practical underpinnings. Concepts and ideas associated with rules have to be taught just the same as any other set of concepts and ideas. For instance, very young children can see the necessity for keeping talk low during downtime, when it is explained that loud talk disturbs students in neighboring classrooms who are still working. Taking turns strikes a chord with older students who have heightened concerns with issues of fairness and justice. Potential injury to self and others can be explained as the reason why movement in a science laboratory has to be done a certain way. One point of caution about teaching rules should be noted, however. When the teachers are explaining rules, they must walk a rather thin line between providing explanations that are helpful to students and sounding patronizing or overly moralistic.

Most movement and discourse procedures have not only a practical dimension but also a skill dimension that must be taught, like academic skills. In Chapter 5 several strategies were described to teach students how to listen to other people's ideas and how to participate in discussions which can be used by beginning teachers to help manage student talking. Student movement skills also need to be taught. Even with college-age students, it takes instruction and two or three practices to make getting into a circle, a fishbowl formation, or small groups move smoothly. Effective classroom managers devote time in the first week or so of the school year to teaching rules and procedures and then provide periodic review as needed. This approach is described more thoroughly in Chapter 13.

Effective classroom managers are consistent in their enforcement of rules and their application of procedures. If they are not, any set of rules and procedures soon dissolve. For example, a teacher may have a rule for student movement that says, when you are doing seatwork and I'm at my desk, only one student at a time can come for help. If a student is allowed to wait at the desk while a first student is being helped, soon several others will be there too. If this is an important rule for the teacher, then whenever more than one student appears, he or she must be firmly reminded of the rule and asked to sit down. Another example would be when a teacher has a rule that no talking is allowed when he or she is giving a presentation or explaining important ideas or procedures. If two students are then allowed to whisper in the back of the room, even if they are not disturbing others, soon many students will follow suit. Similarly, if the teacher wants students to raise their hands before talking during a discussion and then allows a few students to blurt out whenever they please, the hand-raising rule is soon rendered ineffective.

It is difficult for beginning teachers to establish consistency for at least two reasons. One, rule breaking normally occurs when more than one event is going on simultaneously. The novice teacher cannot always maintain total awareness of the complex classroom environment and thus does not always see what is occurring. Two, it takes considerable energy and personal courage to enforce rules consistently. Many beginning teachers find it easier and less threatening to ignore certain student behavior rather than to confront and deal with it. Experienced teachers know that avoiding a difficult situation only leads to more problems later.

PREVENTING DEVIANT BEHAVIOR WITH SMOOTHNESS AND MOMENTUM

A second dimension of preventive classroom management involves pacing instructional events and maintaining appropriate momentum. The research by Doyle and Carter (1984) described how students can delay academic tasks, and Kounin's research (1970) pointed out the importance of keeping lessons going in a smooth fashion. Kounin also explained how teachers sometimes do things themselves that interfere with the flow of activities. For example, sometimes a teacher might start an activity and then leave it in midair. Kounin labels this type of behavior *a dangle*. A dangle occurs, for example, when a teacher asks students to hand in their notes at the end of a lecture and then suddenly decides that he or she needs to explain one more point. Teachers also slow down lessons by doing what Kounin labeled *flip-flops*. A flip-flop is when an activity is started and then stopped while another is begun and then the original started again. A flip-flop occurs, for example, when a teacher tells students to get out their books and start reading and then interrupts the reading to explain a point and then resumes the silent reading. Dangles and flip-flops interfere with the smoothness of classroom activities, cause confusion on the part of some students, and most importantly, present opportunities for noninvolved students to misbehave.

Teachers also do things that slow down the momentum of lessons. Kounin described two types of important slow-down behaviors—*fragmentation* and *over-dwelling*. A teacher who goes on and on after instructions are clear to students is overdwelling. A teacher who breaks activities into overly small units, such as "sit up straight, get your papers out, pass them to the person in front, now pass them to the next person," and so on is fragmenting a set of instructions. Slowing down momentum disrupts smoothness and gives noninvolved students opportunities to interrupt classroom activities. Minimizing disruptive and slow-down behaviors is difficult for beginning teachers to learn, as are many other effective management skills. Smoothness and momentum definitely vary with the nature of individual classes—what may be a dangle in one classroom may not be so in another, or what may be overdwelling with one group of students may be appropriate for another group.

ORCHESTRATING CLASSROOM ACTIVITIES DURING UNSTABLE PERIODS

A third important dimension of preventive classroom management involves planning and orchestrating student behavior during unstable periods of the school day—periods of time when order is most difficult to achieve and maintain.

Opening Class The beginning of class, whether it is the first few minutes of the morning in an elementary classroom or the beginning of a period in secondary schools, is an unstable time. Students are coming from other settings (their homes, the playground, another class) where a different set of behavioral norms apply. The new setting has different rules and procedures as well as friends who have not been seen since the previous day. The beginning of class is also a time in most schools where several administrative tasks are required of teachers, such as taking roll and making announcements.

Effective classroom managers plan and execute procedures that help get things started quickly and surely. For example:

1. They greet their students at the door, extending welcomes to build positive feeling tones, and also to keep potential trouble outside the door.
2. They train student helpers to take the roll, read announcements, and do other administrative tasks, so they can be free to start lessons.
3. They write instructions on the board or on newsprint so students can get started on lessons as soon as they come into the room.
4. They establish routine and ceremonial events that communicate to students that serious work is about to begin.

Transitions Citing research of Gump (1967; 1982) and Rosenshine (1980), Doyle (1986) says that "approximately 31 major transitions occur per day in elementary classrooms, and they account for approximately 15 percent of classroom time" (p. 406). There are fewer transitions in secondary classrooms, but they still are numerous and take considerable time. It is during transition periods (moving from whole group to small groups, changing from listening to seatwork, getting needed materials to do an assignment, getting ready to go to recess) that many disruptions occur. Learning to handle transitions is difficult for most beginning teachers. Prior planning and the use of cuing devices are two techniques that can help.

1. *Planning.* Planning is crucial when it comes to managing transitions. Chapter 3 described how transitions must be planned just as carefully as any other instructional activity. At first, beginning teachers should conceive of each transition as a series of steps they want students to follow. These steps should be written down in note form and in some instances given to the students on the chalkboard or on newsprint charts. For example, making the transition from a whole-class lecture to seatwork might include the following steps:

STEP 1 Put your lecture notes away and clear your desk.

STEP 2 Make sure you have pencils and a copy of the work sheet being distributed by the row monitor.

STEP 3 Begin your work.

STEP 4 Raise your hand if you want me to help you.

As beginning teachers become more experienced with managing transitions, they will no longer need to list the steps for minor transitions and may instead rely on clear mental images of what is required.

2. *Cuing and Signaling.* Cuing and signaling systems are used by effective teachers to manage difficult transition periods. The best way to understand cuing is to think of it as a warning device similar to the yellow light on a traffic signal or the *slow* sign on a curving road. Cues are used by teachers to alert students

that they are about to change activities or tasks and to start getting ready. Some examples of cues would include:

- During a small group activity, a teacher goes around to each group and announces, "You have five minutes before returning to the whole group."
- During a discussion activity, a teacher tells students, "We must end the discussion in a few minutes, but there will be time for three more comments."
- During a laboratory experiment, the teacher says, "We have been working for 20 minutes now, and you should be at least halfway done."
- In getting ready for a guest speaker, the teacher tells the class, "Our speaker will arrive in three minutes, let's straighten up the chairs and get ready to greet her."

Many teachers also develop a signal system for alerting students to a forthcoming transition or for helping them move through the steps of a transition smoothly. Signal systems are particularly effective with younger children and in classrooms where the activities are such that it is difficult to hear the teacher. The band instructor raising his or her baton is an example of a signal for students to get quiet and ready their instruments to play the first note. Figure 6.1 shows a set of hand signals developed by one experienced teacher to alert and assist his students with difficult transitions and with checking with their understanding of what is being taught.

Closing Class The closing of class is also an unstable time in most classrooms. Sometimes the teacher is rushed to complete a lesson that has run over its allocated time; sometimes materials such as tests or papers must be collected; almost always students need to get their own personal belongings ready to move to another class, the lunchroom, or the bus. Effective teachers anticipate the potential management problems associated with closing class by incorporating the following procedures into their classroom organizational patterns:

1. Leaving sufficient time to complete important closing activities, such as collecting books, papers, and the like
2. Making homework assignments early enough so that possible confusion can be cleared up prior to the last minute of class
3. Establishing routine procedures for collecting student work (such as placing a box by the door), so class time does not have to be used for this activity
4. Using alerting and cuing procedures to give students warning that the end of the class is approaching and that certain tasks need to be completed before they leave
5. Teaching older students that class will be dismissed by the teacher, not by the school bell or buzzer

DEVELOPING STUDENT ACCOUNTABILITY

A final dimension of preventive classroom management involves the procedures effective teachers develop to hold the students accountable for their academic work and for their classroom behavior. Carolyn Evertson and Edmund Emmer have identified six areas that teachers should attend to for developing student accountability. These are listed in Figure 6.2.

Managing Inappropriate and Disruptive Behavior

Preactive planning and skilled orchestration of classroom activities can prevent many of the management problems faced by beginning teachers, but not all. As in other social settings, every classroom will have a few students who will choose not to involve themselves in classroom activities and, instead, be disruptive forces. Disruptions can, of course, range from students talking when they are supposed to be listening to the teacher or refusing to go along with a small group activity to yelling at the teacher and stomping out of the room. Managing disruptive behavior calls for a special set of understandings and also a special repertoire of skills.

THE CAUSES OF MISBEHAVIOR

Because beginning teachers have observed disruptive behavior in classrooms for many years, most can readily list the major causes of student misbehavior. Causes appearing on most lists include: (1) students find school work boring and irrelevant and try to escape it; (2) students' out-of-school lives (family or community) produce psychological and emotional problems that they play out in school; (3) students are imprisoned within schools that have authoritarian dispositions, which causes them to rebel, and (4) student rebelliousness and attention seeking are a part of the growing-up process.

Beginning teachers will want to think about the causes of inappropriate behavior, but they should beware of spending too much time on this type of analysis for two reasons. One, knowing the cause of student misbehavior, although helpful in analyzing the problem, does not necessarily lead to any change in that behavior. Two, dealing too much with psychological or sociological causes of misbehavior, particularly those that are not under the teacher's influence, can lead to acceptance and/or resignation. William Glasser (1986) made this point clearly:

> When a student is doing badly in school, we often point our finger at a dismal home when the reason really is that the student does not find school satisfying enough for him to make an effort. There is no doubt that a student who cannot satisfy his needs at home may come to your class hungry for love and recognition and impatient that he can't quickly get what he wants. Rather than become discouraged, you should realize that if he can begin to satisfy his needs in your class, and if you are patient enough with his impatience, he has good a chance to learn enough to lead a productive life despite his home life. (p. 21)

Figure 6.1 Examples of Signals for Communicating with Students

Rhythm or echo clapping can be used to get the attention of the students in the classroom. When the teacher claps four beats, the students respond with a two–clap echo, and this signals that all activity stops.

Bell signaling can be used to gain the attention of the students. Just a short ring will cue the students to stop all activities and listen. (Small hand bell)

Light signaling is often used by teachers and can be effective. The light switch is flicked once, quickly.

Arm signals can be used at times to gain the attention of students without having to use an audible signal. When children are in the hallway, lining up or on the playground, the teacher raises an arm and this will cue the students to do the same and become quiet.

Finger signals can be used effectively in managing small groups, dismissing students or conducting other tasks. When dismissing groups of students by areas, code the groups numerically and dismiss by signals.

Looks are often effective in gaining a student's attention. A quizzical or firm look may be all that is needed.

Charts can signal directions and important messages. Use a smiley face or sad face suspended from the ceiling. Flip to sad face when students' behavior is unacceptable; return to a smiley face when acceptable behavior occurs.

Charts that tell students what to do when they finish work are very useful, and assist students in becoming more independent and involved in purposeful activities. The ideas on these charts should be varied and changed frequently.

Thumb signals can be used to respond to yes—no situations, to signal choices and to communicate when things aren't clear.

Signal with extended thumb

Examples: Do you agree? (Thumbs up); Do you disagree? (Thumbs down); Not clear? (Thumbs sideways) — Is this an example of the problem?

The general approach recommended to beginning teachers for dealing with disruptive behavior is not to search zealously for causes but, instead, to focus on the misbehavior itself and to find ways to change it, at least during the period of time the student is in the classroom. This approach emphasizes the importance of teachers accurately spotting misbehavior and making quick, precise interventions.

Finger signals can be used to respond to numerical answers, multiple-choice and true-false questions. Signal with hand against chest.

Examples: Show us how many tens are in 64.
Which word means land surrounded by water?
1. peninsula 2. island 3. continent
Which word means land surrounded by water on three sides? 1. peninsula 2. island 3. continent
Shape the answer by forming the beginning symbol or letter to the answer with your fingers. (Be as creative as you can in developing signals.)

Think pads/response cards can be used to let every student answer. These responses can be written on scrap paper cut into quarters and placed in envelopes on the children's desks. Children write answers on pads or cards and hold them up to be checked by the teacher. Responses can be adapted to any subject area, and any type of question. This information can serve as a pretest, a check on prior day's work or as a diagnostic informal assessment.

Example: "Write the names of the seven (7) continents on your pads—then let me see."

Whisper signal can provide general feedback to the teacher.

Examples: Point to the word as we all whisper it. Place your finger on the part that proves the answer. Whisper the number of the paragraph where the answer is found.

Head signaling can also be used to respond to a question or direction.

Example: Put your head on your desk and imagine what I am describing. Lift your head when you have the answer.

Help cards can be used to signal for assistance from the teacher or a student. When the student encounters a problem or has difficulty, he/she goes on to the next problem or activity but signals for help by placing a card on the corner of the desk. This signal will alert the teacher or a student helper to provide assistance as soon as possible. Loss of time from waiting with the hand raised is avoided and the student learns to better utilize his or her time.

Example: A student cannot spell a word, posts help card and continues work.

SOURCE: From M. Bozman (1985), Signaling in the classroom. Mimeographed. Salisbury, Md.: Salisbury State College.

THE DESIST INCIDENT

For Kounin (1970), a well-managed classroom is one where there is a minimum of student *deviancy* and a high degree of work *involvement*. Deviancy is student behavior that interrupts the flow of academic work, and good management to Kounin is the way teachers react to deviant behavior and the way they manage the classroom group as a whole.

Figure 6.2   Evertson and Emmer's Procedures for Developing Student Accountability

1. **Clarity of Work Assignments**   The teacher must have a specific set of expectations for student performance, covering such details as the form of student work, expectation regarding neatness, completeness, due dates, and procedures for make-up work. The specific requirements in these areas may vary greatly from teacher to teacher, according to subject matter and age level of the students, and the personal preferences of the teacher. The teacher must decide what is reasonable, given the teaching context, and what will aid students in the development of good work habits. . . .

2. **Communicating Assignments**   Assignments should be clear, so that every student understands what to do. This can be accomplished in several ways. Establishing a routine for posting assignments in a particular place or having students copy assignments onto their worksheet or paper assures that everyone will at least be able to find out what the assignment is, even when the teacher is not available to point it out to them. Grading requirements should be spelled out to students, so that they know exactly what the teacher considers important in assessing achievement. . . .

3. **Monitoring Student Work**   Once assignments are made and students begin work, it is again essential that the teacher be aware of student progress. This can be accomplished by circulating throughout the classroom and systematically checking each student's work. The teacher should scan the class for a minute or two at the beginning of a seatwork activity to make sure that everyone has begun. . . . Once the teacher is sure that everyone understands the task and has begun work, then he or she may circulate around the room and assist individual students. During recitation or discussion activities, as well as small-group work, the teacher should also monitor student involvement.

4. **Checking Work**   Once assignments have been completed, the teacher needs a system for checking work. Assignments that have specific answers may be checked by students. This provides quick feedback to each student, although the teacher should be sure to establish procedures for checking. A procedure is also needed for students to turn in their papers. Certain assignments may be put in a basket at the front of the room, and a special area may be designed for collecting and returning assignments of absent students.

5. **Giving Feedback to Students**   It is through practice and feedback that most instruction begins to pay off in learning. When students receive information about their performance, they obtain the basis for improvement. Regular routines for checking work and returning it to students are useful. It is also helpful if teachers set aside some time after assignments have been returned for the students to review their papers and make corrections. . . . The feedback older students receive is usually tied in with a grading system; therefore, the teacher needs an overall basis for grading consistent with the instructional goals.

6. **Clarity of Instructions**   Most effective managers give clear and specific instructions, which is an instructional and a managerial asset. Clear instruction of academic content helps students succeed and learn; unclear instruction can produce failure, frustration, and task avoidance. Clarity is aided by a number of factors. First, the teacher must have a very good idea of what is to be taught and how. Therefore, planning is essential. Second, the teacher must communicate information so that students understand it. Thus, the teacher's awareness of student comprehension is critical. Third, the precision and clarity of the teacher's oral expression are important. Sloppy speech habits lead to vagueness and confusion.

SOURCE: From C. Evertson and E. Emmer (1982), Preventive classroom management. In D. Duke, (Ed.), *Helping teachers manage classrooms*. Alexandria, Va.: Association for Supervision and Curriculum Development, pp. 28–29. Used with permission.

In classrooms, just as in any social setting, there are some participants who commit deviant acts. An example of deviant behavior on the freeway would be driving more than 5 miles an hour above the speed limit; in church it might be falling asleep during the sermon; in a library it is talking while others are trying to study. Those charged with the responsibility of enforcing rules and procedures may or may not choose to respond to each occurrence of deviancy. For example, most highway patrol officers will not stop a motorist for going 60 miles an hour on the freeway; most ministers will not choose to confront a single parishioner who falls asleep; and those who talk very softly in libraries will probably not elicit a response from the librarian. There are times, however, when those in charge will choose to respond to deviant behaviors. Kounin calls this a *desist incident*, meaning an incident serious enough so that, if not dealt with, it will lead to further and widening management problems. The way that desist incidents are identified and dealt with is the business of classroom management.

RECOGNIZING DEVIANT BEHAVIOR THROUGH WITHITNESS AND OVERLAPPINGNESS

You can all remember a teacher from your own school days who seemed to have "eyes in the back of her head." Kounin calls this skill *withitness*. Teachers who are with-it spot deviant behavior right away and are almost always accurate in identifying the student who is responsible. Teachers who lack this skill normally do not spot misbehavior early and they often make mistakes when assigning blame.

Overlappingness is a second skill teachers use to spot and deal with deviant behavior. Overlapping means being able to spot a student acting inappropriately and inconspicuously deal with it so the lesson is not interrupted. Moving close to an offender is one overlapping tactic effective classroom managers use. Putting a hand on the shoulder of a student who is talking to his neighbor while continuing with instructions about how to do a lab project is another. Integrating a question intended to delay instruction or a "smart" remark right into an explanation about Edgar Allen Poe's syntax is a third example of overlappingness.

With-it and overlapping skills are difficult for beginning teachers to learn because they call for quick, accurate reading of classroom situations and the ability to perform several different teaching behaviors simultaneously.

Teacher Interventions in Desist Incidents Teachers prevent deviant behavior by their ability to run smooth activities and to keep the momentum going. They deal with minor behavior problems through their with-it and overlapping skills. Finally, there are some behaviors that must be confronted and dealt with more firmly. Kounin describes this as a *desist*, that is, a teacher behavior that puts a stop to student deviancy and gets students back to the learning activities. Desist activities by teachers can vary in a number of ways. Kounin identified several teacher desist behaviors in his various studies. Three are illustrated in Figure 6.3.

Figure 6.3 Examples of Teacher Desist Behaviors

Clarity
The degree to which the teacher specifies what is wrong.

Unclear desist:	"Stop that!"
Clear desist:	"Do not sharpen your pencil while I am talking!"

Firmness
The degree to which the teacher communicates "I mean it."

Unfirm desist:	"Please don't do that."
Firm desist:	"I absolutely will not tolerate that from you!"

Roughness
The degree to which the teacher expresses anger.

Unrough desist:	"You shouldn't do that anymore."
Rough desist:	"When you do that I get angry and I intend to punish you."

Extending the research of Kounin and drawing on their own work, Carolyn Evertson and Edmund Emmer provided a set of guidelines for the use of desist behaviors by teachers. Their guidelines are shown in Figure 6.4.

Exhibiting Confidence and Exerting Influence

To be effective in classroom management, a beginning teacher cannot rely totally on rules, procedures, and techniques. There is also a leadership dimension to classroom management that is closely connected to a teacher's interpersonal style and perhaps even to his or her inner strength. This is a difficult dimension to describe and one that is even more difficult for beginning teachers to do something about. An aspect of teaching that has not been studied carefully of late, it is nonetheless important and deserves some attention.

Success in providing leadership to others depends on the degree to which a person exhibits confidence and the degree to which he or she is willing and able to exert interpersonal influence. The precise relationships between these personal traits and effective classroom management have not been studied carefully. However, most principals and others who interview and hire new teachers say they are important.

CONFIDENCE

A high correlation between teacher confidence and effective classroom management was observed in Sanford's research described in Research Summary 6.2. But what does confidence mean, and what are the characteristics of a confident teacher? This is a difficult question to answer precisely. However, some of your own experiences may provide some helpful insights.

Figure 6.4 Evertson and Emmer's Guidelines for Managing Inappropriate Behavior

1. Ask the student to stop the inappropriate behavior. The teacher maintains contact with the child until the appropriate behavior is correctly performed.

2. Make eye-contact with the student until appropriate behavior returns. This is suitable when the teacher is certain the student knows what the correct response is.

3. Restate or remind the student of the correct rule or procedure.

4. Ask the student to identify the correct procedure. Give feedback if the student does not understand it.

5. Impose the consequence or penalty of the rule or procedure violation. Usually, the consequence for violating a procedure is simply to perform the procedure until it is correctly done. When the student understands the procedure and is not complying in order to receive attention or for other inappropriate reasons, the teacher can use a mild penalty, such as withholding a privilege.

6. Change the activity. Frequently, off-task behavior occurs when students are engaged too long in repetitive, boring tasks or in aimless recitations. Injecting variety in seatwork, refocusing the discussion, or changing the activity to one requiring another type of student response, is appropriate when off-task behavior spreads throughout a class.

SOURCE: From C. Evertson and E. Emmer (1982), Preventive classroom management. In D. Duke (Ed.), *Helping teachers manage classrooms*. Alexandria, Va.: Association for Supervision and Curriculum Development, p. 27. Used with permission.

Think for a moment about people you know whom you would consider confident. There is a good chance that you are thinking of a person who always seems to be in charge, who talks with conviction, and who does not shy away from difficult situations. Similarly, if you think about people who lack confidence, you probably think of a person who perhaps is shy, tentative, and indecisive. Beginning teachers obviously vary tremendously in this respect. There is not space here to go into detail about how to build confidence if the reader does not have it. However, it is important to point out some of the characteristics of confident people and list a few actions that help build more confident behaviors if these are lacking. Some common characteristics of confident people include:

Voice: Confident people speak with sufficient volume to be heard and express their ideas and wishes with conviction.
Posture: Confident people stand straight, walk forcefully, and look people in the eye.
Conviction: Confident people believe in themselves, their ideas, and their decisions.
Dress: Confident people use dress to draw attention to themselves.

As with so many other aspects of human behavior, it is important to point out the situational aspects of confidence. For example, a person may feel confident in one setting and not another. Even very confident people will feel less confident in new settings, such as student teaching and the first job, than in more familiar situations. Confidence may also be a function of how other people are perceiving one's behavior. Speaking or dressing in certain ways only projects confidence if other see it that way.

Beginning teachers will find few college classes in building confidence, but there are a variety of community workshops and seminars devoted to this goal. Some that readily come to mind include: public speaking classes, assertiveness training seminars, workshops on dressing for success, support workshops and networks for shy people, acting and stage presence workshops. A beginning teacher who believes he or she lacks confidence and finds this detrimental to effective classroom management should seek out learning experiences of this type.

INTERPERSONAL INFLUENCE

You saw in the Doyle and Carter study described earlier how students used questions and other tactics to delay certain academic work. They were in a sense testing the teacher's instructional system and trying to advance their own agendas. Put another way, students, like people in any social setting, strive to have influence over their environments. In many ways the job of the teacher is one of exerting interpersonal influence over students. Such influence should be used only to achieve positive academic and social goals and never for purposes of personal domination.

Three decades ago, French and Raven (1959) thought about the processes of interpersonal influence and postulated that people have five ways to influence others in social settings: (1) one's ability to control and distribute valued rewards, (2) one's ability to withhold rewards, (3) one's authority legally vested in a position, (4) one's expertise or special knowledge, and (5) one's personal attractiveness or membership in a primary reference group. According to French and Raven, all persons in social situations have some sources of influence, and one of the dominant facts of group life is the subtle but constant negotiation that occurs as individuals play out their own personal agendas and strive to influence a group's goals and procedures. Table 6.1 describes sources of influence for teachers and students in classrooms. These ideas are important for beginning teachers because they describe how teachers can use various kinds of influence to shape classroom events. As can be observed in Table 6.1 teachers have legitimate influence based on the teaching position itself and expert influence based on their greater knowledge and skill. Some teachers, as a result of personal attractiveness and charisma, also have referent influence with students. They can, for example, get students to relate to important goals, impart a sense of importance and urgency about these goals, and give students a sense of personal efficacy.

Much attention has been paid by education to the way teachers use reward and coercive influence. Some ideas emanating from this interest are described here.

Table 6.1 Influence in Classrooms

SOURCES OF INFLUENCE	TEACHERS	STUDENTS
Reward influence	Teachers have control of grades and can reward students with good grades.	Students can control their own behavior and can reward teachers with good behavior.
Coercive influence	Teachers can withhold good grades and special privileges and impose penalties.	Students can withhold involvement and cooperative behavior.
Legitimate influence	The position of teacher has legally vested power.	Students have little legitimate power; they do have considerable rights.
Expert influence	Teachers by training have special knowledge that is valued by many students.	Some students, "the real smart ones," have expert power that can in some instances compete with the teacher's.
Referent influence	Teachers have referent influence with students through their own charisma.	Popular students have a great deal of referent power within the peer culture.

USING REWARDS

A rather well-established principle in psychology is that when certain behaviors are *reinforced*, they tend to be repeated; conversely, behaviors that are not reinforced tend to decrease or disappear. This principle holds true for classrooms and provides teachers with one means for managing student behavior. The key to using reinforcement principles to influence student behavior obviously rests on the teacher's ability to (1) identify desirable behaviors, (2) identify appropriate reinforcers, and (3) skillfully use these reinforcers to strengthen and encourage desired behaviors.

Praise The reinforcer most readily available to the classroom teacher is praise. However, there are important guidelines for the effective use of praise. For example, general praise, such as "great job," "oh, that's wonderful," or "excellent," is not very effective. Nor is insincere praise apt to have the desired effect. Jere Brophy, a researcher at Michigan State University, reviewed a massive amount of research on the subject of praise and came up with the guidelines for teachers described in Figure 6.5.

Rewards and Privileges Teachers can also encourage desirable behaviors through granting rewards and privileges to students. Rewards teachers have at their disposal include:

1. Points given for certain kinds of work or behavior that can enhance a student's grade

Figure 6.5 Brophy's Guidelines for Effective Praise

Effective Praise

1. Is delivered contingently
2. Specifies the particulars of the accomplishment
3. Shows spontaneity, variety, and other signs of credibility; suggests clear attention to the student's accomplishment
4. Rewards attainment of specified performance criteria (which can include effort criteria)
5. Provides information to students about their competence or the value of their accomplishments
6. Orients students toward better appreciation of their own task-related behavior and thinking about problem solving
7. Uses student's own prior accomplishments as the context for describing present accomplishments
8. Is given in recognition of noteworthy effort or success at difficult (for this student) tasks
9. Attributes success to effort and ability, implying that similar successes can be expected in the future
10. Fosters endogenous attributions (students believe they expend effort on task because they enjoy it and/or want to develop task-relevant skills)
11. Focuses students' attention on their own task-relevant behavior
12. Fosters appreciation of, and desirable attributions about, task-relevant behavior after the process is completed

Inneffective Praise

1. Is delivered randomly or unsystematically
2. Is restricted to global positive reactions
3. Shows a bland uniformity that suggests a conditioned response made with minimal attention
4. Rewards mere participation, without consideration of performance processes or outcomes
5. Provides no information at all or gives students information about their status
6. Orients students toward comparing themselves with others and thinking about competing
7. Uses the accomplishments of peers as the context for describing students' present accomplishments
8. Is given without regard to the effort expended or the meaning of the accomplishment (for *this* student)
9. Attributes success to ability alone or to external factors such as luck or (easy) task difficulty
10. Fosters exogenous attributions (students believe they expend effort on the task for external reasons—to please the teacher, win a competition or reward, etc.)
11. Focuses students' attention on the teacher as an external authority figure who is manipulating them
12. Intrudes into the ongoing process, distracting attention from task-relevant behavior

SOURCE: From J. E. Brophy (1981), Teacher praise: A functional analysis. *Review of Educational Research*, Spring: 26. Copyright 1981, AERA, Washington, D.C.

2. Symbols such as gold stars, happy faces, or certificates of accomplishment
3. Special honor rolls for academic work and social conduct

Privileges that are at the command of most teachers to bestow include:

1. Serving as a class leader or helper who takes notes to the office, collects or passes out papers, grades papers, runs the movie projector, and the like
2. Extra time for recess
3. Special time to work on a special individual project
4. Being excused from some required work
5. Free reading time

A carefully designed system of rewards and privileges can help immensely in encouraging some types of behavior and reducing others. However, rewards and privileges will not solve all classroom management problems, and beginning teachers should be given two warnings. First, what is a reward or a privilege for some students will not be perceived as such by others. The age of students obviously is a factor; family and geographical background are others. Effective teachers generally involve their students in identifying rewards and privileges in order to ensure their effectiveness. Second, an overemphasis on extrinsic rewards can interfere with the teacher's efforts to promote academic work for its own sake and to help students practice and grow in self-discipline and management.

COERCIVE PUNISHMENT AND PENALTIES

Rewards and privileges are used to reinforce and strengthen desirable behaviors. Punishments and penalties are used to discourage infractions of important rules and procedures. Socially acceptable punishments and penalties available to teachers are, in fact, rather limited and include:

1. Taking points away for misbehavior which, in turn, affects student grades
2. Making the student stay in from recess or stay after school for detention
3. Removal of privileges
4. Expulsion from class or sending a student to a counselor or administrator

Beginning teachers should to be careful about the types of punishments and penalties they establish. Researchers from the University of Texas offer the guidelines found in Figure 6.6.

WORKING TOWARD SELF-MANAGEMENT

The final classroom management procedure described in this chapter, the Glasser Classroom Meeting, goes beyond planning and orchestrating classroom activities

Figure 6.6   Guidelines for the Use of Penalties

1. Use reductions in grade or score for assignment- or work-related behaviors such as missing or incomplete work. Other penalties, such as detention or fines, are usually not needed. When a problem of missing work becomes chronic, contact the students' parents, talk with the student, and try to get at the source of the problem.

2. Use a fine or demerit system to handle repeated violations of rules and procedures, particularly those involving willful refusal to comply with reasonable requests. Such behaviors might include continued talk during whole-class instruction, or leaving one's seat. You will not need penalties to handle occasional occurrences of these types of inappropriate behaviors . . .; however, students who persist in such behavior need a penalty for a deterrent. Give them one warning, and if the behavior persists, assess a fine or demerit.

3. If you have a student who frequently receives penalties, try to set a more positive tone. Help the student formulate a plan to stop the inappropriate behavior, and be sure he or she understands what is and is not acceptable behavior.

4. Limit the use of penalties such as fines or checks to easily observable behaviors that represent major or chronic infractions of rules and procedures. The reason for this limitation is that penalty systems work only when they are used consistently. In order for this to take place, you must be able to detect the misbehavior when it occurs. If you cannot, you will find yourself constantly trying to catch students who misbehave. For example, don't try to "fine" each student who whispers during seatwork. You can handle such events in simpler ways, and you certainly don't want to spend all your time checking for whispering behavior. However, you could use a fine if the student does not stop when you request it.

5. Keep your classroom positive and supportive. Penalties should serve mainly as deterrents and should be used sparingly. Try to rely on rewards and personal encouragement to maintain good behavior.

SOURCE: From Emmer/Evertson/Sanford/Clements/Worsham, *Classroom management for secondary teachers*, © 1984, p. 64. Adapted by permission of Prentice Hall, Inc. Englewood Cliffs, NJ.

or dealing with specific disruptive acts. It involves planning regular, 30-minute nonacademic periods in which teachers and students can discuss and find cooperative solutions to personal and behavioral problems.

Joyce and Weil's (1972) concept of teaching models was introduced in Chapter 1 as a way of thinking about and categorizing various approaches to teaching along three important dimensions: (1) their instructional effects, (2) their syntaxes, and (3) the structures of their learning environments. These concepts are used now to describe Glasser's Classroom Meeting model.

Instructional Effects of Glasser's Classroom Meeting Model

Trained first as a chemical engineer, and later as a physician and clinical psychologist, William Glasser has devoted much of his professional life to finding ways to make schools more satisfying and productive for students. At the center of Glasser's thought has been his belief that most classroom problems stem from a failure to satisfy the basic needs of students. In his earlier work (1969) he emphasized students' needs for love and feelings of self-worth. These needs are similar to the motives of affiliation and achievement described in Chapter 5. In his later work (1986) Glasser expanded his list of basic needs to include: survival and reproduction, belonging and love, power and influence, freedom and fun. Glasser believes that school structures do not, in most instances, provide ways for these needs to be satisfied. He has proposed the classroom meeting and cooperative learning strategies as structural changes to correct this failure.

The purpose of the classroom meeting is to develop a caring environment for students where they can identify problems, practice self-discipline, and in the process, satisfy their needs for influence and self-worth. It is designed to help students understand themselves and take responsibility for their own behavior and their personal and social development.

Syntax of the Classroom Meeting

Normally a Glasser Classroom Meeting consists of six steps or phases. Each of these phases is described in Table 6.2. Note that for each phase there are specific things teachers need to do to make the meeting go successfully.

Structuring the Learning Environment

When this model is being introduced and taught to students, the teacher keeps the learning environment tightly structured. Although more and more freedom

Table 6.2 Syntax for the Glasser Classroom Meeting

PHASE	TEACHER BEHAVIOR
Phase 1: Set the climate and establish set	Using many of the strategies and procedures described in Chapter 5, the teacher establishes a climate such that all students feel free to participate and to share opinions and feedback.
Phase 2: Identify problems	Teacher asks students to sit in a circle. Either the teacher or the students can bring up problems. Teacher should make sure that problems are described fully and in nonevaluative ways. Specific examples of the problems are encouraged.
Phase 3: Make value judgments	After a specific problem has been identified, the teacher asks students to express their own values about the problem and the behaviors associated with it.
Phase 4: Identify courses of action	Teacher asks students to suggest alternative behaviors or procedures that might help solve the problem and to agree on one to try out.
Phase 5: Make a public commitment	Teacher asks students to make a public commitment to try out the new behaviors or procedures.
Phase 6: Provide follow-up and assessment	At a later meeting, the problem is again discussed to see how effectively it is being solved and whether commitments have been kept.

can be given to students as they become successful in meetings, the teacher must maintain the responsibility for assuring participation, for keeping student problem solving focused, and for providing overall leadership. Normally, the teacher acts as discussion leader and asks students to sit in a circle during the classroom meetings. However, with younger students, participants sometimes sit on the floor, and with older students, the role of discussion leader is sometimes assumed by a student in the class.

SUGGESTIONS FOR STARTING AND RUNNING CLASSROOM MEETINGS

Effective execution of classroom meetings requires specific teacher actions before, during, and after the meeting. As much care and concern must go into planning and executing meetings as any other aspect of instruction.

Planning In preparation for classroom meetings, teachers will need to think through what they want the meeting to accomplish and have some problems ready for discussion in case none come from students. Most important, overall planning must allow time for classroom meetings on a regular basis.

In elementary schools many teachers who use classroom meetings start each day with this activity; others schedule it as a way to close each day; still others schedule classroom meetings on a weekly basis. In most middle and high schools, teachers schedule meetings less frequently, perhaps 30 minutes every other Friday, with special meetings if serious problems arise. The frequency of meetings is not as important as their regularity.

Conducting the meeting On the surface the classroom meeting may look fairly simple and easy to conduct. In reality it is very complex and calls for considerable skill on the part of the teacher. If the beginning teacher is in a school where classroom meetings are common and students already understand their basic purposes and procedures, then the teacher can start meetings at the beginning of school. If not, then the recommendation is for beginning teachers to wait for a few weeks before introducing classroom meetings to students.

Most of the student and teacher skills needed for successful meetings are described elsewhere in *Learning to Teach*, particularly in Chapter 5. Some are repeated here as they specifically relate to each phase of the classroom meeting.

1. *Establishing climate and establishing set.* Before classroom meetings can be successful, the overall climate must be one that encourages participation in free and nonpunitive ways. Students also must be prepared in the appropriate mind-set to make meetings productive. Although classrooms meetings can be used to build this kind of productive environment, some degree of trust must exist before meetings can be implemented. Many of the activities described in Chapter 5 are preludes to implementing classroom meetings.

2. *Identifying problems.* Students who have not been involved in classroom

meetings need to be taught what constitutes a legitimate problem for the meeting. Problem-solving techniques described in Chapters 5 and 12 can be taught, including giving students time to practice stating a problem, giving examples of a problem, and identifying the descriptive and value dimensions of a problem.

3. *Dealing with values*. The values surrounding most classroom behavior problems are very important, especially differences regarding the value of academic work. Put bluntly, some students do not value academic work as much as teachers do. At the same time, teachers may find an amazing similarity of values across racial, ethnic, and social-class lines regarding other aspects of classroom behavior. For examples, most students, even at a very young age, see the moral and practical necessity of such rules as taking turns, listening, and showing respect to others. They also readily embrace most procedures that assure safety and fairness. The classroom meeting can become an important forum for talking about value similarities and differences.

4. *Identifying alternative courses of action*. Except for very young children, most students can readily identify courses of action they, their teacher, or their classmates can take to resolve all kinds of classroom management problems. They know the reasons for rewarding desirable behavior and punishing disruptive behavior and they also know the shortcomings of relying too heavily on these strategies. They even know what sort of alternative actions are available in classroom settings. During this phase of the classroom meeting, the teacher's primary role is to listen to alternative proposals, make sure everyone understands each one, and push for some type of consensus about which action students are willing to take. The teacher must also be clear and straightforward with students if a proposed action is definitely unacceptable, particularly those proposals that go against school policy. However, this does not exclude student efforts to get school policies changed.

5. *Making a public commitment*. A public commitment is nothing more than a promise by students, and in some instances the teacher, that certain attempts are going to be made to correct difficult situations. Many teachers write these promises on newsprint charts so everyone in the class can remember them.

6. *Follow-up and assessment*. Once students have made a commitment to try out a new set of procedures and behaviors, it is very important that these commitments be followed and assessed. Specifically, teachers must remember the public commitments that were made and periodically come back to them in future classroom meetings. If commitments are not being kept or if the planned actions are not solving the problem, then additional time and energy must be given to the problem.

Summary

This chapter focused on the most troublesome problem facing many beginning teachers, classroom management. It emphasized the importance of seeing classroom management as an integral part of a broader repertoire of teaching behaviors that includes both the executive and instructional functions of teaching. It was shown that careful planning of classroom rules and procedures can prevent many of the problems associated with creating order in the classroom. Other problems can be eliminated by skillfully orchestrating unstable periods, such as the opening and closing of class and transitional situations. However, regardless of their planning and orchestration skills, beginning teachers will still be faced with difficult students who will choose to be disruptive forces rather than involve themselves in academic activities. Effective teachers have intervention skills for dealing with disruptive behaviors—skills that can bring quick results in maintaining classroom order so learning can proceed on schedule. However, effective teachers also know that these order-maintaining interventions are stop-gap measures and do not lead to permanent change in the behavior of a disruptive student. Longer-term solutions to disruptive behaviors depend upon creating a satisfying learning environment and in using strategies such as the Glasser Classroom Meeting that provide opportunities for students to learn self-management and self-development skills.

It is very important for beginning teachers to enter their first classroom assignments (student teaching and the first year) armed with a set of concepts for thinking about classroom management and with a repertoire of skills for dealing with student behavioral problems. With classroom management, as with many other aspects of teaching, understanding and a minimum set of skills will prove insufficient for solving the unique problems beginning teachers will face. More complex skills, such as withitness and overlappingness or smoothness and momentum, will come only with practice and reflection.

Books for the Professional

Bramson, R. M. (1981). *Coping with difficult people*. New York: Random House. Classrooms are not the only settings where we find people who are difficult to deal with. This little book describes a variety of strategies for dealing with these people in all aspects of life. It is well written and will give beginning teachers concrete suggestions and also the encouragement of knowing that their problems are not too different from those of managers and leaders everywhere.

Duke, D. L. (Ed.). (1982). *Helping teachers manage classrooms*. Alexandria, Va.: Association for Supervision and Curriculum Development. Daniel Duke is probably the foremost expert on classroom management today. In this book he included readings by a variety of other people who have contemporary views of the problems associated with classroom management, along with concrete recommendations for teachers to follow.

Emmer, E., Evertson, C., Sanford, J., Clements, B., and Worsham, W. E. (1984). *Classroom management for secondary teachers*. Englewood Cliffs, N.J.: Prentice-Hall.

Evertson, C., Emmer, E., Clements, B., Sanford, J., and Worsham, M. (1984). *Classroom management for elementary teachers*. Englewood Cliffs, N.J.: Prentice-Hall. These two volumes, one aimed at secondary teachers, the other for elementary teachers, describe in more detail many of the procedures and techniques described in this chapter. Growing out of a decade of research at the University of Texas, these books offer a comprehensive approach to classroom management from the perspective of teacher effectiveness. They stress the importance of teacher planning and organization as preventive management approaches.

Glasser, W. (1969). *Schools without failure*. New York: Harper and Row. Although 20 years old now, this is still one of the best analyses of why students misbehave and fail in school. Glasser's recommendation that schools themselves need restructuring is presented powerfully, and his description of the use of the classroom meeting model will provide beginning teachers with more details than are presented in this chapter.

Glasser, W. (1986). *Control theory in the classroom*. New York: Harper and Row. Glasser's most recent work extends some of the basic ideas presented in *Schools Without Failure*. Most important are Glasser's recommendations for how schools can be restructured to provide more powerful settings for learning and how teachers can use the learning team and the cooperative learning strategies described in Chapter 10 of *Learning to Teach* to accomplish this restructuring.

CHAPTER 6
LEARNING AIDS FOR PLANNING, OBSERVATION, AND REFLECTION

- Assessing My Classroom Management Skills
- Observing Teachers' Management Behavior
- Observing Students' Influence on Academic Tasks
- Interviewing Teachers About Rules and Procedures
- Observing Management Practices During Unstable Periods
- Observing Teacher Responses to Student Misbehavior

ASSESSING MY CLASSROOM MANAGEMENT SKILLS

PURPOSE: The aids for this chapter begin with an assessment device designed to help you to gauge your level of effectiveness in applying classroom management skills.

DIRECTIONS: Check the level of effectiveness you feel you have attained for each of the following skills.

Skill or Competency	Level of Effectiveness		
	High	Medium	Low
Preventive Classroom Management Through: Establishing and Teaching Rules and Procedures			
Student movement	_____	_____	_____
Student talk	_____	_____	_____
Downtimes	_____	_____	_____
Ensuring Smoothness and Momentum	_____	_____	_____
Orchestrating Unstable Periods			
Planning thoroughly	_____	_____	_____
Cuing and signaling	_____	_____	_____
Developing Student Accountability	_____	_____	_____
Managing Inappropriate and Disruptive Behavior			
Withitness	_____	_____	_____
Overlappingness	_____	_____	_____
Using the desist response	_____	_____	_____
Projecting Confidence	_____	_____	_____
Exerting Interpersonal Influence			
Using rewards	_____	_____	_____
Using punishment	_____	_____	_____
Using the Classroom Meeting Model	_____	_____	_____

OBSERVING TEACHERS' MANAGEMENT BEHAVIOR

PURPOSE: As discussed in the chapter, Kounin has contributed much to our understanding of classroom management. This aid is to help you to develop awareness of the teacher in-class behaviors described by Kounin that have an impact on classroom management.

DIRECTIONS: Observe a teacher for about an hour. As you observe, note instances where the lesson seems to go especially well—students are orderly and on task—and instances where the lesson seems to go especially poorly—students are disorderly and off task. After the observation, answer the questions below.

1. Did the teacher exhibit withitness? _____

   If so, give an example of it that appeared in the lesson. _____

   _____

   Describe how students behaved in this example. _____

   _____

   If not, how might he or she have done so? _____

   _____

2. Did the teacher exhibit overlappingness? _____

   If so, give an example of it that appeared in the lesson. _____

   _____

   Describe how students behaved in this example. _____

   _____

   If not, how might he or she have done so? _____

   _____

3. Did the teacher exhibit smoothness? _____

   If so, give an example of it that appeared in the lesson. _____

   _____

   Describe how students behaved in this example. _____

   _____

   If not, how might he or she have done so? _____

   _____

4. Did the teacher exhibit momentum? _____

If so, give an example of it that appeared in the lesson. _____

_____

Describe how students behaved in this example. _____

_____

If not, how might he or she have done so? _____

_____

5. Did the teacher exhibit group alerting? _____

If so, give an example of it that appeared in the lesson. _____

_____

Describe how students behaved in this example. _____

_____

If not, how might he or she have done so? _____

_____

6. Did the teacher exhibit accountability for students? _____

If so, give an example of it that appeared in the lesson. _____

_____

Describe how students behaved in this example. _____

_____

If not, how might he or she have done so? _____

_____

7. Did the teacher exhibit challenge arousal? _____

If so, give an example of it that appeared in the lesson. _____

_____

Describe how students behaved in this example. _____

_____

If not, how might he or she have done so? _____

_____

_____

8. Did the teacher exhibit variety? _____

If so, give an example of it that appeared in the lesson. _____

_____

Describe how students behaved in this example. _____

_____

If not, how might he or she have done so? _____

_____

Analysis and Reflection: Write a paragraph about how you might apply these management principles while teaching in your own subject area or grade level.

OBSERVING STUDENTS' INFLUENCE ON ACADEMIC TASKS

PURPOSE: Doyle and Carter showed that students can have an impact on what happens in the classroom. It is clearly important for teachers to be aware of the influence students can exert. This aid will help you to develop awareness of the pattern of academic tasks and student influence in the classroom.

DIRECTIONS: Observe in an elementary classroom for at least a half day, or in a secondary classroom for at least three consecutive days. If you can observe longer, you should do so. Keep a running account of what happens in the classroom, what the teacher says and does, what the students say and do, and the amount of time spent on each activity. Obtain copies of all handouts. Immediately after each observation, write down any details you noticed but did not have time to include during the observation itself.

Analysis and Reflection: Read through your notes several times. Look for recurring patterns of behavior. Are there any consistencies in the way the teacher introduces a new task? In the way he or she elaborates or explains the task? In the way students react? In the type of task and the length of time it takes to complete? In the way tasks are ended? You may see patterns in other areas. Write an additional two pages about the patterns you observed and comment on why you think those patterns take the form they do. That is, think about who has influence on academic tasks, based on what you observed, and how that influence is exerted. Does it affect academic tasks in a positive or negative way? Do you think these influences are universal, or are they specific to this particular teacher, group of students, or school? What will you do as a teacher to maintain your awareness of these influences in your own classroom, and what will you do to manage these influences in a positive way?

INTERVIEWING TEACHERS ABOUT RULES AND PROCEDURES

PURPOSE: Teaching and enforcing appropriate rules and procedures can prevent or solve the vast majority of management and discipline problems. This tool is to help you to gain practical knowledge about what kinds of rules and procedures are needed in classrooms and how these are taught and enforced.

DIRECTIONS: Interview one elementary teacher, one middle school or junior high teacher, and one high school teacher, using the questions listed below.

1. What are the rules and procedures in your class that govern student movement?

   _____

   _____

   _____

2. How did you initially teach those rules and procedures? _____

   _____

   _____

3. Which ones seem easiest for students to follow? Why? Which ones seem the hardest? Why?

   _____

   _____

   _____

   _____

4. What do you do to maintain and enforce them? _____

   _____

   _____

5. What are the rules and procedures in your class that govern student talking?

   _____

   _____

   _____

6. How did you initially teach those rules and procedures? _____

   _____

   _____

7. Which ones seem easiest for students to follow? Why? Which ones seem the hardest? Why?

_____

_____

_____

_____

8. What do you do to maintain and enforce them? _____

_____

_____

9. What are the rules and procedures in your class that govern downtime?

_____

_____

_____

10. How did you initially teach those rules and procedures? _____

_____

_____

11. Which ones seem easiest for students to follow? Why? Which ones seem the hardest? Why?

_____

_____

_____

_____

12. What do you do to maintain and enforce them? _____

_____

_____

Analysis and Reflection: What seem to be the common elements of rules and procedures at any grade level? Are there any rules and procedures that occur in each level? Are there any common ways they are taught, maintained, and enforced? Are there any common areas of difficulty? Conversely, what did you uncover about rules and procedures that seems to apply only to a particular age group or a particular teacher's style? How will you apply what you have learned to your own teaching?

Assignment 5

OBSERVING MANAGEMENT PRACTICES DURING UNSTABLE PERIODS

PURPOSE: Unstable periods in classroom life pose the most difficult management challenges. This aid is to help you to gain practical knowledge about how to manage these difficult periods.

DIRECTIONS: Observe in an elementary classroom for a few hours from the opening of the school day, or in a secondary classroom for an entire period. Check the actions you see the teacher take in managing unstable periods.

	Yes	No

1. **Opening Class**

   In order to open class smoothly and efficiently, did the teacher do the following:

   a. Greet students at the door? _____ _____

       If so, give an example: _____

       _____

   b. Use student helpers for routine administrative tasks? _____ _____

       If so, give an example: _____

       _____

   c. Write start-up activities on the board? _____ _____

       If so, give an example: _____

       _____

   d. Use routine or ceremonial events that set the proper tone? _____ _____

       If so, give an example: _____

       _____

   e. Other (specify): _____

2. **Transitions**

   Keep a tally of the number of transitions you observe.

   _____

   Describe one of the transitions you observed.

   _____

   _____

   In order to move students smoothly and efficiently from one activity to the next, did the teacher do the following:

   a. Rely on routinized procedure?   _____ _____

      If so, give an example: _____

      _____

   b. Cue or signal the students in some way?   _____ _____

      If so, give an example: _____

      _____

   c. Other (specify): _____

3. **Closing Class**

   In order to close class smoothly and efficiently, did the teacher do the following:

   a. Leave sufficient time to collect books and papers?   _____ _____
   b. Make assignments early enough to avoid last-minute confusion?   _____ _____
   c. Rely on routine procedures for collecting papers and materials?   _____ _____

      If so, give an example: _____

      _____

   d. Cue students that close of class was approaching?   _____ _____

   e. Other (specify): _____

      _____

Analysis and Reflection: Which elements of effective management of unstable periods did this teacher rely on? Which elements were missing? How might this teacher incorporate these missing elements into his or her management routines? Write a paragraph about how you will manage unstable periods in your own classroom.

Assignments

OBSERVING TEACHER RESPONSES TO STUDENT MISBEHAVIOR

PURPOSE: How to respond to student misbehavior is one of the greatest concerns of beginning teachers. This aid is to help you to gain practical knowledge about how to respond to such misbehavior.

DIRECTIONS: Observe a classroom for 45 to 60 minutes. Whenever you observe an instance of student misbehavior, quickly describe the incident, then use the codes given below to code the type of misbehavior and the teacher's response. (You may use more than one code per incident, if necessary.)

Incidents	Student Misbehavior	Teacher Response
1. _____ _____	_____	_____
2. _____ _____	_____	_____
3. _____ _____	_____	_____
4. _____ _____	_____	_____
5. _____ _____	_____	_____
6. _____ _____	_____	_____
7. _____ _____	_____	_____
8. _____ _____	_____	_____
9. _____ _____	_____	_____
10. _____ _____	_____	_____

Codes:
Student behavior
  A. Minor misbehavior
  B. Serious misbehavior

Teacher responses
  A. Withitness: spotted misbehavior early and accurately
  B. Overlapping: while teaching:
    1. Moved closer to problem student
    2. Made and held eye contact with problem student
    3. Rested hand on student's shoulder
    4. Integrated off-task remark into teaching activities
    5. Other (specify)
  C. Used a desist, i.e., told the student to stop the misbehavior. The desist
    was:
    1. Clear
    2. Firm
    3. Rough
  D. Restated the rule or procedure for the student
  E. Had the student identify the rule or procedure
    1. Gave corrective feedback to the student if he or she did not under-
      stand the rule
  F. Imposed a consequence
  G. Changed activity

Analysis and Reflection: What were the teacher's most common responses to instances of minor misbehavior? Were these successful? Why or why not? What were the teacher's most common responses to instances of serious misbehavior? Were these successful? Why or why not? Think through the range of options you will be likely to have for responding to misbehavior. Write at least two paragraphs about these options, and the kinds of situations in which they would be appropriately applied.

PART 3

The next four chapters of *Learning to Teach* focus directly on what most people think of as teaching—the actual face-to-face interaction between the teacher and the learner. Each chapter considers one of the following four basic approaches to instruction: (1) teaching information through presentation, (2) teaching concepts for higher-level thinking, (3) teaching skills through direct instruction, and (4) teaching social and academic skills through cooperative learning.

These approaches are labeled *teaching models*, although one of several other terms—such as teaching strategies, teaching methods, or teaching principles—could have been chosen. The label teaching model was selected for two important reasons.

First, the concept *model* implies something larger than a particular strategy, method, or procedure. For example, as used here, the term teaching model encompasses a broad, overall approach to instruction rather than a specific strategy, such as discussion or seatwork, that can be used with any of the models. Models of teaching have some attributes that specific strategies and methods do not have. The attributes of a model are a coherent theoretical basis and rationale made explicit by its creators and developers; a point of view and an orientation about what students should learn and how they learn; and recommended teaching behaviors and classroom structures for bringing about different types of learning.

Second, the concept of the teaching model can serve as an important communication device for teachers. Joyce and Weil (1986), as you saw in Chapter 1, classified various approaches to teaching according to their instructional intents, their syntaxes, and the nature of their learning environments. Instructional intents are the types of learning goals the model has been designed to achieve. The use of a particular model helps the teacher achieve some goals, but not others. A model's syntax is the overall flow of a lesson's activity. The learning environment (called *social system* by Joyce and Weil) is the context in which any teaching act must be carried out.

Although there is nothing magic about these words or this classification system, they provide a language for communicating about various kinds of teaching activities, when they should occur, and why. Take the idea of syntax for instance. It is used to define the major steps or phases of a lesson based on a particular model. It specifies what kind of teacher and student actions should occur and in what order. The syntaxes of the various models differ, and it is these differences that must be understood if the models are to be used effectively.

In describing the four models in the chapters that follow, it might appear that there is only one correct way to use a particular model. In some respects this is true. If teachers deviate too far from the model's syntax or environmental demands, they are not using the model.

The Interactive Functions of Teaching

On the other hand, once teachers have mastered a particular model, they often need to adapt it to their own particular teaching styles and to the particular group of students with whom they are working. As with most other aspects of teaching, models are guides for thinking and talking about teaching. They should not be viewed as recipes to follow; each teaching situation is unique.

There is a substantial knowledge base for the interactive functions of teaching that can provide a guide for practice. To carry out the interactive functions of teaching, however, you will also rely on the wisdom that has been accumulated by experienced teachers over the years. You will find that many of the interactive functions of teaching overlap with what has already been described in previous chapters. Part of the excitement and challenge in learning to teach is to figure out the complexities of teaching, which the organizational pattern of a book cannot portray with complete accuracy.

CHAPTER 7

MAIN IDEAS

- The presentation teaching model draws its rationale from three streams of contemporary thought: structure of knowledge, psychology of meaningful verbal learning, and cognitive psychology.
- The primary goal of the model is knowledge acquisition.
- Bodies of knowledge have logical structures from which key concepts and ideas are drawn for teachers' presentations.
- Knowledge can be broken into two categories—declarative and procedural.
- Meaningful verbal learning occurs when teachers present major unifying ideas and connect these ideas to students' prior learning.
- Humans process information by taking it in through the senses and transforming it into working and long-term memory.
- Preinstructional tasks consist of choosing content, planning advance organizers, and matching both to students' prior learning.
- Presenting information effectively requires preparing students to learn, presenting advance organizers and learning materials with clarity and enthusiasm, and attending to specific techniques such as "explaining links," "rule-example-rule," "examples and elaborations," and "verbal transitions."
- Postinstructional tasks consist mainly of finding ways to test and evaluate student knowledge gains.

Teaching Through Presentation

Formal presentations by teachers comprise one-sixth to one-fourth of all classroom time. The amount of time devoted to presenting and explaining information increases at the higher grade levels of elementary school, in middle schools, and high schools (Dunkin and Biddle, 1974). Some educators have argued that too much time is devoted to teachers talking, and over the past two decades considerable effort has gone into creating models aimed at decreasing the amount of teacher talk. Nonetheless, formal presentation of information remains the most popular model of teaching and the amount of time devoted to it has remained relatively stable over time.

The popularity of presenting and explaining is not surprising since the most widely held objectives for education are those associated with the acquisition and retention of information. Curricula in schools have been structured around bodies of information organized as science, mathematics, English, and the social sciences. Consequently, curriculum guides, textbooks, and tests routinely used by teachers are similarly organized. Experienced teachers know that exposition is an effective way of helping students acquire the array of information society believes it is important for them to know.

The purpose of this chapter is to introduce the presentation teaching model and tell how to use it effectively. Judgments will not be made about the ideal amount of time a teacher should devote to this model. Instead, the model will be described as a valuable teaching approach that can be used in all subject areas and at all grade levels. The point of view taken here is that the appropriate use of the presentation model is situational; that is, its use depends on the objective the teacher is striving to achieve and the particular students with whom the teacher is working.

Fortunately, the knowledge base on teacher presentation and explanation is fairly well developed. Beginning teachers can learn this model quite easily. As you read this chapter and study the model, you will find much that is familiar. Some of the material you already know from speech classes taken in high school or college. Some of the difficulties of presenting you know from informal talks or speeches you have made. Although the goals of public speaking and classroom presentations are quite different, many of the basic communication skills are the same. As in previous chapters, this chapter first provides a framework for thinking about presenting and explaining information to students, followed by summaries of some of the research that supports this model. The chapter concludes with a discussion of procedures for teachers and learning aids to help teachers understand and practice the model.

PERSPECTIVE AND RATIONALE

Three complementary ideas have come together over the past three decades to provide the rationale and the pedagogy for the presentation model of teaching. These include: (1) the concept of *structure of knowledge,* (2) the psychology of *meaningful verbal learning*, and (3) ideas from cognitive psychology associated with the *representation and acquisition of knowledge*. It is important to understand the ideas underlying these three topics because they provide the basis on which teachers choose, organize, and present information to students. They also support several features of the other models presented later.

Structure and Organization of Knowledge

Knowledge of the world has been organized around various subject areas called disciplines. History is an example of a discipline that organizes knowledge using temporal concepts; biology organizes information and ideas about living things and physics about the physical world. The clustering of courses by academic departments in college catalogs is one illustration of the wide array of disciplines which currently exist. The classification of books in libraries according to subject matter under the Dewey decimal or Library of Congress systems is another.

The disciplines, as they are defined at any point in time, constitute the resources on which most teachers and curriculum developers draw in making decisions about what knowledge should be taught to students. Over two decades ago Ralph Taylor made this observation in a speech at a conference on curriculum:

> From the standpoint of the curriculum, the disciplines should be viewed primarily as a resource that can be drawn upon for the education of students. Hence, we want to understand these resources at their best. And we, I think properly, are often fearful that some of the second-hand treatment that we get of these subjects really prostitutes them—does not represent them at their best. Certainly these disciplines at their best are not simply an encyclopedic collection of facts to be memorized but rather they are an active effort to make sense out of some portion of the world or of life. (Ford and Pugno, 1964, p. 4)

During the 1950s several scholars and curriculum theorists started to study how disciplines were organized and what that organization meant to instruction. A little book written by Jerome Bruner in 1960 called *The Process of Education* highlighted this research. This inquiry produced the idea that each discipline has a structure consisting of key concepts that define the discipline. Figure 7.1 shows a partial knowledge structure for information about American government.

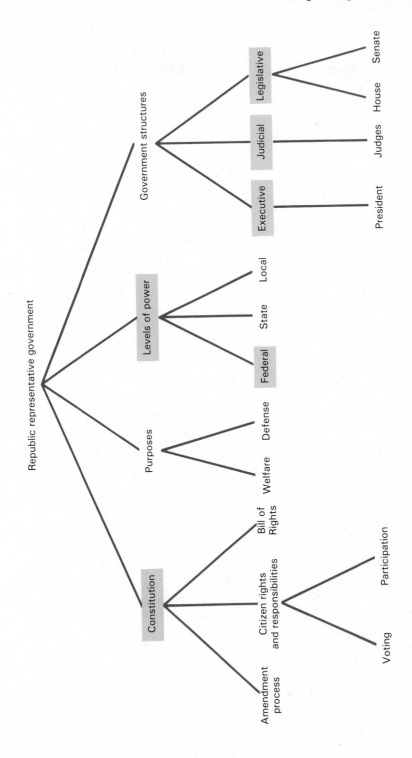

Figure 7.1 A Partial Structure of Knowledge for Representative Government

Note the illustration shows how the structure of government can be viewed as having several major ideas with a variety of subideas such as citizen rights, powers given to the states, and the various branches of government. It is not appropriate here to go into detail about the knowledge structures of various disciplines. However, it is important to emphasize that such structures exist and that they become a means for organizing information about topics, for dividing information into various categories, and for showing relationships among various categories of information.

The teaching implications of this structuring of knowledge are clear—the key ideas supporting each structure should be taught to students instead of lists of disparate facts or bits of information. For example, Bruner (1962) argued that knowing about a house "is not a matter of knowing about a collection of nails, shingles, wallboards, and windows" (p. 77). It is the total concept of house that is significant and important. The same could be said with examples from mathematics, economics, or botany.

Meaningful Verbal Learning

David Ausubel (1963), an educational psychologist, did some interesting ground-breaking work at about the same time. He was particularly interested in the way knowledge is organized hierarchically and how the human mind organizes ideas. He explained that at any point in time a learner has an existing "organization, stability, and clarity of knowledge in a particular subject-matter field" (p. 26). He called this organization a *cognitive structure* and believed that this structure determined the learner's ability to deal with new ideas and relationships. Meaning can emerge from new materials only if they tie into existing cognitive structures of prior learning.

Ausubel saw the primary function of formal education as the organizing of information for students and the presenting of ideas in clear and precise ways. The principal function of pedagogy, according to Ausubel, is "the art and science of presenting ideas and information meaningfully and effectively—so that clear, stable and unambiguous meanings emerge and . . . [are] retained over a long period of time as an organized body of knowledge" (Ausubel, 1963, p. 81) For this learning to occur, according to Ausubel, the teacher should create two conditions. (1) Present learning materials in a potentially meaningful form, with major and unifying ideas and principles, consistent with contemporary scholarship, highlighted rather than merely listed as facts. (2) Find ways to anchor the new learning materials to the learners' prior knowledge and cognitive structures and ready the students' minds so that they can receive new information.

The major pedagogical strategy proposed by Ausubel (1963) is the use of *advance organizers.* It is the job of an advance organizer to "delineate clearly, precisely, and explicitly the principal similarities and differences between the ideas in a new learning passage, on the one hand, and existing related concepts in cognitive structure on the other" (p. 83). More specific details about how to construct and present advance organizers will be provided later in this chapter.

Cognitive Psychology of Learning

A third stream of inquiry that helps explain how information should be presented to students grew out of the rapidly expanding field of cognitive psychology. Its frame of reference is important to teachers because it provides ways for thinking about how knowledge is represented, and it emphasizes that one of the important goals of teaching is to facilitate active thinking and mental processing. As you read the key ideas below, you will observe how they are connected in many ways to Bruner's earlier concept of *structure of knowledge* and Ausubel's ideas about *meaningful verbal learning*.

Ellen Gagné (1985) organized the ideas and research in the field of cognitive psychology that apply directly to teaching. The discussion that follows relies heavily on her important work and her definitions of three concepts: knowledge types, knowledge representation, and information processing.

TWO TYPES OF KNOWLEDGE

Attributing the idea to Gilbert Ryle (1949) and Robert Gagné (1977), Ellen Gagné distinguished between two types of knowledge: declarative knowledge and procedural knowledge. *Declarative knowledge* is knowledge about something or knowledge that something is the case. *Procedural knowledge* is knowledge about how to do something. Examples of declarative knowledge, again using the illustration of government presented in Figure 7.1, would be information about the legislative branch of government, such as that it has two chambers, the House and the Senate, and that senators are elected for six-year terms. Procedural knowledge about the same subject would be knowledge about how to go to the polling place to vote on Election Day or how to write a letter to a senator.

This distinction between the two types of knowledge is an important one for teachers. Declarative and procedural knowledge are acquired differently by students and require different teaching approaches. This chapter, for instance, deals mainly with what teachers do to help students acquire declarative knowledge—new information about some topic, for instance. Conversely, Chapter 9 on direct instruction focuses on helping students acquire procedural knowledge.

KNOWLEDGE REPRESENTATION

Cognitive psychologists say that humans process knowledge in term of basic units, called propositions or ideas. According to Gagné (1985):

> One of the most important characteristics of any given unit of information is its relationship to other units. Our knowledge of such relationships underlies our ability to make analogies and to see other types of connections. Such abilities are important in novel problem-solving situations.
>
> Because the relationships among sets of information are a crucial aspect of intelligence, it is important to have a way of representing them. One way is the form of *propositional networks*, which are sets of interrelated propositions. (p. 40)

Figure 7.2   Hypothetical Propositional Network

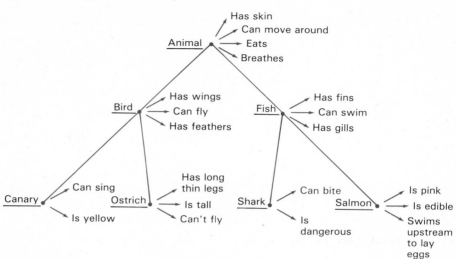

SOURCE: From A. M. Collins and M. R. Quillian (1969), Retrieval time from semantic memory. *Journal of Verbal Learning and Verbal Behavior*, *8*, 241. Used with permission.

Figure 7.2 shows a hypothetical propositional network for information about certain categories of living things.

The illustration in Figure 7.2 is similar to the structure of knowledge concept introduced earlier and to Ausubel's concept of meaningful verbal learning. Without going into further detail on this topic, it is important to note that just as scholars organize academic disciplines according to a structure, so too do learners organize knowledge into propositions and networks. Although psychologists are not in agreement about the exact nature of these networks, the important point for teachers is that information is stored in some type of propositional network and, as will be described later, these networks actively filter new information and thereby determine how well new information presented by teachers will be integrated and retained by learners.

PRIOR KNOWLEDGE: WORKING AND LONG-TERM MEMORY

A final concept from cognitive psychology that is important to teachers as they plan and present new information to students is the concept of working and long-term memory.

New ideas and information enter the mind through one of the senses, eyes or ears for example, and are noted first by the learner's *working memory*. Working memory, according to Gagné (1985), is the "place where conscious mental work is done. For example, if you are solving the problem 26 × 32 mentally, you would hold the intermediate products 52 and 78 in working memory and add them together there" (p. 10). That part of the environment and mental activity of which the learner is actually aware at a particular moment is working memory.

Information in working memory may soon be forgotten unless stored more deeply in *long-term memory*. Long-term memory can be likened to a computer. Information must first be coded before it can be stored and, although stored for perhaps a lifetime, cannot be retrieved unless first given appropriate cues. Information or ideas stored in long-term memory must also be retrieved to working memory before it can be used.

According to Gagné and White (1978) long-term memory stores four types of information: verbal knowledge, intellectual skills, images, and episodes. Verbal knowledge is the declarative and propositional knowledge described above. Intellectual skill is the procedural knowledge for performing intellectual tasks such as the skill to write a sentence. Images and episodes are pictorial representations of certain information and memories of certain events in which the learner has participated. Ellen Gagné (1985) has provided the following illustration (Figure 7.3) for how working and long-term memory interact in instructional settings.

Teaching principles about presenting information growing out of ideas from cognitive psychology are important for teachers in three ways. One, it is important to know that knowledge is organized and structured around basic propositions and unifying ideas. Two, students' abilities to learn new ideas depend on their

---

Figure 7.3   An Example of Working and Long-Term Memory

Suppose that a second-grade teacher wants Joe to learn the fact that the capital of Texas is Austin. The teacher asks Joe, "What is the capital of Texas?" and Joe says, "I don't know." At the same time Joe may set up an expectancy that he is about to learn the capital of Texas, which will cause him to pay attention. The teacher then says, "The capital of Texas is Austin." Joe's ears receive this message along with other sounds such as the other pupils' speech and traffic outside the school.

All of the sounds that Joe hears are translated into electrochemical impulses and sent to the sensory register. The pattern that the capital of Texas is Austin is selected for entry into working memory, but other sound patterns are not entered.

Joe may then code the fact that the capital of Texas is Austin by associating it with other facts that he already knows about Austin (e.g., that it is a big city and that he once visited it). This coding process causes the new fact to be entered into long-term memory. If Joe has already developed special memory strategies (which is somewhat unlikely for a second grader), his executive control process would direct the coding process to use these special strategies.

The next day Joe's teacher might ask him, "What is the capital of Texas?" This question would be received and selected for entry into WM. There it would provide cues for retrieving the answer from LTM. A copy of the answer would be used by the response generator to organize the speech acts that produce the sounds, "Austin is the capital of Texas." At this point Joe's expectancy that he would learn the capital of Texas has been confirmed.

SOURCE: From E. D. Gagné, *The cognitive psychology of school learning*, p. 12. Copyright © 1985 by Ellen D. Gagné. Reprinted by permission of Little, Brown and Company.

prior knowledge and existing cognitive structures. And three, the primary tasks for teachers in helping students acquire knowledge are: (1) thoughtful and skillful organization of learning materials, (2) providing students with advance organizers that will help anchor and integrate new learning, and (3) providing them with cues for drawing information from their long-term to their working memories.

OVERVIEW OF THE PRESENTATION MODEL

The specific presentation model highlighted here is an adaptation of Ausubel's advance organizer model. This model requires the teacher to provide students with advance organizers prior to presenting new information and to make special efforts during and following a presentation to strengthen and extend student thinking. This particular approach was chosen for two reasons. One, the approach is compatible with current knowledge from cognitive psychology about the way people organize, process, and learn new information. Two, various components of the model have been carefully studied over the past 20 years, thus giving the model a substantial, if not always consistent, knowledge base.

As with other models of teaching presented in this book, the presentation model can be described by (1) its instructional effects, (2) its syntax, and (3) the structure of its learning environment. Each of these features was described in the introduction to this section and is used now to organize information about presentations made by teachers.

Instructional Effects of the Model

The instructional effects of the presentation model are clear and straightforward, namely to help students acquire, assimilate, and retain information. The model also helps students build and expand their conceptual structures and develop specific habits for thinking about information and ideas. Table 7.1 provides some examples of the types of objectives a teacher might write for a lesson using the presentation model.

It is evident that all the objectives in Table 7.1 are targeted toward the acquisition of declarative knowledge. None asks for students to be able to do anything procedurally with that knowledge.

Syntax of the Model

There are four phases, or steps, for teachers to follow when presenting information to students. The flow proceeds from the teacher's initial introduction to the lesson by establishing set and presenting his or her objectives, through presentations of the advance organizer and the learning materials, to the conclusion with interactions aimed at extending and strengthening student thinking. Each phase and appropriate teacher behavior is described in Table 7.2.

Table 7.1 **Sample Objectives for a Lesson Using the Presentation Model**

CONTENT AREA	OBJECTIVE
Science	On an exam students will be able to define a tapeworm as a parasite that gains nourishment from a host organism.
History	On an essay examination, the student will be able to correctly list five causes of the American Civil War.
Math	Given pictures of three types of triangles, the student will be able to correctly identify and define each.
Foreign language	Given a list of cultural traits, the student will be able to correctly identify those most closely associated with French culture.
Literature	On an essay examination, the student will be able to define and describe the critical features of a Hemingway short story.

Table 7.2 **Syntax of the Presentation Model**

PHASE	TEACHER BEHAVIOR
Phase 1: Present objectives and establish set	Teacher goes over the objectives of the lesson and gets students ready to learn.
Phase 2: Present advance organizer	Teacher presents advance organizer making sure that it provides a framework for later learning materials and is connected to students' prior knowledge.
Phase 3: Present learning materials	Teacher presents learning materials, paying special attention to their logical ordering and meaningfulness to students.
Phase 4: Extend and strengthen student thinking	Teacher asks questions and elicits student responses to the presentation to extend student thinking and encourage precise and critical thinking.

Structure of the Learning Environment

In the presentation model, the teacher strives to structure the learning environment tightly. Except in Phase 4, where the environment must facilitate student interaction, the teacher is an active presenter and expects students to be active listeners. Successful use of the model requires good conditions for presenting and listening, including appropriate facilities for use of audio and visual aides. The success of the model depends upon students being sufficiently motivated to listen to what the teacher is saying. During formal presentations students should not be sharpening pencils, talking to neighbors, or working on other tasks. Creating an appropriate learning environment for this type of activity can in some settings be a very difficult task.

SAMPLING THE RESEARCH BASE

The knowledge base on presenting and explaining information to learners has been developed by researchers working in several different fields, especially cognitive psychology and information processing, as described in the previous section. Other research comes from the study of teaching and has focused on such topics as set induction, use of prior knowledge, and advance organizers. Still other work has looked at teacher clarity and enthusiasm and how these attributes affect student learning. Since it is impossible to provide full coverage of this extensive research base, three sample studies have been chosen. Together, these studies illustrate the nature of the research on teacher presentation and explanation, and they provide some important guidelines for practice.

Prior Knowledge and Set Induction

Research has been conducted, particularly during the past ten years, on the influence of prior knowledge for learning to read, learning to use new information, and learning to write. In general this research points toward the importance of prior knowledge for learning new information and new skills. For example, a particularly interesting study on the influence of prior knowledge on children's production of narrative was conducted recently by Mosenthal and his colleagues (1985). The researchers selected a representative group of fourth-grade teachers and picked two whose teaching styles were characterized by asking questions to elicit prior learning from students and two who did not do much of this. Each teacher was then asked to conduct a writing lesson in his or her class. The lesson consisted of presenting students with a series of 13 pictures representing a baseball episode and asking students to write a story about the picture sequences. The results from this study showed that students in the classrooms where teachers made use of their students' prior knowledge produced stories that were generally more complex and creative than those produced by students in the other classrooms.

One important teaching skill for helping students use their prior knowledge is a skill called set induction. Set induction is a technique used by teachers at the beginning of a presentation to prepare students to learn and to establish a communicative link between the learners and the information about to be presented. As you will see later, set induction is not the same as an advance organizer, although both serve the similar purpose of using students' prior knowledge. Through set induction, teachers help students retrieve appropriate information and intellectual skills from long-term memory and get it ready for use as new information and skills are introduced. More information about and examples of set induction will be provided later. Research Summary 7.1 describes a study done by Schuck that shows the impact of set induction on the achievement of eighth- and ninth-grade science students.

Using Advance Organizers

As you read in the previous section, Ausubel saw the use of an advance organizer as a means to help make information meaningful to students. For Ausubel, an advance organizer consists of statements made by teachers just prior to actual presentation of the learning materials. These statements are at a higher level of abstraction than the subsequent information. Later in this chapter advance organizers are defined more precisely; however, here it is important to say that advance organizers help students use prior knowledge just as establishing set does. They differ, however, in that they are tied more tightly to the subsequent information and provide an anchor for later learning.

Since 1960, when David Ausubel published a work titled "The Use of Advance Organizers in the Learning and Retention of Meaningful Verbal Material" in the *Journal of Educational Psychology*, psychologists and educational researchers have been actively testing the Ausubel advance organizer hypothesis. Walberg (1986), for example, reported that from 1969 to 1979, advance organizers were the subject of 32 studies. Walberg also described a synthesis of research done by Luiten, Ames, and Aerson (1980) that identified over 135 studies on the effects of advance organizers. Although not all of the studies show the effectiveness of advance organizers, the findings seem to be consistent enough over time to recommend that teachers use advance organizers when presenting information to students. Research Summary 7.2 describes an interesting study done in Australia on this topic.

Teacher Clarity

Using advance organizers, establishing set, and attending to prior learning all affect student learning. Another variable associated with the presentation of information that has been shown to influence student learning is teacher clarity. In a review of the research done in the 1950s and 1960s, Rosenshine and Furst (1973) reported that "teacher clarity" was a specific teaching trait that showed up consistently as having an impact on student achievement. Similarly, when Walberg, Schiller, and Haertel (1979) reviewed the research from 1969 to 1979 they found seven studies that focused on teacher clarity. All seven showed a strong relationship between teacher clarity and student achievement. Research Summary 7.3 is an example of a study that shows the influence of lack of teacher clarity (vagueness) on student performance.

Teacher Enthusiasm

A final aspect of presentation is teacher enthusiasm. This is an interesting concept for two reasons. First, enthusiasm is often confused with theatrics and its associated distractions, and second, the research on the relationship between teacher enthusiasm and student learning is mixed. The topic gives an opportunity to

━━━━━━━━━━━━━━━━━━━ **RESEARCH SUMMARY** ━━━━━━━━━━━━━━━━━
7.1

Schuck, R. F. (1981). The impact of set induction on student achievement and retention. *Journal of Educational Research, 74,* 227–232.

PROBLEM: The researcher was interested in what influence the use of set induction by teachers would have on student achievement and retention.

SAMPLE AND SETTING: The student sample consisted of 120 ninth-grade students who were recruited from two junior high schools in a rural area. The teachers participating in the study were 12 biology teachers involved in an in-service workshop.

PROCEDURES: Students were randomly assigned to 12 groups with ten students in each group. Each of the participating teachers was assigned at random to one of the 12 groups.

- All participating teachers attended a two-hour meeting and were given curricular materials for two biology units: one on respiration, the other on circulation.
- Teachers were then divided into four groups.
- Teachers in experimental groups A and C were given four hours of instruction on set induction techniques.
- Teachers in control groups B and D received no training except for the initial orientation.
- Student achievement was measured using specially designed tests for the units on respiration and circulation.

POINTERS FOR READING RESEARCH: This study employed a particular research method called "Solomon Four Group Design." This is an approach used by some researchers to make sure the effects found are not in fact a result of a pretest given to students. When using this approach, students in one experimental group (group A) are given a pretest; students in the other experimental group (group C) are not. The same is true with the control groups.

provide a concrete example of how conflicting evidence from research on an important aspect of teaching can lead to different guidelines for practice.

EFFECTS OF ENTHUSIASM

In 1970 Rosenshine reviewed the research on teacher enthusiasm and reported that it showed pretty consistent relationships between teacher enthusiasm and student learning. Since that time researchers have tried to study teacher enthusiasm with more precise designs and have developed training programs to help teachers become more enthusiastic in their presentations. For example, Collins (1978) developed and tested a training program that looked at a specific set of enthusiastic

RESULTS: Table 1 summarizes the mean scores for each of the groups and the F ratios related to student achievement both at the end of instruction and 24 to 26 weeks later.

TABLE 1 Summary of Mean Scores and F Ratios Related to Student Achievement and Retention

Variables	Experimental Group		Control Group		F Ratios Experimental vs. Control
	A	C	B	D	
Pretest circulation	12.0	—	11.8	—	.007*
Posttest circulation	34.4	32.8	28.9	27.8	66.600**
Pretest respiration	12.0	—	12.2	—	.005*
Posttest respiration	33.2	32.7	28.9	27.8	53.900**
Retention circulation	27.4	30.2	26.6	25.9	84.700**
Retention respiration	30.6	30.5	26.5	26.7	70.100**

*These F values are not significant, meaning that the groups were about the same prior to instruction.
**These F values are significant, (.01, meaning experimental effects were present.
SOURCE: Adapted from R. F. Schuck (1981), p. 230.

DISCUSSION AND IMPLICATIONS: As can be observed in Table 1 the use of set induction clearly had an impact on student achievement both in the short term and several weeks later. Students taught by teachers using set induction techniques learned more at the end of the units on both respiration and circulation. They also retained this information more than did students taught by teachers who had not been trained in set induction.

Set induction is a rather simple technique to learn. Note that the researchers taught it to their experimental teachers in four hours. Implications for beginning teachers are clear. Learn how to use set induction and know that it will lead (everything else being equal) to higher achievement gains for students immediately and more retention of learning materials at later dates.

behaviors: (1) rapid, uplifting, varied local delivery; (2) dancing, wide-open eyes; (3) frequent, demonstrative questions; (4) varied, dramatic body movements; (5) varied emotive facial expressions; (6) selection of varied words, especially adjectives; (7) ready, animated acceptance of ideas and feelings; and (8) exuberant overall energy (Borg and Gall, 1983, p. 35; also Collins, 1978). Collins found that students in classes of enthusiasm-trained teachers did better than those in classes of untrained teachers.

However, in 1979 Bettencourt, one of Gall's students at the University of Oregon, replicated Collins's study and could find no differences in achievement between enthusiasm-trained and untrained teachers. This led Bettencourt and

---

RESEARCH SUMMARY
7.2

Beeson, G. W. (1981). Influence of knowledge context on the learning of intellectual skills. *American Educational Research Journal, 18,* 363–379.

PROBLEM: Beeson was interested in the influence of knowledge context on the way students learn and transfer certain intellectual ideas and skills. In addition he wanted to find out if ideas learned in "meaningful rather than mechanical ways" would lead to more retention and transfer.

SAMPLE AND SETTING: Six secondary schools were selected at random from schools in the metropolitan area of Melbourne, Australia. In each school the experiment was conducted in tenth-grade classes. A total of 188 students served as subjects in the study.

PROCEDURES: Students were taught a unit in electricity. The unit required learning verbal information and special skills associated with electrical circuits. The 188 students were randomly assigned to three experimental groups:

- *Isolated Elements Group:* In this group, students were taught the ideas in isolation, with minimal verbal instructions but with the same opportunities for practice as students in the other groups.
- *Verbal Instructions Group:* In this group, students were given verbal instruction designed to show relevant subordinate elements of the various skills and to direct their thinking about the skills.
- *Anchoring Idea Group:* Students in this group were given a three-page anchoring idea paper (an advance organizer). The anchoring idea paper related electric circuits to water circuits. Shorter anchoring ideas (advance organizers) were also provided throughout the unit and when appropriate teachers attempted to relate learning to the anchoring ideas.

The researchers tested students on a number of variables. Only those relevant to this illustration will be included.

- *Achievement of Final Task:* This test included problems and questions parallel to those in the teaching materials but with slightly different formats and types of circuit diagrams.
- *Transfer Test:* This test included (1) questions similar to ones on the final task, (2) questions in which the format and orientation of circuit diagrams differed (intermediate transfer), and (3) questions requiring students to solve novel problems related to circuits (far transfer).

To measure short-term achievement and transfer, tests were administered two days after the training program. Long-term tests were administered six to eight weeks later.

POINTERS FOR READING RESEARCH: No new research concepts are introduced in Beeson's study.

RESULTS: Results of Beeson's study are displayed in Table 1. These have been adapted and simplified from the original tables prepared by Beeson.

TABLE 1 Means and Standard Deviations for Short-Term and Long-Term Tests

Test		Learning Program		
		Isolated Elements	Verbal Instructions	Anchoring Idea
Short-Term Tests				
Transfer	*M*	22.6	21.4	30.8
(Whole test)	*SD*	14.8	11.5	14.8
Final task	*M*	19.8	16.1	22.6
(Whole test)	*SD*	11.9	11.1	15.3
Long-Term Tests				
Transfer (far)	*M*	12.3	11.6	13.0
	SD	6.5	5.0	5.6
Final task	*M*	9.8	7.9	12.4
	SD	6.1	6.0	5.9

SOURCE: Adapted from G. W. Beeson (1981), pp. 373–374.

DISCUSSION AND IMPLICATIONS: As can be observed in the data found in Table 1, the anchoring idea treatment produced better achievement by students on the final task and on the transfer tests. For the transfer tests, the researchers reported that the differences between the isolated elements and veral instructions groups were not significant, but the differences found between those groups and the anchoring group were significant at the .05 level of confidence. On the final task test the differences, although favoring the anchoring group, were not statistically signifi-cant. On the long-term tests, the anchoring group produced statistically significant better results than the other two groups.

This study supports the idea that transfer of learning is more likely if students learn ideas within a meaningful context, and with the use of advance organizers. Ideas and skills taught in isolation or mechanically will not be learned very effectively, nor will they be retained or transferred to new situations.

RESEARCH SUMMARY
7.3

Hiller, J. H., Gisher, G. A., and Kaess, W. (1969). A computer investigation of verbal characteristics of effective classroom lecturing. *American Educational Research Journal, 6,* 661–675.

PROBLEM: The researchers were interested in exploring various features of classroom presentation. More specifically, researchers wanted to find out if certain teacher presentation features had any relationship to how well students learned the new information presented.

SAMPLE: Thirty-two high school social studies teachers and their students from the San Franciso area were the subjects. Teachers volunteered for the study. Students were grouped heterogeneously within each class, with 21 the average class size.

PROCEDURES: Teachers participating in the study were asked to deliver two different 15-minute presentations to their students on two successive days.

Lecture 1: The first presentation, on Yugoslavia, was to be based on a 2,500-word article from *Atlantic* magazine. All 32 teachers made this presentation.

Lecture 2: The second presentation, on Thailand, also was to be based on a 2,500-word article from *Atlantic* magazine. This presentation was made by 23 of the 32 teachers.

Teachers were encouraged to make the presentation in their normal fashion, were told not to interject class discussion, and were given half of the test items in advance to facilitate their understanding of the article and of the objectives of the lesson.

Students in the class were tested immediately following the presentation with a ten-item multiple choice comprehension test. The class mean (average of all student scores) formed the criterion (or the measure of student achievement) in the study.

The researchers studied five teacher presentation variables: (1) verbal fluency, (2) amount of information, (3) knowledge structure cues, (4) interest, and (5) vagueness.

POINTERS FOR READING RESEARCH: The independent variables in this study are the five features of presentation described above. The dependent variables are the student achievement scores on two tests: one on the Yugoslavia lesson, the other on the Thailand lesson. The researchers treated their data by looking at the relationships between teacher presentation behaviors and student achievements and used correlation coefficients, a statistic introduced earlier.

RESULTS: Hiller and his colleagues found the correlations between each of the five factors and the criterion measure, the student scores on the test given after the lesson. Table 1 shows the correlation coefficients they found. Table 2 gives examples of teachers who lacked clarity in their presentations and the actual words used by these teachers.

DISCUSSION AND IMPLICATIONS: As can be observed in Table 1 for the Yugoslavia lesson there were significant relationships on two factors—verbal fluency (clarity) and vagueness. Note that the correlation coefficient for vagueness is negative.

TABLE 1 Correlation Coefficients for Five Factors with Criterion

Yugoslavia Presentation ($n = 32$)	Correlation	Signif. Level
1. Verbal fluency	.42	.01
2. Information	−.18	ns
3. Knowledge structure	−.03	ns
4. Interest	.20	ns
5. Vagueness	−.59	.001
Thailand Presentation ($n = 23$)		
1. Verbal fluency	.38	.05
2. Information	.54	.005
3. Knowledge structure	−.23	ns
4. Interest	.41	.02
5. Vagueness	−.48	.001

SOURCE: Adapted from J. H. Hiller, G. A. Gisher, and W. Kaess (1969), p. 667.

TABLE 2 Excerpts from Teacher Presentations Exhibiting Vagueness

Exhibiting vagueness response: "And the young author's name, although this isn't too important a thing to remember, is that it was a young author who wrote this. I'll put his name on the board anyway. Mihajlov wrote these articles. And someone has done something, this is like someone very similar had done, and there was another author whose name is, um let's just remember there's another author . . ."

Repetitive vagueness response: "But at the same time it's a relatively new country, rebuilding you see, and they put a lot of money into building roads and factories and so on and so you don't have a lot of consumer goods—shoes and so on. So, there are not a lot of these things available. There are, is a lot of money and so the dollar becomes worth a lot less."

SOURCE: From J. H. Hiller, G. A. Gisher, and W. Kaess (1969), p. 672.

This means that the more vague the teacher, the less the students achieved. In the Thailand lesson, four of the factors achieved significance: verbal fluency .38, information .54, interest .41, and vagueness −.48.

The researchers concluded that fluency and vagueness were the most significant factors and, as logic would suggest, as fluency scores increased, vagueness scores decreased.

It is clear from this study that teacher clarity and lack of vagueness influence what students learn from a lesson. The researchers suggest that vagueness is present in a lecture when a "speaker commits himself to deliver information he can't remember or never really knew" (p. 670). This, of course, suggests several steps for teachers who are about to present information to their students: (1) make sure the content is thoroughly understood, (2) practice and commit the key ideas to memory prior to presentation, or (3) follow written notes very carefully during presentation.

Gall to go back and review several of the earlier studies on enthusiasm. Borg and Gall (1983) reported the following about this review.

> Four of the previous experiments had demonstrated a positive effect of teacher enthusiasm on student achievement. Only one . . . had found an absence of effect. We discovered that the few experiments with positive results have one feature in common. The comparison treatment (the no-training condition) in each study required the teacher to purposefully act in a non-enthusiastic manner. For example, in one of the comparison treatments the teacher "read an entire speech from a manuscript" and "made no gestures or direct eye contact and held vocal inflection to a minimum" (Coats and Smidchens, 1966). In the two experiments reporting no effect, however, the comparison group were . . . allowed to use their natural teaching style. (p. 38)

It appears that some evidence exists that points to the importance of enthusiasm as an influence on student learning. However, the studies showing effects have pitted enthusiasm against "depressed enthusiasm," not against natural teaching styles. The exact nature of enthusiasm and how much of it to use remains unknown at the present time.

PROCEDURES FOR EFFECTIVE PRESENTATION

Understanding the theoretical and research bases underlying the teacher presentation model is not sufficient for its effective use. That requires expert execution of a set of decisions and behaviors during the preinstructional, interactive, and postinstructional phases of teaching. In this section guidelines for using the presentation model appropriately and effectively are described.

Preinstructional Tasks

Except for people who are really shy, it is quite easy to get up in front of a class of students and talk for 20 to 30 minutes. Talking, however, is not teaching. Making decisions about what content to include in a presentation and how to organize content so it is logical and meaningful to students takes extensive preparation by the teacher. Three planning tasks are most important: (1) choosing objectives and content for the presentation, (2) determining students' prior knowledge and cognitive structures, and (3) selecting appropriate and powerful advance organizers and procedures for set induction.

CHOOSING CONTENT

Most beginning secondary school teachers will still be learning the subjects they teach; many elementary teachers will never completely master all the subjects included in the contemporary elementary curriculum. For teachers who are still in the process of mastering their teaching specialties, the recommendation for choosing content is to rely on the frameworks and structures provided in curriculum guides. Most guides have been written by subject matter specialists to conform to the subject's knowledge structure and are based on experienced teachers' estimates of students' prior knowledge. If good guides do not exist in a particular school system, they can be found in the libraries of most major universities or resource centers within State Departments of Education. Whether beginning teachers use their own knowledge of the subject or knowledge that has been organized by others, several principles can assist in choosing content for a particular presentation or series of presentations.

Economy It has been observed that most presentations by teachers contain too much information and too much information that is irrelevant. Students are hampered from learning key ideas because of verbal clutter. Bruner (1962) says teachers should strive for economy in their presentations and explanations. Economy means being very careful in the amount of information presented at any one time and it means providing concise summaries of key ideas several times during the presentation. The economy principle argues for taking a difficult concept and making it clear and simple for students, not taking an easy concept and making it difficult through vagueness and the use of too many words.

Power Bruner also describes how the principle of power should be applied when selecting content for a presentation. A powerful presentation is one where basic concepts from the subject area are chosen and presented in straightforward and logical ways. It is through logical organization that students come to see relationships between specific facts and the interrelationships among the important concepts that make up any topic. To achieve economy and power in a presentation depends not so much on the delivery style of the teacher as it does on planning. In fact, a carefully organized presentation read in monotone might be more effective in producing student learning than a dynamic presentation void of powerful ideas and logical organization, even though students may enjoy the latter more.

Conceptual Mapping A third idea that is useful in helping decide what to teach is that of conceptual mapping. Posner and Rudnitsky (1986) have written that "conceptual maps are like road maps, but they are concerned with relationships among ideas, rather than places. Conceptual maps . . . help you to 'get your bearings' . . . to clarify the kinds of ideas you want taught—so you can proceed toward your destination of real student learning" (p. 25). To make a conceptual map, you identify the key ideas associated with any topic and arrange these ideas in some logical pattern. Sometimes conceptual maps are hierarchical diagrams, like the one in Figure 7.1 displayed earlier in this chapter. Sometimes they focus on causal relations, such as the conceptual map displayed in Figure 7.4.

Figure 7.4   The Causal Factors Affecting Rice Growing

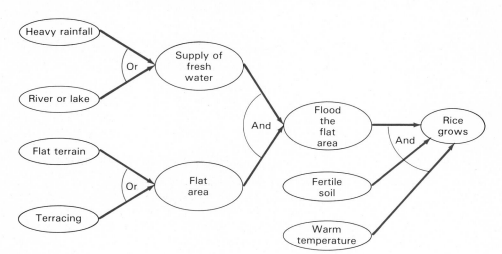

SOURCE: From A. Collins (1977), Processes in acquiring knowledge. In R. C. Anderson, R. J. Spiro, and W. E. Montague (Eds.) *Schooling and the acquisition of knowledge.* Hillsdale, NJ: Lawrence Erlbaum Assoc. Publishers, Fig. 1, p. 341.

Conceptual maps are fun to make. They can help you decide which important ideas to teach and they also can serve as a pictorial to help students understand relationships among various ideas a teacher may want to explain.

MAKING DECISIONS ABOUT GOALS AND OBJECTIVES

Earlier it was explained how a subject's knowledge structure provides one means for making decisions about what kind of information to give to students. Another organizer that aids in making decisions about educational objectives and subject content is Bloom's Taxonomy (classification) of Educational Objectives. Working with colleagues at the University of Chicago in the 1950s, Benjamin Bloom created a scheme that classifies educational objectives according to the type of cognitive processing required of the learner. Bloom's taxonomy has been widely used as an aid in planning, for deciding on what type of information to present to students, as well as for making tests. It also helps guide other classroom procedures, such as questioning strategies (described later in this chapter).

There are six levels to Bloom's classification system. Each level requires students to engage in a different thinking or cognitive process. Table 7.3 presents Bloom's six levels and the associated cognitive tasks expected of the learner.

Bloom's classification system can be very helpful to the beginning teacher who will be faced with all kinds of conflicting goals about education—ranging from promoting critical thinking to assuring mastery of basic facts. Bloom's

Table 7.3 Bloom's Taxonomy of Educational Objectives

LEVEL	STUDENT COGNITIVE PROCESSES
Level 1: Knowledge	The student can recall, define, recognize, or identify specific information presented during instruction. The information may be in the form of a fact, a rule, a diagram, a sound, and so on.
Level 2: Comprehension	The student can demonstrate understanding of information by translating it into a different form or by recognizing it in translated form. This can be through giving a definition in his or her own words, summarizing, giving an original example, recognizing an example, etc.
Level 3: Application	The student can apply the information in performing concrete actions. These actions may involve figuring, writing, reading, handling equipment, etc.
Level 4: Analysis	The student can recognize the organization and structure of a body of information, can break this information down into its constituent parts, and can specify the relationships between these parts.
Level 5: Synthesis	The student can bring to bear information from various sources to create a product uniquely his or her own. The product can take a variety of forms—written, oral, pictorial, etc.
Level 6: Evaluation	The student can apply a standard in making a judgment on the worth of something, a concerto, an essay, an action, an architectural design, etc.

taxonomy helps teachers to think about balancing the range of information provided to students and to be more analytical about what they expect students to do with that information.

DETERMINING STUDENTS' PRIOR KNOWLEDGE

Information given in a presentation is based on teachers' estimates of their students' existing cognitive structures and their prior knowledge of a subject. As with many other aspects of teaching, there are no clear-cut rules or easy formulas for teachers to follow. There are, however, some ideas that can serve as guides for practice and also some informal procedures to be learned from experienced teachers.

Cognitive Structures For new material to be meaningful to students, teachers must find ways to connect the new material to what students already know. Students' present ideas on a particular topic determine which new concepts are potentially meaningful. Figure 7.5 illustrates how a student's cognitive structure might look in relation to a set of concepts about government. Note that this is the same as the illustration in Figure 7.1. Now it is being used to show that some

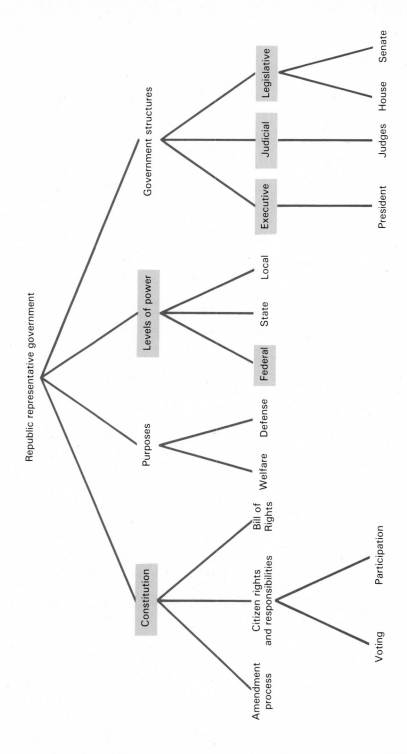

Figure 7.5 An Individual's Cognitive Structure with Respect to Representative Government

concepts have been learned and others have not. Note also the illustrator's judgment about which concepts will be relevant because of the student's prior knowledge.

Intellectual Development Cognitive structures are influenced by students' prior knowledge. They are also influenced by maturation and development. Chapter 2 introduced the idea of emotional and cognitive development and described the developmental stages of teachers. Several theorists have put forth developmental theories, including Hunt (1974), Piaget (1963), and Perry (1969). Space does not allow a full discussion of the similarities and differences among developmental theories, but they agree that learners do go through developmental stages ranging from very simple and concrete structures at early ages to more abstract and complicated structures later. It is important that teachers tailor the information they present to the level of development of the learner.

Ideas about how students develop intellectually can provide assistance to teachers as they plan for a particular presentation; however, they cannot provide concrete solutions for several reasons. As experienced teachers know, development is uneven and does not occur precisely at any given ages. Within any classroom, the teacher is likely to find students at extremely varied stages of development. The teacher will also find some students who have developed to a high level of abstraction in some subjects, say history, and still be at a very concrete level in another subject, such as mathematics.

Another problem facing the teacher striving to apply developmental theories to planning for a particular presentation is the problem of measuring the developmental levels of students. Specific tests exist (such as Hunt's Paragraph Completion Test, or Perry's Test), but these are difficult for teachers to use and are better suited for older students. Most teachers must rely on more informal assessments. For example, teachers can watch students as they approach specific problem-solving tasks and make a rough assessment of the degree to which they use concrete or abstract operations. By listening carefully to students and asking probing questions, teachers can determine whether or not the information they are presenting is meaningful. Watching for nonverbal cues during a presentation, such as silence, or frowns, or expressions of interest, can provide insights into what students are integrating into their knowledge structures. Silence, for example, can mean that students are bored; most often it means they do not understand what the teacher is saying. It may be that part of the "art of teaching" and a major difference between expert and novice teachers is expert teachers' abilities to read subtle communication cues from students and then adapt their presentations so that new learning materials become meaningful.

CHOOSING ADVANCE ORGANIZERS

The third planning task associated with the presentation model is choosing appropriate advance organizers. Remember, advance organizers become the hooks, the anchors, the "intellectual scaffolding" for subsequent learning materials. They must be constructed with care. Two major guidelines are important to consider. The *advance organizer* should be:

- Presented at a *higher level of abstraction* than the content of the learning materials
- Designed to relate to the students' *prior knowledge*

One point should be repeated here: The advance organizer is not the same as other techniques used by teachers to introduce a lesson, such as reviewing past work, establishing set, or giving an overview of the day's lesson. All of the above are important for effective presentations, but they are not advance organizers. Below are three examples of advance organizers teachers have used in particular presentations to give you an idea of what an advance organizer is.

Example 1 Say a history teacher is about to present information about the Vietnam War. After reviewing yesterday's lesson, telling students the goals of today's lesson, and asking students to recall in their minds what they already know about Vietnam (establishing set), the teacher might present the following advance organizer:

> I want to give you an idea that will help you understand why America became involved in the Vietnam War. *The idea is that most wars reflect conflict between peoples over one of the following: ideology, territory, or access to trade.* As I describe for you the United States's involvement in Southeast Asia between 1945 and 1965, I want you to look for examples of how conflict over ideology, territory, or access to trade may have influenced later decisions to fight in Vietnam.

Example 2 Suppose a science teacher is about to present information about foods the body needs to function well. After going over the objectives for the lesson, the teacher might ask students to list all the food they ate yesterday (establishing set) and then present the following advance organizer:

> In a minute I am going to give you some information about the kinds of foods the body needs to function well. Before I do that, however, *I want to give you an idea that will help you understand the different kinds of food you eat by saying they can be classified into five major food groups: fats, vitamins, minerals, proteins, and carbohydrates.* Each food group contains certain elements such as carbon or nitrogren. Also, certain things we eat (potatoes, meat) are the sources for each of the elements in the various food groups. Now as I talk about the balanced diet the body needs, I want you to pay attention to the food group to which each thing we eat belongs.

Example 3 Or, finally, suppose an art teacher is going to show and explain to students a number of paintings from different historical eras. After giving an overview of the lesson and asking students to think for a minute about changes they have observed between paintings done during different historical eras, the following advance organizer is presented:

> In a minute I am going to show and talk about several paintings—some painted in France during the early nineteenth century; others during the late nineteenth and early twentieth century. Before I do that I am going to give you an idea to help you understand the differences you are going to see. *That idea is that a painting reflects not only the individual artist's talent but also the times in which it is created. The "times" or "periods" influence the type of techniques an artist uses as well as what he or she paints about and the type of colors used.* As I show you the various paintings, I want you to look for differences in color, subject of the painting, and specific brush techniques used by the artists and see how they reflect the artist's time.

Conducting the Lesson

It was described previously how the syntax for the presentation model consists of four basic phases. These include (1) explaining goals and establishing set, (2) presenting the advance organizer, (3) presenting the learning materials, and (4) extending and strengthening student thinking. Behaviors associated with effective teaching practice for each of these steps are described below.

1. EXPLAINING GOALS AND ESTABLISHING SET

Effective teaching using any model requires an initial step by the teacher aimed at motivating students to participate in the lesson. Behaviors consistently found effective for this purpose are sharing the goals of the lesson with students and establishing a set for learning.

Explaining Goals Students need a reason for participating in a particular lesson and they need to know what is expected of them. Effective teachers telegraph their goals and expectations by providing abbreviated versions of their lesson plans on the chalkboard or with newsprint charts. Some teachers prefer newsprint charts because they can be made up the night before and posted on the wall, leaving the chalkboard free for other use; then they can be stored for future use. Effective teachers also outline the steps or phases of a particular lesson and the time required for each step. This allows the students to see the overall flow of a lesson and how the various parts fit together. Sharing the time parameters for the lesson also encourages students to help keep the lesson on schedule. Figure 7.6 shows how a social studies teacher shared her goals and the phases of her presentation with a group of eleventh-grade students.

Making students aware of what they are going to learn will help them make connections between a particular lesson and its relevance to their own lives and this motivates them to exert more effort. It also helps students draw prior learning

Figure 7.6 Aims and Overview of Today's Lesson on American Naval Involvement in the Pacific During World War II

Today's Objective: The objective of today's lesson is to help you understand how events and circumstances bring about change in the way people think about things.

AGENDA:

5 minutes	Introduction, review, and getting ready
5 minutes	Advance organizer for today's lesson
20 minutes	Presentation on the demise of the battleship and the concept of decisive engagement
15 minutes	Discussion for critical thinking
5 minutes	Wrap-up and preview of tomorrow's lesson

---

from long-term memory to working memory, where it can be used to integrate new information provided in a presentation.

Establishing Set To get runners ready and off to an even start in a foot race, the command from the starter is "Get Ready. . . . Get *set*. . . . Go!" The *get set* alerts runners to settle into their blocks, focus their attention on the track ahead, and anticipate a smooth and fast start.

Establishing set for a lesson in school is very much the same. Effective teachers have found that a brief review that gets students to recall yesterday's lesson or perhaps a question or anecdote that ties into students' prior knowledge is a good way to get started. Note the words used by the teacher in Figure 7.7 as he establishes set for his students.

Set activities also help students get their minds off other things they have been doing (changing classes in secondary schools; changing subjects in elementary schools; lunch and recess) and begin the process of focusing on the subject of the forthcoming lesson. These activities also serve as motivators for lesson participation. Each teacher develops his or her own style for establishing set, but no effective teacher eliminates this important element from any lesson.

2. PRESENTING THE ADVANCE ORGANIZER

A previous section explained the planning tasks associated with choosing an appropriate advance organizer. Now consider how an advance organizer should be presented.

Effective teachers make sure the advance organizer is set off sufficiently from the introductory activities of the lesson and from the presentation of learning materials. As with the lesson goals, it is effective to present the advance organizer to students using some type of visual format such as a chalkboard, a newsprint chart, or an overhead projector. The key, of course, is that students must understand the advance organizer. It must be taught just as the subsequent

Figure 7.7

Remember yesterday we learned to identify the theme of a story by finding adjectives, verbs, and adverbs that evoked a certain mood. Today we will continue to identify themes, but we will learn to identify them by looking for symbols.

Theme
Mood Symbols

SOURCE: From E. D. Gagné, *The cognitive psychology of school learning*, p. 45. Copyright © 1985 by Ellen D. Gagné. Reprinted by permission of Little, Brown and Company.

information itself must be taught. This requires the teacher to be precise and clear.

3. PRESENTING THE LEARNING MATERIALS

The third phase of the model is the presentation of the learning materials. Remember how important it is for the teacher to organize learning materials in their simplest and clearest form using the principles of power and economy. The key now is to present previously organized materials in an effective manner, giving attention to such matters as clarity, use of examples and explaining links, the rule-example-rule technique, the use of transitions, and finally, enthusiasm.

CLARITY

As described in the research section of this chapter, a teaching behavior that has consistently been shown to affect student learning is the teacher's ability to be clear and specific. Common sense also tells us that students will learn more when teachers are clear and specific rather than vague. Nonetheless, researchers and observers of both beginning and experienced teachers can find many instances of presentations that are vague and confusing. According to Hiller and his colleagues (1969), "Vagueness occurs when a performer . . . does not sufficiently command the facts or the understandings required for maximally effective communication"

(p. 670), or when a speakers tries to present information he or she has forgotten or never really knew.

Clarity of presentation is achieved through planning and organization as already explained. It is also achieved through practice of the suggestions provided by Rosenshine and Stephens (1986) in Figure 7.8. These suggestions are based on the review of the research of Brophy (1980); Emmer et al. (1982); Kennedy, Bush, Cruickshank, and Haefele (1978); and Lard and Smith (1979).

One of the learning aids at the end of this chapter has been designed to help you observe teacher clarity.

EXPLAINING LINKS AND EXAMPLES

Effective presentations contain precise and accurate explaining links and examples. According to Rosenshine (1971a) explaining links are prepositions and conjunctions that indicate the cause, result, means, or purpose of an event or idea. Examples of such links would include: because, since, in order to, if . . . then, therefore,

---

Figure 7.8   Aspects of Clear Presentation

1. Clarity of goals and main points
   a. State the goals or objectives of the presentation.
   b. Focus on one thought (point, direction) at a time.
   c. Avoid digressions.
   d. Avoid ambiguous phrases and pronouns.

2. Step-by-step presentations
   a. Present the material in small steps.
   b. Organize and present the material so that one point is mastered before the next point is given.
   c. Give explicit, step-by-step directions (when possible).
   d. Present an outline when the material is complex.

3. Specific and concrete procedures
   a. Model the skill or process (when appropriate).
   b. Give detailed and redundant explanations for difficult points.
   c. Provide students with concrete and varied examples.

4. Checking for students' understanding
   a. Be sure that students understand one point before proceeding to the next point.
   b. Ask the students questions to monitor their comprehension of what has been presented.
   c. Have students summarize the main points in their own words.
   d. Reteach the parts of the presentation that the students have difficulty comprehending, either by further teacher explanation or by students tutoring other students.

SOURCE: From B. Rosenshine and R. Stephens, Teaching functions. Reprinted with the permission of Macmillan Publishing Company from *Handbook of research on teaching*, 3d ed., M. C. Wittrock, ed. Copyright © 1985 by the American Educational Research Association.

and consequently. The use of explaining links helps students see the logic and relationships in a teacher's presentation and increases the likelihood of understanding.

Examples are another means used by successful presenters to make material meaningful to students. Good examples are, however, difficult for beginning teachers to think up and use. Hunter (1982) has provided the following guidelines that experienced teachers have found useful in selecting examples:

- Identify the critical attribute(s) of the present learning.
- Select from students' own lives some previous knowledge or experience that exemplifies the same critical attribute.
- Check your example for distractors.
- Present the example.
- Label the critical attributes or elements in the example.
- Present exceptions.

Presenting material clearly and using precise and accurate explaining links and examples requires that teachers thoroughly understand both the materials being presented and the structure of the subject area being taught. For the beginning teacher having trouble, no solution exists except studying the content and the subject until mastery is achieved.

RULE-EXAMPLE-RULE TECHNIQUE

A third technique used by effective presenters is the rule-example-rule technique. In this technique:

1. A key rule or principle, such as "prices in a free market are influenced by supply and demand," is presented.
2. Examples of this rule are provided, such as: "When Americans in the 1980s chose to use less oil (decrease in demand), and new oil fields were opened in coastal waters (increase in supply), the price of Middle Eastern oil went down." Or, "When there was a drought in the Midwest (decrease in supply), the price of corn went up."
3. The passage is concluded with a summary and restatement of the original rule: "So, as you can see, the fluctuation of supply along with people's desire for a product influence what the price of a product will be."

MAKING TRANSITIONS

Particularly in longer presentations, which contain several key ideas, effective presenters help learners move from one part of the lesson to another by using transitional statements. Sometimes a transitional statement may be used to alert listeners to important points just made such as, "Now let me summarize the important points for you before I move on." In other instances, a transitional statement telegraphs what is to follow such as, "We have just covered the important eras in Hemingway's life, let's now turn to how his involvement in the Spanish Civil War influenced his writings." Or, "Now that we know the purposes of a conjunction, let's see how they work in some sample sentences." Transitional statements are important because (1) they highlight the relationships among various ideas in a presentation and (2) they help display the internal organization of the information to learners.

ENTHUSIASM

As discussed in the research section, some evidence exists that points to the importance of enthusiasm as an influence on student learning. However, results are somewhat contradictory.

Enthusiasm Versus Theatrics Many teachers, particularly in secondary schools and colleges, argue that the key to effective presentation is for the presenter to use techniques and strategies borrowed from the performing arts. Books, in fact, have been written describing this approach, such as Timpson and Tobin's *Teaching as Performing* (1982). Emphasis is given to wit, energy, and charisma. Presentation is full of drama, anecdotes, and humor. The fact is that this type of presentation can produce a positive evaluation from student audiences without regard for learning outcomes. This was seen in one well-known study where a charismatic lecturer purposely gave an entertaining lecture without any real substance (see Naftulin et al., 1973) and got a very positive evaluation from a student audience. This type of presentation does not, however, necessarily lead to student acquisition of important information.

Although making presentations interesting and energizing for learners is desirable, the beginning teacher who has the skills to make such presentations should consider a note of caution. Too many theatrics may, in fact, detract from the key ideas a teacher is trying to convey and focus students' attention on the entertaining aspects of the presentation. However, this does *not* mean that teachers should not display enthusiasm for their subjects and/or for a particular lesson. There is a fine line between the teacher who uses humor, storytelling, and involvement to get major ideas across to students, and the teacher who uses the same techniques for their entertainment value. A learning aid at the end of this chapter will assist you in observing the use of teacher enthusiasm and in reflecting about this attribute of effective presentations.

4. EXTENDING AND STRENGTHENING STUDENT THINKING

Although an effective presentation will transmit new information to students, that is not the only goal for presenting and explaining information to students. In addition, teachers want students to use and strengthen their existing cognitive structures and to increase their ability to monitor their own thinking. The fourth phase in the syntax of the presentation model is designed to accomplish these important goals.

The best means for extending and strengthening student thinking following presentation of information is through classroom discourse, primarily by asking questions and having students discuss the preceding information. The techniques of asking good questions and conducting effective discussions are among the most difficult for beginning teachers to master and are the subject of the following sections.

QUESTIONING

Asking students questions is a key instructional strategy in most classrooms. Take for instance the following account of teacher questions provided by Gall and his colleagues (1971):

> Certainly teachers ask many questions during an average school day. A half-century ago, Stevens (1912) estimated that four-fifths of school time was occupied with question-and-answer recitations. Stevens found that a sample of high school teachers asked a mean number of 395 questions each day. High frequencies of question use by teachers were also found in recent investigations: ten primary-grade teachers asked an average of 348 questions each day during a school day (Floyd, 1960); twelve elementary-school teachers asked an average of 180 questions each in a science lesson (Moyer, 1966); and fourteen fifth-grade teachers asked an average of sixty-four questions each in a 30-minute social studies lesson (Schreiber, 1967).

As the beginning teacher approaches the task of question-asking, three features of effective questioning should be considered: the cognitive level of questions, the level of difficulty, and appropriate response to student answers.

Cognitive Level of Questions During the past two decades there have been many systems developed for classifying the cognitive level of teacher questions. Most of the classification systems have similarities and all consider questions in terms of the cognitive processing they require of students. Earlier Bloom's Taxonomy of Educational Objectives was introduced as a means for selecting content. This system can also be used by teachers to design questions for classroom discussion, as in Table 7.4. The table shows the six categories of classroom questions and examples for each that have been taken from a course on Higher-Level Questioning developed by the Far West Laboratory for Educational Research.

Using Different Levels of Questions Studies of teacher questions have consistently shown that well over 50 percent of all questions teachers ask are what Bloom would call knowledge or recall questions (Level One). These same studies have shown that less than 20 percent of teacher questions require higher-level thinking (Level Two and above).

Table 7.4   Question Types According to Bloom's Taxonomy

LEVEL	EXAMPLES OF QUESTIONS	COGNITIVE PROCESSES
Level 1: Knowledge	Where is Baghdad on your map? What is the meaning of longitude?	Recalling information
Level 2: Comprehension	What is this poem about? What is the difference between an acid and a base?	Organizing information
Level 3: Application	If Bill has 49 cents, how many 8-cent balloons can he buy?	Applying rules to solve problems
Level 4: Analysis	Why do you think the leaves have shriveled on this plant? What is the author's attitude about growing old?	Explain relationships and make inferences
Level 5: Synthesis	If school was not required, what would happen? If the boys in the story get in a fight, what do you think the parents will do?	Making predictions
Level 6: Evaluation	Should nuclear weapons be used by the United States? If you were mayor, which plan would you select?	Giving opinions and judging merit

SOURCE: Adapted from M. Gall et al. (1971), *Higher cognitive questions: Teachers handbook.* Beverly Hills, Calif.: Macmillan Educational Services, pp. 12–16.

The recommendation to beginning teachers would be to recognize that different questions require different types of thinking and that a good lesson should include both lower- and higher-level questions. One approach is to start by asking simple recall questions to see if students have grasped the basic ideas presented, followed by comprehension and analysis questions ("why" questions), and then concluding with evaluation questions about the content of a presentation and the students' own thinking processes. This latter set of questions will encourage students to look at the subject matter critically and to consider their own abilities to think about it.

Question Difficulty Level of difficulty refers to students' ability to answer questions correctly regardless of cognitive level. Research on this topic has also produced mixed results. The recommendations by Brophy and Good (1986) based on their review of the research were as follows:

1. It seems clear that most (perhaps three-fourths) of teachers' questions should elicit correct answers.

2. Most of the rest [of the questions] should elicit overt, substantive responses

[incorrect or incomplete answers] rather than failures to respond at all. (pp. 362–363)

These recommendations are consistent with practices of experienced, effective teachers. They know that if the level of questions asked is too difficult for most students in the class, they will be faced with either silence or with responses from only two or three of the most precocious students. They also know that when they are striving to extend students' thinking, particularly with complex content, questions must be sufficiently challenging and rewarding to students.

Wait Time A consistent finding in the research on teacher questioning is that many questions go unanswered because teachers, instead of waiting for student response, ask another question. However, research shows that waiting for student response is critical and is highly correlated with student achievement. (See, for example, Rowe, 1974a, 1974b)

There are probably several reasons why teachers do not provide sufficient time for students to respond. One, there is a strong cultural norm against silence. Silence is uncomfortable for many people and, consequently, they jump in to keep the conversation moving. Two, waiting for student response can be perceived by teachers as threatening to the pace and momentum of a lesson. Finally, silence or waiting can give noninvolved students opportunities to start talking or otherwise misbehaving. Although many contextual conditions influence "wait time," the general recommendations would be for beginning teachers to practice waiting at least two or three seconds for a student's response, to ask the question again or in a slightly different way if there is no response, and never to move on to a second question without some closure on the first. The amount of wait time should probably be less for direct recall questions and more for questions aimed at higher-level thinking and more complex cognitive content. A learning aid at the end of this chapter has been designed to help you observe teacher questioning and wait time.

CONDUCTING EFFECTIVE DISCUSSIONS

Teacher questioning is one way to extend student thinking and strengthen cognitive structures; open-ended discussions and interactions with the learning materials is another. The effective teacher should have strategies in his or her repertoire to facilitate student interactions with learning materials in both small groups and also in whole-class settings. Chapter 5 described several small group strategies. Here are some ideas about whole-class discussions.

Whole-Class Discussion Strategies For whole-class discussions to be successful requires some rather sophisticated communication and interaction skills and norms on the part of both teachers and students. As discussion leader, the teacher should be able to clearly focus the discussion, keep it on track by refocusing student digressions, and encourage participation by listening carefully to all ideas and points of view.

1. *Focusing discussions*. Many classroom discussions are characterized by talk and more talk, much of which has little to do with either the main aims of the lesson or with extending student thinking. An effective discussion, just like an effective presentation, is clearly focused and to the point. The teacher must ask a specific question or raise a specific issue associated with the learning materials that students can understand and respond to. Planning the focus question or issue is the key to getting a good discussion started.

2. *Refocusing discussions*. As a whole-class discussion proceeds, many circumstances can get it off the track. In some instances students will purposely try to get the teacher off the topic. One example might be students who want to talk about last Friday's ball game instead of the causes of World War I. This type of discussion is fine if that is the objective of the lesson, but it is not appropriate if the aim is to extend student thinking about the learning materials. A second example of wandering is when a student expresses an idea or raises a question that has nothing to do with the topic. This happens often, particularly with students who have trouble concentrating in school. It is also likely to happen with younger students who have not been taught good listening and discussion skills.

In both instances effective teachers acknowledge what students are doing—"We are now talking about last Friday night's game," or "You say your father had a good time in New York last weekend"—and then refocus the class's attention on the topic with a comment such as, "Talking about the game seems to be of great interest to all of you. I will let you do that during the last five minutes of the class period, but now I want us to get back to the question I posed to you." Or, "I know you are very interested in what your father did in New York, and I would love it if you would spend some time during lunch telling me more. Right now we want to talk about. . . ."

Just as teachers need to learn and practice discussion behaviors, so too do students. For successful classroom discussions to occur, students need to be taught discussion skills, and norms need to be established for discussion time. Many of the skills and procedures described in Chapter 5 are appropriate for use in helping students participate more effectively in whole-class discussions.

Postinstructional Tasks

Chapter 3 described a view of teaching that included preinstructional, during instruction, and postinstructional tasks. The most important postinstructional tasks connected to the presentation model are testing and grading students on the information presented. Tests and grades are perhaps the most important feedback that teachers give to students, to parents, and to others associated with the schools. In the special topic section on testing and evaluation that follows this chapter, some general issues on this topic are described; here the topic is discussed as it directly relates to the evaluation of student acquisition of knowledge.

APPROPRIATE TESTING AND GRADING PROCEDURES FOR THE MODEL

The presentation model is particularly adept at transmitting new information to students and at helping them retain that information. Therefore, the testing of students' knowledge acquisition and retention is the appropriate evaluation strategy for the model. This type of testing lends itself nicely to the paper and pencil tests with which you are very familiar. In testing for student knowledge, however, there are several factors that should be considered. Teachers should test at all levels of knowledge and not for simple recall of information. Go back and look at the various question types found in Table 7.4. Furthermore, teachers should communicate clearly to students what they will be tested on. Finally, it is better to test frequently than to wait for midterm or final testing periods, particularly with younger students.

Summary

This chapter has provided a detailed explanation of a teaching model for presenting and explaining information to students and described many techniques for its effective use. It has also provided important information about the way students process information, which is relevant for all the models of teaching.

The point of view has been taken that presentation by teachers is, and will remain, an important means of conveying new information to students and of helping them develop higher-level thinking skills. The research base on the effectiveness of the model is highly developed and supports specific practices such as using advance organizers, connecting new information to students' prior knowledge, and lecturing with clarity, economy, and power.

Effective use of the model, whether in a short ten-minute talk or a series of hour-long formal presentations, requires extensive preparation by the teacher and critical decisions about what to include and exclude. Awareness of the way knowledge is organized provides one means for making these decisions. Knowledge of students' prior learning and intellectual development provides another.

Clarity of presentation is perhaps the most important element in conducting a lesson aimed at presenting and explaining information. Clarity depends on both the teacher's preparation and the teacher's general mastery of the subject matter being presented. No shortcuts are available for teachers who do not know their subjects well or who are unprepared.

Extending student thinking about information given in a presentation requires classroom discourse, a difficult operation for most beginning teachers. Learning to conduct small group and whole-class discussions is important, and equally important is learning how to teach students the skills of effective classroom discourse.

Students will learn what is expected of them and, consequently, testing of the ideas is very critical. If teacher testing is limited to the recall of specific information, that is what students will learn. If teachers require higher-level cognitive processing on their tests, students will also learn to do that.

Books for the Professional

Bloom, B. S., et al. (Eds.). (1956). *Taxonomy of educational objectives, handbook I: Cognitive domain*. New York: David McKay. The original book on Bloom's taxonomy. It provides a history of the taxonomy's development along with detailed rationale and examples.

Bruner, J. (1960). *The process of education*. Cambridge, Mass.: Harvard University Press. A classic that influenced the curriculum reform movement of the 1960s, particularly in regard to the "structure of knowledge."

Gagné, E. D. (1985). *The cognitive psychology of school learning*. Boston: Little, Brown. An excellent review of the research in cognitive psychology with particular attention on learning and how teachers can use this research in their day-to-day instruction.

CHAPTER 7
LEARNING AIDS FOR PLANNING, OBSERVATION, AND REFLECTION

- Assessing My Presentation Skills
- Lesson Plan for Presentation
- Observing a Presentation
- Observing Teacher Clarity
- Observing Teacher Enthusiasm
- Observing Teacher Use of Questions

Included in Part 3 are learning aids to assist you in thinking about and developing your skill in presenting information. To that end, the first learning aid provides you with an opportunity to assess your overall knowledge and level of skill. Further aids provide opportunities for more refined practice and reflection. For example, the second aid suggests a format for making a lesson plan using this teaching model and asks you to consider its effectiveness and make any modifications that you deem necessary. Another aid (the fourth) focuses on teacher clarity, an important characteristic of effective presentations.

The aids for each chapter in Part 3 follow a similar format: first, a general assessment of your skill level, followed by more focused and refined looks at important components of the model.

ASSESSING MY PRESENTATION SKILLS

PURPOSE: This aid provides an overall indication of your skill in the presentation model. The key components of the model, as given from page 283 to page 293 in the text, have been highlighted here. This could be used just after reading the chapter to pinpoint areas of confusion or after a practice presentation to assess your own performance.

DIRECTIONS: Check the level of skill you perceive that you have for the various teaching tasks associated with the presentation model.

Skill or Competency	Level of Effectiveness		
	High	Medium	Low
Preinstructional Tasks			
Choosing content	_____	_____	_____
Determining prior knowledge of students	_____	_____	_____
Selecting an advance organizer	_____	_____	_____
Instructional Tasks			
Phase 1			
Explaining goals and rationale	_____	_____	_____
Establishing set	_____	_____	_____
Phase 2			
Presenting the advance organizer	_____	_____	_____
Phase 3			
Presenting the learning materials			
Clarity	_____	_____	_____
Explaining links and examples	_____	_____	_____
Enthusiasm	_____	_____	_____
Phase 4			
Extending and strengthening thinking			
Questioning	_____	_____	_____
Conducting discussions	_____	_____	_____
Postinstructional Tasks			
Testing and grading	_____	_____	_____
Assessing my own performance	_____	_____	_____

LESSON PLAN FOR PRESENTATION

PURPOSE: This is a suggested format for making a lesson plan tailored specifically to the presentation model. You can try it out as you plan a presentation microteaching assignment or in field placements. As you do so, maintain an attitude of flexibility and experimentation; revise the format as you see the need.

DIRECTIONS: Follow the guidelines below as you plan a presentation lesson.

Planning Phase

Content to be taught: _____

_____

Advance organizer: _____

_____

Objectives

1. Given _____ , the student will be able to
   (situation)

   _____ with
   (action or behavior)

   _____ .
   (level of performance)

2. Given _____ , the student will be able to
   (situation)

   _____ with
   (action or behavior)

   _____ .
   (level of performance)

Conducting the Lesson

Time	Phase and Activities	Materials
_____	Lesson goals, rationale, and set: _____	
	_____	
	_____	
_____	Advance organizer: _____	
	_____	
	_____	

—— Presenting information: _____

_____

_____

—— Extending student thinking: _____

_____

_____

Pitfalls to Avoid

During Introduction   **During Transitions**   **During Ending**

Analysis and Reflection: How well did this format work for you? Did some elements present seem to be extraneous to you? Did some absent elements seem important? How will you revise this format the next time you give a presentation? Write a paragraph in response to these questions.

OBSERVING A PRESENTATION

PURPOSE: This aid, which highlights the key components of the presentation model, can be used to observe peers in a microteaching class or in field observations and for purposes of providing feedback. It will sharpen your own understanding of what it means to give a good presentation.

DIRECTIONS: As you observe the lesson, make a "tick" for the category you believe best describes the level of performance for each of the teaching moves associated with the presentation model.

Teaching Move or Activity	Level of Performance			
	High	Average	Low	Not Needed
Preinstructional Tasks				
The teacher's choice of content made sense.	_____	_____	_____	_____
Content was tailored to students' prior knowlege.	_____	_____	_____	_____
The teacher had a clear advance organizer.	_____	_____	_____	_____
Instructional Tasks				
Phase 1				
The teacher explained goals and rationale.	_____	_____	_____	_____
The teacher established set.	_____	_____	_____	_____
Phase 2				
The teacher provided the advance organizer.	_____	_____	_____	_____
Phase 3				
The presentation was done with clarity.	_____	_____	_____	_____
The teacher used explaining links and examples.	_____	_____	_____	_____
The teacher had enthusiasm.	_____	_____	_____	_____
Phase 4				
The teacher extended and strengthened student thinking.	_____	_____	_____	_____
Postinstructional Tasks				
The teacher tested and evaluated appropriately.	_____	_____	_____	_____

The teacher assessed his or her own
performance.   _____ _____ _____ _____

Analysis and Reflection: For every item you checked "yes," write out what the teacher actually did or said that showed that task had been accomplished. For every item you checked "no," write what the teacher could have done to have accomplished that task.

OBSERVING TEACHER CLARITY

PURPOSE: This aid refines understanding of how to achieve clarity. As described in the chapter (see page 285 to page 286), clarity has several ingredients, such as checking for student understanding and avoiding vagueness. These ingredients are listed below.

DIRECTIONS: Observe a teacher during a presentation for 10 or 15 minutes, then check how effectively you feel the teacher incorporated these indicators of clarity into his or her presentation.

	Level of Effectiveness			
Indicators of Clarity	High	Medium	Low	Not Done
Stated objectives	_____	_____	_____	_____
Made content organization explicit	_____	_____	_____	_____
Used explaining links	_____	_____	_____	_____
Gave appropriate examples	_____	_____	_____	_____
Used the rule-example-rule technique	_____	_____	_____	_____
Used a variety of media	_____	_____	_____	_____
Made smooth transitions from one point to the next	_____	_____	_____	_____
Checked with students to verify understanding	_____	_____	_____	_____
Avoided vagueness	_____	_____	_____	_____
Other (specify)				
_____	_____	_____	_____	
_____	_____	_____	_____	

Analysis and Reflection: Write specific examples from the teacher's presentation that reflect each indicator of clarity. Can you apply any of these examples to your own subject area or grade level? How might you adapt the others to fit your subject or grade level? Keep these ideas on file for future use.

OBSERVING TEACHER ENTHUSIASM

PURPOSE: As discussed on page 288, enthusiasm is an important part of lecturing, but should not be confused with theatrics. Enthusiasm makes learning exciting, but theatrics can interfere with learning. The following elements of enthusiasm were taken from Collins (1978). This tool is intended to demonstrate in concrete ways how enthusiasm can be communicated to students.

DIRECTIONS: Observe a teacher during a presentation for about 10 to 20 minutes, then check how effectively you feel the teacher incorporated the following elements of enthusiasm.

Elements of Enthusiasm	Level of Effectiveness			
	High	Medium	Low	Not Done
Vocal Delivery Varied, lilting, uplifting intonations, many changes in tone, pitch	____	____	____	____
Eyes Shining, frequently opened wide, eyebrows raised, eye contact with total group	____	____	____	____
Gestures Frequent movements of body, head, arms, hands and face, sweeping motions, clapping hands, head nodding rapidly	____	____	____	____
Movements Large body movements, swings around, changes pace, bends body	____	____	____	____
Facial Expression Changes denoting surprise, sadness, joy, thoughtfulness, awe, excitement	____	____	____	____
Word Selection Highly descriptive, many adjectives, great variety	____	____	____	____
Acceptance of Ideas and Feelings Accepts ideas and feelings quickly with vigor and animation, ready to accept, praise, encourage or clarify in a nonthreatening manner, many variations in responding to pupils	____	____	____	____

Overall Energy   _____ _____ _____ _____
   High degree of spirit throughout lesson

Analysis and Reflection: Did any elements of enthusiasm seem more important than others in communicating excitement for learning? Which elements do you think most easily suit your own personality? Which elements do you think need improvement?

SOURCE: Adapted from M. L. Collins (1978), Effects of enthusiasm training on preservice elementary teachers. *Journal of Teacher Education, 29,* 53–57.

OBSERVING TEACHER USE OF QUESTIONS

PURPOSE: In order to extend and strengthen student thinking, teachers need to have good questioning skills. This aid is to help you analyze teachers' use of questions, such as number of questions asked, cognitive level of questions, and wait time.

DIRECTIONS: There is a column labeled *Code*, another labeled *Question No.*, and other columns labeled *A, B, C,* and *D*. The *Code* column is your key for determining what code goes in each column. For the first question the teacher asks, go to the *Question No.* column and find *1*. Then read across to column *A* and code in that column the level of question that the teacher asked—a knowledge question would be coded *1*, an application question *3*, and so on. Then code in column *B* for question *1* the appropriate wait time code. Follow the same procedure for columns *C* and *D*, and repeat the procedure for each question the teacher asks.

Code

A. Level of question
  1. Knowledge
     Can the students recall what they have seen, heard, or read? E.g., What is the meaning of *longitude*?
  2. Comprehension
     Can the student organize facts in various ways? E.g., What is the main idea in this paragraph?
  3. Application
     Can the student apply techniques and rules to solve problems that have single correct answers? E.g., If Bill has 49 cents, how many 8-cent balloons can he buy?
  4. Analysis
     Can the student explain relationships, make inferences, and find examples to support generalizations? E.g., Religion was the focal point of life in the Middle Ages. What have you read that supports this idea?
  5. Synthesis
     Can the student make predictions, solve problems, or produce original communications? E.g., If school were not required, what would happen?

Question No.	A	B	C	D
1.	___	___	___	___
2.	___	___	___	___
3.	___	___	___	___
4.	___	___	___	___
5.	___	___	___	___
6.	___	___	___	___
7.	___	___	___	___
8.	___	___	___	___
9.	___	___	___	___
10.	___	___	___	___
11.	___	___	___	___
12.	___	___	___	___
13.	___	___	___	___
14.	___	___	___	___
15.	___	___	___	___
16.	___	___	___	___
17.	___	___	___	___
18.	___	___	___	___

Code	Question No.	A	B	C	D
	19.	___	___	___	___
	20.	___	___	___	___

6. Evaluation
   Can the student give opinions about issues, and judge the merit of ideas, problem-solutions, art, and other products? E.g., Do you agree that honesty is always the best policy?
7. Rephrasing the previous question, cuing.

B. Wait time
   1. Teacher paused a few seconds *before* calling on student.
   2. Teacher paused a few seconds *after* calling on student.
   3. Teacher did not pause.
   4. Not applicable; student answered readily.

C. Level of difficulty.
   1. Student response was accepted by teacher.
   2. Response was not accepted by teacher.

D. Teacher response to student answers.
   1. Teacher gave a brief acknowledgment of correct answer.
   2. Teacher gave gushy praise.
   3. Student error was "dignified."
   4. Student error was handled inappropriately.

Comments:

_____

_____

Tallies: Count up the number of codes in each category.

A Totals	B Totals	C Totals	D Totals
1. _____	1. _____	1. _____	1. _____
2. _____	2. _____	2. _____	2. _____
3. _____	3. _____		3. _____
4. _____	4. _____		4. _____
5. _____			
6. _____			
7. _____			

Analysis and Reflection: When you reflect on this observation and the results you obtained, think about whether the questions were appropriate for the lesson. If not, what questions would have been appropriate? Were higher-order questions used? Did you observe wait time? If not, what obstacles do you suspect accounted for this? What can you do to prevent similar obstacles from interfering with your ability to use good questioning skills? Write a paragraph on your thoughts about questioning.

SOURCES: The codes concerning level of questions were adapted from M. D. Gall, B. Dunning, and R. Weathersby (1971), *Higher cognitive questioning*. Beverly Hills, Cal: Macmillan Educational Services, pp. 12–16. The format for the coding system was adapted from *Looking in classroom* by T. L. Good and J. E. Brophy © 1984 by Harper & Row, Inc. Reprinted by permission of the publisher.

Testing and Evaluation

A recent review (Shaefer and Lissitz, 1987) reported that teachers spend as much as 10 percent of their time on matters related to the testing and evaluation of student progress. Many of the matters associated with testing and evaluation, particularly the theory and techniques of measurement, are complex and beyond the scope of this book. There are, however, several features of this important teaching function that are rather straightforward and easy to grasp. Describing key concepts and procedures for testing and evaluating student progress are the purposes of this special topic section.

SCHOOL-WIDE USE OF STANDARDIZED TESTS

Currently, it is common practice for school systems to use standardized tests to diagnose and evaluate student academic progress. In larger school systems whole units of specially trained personnel exist to coordinate and manage this important educational activity. It is a rare school in which students are not tested, at least on a yearly basis, in such topics as study skills, reading, language acquisition, mathematical operations, verbal reasoning, and concept development. Some schools use tests developed and distributed by national test publishers. Others use tests developed and distributed by state or district testing authorities. For example, there appears to be a growing trend to require all students to pass a state-mandated functional literacy test before they are granted a high school diploma. The results of testing are used to make judgments about the effectiveness of schools and teachers and, most importantly, test results are used to decide the future educational and job opportunities available to students.

Most beginning teachers will not be required to select the tests to be used on a school-wide basis, nor will they be held responsible for the administration, scoring, or initial interpretation of these tests. They will, however, be expected to understand the nontechnical nature of the testing program, and they will be expected to use test results and communicate these clearly to students and their parents. This requires beginning teachers to have some understanding of the nature of testing and its key concepts.

Standardized Tests

Standardized tests, as contrasted to tests made by teachers, have been designed and valiadated by professional test makers for specific purposes such as measuring academic achievement or literacy levels. They can normally be administered in many different settings and still produce reliable information. In some instances, standardized tests also describe how some nationwide "norm group" performed on the test, thus providing a basis of comparison for students subsequently taking the test. Examples of standardized tests include the Stanford Achievement Test, the California Achievement Test, or the well-known Scholastic Aptitude Test (SAT) used by many colleges and universities in making entrance selections. Many of you took the SAT and soon will be taking the National Teachers Exam (NTE), which is another example of a standardized test.

Norm-Referenced and Criterion-Referenced Tests

Today, two major types of standardized tests are used to measure student abilities and achievement. These are called norm-referenced and criterion-referenced tests. It is important to understand the differences between these two approaches to testing and to be able to communicate to others the assumptions and the advantages and disadvantages of each approach.

Norm-referenced tests attempt to evaluate a particular student's performance in relation to the performance of some other defined group of students. Most of the achievement tests you undoubtedly took as students were norm-referenced. Your score told you how you performed on some specific topic or skill in comparison with students from a national population who served as the "norming" group for the test. Most norm-referenced tests produce two types of scores—a raw score and a percentile rank. The raw score is the number of items on the test a student answered correctly. The percentile-rank score is a statistical device that shows how a student compares to others, specifically the proportion of individuals who had the same or lower raw scores for a particular section of the test. Table S3.1 shows how raw scores are typically converted to percentile ranks on standardized, norm-referenced tests.

By studying two raw scores in the example above, the relationship between the raw score and percentile rank becomes clear. For example, look at the student who answered 38 out of the 48 test items correctly. You can see that this score gave the student a percentile rank of 71, meaning that 71 percent of the students in the norm group scored 38 or lower on the test. If you look at the student who had a raw score of 30 on the test, you can see this converts to a percentile score of 22, meaning that only 22 percent of the students in the norm group scored 30 or below.

Whereas norm-referenced tests measure student performance against that of other students, *criterion-referenced tests* measure it against some agreed upon level of performance, the performance criterion. To show the major difference between a norm-referenced and criterion-referenced test, take the example of a simple skill

Table S3.1 Conversion of Raw Scores to Percentile Ranks

RAW SCORE	PERCENTILE RANK	RAW SCORE	PERCENTILE RANK
48		34	44
47		33	40
46		32	36
45	99+	31	30
44	96	30	22
43	93	29	18
42	90	28	15
40	81	27	11
39	76	26	7
38	71	25	4
37	65	24	3
36	56	23	1
35	49	22	1−

SOURCE: From W. R. Borg and M. D. Gall (1983), *Educational research: An introduction*. (4 Edition). Copyright © 1983 by Longman Inc. All rights reserved.

like running the 100-yard dash. If a runner was compared to a larger group of runners using concepts from norm-referenced testing, the tester would report that a student who ran the 100-yard dash in 13 seconds was in the 65th percentile for all other students in his or her age group. Using concepts from criterion-referenced testing, the tester would report that the established goal for running a 100-yard dash was 12 seconds, and the student can now run it in 13 seconds.

Normally the content and skills are much more specific on criterion-referenced tests than on norm-referenced tests, and obviously each provides different types of information for teachers to use. Figures S3.1 and S3.2 illustrate some of these differences.

Notice that the criterion-referenced test indicates the level of mastery for very specific word-attack skills as contrasted to the more general category of reading comprehension found in the norm-referenced test. Note also that results from the norm-referenced tests are reported in percentile ranks, whereas the results on the criterion-referenced test show the degree to which a particular student has mastered a specific word-attack skill.

Advantages and Disadvantages of Different Approaches

If the teacher is interested in how his or her students compared to students elsewhere, results from norm-referenced tests are obviously the best to use. Norm-referenced tests allow comparisons within a particular school, district, or state. For example, achievement levels in all third grades in a particular district might be compared with those from other districts. Norm-referenced tests, however, will not tell very much about how well a specified set of school or teacher objectives are being accomplished, nor will they tell how students are currently doing in comparison to past performance on locally derived objectives.

Criterion-referenced tests, on the other hand, can provide information about a student's level of performance in relation to some specified body of knowledge or list of agreed upon objectives. The results of criterion-referenced tests, however, do not allow for comparisons of students in a particular locale with national norms. More and more schools and teachers are using criterion-referenced tests because their information is better for diagnosing student difficulties and for assessing the degree to which school-wide or system-wide purposes are being achieved.

Communication of Test Results

It is important that teachers be able to explain the results of both norm-referenced and criterion-referenced tests in honest and straightforward ways. They may be asked to go over test scores with students, to explain test results to parents and to interpret test scores that are published in the newspaper. Students and their parents need to know that a single score on a test does not pretend to measure all aspects of a person's abilities. At the same time, they need to know how standardized tests scores are used to make decisions that can affect students' lives.

Community members often need to be reminded of the strengths and limitations of particular testing programs and of the assumptions underlying all standardized tests. Educators have not done a very good job of explaining, in nontechnical ways, the assumptions behind norm-referenced tests and the limitations of the tests for judging the effectiveness of a particular school's educational

Figure S3.1   Student Profile on Selected Topics of the California Achievement Test

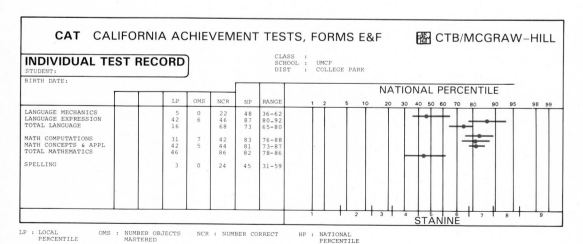

SOURCE: From B. S. Bloom, T. J. Hastings, and G. F. Madaus, *Handbook on formative and summative evaluation of student learning*, p. 104. Copyright 1971 McGraw-Hill. Used with permission.

program. Knowledgeable teachers can find ways to communicate to parents and others that norm-referenced tests only compare students against a norm group and do not necessarily provide a good measure for how well a particular teacher, school, or system is achieving particular objectives. Teachers can also communicate to parents and community members that students' native abilities help determine how well they do on standardized tests and that a school with a predominance of low-ability students will never perform as well as schools with a predominance of high-ability students.

TEACHER TESTING AND GRADING

Beginning teachers have the major responsibility for the testing and grading of students within their classrooms. They must attend to the major purposes of classroom testing and evaluation: diagnosing students' prior knowledge, providing corrective feedback, and making judgments about student achievement. These three purposes have some similarities but also some important differences.

Diagnosing Students' Prior Knowledge

To individualize instruction for specific students or to tailor instruction for a particular classroom group requires reliable information about students' capabilities

Figure S3.2   Level of Mastery of Various Word-Attack Skills

Word-Attack Skills									
	Beginning sounds	Final sounds	Blends	Rhyming	Long–short vowels	Other vowels	Syllabication	Prefixes and suffixes	Root words
Ricardo	Near mastery	Near mastery	Near mastery	Near mastery	Skill not learned yet	Skill not learned yet	Mastery	Skill not learned yet	Near mastery
Anthony	Skill not learned yet	Skill not learned yet	Skill not learned yet	Skill not learned yet	Skill not learned yet	Skill not learned yet	Near mastery	Skill not learned yet	Skill not learned yet
Sharon	Skill not learned yet	Skill not learned yet	Skill not learned yet	Skill not learned yet	Skill not learned yet	Skill not learned yet	Skill not learned yet	Skill not learned yet	Skill not learned yet
Brenda	Skill not learned yet	Skill not learned yet	Skill not learned yet	Skill not learned yet	Near mastery	Skill not learned yet	Near mastery	Skill not learned yet	Mastery
Barbara	Skill not learned yet	Near mastery	Skill not learned yet	Skill not learned yet	Skill not learned yet	Skill not learned yet	Skill not learned yet	Skill not learned yet	Skill not learned yet
Earlie	Near mastery	Skill not learned yet	Skill not learned yet	Skill not learned yet	Skill not learned yet	Skill not learned yet	Skill not learned yet	Skill not learned yet	Near mastery

☐ = Mastery   ■ = Near mastery   ▨ = Skill not learned yet

SOURCE: From B. S. Bloom, T. J. Hastings, and G. F. Madaus, *Handbook on formative and summative evaluation of student learning*, p. 104. Copyright 1971 McGraw-Hill. Used with permission.

and their prior knowledge. It also requires information about the students' existing schema. The previously described norm- and criterion-referenced standardized tests attempt to measure many areas of student achievement but are most highly developed and most readily available in reading, language development, and mathematics. Unfortunately they are less available for other topics.

In many school systems, a beginning teacher will be assisted by test and measurement personnel or by counseling and special education staff who have been specifically trained to help diagnose student capabilities and achievements. In other school systems this type of assistance may not be available. If good, formal diagnostic information is not available, beginning teachers will have to rely on the informal techniques for assessing prior knowledge described in Chapter 7. For example, teachers can observe students closely as they approach a particular task and get some sense about how difficult or easy that particular task is for them. Similarly, by listening carefully to students and asking probing questions, additional cues about students' levels of prior knowledge can be ascertained on almost any topic.

Testing to Provide Corrective Feedback

A second important purpose of testing and evaluation is to provide students with feedback on how they are doing. As with the case of diagnosing students' prior knowledge, this is easier to do for some topics and skills than for others. Test makers have developed sophisticated and reliable procedures for measuring discrete skills such as word recognition or simple mathematical operations. It is also quite easy to collect information on how fast a student can run the 100-yard dash or how long it takes to climb a 30-foot rope. Biofeedback techniques are also available to help students monitor their own physical reactions to stress and certain types of exertion. However, as instruction moves from a focus on basic skills and abilities to more complex thinking and problem-solving skills, the problem of providing corrective feedback becomes more difficult because there are few, if any, reliable tests for them.

Chapter 10 provides some principles for giving feedback to students and explains the importance of feedback for student improvement. It also emphasizes that for corrective feedback to be useful it must be immediate, frequent, and communicated in nonjudgmental ways.

Testing for Reporting

Perhaps it should not be so, but beginning teachers will spend most of their test time and energy on testing students for the purpose of determining grades and reporting progress. Many teachers report that they do not like this aspect of their work, but it must be done and done well for two important reasons. First, as described in Chapter 5, students expect their work to be evaluated. In fact, one very important feature of classroom life is the traditional exchange that takes place there—students performing academic work for grades provided by the teacher. Teachers who take this work-for-grade exchange lightly, or who do it poorly, usually are faced with serious classroom problems.

Second, the larger society has assigned the job of making judgments about student achievement and ability to teachers. How well students perform on tests, the grades they receive, and the judgments their teachers make about their work and ability have important, long-run consequences. These factors can determine whether or not students go to college, the lifestyle they maintain, the type of entry level jobs they eventually obtain, and most important, their self-concepts. Although societies of the future may find other, and perhaps fairer, ways to make these decisions, today this sorting function is placed squarely in the hands of teachers. Teachers who do not take this function seriously are doing their students a great disservice.

Key concepts and procedures associated with the three major purposes of classroom testing are summarized in Table S3.2.

Table S3.2   Similarities and Differences Between Three Testing Purposes

	TYPE OF TESTING		
	DIAGNOSTIC	FEEDBACK	REPORTING
Function	Placement, planning and determining the presence or absence of skills and prior knowledge	Feedback to student and teachers on progress	Grading of students at the end of a unit or semester
When Used	At the outset of a unit, semester, or year or during instruction when student is having problems	During instruction	At the end of quarter, semester, or year's work
Type of Test	Standardized diagnostic tests Observations and checklists	Quizzes and special tests or homework	Final exams
Scoring	Norm- and criterion-referenced	Criterion-referenced	Norm- or criterion-referenced

SOURCE: Adapted from B. S. Bloom, T. J. Hastings, and G. F. Madaus, *Handbook on formative and summative evaluation of student learning*, pp. 91–92. Copyright 1971 McGraw-Hill. Used with permission.

Grading

The logic behind norm-referenced and criterion-referenced testing also applies to the two major approaches to grading. The concept of "grading on a curve" is a commonly used procedure in secondary schools and colleges where students compete with each other for positions along a predetermined grading curve. A teacher following a strict interpretation of the concept "grading on a curve" would give 10 percent of the students A's, 20 percent B's, 40 percent C's, 20 percent D's and 10 percent F's. Under this grading scheme, even students with a high degree of mastery over the testing material sometimes fall into one of the lower grading areas and vice versa.

An alternate approach to grading on a curve is grading to "criterion or mastery." Teachers using this approach define rather precisely the content and skills objectives for their class and then measure student performance against that criterion. For example, in spelling, the teacher might decide that the correct spelling of 100 specified words constitutes mastery. Student grades would then be determined and performance reported in terms of the percentage of the 100 words a student can spell correctly. A teacher using this approach might specify the following grading scale: A = 100 to 93 words spelled correctly; B = 92 to 85 words spelled correctly; C = 84 to 75 words spelled correctly; D = 74 to 65 words spelled correctly; and F = 64 words spelled correctly or below.

Data in Table S3.3 illustrate the differences between these two approaches for a particular group of students.

As can be observed, the approaches produce different grades for individuals within the same class of students. Both grading on a curve and grading on mastery

Table S3.3 Assigning Spelling Grades From Test Scores Using Two Approaches

	GRADING ON A CURVE		GRADING TO CRITERION	
Eric	98	A	98	A
Mary	97		97	
Dick	96	B	96	
John	96		96	
Jordon	96		96	
Sam	95		95	
Denise	92	C	92	B
William	90		90	
Richard	90		90	
Elizabeth	90		90	
Betty	87		87	
Marcos	87		87	
Martha	86		86	
Tom	83		83	C
Bob	80	D	80	
Ruth	78		78	
Beth	73		73	D
Lane	69		69	
Mark	50	F	50	F
Helen	50		50	

present some troublesome dilemmas for teachers. When grading on a curve the teacher is confronted with questions about the relationship of grades to native ability. For example, should 10 percent of a class of very able students be given *F*'s? Should 10 percent of a class of very slow students be given *A*'s? Criterion testing and grading also present troublesome issues for teachers. If criterion levels are set in relation to what is realistic for a particular group of students, then able students should be expected to perform more work and at higher levels than their less talented peers. However, when grades are assigned, the question arises, Should students who complete all work accurately, even though it is at a lower level, be given the same grade as students who complete all work accurately at a higher level?

Some schools and teachers have tried to resolve this dilemma by using a criterion-referenced report card where numbers are assigned or where teachers describe how students are doing for the whole list of objectives for a course. No single grade is assigned. This approach is also not trouble free for teachers. Many parents are accustomed to the five-letter grading scale because it is what they experienced when they were in school. Departures are confusing to them. Also, since a student's GPA is traditionally used to determine admission to colleges and jobs, it is difficult to report a long list of performance measures that people in the outside world can easily interpret.

Guidelines for Testing and Grading Student Progress

This special topic section concludes with four important guidelines that can assist beginning teachers as they approach the task of working out their own testing and grading procedures.

1. TEST AT ALL LEVELS

A common mistake made by some teachers in testing students is to focus most test items on simple recall of information. It is easier to write and score this type of question because there is usually a single correct answer. However, if the teacher wants to extend student thinking and promote higher-level thought processes, then test questions must require higher-level thinking. Bloom's taxonomy, described in Chapter 7, is an excellent device to assist the beginning teacher in constructing test items at various levels.

2. COMMUNICATE CLEARLY TO STUDENTS WHAT THEY WILL BE TESTED ON

A favorite question from students is, "Is this going to be on the test?" Effective teachers make it very clear to students which of the ideas presented in a lecture or found in the textbook will be included on the test. Some teachers will write key ideas from a lecture on the board or give them to students in a handout. Some provide the same type of tool for information in the text. This communicates to students exactly what they are responsible for on the test. Other teachers spend time in review, outlining key ideas to be covered on the test. Still others provide study sheets with sample questions. The goal in each case is to alert students to what is expected of them.

Effective teachers also communicate to students the various levels of knowledge that they will need to demonstrate and the amount of detail expected. If the students are expected to commit a list of facts to memory, they are told so; if they are expected to evaluate one idea and contrast it with another, they are told so. Starting with the fifth or sixth grades, students can be taught Bloom's classification system and can use it as a guide for their own study, just as teachers use it as a guide for test construction.

3. TEST FREQUENTLY

Some teachers will wait until the end of an instructional unit to test students' knowledge acquisition. It is better to test students frequently for two reasons. First, frequent tests pressure students to keep up with what they are learning and provide them with feedback on how they are doing. Second, frequent testing provides the teacher with feedback on how students are doing on the various ideas taught and allows reteaching of ideas students are not learning.

4. MAKE GRADING PROCEDURES EXPLICIT

Regardless of the approach a teacher chooses to use in assigning grades, the exact procedures should be written down and should be communicated clearly to students and to their parents. Taking the mystery out of grading is one way to help students accomplish the work expected of them and also a means of getting students to see the "fairness" of the grading system.

Books for the Professional

Bloom, B. S., Hastings, T. J., and Madaus, G. F. (1971). *Handbook on formative and summative evaluation of student learning.* New York: McGraw-Hill. Although intended for more advanced study, this book is clearly written and contains many helpful examples on issues associated with testing and grading student learning.

TenBrink, T. D. (1986). Evaluation. In J. M. Cooper, (Ed.). *Classroom teaching skills.* (Third edition). Lexington, Mass.: D. C. Heath. This is an excellent presentation of concrete steps for teachers to follow in their efforts to evaluate students.

CHAPTER 8

MAIN IDEAS

- Concepts are the basic building blocks around which people organize their thinking and communication.
- Concept learning is the key to understanding any subject.
- Concept learning involves the acquisition of conceptual knowledge and procedural knowledge.
- The three concept teaching models presented in this chapter are direct presentation, concept formation, and concept attainment.
- None of these approaches to concept teaching is superior to the others. Each has been developed with specific objectives in mind, and each must be adapted to suit the teacher's instructional style and student needs.
- Research shows that the presentation and sequencing of examples and the use of best examples, visual or mental images, and graphic organizers all promote the learning of concepts.
- Teaching concepts effectively requires teachers to match their testing and evaluation programs to the model's particular goals and objectives.

Teaching Concepts for Higher-Level Thinking

RICHARD JANTZ

Most experienced teachers would agree that conveying information to students is very important but that teaching students how to think is even more important. Experienced teachers also know that concepts are the basic building blocks for thinking, particularly higher-level thinking, in any subject. Concepts allow individuals to classify objects and ideas and to derive rules and principles; they provide the foundations for the idea networks that guide our thinking. The process of learning concepts begins at an early age and continues throughout life as people develop more and more complex concepts, both in school and out. The learning of concepts is crucial in schools and in everyday life, because concepts allow mutual understanding among people and provide the basis for verbal interaction.

The focus of this chapter is on concept teaching and how teachers can help students attain and develop the basic concepts needed for further learning and higher-level thinking. The first section deals with the nature of concepts and their importance in education. The next sections provide a brief overview of three approaches to concept teaching and summarize research that underlies and supports these concept teaching models. The final section describes specific teaching and evaluation procedures associated with these three approaches to concept teaching.

PERSPECTIVE AND RATIONALE

"Ball." "Chair." "Box." "Table." "Crayon." Kim is naming things, and placing objects into groups or classes. She is developing concepts. Combining something concrete, such as a ball, with an abstract quality, such as roundness, enables Kim to identify classes of objects that differ from each other. By repeatedly sorting and classifying different balls she can eventually form an abstract concept for these similar objects that allows her to think about them and, eventually, to communicate with others about them.

The Nature of Concepts

In everyday usage the term *concept* is used in several ways. Sometimes it refers to an idea someone has, such as "My concept of how a president should act is straightforward." At other times it is used like a hypothesis, for example, "My concept is that we are always in debt because we spend too much on frills." When the term *concept* is used in connection with teaching and learning it has a more precise meaning and refers to the way knowledge and experience are categorized.

Concept learning is essentially "putting things into a class" and then being able to recognize members of that class (R. M. Gagné, 1985, p. 95). This requires that an individual be able to take a particular case, such as his or her pet dog Lucky Lady, and place it into a general class of objects, in this case a class termed *dog*, that share certain attributes. This process requires making judgments about whether a particular case is an instance of a larger class.

CONCEPTS HAVE DEFINITIONS AND LABELS

All concepts have names or labels and more or less precise definitions. For example, a relatively small body of land surrounded on all sides by water is labeled an island. Labels and definitions permit mutual understanding and communication with others using the concept. They are prerequisites for concept teaching and learning.

CONCEPTS HAVE CRITICAL ATTRIBUTES

Concepts also have attributes that describe and help define them. Some attributes are *critical* and are used to separate one concept from all others. For example, an equilateral triangle is a triangle with three equal sides. The critical attributes are that it must be a triangle and that each of the sides must be equal. Triangles without three equal sides are not equilateral triangles. In addition, if the concept is a subset of a broader concept, then it must also include the critical attributes of the broader concept. An equilateral triangle is a member of the class of concepts called triangles and thus must contain all the critical attributes of a triangle.

CONCEPTS HAVE NONCRITICAL ATTRIBUTES

Some attributes may be found in some but not in all members of the class. These are called *noncritical attributes*. For example, size is a noncritical attribute of an equilateral triangle. All concepts have both critical and noncritical attributes and it is sometimes difficult for students to differentiate between the two. For example, the concept of bird is typically associated in most people's minds with the noncritical attribute, flying. Robins, cardinals, eagles, and most other birds can fly. Flying, however, is not a critical attribute of birds since ostriches and penguins cannot fly. Focusing exclusively on critical attributes and typical members of a class can sometimes cause confusion when learning new concepts. Although flying is a noncritical attribute of birds, it is nonetheless typical of most birds and must be accounted for in teaching about them.

CONCEPTS THEMSELVES CAN BE PLACED INTO CATEGORIES

Concepts, like most other objects or ideas, can be categorized and labeled. Knowing the different types of concepts is important because, as will be illustrated later, different types of concepts require different teaching strategies. One way of classifying concepts is according to the rule structures that define their use.

Some concepts have constant rule structures. The concept of island, for example, always involves land surrounded by water. A triangle is a plane, closed figure with three sides and three angles. The rule structures for these concepts are constant. Their critical attributes are combined in an additive manner and are always the same. This type of concept is referred to as a *conjunctive* concept.

Other concepts are broader and more flexible and permit alternative sets of attributes. Their rule structures are not constant. For example, the concept of a strike in baseball is based upon a number of alternative conditions. A strike may be when a batter swings and misses, when an umpire determines that the pitch was in the strike zone even though the batter did not swing at the ball, or when the batter hits a foul ball. This type of concept is called a *disjunctive* concept, that is, one that contains alternative sets of attributes. The concept *noun* is another example of a disjunctive concept. It may be a person, a place, or a thing, but it cannot be all three at the same time.

A third type of concept is one whose rule structure depends on *relationships*. The concept *aunt* describes a particular relationship between siblings and their offspring. The concepts *time* and *distance* are also relational concepts. To understand either of these concepts, one must know the other, plus the relationship between them. For example, *week* is defined as a succession of days that has as its beginning point day one (usually Sunday) and as its ending point day seven (usually Saturday) and a duration of seven days.

Finally, concepts can be classified as *independent* or *coordinated*. Some concepts have independent rules and can be taught by themselves. Previous examples, such as island and equilateral triangle, fall into the independent category. Many concepts have dependent rules and must be taught simultaneously with other closely related or coordinated concepts. Examples of coordinated concepts include *father*, *mother*, *brother*, and *sister*, all of which must be taught and understood in relationship to each other. *Democracy* is another coordinated concept that must be related to a whole complex set of concepts such as *citizen*, *power*, and *freedom*. A final example of coordinated concepts is *spring*, *summer*, *fall*, and *winter*, which can only be understood in relation to each other and the larger concept *season*.

Concepts having complex rule structures like disjunctive and relational concepts are normally more difficult to teach than those having simple, constant rule structures. Similarly, coordinated concepts are more difficult to teach than independent concepts. This helps explain why some students who never master simple prerequisite concepts have difficulty with more advanced work in just about every subject field.

CONCEPTS ARE LEARNED THROUGH EXAMPLES AND NONEXAMPLES

Learning a particular concept involves identifying both examples and nonexamples. For instance, a cow is an example of a mammal but is a nonexample of a reptile. Australia is an example of a country in the southern hemisphere, but it is a nonexample of a developing country. Cotton and silk are examples of the concept *fabric*, but leather and steel are nonexamples. As will be described later, the way examples and nonexamples are identified and used is important in a concept lesson.

CONCEPTS ARE INFLUENCED BY SOCIAL CONTEXT

The critical attributes of a conjunctive concept, such as *equilateral triangle*, are fixed across social contexts. However, disjunctive or relational concepts such as *poverty* or *literacy rate* change from one social context to another. Concepts with changing critical attributes are often found in the behavioral and social sciences and need an operational definition depending on the social context or cultural environment in which they are used. Consider the concept *aunt*. In some societies, the concept *aunt* or *auntie* refers to any adult in the society who has some responsibility for caring for a particular child and has nothing to do with actual blood relationship. Consider also the geographical concepts *north* and *south* as they relate to climate. Children in the northern hemisphere are taught that as one goes south, the climate gets warmer. Obviously this would not hold true for children in Australia or Argentina. The labeling of concepts is also influenced by context. In England a car's windshield is called a windscreen, and the trunk is called the boot. The concepts are the same; the label is different.

CONCEPT LEARNING INVOLVES THE LEARNING OF BOTH CONCEPTUAL AND PROCEDURAL KNOWLEDGE

Conceptual knowledge is the learner's ability to define a concept based on some criteria (for example, physical characteristics or relationships) and to recognize the concept's relationship to other concepts. It implies understanding of the typical or best instance of the class, based on defining attributes. For example, if you were to identify the typical or best example of the adult male in terms of height, you would probably use as your prototype someone about six feet tall. You would not use the seven-foot-six-inch basketball player or the four-foot-eight-inch jockey.

Procedural knowledge of a concept refers to the student's ability to use the concept in a discriminating fashion. This involves the ability to use a concept's defining attributes to compare and contrast it with similar but different concepts. Procedural knowledge about males would allow comparison with similar concepts such as female, girls, boys, old men, young men, and tall men.

To understand the difference between conceptual and procedural knowledge, think again about the concept *equilateral triangle*. Learning the concept *equilateral triangle* involves both the acquisition of conceptual knowledge and the development of procedural knowledge. Conceptual knowledge exists when a student knows the defining attributes of an equilateral triangle and can speak with clarity about them. A student with a conceptual knowledge of an equilateral triangle would define it as a plane, closed figure with three equal angles and three straight sides of equal length. This student would be able to generalize a single instance of an equilateral triangle to the whole class. The student with procedural knowledge, however, could *apply* the definition and could *discriminate* the class of triangle from other classes of triangles and other closed, simple plane figures, such as rectangles or octagons. The student could also generalize to and discriminate among newly encountered instances of equilateral triangles.

OVERVIEW OF CONCEPT TEACHING

Concept teaching actually involves a number of different models. Three variations of concept teaching along with their instructional effects, syntaxes, and environmental structures are briefly described in this section. Teaching behaviors associated with the three approaches are thoroughly examined later in the chapter.

Instructional Effects of Concept Teaching

Concept teaching models have been developed primarily to teach key ideas that serve as foundations for student higher-level thinking and to provide a basis for mutual understanding and communication. Such models are not designed to teach large amounts of information to students. However, by learning and applying key concepts within a given discipline or subject, students are able to transfer specific learnings to more general areas. In fact, without mutual understanding of certain key concepts, subject area instruction is nearly impossible.

Three Approaches to Concept Teaching

There are numerous approaches to concept teaching, but three basic ones have been selected for this chapter: (1) direct presentation, (2) concept formation, and (3) concept attainment.

DIRECT PRESENTATION

In the direct presentation approach, the teacher provides a carefully sequenced expository and/or interrogatory presentation of the concept, including many illustrative examples. Built upon the work of Tennyson and others (1983), the model includes some of the same principles of instructional design as the presentation model of teaching discussed in the previous chapter. The direct presentation approach to concept teaching makes distinctions about appropriate teacher behavior based upon the nature of the concept being taught.

CONCEPT FORMATION

Based on the work of the late Hilda Taba (1967), this approach is particularly useful when the learning goals include inventing new concepts and developing concept-building strategies. A concept formation lesson includes helping students to differentiate between properties of objects or events, to group these properties based on common elements, and to form their own categories and labeling schemes. Its primary purpose is the development of discrimination and classification skills.

CONCEPT ATTAINMENT

Heavily influenced by the work of Bruner and his colleagues (1956), the concept attainment approach is used when students already have some idea about a particular concept or set of concepts. Through consideration of multiple examples and nonexamples of a particular concept, teachers promote inductive thinking by students and help them monitor their own thinking processes.

Distinctions among these three approaches and specific teaching behaviors will be described in more detail later in this chapter.

Syntax of Concept Teaching

There are four major phases or steps in each of the concept teaching approaches described in this chapter. There are, however, variations in the sequencing of learning activities and the accompanying teacher behaviors in Phases 2 and 3. These variations will be highlighted and described later. The overall sequence of phases, however, is summarized in Table 8.1.

Table 8.1   Syntax for Concept Teaching

PHASE		TEACHER BEHAVIOR
Phase 1:	Present goals and establish set	Teacher explains the goals of the lesson and gets students ready to learn.
Phase 2 or 3:	List, label, define	Teacher names the concept and identifies the critical attributes in direct presentation. In concept formation, teacher helps students differentiate group properties and form identifying labels. In concept attainment, students engage in an inductive process in which they discover the attributes of a concept.
Phase 2 or 3:	Present examples and nonexamples	Teacher presents examples, using concept attainment and direct presentation approaches. In concept formation, students group objects by characteristics.
Phase 4:	Help students analyze thinking and integrate learning	Teacher helps students to think about their own thinking and to integrate new learning.

Structure of the Learning Environment

The learning environment for concept teaching is one that might be described as moderately structured. The teacher makes judgments about which concepts to teach and where concept lessons should be sequenced within a larger unit of study. The teacher also selects the best examples and nonexamples of the concept based on the background and experiences of the students. While conducting a concept lesson, however, there are numerous occasions when the teacher's main role becomes one of responding to student ideas, encouraging student participation, and supporting students as they develop their reasoning abilities. Checking for understanding and giving students opportunities to explore their own thinking processes also call for the teacher's support and encouragement. The learning environment for concept teaching, just as for the presentation model described in Chapter 7, requires students to pay close attention to the lesson. While a concept lesson is in progress, there is no time for talking to neighbors, studying, or any other activity that might take attention away from the lesson.

SAMPLING THE RESEARCH BASE

The research base on concept teaching and learning is very extensive and covers a wide range of topics. This is because concept development and its relation to how the mind works has held the interest of theorists, philosophers, and researchers for centuries. Recently this work has centered mainly in psychology and includes the contributions of Jean Piaget, Jerome Bruner, and David Ausubel, among others. Their studies showed how conceptual thinking develops in children and youth and how certain approaches to concept teaching affect these learning processes. To sample ideas from the research tradition, a few topics of particular importance to teachers have been selected for review.

Human Development and Concept Learning

One important set of ideas underlying concept teaching comes from the field of human development. This research specifies how age and stages of intellectual development interact and influence students' readiness to learn various types of concepts. This research has shown that children begin learning concepts at a remarkably early age. Starkey (1980), for example, identified the beginnings of concept formation with the object-sorting and object-preference behavior found in children between 9 and 12 months of age. These initial sorting activities gradually lead to classifying and generalizing, which are the basis for concept learning. Children around 26 months of age can sort concepts into simple genus-species relationships, such as cats and dogs are animals. At about four-and-one-half years of age they can comprehend hierarchical relationships, such as people-lady-nurse or food-fruit-orange (Welch and Long, 1940).

Research has also shown that young children can develop complex spatial and temporal concepts. Friedman (1980) found that children between three and five years of age could comprehend such spatial terms as *ahead of*, *behind*, *beside*, *together with*, *above*, *between*, and such temporal terms as *before*, *after*, and *at the same time*. Although concept learning continues throughout life, the way concepts are learned is affected by the learner's age, language development, and level of intellectual development.

Bruner (1966) identified three distinct modes of learning: (1) by doing, called the enactive mode, (2) by forming mental images, called the iconic mode, and (3) through a series of abstract symbols or representations, called the symbolic mode. As children grow older and progress through the grades, they depend less on the enactive mode and more on mental imagery and symbolic operations. In general, children under age 7 rely mainly on doing, or the enactive mode, for learning concepts. Children between the ages of 7 and 11 still rely on the enactive mode but begin learning concepts through forming mental images. Older children and early adolescents still use the iconic mode but increasingly rely on abstract symbols and mental imagery.

Presentation and Sequencing of Examples

The research from human development can assist teachers as they make decisions about the types and the complexity of concepts to teach specific groups of students. Other research has focused more specifically on the components of the concept lesson, for example, how to present and sequence examples.

The presentation of examples is common to all concept teaching and can be presented in three formats: (1) expository, (2) interrogatory, or (3) a combination of both. Research seems to indicate that an expository presentation is most effective in the development of conceptual knowledge. This involves the teacher selecting the best examples and making an orderly presentation of them according to their difficulty level. The focus is on labeling and defining the concept.

The use of an interrogatory presentation appears to be most effective when the goal is the development of procedural knowledge. In this situation the teacher develops a series of questions and asks students to selectively compare the presence or absence of critical attributes when presented with new instances of the concept.

When the desired goal is to develop both conceptual and procedural knowledge, both expository and interrogatory presentations are made. This is particularly true when students are learning coordinated concepts. Coordinated concepts, remember, are those that need to be taught simultaneously with other related concepts.

The sequencing of examples is another consideration in concept teaching. Examples can be presented in a fixed sequence or in such a way that they are sensitive to the responses of the learner. It seems that sequencing to match the learner's response usually enhances the learning process.

These ideas on the selection and sequencing of examples and the selection of the proper presentation format are presented in Research Summary 8.1. The study done by McKinney and his colleagues focused on the teaching of a set of coordinated social studies concepts to first graders.

Use of Best Examples

The previous research summary demonstrated the importance of examples and nonexamples and their sequencing when teaching concepts. But what about the examples themselves? What should be their characteristics and how should they be selected and used?

In general, initial examples should be selected on the basis of their familiarity to the class. Students need to clearly see typical examples before they are ready to consider atypical ones. Similarly, students normally find it easier to identify a concept with its most immediate neighbors before relating it to more distant ones. If a robin is used as the best (most familiar) example of the concept *bird*, it is easier for the learner to distinguish close neighbors to robins, such as cardinals, sparrows, or bluebirds, than more distant members, such as ducks, chickens, or penguins.

The importance of best examples was highlighted in an interesting study conducted by Tennyson and his colleagues a few years ago. In a carefully controlled study, the researchers tested the effectiveness of two approaches to teaching the concept *regular polygon* to a sample of third-grade students. Some groups of students received a definition of regular polygon and then were presented with some best examples of this concept, such as the ones in Figure 8.1.

Figure 8.1 Best Examples of Regular Polygons. There are many examples of regular polygons. Here are two best examples.

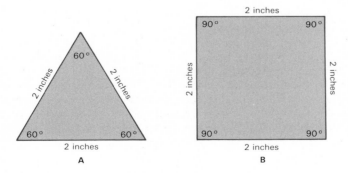

SOURCE: Adapted from R. Tennyson et al. (1983), Concept learning by children using instructional presentation forms for prototype formation and classification-skill development. *Journal of Educational Psychology, 75,* 282. Copyright 1983 by the American Psychological Association. Adapted by permission of the publisher and author.

━━━━━━━━━━━━━━━━ **RESEARCH SUMMARY** ━━━━━━━━━━━━━━━━
8.1

McKinney, C., Burts, D., Ford, M. J., and Gilmore, A. (1985). The effects of the presentation order of examples and non-examples on first-grade students' acquisition of coordinate concepts. *Journal of Educational Research, 78,* 310–314.

PROBLEM: McKinney and his colleagues were interested in teaching students four coordinated social studies concepts and finding out which of two ways of presenting the examples and nonexamples would be more effective.

SAMPLE AND SETTING: The sample consisted of 101 first-grade students who attended one of two elementary schools located in the southern United States. School 1 was located in a large metropolitan area and had a student population consisting of 65 percent black, 10 percent Hispanic and Oriental, and 25 percent white. School 2 was located on the fringe of a small city. Eighty percent of the students were white and 20 percent black.

PROCEDURES: Students were taught four concepts: mountains, hills, tablelands, and plains. The teacher read the definitions aloud. The definitions were accompanied by a line drawing of the four land forms showing how they were related to one another. The teacher pointed to the appropriate land form as each definition was read.

Following each definition, the teacher showed photographs that were examples of each of the four land forms. The teacher identified each photograph and stated why it was an example of the particular concept.

Following this expository presentation, an interrogatory or student practice presentation was conducted. This consisted of the teacher showing students 20 examples (five for each land form) and asking students to identify the land form and to explain their choices.

This part of the lesson was done in two different ways for randomly selected groups of students. A third group of students served as a control group.

▪ *Group 1: Response-sensitive group:* The order in which the 20 examples were presented to students in this group was determined by the students' responses. If a student responded correctly to an example, then the teacher presented one of the remaining examples. However, if the student incorrectly identified the example, the teacher gave the correct response with an explanation. Only after the student could correctly identify the example did the teacher select a new example and call on another student.

▪ *Group 2: Response-insensitive group:* The response-insensitive treatment used the same 20 examples. The presentation order, however, was determined by random ordering of the examples, regardless of student responses.

▪ *Group 3: Control group:* A control group was included to examine whether the students had prior knowledge of the concept.

A 32-item multiple choice test was administered to students in all groups following the treatment. All examples on the test were new examples of the four coordinated concepts: mountains, hills, tablelands, and plains.

POINTS FOR READING RESEARCH: Sometimes the treatment groups in a research study are not equal on some measure of their ability. In this study the Metropolitan

Reading Readiness Test scores were used to determine abilities of the three groups. These scores are listed as the covariate in Table 1. By entering the covariate score into the computations, differences in the abilities of the three groups can be controlled statistically. The covariate score would be similar to a handicap score in golf or bowling. This "handicap score," or covariate, is reflected in the adjusted means. It is the adjusted mean score that researchers examine in comparing the effectiveness of the intervention.

RESULTS: Table 1 displays the results of the study converted to percentages. As can be observed in these data, the response-sensitive group scored statistically significantly higher than both the response-insensitive group and the control group. The response-insensitive group was also statistically significantly higher than the control group.

TABLE 1 **Covariate, Means, and Adjusted Means for Response Sensitive, Response Insensitive, and Control Groups**

Source	n	M Covariate	Unadjusted Mean Percentage	Adjusted Mean Percentage
Response-sensitive	36	54	72%	71%
Response-insensitive	32	50	63%	64%
Control	33	51	31%	31%

SOURCE: Adapted from McKinney et al. (1985), p. 313.

DISCUSSION AND IMPLICATIONS: The data in Table 1 support the use of response-sensitive presentations of examples in the teaching of coordinated concepts. This means that it would appear that matching either a correct response with another example of the concept or matching an incorrect response with a second example facilitates the learning of coordinated concepts. In other words, if a student labels concept A (mountains) incorrectly as hills, the teacher should then give the student examples of concept B (hills) until the student correctly identifies that concept before moving on to another student or another instance of one of the other coordinated concepts.

It would appear from this study that the defining of the coordinated concepts and the selection of instances as examples and nonexamples are very important in learning concepts. Important questions for teachers to ask for this lesson would include: What are the critical attributes that separate hills from mountains and hills from plains? What are the best examples that can be selected to illustrate the concepts of hills, mountains, plains, and tablelands? Expository teaching of the definition and best examples provides the basis for the learner's formation of conceptual knowledge. The interrogatory practice provides the basis for the generalizing and discrimination associated with procedural knowledge of the concepts.

Figure 8.2   Operational Rule for Regular Polygons

Read the following addition to the definition of regular polygons:

Regular polygons have:

1. all sides of equal length
2. all equal angles

They are:

3. planes
4. closed
5. simple

SOURCE: Adapted from R. Tennyson et al. (1983), Concept learning by children using instructional presentation forms for prototype formation and classification-skill development. *Journal of Educational Psychology*, 75, 283. Copyright 1983 by the American Psychological Association. Adapted by permission of the publisher and author.

Another group received a definition of the concept and an operational rule about regular polygons. The operational definition used in the study is shown in Figure 8.2.

The group of students given the best examples achieved higher than did the group given the operational rule. This study clearly showed that the use of best examples can aid the learning of concepts. The use of best examples prevents misconceptions that might occur if more distant or atypical examples are used. It also appears that the use of best examples can minimize classification errors that often occur when students are only given a definition as the basis for making judgments as to whether an instance is a member of the class or not.

Use of Visual or Mental Images

Using visual or mental images also affects the learning of concepts and supports the old adage that "a picture is worth a thousand words." Tennyson (1978) tested three types of pictorial support with elementary children as aids for concept learning. In one case the children were given drawings highlighting the relevant features of the concept. In the second case the students were guided to produce their own drawings highlighting the relevant features. In the third instance students were asked to generate mental images of the relevant features. The students were divided into two groups. The first group received full pretraining in one of the three techniques; the second group was given only practice items without training.

This study concluded that for young children learning concepts and rules can be assisted by providing pictorials or by having students generate their own pictorials to accompany the text and by providing specific instructions for these tasks. This study was conducted with third- and fourth-grade students using mathematical concepts, but it holds promise for other instruction as well. Further, strategies that link mental images with concepts have been shown to increase the recall of key ideas. For example, a series of pictures representing clear differences

RESEARCH SUMMARY
8.2

Jantz, R., and Klawitter, K. (In press). The effects of instruction on the learning of social studies concepts by fourth graders. *Journal of Instructional Psychology.*

PROBLEM: The purpose of this study was to compare the effects of different approaches for teaching students four social studies concepts: government, laws, roles, and responsibilities.

SAMPLE AND SETTING: The subjects for this study consisted of 57 fourth-grade students from a moderate income school district in a major city in south-central Pennsylvania.

PROCEDURES: Students were assigned to one of three treatment groups:

- *Group 1:* This group used study prints and student drawings to supplement the text's presentation of the concepts and to help focus on the relevant features of the concepts.
- *Group 2:* Students in this group were required to generate conceptual webs in their attempt to learn the concepts.
- *Group 3:* The teacher in this group generated webs that illustrated the concepts. The subjects were required to identify textual sentences that supported the teacher-generated webs.

At the beginning of the study there were no significant differences among the three treatment groups in either their reading or social studies achievement scores.

Lessons of 45 minutes each were taught on five consecutive days. The first day consisted of a pretest over the four concepts and a lesson introducing the concepts using an expository approach that combined a conceptual chart and webbing. On days two and three, the subjects experienced guided practice and feedback consistent with the three treatment conditions. The final 15 minutes of each lesson were used by the students to generate pictures, webs, or sentences that were relevant to the concepts studied that day. Day four consisted of independent practice and feedback following the same routine as the lessons on the previous days. On day five students completed a multiple choice posttest to measure their understanding of the concepts.

(cont'd)

---

in the four seasons coupled with instructions that help create images of fall, winter, spring, and summer can help children make the concept *seasons* more concrete and more effectively learned. Likewise, a diagram of the major branches of a city's government could assist a student in developing the concept of city government while reading about it in a social studies text or listening to the teacher explain it.

Webbing is another form of visual representation that can be used by teachers to aid students in learning concepts. Webs can highlight the critical attributes of a concept and help make the concept more concrete for students. Webs can also

━━━━━━━━━━━━━━━ **RESEARCH SUMMARY** ━━━━━━━━━━━━━━━
8.2 (continued)

RESULTS: An examination of the data in Table 1 indicates that the group of students that used mental imagery by generating their own webs (group 2) had an increase of 27.5 percentage points, had the highest concept recall score (89.5 percent), and the highest total concept score (92.8 percent) on the posttest.

TABLE 1 Mean Percentage Scores by Treatment Group and Social Studies Grade Equivalent Grouping

	Concept Score			
Group	Knowledge Pretest	Knowledge Posttest	Recall Posttest	Total Concept Posttest
Treatment				
Study Prints				
(*N* = 19)	72.3%	94.8%	85.5%	90.1%
Student Webbing				
(*N* = 19)	68.5%	96.0%	89.5%	92.8%
Teacher Expository				
(*N* = 19)	77.8%	94.8%	79.0%	86.9%
Total Group				
(*N* = 57)	72.8%[a]	95.3%[a]	84.8%	89.9%

[a] Statistically significant at the $p < .05$ level from pretest to posttest social studies grade equivalent.
SOURCE: Adapted from R. Jantz and K. Klawitter (In press).

DISCUSSION AND IMPLICATIONS: All three treatment groups made significant gains from the pretest to the posttest on knowledge of the four concepts. Students had the opportunity to practice with the concepts by forming visual images of the relationships among the critical attributes through student-generated webs, by student drawings of scenes depicting the key concepts based upon study pictures and textual materials, or by locating sentences in the text that supported the key concepts. This study supports the literature that indicates that focusing on the essential characteristics of concepts, selecting appropriate examples, aiding students in the formation of mental images by such activities as webbing and student-generated pictures and drawings, and providing time for students to practice can all enhance the learning of concepts.

provide the learner with an effective means for retrieving information from long-term memory so new concepts can be more easily understood. More information about webbing will be provided in the next section.

Research Summary 8.2 shows how the idea of helping learners to form visual images as a means of learning key concepts from social studies was tested. The study relied on the work of Tennyson (1978) and employed student practice with charting, webbing, or drawing pictures of the key concepts.

Text Organization

In almost all subject areas, and at all grade levels, teachers rely on textbooks and other printed materials to help students acquire information and conceptual understanding. Chapter 7 explained how the organization of verbal information in presentations and the use of advance organizers can influence student learning. The organization of text materials through the use of advance organizers can also facilitate the learning of concepts.

Advance organizers can be used to progressively differentiate a concept from the general to the specific. They can also be used to present parallel or hierarchical relationships among concepts found in text materials. They can aid in the orderly presentation of the concepts by providing a type of "scaffolding" that helps link newly acquired concepts to the learner's existing schemata. During the processing of text information, the readers' schemata permit the simultaneous examination of abstract and concrete referents of the concept being described. If enough referents are located, readers can process the information and learn the concept. If referents do not exist, the reader cannot process the information adequately and the concept being described will not be learned or will fade from memory very quickly. The use of advance organizers in texts seems to enhance this referral process.

There is some indication that for advance organizers to be effective in the learning of concepts they need to be visual and should be located in the text next to the concept being described. One interesting study on this topic is shown in Research Summary 8.3.

The research on concept teaching and learning indicates that particular teaching strategies can help students learn concepts more effectively. Eight guidelines are offered here from the research just summarized and from the work of Martorella (1982), who did an extensive review of research related to instructional applications of the principles of concept learning:

1. Teachers should begin with a clear definition of the concept.
2. At some point, instruction should include a definition of the concept and a statement of the concept's critical attributes.
3. The teaching of coordinated concepts requires both expository and interrogatory presentations.
4. The use of best examples can increase concept learning.
5. Unless students know the critical attributes of a concept, they should be taught them prior to or concurrently with instruction.

RESEARCH SUMMARY
8.3

Hawk, P. (1986). Using graphic organizers to increase achievement in middle school life science. *Science Education, 70,* 81–87.

PROBLEM: The purpose of this study was to determine the effectiveness of graphic organizers in aiding concept learning among sixth- and seventh-grade students in life science.

SAMPLE AND SETTING: Subjects for this study were seventh graders enrolled in seven classes of life science at four middle schools, and sixth graders enrolled in eight classes of life science at four other middle schools. All eight schools were within the same school system.

PROCEDURES: The life science course in which the subjects were enrolled was the required course of study for seventh graders. In an effort to accelerate the science program in the school system, half of the schools were designated to pilot a revised science curriculum using high-ability sixth graders. This revised curriculum was essentially the seventh-grade life science curriculum. Students were divided into two groups.

▪ *Group 1:* **Sixth graders**—Students were given specially developed graphic organizers to accompany the first seven chapters of a life science text published by Holt, Rinehart and Winston. An example of one of these organizers is found in Figure 1. The content covered in the chapters was the scientific method, the living world, and life support processes. The organizers had been developed by a group of teachers, and teachers in the study were given a two-day workshop on their use.

▪ *Group 2:* **Seventh graders**—Serving as the control group, these students did not receive the graphic organizers during instruction. Teachers in this group were told to teach using their regular methods.

An analysis of covariance design was used to control statistically any initial differences in the students that might confound differences caused by the treatment. Present were an experimental variable (graphic organizers), a covariate

FIGURE 1 Graphic Organizer for Protoplasm

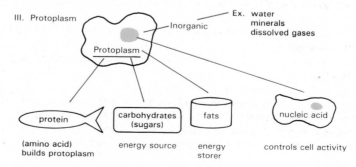

SOURCE: Adapted from P. Hawk (1986), Using graphic organizers to increase achievement in middle school life science. *Science Education, 70,* 84. Used with permission.

variable (pretest), and a dependent variable (posttest). Teachers for both groups were provided with a list of activities to include during the instruction of each chapter and a time line to follow.

Identical pretests and posttests containing 50 items were used in the study. This test is standardized and published by Holt, Rinehart and Winston for use with their life science curriculum.

POINTS FOR READING RESEARCH: All research studies have limitations. One of the limitations of this study was teacher control. All the teachers used their usual pedagogy and obviously they varied in ability and style. This is always a limitation in actual classroom research. However, in the opinions of the system supervisors there was no significant difference in the two groups of teachers. You must decide if you agree with this.

RESULTS: The results in Table 1 clearly support the use of graphic organizers as a teaching strategy for improving concept learning. The 213 students in the sixth-grade classes of life science that used the organizers had an adjusted percentage difference between the pretest and posttest of 43 percent, while the 177 students in the seventh-grade classes that did not use graphic organizers had an adjusted percentage difference of 24 percent. The adjusted percentage difference between the two treatments was statistically significant.

TABLE 1   Mean Percentage Scores for Pretests and Posttests by Treatment Group

Treatment Group	Pretest	Posttest	
	Obtained	Obtained	Adjusted
Graphic	26%	68%	69%
Control	28%	54%	52%

SOURCE: P. Hawk (1986), p. 85.

DISCUSSION AND IMPLICATIONS: The significant findings in this study support previous studies on the effectiveness of using graphic organizers. There are a number of reasons why graphic organizers enhance learning. First, the graphic organizer provides an overview of the material to be learned. It says, "This is where we are going and these are the things we need to know to get there." Second, the graphic organizer provides a framework and reference points that aid the learner in assimilating new vocabulary and in organizing the main concepts into a logical pattern. Third, the graphic organizers cue students as to what to look for as they read printed materials. The organizers direct students to look for cause and effect, for comparison and contrast, for sequence of events, and a variety of other relationships. Fourth, as a review instrument, the graphic organizer is succinct and informative. Its appears to strengthen the learners' retention. Finally, the graphic aspect of the organizers used in this study provided visual aides with specific frameworks to assist in learning new vocabulary and concepts.

It would appear that classroom teachers could aid their students' concept learning by using graphic organizers without changing any other aspects of their pedagogical style except for explaining the use of the organziers.

6. Some opportunities to experiment with identifying examples and nonexamples should be incorporated in a concept lesson, along with feedback on the correctness or incorrectness of the responses.
7. The use of visuals such as graphics, charts, diagrams, and webs can aid in the learning of concepts by making them more concrete and by depicting relationships among concepts and their critical attributes.
8. The use of graphic organizers can facilitate the learning of concepts described in text-based materials.

Many of these principles, as you will see, are incorporated in the specific teaching procedures described in the following section.

PROCEDURES FOR TEACHING CONCEPTS

In the following story, entitled the "League of the Iroquois," two generalizations serve as the focus of the lesson. These two generalizations, or "big ideas," and the key concepts within them permit comparisons of different cultures at different time periods. The key concepts are in italics:

1. *People* unite to form *governments.*
2. *People* take different *roles* and *responsibilities* in their government.

League of the Iroquois

At a meeting of the colonies in Albany, New York, in 1754, Franklin presented a "plan of union." According to his plan, each colony would choose representatives to a "grand council." This council would pass laws that all the colonies would follow. Where did Franklin get the idea for such a plan? Very possibly, from the Iroquois Indians.

About 200 years before the Albany meeting, the six nations of Iroquois joined together to form the League of the Iroquois. The original aim of the League was to promote peace among the Iroquois. Later, joined together in the League, the Iroquois become powerful opponents in war.

Women and men played different parts in this League government. Women chose the men who were the representatives, or chiefs, from each tribe to the Great Council of the Iroquois, called the Longhouse. Women decided what would be discussed at the Great Council. Often the chief had to decide on ways to solve problems. This sometimes involved making rules for the people in all the tribes. If the chiefs did not do their jobs well, women could remove them from the Council.

Benjamin Franklin's plan of government was not accepted by the colonists at the Albany meeting in 1754. But the government of the United States that was formed thirty-three years later was like the Longhouse Council in many ways. Can you think how? (Scott, Foresman Third Grade Social Studies, 1979, p. 194–195.)

Preinstructional Tasks

In order to understand these two generalizations above and use them to solve problems, students must first understand the concept embedded in them. They must understand the concept of role before they can identify the roles and responsibilities that women had in the League of the Iroquois or before they can compare the roles of women today with those of the Iroquois. Consequently, a teacher's first decisions when planning a concept lesson involve selecting, defining, and analyzing concepts to be taught.

SELECTING CONCEPTS

The curriculum is the primary source of key concepts for instruction. These concepts may be embedded in a textbook, listed in the teacher's edition of a text, or contained in local curriculum guides. In the story of "The League of the Iroquois," the concepts of role, responsibilities and government are implied within the text, but they also need to be taught. Reading the text and being able to apply the generalization, "People unite to form governments," is dependent on the learner's conceptual and procedural knowledge of the key concepts.

The teacher's edition for most textbook series provides guidance in selecting key concepts for instruction. For example, in the same third-grade social studies textbook, the teacher's edition identifies the main idea for Lesson Two as "weather and climate can affect your choices." Knowledge of the concepts of weather, climate and choices is crucial to understanding this main idea. In this instance the concepts of weather and climate are clearly stated as learning outcomes (key vocabulary) and are developed within the lesson.

> Just as the location of your community can affect your choices, so can its weather and climate. Suppose, for example, that you plan to go on a picnic Saturday. But, suppose when Saturday comes, it brings "thunder" and "storms." You decide to cancel your picnic because of bad weather. Weather has influenced your choices.
>
> When we talk about weather we mean the day-to-day changes in the hotness, coldness, dryness, and wetness of a place. Climate means the kind of weather a place has over many months or even years.
>
> Here is an example that will show you the difference between weather and climate. Sometimes the weather is very hot in Chicago. The summer Diana, Vito, Gina, and Sammy were asked to describe Chicago, temperatures rose into the high 90s on many days. (Perfect swimming weather!) But, even though the weather sometimes is very hot in Chicago, still we don't say that Chicago has a hot climate. Let's see why not. (Scott, Foresman, Third Grade Social Studies, 1979, p. 105)

Local curriculum guides are another primary source for selecting concepts for instruction. In some cases the key concepts will be listed as vocabulary to be developed in the unit. In other cases concepts will be found within the main ideas or generalizations for a unit of study. For example, the fifth-grade curriculum guide for Howard County Public Schools, Howard County, Maryland, contains a unit on the westward movement. In this unit students study why people migrated west, and in the process, study such key concepts as migration, economic gain, religious freedom, and political freedom. They also examine other concepts related to the unit's objectives such as expansion, self-sufficiency, taming, heterogeneous, frontier, pioneer, pluralism, and terrain. Some of the other concepts for the unit are listed below. Obviously, they cannot all be taught, and the teacher must make decisions about which ones to single out for particular lessons.

trek	blockade	rebellion	neutral
pioneer	frontier	flatboat	canal
territory	fertile soil	acre	treaty
Conestoga wagon	compromise	besiege	expedition
harsh	treaties	reservations	turnpikes

Teachers need to make decisions about which of the new vocabulary words need to be directly taught as concepts. Judgments are constantly being made as to which new terms are essential to understanding the important ideas of a lesson or a unit. If key concepts within a generalization or main idea are not known by the students, then a lesson on the unknown concept(s) should be taught. Merrill and Tennyson (1977) summarized the major conditions under which concept lessons are appropriate.

Does the material involve *new terms?* If so, prepare a concept lesson for each important new term or related set of new terms.

Does the material require the student to define *new words?* If so, prepare a concept lesson for each important new word or related set of new words.

Does the content involve *rule using?* If so, prepare a concept lesson for each component in the rule.

Does the content involve a series of steps or events? If so, examine each step or event as a potential concept and prepare a concept lesson for those steps or events that are concepts.

Does the material require identification of parts? If so, decide if some parts should be taught as concepts and prepare a concept lesson for those that should be taught. (pp. 21–22)

DEFINING CONCEPTS

Critical attributes, as you read earlier, are those attributes that are present in every example of a concept and distinguish it from all other concepts. For example the concept *tree* might be defined as a "plant that lives for many years and has a single main stem that is woody." This definition includes the critical attributes of *plant, lives for many years, single main stem,* and *woody.* These critical attributes define a concept and, consequently, students must understand them. However, noncritical attributes also enter into the picture. For example, size, shape, and color are noncritical attributes of trees. Blue lagoons, sandy beaches, and palm trees may be desirable on an island but they are noncritical attributes. When learning concepts, students must not confuse the noncritical attributes, no matter how common, with the critical attributes of the concept.

The source of the definition for a concept and its critical attributes is also important. In some instances concepts are defined in the glossaries of the students' textbooks, but in other cases they may be defined in the curriculum guides published by the local school districts. These definitions and critical attributes should be examined carefully. Markle (1975) warned that "some of the words in many definitions are irrelevant to classifying tasks. For instance, Webster's says under 'dog,' that these were 'kept in domesticated state since prehistoric times,' an interesting fact, perhaps, but without utility in the identification task" (p. 7). Markle also cautioned against using synonyms as critical attributes and against using the illustrations in dictionaries and texts as defining examples. The best sources of definitions stem from the specialists within a particular subject area. Economists, anthropologists, mathematicians, chemists, and geographers, for example, are apt to provide more exact definitions and attributes of concepts in their fields than other less specialized sources.

Merrill and Tennyson (1977) offered the following three steps in defining concepts for instruction:

1. Identifying the concept's name. A name is a word or symbol that is used to refer to the class as a whole or to examples of the class, for example the word *island*.

2. List critical and noncritical attributes. A critical attribute is a characteristic shared by all members of a class, whereas a noncritical attribute is a characteristic shared by some, but not all, members of the class. In the example of an island, the identifying characteristics are *land mass*, *water*, and *surrounding*.

3. Write a concise definition. A definition is a statement identifying each of the critical attributes and indicating how these attributes are combined. For example, *an island is a land mass that is smaller than a continent and is surrounded by water*. (p. 30)

When translating definitions from particular academic subjects into instructional definitions, it is important not to distort or eliminate the critical attributes. The result might be to teach a false concept. It is also important to remember that memorizing a definition does not equal concept learning.

ANALYZING CONCEPTS

Once a concept has been selected and defined in terms of its critical attributes, the concept needs to be analyzed for examples and nonexamples. The selection of examples and nonexamples, based on the critical attributes, is probably the most difficult and important task teachers perform in the preinstructional phase of concept teaching. Examples serve as the connectors between the concept's abstraction and the learner's prior knowledge and experiences. Examples must be meaningful to the learner and must be as concrete as possible.

Charts, diagrams, and webs, as well as pictures, can be employed as visual examples of abstract concepts. They can also aid the teacher in analyzing the concept for instructional decisions. Table 8.2 contains an analysis of a set of coordinated concepts. As illustrated in Table 8.2, numbering the critical attributes and using the word *and* can be a reminder that all of the critical attributes must be present to have an example of the concept.

If you look at the example *Hawaii* in the table it (1) is a land mass not as large as a continent, (2) there is a body of water nearby, and (3) the water completely surrounds it. Each of the three critical conditions of an island is met, therefore, it is an example of the concept. Teachers might also look at Florida as a nonexample of island. Land and water are present, but the land is not completely surrounded by water. All of the criteria are not met, therefore, Florida is not an example of an island.

The isolation of the attributes is critical to the analysis and teaching of concepts. The teacher needs to decide if the attributes are critical and should be presented when matching examples and nonexamples such as Hawaii and Florida,

Table 8.2   Analysis of Coordinated Concepts

CONCEPT	DEFINITION	EXAMPLE	NONEXAMPLE	CRITICAL ATTRIBUTES
Island	A land mass not as large as a continent, surrounded by water.	Hawaii Cuba Greenland	Florida Lake Erie Australia	1. Land mass (not continent), AND 2. Water, AND 3. Land surrounded by water.
Lake	A large inland body of water surrounded by land	Lake Huron Great Salt Lake Big Lake	Ohio River Hawaii pond	1. Large inland body of water, AND 2. Land, AND 3. Water surrounded by land.
Peninsula	A land area almost entirely surrounded by water, but having a land connection to a larger land mass.	Florida Italy Delmarva	Cuba Hudson Bay Big Lake	1. Land connected to larger land mass, AND 2. Water, AND 3. Land surrounded almost entirely by water.
Bay	A body of water partly surrounded by land, but having a wide outlet to the sea.	Chesapeake Hudson Green Bay	Florida lake gulf	1. Body of water connected to the sea by a wide outlet, AND 2. Land, AND 3. Water partly surrounded by land.

or if the attributes are noncritical and are best used in divergent examples after clear instances of the concept are presented.

It is also important in the process of isolating attributes to make some judgment as to the difficulty of the examples. What is meaningful to the teacher may be too difficult and not within the experiences of the learner. Merrill and Tennyson (1977) illustrated easy, medium, and difficult examples for teaching the concept *adverb*. They indicated that an "adverb is a word that modifies a verb, an adjective, or another adverb and answers one of these questions: When? How? Where? or To What Extent?" The critical attributes are *modifies another word* and *function*. Figure 8.3 presents examples and nonexamples of the concept *adverb*.

Webbing can also be used to analyze a concept. A semantic web provides a visual image of the characteristics and relationships generating from the core idea of the concept. Figure 8.4 is a web of the concept *equilateral triangle*.

There are normally four steps in constructing a semantic web for a particular concept (Freedman and Reynolds, 1980).

STEP 1: Create the core, which is the focus of the web. This would be the name of the concept.

STEP 2: Construct strands branching out from the core. These strands are critical attributes of the concept.

STEP 3: Draw strand supports, which connect the critical attributes to the concept.

STEP 4: Identify the strand ties, which may show relationships among the various attributes.

Figure 8.3 List of Easy and Difficult Examples and Nonexamples of Adverbs

EASY EXAMPLES

1. You are so happy.
2. She has been absent lately.
3. Slowly, she walked home.
4. The train chugged loudly.

MEDIUM EXAMPLES

5. Are you fighting mad?
6. Clouds gathered threateningly.
7. It was not difficult to explain.
8. The most dangerous weapon is a gun.

DIFFICULT EXAMPLES

9. The small floral print looked pretty.
10. Cats are my No. 1 favorite pet.
11. He wants the dark purple bicycle.
12. The book had three color pictures.

EASY NONEXAMPLES

13. Sewing makes you happy
14. She has been late.
15. She is slow.
16. The loud train chugged.

MEDIUM NONEXAMPLES

17. Do you fight?
18. The threatening clouds gathered
19. It is difficult to explain that *not* is a negative word.
20. Most guns are dangerous weapons.

DIFFICULT NONEXAMPLES

21. The small print looked pretty.
22. One special cat is my favorite pet.
23. He wants the dark trim to match.
24. The book had three pictures.

SOURCE: Adapted from M. D. Merrill and R. D. Tennyson (1977), *Teaching concepts: An instructional design approach.* Englewood Cliffs, N.J.: Educational Technology, pp. 50–51.

Figure 8.4   Web of the Concept Equilateral Triangle

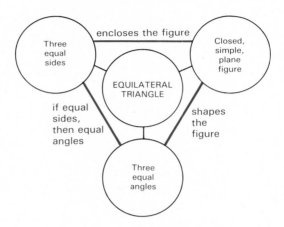

Learning aids have been included at the end of this chapter to provide you with practice in analyzing and webbing concepts.

DECIDING ON WHICH APPROACH TO USE

A final preinstructional decision involves choosing which approach (direct presentation, concept formation, or concept attainment) to use. This decision is related to both the goals sought by the teacher and to the nature of the concept. In general, the concept formation approach is an inventive act in which new categories and new concept labels are formed. Concept attainment is a search for critical attributes in which the concept is known by the teacher. The direct presentation approach is a teacher-directed activity with highly structured expository and interrogatory presentations based on best examples. In both the concept attainment and direct presentation approaches one important goal is mastery of the concept. Some instructional goals commonly associated with the three fundamental approaches are shown Table 8.3.

Conducting the Lesson

The four phases of a concept-teaching lesson were outlined in Table 8.1. These were: (1) presents goals and establishes set, (2 or 3) lists/labels/defines, (2 or 3) presents examples and nonexamples, and (4) helps students analyze thinking and integrate learning. Teacher behavior associated with each phase is described in some detail below.

PRESENTS GOALS AND ESTABLISHES SET

Teachers select the concepts to be learned and match the approach with their goals for a concept lesson. At the beginning of a concept lesson, just as with all

Table 8.3 Learning Goals Associated With Three Approaches to Concept Teaching

LEARNING GOALS	APPROACH
To develop skills in listing, grouping, and labeling	Concept formation
To distinguish examples from nonexamples	Concept attainment Direct presentation
To invent new concepts based on regrouping of the critical attributes	Concept formation
To acquire new concepts through inductive strategies	Concept attainment
To acquire new concepts with maximum efficiency	Direct presentation
To analyze thinking processes for concept learning	Concept attainment
To develop concept-building strategies	Concept formation Concept attainment
To learn about the nature of concepts	Concept formation Concept attainment Direct presentation

types of lessons, the teacher needs to communicate clearly to students the objectives for the lesson and how the class will proceed. For example, if the class is engaging in a concept formation activity and the learning objectives focus on the skills of listing, grouping, and labeling, the teacher might tell the students that they are going to look at a collection of objects and put some of them into groups, being as creative as possible. Similarly, with a direct presentation lesson, the teacher might want to go over the steps of the lesson and give students reasons why the concepts about to be taught are important to learn.

Establishing set for a concept lesson requires procedures no different from those described in Chapter 7. Teachers get students ready to learn with a brief review, questions about yesterday's lesson, or an interesting anecdote that ties the forthcoming lesson into students' prior knowledge.

LABELING, DEFINING, AND USING EXAMPLES

The exact sequence for defining and labeling a concept or for presenting examples and nonexamples varies according to the particular approach being used by the teacher. It is this internal arrangement and flow of activities that gives each of the three approaches its unique character and allows each one to accomplish the particular goals for which it was designed.

Direct Presentation In the direct presentation approach the internal flow of the lesson includes:

1. Naming the concept and providing students with a definition

2. Identifying the critical attributes
3. Showing best examples through expository presentation
4. Working with the concept through interrogatory presentation

Taking the concept *island* as analyzed in Table 8.2, a teacher using the direct presentation approach might proceed as follows:

1. Tell students that they are going to learn the concept *island* and write the name of the concept on the board so that students can see the word. Define island as a land mass, not as large as a continent, surrounded by water.
2. List the critical attributes:
   a. Land mass (not a continent)
   b. Water
   c. Land surrounded by water
3. Show a simple drawing that contains only the critical attributes, pointing out each critical attribute and the fact that the land is surrounded by the water. This could be followed by pictures of best examples, such as Hawaii, Greenland, or Cuba. As each picture is presented, point out the critical attributes again.
4. Show students both examples and nonexamples of the concept, and ask questions that force judgments about whether a new instance is an example or nonexample of the concept.

To show the difference between an expository and interrogatory presentation of examples consider the illustration in Figure 8.5.

Concept Formation Concept formation is a more inventive approach in which the central activity centers on listing and grouping examples and nonexamples of concepts into categories. Concept lessons using this approach include the following steps:

1. Ask students a question that generates a list of objects or ideas.
2. Ask students to group the objects into classes.
3. Ask students to label the various classes of objects.

Using the concept *island* again, a teacher using the concept formation approach might proceed as follows:

1. Ask students to name places they know about where land and sea meet. List these on the board.
2. After several places are listed, discuss with students how these places should be grouped. They may group together those instances where the land is surrounded by water, leaving those instances where the land is only partially surrounded to form another group. It is possible they might group these places using other criteria.

Figure 8.5   Expository and Interrogatory Presentation of Examples

Expository Presentation of Examples

Look carefully at these figures

Figure 9 is *not* an equilateral triangle because it shows a solid figure. Equilateral triangles are flat.

Figure 10 *is* an equilateral triangle.

Figure 11 is *not* an equilateral triangle because it is a complex figure. Equilateral triangles are simple.

Figure 12 *is* an equilateral triangle.

Interrogatory Presentation of Examples

You will now see some figures.   Your job will be tell if the figure is an equilateral triangle. Each time you see a figure, ask yourself the following five questions. If you answer YES to all five questions, it is an equilateral triangle. If you answer NO to any of the five questions, it is not.

Be sure to circle YES or NO to each of the five questions. Then circle YES or NO after the questions: Is it an equilateral triangle?

1. Does it have three straight sides of equal length?	YES NO
2. Does it have three equal angles?	YES NO
3. Is it a plane figure?	YES NO
4. Is it a closed figure?	YES NO
5. Is it a simple figure?	YES NO

Is it an equilateral triangle?   YES   NO

1. Does it have three straight sides of equal length	YES NO
2. Does it have three equal angles?	YES NO
3. Is it a plane figure?	YES NO
4. Is it a closed figure?	YES NO
5. Is it a simple figure?	YES NO

Is it an equilateral triangle?   YES   NO

1. Does it have three straight sides of equal length?	YES NO
2. Does it have three equal angles?	YES NO
3. Is it a plane figure?	YES NO
4. Is it a closed figure?	YES NO
5. Is it a simple figure?	YES NO

Is it an equilateral triangle?   YES   NO

SOURCE: Adapted from R. Tennyson and M. Cocchiarella (1986), An empirically based instructional design theory for teaching concepts. *Review of Educational Research, 56,* 48–49. Copyright 1986, AERA.

3. Finally, ask students to provide a label or name for the groups they have constructed. Sometimes students may come up with labels the teacher has in mind; other times they will not. It is usually not important that students name the concept the same as the teacher. However, if the concept and its name are important for further study, the teacher will want to teach it using the direct presentation approach.

In the concept formation approach, teachers help students primarily through questioning and dialogue. Some questions and purposes for them follow:

1. To develop criteria for grouping.	1. What are some ways in which we can put these items together?
2. To help students see relations between items.	2. What items belong together?
3. To explore similarities.	3. What are some reasons why you put these together?
4. To explore differences.	4. Are there other relationships among the items that would justify organizing them into different groups?
5. To explore characteristics of various items.	5. Why does this item go here?

Concept Attainment In concept attainment, students already have some grasp of a concept or set of concepts and are asked to make decisions about whether or not particular examples are instances of a class. Teachers using the concept attainment approach would proceed through the following steps:

1. Provide students with examples, some that represent the concept and some that do not. Best examples are clearly labeled *yes*, and carefully selected nonexamples are clearly labeled *no*.
2. Urge students to hypothesize about the attributes of the concept and to record reasons for their speculation. The teacher may ask additional questions to help focus student thinking and to encourage them to compare attributes of the examples and nonexamples.
3. When students appear to know the concept, they name (label) the concept and describe the process they used for identifying it.
4. Check to see if the students have attained the concept by having them identify additional examples as YES or NO and by asking them to generate examples and nonexamples of their own.

Concept attainment is an inductive process that assists learners in organizing data according to previously learned concepts. Unlike the direct presentation approach, the teacher provides a label and definition only after the students have engaged in the discovery of the critical attributes, and it differs from the concept formation approach in which students are required to organize data to form new concepts.

To illustrate the concept attainment approach, consider the following lesson, again using the concept *island*.

1. The teacher shows a picture of an island and tells students this is an example of the concept. He or she would then show a picture of a land form that is not an island and say, this is a nonexample of the concept.

2. The teacher would continue displaying pictures of islands and of other land forms, telling students which are examples and which are not. Students would be asked to hypothesize what they think the concept is. All hypotheses and ideas would be listed on the chalkboard. The teacher would continue to present examples and nonexamples and to ask students to reconsider their original hypotheses.

3. Students would be asked to state a definition of the concept and, if possible, label it.

4. The teacher would then show additional pictures of islands and other land forms and ask students to identify each as a *yes* or *no*. He or she would also ask students to provide examples of islands they know about and instances of land forms that would not be considered islands.

The major roles for the teacher during this aspect of a concept attainment lesson are (a) to record student hypotheses and any critical attributes identified, (b) to cue students, and (c) to provide additional data if necessary.

Each of the three approaches to concept teaching has its own goals and its own internal structure for accomplishing these goals. The direct presentation approach is the most straightforward and probably the most efficient for teaching abstract concepts about which students have little prior knowledge. When using this approach the teacher defines and labels the concept at the beginning of the lesson and then proceeds with promoting student understanding through careful presentation of examples and nonexamples. Concept formation lessons are the most inductive and require students to generate lists of objects and ideas from their own information bases before concerning them with concept definition and labeling. Concept attainment lessons provide examples and nonexamples first and then engage students with hypothesizing about critical attributes of the concepts. The concept is defined and labeled only after student interaction and engagement.

ANALYZING THINKING PROCESSES AND INTEGRATING LEARNING

The final phase of all three approaches to concept teaching emphasizes teacher-directed activities aimed at helping students to analyze their own thinking processes in order to integrate newly acquired conceptual knowledge. To accomplish this, teachers ask students to think back and recount what was going through their minds as they were considering the concepts. What criteria did they use for listing items in a concept formation lesson? When did they first figure out the concept in the concept attainment lesson? Why? What was confusing in the direct presentation lesson? How does the concept relate to other concepts they know about? Were they focusing on the concept as a whole or on a particular attribute? How did noncritical attributes affect discovering the concept? If they were going to teach the concept to a student younger than them, what would they do?

The intent of this type of questioning is to get students to think about their own thinking (termed metacognition) and to discover and consider the patterns they use to learn and integrate new concepts into their cognitive frameworks. This phase of a concept lesson relies, obviously, on student discussion and participation. The guidelines for encouraging and facilitating student discussion and participation provided in Chapters 5 and 7 can also be used for this final phase of a concept-teaching lesson.

Postinstructional Tasks

Many of the same ideas and strategies used in defining and analyzing concepts can be employed in evaluating students' understanding of concepts. The critical attributes become the basis for knowing a concept. A concept analysis separates the critical attributes from the noncritical attributes, permitting discriminations and classifications to take place.

To attain the higher levels of concept learning advocated by Klausmeier (1980), the learner should (1) define the concept and know its critical attributes, (2) be able to recognize examples and nonexamples, and (3) evaluate examples and nonexamples in terms of their critical attributes. For example, with the concept *island*, the learner, when given examples of islands, bays, lakes, and peninsulas could (1) properly name and identify the islands, (2) name the critical attributes of islands and discriminate them from noncritical attributes, and (3) evaluate how the islands differ from bays, lakes, and peninsulas; in terms of the critical attributes of islands, for examples, peninsulas are not completely surrounded by water.

Klausmeier (1980) provided examples of multiple-choice test items for assessing students' understanding of concepts.

1. Item to measure knowledge of the definition of the concept *inferring:*

Which of the following is the best definition of *inferring?*

a. Using one or more of the senses to examine things carefully and to draw a conclusion.

b. Relating a scientific observation to something which is known, and drawing a conclusion about what was observed.

c. Drawing a conclusion about what will happen without making a scientific observation.

d. Relating a scientific fact to something which is observed, and predicting the scientific outcome.

2. Item to measure the ability to discriminate the critical attributes of *inferring*:

For the following questions, blacken the letter of the correct answer on your answer sheet.

Which of the following tells about someone relating a scientific observation to something which is known?

    a. Tom looked up information about African wildlife and gave a report on lions.

    b. Mary drew pictures of three different types of clouds in the sky.

    c. Bill saw some blue speckled eggs in a nest. He knew that robins lay blue speckled eggs.

    d. Pam heard a noise in the dark room. She thought, "It must be a monster."

3. Item to measure the ability to recognize examples and nonexamples of the concept *inferring*:

Some of the following stories describe inferring. Some stories do not. You must read each story carefully and then decide whether or not the person inferred. If the story describes inferring, blacken in the space for "Yes" on your answer sheet; if the story does not, blacken the space for "No."

    a. Sandy observed many acorns underneath a tall tree. She knew that acorns fall from oak trees. Sandy concluded that the tall tree was an oak.

    b. Don looked carefully at a slice of bread and saw something green growing there. Don knew that bread mold was green.

    c. Sam went to visit his uncle on the farm. He looked in the barn to see if his uncle was there, but he did not see his uncle. Sam did not see the cows either.

    d. Joe baked a cake. The cake did not rise. Joe knew that baking powder makes cakes rise. He concluded that he had left the baking powder out of his cake. (pp. 127–130)

When evaluating students' understanding of a concept, it is important that teachers ask the students to do more than merely define the concept with words. They should also ask students to demonstrate knowledge of the critical attributes and their relationships. For example, the concept *sidewalk* might be defined as "a walkway *beside* a street." To demonstrate knowledge of the concept, the learner might "(1) identify a walkway by pointing to an actual picture of a walkway, (2) identify the street in a similar fashion, and (3) demonstrate *beside* by correctly relating the walkway to the street in the correct spatial relationship" (Gagné and Briggs, 1979, p. 66).

There are a number of principles that teachers should consider when constructing tests of the students' behaviors in the learning of concepts. For example, test items should include examples that measure the students' abilities to generalize to newly encountered examples of a concept. The test items should also assess students' abilities to discriminate among examples and nonexamples. Tests might employ different formats such as true-false, multiple choice, matching, short answer, or short essay. Practice assessment activities such as a variation of

"Twenty Questions" can be used to provide practice on the students' knowledge of concepts.

Tests for concept learning can also be employed for diagnostic purposes. An analysis of students' errors can indicate whether students have misconceptions about a concept, overgeneralize the concept to include closely related nonexamples, or undergeneralize by labeling some examples as nonexamples. If any of these three conditions exists, *reteaching* should take place. Merrill and Tennyson (1977) suggested the following guidelines:

1. If a student makes an overgeneralization error, additional instruction should consist of *matched* example-nonexample pairs that emphasize the absence of the critical attribute.
2. If a student makes an undergeneralization error, additional instruction should consist of more *difficult* examples that focus attention on the presence of the critical attribute.
3. If a student makes a misconception error, additional instruction should consist of matched example-nonexample pairs that are *divergent* on the noncritical attribute causing the confusion. Attribute isolation should focus the student's attention on the noncritical nature of this attribute. (p. 82)

Summary

Concept learning and logical thinking are critical goals for almost every subject taught in schools. Concepts, in most instances, form the core of academic subjects, and they become important scaffolding for building student understanding of any topic. They also serve as the road maps that allow human communication and understanding. The strong research base on concept teaching and learning provides teachers with good information about how people at various ages and levels of intellectual development acquire concepts and also about the relative effectiveness of various approaches to concept teaching. This research shows how conceptual understanding moves from the concrete to the abstract, and it emphasizes the importance of using best examples, conceptual webbing, and graphic organizers to promote concept development, particularly with younger students.

There are numerous approaches available to teachers who want to teach concepts and higher-level thinking to their students. Three approaches have been emphasized in this chapter—direct presentation, concept formation, and concept attainment. Although each approach starts with the teacher establishing set and ends with an effort to extend student thinking about their own thinking, the internal sequencing of the three approaches differs. Direct presentation emphasizes teachers' labeling and defining the concept to be learned early in the lesson followed by presentation of best examples and working for student understanding through exposition and questioning. The concept formation approach is inductive and involves students in listing and grouping objects and ideas and, in some instances, even naming and defining their own concepts. The concept attainment approach starts with a presentation of examples and nonexamples of a particular concept and saves defining and labeling until the end.

No one approach is more desirable than the others. Each has been designed to meet its own set of goals. Each approach also has to be adapted by teachers to complement their own teaching styles and to meet the needs of a particular group of students. Finally, as with all the models presented in this text, teaching effectiveness requires teachers to match their testing and evaluation programs to the model's particular goals and objectives.

Books for the Professional

Bolton, N. (1977). *Concept formation*. Oxford: Pergamon Press. A general introduction to the study of concept formation.

Klausmeier, H. (1980). *Learning and teaching concepts*. New York: Academic Press. This book includes reports on experiments and test construction for concept learning. It also contains suggestions for adapting concept teaching for individual differences.

Merrill, M., and Tennyson, R. (1977). *Teaching concepts: An instructional design guide*. Englewood Cliffs, N.J.: Educational Technology. Outlined in this text are specific steps for such activities as selecting concepts, defining concepts, selecting an example pool, and teaching strategies. The final section tells how to put it all together.

=============== **CHAPTER 8** ===============
LEARNING AIDS FOR PLANNING, OBSERVATION, AND REFLECTION

- Assessing My Skills for Concept Teaching
- Observing a Concept Attainment Lesson
- Concept Analysis
- Webbing Exercise
- Analyzing Curriculum Guides for Concept Lessons

ASSESSING MY SKILLS FOR CONCEPT TEACHING

PURPOSE: The purpose of this aid is to give you an opportunity to assess your current level of effectiveness or understanding of concept teaching.

DIRECTIONS: Check the level of effectiveness or understanding you feel you have for the teaching tasks listed below that are associated with concept teaching.

	Level of Effectiveness		
Skill or Competency	High	Medium	Low
Preinstructional Tasks			
Selecting concepts	——	——	——
Defining concepts	——	——	——
Analyzing concepts	——	——	——
Deciding on which approach	——	——	——
Instructional Tasks			
Directed Presentation			
Present goals and establish set	——	——	——
Name concept and provide definition	——	——	——
Identify critical attributes	——	——	——
Show examples—expository presentation	——	——	——
Develop concept—interrogatory presentation	——	——	——
Analyze thought processes and/or integrate learning	——	——	——
Concept Formation			
Present goals and establish set	——	——	——
Ask a question that will generate examples	——	——	——
Have students group examples into categories	——	——	——
Have students label categories	——	——	——
Analyze thought processes and/or integrate learning	——	——	——

Concept Attainment

   Present goals and establish set   _____   _____   _____

   Present examples and nonexamples of concept   _____   _____   _____

   Facilitate students' hypothesizing about concept
      and comparing attributes   _____   _____   _____

   Facilitate students' describing how they arrived
      at the label for the concept   _____   _____   _____

   Check for student understanding   _____   _____   _____

   Analyze thought processes and/or integrate
      learning   _____   _____   _____

Postinstructional Tasks

   Testing for concept learning   _____   _____   _____

OBSERVING A CONCEPT ATTAINMENT LESSON

♯ 9

PURPOSE: Good examples are critical to promote understanding of concepts. This aid will help provide you with an example of a concept attainment lesson. By observing how one teacher performs concept attainment, you will get a better idea about how you might conduct such a lesson yourself.

DIRECTIONS: Observe a concept attainment lesson, and as you do so, circle the term that best describes the teacher's behavior—(1) thoroughly, (2) partially, (3) missing, or (4) not needed. When there is time during or after the lesson, jot down the words the teacher used to convey each step. The latter is an important activity— it will help you move from having a general idea about concept attainment to knowing how it is actually implemented.

1. Did the teacher state the purpose of the lesson? 1 2 3 4

    _____

2. Did the teacher explain the function of the *yes* and *no* categories? 1 2 3 4

    _____

3. Did the initial *yes* clearly contain the essential characteristics? 1 2 3 4

    _____

4. Did the teacher ask questions that focused students' thinking on the essential attributes? 1 2 3 4

    _____

5. Did the teacher ask the students to compare the *yes* examples? 1 2 3 4

    _____

6. Did the teacher ask the students to contrast the characteristics of the *yes* examples with those of the *no* examples? 1 2 3 4

    _____

7. Did the teacher label each example *yes* or *no*? 1 2 3 4

    _____

8. Did the teacher ask the students to generate hypotheses and test them against the *yes* examples? 1 2 3 4

    _____

9. Did the teacher ask the students to name the concept? 1 2 3 4

    _____

10. Did the teacher ask the students to state the essential charac-   1 2 3 4
    teristics of the concept?

    _____

11. After the concept was agreed upon, did the teacher present   1 2 3 4
    additional examples and ask whether they contained the con-
    cept?

    _____

12. Did the teacher ask the students to justify their answers?   1 2 3 4

    _____

13. Were the students able to supply their own examples to fit the   1 2 3 4
    concept?

    _____

14. Did the teacher ask the students to justify their examples by   1 2 3 4
    identifying the essential characteristics (that is, critical attri-
    butes)?

    _____

15. Did the teacher ask the students to describe the thinking proc-   1 2 3 4
    esses they used in attaining the concept?

    _____

16. Did the teacher ask the students to evaluate the effectiveness   1 2 3 4
    of their strategies?

    _____

_____

Analysis and Reflection: Think of a concept you are very familiar with and might
someday teach. Write an outline of a concept attainment lesson for this concept
containing a statement for each of the steps listed above. You can use the words
of the teacher you have observed as a guide, if you wish. Think the lesson through.
Where are the awkward spots? Revise these until the outline seems smooth.

CONCEPT ANALYSIS

PURPOSE: It is imperative that the teacher carefully analyze any concept that he or she is planning to teach. In order to communicate clearly to students what the concept is, what its attributes are, and what constitutes an example or nonexample, the teacher needs to have an unshakably clear grasp of the concept. This aid is a planning guide to assist you in concept analysis.

DIRECTIONS: Select a concept for analysis that it is likely you will want to teach some day. Follow the steps listed below to analyze this concept.

1. Name the concept. _____

_____

2. Define or state the rule for the concept. _____

_____

_____

3. List the critical attributes of the concept. _____

_____

_____

4. List the noncritical attributes that are related to the concept. _____

_____

_____

5. Select examples that highlight the critical attributes of the concept. _____

_____

_____

6. Select nonexamples that are closely related to the concept. _____

_____

Analysis and Reflection: Try teaching your concept informally to a few friends. Did you discover any parts that were difficult for them to understand? Based on your friends' feedback, refine your definition, attributes, and examples. Write a paragraph on what you learned about forming clear definitions, attributes, and examples.

SOURCE: Adapted from P. Martorella (1985), *Elementary social studies: Developing reflective, competent, and concerned citizens*. Boston: Little, Brown, p. 83.

WEBBING EXERCISE

PURPOSE: Webbing can be a useful tool for analyzing concepts. This aid is a planning guide to help you construct a semantic web for a concept of your choice.

DIRECTIONS: Select a concept for analysis that it is likely you will want to teach some day. Follow the steps in constructing a concept web.

Step 1: Place the concept a circle (the core) on the bottom of this page and label it.

Step 2: Draw strands branching out from the core. These are the critical attributes. Give each a name.

Step 3: Draw lines connecting the various strands to show how the attributes and dimensions are differentiated from one another.

Step 4: Tie the various strands together to show relationships among the attributes.

A Web for the Concept _____

ANALYZING CURRICULUM GUIDES FOR CONCEPT LESSONS

PURPOSE: There are always more concepts that could be taught than there is time to teach. The purpose of this aid is to give you practice in making concept selection decisions.

DIRECTIONS: Obtain a teacher's guide to a textbook in your subject area or grade level. Assume that you are planning a three-week unit on a major topic presented in the text. Select five concepts associated with this topic for inclusion in the unit and answer the questions below.

1. What is the first concept that you will teach in this unit? _____

   _____

   Why did you choose this concept to be first? _____

   _____

   Which model of concept teaching will you use to teach this concept?

   _____

   Why? _____

   _____

2. What is the next concept that you will teach in this unit? _____

   _____

   Why did you choose this concept to be next? _____

   _____

   Which model of concept teaching will you use to teach this concept? _____

   _____

   Why? _____

   _____

3. What is the next concept that you will teach in this unit? _____

   _____

   Why did you choose this concept to be next? _____

   _____

   Which model of concept teaching will you use to teach this concept? _____

   _____

Why? _____

_____

4. What is the next concept that you will teach in this unit? _____

_____

Why did you choose this concept to be next? _____

_____

Which model of concept teaching will you use to teach this concept? _____

_____

Why? _____

_____

5. What is the next concept that you will teach in this unit? _____

_____

Why did you choose this concept to be next? _____

_____

Which model of concept teaching will you use to teach this concept? _____

_____

Why? _____

_____

_____

Analysis and Reflection: What factors did you consider in making these decisions? Was the time available an important consideration? Students' prior knowledge? Availability of resources? Other considerations? Did you overlook any factors you should have weighed? Write a paragraph about the factors that enter into concept decisions.

CHAPTER 9

MAIN IDEAS

- The model grew out of systems analysis and training psychology, with applications made first in industry and the military.
- Studies in classrooms have shown the effectiveness of the model for raising student achievement, particularly with elementary students from low socioeconomic backgrounds.
- The model is specifically designed to promote mastery of simple and complex skills and knowledge that can be defined and taught in a step-by-step fashion.
- The syntax of the model and the learning environment needed for its use are highly structured, which does not mean it is necessarily authoritarian or uncaring.
- The model's theoretical base is social learning theory and the research base on the efficacy of demonstration, practice, feedback, and transfer of learning.
- Preinstructional tasks associated with the model put emphasis on careful preparation of objectives and performing task analysis.
- Conducting a lesson using the model requires the teacher to be clear about rationale, to demonstrate and model precise behaviors, and to provide for practice, monitoring performance, and feedback.
- Postinstructional tasks emphasize practice under more complex conditions and the use of performance tests that can accurately measure skills and provide feedback.

Teaching Through Direct Instruction

Sometimes it is easy for teachers to forget that the basis for all other types of learning is basic skills. Skills—cognitive and physical—are the foundations on which more advanced learning (including learning to learn) are built. Before students can discover powerful concepts, think critically, solve problems, or write creatively they must first acquire basic skills and information. For example, before students can acquire and process large amounts of information, they must be able to decode and encode spoken and written messages, to take notes, and to summarize. Before students can think critically, they must have basic skills associated with logic, such as drawing inferences from data and recognizing bias in presentation. Before students can write an eloquent paragraph, they must master basic sentence construction, correct word usage, and the self-discipline required to keep on a writing task. In essence, in any field of study, "We must learn the *mechanics before the magic*."

In fact, the difference between novices and experts in almost any field is that experts have mastered certain basic skills to the point where they can perform them unconsciously and with precision, even in new or stressful situations. For example, expert teachers seldom worry about classroom management because after years of experience they are confident of their group control skills. Similarly, top NFL quarterbacks read every move of a defense without thinking and automatically respond with skillful actions to a "safety blitz" or double coverage of prize receivers, something novice quarterbacks cannot do.

This chapter focuses on a teaching model aimed at helping students learn basic skills and knowledge that can be taught in a step-by-step fashion. For purposes here, the model is labeled the *direct instruction model*. As you will see later, this model does not always have the same name. Sometimes it is referred to as a training model. Good, Grouws, and Ebmeier (1983) called their model *active teaching*. Hunter (1982) labeled hers *mastery teaching*. Recently, Rosenshine and Stephens (1986) called this approach *explicit instruction*.

Even though you may never have thought about this model in any systematic way, you will undoubtedly be familiar with certain aspects of it. The rationale and procedures underlying this model were probably used by adults to teach you to drive your first car, to brush your teeth, to hit a solid backhand, to write a research paper, or to solve algebraic equations. This model may have been used to correct your phobia about flying or to wean you from cigarettes. The direct instruction model is rather straightforward and can be mastered in a relatively short time. It is a "must" in the repertoire of the beginning teacher.

PERSPECTIVE AND RATIONALE

Several historical and theoretical roots provide the rationale for the direct instruction model, including the ideas from cognitive psychology and information processing discussed in Chapter 7. Joyce and Weil (1980) have emphasized the contributions from training and behavioral psychology. Madeline Hunter (1987) credits the work of Gagné (1977) as the basis for the components included in her lesson design. Rosenshine and Stephens (1986) wrote that they found a book published by the War Manpower Commission in 1945 titled *How to Instruct* that included many of the ideas and steps associated with direct instruction. Much of the research presented in Chapter 4 on time and learning also supports the model, as you will soon see. Short discussions about the contributions of systems analysis, training psychology, and studies of effective teaching follow.

Systems Analysis

Systems analysis has its roots in many fields and it has influenced research on many aspects of human development—biology, organizational theory, social theory, and learning. Basically, it is the study of the various relationships that exist between the interdependent parts of some whole. Examples of two well-known *systems* are the intricate relationships among the various living organisms that make up an ecosystem, or the relationships between the production, distribution, and communication parts of the incredibly complex system of international trade. People generally become aware of the part-whole relationships of systems only when they break down. For example, overpopulation of rabbits developed in Wyoming after the coyote population was systematically eliminated in that area. Similarly, there are instances when purchasers are unable to buy a Japanese car in Chicago because East Coast dock workers are on strike.

In the area of instruction and learning the systems approach has emphasized how to systematically separate complex skills and ideas into their component parts so they can be taught and learned more effectively. Two theorists and instructional designers, Gagné and Briggs (1979), represent the systems point of view in education:

> Systematically designed instruction can greatly affect individual human development. Some educational writings . . . indicate that education would perhaps be best if it were designed simply to provide a nurturing environment in which young people were allowed to grow up in their own ways, without the imposition

of any plan to direct learning. We consider this an incorrect line of thinking. Unlearned and undirected learning, we believe, is very likely to lead to the development of many individuals who are in one way or another incompetent to derive personal satisfaction from living in our society of today or tomorrow. (p. 5)

Later you will see how the ideas of directed learning and task analysis (a tool used by systems analysts) have contributed to the direct instruction model.

Training Psychology

If systems analysis has provided the rationale and theory for the precision of the direct instruction model, training psychology, as applied in military and industrial settings, has motivated much of the direct application. With the rise of modern organizations, many jobs require performance of tasks far more complex than those required in earlier periods. Modern warfare has also created a demand for personnel who can operate complex and sophisticated weapon systems. For example, it is reported that the Air Force's B-1 bomber requires over 7,000 manuals totaling over a million pages to guide the 1,577 personnel who fix and fly this plane (*Washington Post*, August 18, 1985). Obviously, since no one person can fix or even understand such complexity, a continuing problem for educators in military and industrial settings is how to prepare personnel who can master particular pieces of large complex tasks. Since traditional educational methods failed to produce the necessary precision and mastery, training methods gradually evolved.

Studies of Effective Teaching

Teachers discovered that these methods could be adapted to the teaching of basic academic skills such as reading, mathematics, writing, and various science and social science skills. Much of the evidence of the model comes from studies where researchers found effective teachers who were using this model on their own. When the achievement of their students was compared to that of students in classrooms where the teachers were not so direct in their instructional approaches, researchers found that the former were doing better, particularly in reading and mathematics at the elementary level.

OVERVIEW OF DIRECT INSTRUCTION

The direct instruction model can be described by its instructional effects, its syntax, and the structure of its learning environment. After providing an overview of the model and presenting a sample of the research associated with it, teaching behaviors required to successfully execute this model are examined.

Instructional Effects

In Chapter 7, the concepts of declarative and procedural knowledge were introduced. Declarative knowledge, remember, is knowledge learners have about something, whereas procedural knowledge is knowledge about how to do something. The direct instruction model has been specifically designed to promote student learning of the procedural knowledge needed to perform simple and complex skills and for declarative knowledge that is well structured and can be taught in a step-by-step fashion. The models described previously focused primarily on acquisition of declarative knowledge; in contrast, the direct instruction model makes important contributions to the teaching of skills. Table 9.1 contrasts the instructional objectives of models aimed at promoting knowledge acquisition with those of models aimed at teaching skills.

Differences can easily be observed in the two sets of objectives listed in Table 9.1. For instance in the first set of objectives, the student is expected to know ice hockey rules. This is important declarative knowledge for students in a physical education class. However, being able to identify the rules does not necessarily mean that the student can perform any skills associated with ice hockey, like passing while on the move, the content of the procedural knowledge objective found in column 2. Another example illustrating the differences in the two types of objectives could be from the field of music. Many people can identify a French horn; some are even familiar with the history of the instrument. Few, however, have sufficient procedural knowledge to play a French horn well.

Syntax of Direct Instruction

There are five essential phases or steps in the direct instruction model. The model begins with the teacher providing rationale and establishing set; next it requires demonstration of the skill or knowledge being taught; and it concludes with opportunities for students to practice and receive feedback on their progress. It

Table 9.1 Contrasting Objectives for Knowledge Acquisition and Skill Development

KNOWLEDGE ACQUISITION	SKILL DEVELOPMENT
1. The student will be able to list the basic rules of ice hockey.	1. The student will be able to pass while moving.
2. The student will be able to identify the subjects in the following sentences: a. Whose brother are you? b. Ralph always walked to school. c. Josie loves to read mysteries.	2. The student will supply an appropriate verb in the following sentences: a. Where _____ you? b. Ralph always _____ to school. c. _____ the apples to your sister.
3. Given the equation, $y = 2.6x + 0.8$, the student will correctly select the number corresponding to the y intercept.	3. The student will be able to solve for x in the equation, $9 = 2.6x + 0.8$

Table 9.2   Syntax of the Training Model

PHASES		TEACHER BEHAVIOR
Phase 1:	Provide objectives and establish set	Teacher goes over objectives for the lesson, gives background information, and explains why the lesson is important. Gets students ready to learn.
Phase 2:	Demonstrate	Teacher demonstrates the skill correctly or presents step-by-step information.
Phase 3:	Provide guided practice	Teacher structures initial practice.
Phase 4:	Check for understanding and provide feedback	Teacher checks to see if students are performing correctly and provides feedback.
Phase 5:	Provide extended practice and transfer	Teacher sets conditions for extended practice with attention to transfer of the skill to more complex situations.

is always important for teachers to promote transfer to other "real life" settings for skills taught in classrooms. The five phases of the training model are summarized in Table 9.2. A more detailed discussion of these steps is presented in the last section of this chapter.

Structure of the Learning Environment

Of all the models described, the direct instruction model requires the most careful structuring and orchestration by the teacher. To be effective, the model requires attention to every detail of defining the skill or content to be taught and the nature of the demonstration, as well as to the practice schedules provided for students. Even though there are opportunities for teachers and students to jointly identify goals, the model is primarily teacher directed. This does not mean, as most developers of the model point out, that the learning environment has to be authoritarian, cold, or free from humor. It does mean that the environment is task oriented with high expectations for student accomplishment.

SAMPLING THE RESEARCH BASE

The research base for the direct instruction model and its various components comes from many fields. Three areas are highlighted here, including studies that provide some insight into the knowledge base and the nature of the research associated with this model.

Overall Effects

Much of the research that provided the empirical base for the direct instruction model has already been introduced. Chapter 4 described the Stallings and

Kaskowitz (1974) study in which the researcher found that classrooms in Project Follow Through that emphasized structured learning of basic skills produced stronger learning gains than classrooms using informal approaches. You also read about studies showing strong relationships between structured situations where students had high time-on-task ratios and student achievement, particularly in the area of basic skills. Many of these studies used procedures that identified two groups of teachers: those who were effective in producing student achievement and those who were not. Observing these teachers in naturalistic settings gave some insight into what the effective ones were doing to promote higher student achievement; in this instance they were applying direct instruction procedures.

Some researchers started to list the behaviors used by effective teachers and to develop programs that could be used to train teachers and to test the cause and effect relationships between specific teacher behaviors and student achievement under experimental conditions.

One such experiment was done by Good and Grouws at the University of Missouri. Based on earlier research, Good and Grouws developed a program for teaching mathematics in elementary schools following the procedures in Figure 9.1.

Note how closely the steps in Good and Grouws's approach follow the syntax of the direct instruction model. More information about Good and Grouws's study is found in Research Summary 9.1.

Behavioral Modeling and Demonstration

Some of the conceptual underpinnings for the direct instruction model come from Albert Bandura's social learning theory, which says that much of what we learn is through modeling. Bandura (1977) wrote:

> Learning would be exceedingly laborious, not to mention hazardous, if people had to rely solely on the effects of their own actions to inform them what to do. Fortunately, most human behavior is learned observationally through modeling: from observing others one forms an idea of how new behaviors are performed, and on later occasions this coded information serves as a guide for action. Because people can learn from example what to do, at least in approximate form, before performing any behavior, they are spared needless errors. (p. 22)

Given the confines of the classroom, demonstration is usually the most practical strategy for teachers to use in promoting learning through modeling. However, demonstrations must be carefully planned and executed as described later. They must also be structured so the learner will, according to Bandura (1977), "attend to, and perceive accurately, the significant features of the modeled behavior" (p. 24). This proposition has been studied in a variety of formats and contexts over the years, including studies that date back to the 1930s and 1940s. The key principles that come out of all this research are: (1) effective demonstrations

Figure 9.1   Summary of Key Instructional Behaviors

Daily Review (first 8 minutes except Mondays)
1. Review the concepts and skills associated with homework
2. Collect and deal with homework assignments
3. Ask several mental computation exercises

Development (about 20 minutes)
1. Briefly focus on prerequisite skills and concepts
2. Focus on meaning and promote student understanding by using lively explanations, demonstrations, process explanations, illustrations, etc.
3. Assess student comprehension
   (a) using process/product questions (active questions)
   (b) using controlled practice
4. Repeat and elaborate on the meaning portions as necessary

Seatwork (about 15 minutes)
1. Provide uninterrupted successful practice
2. Momentum—keep the ball rolling—get everyone involved, then sustain involvement
3. Alerting—let students know their work will be checked at end of period
4. Accountability—check the students' work

Homework Assignment
1. Assign on a regular basis at the end of each math class except Fridays
2. Should involved about 15 minutes of work to be done at home
3. Should include one or two review problems

Special Reviews
1. Weekly review/maintenance
   (a) conduct during the first 20 minutes each Monday
   (b) focus on skills and concepts covered the previous week
2. Monthly review/maintenance
   (a) conduct every fourth Monday
   (b) focus on skills and concepts covered since the last monthly review

SOURCE: From T. L. Good and D. A. Grouws (1979), The Missouri mathematics effectiveness project: An experimental study in fourth-grade classrooms. *Journal of Educational Psychology*, *71*, 357. Copyright 1979 by the American Psycological Association. Reprinted by permission of publisher and author.

---

require careful attention by teachers to make sure all behaviors being demonstrated are accurately modeled, (2) conditions are present so learners can clearly perceive what is going on, and (3) explanation and discussions during demonstrations enhance later student performance. Procedures for giving effective demonstrations are elaborated later in the chapter.

Practice and Transfer

A critical feature of the direct instruction model is the use of practice, particularly practice to facilitate transfer. Fortunately, this topic has been studied rather extensively, so a solid base exists from which to operate. The syntax for this model brings practice into focus two times. First, when the teacher provides

─────────────────────── **RESEARCH SUMMARY** ───────────────────────
9.1

Good, T. L., and Grouws, D. A. (1971). The Missouri mathematics effectiveness project: An experimental study in fourth-grade classrooms. *Journal of Educational Psychology, 71,* 355–362.

PROBLEM: Based on a previous study they had done on effective mathematics teachers (those who consistently produced good achievement results), Good and Grouws decided to investigate the effectiveness of a mathematics teaching program on student achievement.

SAMPLE AND SETTING: From the Tulsa, Oklahoma, public schools, 40 classroom teachers volunteered from 27 schools that used semidepartmental structures for teaching mathematics. Good and Grouws report that most of the schools were in low socioeconomic areas of the city.

PROCEDURES: The researchers met with all the teachers in the fall of the year and randomly assigned them to two groups. Schools were used as the units for random assignment.

- *Experimental Group:* The program was explained to the teachers in this group and they were provided with a short training session and a 45-page manual explaining the key teaching behaviors of the program. These behaviors are the same as those summarized in Figure 9.1.
- *Control Group:* Teachers in this group were told they would not get any information about the program or the study until it was over. Their job was to continue to teach mathematics in their own style. The researchers strived to create a strong Hawthorne condition with control teachers by emphasizing how important it was to improve achievement in mathematics.

Student achievement was measured with a specially designed test of the content covered by teachers in the school system with the mathematics subtest of Science Research Associates' standardized achievement test. Students were tested in September at the beginning of the project and again in December and January.

RESULTS: The researchers observed all the teachers in the study and reported that the program as defined was implemented "reasonably well." Table 1 shows the impact of the experimental program on student achievement.

───

initial practice to see if students understand specific topics or skills, and second, when independent practice is assigned under different or more complex conditions. Both kinds of practice are intended to promote transfer of learning.

Transfer of learning is an important concept because the intention of most school learning is to promote transfer to nonschool settings. Teachers want their students to read a first-grade primer so that they can later read newspapers, magazines, and works of literature. Teachers want students to solve mathematical problems in textbooks so that later they can perform real-world mathematical functions, or can think mathematically in problem situations.

TABLE 1   Preproject and Postproject Means and Standard Deviations for Experimental and Control Classes on the SRA Mathematics Test

Group	Preproject data			Postproject data			Postproject gain		
	Raw Score	Grade Equivalent	Percentile	Raw Score	Grade Equivalent	Percentile	Raw Score	Grade Equivalent	Percentile
	All treatment and all control teachers								
Experimental									
M	11.94	3.34	26.57	19.95	4.55	57.58	8.01	1.21	31.01
SD	3.18	.51	13.30	4.66	.67	18.07			
Control									
M	12.84	3.48	29.80	17.74	4.22	48.81	4.90	.74	19.01
SD	3.12	.48	12.43	4.76	.68	17.45			

SOURCE: Adapted from T. L. Good and D. A. Grouws (1979), p. 359.

DISCUSSION AND IMPLICATIONS: As can be observed in Table 1 students in the experimental group began the program will lower scores than did students in the control group. Note, however, that by the end of the program students in the experimental group had gained significantly—11.94 to 19.95 on number of questions answered correctly, as contrasted with a gain for the control group students of 12.84 to 17.74. Data in Table 1 also show the impressive gain in terms of national norms or percentile ranking. The achievement gains by students in the experimental group were statistically significant.

This study, among several others done since that time, supports that direct instruction and training can produce fairly impressive results for the type of learning the model is aimed to accomplish. The Good and Grouws study is also important because it shows that achievement can occur, given the right instruction, in urban, low income schools. Good and Grouws are themselves quick to point out that all mathematics instruction should not necessarily follow this approach, because other goals can be better achieved by different approaches.

The concept of time for learning, introduced in Chapter 4, is also associated with practice and transfer. Researchers have studied such questions as: How much time should be devoted to practice? Should the time be spread out or concentrated? How much time should pass between practice sessions? Later in the chapter several of these issues are discussed in some detail; here, Research Summary 9.2 relates a study that explored how much time and practice are needed to master several different types of learning tasks. This study is interesting because it serves as a reminder that some learning tasks take more time and practice to learn than do others.

━━━━━━━━━━━━━━━━ **RESEARCH SUMMARY** ━━━━━━━━━━━━━━━━
9.2*

Lyon, M. and Gettinger, M. (1985). Differences in student performance on knowledge, comprehension, and application tasks: Implications for school learning.
Journal of Educational Psychology, 77, 12–19.

PROBLEM: A number of studies have investigated the importance of time for practice
and for learning. But are all types of tasks alike in terms of the time needed for
learning? Do students differ in terms of the time they need to learn? How should
a teacher allocate practice time among different types of tasks? This study
investigated the time needed to learn three types of tasks: knowledge, comprehension, and application.

SAMPLE AND SETTING: The learning task used by the researchers was three fictitious
reading passages, each followed by 15 multiple-choice questions. Five questions
assessed knowledge, five comprehension, and five application. The students were
asked to read a given passage while it was being read to them. They were then
asked to turn the written passage over and answer the questions. This procedure
was repeated five times for each passage, although the questions were in a
different order each time. Time needed to learn was assessed by the number of
trials necessary for a child to achieve a certain level of accuracy. Five days later,
the students were asked to complete the same task, but without reading the
passages.

RESULTS: There was wide variation in the number of trials the students needed to
reach the criterion level of accuracy: some students needed only one trial, while
others needed as many as five. A few students were never successful in performing
some of the tasks. Table 1 provides information on the average scores on each
type of task and trial and the range.

DISCUSSION AND IMPLICATIONS: As can be observed in Table 1 knowledge questions
were answered more accurately at the time of the experiment and five days later
than were comprehension and application questions. Further, comprehension
questions were answered more accurately than application questions. It would
appear that application tasks take more time to master than comprehension tasks,
and both take longer than knowledge tasks. Further, different children require
different amounts of time to complete a task to a criterion level.

The researchers were, in part, testing some assumptions inherent in Bloom's
taxonomy: that there is a hierarchy of tasks that become progressively more
difficult and time-consuming. (See Chapter 7 for explanation of Bloom's work.)
Unfortunately, the time-needed-to-learn measurement in this study was based on

_____

* This report was summarized by Virginia Richardson-Koehler.

TABLE 1 Descriptive Statistics for Individual Trial Scores, Total Gain Scores, Time to Learn (TTL) Scores, and Retention Scores

Variable	M	SD	Range
Trial 1			
Knowledge	10.43	2.16	3–14
Comprehension	9.91	2.46	5–15
Application	9.78	2.38	2–15
Trial 2			
Knowledge	12.52	1.84	6–15
Comprehension	11.49	2.25	4–15
Application	10.26	2.29	3–15
Trial 3			
Knowledge	13.30	1.43	9–15
Comprehension	11.84	2.12	5–15
Application	10.61	2.09	3–15
Trial 4			
Knowledge	13.49	1.37	8–15
Comprehension	12.18	2.18	5–15
Application	10.74	2.09	2–15
Trial 5			
Knowledge	13.66	1.48	6–15
Comprehension	12.38	2.12	4–15
Application	10.90	2.27	2–15
Total gain			
Knowledge	3.13	0.20	−2–8
Comprehension	2.47	0.24	−2–8
Application	1.11	0.23	−4–6
TTL score			
Knowledge	2.61	1.51	1–6
Comprehension	3.75	1.93	1–6
Application	4.89	1.81	1–6
Retention score			
Knowledge	13.44	1.77	7–15
Comprehension	12.89	1.99	5–15
Application	12.13	2.22	2–15

SOURCE: From M. Lyon and M. Gettinger (1985), p. 15.

the number of trials required to successfully complete a task, rather than a time measurement. Further, as is the case in many studies of this type, the sample was small and specialized. Nonetheless, the study was conducted in a real classroom setting and the results indicate that the allocation of time and practice for the mastery of a task must take into account the type of task and the differential rates at which students successfully complete it. It also requires understanding of students' prior knowledge.

PROCEDURES FOR USING DIRECT INSTRUCTION

Expert execution of the direct instruction model requires specific behaviors and decisions by teachers during the preinstructional, interactive, and postinstructional stages. Some of these required behaviors you have already learned from studying the previous models; some, however, are unique. The unique features are emphasized here.

Preinstructional Tasks

Although the direct instruction model is applicable to any subject, it is most appropriate for the performance-oriented subjects, such as reading and writing or physical education, and for the skill components of the more informationally oriented subjects like history or science. It is also effective for teaching those aspects of any subject in which the information or skill is well-structured and can be taught in the step-by-step fashion. The direct instruction model is not appropriate for teaching creativity, higher-level thinking skills, or abstract concepts and ideas, nor for teaching attitudes, appreciation, or understanding of important public issues. Table 9.1 illustrated the kinds of objectives for which the direct instruction model is most appropriate. In this section more detail is provided in how to prepare objectives for this model.

PREPARING OBJECTIVES WHEN USING THE MODEL

Previous chapters described the characteristics of objectives in some detail. In general, conceptualizing objectives for a lesson using the direct instruction model follows the same general guidelines. Remember, a good objective is student based and specific, describes the testing situation, and specifies the level of performance expected. The major characteristic of objectives for lessons that are skill oriented is that the objectives for these types of lessons normally represent easily observed behaviors that can be stated precisely and measured accurately. For example, if the objective is to have students climb a 15-foot rope in seven seconds, that behavior can be observed and timed. If the objective is to have the student go to the world globe and point out Kuwait, that behavior can be observed. On the other hand, performance tests for more complex skills (such as your use of the various models of teaching described in this book) are very difficult to construct and sometimes nearly impossible. A learning aid at the end of this chapter has been designed to help you gain further clarity about the nature of basic skill objectives deemed important in schools.

PERFORMING TASK ANALYSIS

Task analysis is one tool used to define with some precision the exact nature of a particular skill or well-structured bit of knowledge. Some people believe that task analysis is something that is unreasonably difficult and complex, when in fact it is a rather straightforward and simple process, particularly for teachers who know their subjects well. The central idea behind task analysis is that complex understandings and skills cannot be learned at one time or in their entirety.

Instead, for ease of understanding and mastery, complex skills and understandings must first be divided into significant component parts.

Task analysis helps the teacher define precisely what it is the learner needs to do to perform a desired skill. It can be accomplished through the following:

STEP 1: Find out what a knowledgeable person does when the skill is performed.

STEP 2: Divide the overall skill into subskills.

STEP 3: Put subskills in some logical order, showing those that might be prerequisite to others.

STEP 4: Design strategies to teach each of the subskills and how they are combined.

Figure 9.2 shows a simple task analysis for an objective in mathematics, subtracting whole numbers.

Figure 9.2 Task Analysis for Subtracting Whole Numbers

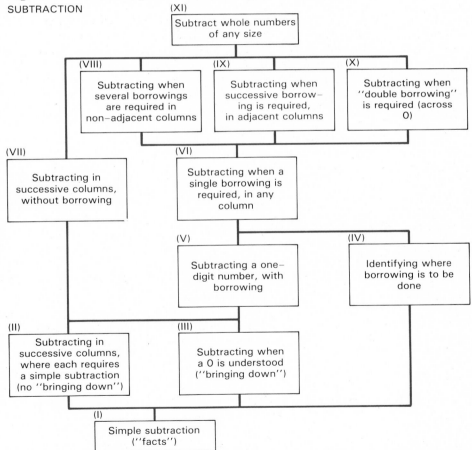

SUBTRACTION

SOURCE: From *Principles of instructional design*, R. M. Gagné and L. J. Briggs (1979) © Holt, Rinehart and Winston. Reprinted by permission of Holt, Rinehart and Winston Inc.

Sometimes a task analysis can take the form of a flow chart. This allows the skill and the relationships among subskills to be visualized. It also can show the various steps that a learner must go through in acquiring the skill. Figure 9.3 is a task analysis done this way. It shows the steps and subskills needed to perform a set of skills associated with playing ice hockey.

It would be a mistake to believe that teachers do task analysis for every skill they teach in the detail found in Figures 9.2 or 9.3. Even though the process is not difficult, it is time-consuming. Effective teachers do, however, rely on the main concept associated with task analysis, that is, that most skills have several subskills and that learners cannot learn to perform the whole skill well unless they have mastered the parts.

As a final note about task analysis, think about the way information and tasks associated with using the various teaching models are organized in this book. First it is stated that there are a number of tasks that must be performed: planning

Figure 9.3   Flow Chart of Skills for Ice Hockey

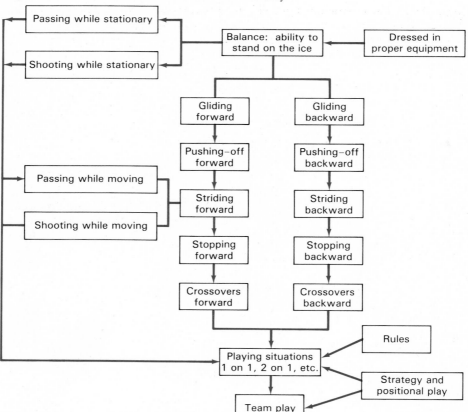

tasks in the preinstructional phase, specific tasks associated with conducting the lesson, and tasks connected to postinstructional activities. A teacher who cannot perform all tasks well cannot use the model effectively. On the other hand, even if all tasks can be performed well, a lesson will not be well taught unless the teacher can creatively combine all the parts into a meaningful whole.

Conducting the Lesson

As outlined in Table 9.2, the direct instruction model breaks down into the following five steps: (1) providing objectives and establishing set, (2) demonstrating the skill or understanding that is the focus of the lesson, (3) providing guided practice, (4) checking for understanding and providing feedback, and (5) assigning independent practice. The first four steps, which take place in the classroom, are described below. The fifth step is dealt with as a postinstructional activity.

PROVIDING OBJECTIVES AND ESTABLISHING SET

Regardless of the instructional model being used, good teachers begin their lessons by explaining their objectives and establishing a learning set. As previously described, an abbreviated version of the objectives should be written on the chalkboard or printed and distributed to students. In addition, students should be told how a particular day's objective ties into previous ones and, in most instances, how it is a part of longer-range objectives or themes. They should also be informed about the flow of a particular lesson and about how much time the lesson is expected to take. Figure 9.4 is an example of what a science teacher provided for her students prior to a lesson on microscopes.

Giving the rationale and overviews for any lesson is important, but particularly so for skill-oriented lessons. Such lessons typically focus on discrete skills that students may not perceive as important but that require substantial motivation and commitment to practice on the part of students. Knowing the theory behind a particular skill and why it is being taught helps to motivate and bring the desired commitment, as contrasted to such general statements as, "It's good for you," "You'll need it to find a job," or, "It is required in the curriculum guide."

Figure 9.4   Aims and Overview of Today's Lesson on Microscopes

Today's objective: The objective of today's lesson is to learn how to bring into focus the lens on a compound light microscope so you can make an accurate observation of plant cells.

Agenda:

5 minutes	Introduction, review, and objectives
5 minutes	Rationale
10 minutes	Demonstration of how to adjust lens on microscope—questions and answers
20 minutes	Practice with your microscope (I'll come around and help)
10 minutes	Wrap-up and assignment for tomorrow

CONDUCTING DEMONSTRATIONS

The direct instruction model relies heavily on the proposition that much of what is learned and much of the learner's behavioral repertoire comes from observing others. Bandura's social learning theory specifically demonstrated and argued that it is from watching particular behaviors that students learn to perform them and to anticipate their consequences. The behaviors of others, both good and bad, thus become guides for the learner's own behavior. Needless to say, this form of learning by imitation saves students much needless trial and error. It can also allow them to learn inappropriate or incorrect behaviors.

Demonstrating a particular concept or skill requires teachers to (1) acquire a thorough understanding or *mastery* of the concept or skills prior to the demonstration and (2) carefully *rehearse* all aspects of the demonstration prior to the actual classroom event.

Understanding and Mastery To ensure that students will observe correct rather than incorrect behaviors, teachers must attend to exactly what goes into their demonstrations. The old adage often repeated to children by parents, "Do as I say, not as I do," is not sufficient for teachers trying to teach precise basic information or skills. Examples abound in every aspect of human endeavor where people unknowingly perform a skill incorrectly because they observed and learned the skill from someone who was doing it wrong. The important point here is that if teachers want students to do something "right," they must ensure that they demonstrate it correctly.

Rehearsal It is exceedingly difficult to demonstrate anything with complete accuracy. The more complex the information or skill the more difficult it is to be precise in classroom demonstrations. To ensure correct demonstration and modeling requires practice ahead of time. It also requires that the critical attributes of the skill or concept be thought through clearly and distinctly. For example, suppose you want to teach your students how to use the card catalog to locate information in the library and you are going to demonstrate how call numbers on a particular card corresponds to a book's location. It is important to prepare and rehearse so the numbering system demonstrated is consistent with what students will find in their particular library. If the demonstration consists of such steps as going to the card catalog, looking up the book, writing down the call number, and then proceeding to the stacks, it is important that these steps be rehearsed to the point that none (such as writing down the call number) is forgotten during the actual demonstration.

PROVIDING GUIDED PRACTICE

Common sense says that "practice makes perfect." In reality, this principle does not always hold up. You all know people who drive their cars every day but who are still poor drivers, or people who have many children but who are poor parents.

All too often the assignments teachers give students do not really provide for the type of practice that is needed. Writing out answers to questions at the end of a chapter, doing 20 mathematics problems, or writing an essay do not always help students master important understandings and skills.

A critical step in the direct instruction model is the way the teacher approaches practice. Fortunately for the beginning teacher, a considerable amount of research evidence now exists that can guide efforts to provide practice. For example, it is known that active practice can increase retention, make learning more automatic, and enable the learner to transfer learning to new or stressful situations. The following principles can help teachers provide for practice.

Assign Short, Meaningful Amounts of Practice In most instances, particularly with a new skill, it is important to ask students to perform the desired skill for short periods of time and, if the skill is complex, to simplify the task at the beginning. Briefness and simplification, however, should not distort the pattern of the whole skill. Look again at the example of a teacher using the direct instruction model to help students learn how to use the card catalog in the library. After sufficient explanation and demonstration the teacher now wants students to practice the skill. One approach would be to send students to the library to locate 20 books listed on a work sheet. Probably a more efficient and controlled way would be to have sample sets of catalog cards in the room (simplifying the complexity of the whole catalog system) and have students look up one book at a time in the card index (shortening the practice).

Assign Practice to Increase Overlearning For skills that are critical to later performance, practice must continue well beyond the stage of initial mastery. Many skills associated with the performing arts, athletics, reading, and typing have to be overlearned so they become automatic. It is only through overlearning and complete mastery that a skill can be used effectively in new and novel situations or under stress. This ability to automatically perform a skill or combination of skills is what separates the novice from the expert in all fields. Teachers must be careful, however, because efforts to produce overlearning can become monotonous and actually decrease students' motivation to learn.

Be Aware of the Advantages and Disadvantages of Massed and Distributed Practice Many schools in the United States have homework policies—the rule of thumb is about 30 minutes per night per subject for older students and at least a few minutes a night for younger students. Although homework can be valuable for extending student learning, a required amount of time each night can be harmful. The amount and timing of practice depend upon many factors. Normally psychologists have defined this issue as massed (continuous) practice versus distributed (divided into segments) practice. Although the research literature does not give direct principles that can be followed in every instance, massed practice is usually recommended for learning new skills, with the caution that long periods of practice can lead to boredom and fatigue. Distributed practice is most effective for refining already familiar skills with, again, the caution that the interval of time between practice segments should not be so long that students forget or regress and have to start over again.

Attend to the Initial Stages of Practice The initial stages of practice are particularly critical since it is during this period that the learner can unknowingly start using incorrect techniques that later must be unlearned. It is also during the initial stages of practice that the learner will want to measure success in terms of his or her performance as contrasted to technique. This issue will be described more completely below.

CHECKING UNDERSTANDING AND PROVIDING FEEDBACK

Without knowledge of results, practice is of little value to students. In fact, the most important task of teachers using the direct instruction model is providing students with meaningful feedback and knowledge of results. Feedback to students can be done in many ways, such as verbal feedback, video- or audio-taping of performance, tests, or written comments. Without specific feedback, however, students will not learn to write well by writing, read well by reading, or run well by running. The critical question for teachers is how to provide effective feedback for large classes of students. Guidelines deemed important include the following:

GUIDELINE 1: Provided feedback as soon as possible after the practice.

It is not necessary that feedback be provided instantaneously, but it should be close enough to the actual practice so that students can remember clearly their own performance. This means that teachers who provide written comments on essays should be prompt in returning corrected papers. It means that tests gauged to measure performance should be corrected immediately and gone over with students. It also means that arrangements for verbal feedback or feedback using video or audio devices should be such that delay is kept to a minimum.

GUIDELINE 2: Make feedback specific.

In general, feedback should be as specific as possible to be most helpful to students. For example:

"Your use of the word *domicile* is pretentious; *house* would do nicely."

Instead of:

"You are using too many big words."

Or:

"Your hand was placed exactly right for an effective backhand."

Instead of:

"Good backhand."

Or:

"Three words were spelled incorrectly on your paper: *pleistocene*, *penal*, and
recommendation."

Instead of:

"Too many misspelled words."

GUIDELINE 3: Concentrate on behaviors and not intent.

Feedback is most helpful to students and raises less defensiveness if it is
aimed directly at some behavior as contrasted to one's perception of the intent
behind the behavior. For example:

"I cannot read your handwriting. You do not provide enough blank space
between words and you make your *O*'s and *A*'s identically."

Instead of:

"You do not work on making your handwriting neat."

Or:

"When you faced the class in your last speech, you spoke so softly that
most students could not hear what you were saying."

Instead of:

"You should try to overcome your shyness."

GUIDELINE 4: Keep feedback appropriate to the developmental stage of the
learner.

As important as knowledge of results is, feedback must be administered
carefully to be helpful. Sometimes, students can be given too much feedback or
feedback that is too sophisticated for them to handle. For example, a person trying
to drive a car for the first time can appreciate hearing that he or she "let the
clutch" out too quickly which caused the car to jerk. The beginning driver,
however, is not ready for explanations about how to drop the brake and use the
clutch to keep the car from rolling on a steep hill. A young student being taught
the "i before e" rule in spelling probably will respond favorably to being told that

he or she spelled *brief* correctly, but may not be ready to consider why *recieve* was incorrect.

GUIDELINE 5: Emphasize praise and feedback on correct performance.

You all know from your own experiences that you like to receive positive more than negative feedback. In general, praise will be accepted whereas negative feedback may be denied. Teachers, therefore, should try to provide praise and positive feedback particularly when students are learning new concepts and skills. However, when incorrect performance is observed, it must be corrected. Characteristics of effective praise were given in Chapter 6. Here is a sensible approach to the dealing with incorrect responses and performances provided by Madeline Hunter (1982 pp. 85–90). She recommended the following three teacher behaviors:

1. Dignify the student's incorrect response or performance by giving a question for which the response would have been correct. For example, "George Washington would have been the right answer, if I had asked you who was the first president of the United States."
2. Provide the student with an assist, hint, or prompt. For example, "Remember, the president in 1828 had also been a hero in the War of 1812."
3. Hold the student accountable. For example, "You didn't know President Jackson today, but I bet you will tomorrow when I ask you again."

A combination of positive and negative feedback is best in most instances. For example, "You did a perfect job of matching subjects and verbs in this paragraph, except in the instance where you used a collective subject." Or, "You were holding the racket correctly as you approached the ball, but you had too much of your weight on your left foot." Or, "I like the way you speak up in class, but during our last class discussion you interrupted Ron three different times when he was trying to give us his point of view."

GUIDELINE 6: When giving negative feedback, show how to perform correctly.

Knowing that something has been done incorrectly does not help students do it correctly. Negative feedback should be accompanied with actions by the teacher demonstrating correct performance. If a student is shooting a basketball with the palm of the hand, the teacher should point that out and demonstrate how to place the ball on the fingertips; if a writing sample is filled with words used incorrectly, the teacher should pencil in words that would be more appropriate; if students are holding their hands incorrectly on the computer keyboard, the correct placement should be modeled.

GUIDELINE 7: Help students to focus on "process" rather than outcomes.

Many times beginners want to focus their attention on measurable performance. "I just typed 35 words per minute without any errors." "I wrote my essay in an hour." "I drove the golf ball 75 yards." "I cleared the bar at 4 feet 6 inches." It is the teacher's responsibility to get students to look at the "process" or technique behind their performances and to understand that incorrect techniques may achieve immediate objectives but will probably inhibit later growth. For example, a student may type 35 words per minute using only two fingers but will probably never reach 100 words per minute using this technique. Starting the approach on the wrong foot may be fine for clearing the high jump bar at 4 feet 6 inches, but will prevent ever reaching 5 feet 6 inches.

GUIDELINE 8: Teach students how to provide feedback to themselves and how to judge their own performances.

Chapter 2 described how important it is for beginning teachers to learn how to assess and judge their own performances by submitting their own teaching to self-review and reflection. The same advice can be given to students to help them learn and progress. Teachers can help students judge their own performances in many ways. They can explain the criteria used by experts in judging performance; they can give students opportunities to judge peers and assess their own progress in relation to others; and they can emphasize the importance of self-monitoring and goal setting and the importance of not being satisfied with only "extrinsic" feedback from the teacher.

The process of assigning practice and providing feedback to students is very important for teachers and requires learning a complex set of behaviors. A learning aid at the end of this chapter has been designed to assist your observation of how experienced teachers use practice and provide feedback.

Postinstructional Tasks

Postinstructional tasks associated with the direct instruction model consist of the final phase in the syntax, providing for independent practice and testing student understanding and skill.

INDEPENDENT PRACTICE

Most independent practice for students provided by teachers using the direct instruction model is done through homework. Considerable attention about how to assign and use homework to extend learning time was provided in Chapter 4 and does not need to be repeated here. It is, however, worth mentioning again that homework or independent practice is an opportunity for students to perform newly acquired skills on their own and, as such, should not involve the continuation of instruction, but instead the continuation of the practice. Also, feedback should be provided for independent practice in the same fashion as recommended for initial practice.

TESTING

Previous chapters emphasized the importance of matching testing and evaluation strategies to the goals and objectives for particular lessons and the inherent purposes of a particular model. Since the direct instruction model is used most appropriately for teaching skills and knowledge that can be taught in a step-by-step fashion, evaluation should focus on performance tests measuring skill development rather than paper and pencil tests of declarative knowledge. For example, being able to identify the characters on the typewriter's keyboard obviously does not tell us much about a person's ability to type. It takes a timed typing test. Being able to identify verbs in a column of nouns does not mean that the person can write a sentence. It takes a test that requires the student to write a sentence. Writing the correct steps in any of the teacher models described in this book does not tell us whether a teacher can use the model in front of 30 students. It takes a classroom demonstration.

Many times, performance tests are difficult for teachers to devise and to score with precision, and they can also be very time-consuming. However, if you want your students to master the skills you teach, nothing will substitute for performance-based evaluation procedures. Table 9.3 has examples adapted from Ellen Gagné (1985) of the type of test items that would be included on a skills test and contrasts those with items on the same topic that one would find on a knowledge test. You will note that the test items correspond to the sample objectives in Table 9.1.

Table 9.3   Items for Knowledge Test and Skill Test

KNOWLEDGE TEST	SKILL TEST
1. How many players are there on an ice hockey team? a. 6 b. 8 c. 10 d. none of the above	1. Demonstrate a pass while moving.
2. What is the subject of the following sentence? *Mary's mother is an artist.* a. Mary b. mother c. an d. artist.	2. Correct the verbs, as needed, in the following sentences: a. Kim ran slowly to the store. b. Tommy said it was time to go. c. Levon sat joyfully to greet her dad. d. "Please be noisier," said the teacher.
3. At what point is the intercept located? a. 1 b. 2 c. 3 d. 4	3. Solve for x in the following equations: a. $2 = x + 4$ b. $5x = 1 + (x/2)$ c. $14 = 2x + 9x$ d. $x/3 = 9$

Summary

Basic information and student skill development are important objectives for every subject taught in schools. The direct instruction model is one approach for promoting these objectives. The model has a strong theory and research base and has been widely used and tested in nonschool settings, particularly industry and the military. More recently, its efficacy has been determined in school settings.

Being clear about objectives and the various parts of any skill are tasks for teachers in the preinstructional phase of the model. Becoming proficient in demonstrating complex skills, providing students with a reason for learning, and setting up appropriate conditions for practice and feedback comprise the critical features of conducting a lesson using this model. Postinstructional tasks require paying attention to the type of independent homework assignments given and constructing good performance-based tests, which are sometimes difficult even for experts.

Although the basics of the model can be readily understood by the beginning teacher, it takes considerable practice to incorporate these basics (for example, conducting demonstrations, providing for feedback, and using performance-based evaluation strategies) into the beginning teacher's repertoire. Reading and having declarative knowledge about the model is insufficient. For beginning teachers to master the various understandings and skills needed to perform the model effectively requires the same set of behaviors as learning any other skill, such as watching other teachers demonstrate the model, practicing the model in laboratory and classroom settings, and receiving feedback on performance.

Books for the Professional

Gagné, R. M., and Briggs, L. J. (1979). *Principles of instructional design*. New York: Holt, Rinehart and Winston. Very good chapters on designing instruction, particularly in understanding task analysis and assessing student performance.

Garner, R. (1987). *Metacognition and Reading Comprehension*. Norwood, N.J.: Ablex. Although the focus is on reading, this book contains a good review of the research on metacognition and many ideas on how teachers can promote better student learning through direct and explicit instructional strategies.

Good, T. L., Grouws, D. A., and Ebmeier, H. (1983). *Active mathematics teaching*. New York: Longman. Reports, for the general audience, the work of the Missouri Mathematics Program, including a summary of several research projects. Implications for teachers interested in the direct instruction model are described.

Hunter, M. (1982). *Mastery teaching* El Segundo, Cal.: TIP Publications. A brief account of specific strategies developed by Hunter, many of which are consistent with the focus of the direct instruction model.

Posner, G. J., and Rudnitsky, A. N. (1986). *Course design. A guide to curriculum development for teachers*. (Third edition). New York: Longman. A very readable book on many aspects of course design. Particularly helpful in explaining how to break complex information and skills into teachable units.

CHAPTER 9
LEARNING AIDS FOR PLANNING, OBSERVATION, AND REFLECTION

- Assessing My Skills for Using the Direct Instruction Model
- Lesson Plan Format for a Direct Instruction Model Lesson
- Observing Key Phases in a Direct Instruction Model Lesson
- Observing Teacher Use of Practice
- Reviewing Curriculum Guides for Skill Objectives

ASSESSING MY SKILLS FOR USING THE DIRECT INSTRUCTION MODEL

PURPOSE: To help you gain insight into your level of skill in using the model, use this aid after reading the chapter or after a microteaching or field assignment.

DIRECTIONS: Check the level of skill you perceive yourself having for the various teaching tasks associated with the training model.

Skill or Competency	Level of Effectiveness		
	High	Medium	Low
Preinstructional Tasks			
Writing clear objectives	———	———	———
Performing task analysis	———	———	———
Preparing skill lessons	———	———	———
Preparing for demonstration	———	———	———
Instructional Tasks			
Phase 1			
Explaining objectives and set	———	———	———
Phase 2			
Conducting demonstration	———	———	———
Phase 3			
Designing guided practice	———	———	———
Phase 4			
Checking for understanding	———	———	———
Providing feedback	———	———	———
Postinstructional Tasks			
Phase 5			
Designing independent practice	———	———	———
Designing performance test items	———	———	———

LESSON PLAN FORMAT FOR A DIRECT INSTRUCTION MODEL LESSON

PURPOSE: This is a lesson plan format suggested for use with the model. As with the formats suggested for other teaching models, experiment with this format to determine if it meets your requirements. Be flexible and modify it as the need arises.

DIRECTIONS: Use the following suggested format as a model for writing a training lesson.

Planning Phase:

Content or skill to be taught: _____

_____

Objectives:

1. Given _____, the student will be able to
                        (situation)

   _____ with
                (action or behavior)

   _____
                (level of performance)

2. Given _____, the student will be able to
                        (situation)

   _____
                (action or behavior)

   _____
                (level of performance)

Conducting the Lesson:

Time	Phase and Activities	Materials
_____	Lesson objectives and set: _____	
	_____	
_____	Lesson demonstration: _____	
	_____	
	_____	
_____	Initial guided practice: _____	
	_____	
	_____	

_____ Checking for understanding and providing feedback: _____

_____

_____

_____ Independent practice activities: _____

Pitfalls to Avoid

During Introduction   During Transitions   During Ending

OBSERVING KEY PHASES IN A DIRECT INSTRUCTION MODEL LESSON

PURPOSE: This aid can be used in observing fellow students during a microteaching assignment or in observing teachers in the field. In either case it will help sharpen your understanding of the model.

DIRECTION: As you observe the lesson, make a "tick" for the category you believe best describes the level of performance for each of the teaching moves associated with the model.

Teaching Move or Activity	Level of Performance		
	High	Average	Low
Preinstructional Tasks			
The teacher had clear objectives	_____	_____	_____
The teacher had performed task analysis and divided skills into appropriate components	_____	_____	_____
It was clear that the teacher was prepared	_____	_____	_____
Instructional Tasks			
Phase 1			
The teacher explained objectives and set	_____	_____	_____
Phase 2			
The teacher conducted a demonstration	_____	_____	_____
Phase 3			
The teacher provided for appropriate practice	_____	_____	_____
Phase 4			
The teacher checked for understanding	_____	_____	_____
The teacher provided feedback	_____	_____	_____
Phase 5			
The teacher promoted transfer	_____	_____	_____
The teacher provided for independent practice	_____	_____	_____
Postinstructional Tasks			
The teacher designed performance test items	_____	_____	_____
The teacher assessed own performance	_____	_____	_____

Comments and Analysis:

#19

OBSERVING TEACHER USE OF PRACTICE

PURPOSE: As emphasized on pages 378 to 383, practice is an important element in the direct instruction model and requires finesse to manage properly. Use this aid in the field to help refine your understanding of the use of practice.

DIRECTIONS: Observe a teacher each day for several days during skill lessons. Stay in the same subject area, and try to observe from the first day a skill is introduced to the last day it is covered. For example, you may watch a teacher introduce, develop, and review the skill of writing a business letter, or multiplying by fives, or cleaning a carburator. Whatever the skill, pay close attention to how the teacher handles giving the students practice. Use the questions below to guide your observation and reflection.

1. On the first day the skill was introduced, what type of practice assignment did the teacher make—guided practice, independent practice, or both? _____

    How much time was devoted to the practice segment in class? _____as homework? _____

    What proportion of the total lesson was devoted to practice? _____

    Describe the teacher's behavior during the practice segment. _____

    _____

    Describe the students' behavior during the practice segment. _____

    _____

2. As the skill was developed over one or a few days, what type of practice assignment did the teacher make—guided practice, independent practice, or both? _____

    How much time was devoted to the practice segment in class? _____as homework? _____

    What proportion of the total lesson was devoted to practice? _____

    Describe the teacher's behavior during the practice segment. _____

    _____

    Describe the students' behavior during the practice segment. _____

    _____

3. As the skill was reviewed, what type of practice assignment did the teacher make—guided practice, independent practice, or both? _____

How much time was devoted to the practice segment in class? _____as homework? _____

What proportion of the total lesson was devoted to practice? _____

Describe the teacher's behavior during the practice segment. _____

_____

Describe the students' behavior during the practice segment. _____

_____

Analysis and Reflection: How did the teacher portion out practice? In other words, did you see massed or distributed practice, or both? _____ At what points in the development of the skill were these observed—early on, during the development phase, or during review? _____

Did the teacher give an indication that practice assignments were being matched to students' developing ability to perform the skill? ___ If so, how did the teacher gauge student performance? _____

What kinds of teacher behavior characterized earlier skill lessons? _____ _____ Later skill lessons? _____

What kinds of student behavior characterized earlier skill lessons? _____ _____ Later skill lessons? _____

Do you think this teacher made wise decisions concerning provision for student practice? _____

Why/why not? _____

_____

REVIEWING CURRICULUM GUIDES FOR SKILL OBJECTIVES

PURPOSE: This aid is designed to familiarize you with common skill objectives in your area or grade level, and to give you practice with task analysis, discussed on page 374 in the chapter.

DIRECTIONS: Examine several curriculum guides in your subject area or grade level. List the skill objectives they contain. If any occur more than once, put check marks by them to keep a runing tally.

1. _____

_____

_____

_____

_____

2. _____

_____

_____

_____

_____

3. _____

_____

_____

Analysis and Reflection: Which objectives occur most frequently? _____

_____

Think through a task analysis for the three most common objectives.

by LINDA B. GAMBRELL

Empowering Students: Teaching Comprehension and Composition Strategies

The success of students in school rests, to a large extent, on their proficiency in reading and writing increasingly complex information. Helping students develop independence in the use of specific reading and writing strategies is an important goal for every teacher at every grade level, and these skills should be explicitly taught. Research over the last decade, however, suggests that there is not very much explicit instruction in these skills currently going on. Durkin (1978–1979), for example, reported that teachers in the elementary reading classes that she observed could best be described as "mentioners" and "assignment givers." She found little evidence that teachers provided explicit instruction to students about how to employ specific strategies for comprehending text. Other researchers have provided similar pictures of what goes on in middle schools and high school classes (Sirotnik, 1983). In short, if students are to develop independent strategies for reading and writing, they must be provided with explicit instruction that shows them what strategies are appropriate, why it is important to employ them, how to use them, and when to use them.

A basic concept underlying the development of reading and writing strategies is that students must actively monitor their own reading and writing performances. They must be aware of difficulties as they arise and be able to employ corrective strategies. This ability to monitor one's own information processing is called *metacognition* and is fundamental to becoming a *strategic* reader or writer.

HELPING STUDENTS BECOME STRATEGIC READERS AND WRITERS

A strategy is a specific plan of action. A comprehension strategy is a plan for obtaining meaning from text, whereas a composition strategy is a plan for expressing meaning in written form. Independent strategy employment is unlikely to occur unless students are aware of the utility of the strategy and are motivated to use it. They must also perceive that the strategies being taught are both sensible and useful plans of action for them (Paris, 1986).

Proficient readers and writers are strategic (that is, they use specific strategies) in their reading and writing behaviors. They realize when comprehension and composition break down, and they use specific strategies to resolve the failure.

For example, when a text passage does not make sense to a reader, he or she must put on the mental brakes and apply some corrective action, such as rereading the passage. The same kind of self-monitoring and corrective action takes place when the proficient writer realizes that a composition is unclear. However, it is one thing to know that what is being read or what is being written does not make sense; it is another thing to know what strategy to employ to resolve the difficulty.

STRATEGY INSTRUCTION

Several procedures for teaching students specific comprehension and composition strategies have been developed, such as Direct Instruction (Roehler and Duffy, 1984), Explicit Instruction (Taylor, Harris, and Pearson, 1988), Informed Strategies for Learning (Paris, 1986), and Guided Strategy Instruction (Wilson and Gambrell, 1987). These procedures have been designed to teach students how to independently employ specific strategies; all emphasize four instructional phases. You will notice how similar this approach is to the direct instruction model described in Chapter 9.

1. *Explanation.* Students can be explicitly informed about strategies that can enhance text processing. The explanation step focuses on giving students a *description* and a *rationale* for the use of the strategy which is being taught.

2. *Demonstration.* In demonstration, students are shown how to use specific strategies. Some strategies, however, are more easily demonstrated than others. Teachers can use *think-alouds* and *think-links* to demonstrate and more explicitly inform students about strategy employment. These procedures are described later.

3. *Guided practice.* Guided practice allows students to apply particular strategies under teacher supervision. This step is characterized by teacher feedback and peer interaction, both of which provide opportunities for the student to explain and, consequently, to understand how specific strategies pay off.

4. *Independent application.* Ultimately, students must learn how to use specific strategies independently. Providing instruction that gradually shifts the responsibility from the teacher to the student helps students develop ownership of strategies for enhancing comprehension and composition. This transfer process, which Jones (1985) has labeled *expert scaffolding*, is essential in helping students become independent, self-directed learners (Paris, 1986).

COMPREHENSION STRATEGIES

Proficient readers employ various strategies for comprehending text. Less proficient readers, however, seem to be unaware of specific strategies required for the complex task of comprehending. Instruction in specific comprehension strategies can help less proficient readers learn how to improve their reading comprehension. Although there are many comprehension strategies that readers can use, this discussion focuses on three strategies that encourage students to focus their attention on text comprehension and that lend themselves particularly well to explicit teacher instruction.

Visual Imagery

When students make *visual images* about what they have read, the "pictures" provide a framework for organizing and remembering the information. There is considerable evidence that comprehension and memory are increased when students employ visual imagery (Pressley, 1976; Gambrell and Bales, 1986). However, it appears that students do not spontaneously use visual imagery to enhance their comprehension (Gambrell and Bales, 1986). One reason students may not view visual imagery as a specific comprehension strategy is that it is most frequently associated with aesthetic appreciation of prose and is not directly taught as a comprehension strategy (Belcher, 1981). It is clear that students need explicit instruction in how and when to apply this strategy.

The old saying "A picture is worth a thousand words" may explain why visual imagery is a strategy that enhances reading comprehension. When students make visual images, the "pictures" may provide the framework for organizing and remembering information. Following are some suggestions for providing explicit instruction in using visual imagery as a comprehension strategy.

1. *Explanation.* Inform students that "making pictures in your mind" is a comprehension strategy that can help them understand and remember what a story or passage is about.

2. *Demonstration.* The *think-aloud* procedure can be used to demonstrate how visual imagery is used by the reader. The teacher selects an appropriate passage such as the one below.

The Desert Man

The old man was hot and tired. His long white robe billowed in the dry desert wind. He wiped his brow as he started to trudge up yet another of the endless dunes of the desert. He saw only a sea of sand surrounding him.*

The teacher then proceeds to take the role of the reader and verbalizes (thinks out loud) about reader-text interaction and the process of making visual images about the incoming text information.

TEACHER: The title, *The Desert Man*, brings pictures of a vast, dry desert to mind. I can see miles and miles of sand . . . it's blazing hot . . . there is very little vegetation. Let me read on, *The old man was hot and tired. His long white robe billowed in the dry desert wind.* The picture in my head is of a very old man. . . .

---

* SOURCE: From Wilson, R. M. and Gambrell, L. B. (1987). *Teaching reading comprehension in the elementary school.* Boston, Mass.: Allyn and Bacon.

He is dressed in a long white robe that provides some protection from the sun. The fabric is light and airy. . . . I can see the wind blowing his robe.

The teacher continues to read and to verbalize about the visualization process in order to make the strategy more explicit for students.

3. *Guided practice.* At this stage the teacher provides short passages, appropriate for visualizing, for the students to practice with. Students share ideas about the use of visual imagery by reading the passages aloud and verbalizing their own visual images, just as the teacher did.

4. *Independent application.* Opportunities should be provided for students to use visual imagery in their independent reading. Since students do not appear to use visual imagery unless specifically directed to do so (Gambrell and Bales, 1986), it is particularly important that teachers provide opportunities for and encourage independent application of the visual imagery strategy.

Prediction

Schema theory has been a dominant theme in reading comprehension research for the last decade. A reader's schemata consist of knowledge already stored in memory or the prior knowledge a reader has about a subject or topic. According to Anderson and Pearson (1984), the term *comprehension* refers to the interaction of new information with the reader's prior knowledge. Simply stated, what a reader already knows is a principal determinant of what that reader can comprehend from text.

Proficient readers know how to access, or bring up, their relevant prior knowledge in order to enhance their comprehension. Some younger and less proficient readers have difficulty with this task. One specific strategy that facilitates the integration of prior knowledge and text information is called *prediction.*

Students need to be informed that the use of the prediction strategy can help them read with better comprehension. Specifically, the teacher might say, "One strategy you can use to strengthen your reading comprehension is to make predictions about what you think the passage might be about."

The prediction strategy involves students in making personal statements about what they believe will happen in a text passage based on their own prior knowledge and on some bit of text information, such as the title of the passage, a picture in the text, or the first paragraph of the passage. The prediction strategy encourages students to take risks by piecing together their own prior knowledge with the information provided in the text. The basic steps in the prediction strategy are activate, predict, read, and verify. Consider the following example.

1. *Activate* prior knowledge based on text clues (title, headings, pictures, lead sentences, or charts and graphs). For a story with the title *The Flying Trapeze*, the reader should ask, "What do I already know about trapeze performers?" The reader, for example, might already know that trapeze artists perform dangerous acts on trapeze bars and that they usually work with traveling circuses.

2. *Predict* what you think the passage will be about. The reader might predict, based upon prior knowledge and the title, that the story probably takes place in a circus, and that the major character or characters probably perform in a trapeze act in the circus.

3. *Read* to confirm or reject your prediction(s). The reader, at this step of the prediction process, proceeds to read the passage:

The Flying Trapeze

A beam of light shot up to the platform raised high above the circus audience. Young Steve Renaldi stood bathed in light—the center of attention. His legs were bent, his body poised. He reached for the bar of his trapeze and sent himself into space.

Tony Renaldi swung back and forth, his legs wound around his trapeze, waiting to catch Steve.

"Please, Tony, don't miss!" Steve said silently.*

4. *Verify* your prediction(s) in light of the information you gained from reading the text. The reader now reflects on the predictions that were made based on the title. The prediction that the story takes place in a circus was not completely confirmed but appears to be on target. The prediction that the characters perform a trapeze act does appear to be accurate based upon what was conveyed in the text thus far.

At this point the cycle begins again as the reader continues to (1) activate prior knowledge as new information is forthcoming, (2) make predictions, (3) read, and (4) verify predictions. For example, an obvious prediction based upon the passage about Tony and Steve Renaldi would be that something is going to happen to Tony. Successful use of the prediction strategy is based on the *continuous* process of activating prior knowledge predicting, reading, and verifying.

Self-Questioning

The *self-questioning strategy* involves students in posing questions about the content of the text during the reading process. It is known that good readers pose questions about what they are reading and that these self-questions guide them in the search for understanding (Olshavsky, 1976–1977). Furthermore, there is evidence that suggests that training students to ask self-questions can improve their comprehension performance significantly (Andre and Anderson, 1978–1979; Dreher and Gambrell, 1985).

There is a close relationship between the prediction strategy and the self-questioning strategy. Both strategies engage students in posing questions, but the self-questioning strategy involves students in asking more specific questions about the content of the text. For example, in a unit on mountains the student might see the heading, "Mountain Ranges of North America," and turn the heading into a specific question such as, "What are the names of the mountain ranges of

---

* SOURCE: From the Laidlaw Reading Program (1980). *Spotlights.* The Flying Trapeze by Howard Goldsmith. Irvine, Calif.: Laidlaw Brothers, p. 85.

North America?" For some materials, such as narrative stories, the more general prediction strategy may work best; for other materials, such as expository text, it may be more appropriate to generate self-questions.

COMPOSITION STRATEGIES

Composition strategies are used by writers to organize and clarify the meaning of written compositions. In order to develop independence in written composition it is important that students develop a repertoire of strategies that facilitate the organization, elaboration, and communication of ideas. Two important strategies can assist with this process.

Think-Links

Think-links involve the development of graphic configurations that represent ideas the writer wishes to convey. In short, they provide a concrete prewriting activity that helps the writer organize information. The development of a think-link can help the writer see how ideas are most logically organized and presented. Figure S4.1 is a think-link which was developed by a student prior to writing a passage about trees.

The think-link provides a graphic outline that is then used in writing the passage. Many prewriting and drafting activities take place as the writer plays around with the organization of ideas in the development of the think-link. The

Figure S4.1   Think-Link About Trees

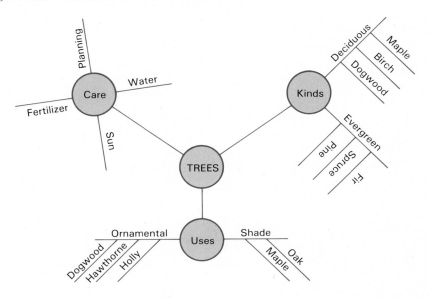

use of think-links is an efficient writing strategy because revision and elaboration can be done prior to the drafting of ideas in passage form.

Summarizing

Summarizing is a skill that is frequently used by writers; however, many students at all grade levels are unfamiliar with the basic elements of well-formed summaries. Teaching students to produce well-formed summaries should start with having the teacher modeling the process. The following example provides a sample passage and three teacher-formulated summaries that are used to provide explicit instruction for students on the features of a well-formed summary.

The Vikings

Vikings were the fearless sailors of a thousand years ago who raided other countries. Guided by the stars and powered by the wind, the daring Vikings crossed dangerous seas. On land, the Viking sailors became soldiers, attacking town after town. Each town was sacked of its treasures and then destroyed.

In battle the Vikings carried iron swords that gleamed with copper and silver. They used shields covered with beautiful designs. They wore helmets carved with figures of animals and heroes. At home the Vikings dressed in fine clothing. They trimmed their clothes with gold and colored ribbons. They fastened their cloaks with heavy gold pins. They wore beautiful gold bracelets and chains. The Vikings were outlaws and robbers who prized both power and beauty.

As time went by the ways of the Vikings became more peaceful. They began to trade with other people instead of raiding their towns. Many Vikings sailed to far-off places and made new homes for themselves. They took with them three of their greatest treasures—strength, courage, and love of beauty.*

TEACHER: A well-formed summary for the passage, *The Vikings*, would: (1) contain the main idea(s), (2) be brief, and (3) omit details. Read the following summaries and decide which of the three—A, B, or C—meets the criteria for a well-formed summary.

SUMMARY A: The Viking sailors became soldiers when they landed. The Vikings were frightening. They loved beauty. They wore fancy helmets and carried shields covered with designs. At home they wore fine clothing and gold bracelets and chains. As time went by, the Vikings became more peaceful traders. Many of them eventually sailed off to make new homes for themselves in other countries.

SUMMARY B: The Viking sailors were outlaws and robbers who raided and destroyed many towns. They prized beauty and power. Later, when the Vikings made new homes for themselves in other countries they took with them their three greatest treasures—strength, courage, and love of beauty.

SUMMARY C: When the Vikings became peaceful many of them sailed away and made new homes in other countries.

* SOURCE: Adapted from the Abracadatlas. (1982). Cambridge, Mass.: Addison-Wesley, pp. 185–186.

By using this approach, the teacher can engage students in determining which of the above summaries is well-formed. Teacher-led discussions would focus on (1) Which summary is most appropriate and why? (2) What makes summary A and C inappropriate? and (3) What are the features of a well-formed summary? As students develop an understanding of summaries, they should be provided with opportunities to generate their own after reading typical course materials.

Summarizing is a skill that individuals are frequently called upon to use both in the classroom and in everyday life. Explicit instruction that makes use of teacher modeling and the discrimination procedure can help students develop and refine their composition skills.

Summary

Empowering students with strategies that enhance comprehension and composition requires a commitment from teachers to provide instruction that makes strategy employment explicit. The goal of comprehension and composition strategy instruction is for the student to possess ownership of a variety of strategies. *Ownership* means that the student is able to determine *how* and *when* to implement specific comprehension and composition strategies to enhance reading and writing performance in all areas of the curriculum.

Books for the Professional

Duffy G. G., Roehler, L. R., & Mason, J. (Eds.). (1984). *Comprehension instruction*. New York: Longman. This edited volume examines reading comprehension as an interactive process. The complexities of providing comprehension instruction are discussed and perspectives and suggestions useful to classroom teachers are provided. Of particular interest is the summary chapter, "A Practitioner's Model of Comprehension Instruction."

Irwin, J. W. (1986). *Teaching reading comprehension processes*. Englewood Cliffs, N. J.: Prentice-Hall. This is a practical book intended for teachers who are interested in helping students become better comprehenders. The pedagogy suggested in this book is soundly based in the processing research of the last decade in the areas of reading, cognitive psychology, information processing, and psycholinguistics. The book contains information about the factors influencing comprehension processes and general instructional approaches.

Raphael, Taffy E. (Ed.). (1986). *The contexts of school-based literacy*. New York: Random House. This book deals with improving the outlook of the development of literacy in schools today. Included in the volume are articles that deal with reading and writing instruction and the social aspects of learning. Four questions are specifically addressed: 1. What is the contextual view of the development of literacy? 2. How can contexts for learning to read and for developing strategic readers be characterized? 3. How can contexts for developing children's understanding and use of the writing process be characterized? 4. What influences the development of appropriate contexts for learning to read and write?

CHAPTER 10

MAIN IDEAS

- The cooperative learning model grew out of an educational tradition emphasizing democratic thought and practice, active learning, cooperative behavior, and respect for pluralism in multicultural societies.
- The model aims at instructional effects beyond academic learning, specifically, at intergroup acceptance, broader peer liking patterns, and self-esteem and efficacy.
- The syntax for the cooperative learning model relies on small group work as contrasted to whole class teaching.
- The model's learning environment requires cooperative rather than competitive task and incentive structures.
- A strong research base supports the use of cooperative learning for the following educational objectives: cooperative behavior, academic learning, improved race relationships, and improved attitudes toward handicapped children.
- Preinstructional tasks associated with cooperative learning emphasize organizing students for small group work and collecting a variety of learning materials.
- Three variations of the basic model can be used: Student Teams Achievement Divisions (STAD), Jigsaw, and Group Investigation.
- Conducting a cooperative learning lesson changes the teacher's role from that of center stage performer to choreographer of small group activity.
- Postinstructional tasks, particularly evaluation, stress individual and group rewards, along with new forms of recognition, rather than traditional competitive approaches.

Teaching Through Cooperative Learning

The three models of teaching described previously—presentation, concept teaching, and direct instruction—are used by teachers primarily (1) to help students acquire new information, (2) to process information already acquired from prior learning, and (3) to learn important skills. It has been emphasized that academic learning (acquiring information and thinking about that information), although extremely important, does not represent the only set of objectives for student learning. Chapter 10 presents a model of teaching called cooperative learning that goes beyond helping students learn academic content and skills to address important social goals and objectives.

PERSPECTIVE AND RATIONALE

The cooperative learning model is not the result of any single stream of pedagogical thought. Its roots go back to the early Greeks, and contemporary developments started with early-twentieth-century educational psychologists and pedagogical theorists.

John Dewey, Herbert Thelen, and Democratic Classrooms

In 1916 John Dewey, then at the University of Chicago, wrote a book called *Democracy and Education*. Dewey's conception of education was that the classroom should mirror the larger society and be a laboratory for real-life learning. Dewey's pedagogy required teachers to create within their learning environments a social system characterized by democratic procedures and scientific processes. Their primary responsibility was to engage students in inquiry into important social and interpersonal problems. The specific classroom procedures described by Dewey (and his latter-day followers) emphasized small, problem-solving groups of students searching for their own answers and learning democratic principles through day-to-day interaction with one another.

Many years after Dewey, Herbert Thelen (1954; 1960), who was also at the University of Chicago, developed more precise procedures for helping students work in groups. Like Dewey, Thelen argued that the classroom should be a laboratory or miniature democracy for the purpose of study and inquiry into important social and interpersonal problems. Thelen, with his interest in group dynamics, put more structure on the pedagogy of group investigation and, as will be described later, provided the conceptual basis for contemporary developments in cooperative learning.

Cooperative group work for Dewey and Thelen went beyond improving academic learning. Cooperative behavior and processes were viewed as basic to human endeavor, the foundation on which strong democratic communities could be built and maintained. The logical way to accomplish these important educational objectives for Dewey and Thelen was to structure the classroom and the students' learning activities so that they would model the desired outcomes.

Gordon Allport and Intergroup Relations

In 1954 the Supreme Court issued its historic *Brown* v. *Board of Education of Topeka* decision in which the Court ruled that public schools in the United States could no longer operate under a "separate but equal" policy, but must become racially integrated. This led to subsequent decisions and actions by judicial and legislative bodies all across the country calling for public school authorities to submit plans for desegregation.

At the time, thoughtful theorists and observers warned that putting people of different ethnic or racial backgrounds in the same location would not, in and of itself, counteract the effects of prejudice or promote better intergroup acceptance. They knew, for example, that the cafeteria in an integrated school might still be characterized by black students sitting on one side of the room and white students on the other. They also knew that a community might be highly integrated but still have restaurants or churches patronized by an all-white or all-black clientele.

A leading sociologist of the time, Gordon Allport, argued that laws alone would not reduce intergroup prejudice and promote better acceptance and understanding. Sharan (1981) summarized three basic conditions formulated by Allport to counteract racial prejudice: "(1) unmediated interethnic contact, (2) occurring under conditions of equal status between members of the various groups participating in a given setting, and (3) where the setting officially sanctions interethnic cooperation" (p. 2).

Some of the interest in the cooperative learning model in recent years has grown out of attempts to structure classrooms and teaching processes according to these three conditions. Some of Robert Slavin's work, which will be described later, was conducted in the inner cities on the eastern seaboard as part of integration efforts. The work of Sharan and his colleagues in Israel was prompted by that country's need to find ways to promote better ethnic understanding between Jewish immigrants with European backgrounds and those with Middle Eastern backgrounds. The work of the Johnsons at the University of Minnesota explored how cooperative classroom environments might lead to better learning by and more postive regard toward handicapped students mainstreamed (integrated) into regular classrooms.

Social Psychology and Small Group Theory

Chapters 3 through 6 provided many ideas about the nature of classroom life and a set of concepts for viewing classrooms as complex social settings where teachers perform important executive functions. Concepts from group dynamics theory and research were described as guides for teachers' work with classroom groups. The importance of group processes on students' academic learning and socialization was discussed in some detail. Here, a few of these concepts are extended for the purpose of showing how social psychology and small group theory provide the third intellectual tradition for the cooperative learning model.

GROUP EFFECTS ON INDIVIDUAL PERFORMANCE

In the early part of this century social psychologists began research on a topic most commonly referred to as "social facilitation." Classic studies in this tradition, such as Allport (1924) and Dashiell (1935), compared the performances of individuals performing both physical and intellectual tasks alone with individuals performing the same tasks with others present. The research showed that having others present has important effects on performance in some instances. Some developers of cooperative learning have used their knowledge of this research to plan specific strategies and procedures.

COOPERATION VERSUS COMPETITION

Interest in the effects that cooperative versus competitive situations have on individual and group performance also dates back to the early part of the twentieth century. Experiments conducted in laboratories, work organizations, and classrooms have consistently shown that cooperative goal structures (activities where persons are working together toward common group goals) are more productive than competitive structures. Many studies conducted across diverse settings suggest that under cooperative conditions where individuals are rewarded for group success three things happen:

1. Interdependent relationships, in which cooperation is rewarded, lead to strong motivation to complete a common task.
2. Group work develops considerable friendliness among group members.
3. Cooperation develops a highly effective communication process that tends to promote maximal generation of ideas and greater mutual influence.

This cooperative versus competitive hypothesis has been tested more directly during the past decade, specifically in field tests of cooperative learning strategies, and this research will be described in detail later in this chapter.

Experiential Learning

A fourth intellectual tradition behind the cooperative learning model comes from theorists and researchers who are interested in how children learn from experience. This group rejects the idea that children (or adults for that matter) should be passive learners under the domination of the teacher. In Chapter 2, some of the principles and practices associated with experiential learning were introduced. The central principle introduced was that experience accounts for much of what students learn, but for best results, experience must be accompanied by systematic analysis and reflection. Cooperative learning also embraces this principle, particularly the models developed by Sharan in Israel and the Johnsons at the University of Minnesota. Sharan (1976) takes the position that the teacher's task is "to increase the child's sense of efficacy by teaching him to control more of his opportunities for learning. . . . Active learning which organizes and assimilates experience through interaction with the environment will help to develop logical thought and higher order verbal communication skills" (p. x).

OVERVIEW OF COOPERATIVE LEARNING

Cooperative learning is a model of teaching with a set of common attributes and features. It also has several variations which will be described in this section along with explanations of the model's instructional effects, syntax, and environmental structure. After presenting an overview and the research base for the model, the teaching behaviors required to effectively teach a cooperative learning lesson are examined more thoroughly.

Common Features of Cooperative Learning

The models described in Chapters 7, 8, and 9 are characterized by task structures where teachers are working with a whole class of students at the same time or where students are working individually to master academic content or skills. Their reward systems are based on individual effort and performance, and their reward structures on individual competition. The cooperative learning model uses different task and reward structures.

Slavin (1984) explained that there are two important components in all cooperative learning methods: *a cooperative incentive structure* and *a cooperative task structure*. According to Slavin, "the critical feature of a cooperative incentive structure is that two or more individuals are interdependent for a reward they will share if they are successful as a group. . . . Cooperative task structures are situations in which two or more individuals are allowed, encouraged, or required to work together on some task, coordinating their efforts to complete the task" (p. 55).

Cooperative learning is described as having the following essential features:

- Students work in teams to master academic materials.
- Teams are made up of high, average, and low achievers.
- Teams are made up of a racially and sexually mixed group of students.
- Reward systems are group oriented rather than individually oriented.

All of these features are explained more fully later in the chapter.

Instructional Effects of Cooperative Learning

The cooperative learning model has been developed to achieve at least four important instructional objectives.

ACADEMIC ACHIEVEMENT

Cooperative learning aims at improving student performance on important academic tasks. The belief is that the model's cooperative incentive structure raises the value placed on academic learning and changes the norms associated with achievement. You remember the work of Coleman (1961), described in Chapter 5, which emphasized the importance of student norms on the quality of academic work. Slavin (1984) relied on these ideas in the development of his cooperative learning models. For example, he wrote that often "students do not value their peers who do well academically, while they do value their peers who excel in sports. . . . This is so because sports success brings benefits to groups (the team, the school, the town), while academic success benefits only the individual. In fact, in a class using grading on the curve or any competitive grading or incentive system, any individual's success reduces the chances that any other individual will succeed" (p. 54).

In addition to changing norms associated with achievement, cooperative learning can benefit both low-achieving and high-achieving students who work on academic materials together. High achievers tutor low achievers, thus giving the latter special attention. In the process, high achievers gain academically because serving as a tutor requires thinking deeply about the relationships and meanings of a particular subject.

IMPROVED RACE RELATIONS

A second important effect of the cooperative learning model is wider acceptance of persons of other races or persons with handicapping conditions. Following the premises outlined by Allport (1954), it is known that mere physical contact among different racial or ethnic groups or mainstreamed children is insufficient to reduce prejudice and stereotyping. Cooperative learning presents opportunities for students of varying backgrounds and conditions to work interdependently on common tasks and, through the use of cooperative reward structures, learn to appreciate each other.

COOPERATIVE PROBLEM-SOLVING SKILLS

A final and very important effect of cooperative learning is that students learn skills of cooperation and collaboration. These are important skills in a society where much adult work is carried out in large, interdependent organizations and where communities become much more global in their orientations.

Syntax of Cooperative Learning

There are six major phases or steps in the cooperative learning model. These are described briefly in Table 10.1

Different Approaches to Cooperative Learning

Although the basic principles of cooperative learning do not change, there are several variations of the model. Three approaches that should be part of the beginning teacher's repertoire are described. The recommended readings at the end of this chapter provide information about several other variations.

STUDENT TEAMS ACHIEVEMENT DIVISIONS (STAD)

STAD was developed by Robert Slavin and his colleagues at the Johns Hopkins University and is perhaps the simplest and most straightforward of the cooperative learning approaches. Teachers using STAD present new academic information to students each week, either through verbal presentation or text. Students within

Table 10.1 Syntax of the Cooperative Learning Model

PHASES	TEACHER BEHAVIOR
Phase 1: Provide objectives and set	Teacher goes over objectives for the lesson and establishes learning set.
Phase 2: Present information	Teacher presents information to students either through verbal presentation or with text.
Phase 3: Organize students in learning teams	Teacher explains to students how to form learning teams and helps groups make efficient transition.
Phase 4: Assist team work and study	Teacher assists learning teams as they do their work.
Phase 5: Test	Teacher tests knowledge of learning materials or groups present results of their work.
Phase 6: Recognize achievement	Teacher finds ways to recognize both individual and group effort and achievement.

a given class are divided into four- or five-member learning teams, with representatives on each team of both sexes, of the various racial or ethnic groups, and of students who are high, average, and low achievers. Team members use work sheets or other study devices to master the academic materials and then help each other learn the materials through tutoring, quizzing one another, or carrying on team discussions. Individually, students take weekly or biweekly quizzes on the academic materials. These quizzes are scored and each individual is given an "improvement score." This improvement score is based not on a student's absolute score, but instead on the degree to which the score exceeds a student's past averages.

Each week, through a short (normally one page) newsletter or some other device, teams with the highest scores and students who have high improvement scores or who have perfect scores on the quizzes are recognized. Sometimes all teams who reach a certain criterion are recognized, as explained later.

JIGSAW

Jigsaw was developed and tested by Elliot Aronson and his colleagues (1978) at the University of Texas and then adapted by Slavin and his Johns Hopkins colleagues. In Jigsaw, students are assigned to five- or six-member heterogeneous study teams. Academic materials are presented to the students in text form, and each student has the responsibility to learn a portion of the material. For example, if the textual material was on cooperative learning, one student on the team would be responsible for STAD, another for Jigsaw, another for Group Investigation, and perhaps the other two would become experts in the research base and history of cooperative learning. Members from different teams with the same topic (sometimes called the expert group) meet to study and help each other learn their topic. Then students return to their home team and teach other members what they have learned. Following home team meetings and discussions, students take quizzes individually over the learning materials. In the Slavin version of Jigsaw, team scores are formed using the same scoring procedures used in STAD. High scoring teams and individuals are recognized in the weekly class newsletter or by some other means.

GROUP INVESTIGATION

Many of the key features of the Group Investigation (G-I) approach were designed originally by Herbert Thelen. More recently, this approach has been extended and refined by Shlomo Sharan and his colleagues at Tel Aviv University. The group investigation approach to cooperative learning is perhaps the most complex of the cooperative learning approaches and the most difficult to implement. In contrast to STAD and Jigsaw, students are involved in planning both the topics for study as well as how to proceed with their investigations. This requires more sophisticated classroom norms and structures than do approaches that are more teacher centered. It also requires that students be taught the communication and group process skills described in Chapter 5.

Teachers who use the G-I approach normally divide their classes into five- or six-member heterogeneous groups. In some instances, however, groups may form around friendships or around an interest in a particular topic. Students select topics for study, pursue in-depth investigations of chosen subtopics, and then prepare and present a report to the whole class. Sharan et al. (1984) described the following six steps of the G-I approach:

1. *Topic selection.* Students choose specific subtopics within a general problem area, usually delineated by the teacher. Students then organize into small two- to six-member task-oriented groups. Group composition is academically and ethnically heterogeneous.
2. *Cooperative planning.* Students and teacher plan specific learning procedures, tasks, and goals consistent with the subtopics of the problem selected in Step 1.
3. *Implementation.* Pupils carry out the plan formulated in Step 2. Learning should involve a wide variety of activities and skills and should lead students to different kinds of sources both inside and outside the school. The teacher closely follows the progress of each group and offers assistance when needed.
4. *Analysis and synthesis.* Pupils analyze and evaluate information obtained during Step 3 and plan how it can be summarized in some interesting fashion for possible display or presentation to classmates.
5. *Presentation of final product.* Some or all of the groups in the class give an interesting presentation of the topics studied in order to get classmates involved in each other's work and to achieve a broad perspective on the topic. Group presentations are coordinated by the teacher.
6. *Evaluation.* In cases where groups pursued different aspects of the same topic, pupils and teachers evaluate each group's contribution to the work of the class as a whole. Evaluation can include either individual or group assessment, or both. (pp. 4–5)

Structure of the Learning Environment

The environment for cooperative learning is characterized by democratic processes and by active roles for students in deciding what should be studied and how. The teacher provides a high degree of structure in forming groups and defining overall procedures, but students control the minute-to-minute interactions within groups. To be successful with a cooperative learning lesson, extensive resource materials must be available in the teachers' room or in the school's library or media center. Success also requires good working relationships between the classroom teacher and resource specialists in the school.

SAMPLING THE RESEARCH BASE

Cooperative learning has a substantial research base, particularly in the field of social psychology. The study of small group dynamics, social facilitation, and the effects of cooperative versus competitive behavior on performance provide a substantial supporting literature for the knowledge of cooperative learning. This section, however, will rely on a more recent literature, particularly the research on classroom effects of cooperative learning on (1) cooperative behavior and interethnic cooperation, (2) interactions with handicapped children, and (3) academic learning. As in previous chapters, studies have been selected that are illustrative of research in the field and that represent the work of major theorists and researchers.

Effects on Cooperative Behavior

Twentieth-century living is characterized by global, interdependent communities and by complex social institutions which require high degrees of cooperation among members. Consequently, most people prize cooperative behavior and believe it to be an important goal for education. Many of schools' extra-curricular activities, such as team sports and dramatic and musical productions, are justified on this basis. But what about activities within the academic classroom? Do certain types of activities, such as those associated with cooperative learning, have effects on students' cooperative attitudes and behaviors?

To find an answer to this question, portions of a large and significant piece of research done by Shlomo Sharan and his colleagues at Tel Aviv University in Israel are highlighted here. The Sharan study looked at the effects of cooperative learning on academic achievement, social attitudes, ethnic relationships, and cooperative behavior. His study is much too large and complex to summarize in its entirety. The portion of the study that investigated the relationships between teachers' uses of cooperative learning strategies and students' cooperative behavior are presented in Research Summary 10.1.

Promoting Positive Interactions with Handicapped Children

Two decades after the Supreme Court ended "separate but equal" public schools, the Ninety-fourth Congress passed an equally historic piece of integration legislation. Titled the "Education for All Handicapped Children Act," and soon to be known as Public Law 94–142, this legislation required handicapped students to be placed, whenever possible, into "least restrictive" environments. Instead of placement in special schools or classrooms (the approach used for most of the twentieth century), children with handicapping conditions (approximately 12 percent of the student population) would be "mainstreamed" into regular classrooms. Obviously, this meant that regular classroom teachers would now have children with physical, emotional, and mental disabilities in their classrooms.

Just as theorists knew that racial integration would not end prejudice, there was considerable evidence in 1974 that placing handicapped people (who have traditionally been perceived negatively by nonhandicapped peers) in close proximity to others would not end negative attitudes. In fact, some researchers argued that closer contact might even increase prejudice and stereotyping. A critical

=============== **RESEARCH SUMMARY** ===============
10.1

Sharan, S., et al. (1984). *Cooperative learning in the classroom: Research in desegregated schools*. Hillsdale, N.J.: Lawrence Erlbaum Associates.

PROBLEM: For over a decade Shlomo Sharan and his colleagues at the Tel Aviv University developed and tested cooperative learning models in Israel. The investigators wanted to find out the effects of three instructional methods on student academic learning, social relations, and cooperative and competitive behavior. They were particularly interested in the ability of cooperative learning to improve social relations among different Jewish subgroups in Israel, particularly those who had Western and those who had Middle Eastern ethnic backgrounds. The three methods compared in the study were: (1) whole-class or presentation-recitation teaching, (2) group investigation (a cooperative learning strategy developed by Sharan), and (3) student teams and academic division (STAD, developed by Slavin and his colleagues).

SAMPLE: From a group of junior high schools in Israel that had both Western and Middle Eastern Jews, the investigators recruited 33 English and literature teachers and their students for the study.

PROCEDURES: Teachers were randomly assigned to one of three groups and received equal amounts of training in a three-day summer workshop and additional evening workshops during the school year. The three groups included:

▪ *Group 1: Whole Class Teaching*—Teachers were taught how to "fine tune" their traditional teaching skills through the application of Bloom's taxonomy to questioning and task design, development of teaching aids and materials, and attention to the research on teaching.
▪ *Group 2: Student Teams (STAD)*—Teachers were introduced to the student team learning model and prepared learning materials for use with this model in their classrooms.
▪ *Group 3: Group Investigation*—Teachers were introduced to the group investigation model and taught how to work with groups and how to facilitate better communication and group processes in their classrooms.

The investigators collected a massive amount of information before, during, and after the experiment, including data from achievement tests, classroom observations, and cooperation-game and group-interaction tasks. For purposes here, only the cooperation tasks are described.

factor in producing more positive attitudes and behaviors seemed to be the way the interaction between handicapped and nonhandicapped students was structured. David and Roger Johnson and several of their colleagues at the University of Minnesota studied how goal structures influence interaction in a unique and interesting way. Their study is summarized in Research Summary 10.2

Students were selected from classrooms using each of the three instructional methods. They were asked to engage in a task called Lego man. In six-member teams (each with three Western and three Middle Eastern members), students were asked to plan how they would carry out a joint task which consisted of constructing a human figure from 48 pieces of Lego. Trained observers (kept naive as to the instructional methods of the students' classrooms and to the goals and methods of the study) recorded a variety of behaviors including: verbal cooperation, nonverbal cooperation, competition, and individualistic behavior.

POINTERS FOR READING RESEARCH: Note that Table 1 includes means and standard deviations for each of the experimental conditions and uses analysis of variance as the statistic to make comparisons among groups. The F ratio, remember, is a statistical value that allows the researchers to determine whether or not their results are significant beyond chance.

RESULTS: Table 1 describes the results of the cooperative and competitive behavior portion of the Sharan study. These data have been adapted (simplified) for ease of presentation and discussion.

TABLE 1 Mean Percentages, Standard Deviations, and F Ratios for Three Experimental Conditions

Category		Group Investigation ($n = 21$)*	STAD ($n = 26$)	Whole Class ($n = 18$)	F
		Instructional Method			
Verbal Cooperation	Mean %	41.52	35.95	29.49	b**
	SD	8.60	8.18	9.93	9.06
Nonverbal Cooperation	Mean %	43.55	36.66	26.03	b**
	SD	7.76	9.51	10.19	17.78
Competition	Mean %	8.30	13.82	31.60	b**
	SD	7.76	11.50	15.54	20.49
Individualistic Behavior	Mean %	6.60	13.57	12.88	a**
	SD	6.97	10.07	9.06	4.03

* Represents the number of six-member groups. Mean scores are converted to percentages to establish uniformity across treatments in terms of total number of events being compared.
** a = $p < .05$; b = $p < .001$.
SOURCE: Adapted from S. Sharan et al (1984), p. 85.

(cont'd)

Effects on Academic Achievement

One of the important aspects of cooperative learning is that while it is helping promote cooperative behavior and better group relations among students, it is simultaneously helping students with their academic learning. Recently, Slavin (1986) reviewed research and reported that 45 studies had been done between 1972 and 1986, investigating the effects of student team learning on achievement.

━━━━━━━━━━ **RESEARCH SUMMARY** ━━━━━━━━━━
10.1 (continued)

DISCUSSION AND IMPLICATIONS: Looking at the mean percentage scores in Table 1 shows clearly that the instructional methods influenced the students' cooperative and competitive behavior. As can be observed, group investigation generated more cooperative behavior, both verbal and nonverbal, than did whole-class teaching or STAD. STAD, however, produced more cooperative behavior than whole-class teaching. Students from both cooperative learning classrooms showed less competitive behavior than those who came from whole-class teaching classrooms.

In other analyses done on these data, Sharan showed that the cooperative learning approaches also increased the cross-ethnic cooperation during the Lego task as compared to whole-class teaching.

Sharan and his colleagues warn us to be careful of this particular aspect of their study. The Lego-man task was one that asked for cooperation and did not reward competitive behavior. However, they concluded that the study holds the following implications for teaching.

Cooperative learning in the classroom . . . promoted prosocial behavior in general among classmates, as well as among classmates from different ethnic groups. (p. 95)

The data reported here lend clear support to the widely asserted claim about the relatively competitive effects of traditional whole-class instruction on children's social relations. (p. 95)

Restructuring of interpersonal relations among schoolchildren engaged in learning tasks, so that these relationships embody the behavior patterns we strive to foster, can lead to significant changes in the way children interact, regardless of ethnic background. (p. 95)

These studies were done at all grade levels and included the following subject areas: language arts, spelling, geography, social studies, science, mathematics, English as a second language, reading, and writing. Studies he reviewed were conducted in urban, rural, and suburban schools in the United States and in Israel, Nigeria, and Germany. Out of the 45 studies, 37 of them showed that student team learning classes significantly outperformed control group classes in academic achievement. Eight studies found no differences. None of the studies showed negative effects for cooperative learning.

The final study reported in this chapter was done by Robert Slavin and one of his colleagues on the effects of cooperative learning on academic achievement in mathematics. This study is summarized in Research Summary 10.3.

RESEARCH SUMMARY
10.2

Johnson, R., Rynders, J., Johnson, D. W., Schmidt, B., and Haider, S. (1979). Interaction between handicapped and nonhandicapped teenagers as a function of situational goal structuring: Implications for mainstreaming. *American Educational Research Journal, 16,* 161–167.

PROBLEM: The researchers wanted to find out the effects of various goal structures on the interactions between nonhandicapped junior high students and trainable mentally retarded students in a learning situation, in this instance, bowling classes.

SAMPLE: Subjects in the study were 30 junior high students (ages 13 to 16, including 15 boys and 15 girls) from three midwestern junior high schools. Nine nonhandicapped students came from a public junior high school; nine other nonhandicapped students came from a private Catholic school. The 12 handicapped students were from a school for the handicapped. The handicapped students were classified as trainable mentally retarded. This meant that they were able to communicate and understand instructions and that they did not have any physical handicaps that would prevent them from bowling.

PROCEDURES: Students were divided randomly into learning teams of five. Each team contained three nonhandicapped students and two handicapped students. Each of the learning teams was then assigned to one of three experimental conditions.

■ *Group 1—Cooperative Condition:* Team members were instructed to "maximize" their team's bowling score at a criterion of 50 points improvement over the prior week. They were to help each other in any way possible.
■ *Group 2—Individualistic Condition:* Students in these teams were instructed to "maximize" their individual scores by 10 points over the previous week and to concentrate only on their own performance.
■ *Group 3—Laissez-Faire Condition:* Students were given no special instructions.

The three bowling instructors in the study were told what to say and were rotated across groups. All groups received the same amount of training over a six-week period.

Trained observers, who were kept naive about the purpose of the study, watched the students bowl and recorded interactions among students into three categories: positive, neutral, and negative. Observations focused on the period of time from when a bowler stepped up to bowl until he or she stepped down from the bowling line.

POINTERS FOR READING RESEARCH: The researchers used the chi square (χ^2) to test the significance of their results. This statistic is used by researchers when their data are of a particular type. It serves the same purpose as other tests of significance introduced earlier. The results as reported in this study are straightforward and easy to read and understand.

RESULTS: Tables 1 and 2 show the results of the bowling study. Table 1 displays the frequency of homogeneous and heterogeneous interactions among the stu-

(cont'd)

RESEARCH SUMMARY
10.2 (continued)

dents in the three conditions. Table 2 displays data on "group cheers" for handicapped students who threw strikes and spares over the course of the study.

TABLE 1 **Frequency of Homogeneous and Heterogeneous Interactions Within Conditions**

	Positive		Neutral		Negative		
	Homo	Hetero	Homo	Hetero	Homo	Hetero	Total
Cooperative	495	336	67	47	4	10	959
Individualistic	243	92	61	17	15	11	439
Laissez-faire	265	136	75	49	9	6	540
Total	1003	564	203	113	28	27	1938

$\chi^2 = 86.87$, $p < .01$
NOTE: Homogeneous interactions took place between nonhandicapped students and between handicapped students; heterogeneous interactions took place between handicapped and nonhandicapped students.
SOURCE: Adapted from R. Johnson et al. (1979), p. 165.

TABLE 2 **Frequency of Group Cheers Within Conditions**

Condition	Frequency
Cooperative	55
Individualistic	6
Laissez-faire	3

SOURCE: Adapted from R. Johnson et al. (1979), p. 165.

DISCUSSION AND IMPLICATIONS: The data presented in Tables 1 and 2 are clear and straightforward. There were more interactions among students in the cooperative bowling team, and more important, more positive interactions that were both heterogeneous and homogeneous. Further study of their data revealed that: "Each handicapped student on the average participated in 17 positive interactions with nonhandicapped peers per hour in the cooperative condition, 5 in the individualistic condition, and 7 in the laissez-faire condition" (p. 164).

The number of cheers given to handicapped students in the cooperative condition gives additional support to the idea that cooperative goal structure is a means for getting positive response from nonhandicapped students toward their handicapped peers.

This study, along with others that have produced similar results, has two important implications for teachers:

Individualistic and competitive goal structures associated with so many classroom learning tasks do not encourage positive interactions among people from differing backgrounds and conditions. Redefining the goal structure and making it more cooperative seems to help.

Severely handicapped students, given the appropriate conditions, can be mainstreamed into learning settings with nonhandicapped students in ways that can benefit all.

RESEARCH SUMMARY
10.3

Slavin, R. E., and Karweit, M. L. (1984). Mastery learning and student teams: A factorial experiment in urban general mathematics classes. *American Educational Research Journal, 21,* 725–736.

PROBLEM: The researchers were interested in testing the separate and combined effects of mastery learning and team (cooperative) learning on student achievement in mathematics.

SAMPLE AND SETTINGS: The sample consisted of 588 ninth-grade general mathematics students from junior and senior high schools in inner city Philadelphia and their teachers. Approximately 76 percent of the students were black, 19 percent were white, and 7 percent were Hispanic-American or Asian-American. Achievement level of the students was very low.

PROCEDURES: Teachers and their students were randomly assigned to one of four treatment conditions:

- *Group 1—Mastery Learning:* Students were taught general mathematics using mastery learning principles developed by Block and Anderson (1975).
- *Group 2—Teams:* Students were taught general mathematics using Slavin's STAD approach.
- *Group 3—Teams and Mastery:* Students were taught general mathematics using a combination of mastery and team approaches.
- *Group 4—Control Group:* Students were taught general mathematics using a focused instruction approach, but with no inclusion of mastery learning or cooperative learning principles.

Classes in all four groups used the same curriculum materials and spent about the same time on mathematics each day. Trained observers visited classrooms to make sure teachers were correctly implementing the various teaching approaches. Student achievement was measured before the various treatments and again after the experiment with a version of a well-accepted test of mathematics basic skills.

POINTERS FOR READING RESEARCH: This is perhaps the most complicated study encountered to date. All of the statistical concepts used by Slavin and Karweit are too complicated to explain in a few words. To make sure results could be attributed to the experimental conditions, the researchers used a two-step process. First they determined that the groups were somewhat equivalent in achievement when the

(cont'd)

RESEARCH SUMMARY
10.3 (continued)

experiment began, and then they used the students' pretest scores as a covariate in their analysis. This means that student ability at the beginning is figured into the final calculations.

RESULTS: Table 1 shows the results of the study. The data have been simplified for ease of demonstration and discussion.

TABLE 1   Means and Approximate Grade Equivalents by Treatments, Mathematics Achievement

	Mastery			No Mastery		
	Teams and mastery			Teams		
		Pre	Post		Pre	Post
Teams	$\bar{X}$	14.28	17.11	$\bar{X}$	14.90	17.54
	GE	4.2	5.0	GE	4.4	5.1
	N of classes 9			N of classes 10		
	N of students 125			N of students 138		
	Mastery			Focused instruction		
		Pre	Post		Pre	Post
No teams	$\bar{X}$	14.50	16.19	$\bar{X}$	14.49	16.10
	GE	4.3	4.7	GE	4.3	4.7
	N of classes 14			N of classes 11		
	N of students 165			N of students 160		

SOURCE: Adapted from: R. E. Slavin and N. L. Karweit (1984), p. 731.

DISCUSSION AND IMPLICATIONS: An inspection of the mean scores and grade equivalents in Table 1 shows that student achievement in each of the experimental conditions and the control groups was essentially equivalent at the beginning of the experiment. The analysis performed by Slavin and Karweit indicated that classes that used team (cooperative) learning made greater progress in mathematics than classes in any of the other conditions.

The researchers concluded that "the results of the present study and others support the utility of student team learning for increasing student achievement, primarily because of the effect of team incentives on student motivation" (p. 734). More details about this consistent research finding and its implications for teaching are explored in the next section of this chapter.

PROCEDURES FOR USING COOPERATIVE LEARNING

Preinstructional Tasks

Many functions of teacher planning described previously can be applied to cooperative learning lessons. However, there are also some unique aspects of planning when using this model. For example, time spent organizing or analyzing specific lesson skills may instead be spent gathering resource materials, texts, or work sheets so that small groups of students can work on their own. Instead of planning for the smooth flow and sequencing of major ideas, the teacher may work on how to make smooth transitions from whole-class to small group instruction.

CHOOSING APPROPRIATE CONTENT

As with any lesson, one of the primary planning tasks for teachers is choosing content that is appropriate for the students given their interests and prior learning. This is particularly true for cooperative learning lessons, because the model requires a substantial amount of student self-direction and initiative. Without interesting and appropriately challenging content, a cooperative lesson can quickly break down.

Obviously, veteran teachers know from past experience which topics are most suited for cooperative learning just as they know the approximate developmental levels and interests of students in their classes. Beginning teachers must depend on curriculum guides and textbooks for appropriate subject content. However, there are several questions that beginning teachers can use to determine the appropriateness of subject content.

Have the students had some prior contact with the subject matter or will it require extended explanation by the teacher?

Is the content likely to interest the group of students for whom it is being planned?

If the teacher wants to use text, does it provide sufficient information on the topic?

For STAD or Jigsaw lessons, does the content lend itself to objective quizzes that can be administered and scored quickly?

For a Jigsaw lesson, does the content allow itself to be divided into several natural subtopics?

For a Group Investigation lesson, does the teacher have sufficient command of the topic to guide students into various subtopics and direct them to relevant resources?

FORMING STUDENT TEAMS

A second important planning task for cooperative learning is deciding how student learning teams are to be formed. Obviously, this task will vary according to (1) the goals teachers have for a particular lesson, and (2) the racial and ethnic mix and the ability levels of students within their classes. Below are some examples of how teachers might decide to form student teams:

- A fifth-grade teacher in an integrated school might use cooperative learning for the purpose of helping students to better understand peers from different ethnic or racial backgrounds. He or she might take great care to have racially or ethnically mixed teams in addition to matching for ability levels.

- A seventh-grade English teacher in a mostly middle-class, white school might form student teams according to students' achievement levels in English.

- A tenth-grade social studies teacher with a homogeneous group of students might decide to use Group Investigation and form teams according to student interest in a particular subtopic but also keep in mind mixing students of different ability levels.

- A fourth-grade teacher with several withdrawn students in her class may decide to form cooperative teams based on ability but also to find ways to integrate the isolates with popular and outgoing class members.

- Early in the year a teacher with several students new to the school might form learning teams on a random basis, thus ensuring opportunities for the new students to meet and work with students they don't yet know. Later students' abilities could be used to form learning teams.

Obviously, the composition of teams has almost infinite possibilities. During the planning phase, teachers must delineate clearly their academic and social objectives. They also need to collect adequate information about their students' abilities so that, if heterogeneous ability teams are desired, they will have the needed information. Finally, teachers should recognize that some features of group composition may have to be sacrificed in order to meet others.

DEVELOPING MATERIALS AND DIRECTIONS

When teachers prepare for a whole-class presentation, a major task is to gather materials that can be translated into meaningful verbal messages. Although teachers provide verbal information to students in a cooperative learning lesson, this information is normally accompanied by text, work sheets, and study guides.

If students are to be given text, it is important that it be both interesting and at an appropriate reading level for the particular class of students. Using materials from a college textbook or other advanced text is normally inappropriate for school-aged students except, perhaps, those in advanced high school classes. If study guides are to be developed by teachers, these should be designed to highlight the content deemed most important. Good study guides and materials take time to develop and cannot be done well the night before a particular lesson is to begin.

If teachers are using the Group Investigation method, an adequate supply of materials will have to be collected for use by student learning teams. In some schools, a beginning teacher can rely on the school librarian and media specialists for gathering materials. This normally requires the teacher to communicate clearly about the goals and objectives of a particular lesson and to be precise about how many students will be involved. For librarians and media specialists to be of maximum assistance requires enough lead time for them to do their work. Again, a beginning teacher should be cautioned about last-minute requests. One of the learning aids at the end of this chapter provides you with a chance to explore the library and media resources in a school with an eye toward future cooperative learning lessons. The following guidelines are offered to get maximum assistance from school support staff when planning a cooperative learning lesson:

- Meet with the school librarian and media specialists at least two weeks prior to the lesson and go over your lesson objectives. Ask for their ideas and assistance.
- Follow up the meeting with a brief memo summarizing ideas, time lines, and agreements.
- Check back a few days before materials are needed to see if things are coming along as you expected and offer your assistance to help if that is needed.
- If the materials are to be used in your room, ask the specialist to help you design a system for keeping track of materials. You may also ask the specialist to come into your room and explain the system to your students.

Finally, it is important that students have a clear understanding about their roles and the teacher's expectations for them as they participate in a cooperative learning lesson. If other teachers in the school are using cooperative learning, this task will be easier because students will already be aware of the model and their role in it. In schools where few teachers use the cooperative learning approach, beginning teachers will have to spend time describing the model to students and working with them on requisite skills. Chapter 5 described procedures to increase communication within classroom groups and also activities to build group cohesion. These are critical skills for students in classrooms where teachers plan to use cooperative learning.

An important thing to remember for beginning teachers who have not used cooperative learning before and who are using it with students who are not familiar with the model is that at first it may appear not to be working. Students will be confused about the cooperative reward structure. Parents may also object. Also, students may not at first be very enthusiastic about the possibilities of small-group interactions on academic topics with their peers. Chapter 11 provides additional information about why this happens and what can be done about it.

Finally, special directions about the goals and activities of a particular cooperative learning lesson should be given to students in writing—on tag board displays for younger children and as handouts for older students. Included in these directions would be information about:

- The goals of the lesson
- What students are expected to do while working in learning teams
- Time lines for completion of particular work or activities
- Dates of quizzes when using STAD or Jigsaw
- Dates for major presentations when using Group Investigation
- Grading procedures—both individual and group rewards
- Format for presentation of reports

Using the cooperative learning model can be most difficult for the beginning teacher because it requires the simultaneous coordination of a variety of activities. On the other hand, this model can achieve some important educational goals that other models cannot, and the rewards of this type of teaching can be enormous for the teacher who plans carefully.

Conducting the Lesson

In Table 10.1 the syntax for the cooperative learning model was divided into six steps: (1) presenting the goals for the lesson and establishing set; (2) presenting information to students through verbal presentation, text, or other forms; (3) making the transition into learning teams; (4) managing and helping students during team study and seatwork; (5) testing over team presentation of materials; (6) recognition of student achievement. The first four steps will be discussed in this section. Testing and student recognition will be described as postinstructional tasks.

PRESENTING GOALS AND ESTABLISHING SET

Some aspects of presenting goals and establishing set are not different for cooperative learning than they were for other models. Effective teachers begin all lessons by reviewing, by explaining their objectives in understandable language, and by showing how the lesson ties into previous learning. Because many cooperative learning lessons extend beyond a particular day or week and because the goals and objectives are multifaceted, the teacher normally puts special emphasis on this phase of instruction.

For example, when teachers are introducing a group investigation lesson for the first time, they will want to spend sufficient time with students to make sure specific steps and roles are clearly understood. This can also be the time when a teacher may want to talk about how students can take responsibility for their own learning and not rely solely upon the teacher. It may also be a time to discuss how knowledge comes from many sources such as books, films, and one's own interactions with others.

If a teacher is about to introduce Jigsaw, he or she may want to discuss how people are required to work interdependently with others in many aspects of life and how Jigsaw gives students an opportunity to practice cooperative behaviors. Similarly, if the teacher's main objective is to improve relations between students from different ethnic backgrounds or races, he or she may want to explain this idea to students and discuss how working with people who are different from us provides opportunities to know one another better.

The important point with all these examples is that students are more likely to work toward important goals and objectives if the rationale for the lesson has been explicitly discussed. It is difficult for students to perform a task well if they are unclear about why they are doing it or if the criteria for success are kept secret.

PRESENTING INFORMATION VERBALLY OR IN TEXT

Procedures and guidelines for presenting information to students will not be repeated here because that subject was covered extensively in Chapter 7. It is important, however, to provide some information about the use of text. Most of what is described here is not unique to the cooperative learning model and can be used by the beginning teacher in many situations involving text.

Assuming Responsibility for Teaching Reading Teachers of young children know that relying on text to transmit content involves helping the children learn to read the assigned materials. Teachers in the upper grades and secondary schools (and college for that matter) often assume their students can read and comprehend the assigned materials. Many times this is an incorrect assumption. If a cooperative learning lesson requires students to read text, then effective teachers, regardless of the age level of their students or the subject taught, will assume responsibility for helping students become better readers. The special topic section on teaching reading and writing highlights several important guidelines on this topic.

MAKING TRANSITIONS FROM WHOLE CLASS TO LEARNING TEAMS

The process of getting students into learning teams and getting them started on their work is perhaps one of the most difficult steps for teachers using cooperative learning. This is the phase in a cooperative learning lesson where bedlam can result unless the transition is carefully planned and managed. There is nothing more frustrating to teachers than transitional situations where 30 students are moving into small groups, not sure of what they are to do, and each demanding the teacher's attention and help. Three simple but important strategies can be used by teachers to make transitions go smoothly.

1. Write key steps on the chalkboard or on charts. Visual cues assist large groups of students as they move from one place in the room to another. Think of these as signs similar to those provided for people lining up to purchase theater tickets to a popular play or queuing procedures used at public events such as football games. Below is an example of such a display:

STEP 1 Move quickly to the location where your team's name has been posted on the wall.

STEP 2 Choose one team member to come up to my desk to gather needed learning materials.

STEP 3 Spend 10 minutes reading your particular assignment.

STEP 4 At my signal, begin your discussions.

STEP 5 At my signal return to your learning team and start presenting your information.

2. State directions clearly, and ask two or three students to paraphrase the directions. Getting several students to repeat the directions helps everyone to pay attention and also gives the teacher feedback on whether or not the directions are understood.

3. Identify a location for each learning team and have that clearly marked. Left to their own devices, students at any age (even adults) will not evenly distribute themselves around a room. They will tend to cluster in areas of the room that are most easily accessible. For effective small-group work, teachers should clearly designate those parts of the room they want each team to occupy and insist that teams go to that particular location.

A learning aid has been included at the end of this chapter to study and reflect upon the transition process in a cooperative learning lesson.

MANAGING AND HELPING STUDENTS DURING TEAM WORK

Some rather uncomplicated cooperative learning activities allow students to complete their work with minimum interruption or assistance by the teacher. For other activities, the teacher may need to work closely with each of the learning teams, reminding them of the tasks they are to perform and the time allocated for each step. When using the Group Investigation method, the teacher must remain constantly available to assist with resource identification. There is a fine line for the teacher to follow during this phase of a cooperative learning lesson. Too much interference and unrequested assistance can be annoying to students. It can also take away opportunities for student initiative and self-direction. At the same time, if the teacher finds that students are unclear about the directions or that they cannot complete planned tasks, then direct intervention and assistance are required. A learning aid at the end of this chapter has been designed for beginning teachers who want to learn more about how students interact with one another during small group work.

Postinstructional Tasks

For each of the models of teaching described previously, the importance of using evaluation strategies that are consistent with the goals and objectives of a particular lesson and consistent with the model's overall theoretical framework has been emphasized. For example, if the teacher is using presentation and explanation to help students master important ideas and to think critically about these ideas, then test questions asking students both for recall and for higher-level responses are required. If the teacher is using the direct instruction model to teach a specific skill, a performance test is required to measure student mastery of the skill and to provide corrective feedback. All of the examples and suggestions given in previous chapters, however, are based on the assumption that the teacher is operating under a competitive or individualistic reward system. The cooperative learning model changes the reward system and, consequently, requires a different approach to evaluation and recognition of achievement.

For STAD and the Slavin version of Jigsaw, the teacher requires students to take quizzes over the learning materials. Test items on these quizzes must, in most instances, be of an objective type so they can be scored in class or soon after. Figure 10.1 illustrates how team and individual scores are determined.

Slavin (1983), the developer of this scoring system, described it this way:

> The amount that each student contributes to his or her team is determined by the amount the student's quiz score exceeds the student's own past quiz average. . . . Students with perfect papers always receive the . . . maximum, regardless of their base scores. This individual improvement system gives every student a good chance to contribute maximum points to the team if (and only if) the student does his or her best, and thereby shows substantial improvement or gets a perfect paper. This improvement point system has been shown to increase student academic performance even without teams (Slavin, 1980), but it is especially important as a component of STAD since it avoids the possibility that low performing students will not be fully accepted as group members because they do not contribute many points. (p. 24)

Figure 10.1   Scoring Procedures for STAD and Jigsaw

Step 1: Establish Base Line

Each student is given a base score based on averages on past quizzes.

Step 2: Find Current Quiz Score

Students receive points for the quiz associated with the current lesson.

Step 3: Find Improvement Score

Students earn improvement points to the degree to which their current quiz score matches or exceeds their base score, using the scale provided below.

More than 10 points below base . . . . 0 points
10 points below to 1 point below base . . . . 10 points
Base score to 10 points above base . . . . 20 points
More than 10 points above base . . . . 30 points
Perfect paper (regardless of base) . . . . 30 points

SOURCE: From R. Slavin (1986), *Student team learning* (Third edition). Center for Research on Elementary and Middle Schools, p. 19. © Johns Hopkins.

Figure 10.2 shows an example how a quiz scoring sheet might look.

An elaborate scoring system does not exist for the Group Investigation approach. The group report or presentation serves as one basis for evaluation and students should be rewarded for both individual contributions and the collective product. The teacher has to be careful with the evaluation process for group investigation activities. Consistent with the concept of cooperative reward structure, it is important for the teacher to reward the group product. However, this can cause two kinds of problems. One, a few ambitious students may take on a larger portion of the responsibility for completing the group project and then be resentful toward classmates who made only minor contributions yet received the same evaluation. Similarly, students who have neglected their responsibilities to the group effort may develop cynicism toward a system that rewards them for work not accomplished. No place in the literature has been found where this problem is directly addressed.

Figure 10.2 Quiz Score Sheet (STAD and Jigsaw)

Student	Date: May 23 Quiz: Addition with Regrouping			Date: Quiz:			Date: Quiz:		
	Base Score	Quiz Score	Improvement Points	Base Score	Quiz Score	Improvement Points	Base Score	Quiz Score	Improvement Points
Sara A.	90	100	30						
Tom B.	90	100	30						
Ursula C.	90	82	10						
Danielle D.	85	74	10						
Eddie E.	85	98	30						
Natasha F.	85	82	10						
Travis G.	80	67	0						
Tammy H.	80	91	30						
Edgar I.	75	79	20						
Andy J.	75	76	20						
Mary K.	70	91	30						
Stan L.	65	82	30						
Alvin M.	65	70	20						
Carol N.	60	62	20						
Harold S.	55	46	10						
Jack E.	55	40	0						

SOURCE: From R. Slavin (1986), *Student team learning.* (Third edition). Center for Research on Elementary and Middle Schools, p. 20. © Johns Hopkins.

Some experienced teachers have found a solution by providing two evaluations for students—one for the group's effort and one for each person's individual contribution. The latter is sometimes difficult to ascertain. This procedure also prevents less able students from making as significant contributions as are possible with the scoring system of STAD and Jigsaw based on individual improvement.

RECOGNITION OF EFFORT

A final important postinstructional task unique to cooperative learning is the emphasis given to recognizing student effort and achievement. Slavin and the Johns Hopkins developers created the concept of the weekly class newsletter for use with STAD and Jigsaw. The teacher (sometimes the class itself) reports on and publishes the results of team and individual learning in this newspaper. An example of a weekly newsletter is shown in Figure 10.3.

More recently, the Johns Hopkins group have tended to play down the competition among teams and instead of determining winning teams they recommend pitting teams against preestablished criteria to evaluate team achievement. Figure 10.4 shows the criteria used by some teachers and recommended by Slavin.

Figure 10.5 gives an example of a Team Summary Sheet that can be used by teachers to determine team scores and also an example of a certificate of congratulations to a team that has achieved SuperTeam status.

The developers of the Group Investigation approach recognize team efforts by highlighting group presentations and by displaying the results of group investigations prominently in the room. This form of recognition can be emphasized even more by inviting guests (parents, students from another class, or the principal) to hear final reports. Newsletters summarizing the results of a class's group investigation could also be produced and sent to parents and others in the school and community.

Summary

Cooperative learning is unique among the models of teaching because it uses a different task and reward structure to promote student learning. This model also facilitates important educational goals that go beyond academic achievement to aim at better understanding between members of different ethnic and racial groups and more cooperation among people. The task structure of cooperative learning requires students to work together on academic tasks in small groups. The reward structure recognizes collective as well as individual effort.

The model's intellectual roots go back to John Dewey and his concept of democratic classrooms, although contemporary approaches, such as STAD, Group Investigation, and Jigsaw, have been developed during the past decade. Developers of cooperative learning strategies have also been researchers. This has led to

Figure 10.3   Sample Weekly Newsletter

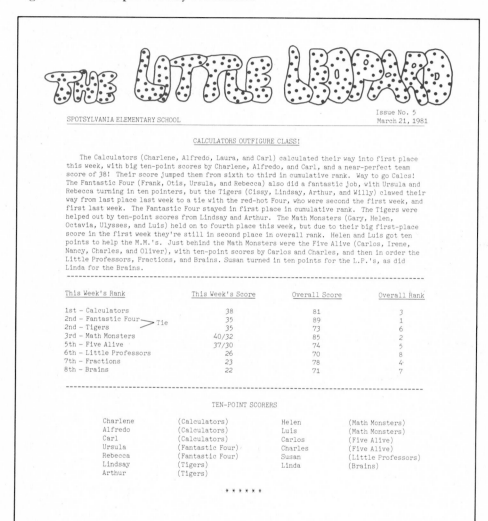

SOURCE: From R. Slavin (1986), *Student team learning* (Third edition). Center for Research on Elementary and Middle Schools, p. 25. © Johns Hopkins.

extensive field testing and a substantial research base for the model. When contrasted to other approaches, evidence supports the effectiveness of cooperative learning in promoting higher student achievement, better group relationships, and higher degrees of cooperative behavior.

Preinstructional, instructional, and postinstructional tasks required of the cooperative learning teacher cast the teacher in a role different from that required

Figure 10.4   Determining and Rewarding Team Scores

Step 1: Determining Team Scores

Team scores are figured by adding each member's individual improvement points and dividing by the number of members on the team.

Step 2: Recognizing Team Accomplishments

Each team receives a particular certificate based on the following point system.

Team Average	Award
15 points	Good Team
20 points	Great Team
25 points	Super Team

SOURCE: From R. Slavin (1986), *Student team learning* (Third edition). Center for Research on Elementary and Middle Schools, p. 19. © Johns Hopkins.

by other models. Teacher planning time is spent primarily in gathering learning materials and forming student learning teams. During the lesson itself, little time is spent presenting or demonstrating learning materials; instead, time is spent helping students form groups and work together. Cooperative reward structures change the ways teachers evaluate students from relying totally on rewards for individual effort to the incorporation of rewards for group effort as well.

Books for the Professional

Aronson, E., Blaney, S. C., Sikes, J., and Snapp, M. (1978). *The jigsaw classroom*. Beverly Hills, Cal.: Sage Publications. This book presents an in-depth discussion of the jigsaw approach to cooperative learning, including results from research and detailed directions for teachers interested in the approach.

Davidson, N. (Ed.). (in press). *Small group cooperative learning in mathematics: A handbook for teachers*. Reading, Mass.: Addison Wesley. This is a book of readings on cooperative learning strategies, written specifically for teachers and representing most of the major cooperative learning theorists and researchers.

Johnson, D. W., and Johnson, R. T. (1975). *Learning together and alone. Cooperation, competition, and individualization*. Englewood Cliffs, N.J.: Prentice-Hall. This book gives a detailed rationale for the goal and reward structures required of cooperative learning. Also provides many good ideas for teachers who want to implement cooperative learning in their classrooms.

Kagan, S. (1985). *Cooperative learning: Resources for teachers*. Riverside, Cal.: University of California. This book is filled with practical ideas and resource materials to assist teachers with cooperative learning lessons.

Slavin, R. (1983). *Cooperative learning*. New York: Longman. This book provides detailed rationale behind cooperative learning along with summaries of Slavin's research.

Slavin, R., Sharan, S., Kagan, S., Hertz-Lazarowitz, R., Webb, C., and Schmuck, R. (Eds.). (1985). *Learning to cooperate, cooperating to learn*. New York: Plenum Press. This is a book of readings by the major theorists and developers of cooperative learning. Rich in theory, it also provides practical approaches for teachers to follow.

Figure 10.5 Team Summary Sheet and Certificate of Congratulations

Team name _Fantastic Four_

Team members	1	2	3	4	5	6	7	8	9	10	11	12	13	14
Sara A.	30													
Eddie E.	30													
Edgar I.	20													
Carol N.	20													
Total team score	100													
Team average*	25													
Team award	Super Team													

*Team average = a total team score ÷ number of team members

THEY'RE GR-R-REAT!

A GREATTEAM

_____ team

did a GREAT JOB

this week

_____ date

SOURCE: R. Slavin (1986), *Student team learning* (Third edition). Center for Research on Elementary and Middle Schools, p. 85. © Johns Hopkins.

CHAPTER 10
LEARNING AIDS FOR PLANNING, OBSERVATION, AND REFLECTION

- Assessing My Skills for Using Cooperative Learning
- Observing Key Phases in a Cooperative Learning Lesson
- Observing Small-Group Interaction
- Observing Transitions and Group Management
- Visiting the School's Library and Media Center

ASSESSING MY SKILLS FOR USING COOPERATIVE LEARNING

PURPOSE: To help you assess your level of skill in using cooperative learning, this aid can be used either after reading the chapter or after a microteaching or field assignment.

DIRECTIONS: Check the level of skill you perceive that you have for the various teaching tasks associated with the cooperative learning model.

Skill or Competency	Level of Effectiveness		
	High	Medium	Low
Preinstructional Tasks			
Choosing appropriate content	_____	_____	_____
Deciding on composition of learning teams	_____	_____	_____
Developing and/or gathering needed materials	_____	_____	_____
Writing clear directions	_____	_____	_____
Instructional Tasks			
Phase 1			
Explaining objectives and establishing set	_____	_____	_____
Phase 2			
Presenting information (lecture and/or text)	_____	_____	_____
Phase 3			
Making transition to learning teams	_____	_____	_____
Phase 4			
Helping students during team study	_____	_____	_____
Postinstructional Tasks			
Phase 5			
Constructing appropriate tests	_____	_____	_____
Scoring tests for individuals and groups	_____	_____	_____
Phase 6			
Devising means to recognize student achievement	_____	_____	_____

OBSERVING KEY PHASES IN A COOPERATIVE LEARNING LESSON

PURPOSE: This aid helps you refine your understanding of the cooperative learning model. Use it as a guide to providing feedback in a microteaching setting or for observations in the field.

DIRECTIONS: As you observe the lesson make a "tick" for the category you believe best describes the level of performance for each of the teaching moves associated with the cooperative learning model.

Teaching Move or Task	Level of Performance		
	High	Average	Not Needed
Preinstructional Tasks			
The teacher chose appropriate content	_____	_____	_____
The teacher formed teams appropriately	_____	_____	_____
The teacher had developed and/or gathered needed materials	_____	_____	_____
The teacher had prepared clear directions	_____	_____	_____
Instructional Tasks			
Phase 1			
The teacher explained objectives and established set	_____	_____	_____
Phase 2			
The teacher presented information	_____	_____	_____
Phase 3			
The teacher made smooth transition to learning teams	_____	_____	_____
Phase 4			
The teacher helped students during team study	_____	_____	_____
Postinstructional Tasks			
Phase 5			
The teacher provided appropriate tests	_____	_____	_____
The teacher scored groups and students appropriately	_____	_____	_____
Phase 6			
The teacher recognized student achievement	_____	_____	_____

Comments and reflection of lesson just observed:

_____

OBSERVING SMALL-GROUP INTERACTION

PURPOSE: For cooperative learning to be a success, students must help each other learn. This tool will focus you on how students behave when in their teams, and will enhance your ability to spot off-task behavior.

DIRECTIONS: Observe a class during the team study phase of a cooperative learning lesson. Watch one of the teams; every 15 seconds, check off which of the following behaviors it exhibits.

Frequency	Group Activity
_____	1. Reading (finding information and so forth)
_____	2. Manipulating equipment
_____	3. Task discussion, general participation
_____	4. Task discussion, one or two students dominate
_____	5. Procedural discussion
_____	6. Observing
_____	7. Nontask discussion
_____	8. Procedural dispute
_____	9. Substantive discussion, task relevant
_____	10. Silence or confusion
_____	11. Other (specify) _____

Analysis and Reflection: Were the students more often on or off task? _____

If on task, what did the teacher do that contributed to on-task behavior? _____

If off task, what could the teacher have done to prevent the off-task behavior?

_____

SOURCE: Adapted from *Looking in classrooms* by T. L. Good and J. E. Brophy © 1984 by Harper & Row, Inc. Reprinted by permission of the publisher.

OBSERVING TRANSITIONS AND GROUP MANAGEMENT

PURPOSE: As noted on page 423 in the chapter, managing the transition from large- to small-group work can be trying. This aid will help you focus on teacher behaviors that smooth transition periods.

DIRECTIONS: Make a check when you observe the teacher performing the indicated behaviors.

_____ Teacher wrote key steps of the activity on the chalkboard or on charts.

_____ Teacher stated directions clearly.

_____ Teacher summarized directions.

_____ Teacher had one or two students summarize directions.

_____ Teacher used hand signals, or other visual signals (flicking light switch, for example), or auditory signals (ringing a small bell) to cue students.

_____ Teacher directed teams to the areas of the room where they were to work.

_____ Teacher labeled team work areas clearly.

_____ Other (specify) _____

Analysis and Reflection: What key thing did the teacher do to help with transitions? What could the teacher have done to make transition go more smoothly? Why?

Assignment 8

VISITING THE SCHOOL'S LIBRARY AND MEDIA CENTER

PURPOSE: A vital component of the Group Investigation approach to cooperative learning is an adequate supply of resources that students can comb for information. This aid is designed to assist you in evaluating a library's resources.

DIRECTIONS: Visit a school library or other resource facility and interview resource specialists. Find answers to the following questions.

1. Does the library have a substantial or minimal collection of print materials for student use? _____

   _____

2. To what degree does the media center have nonprint materials available for student use? _____

   _____

3. If you were an (elementary or secondary) student, would you find the library and/or the media center a pleasant and conducive place to study? Why? Why not? _____

   _____

4. What types of procedures does the librarian or media specialist prefer when working with a teacher on group investigation projects? Concerning

   a. Deadlines? _____

      _____

   b. Policy about taking materials to the classroom? _____

      _____

   c. Policy about small groups of students coming to library on their own? ____

      _____

   d. Policy about resource specialists coming into the room and assisting students with their group investigations? _____

      _____

5. What would be the main logistical drawbacks or weaknesses of the library or media center as a support system for group investigation? _____

   _____

PART 4

Part 4 of *Learning to Teach* is devoted to the organizational functions of teaching. Teachers, like other professionals, are expected not only to perform their primary function (in this case providing instruction to students) but also to provide leadership to the organization as a whole. For teachers this means working alongside others in the school—colleagues, administrators, parents, and students themselves—to help set school-wide expectations and gain clarity of purposes and actions.

The chapters that follow focus on three specific organizational functions that are important for beginning teachers: working with other members of the school community, helping schools improve, and surviving and flourishing as a professional. To perform these functions effectively requires understanding the nature of the school not only as a place where children come to learn but also as a

place where adults work. It also requires specific organizational skills aimed at making work with others in the school productive.

As you read and study these topics, you will discover two reasons why they are so important. One, there appears to be a certain synergy at work in schools in which teachers and others have come together and made agreements about what is going to be taught and how that makes a difference in how much students learn. Two, your ability to relate to and to work with others within the school and larger professional community will have a significant impact on your career. It is in this arena (not inside the classroom) that you will become known to others and will build your professional reputation. Teachers who grow and progress in their careers are those who can enter into school-wide dialogue about educational and professional issues.

The Organizational Functions of Teaching

CHAPTER 11

MAIN IDEAS

- Schools are social organizations and, as such, are adult workplaces as well as places where students come to learn.
- Schools have individual histories and cultures whose norms and roles influence school goals and the way people organize and communicate in regard to those goals.
- Although schools, like other social organizations, are characterized by goals and control structures, they also have special features, such as goal ambiguity, compulsory attendance, political visibility, and limited resources.
- Some of the work of schools is carried out through small groups whose combined efforts are needed to make schools effective as a whole.
- A moderately strong research base exists that helps explain why some schools are more effective than others. Some aspects of this research are still controversial.
- The research on effective schools provides beginning teachers with perspectives for working with various members of the school staff as well as with students and parents.

The School as Workplace

Previous chapters described what teachers do as they plan for and deliver instruction and as they manage complex classroom settings. Providing leadership and teaching students in classrooms, however, are not the only aspects of a teacher's job. Teachers are also members of an organization called *school* and as such are asked to perform important leadership and organizational functions including working with colleagues, serving on committees, and working with administrators and parents. The way these organizational functions are performed by teachers makes a significant difference in how students behave and what they learn. The way particular teachers carry out these functions also makes a significant difference in their own professional careers.

The aim of this chapter is to describe the work environment of schools and the corresponding culture of teaching. An important idea that is emphasized is that schools are not only places where students come to learn; they are also places where adults work. After providing a conceptual framework for viewing schools as workplaces, the emerging knowledge base on the nature of teachers' work behavior and what makes some schools more effective than others will be summarized. The chapter concludes with a discussion of several important organizational skills that beginning teachers need as they become fully involved in their first school and community. Learning aids at the end of the chapter have been designed to assist you with study and reflection about some aspects of the school that you may not have considered before.

PERSPECTIVE AND RATIONALE

At this point in your career it is likely that your view of schools stems mainly from many years of being a learner in classrooms. You are familiar with the classroom portion of the teacher's role, with the role of student, and with how students and teachers interact around academic tasks. However, you may not have had much chance to observe or reflect about schools as social organizations or about the various nonteaching functions performed by teachers. In fact, many people (including those in the media) rarely view schools from the perspective of the complex social organizations they are. This is unfortunate because views of schools, stemming only from experiences as students, have caused misunderstandings on the part of many (teachers, parents, and policymakers) regarding school improvement efforts. Unrealistic views also have led to disillusionment on the part of many beginning teachers. The section that follows provides a view of schools from behind, instead of in front of, the teacher's desk.

Schools Are Social Systems

In discussing schools, both the research literature and the wisdom of experienced educators are utilized. The set of understandings described here can best be labeled a *social systems perspective*. This perspective looks at the complex structure of the school and how its various interactions (including those within the classroom) are shaped by the larger social context.

When schools are called social systems this means that they are not simply places where individuals act in totally free and disconnected ways but, instead, in more or less interdependent and predictable ways. Although individuals come together in schools to promote purposeful learning, each person does not chart his or her own course alone, nor do the actions of each have consequences only for that person. Also, as will be described later, the synergy developed by teachers acting in concert can have important consequences for student learning. To understand the social system view of schools, think for a moment about the number of interdependent actions required to bring about a day's worth of instruction for students:

- Paper, pencils, and chalk have been ordered
- Rooms have been cleaned
- Curriculum guides have been prepared and textbooks ordered
- Parents have chosen to send their children to school
- Teachers have chosen to be professionally trained
- Buses have been driven and breakfasts and lunches prepared
- Schedules have been determined and children assigned to classes

This list could go on and on. The point, however, is that the contempory school is a complex social system requiring its members to perform important functions in interdependent ways.

Schools Have Histories and Cultures

Schools, like other organizations, have histories and cultures consisting of values, beliefs, and expectations that have developed and grown over time. The history of a school provides traditions and a multitude of routines (some good and some not so good) that are taken for granted by organizational members. The culture of a school provides the organizational arrangements that hold it together and give it power as a social entity. Lortie (1975) has referred to culture as the "way members of a group think about social action; culture encompasses alternatives for resolving problems in collective life" (p. 216). Others have provided similar definitions, although they sometimes use different labels. Rutter et al. (1979), for example, refer to the common set of values, beliefs, and ways of doing things as the school's *ethos;* Glass (1981) has called it *tone;* Joyce and his colleagues (1983) prefer the word *community.* Regardless of how it is labeled, culture greatly influences what goes on in schools and determines expectations and roles for beginning teachers.

Schools Have Common Features With Other Organizations

In some ways schools are similar to other organizations in society. For example, as in other organizations, members are directed toward the accomplishment of some goal. In a textile plant, the goal may be the production of men's shirts; IBM says information is its business. The overriding goal for schools is to provide *purposeful learning* experiences for students. Members of schools—principals, teachers, and students—are rewarded, as are members in other organizations, when they strive for and accomplish common organizational goals. Similarly, they are punished when they fail. An example of reward would be experiments in some states in which teaching faculties are given merit increases if, as a group, they can lift achievement in their school above a set criterion. An example of punishment would be instances in which beginning teachers are dismissed if they cannot provide purposeful learning activities.

Another organizational feature of schools is their division of labor and the resulting coordination efforts that are needed. Some teachers specialize according to subjects taught, whereas others specialize by grade level. In addition to teachers, school staffs include curriculum coordinators, administrators, nurses, counselors, janitors, and other support personnel. Most of the people in schools, however, are students, and they too must be considered organizational members. Because school roles are specialized, normative routines and structures are created to help members carry out their special tasks in ways that will more or less facilitate what others are doing. The reason why coordination of effort is not easy to accomplish in schools is described later.

Finally, the people in schools are pretty much like people in other organizations. They not only have jobs to perform, they also have psychological needs and motives to satisfy. In Chapter 5 a particular view of motivation was described in relation to students. This same perspective can help you understand adults in schools. This perspective, you remember, says that people are motivated to invest energy in three domains: achievement, affiliation, and influence. Achievement manifests itself in teachers and other adults in schools as they strive to provide good instruction and act as competent professionals. Affiliative motives become important when teachers come to value their peers for support, friendship, and collegiality. Influence motives are evident in schools as teachers strive to have a larger say in the way schools are run. Organizational members' feelings of self-esteem are related to the feelings they have about their competence, affiliation, and influence. Students who have these emotional states frustrated by the school may become less involved in the school. Similarly, when these states are frustrated for teachers, they are likely to feel incompetent, lonely, and powerless.

These three motivational domains (achievement, affiliation, and influence), while central to each individual in the school, are also central to the school as an organization. A school's ability to provide targeted learning cannot be accomplished without strong achievement motivation on the part of teachers and students. Likewise, affiliation and influence are directly needed to coordinate and manage the academic activities of schools and to make the schools a pleasant place to be. Two learning aids at the end of this chapter have been designed to help you think about your own motives in the three domains and to study a particular school to see what it is doing to help satisfy both student and adult psychological needs.

Schools Have Special Features

Just as schools have features in common with other organizations, so too they have features that are special. In some ways it is the special features of schools that are most significant for beginning teachers to understand.

AMBIGUOUS AND CONFLICTING GOALS

It has been stated several times in this book that the overriding goal of schools is to facilitate purposive learning for students. Stated at this level of abstraction, most people would readily agree with this goal. However, when people in schools speak more precisely about what purposive learning means, many of their statements may seem ambiguous and may conflict with the aims of one group or another in the community.

Goal ambiguity can be illustrated with reference to citizenship education. Most people in Western societies believe that the schools should socialize students as good citizens who accept the values of democratic political systems and who embrace some degree of freedom in their own economic activities. However, how do school people, parents, and others know whether or not this goal is being accomplished? Parents, for example, are never sure their sons or daughters are embracing the values parents desire for them. Teachers seldom know how their former students behave as adult citizens. Do they vote, and are they participating community members?

As for goal conflict, first of all, do citizenship goals compete with academic learning goals? Which are most important and how should time be allocated between the two? Second, what constitutes good citizenship? Some argue that the most important aspect of citizenship education is the socialization of students into traditional values and beliefs. Some church-related and private schools are inclined toward this position. On the other hand, others argue that this approach to citizenship education is simply indoctrination and leads to narrowness and conformity. The good citizen, from this point of view, might be the critical thinker who questions existing values and structures and attempts to modify them.

COMPULSORY ATTENDANCE

A second special feature of schools is that their clients are required to be there. All states have compulsory attendance laws that require parents to send their children to school, normally until age 16. Although most people support these laws because they guarantee a minimum education for all children and help prevent forced child labor, they do create the problem of keeping unmotivated students involved in school life. Schools with large numbers of academically unmotivated students are normally schools where teachers choose not to work. Recent innovations in some school systems, such as the creation of alternative and magnet schools, have attempted to combat the compulsory nature of schooling by giving students and their parents more choices as to the type of school the students attend. The fact still remains, however, that students *must* go to school.

POLITICAL VISIBILITY AND LIMITED RESOURCES

Finally, schools are highly visible and political in most communities but have very few extra resources for taking the initiative or answering their critics. Many people take an active interest in their schools and, given local control, schools offer one of the few opportunities where citizens feel their voices can be heard. For example, it is quite easy in many communities to stay informed about school events since large portions of the daily newspapers are devoted to school news, including the school's budget. It is also easy to attend local school board or council meetings and voice opinions, just as it is easy to walk directly into most principals' offices without an appointment. The whole system is open and permeable. Some aspects of this situation are positive. Local control and the openness of the educational system has helped maintain strong support for education over the past century. At the same time, this situation leaves the school and those who work there vulnerable to political whims and sometimes unfair attacks. And, as with most nonprofit, public service agencies, local political control tends to leave schools underfunded and always striving to satisfy demands for services without sufficient resources to provide them.

Norms, Roles, and the Culture of Teaching

Another way to think about schools is to think about the norms, roles, and organizational arrangements that exist for the purpose of getting work accomplished. These will have strong influences on the experiences that beginning teachers have both during student teaching and their first year.

NORMS

Norms are the expectations that people have for one another in particular social settings. They define the range of social behaviors that are allowed in given situations. Some norms are informal, such as the norm that prescribes a swimsuit rather than a cocktail dress on the beach. Some norms, however, are formal. For example, a person might not be arrested if he wore a tuxedo to the beach, but he would be if he broke the local ordinance that restricts bathing in the nude.

In schools many formal and informal norms exist that affect organizational members, including new teachers. For example, in some schools new teachers will find norms supporting friendliness and openness which will make them feel welcome. In other schools people may act toward one another in more reserved and formal ways. In some schools norms to encourage experimentation may make beginning teachers feel comfortable in trying out new ideas, whereas in other schools few risks will be encouraged. Two important norms associated with schools and the culture of teaching need highlighting because they affect the lives of beginning teachers most directly.

Autonomy Norm In some ways teachers have relatively little power and influence in the larger school system. They do, however, have a great deal of influence in their own classrooms, supported by what has been labeled the *autonomy norm*. Teachers, including beginning teachers, do pretty much what they want to once they are in their classrooms and their doors are closed. They alone are responsible for the day-to-day curricula and make almost all instructional decisions for themselves.

The "Hands-Off" Norm Closely paralleling the autonomy norm is a norm labeled by Lortie (1975), Sarason (1982), and Joyce, Hersh, and McKibbin (1983) as the *hands-off norm*. Not only are teachers given autonomy in their classrooms, but strong sanctions exist against interfering with other teachers in any but the most superficial ways. It is not appropriate according to Lortie (1975) for teachers to ask for help, for example. Such a request would suggest that the teacher is failing. Similarly, according to Feiman-Nemser and Floden (1986), it is not permissible for teachers to tell a peer what to do or to suggest that he or she teach something differently.

This is not to suggest to beginning teachers that colleagues within a particular school will be unfriendly or unsupportive. Teachers socialize a great deal with one another and on an emotional level are concerned and supportive of one another. Even so, according to Feiman-Nemser and Floden (1986), teachers will "avoid talking about instructional practices." Talk will deal instead with "politics, gripes, home life, and the personalities and family background of students rather than curriculum, instructional content, or teaching methods" (p. 509).

ROLES AND ROLE SYSTEMS

A cluster of norms detailing the way a particular job should be performed is called a *role*. The teacher's role, for example, includes norms about (1) how teachers should behave toward students and students toward them, (2) how teachers should interact with each other and with the principal, and (3) how much teachers should participate in school-level problem solving and decision making. The way various roles are interconnected within a particular setting is called a *role system*. People in schools learn roles and role systems from interaction with each other.

Many aspects of the teacher's role are clear and straightforward. For example, it is clear that teachers should teach academic content to students and evaluate their students' progress. Some aspects of the teacher's role, however, are not so clear and sometimes provide contradictory expectations. Contradictions in role expectations cause anxiety and trouble for beginning teachers.

One of the most basic contradictions in the teacher's role stems from strong expectations that teachers should treat each child as an individual even though schools are organized so that teachers must deal with students in groups. This conflict is particularly acute with secondary teachers who face as many as 150 to 180 students a day for rather brief periods of time. This role conflict, according to Lieberman and Miller (1984), is what makes teaching so personal because to deal with the contradictory demands of individualization and group instruction requires the development of a teaching style that is "individual and personal."

A second basic contradiction in the teacher's role involves the degree of distance between teacher and students. On the one hand, teachers are expected to maintain a certain social distance from students so authority and discipline can be maintained. In fact, as described in Chapters 2, 5, and 6, control is an overriding concern for beginning teachers, since they know they are being heavily judged on this score. On the other hand, most teachers know that they must form some type of bond with students in order to motivate them and help them to learn. Beginning teachers manifest the tensions of this role contradiction in a number of ways. They worry whether or not they should allow students to call them by their first name or how friendly they should become with a particular student they really like and so on. Such tensions are quite normal and only experience provides the means for dealing with the many contradictions built into the teacher's role.

ORGANIZATIONAL ARRANGEMENTS

Compared to most other organizations, schools are rather flat organizations. In elementary schools there are mainly teachers and a principal, and in most secondary schools one additional role, the department chair, is added. Lortie (1975) described the school's organizational structure as "cellular," that is, each classroom can be regarded as a cell within which the teacher is responsible for organizing the students, managing discipline, and teaching academic content. This organizational scheme, coupled with the hands-off norm, creates an isolated work situation for teachers. They make independent decisions about when and how to teach each subject and they do not ask other teachers for help. Joyce et al. (1983) have observed that this situation has made it customary for principals to relate to the teachers on a diadic basis, that is, in a one-to-one relationship rather than as an organized faculty prepared to take collective responsibility. This professional isolation has led some observers, such as Lortie, to refer to teaching as a "lonely profession." With the addition of many new roles in schools over the past few years, such as special teachers and lead teachers of one kind or another, it may be that the cellular structure of schools is changing. Currently, it remains the most common arrangement.

LOOSELY COUPLED

The school's cellular structure also causes an organizational arrangement that Weick (1976) has labeled *loosely coupled*. This means that what goes on in classrooms is not very tightly connected to what goes on in other parts of the school. Teachers can and do carry out their own instructional activities independently of administrators and others. The central office may initiate new curricula or new teaching procedures, but if teachers choose to ignore these initiatives, they can. On the positive side, loose coupling allows considerable room for individual teacher decision making in situations were a substantial knowledge about "best" teaching practice is lacking. Conversely, loose coupling can stymie efforts to establish common goals and coordinated activities, something that is important for effective schooling, as you will see later.

SMALL GROUPS AND SUBSYSTEMS

A final observation regarding the social arrangements of schools is that some of the work is carried out in small groups or subsystems. Examples of subsystems in schools would be a team of first- and second-grade teachers in an elementary school, an academic department in a secondary school, the principal's administrative team, or all the social studies teachers in a school district. Special task forces, or committees to improve the science curriculum, to select a new basal reading series, or to come up with school-wide guidelines for student conduct would be other examples, as would student councils, the football team, and the school band.

Important organizational goals are accomplished through these subsystems and their effective functioning is crucial for effective schooling. But what makes for effective functioning of small groups and subsystems? Effective subsystems are those whose members have good interpersonal and group skills that enable them to communicate with one another, establish goals, uncover conflict and work with it, hold effective meetings, solve problems, make decisions, and assess progress toward goals. This topic will be discussed in more detail in the next chapter when ways beginning teachers can improve schools by helping small groups become more effective are described.

SAMPLING THE RESEARCH BASE ━━━━━━━━━━

Educators have for many years thought about the school as a formal organization. In fact, a very important book written by Waller in 1932 on the sociology of teaching provided many important insights into the nature of schools and of teaching. However, it is only in the last two decades that educators and educational researchers have started to highlight the importance of schools as workplaces and the importance of the organizational functions of teaching. This section provides examples from fairly recent research about the nature of the work teachers do in schools and about why some schools seem to be more effective than others.

The Nature of Teachers' Work

Many people think teaching is an easy job, with short work days and long summer vacations. They also think that it consists mainly of working with students during the time they are in school from 9:00 A.M. to 3:00 P.M. Experienced teachers do not agree with this perception. They know that teachers do many other things in addition to directly working with students. They also know that the time demands of teaching are very great. Until recently, the exact nature of the work behavior of teachers and the time they spend on various aspects of their work was not fully known. The investigators whose work is summarized in Research Summary 11.1 tackled this lack of information head-on when they went to a high school and actually observed the work behavior of teachers.

Effective Schools

Most beginning teachers are primarily concerned about what goes on in their own classrooms and with their own students. Although this is natural and healthy, you should be aware that it is the overall culture or ethos of the school that contributes a great deal to student learning and not only one's individual teaching performance. It is only in the last decade that educators and educational researchers have started to discover this important principle. This section provides an example of what has come to be called school effectiveness research. Most of this research has been done over the past 10 or 15 years and is in response to earlier studies, such as Coleman et al. (1966) and Jencks et al. (1972), whch argued that schools did not make much difference. This is a rather new field of study and some of the results remain controversial. Nonetheless it points toward the importance of the organizational functions of teaching. As you will see, this research suggests that the behavior of teachers, administrators, students, and parents within the school setting (not just the classroom setting) can make a difference in how much students learn.

This research also points to the importance of participants coming together and making school-wide agreements about what is taught and how it is taught. It seems that there is a certain synergy working in schools that produces results that cannot be achieved when each teacher works alone on particularistic goals. Finally, this research emphasizes the people aspect of schooling. The quality of teaching and the climate of the school has been found to be much more important than the amount of money spent on concrete, books, or paper. School effectiveness

========= **RESEARCH SUMMARY** =========
11.1*

Cypher, T., and Willower, D. J. (1984). The work behavior of secondary school teachers. *Journal of Research and Development, 18,* 17–24.

PROBLEM: Cypher and Willover tried to find answers to two important questions: (1) How can we determine how much time a teacher spends working? and (2) How is that time spent? One way to determine how teachers spend their workdays would be to ask them, but unfortunately, such studies have not yielded very accurate information. The purpose of Cypher and Willower's study, then, was to determine how teachers spend their time in school (not just in the classroom) by observing them from the moment they entered until they left.

SAMPLE AND SETTING: Five secondary teachers were randomly selected from a list of teachers representing different socioeconomic and geographical distributions of schools and different subject matter areas. Two teachers taught Engish, one math, one social studies, and one biology. Their levels of experience varied from 6 to 18 years.

PROCEDURES: Each teacher was observed for five full days. In addition, work done after school was recorded by each teacher in diary form.

POINTERS FOR READING RESEARCH: The data presented in Table 1 is straightforward. No new concepts are introduced. A major problem with this type of study is that it only involved five teachers. However, such in-depth methods of collecting data (observing each of the teachers every minute of the school day for five days each, and maintaining complex records on their activities) are labor intensive and cannot be done on a large scale without considerable expense.

RESULTS: Table 1 indicates the different types of in-school activities with the mean number of minutes and the percentage of total time spent on each activity per day. Also included is the range of total percentages, to indicate that teachers differed quite considerably in their use of time.

DISCUSSION AND IMPLICATIONS: This research showed that teachers averaged 38 hours per week in in-school activities, and an additional 10.5 hours in after-school work. They spent 38.6 percent of their time on instruction-centered activities. They gave short, frequent quizzes rather than longer tests, and used no audiovisual equipment during instruction.

Noninstructional activities took a considerable amount of time. Little time was spent at scheduled meetings, but 10 percent of the time was taken up with unscheduled meetings (those exchanges which lasted more than one minute).

TABLE 1   Time Spent for Each Activity and Percentage of Total Time per Teacher, per Day.

Activity	Total Time in Minutes	% Total Time and Range
Instruction Centered		
Direct instruction	95.40	20.6% (12.8 – 37.6)
Organizing	15.85	3.4 (2.7 – 4.2)
Reviewing	21.00	4.5 (0 – 13.7)
Testing	22.96	5.0 (0.1 – 11.9)
Monitoring	23.60	5.1 (0.1 – 7.7)
Scheduled Meetings	2.68	0.6 (0 – 0.9)
Unscheduled Meetings	46.52	10.0 (5.3 – 17.8)
Exchanges (out of class)	67.52	14.6 (11.8 – 17.8)
Study Hall Supervisor	17.40	3.8 (0 – 6.4)
Monitoring Assemblies, Clubs	5.88	1.3 (.9 – 4.3)
Control and Supervision	12.68	2.7 (.2 – 9.3)
Desk Work	57.24	12.3 (7.9 – 19.9)
Routine Tasks	34.60	7.5 (3.7 – 14.2)
Travel Time	24.60	5.3 (3.2 – 10.7)
Private Time	16.16	3.5 (.8 – 5.3)

SOURCE: Adapted from T. Cypher and D. Willower (1984), pp. 19–20.

Desk work—planning, marking papers, etc.—took up 12.3 percent of their time, and routine tasks such as running off dittos took 7.5 percent. Private time, such as going to the rest room, was extremely brief—3.5 percent.

In a different cut at these time data, the researchers concluded that instructional activities took 34.4 percent of the time, classroom support, 27.8 percent, pupil control, 19.3 percent, private-personal (including talking to other teachers on nonschool related topics at lunch), 11.6 percent, travel (time from class to class), 5.3 percent, and extra-curricular, 1.8 percent.

What this study indicates is that teaching is extremely active and it involves many interactions with many students and other adults in the school. The daily schedule largely dictates the teachers' use of time. From the researchers' standpoint, teachers in the study used their time efficiently. Even with the rigid schedule, teachers made judgments about what was important and what was not. They were seldom supervised.

Individuals thinking about entering teaching must be able to maintain a high activity level, and be willing to be interrupted and change thought patterns often and quickly. They must also recognize that there are many aspects to a teacher's job beyond actual face-to-face instruction of students.

* This report was summarized by Virginia Richardson-Koehler.

research does not say that resources are not important; it does say that the amount of money spent on the school library collection or on the physical plant takes a back seat to other conditions that people within school can create.

To illustrate these principles a study conducted in Great Britain in the late 1970s is discussed in Research Summary 11.2. It is important because it was one of the first to provide data supporting the importance of whole school environments and because it provided a model for other researchers to follow.

EFFECTIVE SCHOOLS AND THE BEGINNING TEACHER

Since Rutter's ground-breaking study, several other researchers have conducted similar studies (Brookover et al., 1979, for example) with schools in the United States and with elementary as well as secondary schools. Several of these studies have produced similar results and conclusions, namely, that some schools develop norms and expections that support student learning whereas other schools do not. More specifically, some norms and expectations appear to make some schools more effective than others.

Attributes of Effective Schools

Richard Hersh (1982) reviewed the school effectiveness literature and provided a helpful list of the features that characterize effective schools. These are described here and they will serve as a springboard for considering the organizational skills needed by beginning teachers.

Hersch says that attributes of effective schools can be divided into two categories—those having to do with the school's social organization and those having to do with the school's instructional and curriculum patterns. These attributes are listed in Table 11.1.

Table 11.1 Attributes of Effective Schools

SOCIAL ORGANIZATION	INSTRUCTION AND CURRICULUM
Clear academic and social behavior goals	High academic learning time
Order and discipline	Frequent and monitored homework
High expectations	Frequent monitoring of student progress
Teacher efficacy	Coherently organized curriculum
Pervasive caring	Variety of teaching strategies
Public rewards and incentives	Opportunities for student responsibility
Administrative leadership	
Community support	

SOURCE: From *The structure of school improverment*, p. 25, by B. Joyce et al. Copyright © 1983 by Longman, Inc. All rights reserved.

SOCIAL ORGANIZATION

Hersh's definitions of the social organizational attributes are:

Clear academic and social behavior goals Academic achievement is constantly emphasized, and teachers, parents, and students share common values and understandings about the school's achievement goals.

Order and discipline Basic rules of conduct have been agreed upon throughout the school, and teachers feel responsibility for enforcing behavioral norms both in their own particular classes and across the school.

High expectations Teachers and other staff hold high standards for students. They convey to students an "I care" and "can do" attitude and demand that each student aspire to excellence.

Teacher efficacy Teachers also have high expectations for themselves and a strong belief that they can teach every child.

Pervasive caring Teachers and other adults in the school develop a caring atmosphere. Their demands on students are not viewed as cruel and judgmental but as fair and caring. They communicate and celebrate student achievement.

Public rewards and incentives Effective schools have devised ways to publicly reward student successes and achievements. Student work is displayed, honor rolls are published, and active communication exists between the school and parents.

Administrative leadership Principals in effective schools care deeply about the school's academic programs. They support teacher and student efforts and they help set the tone for high expectations and pervasive caring.

Community support Staff in effective schools find ways to involve parents and community in the school's programs. This involvement goes beyond open houses to include such activities as school beautification, tutoring, and active fund rasing for the school.

INSTRUCTION AND CURRICULUM

Hersh's description of attributes associated with the instructional curriculum of effective school's include:

High academic learning time Teachers in effective schools have found ways to maximize the time devoted to academic learning. They waste little time getting classes started and moving smoothly from one activity to another with minimum disruption. School-wide, they have found ways to keep administrative disruptions to a minimum.

Frequent and monitored homework Homework is required and is checked by the teachers in effective schools. Checking and giving feedback to students is one way for teachers and other adults in the school to tell students they have high expectations and that they care.

Frequent monitoring of student progress Through tests, quizzes, and informal

RESEARCH SUMMARY
11.2

Rutter, M., Maughan, B., Mortimore, P., Ouston, J., and Smith, A. (1979). *Fifteen thousand hours: Secondary schools and their effects on children.* Cambridge, Mass.: Harvard University Press.

PROBLEM: During the late 1960s and early 1970s several influential books, such as James Coleman's (1966) *Equality of Educational Opportunity* and Christopher Jencks's (1972) *Inequality: A Reassessment of the Effect of Family and Schooling in America,* presented information that led many to believe that schools made little difference in the education of children. One accepted hypothesis, at that time, was that most student achievement could be attributed to factors outside the school such as family background, heredity and just plain luck. Michael Rutter, an English child psychiatrist, set out to investigate if schools did make a difference in student behavior and in educational attainment.

SAMPLE AND SETTING: Rutter chose to study 12 secondary schools in inner city London, England. Schools participating in the study according to Rutter (1) were in neighborhoods that were a bit "rundown or drab," (2) had a predominance of families from working-class backgrounds, (3) had a substantial number of families from immigrant backgrounds, and (4) included boys' schools, girls' schools, and coeducational schools. These schools had similar and varied external characteristics in terms of size, space, resources, experience of the teachers, and educational aims as expressed by teaching staff.

PROCEDURES: Rutter and his colleagues systematically collected information about a group of students who were to enter the 12 schools while they were still in primary schools. This information included:

▪ Ability and achievement data in math, English, and verbal reasoning
▪ Parental occupations
▪ Emotional and behavioral difficulties

The researchers then followed the students during secondary school and collected outcome measures on four variables:

▪ Behavior in school
▪ Achievement
▪ Attendance
▪ Delinquency

The researchers also gathered data on what they called physical and administrative features of the schools and on "school processes." Measures of administrative features included:

▪ Status and sex of staff
▪ Age of building and number of sites
▪ Internal organization of staff
▪ Size and space of building
▪ Staff provision and class size

School process variables included:

- Academic emphasis
- Rewards, punishments, and praise
- Responsibility and participation
- Stability of teaching and friendship groups
- Teacher's actions in lessons
- Pupil conditions
- Skills of teachers

POINTERS FOR READING RESEARCH: In the preceding chapters, particularly those in Part 2, the research summaries focused mainly on relationships among particular models or procedures of teaching and student achievement. This study focuses on school effects. Good school effects studies are large and complex, and it is difficult to describe every detail of the researchers' methods. It is also impossible to summarize all the results of these large studies. It is important to point out, however, that the collection of data in Rutter's study was very carefully done and included such features as: (1) a researcher who worked in each school, (2) observations in schools done in pairs to ensure reliable data, (3) observations conducted both in schools and in classrooms, (4) in-depth interviews with staff, administrators, and students, (5) a wide range of information collected over an extended period of time.

Results: Two aspects of Rutter's study are highlighted here. Table 1 compares the 12 schools on three of the four important outcome measures in the study: student attendance, student behavior, and academic attainment. The important thing to observe in these data is that, on the whole, schools that have high levels on one measure also have high levels on the others, and vice versa.

TABLE 1 A Comparison of Different Outcome Measures: Attendance, Behavior, and Academic Attainment in 12 Schools.

Attendance	Academic	Behavior
1	1	1
2	2	4
3	6	3
4	5	5
5	8	10
6	4	6
7	10	11
8	9	9
9	3	8
10	7	7
11	12	12
12	11	2

NOTE: Rank: 1 = best school; 12 = worst school
SOURCE: Adapted from M. Rutter, et al. (1979), p. 93.

(cont'd)

RESEARCH SUMMARY
11.2 (continued)

Remember that Rutter chose to collect information on a variety of schools, about their physical and administrative arrangements and about the schools' social processes. On such things as size and space of school, age of building, class size, and administrative organization, Rutter found no relationship between these variables and his outcome measures.

However, when he collected information about the school's academic emphasis, such as high expectations, homework, library use, teacher reporting on progress, teacher actions in class, use of time, rewards and punishments, display of students' work, opportunities for student responsibility and participation, he found the relationships described in Figure 1. Note the high correlations between school processes and academic attainment.

DISCUSSION AND IMPLICATIONS: The Rutter study was large and complex and the details of all results cannot be summarized here. The main conclusions, however, are as follows:

▪ The behavior and achievement of students in London secondary schools varied markedly from school to school
▪ Students were more likely to show good behavior and higher achievement in some schools than others.
▪ Differences in outcomes produced by schools remained stable over time.
▪ Schools performed similarly on all outcome measures. That is, schools which produced good behavior also produced higher achievement and vice versa.
▪ Outcomes were not related to physical factors (size, building, library) but instead related to characteristics of the school as a social organization.

The important implication for teachers made by Rutter was that individual actions of teachers and others combine to create a particular ethos, or set of values, attitudes, and behaviors that become characteristic of the school as a whole, and it is this total pattern that makes some schools more effective than others.

FIGURE 1 Relationships Between Combined Process Measures and Student Academic Outcome

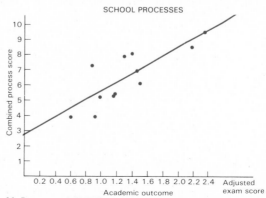

SOURCE: Adapted from M. Rutter et al. (1979), p. 143.

devices, teachers keep track of student progress and give students and parents helpful feedback on this progress.

Coherently organized curriculum The curriculum in effective schools is closely connected to the goals and objectives of the schools and is linked to the major evaluation and testing procedures. Teachers know what teachers at other levels or in other subjects are teaching and match their own instruction accordingly.

Variety of teaching strategies Teachers in effective schools have broad repertoires of teaching strategies and employ these to help meet the school's instructional goals.

Opportunities for student responsibility The adults in effective schools find ways to engage students in running their school through devices such as student government, and they encourage peer tutoring, hall monitoring, and other opportunities for students to engage in leadership behaviors.

Using the Effective Schools Research

The effective schools research can be helpful to beginning teachers in two ways. First, it can help round out your understanding of schools as social organizations, and second, it can serve as a reminder that your own classroom will be but part of a larger school effort. This research also draws attention to several contradictions that stem from the way schools have been organized. On the one hand, it appears that effective schools are places where people have common goals, have organized their curriculum coherently, and where common rules and norms guide teachers' expectations for students, homework policies, and discipline. On the other hand, the cellular structure of schools and traditional norms that support teacher autonomy make it difficult for people in a school to create the conditions that will make their school effective. This dilemma is treated more fully in Chapter 12 where actions teachers can take to improve classrooms and schools are described. Learning aids at the end of this chapter have been designed to help you explore the concept of effective schools in more detail.

Organizational Functions and Skills for Teachers

Detailed accounts of teachers at work, particularly work connected to the organizational functions of their schools, can provide information about specific skills related these functions.

WHAT TEACHERS DO

Following are examples of what three beginning teachers typically do on any given day, including the organizational function they perform:

Neil is a third-grade teacher at Holbrook Elementary School; he usually arrives at school about 7:30 A.M. This particular morning Neil opens his room then joins other third- and fourth-grade teachers who are planning a field trip to the local airport for their students. Back in his room in time to start class at 8:35 A.M., Neil spends the rest of the morning with his third graders. However, he is joined at several points by other adults. The principal drops in for a few minutes to observe and see if Neil needs any help; two mothers join the class at 9:30 A.M. to assist Neil with his reading groups, and they stay through morning recess. The reading specialist in the school comes by and tests a student who Neil thinks is having a severe word recognition problem; the special education resource teacher joins Neil's classroom to work for 30 minutes with two mildly handicapped students mainstreamed in Neil's room.

Over lunch, Neil talks with two second-grade teachers, and they exchange ideas with Neil about students who were in their classrooms last year. Neil drops by the library on his way back to his classroom to pick up a film he plans to show as part of his social studies class and to remind the librarian that he will be bringing a small group of students to the library next Tuesday.

School is out at 2:45 P.M.; Neil drops by the reading specialist's office to discuss the results of her testing before heading to a meeting at the central office to participate on a science textbook selection committee. Neil was appointed to this committee by his principal because the principal knew that he had a very strong background in science and had worked at the Marine Biology Research Center for the past two summers.

Helen, another new teacher, teaches tenth-grade English at Madison High School. She, too, arrives at school about 7:30 A.M., and she meets with another new teacher to have a cup of coffee and discuss an exchange of teaching materials. Helen teaches three classes of sophomore English in the morning. Just before lunch she is visited by her department chairperson who is conducting one of his required formal observations of new teachers.

During her afternoon planning period, Helen and the department chair meet and he gives her feedback on her lesson, pointing out that her lecture was brilliant, but that her students took a long time getting to work in the small-group exercise she had planned.

After school Helen meets for a few minutes with members of the school's debate team for whom she serves as advisor, then dashes home to have a quick dinner. This particular night is the school's open house, and Helen has scheduled meetings with several parents to discuss their children's work.

Mark is a new teacher at Broadbent Middle School. His day begins with a meeting of his "house" (a group of students assigned to Mark for advising and counseling). These students will stay in Mark's house throughout their middle school careers. On this particular morning, Mark spends 20 minutes going over the students' schedules for next semester and talking to one student who has missed school regularly over the past month.

Mark does not teach his regular classes on this particular day. Instead, a substitute has been provided so he can attend a full-day seminar for new teachers.

At the seminar, Mark learns some new classroom management strategies, and he gets a chance to discuss mutual concerns with other new teachers in the district.

Mark enjoys the new teacher seminars, although he always worries about whether or not the substitute will be able to follow his lesson plans and whether or not his students will behave themselves and not cause him any embarrassment. On this day Mark leaves the seminar a bit early because he wants to participate in the discussion on student advising planned for this week's faculty meeting.

After the faculty meeting, Mark finds a note from the substitute teacher telling him that two of his third-period students were acting up and she referred them to the vice principal. Mark drops by the vice principal's office and talks with her about the problem. They plan steps to get the two students more involved and motivated in learning.

Analyzing these typical days in the lives of three beginning teachers illustrates that they do many things in addition to interacting with students in classrooms: They meet with students about nonacademic tasks; they meet with fellow teachers and specialists within the school; they go to meetings; they work with parents; and they attend to their own learning. These are what are called the organizational functions of teaching. The sections that follow discuss three of these functions in some detail and describe some specific skills and procedures related to them.

WORKING WITH COLLEAGUES

Establishing good working relationships with colleagues is an important challenge for the beginning teacher. To be successful in this endeavor requires an understanding of important norms governing collegiality and specific actions that can be taken.

Norms When beginning teachers enter their first school they should be aware of the norms that will govern many of the relationships between themselves and their colleagues. The hands-off norm, which allows colleagues within the school to be friendly and supportive but discourages specific suggestions about instructional practices, has already been described. The beginning teacher is likely to be included in lunchroom talk about school politics and the personalities of individual students, but will not find much talk about curriculum or teaching methods. Beginning teachers will find they can ask colleagues to provide assistance in finding a place to live or locating a good doctor; they will not, however, be able to ask for help (at least very directly) if they are having a classroom management problem.

The cellular structure of most schools means that beginning teachers may be expected to work alone. They will not be observed by other teachers, nor will they be invited to observe their peers. Teaching success will be known only to students, spouses, or close friends; failures will be kept secret.

Possible Actions All schools will not reflect the norms described above in exactly the same way. Some schools, in fact, may have norms that support professional collegiality. Regardless of the situation, beginning teachers do have some latitude for working with colleagues in open and constructive ways. However, it may require well-planned initiatives on their part. The following activities are usually possible:

1. *Observing other teachers.* This book has stressed the importance of focused observation and reflection in the process of learning to teach. This process should continue for first-year teachers. In fact, many of the observation schedules provided can be used again and again—during early field experiences, during student teaching, and in the beginning years.

Beginning teachers who want to observe other teachers should inquire early about whether or not classroom visits and observations are acceptable practice in their schools. If they are, principals, department chairs, or lead teachers can facilitate observation opportunities. If norms prevent collegial observations, it is still likely that these can be done in other schools where the beginning teacher is not known. These visits will have to be arranged by principals or by system-level curriculum specialists because they will require substitute teachers. Procedures to follow and courtesies to extend when visiting teachers' classrooms in other schools are the same as those described in Chapter 2.

2. *Discussing educational issues with colleagues.* Even if school norms prevent widespread collegial interaction concerning the problems of teaching, most schools have at least a handful of teachers who would like more discussion and collegiality. The beginning teacher can take the initiative in seeking out these teachers and promoting this type of exchange. Initial discussions may eventually lead to exchanges of materials and perhaps exchanges of classroom visits and observations.

Finally, beginning teachers can seek out other beginning teachers who have not yet been socialized into the hands-off norm and who are probably suffering from many of the same problems and concerns. Instances have been reported where beginner teachers have established their own weekly study and support group where mutual concerns and teaching strategies are shared.

3. *Working in small groups and at meetings.* It will be a rare school where the beginning teacher will not find at least a few meetings at which teachers come together for the purpose of mutual planning. Some beginning teachers may not feel comfortable speaking up at faculty assemblies, but they can seek out membership within numerous small groups in the school. In these small group settings, they can promote collegial norms through modeling good group behavior such as open communication and effective problem solving and decision making.

WORKING WITH ADMINISTRATORS AND LEADERSHIP PERSONNEL

A second group of people beginning teachers need to relate to is the leadership personnel within the school. School norms govern these relationships also, and specific actions are required.

Norms Most careful observers (Walcott, 1973; Feiman-Nemser and Floden, 1986) of teachers' relationships with principals and other school leaders have pointed out that norms governing these relationship are somewhat ambiguous. On the one hand, the school's professional ethos supports the concept of the principal serving as the school's instructional leader and as a role model for teachers. On the other hand, the hands-off norm applies to principals and other leadership personnel as well as to other teachers. Often this norm inhibits direct participation by principals in matters of curriculum or teaching strategies. Teachers, according to Feiman-Nemser and Floden (1986), want the principal to act as a "buffer between themselves and outside pressures from district administrators, parents, and other community members. . . . In addition, they want the principal to be a strong force in maintaining student discipline—backing the teachers in their classroom discipline policies and maintaining consistent school-wide policies. In return for these services, the teachers are willing to cooperate with the principal's initiatives" (p. 509). Most school norms do not support, however, the direct involvement and participation of the principle in instructional activities.

Possible Actions Obviously, principals vary greatly in their educational beliefs and management styles. Some will be very supportive; some will not. Some will have excellent organizational and interpersonal skills, and some will not. One principal's priorities and values will be different from those of others. In some instances these values and priorities will be consistent with the values and beliefs of the beginning teacher; in other cases they will be diametrically opposed.

Several specific actions can be taken by beginning teachers to gain the support of principals and to establish positive working relationships, regardless of the type of person he or she turns out to be. These incude:

1. Initiate regular weekly meetings with the principal during the first few weeks to discuss expectations for teacher and student behavior, academic goals, and other features of the school. Find out the principal's thoughts on the attributes of effective schools and effective teaching.
2. Keep the principal informed in writing about what you are doing in your classroom, particularly on such topics as (1) special successes you have had, such as a good lesson; (2) a complimentary note from a parent; (3) any conflicts that arise with students or parents; (4) special events such as guest speakers, field trips, or parties you are planning.
3. Invite the principal to your classroom, particularly for a lesson that is unique or special, and for parties in elementary schools or special celebrations in secondary schools.
4. Write complimentary notes to the principal when he or she has done something that you liked or something that was particularly helpful to you or one of your students.

All of these suggestions fall under the category of building positive communication channels between the beginning teacher and the principal. They are efforts by beginning teachers to get clear about the principal's expectations on the one hand, and on the other, to make sure the principal understands your instructional program and activities.

Other School Leaders In many schools beginning teachers will work with other school leaders besides the principal. Roles might include: counselors, reading specialists, special education resource teachers, librarians, media specialists, and curriculum specialists. The beginning teacher should remember that roles within organizations are governed by norms that role holders shape as they interact with each other. This means that beginning teachers will have some latitude in their interactions with leadership personnel. These interactions could range from ignoring them completely to actively seeking out their support and assistance. The latter is recommended in most instances.

Beginning teachers should strive, in the very early weeks of school, to build positive working relationships with school leaders for several reasons. First, unlike teacher colleagues, leadership personnel are expected to help beginning teachers and to provide that help in confidential ways free of evaluation. Second, most counselors and resource teachers got to their current positions because they were effective classroom teachers who received advanced training. This means they probably possess important knowledge that can be passed along to beginning teachers if appropriate relationships are established. Finally, resource personnel have more time to provide assistance and support than do principals or other teachers in the school. Beginning teachers should set up regular meetings with resource personnel to discuss roles and expectations, and they should try to keep these persons informed of their classroom programs and activities.

WORKING WITH PARENTS

A final set of important organizational members with whom beginning teachers will want to establish positive relationships are parents.

Norms Teachers want the norms governing their relationships with parents to include both concern for the child and support for their instructional program. At the same time, many teachers do not want parents to interfere with their classrooms (see Feiman-Nemser and Floden, 1986). On the whole, teachers tend to keep a good distance between themselves and parents and, in fact, have little interaction with them. This is particularly true of teachers in middle and secondary schools.

Working with and for parents is an important organizational function of teaching and, when done properly, can create a strong support system for beginning teachers and their students. It can also be a very rewarding aspect of the teacher's work. Following are several ways beginning teachers can build positive, supporting relationships with parents or other significant adults in students' lives. It should be remembered that, as with other aspects of teaching, guidelines for working with parents will vary from one context to another. You need to remain sensitive to the fact that in many communities the two-parent home may no longer be the norm. You also need to recognize that even when two parents or adults live in the same home, it is likely that both are working.

Possible Actions Teacher-parent interactions can take several forms, including reporting to parents, holding conferences with parents, and enlisting parents' help in school and at home.

1. *Reporting to parents.* Parents of children at any age want to know how their children are doing in school. The traditional report card is one means of giving parents this information. Experienced teachers, however, often use additional means to keep parents informed because the formal report card is only issued on a quarterly basis and only summarizes progress in general terms.

Some teachers, particularly of younger children, try to make weekly or biweekly contacts with parents through notes or through telephone calls. Such contacts allow teachers to explain what is going on in their classrooms and how the parent's child is doing on specific lessons. Such frequent and regular contact provides the teacher with a natural means for communicating children's successes, not just their deficiencies, which often dominate more formal reports.

Another means of parent communication—one that works well for middle and high school teachers who have many students—is the use of a weekly or monthly newsletter. The use of newsletters was described in the chapter on cooperative learning and here additional guidelines are offered. Jane Bluestein (1982) has suggested the following guides to the production and circulation of classroom newsletters:

- Newsletters can be either formal or informal. They can be in handwritten letter format, on a ditto sheet or typed with headings in a newspaper format.

- Newsletters should be sent home consistently, at least once every four to six weeks.

- Newsletters should give the parents information such as: what the class is studying this week or month, changes in format, grouping, environment, new goals and directions, special events or projects, special contributions of students, upcoming programs, projects or events.

- The content and language of the newsletters should "fit" the community and be written with the parent's interest in mind.

- Newsletters can directly involve parents by inviting them to participate in activities, attend programs or presentations, contribute materials for school activities, or remind students to do certain things or bring in certain items.

- Newsletters may contain samples of students' work, such as poems or writings that illustrate current topics and concepts. If student work is included, be sure each child is featured eventually.

▪ Share newsletters with students and make sure the principal gets a copy. (pp. 183–184)

2. *Holding conferences with parents.* Most beginning teachers will be involved with parent conferences. Teachers of younger children are sometimes required to make a home visit early in the school year and to hold quarterly in-school meetings with parents. Teachers of older students are normally given more latitude to initiate conferences as needed or when parents request them. In either event, holding parent conferences is an important organizational function of teaching and can provide valuable experiences for the teacher and the parents if done properly. This is also a function that some beginning teachers feel somewhat nervous about.

Jane Bluestein (1982), using information from the New Mexico Institute for Parent Involvement, suggested the following strategies for teachers to use for parent conferences:

Preconference preparations include the following:

1. Notify: Purpose, place, time, length of time allotted. Consider the parent's schedule and availability; offer choices of time whenever possible.
2. Prepare: Review child's folder, gather examples of work, and prepare materials. Be very familiar with the student's performance and progress before the parent arrives.
3. Plan agenda: List items for discussion and/or presentation.
4. Arrange environment: Comfortable seating, eliminate distractions. The parent is at an immediate disadvantage by being on your "turf." To help avoid power implications, arrange the environment so that you and the parent are on equal planes (same-sized chairs), sitting side-by-side at a table, as opposed to face-to-face across your desk.

The actual conference includes the following:

1. Welcome: Establish rapport.
2. State: Purpose, time limitation, note taking, options for follow-up. This is where you share information and present data. You may find note taking during the conference useful in recording your interactions—particularly the parent's feedback and responses. In addition, discuss various avenues you (each) may follow in future dealings with the student, including directions for your instruction and expectations.
3. Encourage: Information sharing, comments, questions.
4. Listen: Pause once in a while. Look for verbal and nonverbal cues. The above two recommendations support the concept of a conference being an *exchange* between the teacher and the parent.
5. Summarize.
6. End on a positive note.

Postconference steps and recommendations include the following:

1. Review conference with child, if appropriate.
2. Share information with other school personnel, if needed.
3. Mark calendar for planned follow-up. (pp. 385–386)

3. *Enlisting parents' help in school and at home.* A final way that beginning teachers can work with parents is through involving them as teachers and assistants, both in school and at home. This practice is more common in elementary and middle schools than in high schools. It is also easier in communities where *not* all the parents hold jobs. Regardless of the situation, beginning teachers will always find some parents willing to help if proper encouragement is given. Some guidelines for involving parents include:

- *To assist with small groups* Conducting small-group activities is difficult for teachers because there are so many simultaneous demands in the classroom. Effective teachers sometimes find parents who will come to the school and help on a regular basis. If beginning teachers choose to use parents in this way, they should remember that parents' schedules will have to be considered and that some training will be needed so parents know what is expected of them.

- *To assist with field trips and other special events* Field trips and many other special events such as parties or celebrations take an extra set of hands. Again, with proper encouragement and training, parents can be most useful during these times.

- *As teacher aides* Some teachers have found ways to use parents as aides in their classrooms, thus getting valuable assistance in correcting papers, writing and publishing class newsletters, organizing parties, and the like.

- *To help with homework* Most parents feel a responsibility for helping their children with homework. Unfortunately, many do not know how to be helpful. Effective teachers (sometimes this is done on a school-wide basis) teach parents how to teach their own children. This normally requires holding special evening sessions where the teacher explains to parents what the homework is trying to accomplish, shows them how to help students practice, and provides them with guidelines for giving students feedback. Many of the skills described in Chapters 7 to 10 can be taught to parents. Teaching parents teaching skills may be time-consuming, but it can extend the teacher's influence over student learning, perhaps more than any other single action.

Summary

This chapter has been about the organizational functions of teaching. Presented from the perspective that schools are social organizations, the chapter used a set of social system concepts to show how a school's history and culture (that is, its beliefs, norms, and roles) influence the behavior of those who work there, particularly beginning teachers.

A review of the research on effective schools showed that, while the teaching performance within individual classrooms is very important, it is the way that principals, teachers, parents, and students all come together to define common goals, expectations, and procedures that makes the most difference in what students learn.

Three specific organizational functions of teaching—working with colleagues, working with school leaders, and working with parents—have been described in some detail. Guidelines and behaviors for performing these functions effectively were presented along with an explanation of why these aspects of the teacher's work are just as important as day-to-day interaction with students.

Books for the Professional

Boyer, E. L. (1983). *High school: A report on secondary education in America*. New York: Harper and Row. This book reports the results of a major study of the American high school sponsored by the Carnegie Foundation for the Advancement of Teaching. It is a thorough look at the people who participate in schools (students, teachers, and principals) and what happens in secondary school classrooms.

Goodlad, J. I. (1984). *A place called school: Prospects for the future*. New York: McGraw-Hill. This book reports a comprehensive study of the American school. It looks inside classrooms and schools with insightful detail and proposes ways effective schools can be achieved.

Jackson, P. W. (1968). *Life in classrooms*. New York: Holt, Rinehart and Winston. *Life in Classrooms* is just what its name implies, a very careful description of what happens in elementary classrooms. Scholarly yet easy to read for beginning teachers.

Lortie, D. C. (1975). *School-teacher. A sociological study*. Chicago: University of Chicago Press. This book is now considered a classic work on the nature and ethos of the teaching profession. Lortie defined many of the concepts that now have become commonplace in educational discussions.

══════════════ CHAPTER 11 ══════════════
LEARNING AIDS FOR PLANNING, OBSERVATION, AND REFLECTION

- Assessing My Workplace Skills
- Measuring My Needs for Achievement, Affiliation, and Influence
- Diagnosing the School's Ability to Meet Personal Needs
- Interviewing Teachers About Resolving Role Conflict
- Observing Attributes of Effective Schools
- Interviewing Teachers About Using Parents as Helpers

ASSESSING MY WORKPLACE SKILLS

PURPOSE: Norms in schools, as in any organization, are powerful forces that shape teacher, administrator, student, and even parent behavior. It is possible for teachers to influence these norms in a positive way. In this aid, you have the opportunity to assess what you consider your level of effectiveness might be in helping develop positive norms of collegiality.

DIRECTIONS: Mark the response that you think reflects what your level of skill or understanding would be in each area. If you discover that you feel a weakness in any, discuss with other students or practicing teachers how it might be overcome.

Skill or Competency	Level of Effectiveness		
	High	Medium	Low
Developing collegiality in my work with colleagues			
Observing teachers	_____	_____	_____
Discussing educational issues	_____	_____	_____
Working in small groups	_____	_____	_____
Developing collegiality in my work with administrators			
Meeting with principal	_____	_____	_____
Informing principal of classroom activities	_____	_____	_____
Inviting principal to observe my class	_____	_____	_____
Writing complimentary notes to principal	_____	_____	_____
Seeking out support from other school and district leaders	_____	_____	_____
Developing collegiality in my work with parents			
Reporting classroom activities to them	_____	_____	_____
Holding conferences	_____	_____	_____
Using parents as helpers	_____	_____	_____

MEASURING MY NEEDS FOR ACHIEVEMENT, AFFILIATION, AND INFLUENCE

PURPOSE: The purpose of this aid is to illuminate your own pattern of needs. As discussed on pages 443 and 444, the way personal needs for achievement, affiliation, and influence are met or not met within a school can have a big impact on the smooth functioning of the school and its ability to foster student learning. It is important for you to understand your needs for two reasons: First, self-understanding will increase your ability to meet those needs; and second, you will be better able to see those needs operating in others and to respond appropriately.

DIRECTIONS: This questionnaire consists of 48 pairs of statements about things you may or may not like. For each pair, decide which of the two statements is more characteristic of what you like. You may like both statements in the pair. In that case, choose the one that you like better. If you dislike both statements, choose the one that you dislike less. Your choices should be in terms of what you really like, not what you think you shoud like. Read each pair of statements and circle the (a) or (b) corresponding to the one that better describes what you like. Directions for scoring follow the questionnaire.

1. (a) I like to be independent of others—do my own thing rather than have others tell me what to do.
   (b) I like to work hard at any job I undertake.

2. (a) I like to accomplish tasks that others recognize as requiring skill and effort.
   (b) I like to take strong forceful actions with regard to myself and others.

3. (a) I like to give suggestions and advice and to get other people to do things the way I think they should be done.
   (b) I like to be able to say that I have done a difficult job well.

4. (a) I would like to accomplish something of great significance.
   (b) I like to be recognized and regarded by others as a leader.

5. (a) I like to take strong forceful actions with regard to myself and others.
   (b) I like to work hard at any job I undertake.

6. (a) I like to accomplish tasks that others recognize as requiring skill and effort.
   (b) I like to give suggestions and advice and to get other people to do things the way I think they should be done.

7. (a) I like to be recognized and regarded by others as a leader.
   (b) I like to be able to say that I have done a difficult job well.

8. (a) I like to be independent of others—do my own thing rather than have others tell me what to do.
   (b) I would like to accomplish something of great significance.

9. (a) I like to give suggestions and advice and to get other people to do things the way I think they should be done.
   (b) I like to work hard at any job I undertake.

10. (a) I like to accomplish tasks that others recognize as requiring skill and effort.
    (b) I like to be recognized and regarded by others as a leader.

11. (a) I like to be independent of others—do my own thing rather than have others tell me what to do.
    (b) I like to be able to say that I have done a difficult job well.

12. (a) I would like to accomplish something of great significance.
    (b) I like to take strong forceful actions with regard to myself and others.

13. (a) I like to work hard at any job I undertake.
    (b) I like to be recognized and regarded by others as a leader.

14. (a) I like to be independent of others—do my own thing rather than have others tell me what to do.
    (b) I like to accomplish tasks that others recognize as requiring skill and effort.

15. (a) I like to be able to say that I have done a difficult job well.
    (b) I like to take strong forceful actions with regard to myself and others.

16. (a) I like to give suggestions and advice and to get others to do things the way I think they should be done.
    (b) I would like to accomplish something of great significance.

17. (a) I like to be independent of others—do my own thing rather than have others tell me what to do.
    (b) I like to do things with my friends rather than by myself.

18. (a) I like to share things with my friends.
    (b) I like to take strong actions with regard to myself and others.

19. (a) I like to give suggestions and advice and to get other people to do things the way I think they ought to be done.
    (b) I like to have strong attachments with my friends.

20. (a) I like to participate in groups in which the members have warm and friendly feelings toward one another.
    (b) I like to be recognized and regarded by others as a leader.

21. (a) I like to do things with my friends rather than by myself.
    (b) I like to take strong forceful actions with regard to myself and others.

22. (a) I like to give suggestions and advice and to get other people to do things the way I think they should be done.
    (b) I like to share things with my friends.

23. (a) I like to have strong attachments with my friends.
    (b) I like to be recognized and regarded by others as a leader.

24. (a) I like to be independent of others—to do my own thing rather than have others tell me what to do.
    (b) I like to participate in groups in which the members have warm and friendly feelings toward one another.

25. (a) I like to give suggestions and advice and to get other people to do things the way I think they should be done.
    (b) I like to do things with my friends rather than by myself.

26. (a) I like to share things with my friends.
    (b) I like to be recognized and regarded by others as a leader.

27. (a) I like to be independent of others—do my own thing rather than have others tell me what to do.
    (b) I like to have strong attachments with my friends.

28. (a) I like to participate in groups in which the members have warm and friendly feelings toward one another.
    (b) I like to take strong forceful actions with regard to myself and others.

29. (a) I like to do things with my friends rather than by myself.
    (b) I like to be recognized and regarded by others as a leader.

30. (a) I like to be independent of others—do my own thing rather than have others tell me what to do.
    (b) I like to share things with my friends.

31. (a) I like to have strong attachments with my friends.
    (b) I like to take strong forceful actions with regard to myself and others.

32. (a) I like to give suggestions and advice and to get other people to do things the way I think they should be done.
    (b) I like to participate in groups in which the members have warm and friendly feelings toward one another.

33. (a) I like to work hard at any job I undertake.
    (b) I like to do things with my friends rather than by myself.

34. (a) I like to share things with my friends.
    (b) I like to accomplish tasks that others recognize as requiring skill and effort.

35. (a) I like to be able to say that I have done a difficult job well.
    (b) I like to have strong attachments with my friends.

36. (a) I like to participate in groups in which the members have warm and friendly feelings toward one another.
    (b) I would like to accomplish something of great significance.

37. (a) I like to do things with my friends rather than by myself.
    (b) I like to accomplish tasks that others recognize as requiring skill and effort.

38. (a) I like to be able to say that I have done a difficult job well.
    (b) I like to share things with my friends.

39. (a) I like to have strong attachments with my friends.
    (b) I would like to accomplish something of great significance.

40. (a) I like to work hard at any job I undertake.
    (b) I like to participate in groups in which the members have warm and friendly feelings toward one another.

41. (a) I like to be able to say that I have done a difficult job well.
    (b) I like to do things with my friends rather than by myself.

42. (a) I like to share things with my friends.
    (b) I would like to accomplish something of great significance.

43. (a) I like to work hard at any job I undertake.
    (b) I like to have strong attachments with my friends.

44. (a) I like to participate in groups in which the members have warm and friendly feelings toward one another.
    (b) I like to accomplish tasks that others recognize as requiring skill and effort.

45. (a) I like to do things with my friends rather than by myself.
    (b) I would like to accomplish something of great significance.

46. (a) I like to work hard at any job I undertake.
    (b) I like to share things with my friends.

47. (a) I like to have strong attachments with my friends.
    (b) I like to accomplish tasks that others recognize as requiring skill and effort.

48. (a) I like to be able to say that I have done a difficult job well.
    (b) I like to participate in groups in which the members have warm and friendly feelings toward one another.

SCORING KEY FOR PERSONAL PREFERENCE QUESTIONNAIRE

DIRECTIONS: Make a mark through each choice you made. Total the marks in each column, and add the three columns for Achievement, the three for Influence, and the three for Affiliation.

	ACH	INF	AFF			ACH	INF	AFF			ACH	INF	AFF
1.	b	a			17.		a	b		33.	a		b
2.	a	b			18.		b	a		34.	b		a
3.	b	a			19.		a	b		35.	a		b
4.	a	b			20.		b	a		36.	b		a
5.	b	a			21.		b	a		37.	b		a
6.	a	b			22.		a	b		38.	a		b
7.	b	a			23.		b	a		39.	b		a
8.	b	a			24.		a	b		40.	a		b
9.	b	a			25.		a	b		41.	a		b
10.	a	b			26.		b	a		42.	b		a
11.	b	a			27.		a	b		43.	a		b
12.	a	b			28.		b	a		44.	b		a
13.	a	b			29.		b	a		45.	b		a
14.	b	a			30.		a	b		46.	a		b
15.	a	b			31.		b	a		47.	b		a
16.	b	a			32.		a	b		48.	a		b

TOTALS _____ 0   0   0

TOTAL ACHIEVEMENT _   Very High Score 27–32   Low Score 6–12
TOTAL INFLUENCE _____   High Score 20–26   Very Low Score 0–5
TOTAL AFFILIATION ____   Medium Score 13–19

Analysis and Reflection: Which of the three needs was highest? Which lowest? What are the implications of this result for your teaching? For your role as a member of a school organization? How do you respond when your needs are not met? Imagine you are teaching in a school which is structured in such a way that it is difficult to meet your motivation needs. Write a paragraph about what you could do to get those needs met.

SOURCE: From Arends, R. et al. (1981), *School life and organizational psychology.* New York: Teachers College Press, pp. 14–20. Used with permission.

DIAGNOSING THE SCHOOL'S ABILITY TO MEET PERSONAL NEEDS

PURPOSE: The purpose of the previous aid was self-understanding about personal needs. The purpose of this aid is organizational understanding. It is intended to increase your ability to see the ways schools can operate so as to help or hinder their members in meeting their needs for achievement, affiliation, and influence.

DIRECTIONS: Use the questions below to interview teachers or administrators about their schools. Be sure to probe for specific examples.

SCHOOL INTERVIEW SCHEDULE

Our _____ class has been studying some aspects of organization psychology. We have been learning about how organizations can serve as vehicles to satisfy such basic human needs as:

1 *Affiliation:* the need for friendship, for working with others, for warmth and caring
2 *Influence:* the need for power, for having control over one's life and one's destiny
3 *Achievement:* the need to experience success, to do well in work, to find new and better ways of doing things.

We are trying to find out how this school provides opportunities to experience friendship, influence, and success to the people who come here every day to work and learn. We appreciate your willingness to give us your views on this topic.

Let's start with some questions regarding you and the way you experience the school as a (principal, vice principal, teacher).

1. Over what aspects of your work do you feel most influential? (Probe to get the person to list specific tasks such as, "I feel I have a great deal of influence when I make out the daily schedule or when I determine which textbook to use in my class.")

    a. _____

    b. _____

    c. _____

    d. _____

2. Over what aspects do you feel least influential?

    a. _____

    b. _____

    c. _____

    d. _____

3. Can you name two or three things (pertaining to work here at school) that you have done in the past year that gave you a real sense of accomplishment?

   a. _____

   b. _____

   c. _____

   d. _____

4. What happens here at school that makes you feel close and warm toward others or that enables you to experience feelings of closeness and warmth from others?

Now let's turn to the school in relation to experiences provided for students.

5. From your viewpoint, which experiences provided here at _____ give students the best chance to feel influential?

   a. _____

   b. _____

   c. _____

   d. _____

6. From your viewpoint, is _____ a place where students have a lot of friends and like being involved with others? (If yes, ask for examples; if no, probe for reasons.)

7. From your viewpoint, is _____ a place where most students take pride in their work and strive to do well? (If yes, ask for examples: if no, probe for reasons.)

8. What ideas or suggestions do you have that could make _____ a place where students would experience more friendship, greater influence, and more success?

Analysis and Reflection: Write a paragraph responding to the following questions: What are your reactions to the activities teachers mentioned as contributing to their influence, achievement, and affiliation needs? Would these kinds of activities satisfy you? Why or why not?

SOURCE: Adapted from Arends, et al. (1981), *Teacher handbook for school life and organizational psychology*. New York: Teachers College Press, p. 32. Used with permission.

INTERVIEWING TEACHERS ABOUT RESOLVING ROLE CONFLICT

PURPOSE: Teachers work under many role expectations, some of which are clear and straightforward, and some of which conflict with each other. Teachers wrestle with how to resolve conflicting role expectations, and arrive at different strategies for accomplishing it. This aid is to give you some ideas about how you might achieve your own resolution of role conflict by discovering how other teachers have achieved it.

DIRECTIONS: Use the following questions to guide you in interviewing one or two teachers about role conflict.

1. Do you value treating students as individuals?
2. What do you do to show students that you value them as individuals and are attempting to tailor instruction to their needs?
3. How many students do you teach every day? Do you teach mostly to groups of students or individuals?
4. How do you resolve the dilemma between treating students as individuals and teaching that many students every day?
5. Do you think it is important to be on close terms with students in order to better teach them?
6. Do you think it is important to maintain some social distance from students in order to maintain discipline?
7. How do you resolve the dilemma between fostering closeness with students for teaching purposes and yet maintaining distance for discipline purposes?

Analysis and Reflection: Using these teachers' responses as a jumping-off place, write a paragraph about how you might initially try to deal with resolving these conflicting role expectations for yourself.

OBSERVING ATTRIBUTES OF EFFECTIVE SCHOOLS

PURPOSE: Listed on page 453 in the chapter are the social and instructional attributes of effective schools. The purpose of this aid is to help you recognize these attributes in practice. Refer to pages 452 to 453 for definitions of these attributes.

DIRECTIONS: Spend a half day visiting a school—observe in several classrooms, the library, cafeteria, outdoor activity areas, and so forth. Read fliers and newsletters sent home. Then if you observe one of the following effective school attributes, make a tally mark in the "Yes" column. Next, write under "Evidence" what you observed that led you to conclude the attribute was present. Conversely, mark the "No" column if you observed something that led you to conclude that the attribute was absent. For example, if you see student work prominently displayed in hallways, then you would check "Yes" for "Public rewards and incentives," and write under "Evidence" that "student work was displayed."

Attributes	Yes	No	Evidence
Social Organization			
Clear academic and social behavior goals	___	___	_____
Order and discipline	___	___	_____
High expectations	___	___	_____
Teacher efficacy	___	___	_____
Pervasive caring	___	___	_____
Public rewards and incentives	___	___	_____
Administrative leadership	___	___	_____
Community support	___	___	_____
Instruction and Curriculum			
High academic learning time	___	___	_____
Frequent and monitored homework	___	___	_____
Frequent monitoring of student progress	___	___	_____
Coherently organized curriculum	___	___	_____
Variety of teaching strategies	___	___	_____
Opportunities for student responsibility	___	___	_____

Analysis and Reflection: While research shows the above attributes to be associated with effective schools, there is still some controversy around it. What is your impression of the validity of these attributes? Did you think that the attributes you observed during your visit were contributing to student achievement in the school? Think back to your own schooling—to what extent were these attributes present, and were they contributing to student achievement in your school? Write a paragraph in response to these questions.

INTERVIEWING TEACHERS ABOUT USING PARENTS AS HELPERS

PURPOSE: Establishing good working partnerships with parents is very important. One way this can be done is by using parents as helpers in the classroom. The purpose of this aid is twofold: to help you develop an awareness of the things parents can do, and to alert you to how you can plan to make parent helping go smoothly.

DIRECTIONS: Use these questions as a guide in talking with teachers about using parents as helpers.

1. In what ways do you use parents as helpers?

   _____ In class, conducting small groups

   _____ As assistants for field trips

   _____ As assistants for special events in school

   _____ As teacher aides (correcting papers, putting out newsletter, and so on)

   _____ At home, helping with homework

   _____ Other (Specify)

   _____

   _____

   _____

2. How did you locate parents for these tasks? _____

   _____

   _____

   _____

   _____

3. Was it necessary to train parents for these tasks? If so, what did the training consist of? Who conducted the training? How long did it last? _____

   _____

   _____

4. What sorts of problems have you run into in using parents? How have you solved these problems? _____

   _____

   _____

5. How have you provided recognition to parents for their efforts?

_____

_____

_____

6. What benefits have accrued to you, to parents, and to students as a result of using parents as helpers?

Benefits for teacher: _____

_____

_____

Benefits for parents: _____

_____

_____

Benefits for students: _____

_____

_____

_____

Analysis and Reflection: Consider your own subject area or grade level. In light of what this teacher has told you about using parents for helpers, how might you utilize parent help? What kind of training will parents need? How will you arrange for parent training? How will you arrange for parent recognition? Write a paragraph in response to these questions.

CHAPTER 12

MAIN IDEAS

- Educational change is needed because schools, in many instances, are out of phase with the needs of today's youth or do not live up to rising expectations for schooling.

- Problems requiring reform include the school's inability to provide equal education opportunities to all youth, develop each person's talents to their potential, and keep curricula and approaches up-to-date.

- Many previous change efforts failed because reformers had inadequate conceptualizations about schools and about the processes of change.

- Research on change establishes how change is experienced by individuals who work in schools, and how schools change as social systems.

- Future change efforts are likely to be more successful because of new understandings that now exist about the processes of change.

- Beginning teachers who choose to work toward school improvement can do so by using action research, by being thoughtful and informed about change initiatives, and by helping to create conditions for change with colleagues and students.

Improving Classrooms and Schools

"The more things change the more they stay the same," quoted Seymour Sarason (1971) after ten years of observing reform in American education. In this one sentence, Sarason captured both the hope and the frustration many have with school reform. On the one hand, numerous lay and professional groups have worked hard over the years and have spent enormous resources to make schools and classrooms better. On the other hand, many of these change initiatives have not met the expectations of reformers and consequently, many people feel today's schools are about the same as they have always been.

A chapter on school improvement and change is included in this book for three reasons. First, it is here because of the belief (supported with considerable evidence) that without continuous rejuvenation and attention to change, social organizations such as schools tend to deteriorate. Second, helping to improve classrooms and schools is as much a part of teaching as are planning and delivering instruction, even though this function may not have been emphasized traditionally. Many educators today believe that if educational improvement is to happen, it will require strong involvement and leadership on the part of tomorrow's teachers. Finally, most beginning teachers have strong idealistic tendencies; you want to make schools and classrooms better places for students to learn. Memories of incompetent teachers, of unfair school rules, or possibly general dissatisfaction with the educational system provide most beginners with an interest in school change. However, these tendencies need to be supported with a set of understandings and skills that will help make school improvement efforts successful. This chapter shows beginning teachers how to go about the business of improving their classrooms and their schools.

PERSPECTIVE AND RATIONALE

This chapter does not try to promote specific educational innovations or to convince beginning teachers to serve as a radical force for school reform. Neither is it based on the belief that changing schools will be *the* major concern for most beginning teachers. Few beginning teachers will have the time, energy, or confidence to assume leadership roles in this area. However, you should understand that improving instruction and schools is part of a teacher's job and that this involvement in improvement processes, if only in a very small way, should start early in one's career. Thoughtful beginning teachers will want to consider three important questions about educational change: (1) Why is educational change needed? (2) What are the emerging problems requiring reform? and (3) Why have many past attempts at reform failed?

Why Is Educational Change Needed?

Per Dalin (1978), a Norwegian researcher, wrote that from a historical perspective "dissatisfaction with schools is not a new phenomenon. Schools have been the focus of public concern for nearly as long as they have existed" (p. 1). Michael Fullan (1982), a Canadian educational sociologist and perhaps the foremost expert on the processes of educational change, made the same observation, noting that desire for change is neither new nor localized. In fact, "Dissatisfaction with and interest in improving current efforts at bringing about educational change is a worldwide phenomenon" (p. xi).

Schools as they exist today assumed their basic design in the early 1800s. Curiously, people in most developed countries are ambivalent about this design. Although most citizens are comfortable with the familiar patterns of the schools they experienced as children and get upset with changes that challenge these patterns, they are quick to find fault with the schools when they fail to live up to contemporary expectations. Bruce Joyce and his colleagues (1983) caught the essence of this paradox when they wrote:

> Throughout history . . . [critics] . . . have found [the school] both too backward and too advanced. It falls behind the times and fails to keep us in simultaneous cadence. . . . Most citizens are cautious about educational innovation. People like the familiar old schoolhouse as much as they criticize it. They tend to believe that current problems in education are caused by changes (perceived as "lowering of standards") rather than because the old comfortable model of the school may be a little rusty and out-of-date. In fact, our society has changed a great deal since the days when the familiar and comfortable patterns of education were established, and many schools have become badly out of phase with the needs of children in today's world. (pp. 3–4)

Joyce and his colleagues are right. The world has changed considerably since the idea of formal schooling was first conceived. During the past two decades, for example, many aspects of peoples' lives and of their social institutions have been drastically transformed. A shrinking world produced by new communication and transportation technologies has replaced older parochial views with more cosmopolitan outlooks and interests. Shifting population patterns have made diverse, multicultural communities the norm and have greatly increased social sensitivity. Diminishing natural resources have also impacted significantly on the values people hold and their lifestyles.

Similarly, information technologies that include telecommunication satellites, word processors, microcomputers, and information retrieval systems have substantially changed the way information can be thought about and used. The printing technologies that only came into being during the last 200 years, making possible the current system of schools and libraries, must now compete with electronic communications. It is possible right now, and affordable in the near future, for every classroom and home to have electronic access to the information and wisdom stored in the major libraries of the world.

It is important to keep these changing conditions in mind when discussing educational change because they provide the context in which education and schools must operate. They also influence the values and interests of the youth found in classrooms, including the values and beliefs you have about teaching and about schools.

Emerging Problems Requiring Reform

Schools in most developed countries provide educational opportunities far surpassing those provided in earlier eras. Despite this fact, serious observers such as Michael Fullan (1982) and Per Dalin (1978) report that there is a general dissatisfaction with schools. Perhaps schools have not failed in some absolute sense so much as they have failed to live up to the rising expectations people have for them. Some of these unrealized educational goals exist because educational procedures have become antiquated, and others exist because of emerging problems.

These problems can be divided into three general areas: (1) the inability to achieve equal educational opportunity, (2) the inability to develop each person's unique talents to their fullest, (3) outdated curricula that fail to provide relevant experiences for a large portion of students. This list of challenges is not altogether new nor is it unique to a single educational system. It represents a challenge faced in North America, Europe, and the developed countries on the Pacific rim.

UNEQUAL EDUCATIONAL OPPORTUNITIES

Per Dalin (1978) wrote, "After World War II, education was looked upon as the main instrument for individual and economic development as well as the major social force for equalization of opportunity . . . and most educational systems were quite successful in 'expanding,' that is, in making the same opportunities available for more individuals" (pp. 2–3). He also wrote, "In most countries, particularly in America, Canada, the Scandinavian countries and the United Kingdom, we experienced two decades (1950–1970) of active, innovative activities" (p. 3). This growth and the educational innovations of those two decades, however, failed to live up to some of the hopes held for them regarding "equal opportunities," and most countries were left after two decades of experimentation with conditions about the same as when they started. In other words, even though educational opportunities were expanded quite extensively, the promise of equal education for all remained elusive.

DEVELOPMENT OF EACH PERSON'S TALENTS

Even though this educational goal has been around for some time, it still has not been fully achieved. School organization that is keyed to academic disciplines and divided into brief class periods makes it difficult for teachers to develop a sense of personal responsibility for students' total development. Instead, it has been the norm to stick with a common curriculum and traditional strategies regardless of developmental levels, motivation, and unique learning styles of particular groups of students. The number of students staying in school to finish rather than dropping out has not increased over the past three decades. In fact, fewer students are staying in school today to develop their talents than ten years ago. Many believe this is unfortunate because today it is more important than ever for each person to use every ounce of potential that he or she possesses.

OUTDATED CURRICULA

A third challenge is the inability to keep school curricula up-to-date and relevant. In 1939, J. A. Peddiwill (a pen name for Harold Benjamin) wrote a little book titled the *Saber-Tooth Curriculum.* In it he described a mythical society whose educational system prepared its young to fight off saber-toothed tigers with fire clubs, catch fish with their bare hands, and club horses with large sticks. Then, as a result of an ice age, the society changed; the saber-toothed tigers and horses became extinct and were replaced in nature's scheme by antelope. The fish disappeared into the muddy waters of glacial pools. The traditional skills of the old educational program were no longer needed and soon students started to complain that they could not see the relevance of learning tiger scaring, horse clubbing and fish catching. After ample debate and discussion, the elder members of the society, who were responsible for the educational program, declared:

> We don't teach fish-grabbing to grab fish; we teach it to develop generalized agility which can never be developed by mere training. We don't teach horse-clubbing to club horses; we teach it to develop a generalized strength in the learner which he can never get from so prosaic and specialized things as antelope-snare-setting. We don't teach tiger-scaring to scare tigers; we teach it for the purpose of giving noble courage which carries over into all the affairs of life. (Peddiwill, 1939, pp 42–43)

Peddiwell was poking fun at the school curriculum of fifty years ago. His point about relevancy, however, has a timeless quality. The curriculum in schools is too often organized around obsolete concepts that fail to meet the needs and demands of youth. This will be a continuing problem for educators living in a society where knowledge and institutions are constantly expanding and changing. It is exceedingly difficult to keep up in any field today and the answer to the question about how best to prepare youth for a world that will certainly be different from the one they now experience will remain elusive, particularly when no one can predict future changes with certainty.

Social changes are also accompanied by changes in childhood and adolescence. Youth mature sooner than in earlier times and each generation is confronted with a different set of questions and priorities that must be addressed. Some years ago, James Coleman (1972), an American sociologist, illustrated this problem in an article he wrote entitled "The Children Have Outgrown the Schools." In this article, he put forth the argument that schools fail students because they are pursuing the wrong goals with inappropriate experiences. Schools were created at a time in history when the society, according to Coleman, was "information poor and action rich." This meant that people, including youth, had plenty of things to do but little information to assist them. Over time, however, society has become "information rich but action poor"—people now have access to all kinds of information, but fewer opportunities exist, particularly for applying and taking action on the information. Coleman suggested that modern curricula should require more opportunities for active learning and involvement rather than providing exposure to more and more information. He argued that it is no longer sufficient to view the transmitting of information as the only purpose of schooling. Programs are needed that provide youth with realistic links between education and daily living. How to do this, however, is a difficult and perplexing problem.

Why Have Previous Change Efforts Failed?

Certainly no one will deny that schools have changed. If, for instance, you returned to your high school, you would be likely to find noticeable changes in school policies, educational programs, and in the topics of student conversations. Similarly, you can pick up almost any newspaper and find an account of a new educational program in one of the local schools. If you chose to study educational change more systematically, you would find many innovations, as did Mann (1981), who found that New York City schools tested 781 innovative programs between 1979 and 1981 (Fullan 1982, p. 4).

But have schools really changed? Some would argue that most changes have been only on the surface. Earlier you read Sarason's observation that in education "the more things change, the more they stay the same." Others who have looked for new and potentially exciting practices in schools have come away equally disappointed (see Goodlad and Klein, 1970; Goodlad, 1975 and 1984; Silberman, 1970; Sizer, 1984). All concluded that schools do appear to change over time, but the amount of change is modest, given the time and energy required. Lortie (1975) summarized the situation in this way: "If there has been a revolution . . . it has occurred in people's expectations for schools, not the practice: the gap between the possible and the actual has become an issue" (p. 216).

Perhaps part of the reason for the lack of significant change and improvement can be attributed to inadequate conceptualizations about the nature of schools and the role of teachers in the process of educational change. Often it has been assumed that externally imposed change could be accomplished if careful plans were devised and adequate resources provided. Also, reformers have frequently based change efforts on short-term strategies that by-passed teachers in favor of "teacher-proof" strategies and curricula. This is not to imply that changes imposed from outside the school will not help with school reform. It just means that external rules and regulations alone will not get the job done.

Perhaps reformers have also underestimated the complexities of the school as a social organization and have failed to realize the time span needed for successful change to occur. During the past decade, a knowledge base has been created that can help support school improvement efforts. This research base is discussed in the next section of this chapter.

SAMPLING THE RESEARCH BASE

Two major longstanding theoretical orientations have guided research into the nature and processes of change in educational settings. One orientation stems from psychology and focuses on how individuals react to change. The other is based on systems theory applied to organizations and focuses on the nature of the school as a social system and how organizational norms, roles, and culture restrain educational change. Both orientations are discussed in this section along with representative studies.

The Process of Change for Individuals

Michael Fullan (1982) wrote, "We have become so accustomed to the presence of change that we rarely stop and think what change means as we are experiencing it at the personal level . . . [and] more important, we almost never stop to think what it means for those others around us who might be in change situations" (p. 82). Fullan pointed out that the "crux of change" in education is how individuals within schools come to grips with new realities, expectations, and behaviors.

If you stop and think for a moment, your own experiences will probably confirm Fullan's ideas. Many of you have experienced the changes associated with leaving home and going away to college; others have experienced the death of a loved one or a happier experience such as marriage or having a first child. Some of you have experienced jobs where duties and responsibilities were suddenly and radically restructured. All of these changes probably caused anxiety, a sense of loss, and a struggle to adapt and find meaning in the new set of circumstances.

Drawing on the work of others, Fullan (1982) also explained more fully why and how individuals react to new situations. He said, "New experiences are always initially reacted to in the context of some 'familiar, reliable construction of reality' in which people must be able to attach personal meaning to the experiences regardless of how meaningful they might be to others" (p. 25). Combs (1965), writing several years earlier, presented a similar point of view. He said that people's behaviors are a result of the "world view" they hold. This world view evolves over a very long period of time as each person strives to make meaning our of experience. As people grow older, their world view becomes more and more consistent and their behavior more patterned. Therefore, according to Combs (1965), when one thinks about teachers or students changing their behavior the importance of their current beliefs and patterns must be recognized, and the importance of involving them in the change process must be considered:

> [Changing] must concern itself with the inner life. Simple exposure to subject matter (or new information or ways of doing things) is not enough. The maturation of an effective professional worker requires changes . . . in perceptions—his feelings, attitudes, and beliefs and his understanding of himself and his world. This is no easy matter, for what lies inside the individual is not open to direct manipulation and control. It is unlikely to change except with the active involvement of the . . . [person] in the process. (p. 14)

These concepts allow three predictions about the process of change within schools. First, change will be slow because it will come about only as individuals change their perceptions about new experiences and their relationships to self. Take for instance the beginning teacher who chooses to use the cooperative learning model described in Chapter 10. If this model has not been used in the school before, it is likely that students will at first resist key features of the model, such as working in groups and sharing rewards with other students. It will take time for students to adjust to the new realities and to find personal meaning in this novel educational experience.

Second, adjustments are most likely to occur in areas that are personally meaningful and least likely to occur in unfamiliar areas. Again, using cooperative learning as an example, its introduction into the classroom will probably necessitate the spending of a considerable amount of time explaining its rationale and advantages to students and other school staff.

Finally individuals in schools will change only as a result of experiences that help them perceive themselves in new or different ways or help them see events from a new perspective. Change in self follows changed perceptions of others. In practice this means that most poeple cannot change simply as a result of new information or admonitions about the value of some new thing. It is only through first-hand experience that they are able to replace old realities with new ones.

STAGES OF CONCERN

Gene Hall and his colleagues while at the University of Texas conducted research on change and developed a framework for viewing the change process. Their approach is called the Concerns-Based Adoption Model (CBAM). Like Fullan and

Combs, Hall and his colleagues concluded that change has not occurred unless individuals (teachers, principals, or students) have altered their behavior in relation to some particular innovation. Innovation is defined as some new way of doing something. They also argued that change is a highly personal experience and that individuals go through a developmental cycle in the process of changing.

Drawing on the developmental work of Francis Fuller (1969) (described in Chapter 2), the Texas researchers identified six stages of concern that teachers experience as they strive to find meaning in some innovation. Figure 12.1 describes Hall's six stages of concern.

LEVELS OF USE

Hall and his colleagues also found out that individuals do not immediately use an innovation in its entirety. Instead, when people start to do something new they do it a bit at a time. Total use does not come until people understand the

---

Figure 12.1   Stages of Concern About an Innovation

0 **Awareness:** Little concern about or involvement with the innovation is indicated.

1 **Informational:** A general awareness of the innovation and interest in learning more detail about it is indicated. The person seems to be unworried about himself/herself in relation to the innovation. She/he is interested in substantive aspects of the innovation in a selfless manner such as general characteristics, effects, and requirements for use.

2 **Personal:** Individual is uncertain about the demands of the innovation, his/her inadequacy to meet those demands, and his/her role with the innovation. This includes analysis of his/her role in relation to the reward structure of the organization, decision making and consideration of potential conflicts with existing structures or personal commitment. Financial or status implications of the program for self and colleagues may also be reflected.

3 **Management:** Attention is focused on the processes and tasks of using the innovation and the best use of information and resources. Issues related to efficiency, organizing, managing, scheduling, and time demands are utmost.

4 **Consequence:** Attention focuses on impact of the innovation on students in his/her immediate sphere of influence. The focus is on relevance of the innovation for students, evaluation of student outcomes, including performance and competencies, and changes needed to increase student outcomes.

5 **Collaboration:** The focus is on coordination and cooperation with others regarding use of the innovation.

6 **Refocusing:** The focus is on exploration of more universal benefits from the innovation, including the possibility of major changes or replacement with a more powerful alternative. Individual has definite ideas about alternatives to the proposed or existing norm of the innovation.

SOURCE: Adapted from G. E. Hall et al. (1973), *A developmental conceptualization of the adoption process within educational institutions.* Austin, Tex.: Research and Development Center for Teacher Education. The University of Texas, p. 4.

innovation fully and until they gain confidence with the required new behaviors. Hall and his colleagues found that the degree to which people use an innovation goes through developmental stages similar to those associated with concerns. Hall's Levels of Use stages are described in Figure 12.2.

Hall and his colleagues used this developmental model to guide several investigations in educational change. One of their studies is described in Research Summary 12.1.

Schools as Social Systems

The impact of change rests mainly on the individuals who work in schools, and their responses will ultimately determine the success or failure of nearly all educational innovations. However, unless a climate that is conducive to change and innovation exists within the school and its surrounding environment, few

---

Figure 12.2   Levels of Use of an Innovation

0 **Nonuse:** State in which the user has little or no knowledge of the innovation, no involvement with the innovation, and is doing nothing toward becoming involved.

1 **Orientation:** State in which the user has recently acquired or is acquiring information about the innovation and/or has recently explored or is exploring its value orientation and its demands upon user and user system.

2 **Preparation:** State in which the user is preparing for first use of the innovation.

3 **Mechanical Use:** State in which the user focuses most effort on the short-term, day-to-day use of the innovation with little time for reflection. Changes in use are made more to meet use needs than client needs. The user is primarily engaged in a stepwise attempt to master the tasks required to use the innovation, often resulting in disjointed and superficial use.

4A **Routine:** State in which use of the innovation is stabilized. Few if any changes are being made in ongoing use. Little preparation or thought is being given to improving innovation use or its consequences.

4B **Refinement:** State in which the user varies the use of the innovation to increase the impact on clients within immediate sphere of influence. Variations are based on knowledge of both short- and long-term consequences for clients.

5 **Integration:** State in which the user is combining own efforts to use the innovation with related activities of colleagues to achieve a collective impact on clients within their common sphere of influence.

6 **Renewal:** State in which the user reevaluates the quality of use of the innovation, seeks major modification of or alternatives to present innovation to achieve increased impact on clients, examines new developments in the field, and explores new goals for self and the system.

SOURCE: Adapted from G. E. Hall and S. F. Loucks (1977), A developmental model for determining whether the treatment is actually implemented, *American Educational Research Journal, 14,* 266–267. Copyright 1977 AERA, Washington, D.C. Used with permission.

RESEARCH SUMMARY
12.1

Hall, G. E., and Loucks, S. F. (1977). A developmental model for determining whether the treatment is actually implemented. *American Educational Research Journal, 14,* 263–276.

PROBLEM: Hall and Loucks were interested in verifying their theory that when teachers were expected to implement an innovation their level of use of the innovation would indeed vary.

SAMPLE OF SETTING: The Texas researchers chose to study two samples of teachers. In sample 1, they studied 371 elementary teachers from the states of Texas, Nebraska, and Massachusetts who were associated with efforts to implement team teaching. In sample 2, they studied teachers in twelve colleges and universities from several different states. Teachers in sample 2 were involved in the study and implementation of new instructional modules in their institutions' teacher education programs.

PROCEDURES: Subjects in the study were interviewed with an interview schedule developed to measure their level of use of a particular innovation. Interviewers asked subjects what they were doing in relation to their particular innovation. The interview took approximately 20 minutes to conduct and is reported to be reliable. Subjects were chosen using a sampling technique called cross-sectional sampling. This means that subjects were selected according to the number of years of experience they had had with the innovation and were divided into one of the five groups:

- *Group 1:* subjects with no experience or training with the innovation
- *Group 2:* subjects with 1 year of experience with the innovation
- *Group 3:* subjects with 2 years of experience with the innovation
- *Group 4:* subjects with 3 years of experience with the innovation
- *Group 5:* subjects with 4 or more years with the innovation.

POINTERS FOR READING RESEARCH: The data presented from this study are straightforward and no new research concepts are introduced.

RESULTS: Table 1 shows the distribution of the overall level of use for the various groups studied by Hall and Loucks.

Note that for both innovations, individuals were identified at each of the Levels of Use categories. However, these distributions are not uniform. More than 50 percent of the users of teaming are at routine use or higher, whereas over 50 percent of the higher education teachers are below the routine use category.

Table 2 shows the Levels of Use of for each innovation plotted against how many years the users had had experience with the innovation.

TABLE 1 Percentage Distribution of Overall Level of Use for *Individuals Involved in Cross-Sectional Studies of Two Innovations*

Level of Use		Study of Teaming in Elementary Schools* N = 371	Study of Modules in Teacher Education Institutions* N = 292
0	Nonuse	7	10
I	Orientation	9	31
II	Preparation	3	9
III	Mechanical Use	19	8
IVA	Routine	52	22
IVB	Refinement	6	11
V	Integration	3	8
VI	Renewal	2	2

* In percentages
SOURCE: Adapted from G. E. Hall and S. F. Loucks (1977), p. 270.

TABLE 2 Distribution of Users Within Each Level of Use by *Years of Experience for Two Innovations*

Years of Experience With Teaming*

Levels of Use		1st Year	2nd Year	3rd Year	4th Year or More
III	Mechanical	41	16	11	10
IVA	Routine	51	80	73	72
IVB	Refinement	6	0	9	10
V	Integration	2	4	7	3
VI	Renewal	0	0	0	5
		N = 87	N = 25	N = 70	N = 101

Years of Experience With Modules*

Levels of Use		1st Year	2nd Year	3rd Year	4th Year or More
III	Mechanical	22	10	11	15
IVA	Routine	40	54	37	37
IVB	Refinement	22	21	33	15
V	Integration	12	10	11	30
VI	Renewal	4	5	7	4
		N = 50	N = 39	N = 27	N = 27

* In percentages
SOURCE: G. E. Hall and S. F. Loucks (1977), p. 271.

(cont'd)

═══════════════════ **RESEARCH SUMMARY** ═══════════════════
12.1 (continued)

DISCUSSION AND IMPLICATIONS: As can be observed in Tables 1 and 2, Hall and Loucks' data tend to confirm that individuals vary in their level of use of an innovation and that these levels are associated with experience. Take for example the teachers using teaming. It is apparent that more individuals are at Level 3 (mechanical use) in their first year as contrasted to later years, and that use at Level 4 (routine use) and above increases after the first year of experience. The same overall pattern can be observed with the teachers in higher education implementing new instructional modules.

The implications of this study and others like it are numerous.

It confirms ideas we have that people respond to change differently and that their use of something new will likely proceed through stages from nonuse to higher levels of use characterized by refinement and renewal.

Those who advocate new approaches should anticipate that many teachers or students will make only mechanical use of the new approach during the first year.

Those who are on the receiving end of an innovation should be cognizant of their need to move slowly and know this is likely consistent with the responses of others.

It helps confirm the research on change that says "change takes time," and individuals who are expected to change need support consistent with their levels of concern and use.

innovations that are programmatic or organizational in nature will succeed. Despite the fact that individual teachers or students are taught new skills and new ways of perceiving their world, these new behaviors are often not observed in the school setting because the school as an organization has failed to change its norms, routines, and culture in ways that support the new behaviors. Examples of past educational innovations that have failed on occasion for this reason include:

- *Team teaching* The program flexibility and the time needed for planning were never provided to teachers, and students were not taught how to learn from a teaching team in contrast to a single teacher.

- *Open-space schools* New routines and structures to account for student control and movement were not developed. The hands-off norm was not changed.

- *Complex curriculum* Teachers were not given the facilities and assistance needed to store, to purchase, and to use the materials required in these curricula.

A view of schools as complex social systems helps us understand these phenomena. Theorists and researchers in this tradition (Miles, 1964; Lortie, 1975;

Rutter et al., 1979; Sarason, 1971; Schmuck, Runkel, Arends, and Arends, 1977; Schmuck and Runkel, 1986) view school life as a process of individuals interacting in predictable patterns within a group setting. This view of patterned interaction provides a means to understand the stability of schools over time and their resistance to change. It also provides a set of concepts for thinking about the school as a complex social system that in many ways resembles a spider's web or a geodesic dome in which each strand or part is related to all the others. When one strand is affected or changed all other parts must too be changed. Organizational development as a strategy for helping schools change has been based on this set of principles.

Research in this tradition looks at school innovation from the standpoint of how the school's overall social system responds to change as opposed to how individuals within the school respond. A classic study in this tradition is summarized in Research Summary 12.2. This study was conducted by Seymour Sarason and his colleagues during the 1960s. This is a very important study because Sarason's interpretations of the problems associated with educational change research greatly influenced subsequent research in the field.

SCHOOL IMPROVEMENT SKILLS FOR BEGINNING TEACHERS

As a beginning teacher encountering your first classroom, it is likely that you will be faced with many dilemmas and unanswered questions. It is also likely that some of the discrepancies between professional ideals and the realities you find may be troublesome. Some beginning teachers have been known to accept these realities with a sense of resignation or defeat. Others have faced the complexities of teaching with a desire for improvement. There are some concrete things teachers can do, even in their beginning years, that will establish healthy patterns and contribute to school improvement.

Improving Classrooms Through Action Research

The point has repeatedly been made that when the "classroom doors" are closed, teachers are pretty much in charge of what goes on. Teachers report that they set their own objectives, procedures, and approaches to instruction and most observers (Goodlad and Klein, 1970; Lortie, 1975; and Goodlad, 1984) concur with the accuracy of these reports. Although this situation has its drawbacks, it does provide freedom for beginning teachers to work toward change and improvement in their own classrooms.

Two aspects of classroom life that teachers can directly control are classroom environments and instructional strategies. However, because the classroom is so complex, working toward improvement can be a difficult process. Action research is one tool that can be used by beginning teachers.

━━━━━━━━━━━━━━━━━ **RESEARCH SUMMARY** ━━━━━━━━━━━━━━━━━
12.2

Sarason, S. (1971). *The culture of school and the problem of change.* Boston: Allyn and Bacon.

PROBLEM: For many years Seymour Sarason studied and wrote about schools. For a ten-year period during the 1960s he was director of the Yale Psycho-Educational Clinic where he studied the problems of change, particularly how the school's culture affects the change process.

SAMPLE AND SETTING: The conclusions reached by Sarason in this book came from a number of studies. The one that will be described here focused on the implementation of a new math curriculum in three suburban school districts.

PROCEDURES: A new math curriculum was introduced in three suburban school districts in the late 1950s and early 1960s. Sarason and his colleagues were already intimately involved in classrooms in these systems through their work on a number of projects. In 1968, approximately ten years after the new math was introduced, E. K. Sarason and S. B. Sarason did an observational study of the teaching of the new math. Over a period of six weeks, they observed six classrooms, two in each of three school systems. Sixth-grade classrooms were observed at least three times a week. Two schools were using the School Mathematics Study Group (SMSG) program. The third school used the Addison-Wesley program.

POINTERS FOR READING RESEARCH: Saraon's study, unlike many of the others described in this book, was a result of his personal experiences and both formal and informal observations. He has no numbers to report, but instead reports from his field notes and observations. His own words best illustrate what he discovered about the process of change in schools. They also give insights into the type of conclusions researchers using observational methods draw from their research.

RESULTS: Sarason's overall conclusion was that, even though millions of dollars were spent in developing the new mathematics curriculum, it was really never implemented in the schools. He argued that the reasons for this state of affairs were many, but most important was that the people who were trying to change the schools—both the insiders and the outsiders—were ignorant about school culture and had no theory about the change process. As a result, all parties involved "unwittingly" worked in self-defeating ways. Here are the aspects of the process leading Sarason to his conclusions:

1. *The Context of the New Math Curricula* Sarason began by explaining how the development of the new math curricula grew out of social concerns in the post–World War II era and the Russian launching of Sputnik in 1957. Critics thought the way math was taught was extinguishing students' interest in the topic and thus making America fall behind the Soviets in math and science. Those, however, who were dissatisfied were not the teachers and students, according to Sarason. Instead: "The most vocal critics, as well as those who were developing new curricula, were not indigenous to the school culture; they were mostly university people" (p. 34). From this concern came a new math curricula, developed mainly by university mathematicians.

2. *How the New Curricula Were Introduced in the School* According to Sarason, it was not only the outside university critics who were involved, but also supervisory personnel within the school system, particularly math supervisors. These supervisors, who were once mathematics teachers, were now doing graduate work at the university and accepted the university's culture more than the culture of the schools experienced by teachers.

3. *Implementation at the Local Level* The development of the new math, thus, had been done at the university level and its initial adoption was made by mathematics curriculum specialists. Together they planned to introduce the new curricula to teachers who up to this point had not been informed or consulted. This was accomplished mainly through short summer workshops

> taught (by supervisors and outside experts) in precisely the same ways that teachers had been criticized for in their teaching of children. There was little sensitivity to the plight of the teachers—they were being asked to learn procedures, vocabulary, and concepts that were not only new but likely to conflict with highly overlearned attitudes and ways of thinking. Many of the teachers were unable to voice their uncertainties and lack of understanding. The pressure and tension stemmed not only from being in a group learning situation with peers but also from the scary knowledge that in several weeks they would have to teach the new math to their pupils (p. 42)

It had been planned for teachers to get help and support once the school year began, and this was to be provided through individual meetings with the math supervisors, as well as group meetings:

> Two things became clear to the supervisors after the close of the workshop. First, the number of supervisors was inadequate to meet the individual needs and problems of the teachers. Second, the supervisors had seriously underestimated the difficulty teachers would have learning the new material to a degree of mastery comparable to that they had attained with the old curriculum. (p. 43)

Therefore, as the school year progressed:

> Teachers generally were anxious, angry, and frustrated; many children were confused and many parents began to raise questions about what was going on and about their own inability to be of help to their children. (p. 44)

4. *Outcomes—Ten Years Later* Sarason described what he observed going on in new math classrooms ten years later and concluded as follows:

> One of the bothersome features of the old curriculum was that children did not enjoy the world of numbers; they found it dull, unstimulating, and a chore. .... The two observers [Sarason and Sarason] came away with the impression that enjoyment was one of the last words they would use to characterize their impressions of the feeling of the children. Struggle was certainly one way of characterizing what was going on but it was not

(cont'd)

═══════════════════ **RESEARCH SUMMARY** ═══════════════════
12.2 (continued)

that kind of intellectual struggle which generates its own sources of internal reinforcement or elicits such reinforcement from others—in this case the teacher. At no time in our discussion did any of the six teachers say anything which disconfirmed our opinion that neither children nor teachers enjoyed what they were doing in the sense of feeling intellectual excitement, a desire to persist, and a joy of learning. One had the overwhelming impression of a task having to be done not because children desired to do it but because that is the way life is. Using the "joy of learning" as a criterion there appears to be no difference between the new and old math. . . .

It is fair, we think, to say that one of the major aims of the new math concerned not only schools and children but our entire society in the sense that the new math was viewed as one important way of helping to produce more and better mathematicians and scientists because that is what our society was viewed as needing. If our observations and those of others have validity and generality, one would have to predict that the goal of more and better mathematicians and scientists relative to the total population—or the number of college students majoring in math or physics—will not be met.

It is perhaps too charitable to conclude that "the more things change the more they remain the same," if only because so many people continue to be unaware that basically nothing has changed; in addition, and perhaps more to the point, many of those who are aware that intended outcomes have not been achieved have no clear understanding of the factors contributing to failure. It is unlikely that in the future we will be spared the development of newer curricula, that is, new programs, attractively bound, surrounded by evangelism and the spirit of reform, and unrelated to the realities of the school culture. (pp. 45–46)

DISCUSSION AND IMPLICATIONS: The results of the Sarason study were among the first of many to show that simply having a good idea and good intentions will not achieve meaningful change in schools. Sarason's work with the new math shows us that attempts by outsiders to introduce change in school will not work unless the reformers are aware of the school's culture and the regularities within that culture. His work also pinpoints the necessity of involving teachers and other school participants in the change process.

The evidence from this study and others suggests that change efforts initiated or imposed from the outside are likely to fail. Better results seem to occur when change projects are based on information or methods already known to local participants. Local actors—in a single community or district—are likely to be skeptical about the reported success of methods that had been tried elsewhere. They rely instead on the advice of those believed to be knowledgeable about local conditions. Teachers in "other" schools, personnel from the district office, and consultants from the state departments or universities will lack credibility because they do not "belong" to the school where the project is being tried. From a social systems perspective those who do belong, like teachers and other local personnel, have a much better chance to bring about change and improvement.

RATIONALE FOR ACTION RESEARCH

This book has taken the point of view that educational research is an important resource for teachers and that beginning teachers should be able to apply research findings to their own teaching. This research orientation is now carried even further by describing how you can conduct your own classroom research for the purpose of making your classroom teaching better. This type of research is commonly called "action research." Chris Argyris and his colleagues (1985) described action research as a process of seeking "knowledge that will serve action" (p. 36).

Action research is based on several premises about the processes of change and the role of valid information in helping bring about change. Previous sections described how change in individuals comes about only as they construct new realities to replace existing ones and thereby make the proposed changes meaningful to themselves. Action research is a way for teachers to:

- Collect *valid information* about their classrooms
- Use this information to make *informed choices* about learning activities and classroom procedures
- Share the information with students in order to gain their ideas and *internal commitment* to specified learning activities and procedures*

Action research as conceptualized and practiced today is the outgrowth of over a half century of thought that has been most influenced by the early traditions of John Dewey, Kurt Lewin, and Corey and his associates at Teachers College. More recently the field has been influenced by Donald Schön and Chris Argyris. Schön's ideas about reflective practice, you remember, were introduced in Chapter 2. Argyris and colleagues (1985), who studied the traditions of action research, pointed out the importance of Dewey's contributions:

> Dewey (1929, 1933) was eloquent in his criticism of the traditional separation of knowledge and action, and he articulated a theory of inquiry that was a model both for scientific method and for social practice. He hoped that the extension of experimental inquiry to social practice would lead to an integration of science and practice. He based his hope on the observation that "science in becoming experimental has itself become a mode of directed practical doing" (1929, p. 24). This observation that experimentation in science is but a special case of human beings testing their conceptions in action, is at the core of the pragmatist epistemology. For the most part, however, the modern social sciences have appropriated the model of the natural sciences in ways that have maintained the separation of science and practice that Dewey deplored. Mainstream social science is related to social practice in much the same way that the natural sciences are related to engineering. This contrasts sharply with Dewey's vision of using scientific methods in social practice. (pp. 6–7)

---

* The concepts of valid information, informed choice, and internal commitment come from Argyris's (1970) framework for individual and organizational change.

Action research is in some ways like any other research. It is a process of asking questions and seeking objective answers. In some ways, however, it differs. As Argyris and Dewey pointed out, action research tries to produce knowledge that has immediate application—in this instance by teachers or their students. And, unlike some researchers, the action researcher is more interested in "knowledge" about a specific situation than about results with general application.

ACTION RESEARCH PROJECTS

Teacher-initiated action research projects can range from very informal to very formal. The more informal end of the scale might include efforts to collect information about classroom climate or some other aspect of classroom life using observational or questionnaire instruments such as those provided in the learning aids section of this chapter and in Chapter 5. Another informal example would be giving evaluation questionnaires to students that ask their opinions about a particular aspect of the classroom, about the teacher, or about a specified learning activity. Most beginning teachers have filled out such evaluation instruments in their own college classes and know these devices are rather straightforward in their construction and use. Frank Lyman (1984) has helped many student teachers and beginning teachers launch more formal action research projects using a seven-step process. These steps are listed in Figure 12.3.

Many of the understandings required to carry out the steps in the action research project outlined in Figure 12.3 have already been described, particularly in the special topic section on understanding research. Perhaps the most difficult part of an action research project is identifying a good problem for study and defining carefully the variables involved. Remember that the special topic section on research described how a good research problem should be (1) stated in question form, (2) focused on relationships between two or more variables, and (3) have the possibility of empirical testing. Remember also the distinctions made between independent and dependent variables. An independent variable refers to some aspect or property of the problem that is the presumed *cause* (teaching behavior, for instance); a dependent variable is a *consequence* such as student learning or self-esteem.

The beginning teacher is, of course, confronted with literally hundreds of problems that could be topics for action research. In the beginning, however, teachers should draw questions from their own experiences, questions that can be tested with rather straightforward designs. Below are some questions tackled by beginning teachers working with Frank Lyman on action research.

1. If the teacher of a seventh-grade social studies class uses the think-pair-share strategy after films, written material, or questions from the teacher, how will the results (in terms of individual participation and test scores) compare to a unit of work on the same topic using the traditional approach?

Figure 12.3   Steps in Action Research

Step 1: Consider your present classroom, and isolate a problem you think would be improved by a different approach or teaching strategy.

Step 2: Frame a question that includes the independent variable and dependent variable(s).

Step 3: Note that the difference or differences you are looking for are the dependent variable(s).

Step 4: Decide what the indicators of the dependent variables are. (For example, accuracy could be indicated by the number of words written and by the correctness of their spelling. Number of student questions could be tabulated in a discussion).

Step 5: Design your experiment to keep constant as many variables as possible (for example, the same group of children, at the same time of day).

Step 6: Arrange for someone to help with the data collection (for example, a cooperating teacher or a teacher next door to count the number of questions asked by students).

Step 7: Organize and write up the results to share with others, particularly with colleagues and students.

SOURCE: Adapted from F. Lyman et al. (1984), Action research by student teachers and beginning teachers: An approach to developing problem solving in classrooms. Mimeographed. College Park, Md.: University of Maryland, p. 42.

---

2. If a teacher of a distractible and uninvolved first-grade child makes a contract involving a point/reward system with him, how will his participation in large and small group activities be affected?

3. If a third-grade teacher provided manipulatives and pair time for exploring measurement concepts for one group of math students in addition to auditory and visual presentation, how will that group's test results compare to those of a group that does not use manipulatives and has a more controlled presentation period?

USING INFORMATION FROM ACTION RESEARCH

The final step in the seven-step action research process described in Figure 12.3 is to organize the results from a project and share it with others. Some teachers share the results with colleagues and use the data they have collected as a springboard for discussions about different approaches to teaching. Other teachers choose to share the results of an action research project with their students. The information collected in many projects can provide students with insights about their classroom and the teaching approaches being used by the teacher. This type of information can also help students gain commitment to learning activities found effective and provide a vehicle for them to think about and help plan classroom activities.

Working at the School Level

Most beginning teachers will be mainly interested in how they can improve their own classrooms. However, opportunities for taking action at the school level will also occur as they work with others in the school.

RESPONDING TO CHANGE INITIATIVES

A beginning teacher's role in school-wide improvement efforts at first involves being a thoughtful participant in proposals that come from others. Such proposals may involve policies for beginning teacher evaluation created by the state legislature, a new science curriculum adopted by the school district, or perhaps new approaches for classroom management offered by the principal. In all of these instances beginning teachers will be primarily on the receiving end. According to Fullan (1982), when teachers are faced with new proposals they should ask three questions before commiting themselves or deciding to throw their energies into a new approach:*

1. *Is the change needed?* "Does it address an important educational goal which is currently not being achieved adequately, and does the particular change offer some potential for accomplishing the goal more effectively? . . . Being self-critical (analytic) is necessary in order to avoid the problem of false clarity, when a teacher superficially assumes that the goal is already being addressed but in reality is not employing teaching resources and behaviors which would maximize attainment. Related to this issue is the current tendency for many teachers to reject all external changes (particularly if they come from certain sources, such as governments). Rejecting all proposed changes out of hand may be just as regressive as accepting them all. However, even if the change is desired and needed, it will also be necessary to determine its priority. Since teachers are often faced with too many changes at once, they individually or jointly must choose where to put their efforts. If everything is attempted (or rejected), nothing will succeed. In one sense, the best a teacher can do is work hard on one or two of the most important priorities at one time, and cope with the others as well as possible." (pp. 123–124)

2. *Is the administration endorsing the change and why?* "Some form of active commitment by administrators will be necessary for freeing up necessary resources (reducing the cost) for the innovation to succeed. It may be still possible to go it alone, if the specific change is highly valued by the teacher, but it will be difficult unless there is some support from the administration. It is also important that teachers should not automatically accept apparent lack of interest on the part of an administrator at face value. Administrators have their own worlds of pressure, which they frequently keep private. . . . It

---

* Quotations from Fullan, *The Meaning of Educational Change* (1982), beginning on this page and on page 510 are used with permission of Teachers College Press, New York.

may be that individual or group-based teacher initiative and negotiation with the administration could lead to significant changes in support in some cases. Untested assumptions are fertile ground for false attribution of motives and intentions. Apparent lack of attention by the administrator may or may not mean lack of interest" (p. 124).

3. *Do fellow teachers show an interest in the change?* "If collegiality among teachers in a school is already strong, the degree of teacher interest can usually be found out quite quickly. As before, one should not assume lack of interest. Because of the isolation of teachers from each other, there may be a lot of 'pluralistic ignorance'—that is, each one assumes that no one else is interested, everyone is making the same assumption, but no one bothers to test it out. In any case, if peer interests exists or can be stimulated, it can represent one of the most satisfying (and necessary) aspects of the change process" (p. 124).

HELPING TO ESTABLISH CONDITIONS FOR CHANGE*

You remember from Chaper 11 that many aspects of the school culture are determined by the way members of the school staff interact with one another in face-to-face settings, both formal settings such as meetings and informal settings such as the faculty room. It is in these settings that communication among colleagues occurs and where problems are solved and decisions made. As members of informal and formal faculty groupings, beginning teachers can help influence important organizational processes that facilitate or restrain improvement effort. Five important processes and what can be done to improve them are described below. It is important to note that beginning teachers by themselves cannot affect these processes substantially. They can, however, working in subtle ways, help others in the school see how important these processes are and perhaps enlist their support for improvement.

1. Communication Processes Many things that go on in schools are affected by subtle and complex communication processes. These processes include verbal and written messages as well as nonverbal expressions, signals, and postures, and they often dictate who speaks to who, when, and why.

Norms: Because communication is such a complex process, the possibility of breakdown is always present. Sometimes communication may not occur at all; at other times—particularly during stress or when emotional topics are being discussed—miscommunication can occur. Poor communication exists in a school when unproductive norms such as the following are observed:

▪ Group members continually restate the merits of their own position and refuse to hear what others say.

* Part of this discussion follows Arends and Arends (1977).

- Group members ignore each other's feelings.
- Everyone is expected to talk loudly and emphatically, no matter what the issue.
- People are willing to discuss trivial issues, but withdraw when certain topics are mentioned.

On the other hand, communication processes in some schools are guided by more productive norms, such as these:

- Group members continually check to make sure they understand what others are saying.
- Everyone is expected to show concern for the feelings of others by monitoring nonverbal cues and checking their impressions.
- Voices typically remain calm, but people are heard—even when they express strong emotions.
- Important and fundamental issues are publicly discussed with everyone concerned.

Improving communication processes: It is unrealistic to believe you can change unproductive communication processes to productive ones either by yourself or overnight. Nonetheless, modeling good communication and using the communication skills described in Chapter 5 can launch a slow process of improvement. Others in the school will begin to see that tasks can be accomplished more effectively if good communication exists and that work in schools can be more rewarding when people are talking with and understanding one another.

2. Goal-Setting Processes Chapter 11 described one of the characteristics of effective schools as the degree to which members of the school had clear goals and expectations. Goal setting is an important process within schools because it is basic to problem solving and change, and it often figures prominently in interpersonal communication and conflict. There are two important features of school goals: the degree to which they are clear and the degree to which they are shared.

Norms: Some schools lack clear and shared goals, particularly those schools in which the following norms apply:

- Goals are taken for granted rather than being discussed or written down.
- People are rewarded for keeping goals unclear.
- No one expects that progress toward goals will be carefully assessed.
- People harbor different versions of goals that are supposedly shared.

Conversely, people can learn to uncover and share goals or sharpen vague goal statements when norms such are the following exist:

▪People monitor how much others are committed to written goals.

▪People expect goals to be precisely stated, even when being clear makes it harder to avoid talking about conflict.

▪Many kinds of informal and formal procedures are used to assess progress toward goals.

Helping improve goals: Beginning teachers can help group members clarify their goals by merely asking questions such as, "What are we trying to accomplish?" "Are you sure that is what we really want to do?" "What goal are we trying to achieve?"

There are also many techniques for helping groups state and agree on goals. One technique is labeled "Ten Years from Now," a procedure that asks group members to fantasize in writing what life in their school should be like in ten years. These descriptions can illustrate themes such as what I do every day, what my responsibilities are, or what the outputs of our group should be. Another technique for defining goals and expectations is by imagining what things would look like if goals were successfully being accomplished. Steps to use with this process are described in Figure 12.4.

Even when all members of a group are clear about their goals, they can still have problems working together to reach them. Movement toward one goal may actually inhibit movement toward another, or differences in priorities can cause poorly coordinated action. Using procedures such as the one described above in a group setting can help people become clearer about important goals they share.

Figure 12.4 Imagining Success (Defining Goals and Expectations)

Before setting any goals, ask yourself two questions:

1. What knowledge, attitude, or behavioral changes do I want to see achieved by whom (students, teachers, parents)?
2. What do I want my classroom, school, or district to look like when implementation is complete?

To clarify your answer to the second question, imagine you are hovering over your school in a helicopter. What you see is a close-to-ideal version of the new activity (for instance, use of microcomputers). Now ask yourself:

1. What is going on in the classroom?
2. How is the room organized?
3. What materials and equipment are available or in use?
4. Who is working with whom?
5. What are teachers doing?
6. What are the students doing?

SOURCE: Adapted from S. Loucks-Horsley and L. F. Hergert (1985), *An action guide to school improvement.* Alexandria, Va.: Reprinted with permission of the Association for Supervision and Curriculum Development. Copyright © 1985 by the Association for Supervision and Curriculum Development. All rights reserved.

3. Problem-Solving Processes In some ways, the ultimate test of an effective school is its ability to solve the problems it encounters. For effective problem solving to occur, school members must be able to identify discrepancies between actual and ideal conditions, and once a problem is defined, group members must then develop solutions that move them toward their ideals.

Norms: Ineffective problem solving in schools is often characterized by the following norms:

- Group members ignore problems or fail to state them properly.
- People expect others to solve their problems instead of organizing for that purpose.
- Problem solving either fails to follow systematic procedures or follows overly rigid procedures that block creative solutions.

Conversely, examples of norms that tend to promote effective problem solving include:

- Group members state problems precisely and directly, accepting any discomfort as temporary and solvable.
- People organize quickly into groups to inquire jointly into common problems.
- Everyone understands and is expected to follow flexible, agreed-on procedures.
- People are rewarded for viewing problems as normal and for viewing logical problem solving as a springboard to creative action.

Helping with problem solving: One small way to help people in school improve their problem-solving capabilities is to help members clearly define the problems confronting them and to develop workable plans in collaborative ways. Strategies that aim toward this kind of goal can make an important difference and can be used by beginning teachers as they work with students and colleagues.

There are many approaches to problem solving for individuals and groups. Some include a linear sequence of phases such as the one illustrated in Figure 12.5

Other approaches emphasize the closed-loop nature of problem solving in which a group may start at any step in the process and recycle as needed. Some problem-solving technologies are designed to find the best route to a specified goal; others are designed to find answers concerning why things are happening as they are; and still others to sort out conflicting goals.

An extremely simple and very powerful model developed by Fred Fosmire and Richard Wallen (1971) distinguishes three kinds of problem-related information.

1. Situational Information—that which describes the current situation or condition

Figure 12.5   Phases of Problem Solving

Identify problem or assess needs
↓
Agree on objectives
↓
Search for alternative solutions
↓
Choose a means to reach the objective
↓
Implement the chosen plan
↓
Evaluate what happens

---

2. Target Information—that which describes a preferred state of affairs
3. Proposal Information—that which describes ways to move from the current situation to one or more targets

A problem using this model exists any time there is a discrepancy between a situation and a target. A problem is identified any time people say, "Existing conditions are not what we want." Groups using this procedure normally tape three pieces of butcher paper on the wall and proceed in their problem solving by listing ideas and information under each of the categories.

4. Decision-Making Processes Creative efforts to solve problems include choosing among alternative goals, procedures, resources, and solutions. Even when only one solution is thought of or is possible, problem solving always ends with the choice of acting or not acting. This process is important because it can produces much conflict among people, particularly if decision-making processes are not clear.

Norms: Norms like these often inhibit the way people exert or accept influence and make their decisions:

- Only those with legitimate authority are expected to make decisions.
- Responsibilities for decision making are vague or unclear.
- Group members are locked into a single method of group decision making—majority voting for example.
- Even decisions that require everyone's understanding and commitment are made by one person or majority vote.

It is possible to change unproductive school norms into productive ones like the following:

- The best-informed people make decisions because decision quality is viewed as more important than who makes it.
- Everyone has clear expectations about who normally makes what decisions.

- Procedures for making a decision are carefully matched to the kind of decision being made.
- Those who must understand and be committed to a decision are rewarded for participating in it.

Helping clarify decision-making procedures: Teachers report that sometimes they are confused about how much different role groups in schools should be involved with various decisions. Although beginning teachers cannot be expected to clarify decision making in a school, the matrix shown in Table 12.1 can at least provide a model for thinking about this issue. This sample matix lists different role groups found in schools across the top and examples of various decision areas down the side. The letter codes provided can be put in each cell to indicate the kind of influence each member in the school exerts on each kind of decision.

This procedure can help people think about who does what to whom in a school. It can also provide a vehicle for discussion of decision making in classrooms and in faculty meetings. It is a good device for members of a teaching team to use to get clarity about who on the team is responsible for what kinds of decisions.

5. Meetings Processes All beginning teachers will attend meetings and in many schools these offer the best opportunity for influencing needed improvements. Meetings are the places where much of the collaborative work of the school occurs.

Table 12.1   Decision-Making Matrix

	ADMINISTRATORS	TEACHERS	SCHOOL PSYCHOLOGIST AND COUNSELORS	STUDENTS
Determining curriculum				
Ordering supplies				
Scheduling students				
Evaluating teachers				

CODES:

I = must be informed of the decision
C = must be consulted and allowed to influence the decision
P = must participate in the decision, has a vote
V = has veto power, must agree
A = has sole authority to make the decision

SOURCE: Adapted from R. Arends and J. Arends (1977), *Systems change strategies in educational settings.* New York: Human Science Press, p. 78.

Norms: In some schools, meetings will be terrible, particularly if they are characterized by the following norms:

- People straggle in and leave early, and no one pays enough attention to fill them in later.
- Certain people always convene the meeting or take minutes.
- Everyone talks at once or certain persons dominate the discussions.
- Everything is "all business"; no one is sensitive to others as people or to the way in which the work is accomplished.

In contrast, some schools have meeting norms that are much more productive, such as these:

- Expectations about starting and ending times are clear, and people help those who cannot meet them.
- Convening and recording functions are shared or rotated so that everyone has a chance to participate equally.
- Discussions encourage participation by all those who want to speak.
- Certain times are set aside to review the meeting including any interpersonal feelings it created.

Helping improve meetings: A beginning teacher can help improve the quality of meetings by taking the following actions:

- Being an effective group member—As a group member, beginning teachers can bring about improvement primarily by modeling. For example, the teacher in a large high school might improve the effectiveness of his or her group by continuously clarifying what others are saying. If clarification statements begin increasing, the modeling will have been successful. A beginning teacher can also set an example by always getting to meetings on time and encouraging others to do the same.
- Serving as a group convener—Often groups can be helped a great deal by those who agree to serve as chairpersons or conveners. A beginning teacher can volunteer for this role and perhaps show a disorganized group how to set an agenda such as the one in Table 12.2 which identifies topics for action and times associated with each.

Summary

This chapter has taken the point of view that helping to improve classrooms and schools is as much a part of the teacher's job as are planning and delivering instruction directly to students. The reasons for change and improvement have

Table 12.2 Sample Agenda for a Meeting

TIME	AGENDA ITEM	PERSON	REQUIRED ACTION
5 min	Announcements	Dick	Information only
15 min	Search committee 7th-grade teacher	Pat	Decision
20 min	Student conduct in B wing	Dick	Discussion only at today's meeting
15 min	Reading text for next year	Donna	Decision (remember our discussion last week)
5 min	United Way	Sharon	Information
10 min	Debrief	All	Discussion

been described, as have the difficulties involved in this process. Although it is unrealistic to think you can bring about major change in schools immediately or by yourself, there are nonetheless several small steps that you can take to help improve your own classroom and your first school. A list of "dos and don'ts" provided by Fullan (1982) serves as a good chapter summary and also as a final reminder that improvement in schools and classrooms is possible if the process of change is approached with understanding and skill. The list is also a reminder that working toward improvement may be a difficult and frustrating process. Here are Fullan's dos and don'ts:

1. Do not assume that your version of what . . . [needs changing] . . . is the one that should or could be implemented. On the contrary, assume that one of the main purposes of the process of implementation is to exchange your reality of what should be through interaction with . . . others concerned.

2. Assume that any significant innovation, if it is to result in change, requires individuals . . . to work out their own meaning. Significant change involves a certain amount of ambiguity, ambivalence, and uncertainty for the individual about the meaning of the change.

3. Assume that conflict and disagreement are not only inevitable but fundamental to successful change. Since any group of people possess multiple realities, any collective change attempt will necessarily involve conflict.

4. Assume that people need pressure to change . . . but it will only be effective under conditions which allow them to react, to form their own position, to interact with others . . .

5. Assume that effective change takes time. It is a process of "development in use." Unrealistic or undefined time-lines fail to recognize that implementation occurs developmentally . . .

6. Do not assume that the reason for lack of implementation is outright rejection of the values embodied in the change, or hard-core resistance to all change. Assume that there are a number of possible reasons.

7. Do not expect all or even most people or groups to change. The complexity of change is such that it is totally impossible to bring about widespread reform

in a large social system. Progress occurs when we take steps . . . which increase the number of people affected. Our reach should exceed our grasp but not by such a margin that we fall flat on our face. Instead be encouraged by all that remains to be done, be encouraged by what has been accomplished by way of improvement resulting from your actions.

8. Assume that you will need a plan which is based on the above assumptions and which addresses the factors known to affect implementation . . . Knowledge of the change process is essential. Careful planning can bring about significant change on a fairly wide scale over a period of two or three years . . .

9. Assume that no amount of knowledge will ever make it totally clear what action should be taken. Action decisions are a combination of valid knowledge, political considerations, on-the-spot decisions, and intuition. Better knowledge of the change process will improve the mix of resources on which we draw, but it will never and should never represent the sole basis for decisions.

10. Assume that change is a frustrating, discouraging business. If all or some of the above assumptions cannot be made (a distinct possibility in some situations for some changes), do not expect significant changes as far as implementation is concerned. (pp. 91–92)

Books for the Professional

Fullan, M. (1982). *The meaning of educational change.* New York: Teachers College Press. This is an excellent book on educational change. It reviews the research on this topic and in addition provides concrete actions educators can take to get new educational programs to work.

Joyce, B., Hersh, R., and McKibbon, M. (1983). *The structure of school improvement.* New York: Longman. Based on the effective schools research, this book provides an insightful analysis of the change process and step-by-step directions for educators interested in improving schools from the inside.

Loucks-Horsley, S., and Hergert, L. F. (1985). *An action guide to school improvement.* Alexandria, Va.: The Network and Association for Supervision and Curriculum Development. Based on over a decade of research on school improvement and effective schooling, this book provides practical, concrete suggestions for embarking on and completing school improvement projects.

Schmuck, R. A., and Runkel, P. J. (1985). *The handbook of organization development in schools.* (Third Edition) Palo Alto, Cal.: Mayfield. Based on 20 years of research on school improvement at the University of Oregon, the handbook describes the theory and technology that guide organization development in educational settings and provides hundreds of concrete suggestions for educators who want to improve small group and organizational functioning.

============================== **CHAPTER 12** ==============================
LEARNING AIDS FOR PLANNING, OBSERVATION, AND REFLECTION

- Assessing My Skills for Improving Schools
- Observing a Staff Meeting
- Clarifying Goals
- Checking My Group Behavior
- Change Process Interview

ASSESSING MY SKILLS FOR IMPROVING SCHOOLS

PURPOSE: The purpose of this aid is to help you assess your level of effectiveness in school improvement skills.

DIRECTIONS: Check the level of understanding and/or effectiveness you feel you currently have in these school improvement skills that were discussed in the chapter.

Skill or Competency	Level of Effectiveness		
	High	Medium	Low
Conducting Action Research Projects			
Isolating a problem	———	———	———
Identifying the independent and dependent variables	———	———	———
Framing a question	———	———	———
Selecting the indicator(s) of the dependent variable	———	———	———
Gathering data	———	———	———
Analyzing the results	———	———	———
Organizing and writing up the results	———	———	———
Working at the school level to help improve			
Communication	———	———	———
Goal setting	———	———	———
Problem solving	———	———	———
Decision making	———	———	———
The effectiveness of meetings	———	———	———

OBSERVING A STAFF MEETING

PURPOSE: For a school staff or any work group to be effective, the members of the group must perform certain task and process functions. This aid is to help you gain practical experience in understanding what these group effectiveness skills are.

DIRECTIONS: Use the following matrix to keep track of task and process functions while observing a faculty meeting, committee meeting, or some other work group. Label the columns with the initials of the group members. Every time you see them execute one of the listed functions, make a tally mark. Then in the Comments column, note exactly what they said.

Function	Member 1 2 3 4 5 6 7	Comments
Task		
Initiating		
Information seeking		
Information giving		
Clarifying/elaborating		
Summarizing		
Consensus testing		
Process		
Encouraging		
Expressing group feelings		
Harmonizing		
Compromising		
Gate keeping		
Setting standards		

Analysis and Reflection: Do you think the meeting you observed was effective? Write a paragraph about why or why not. Link your evaluation to the group behaviors that were present or absent. For example, this may have been an ineffective group because the harmonizing function was absent, even though the information-giving function was present.

CLARIFYING GOALS

PURPOSE: Arriving at clear goals is an important component of school improvement. The purpose of this aid is to give you practice in clarifying goals.

DIRECTIONS: This aid is an elaboration of the suggestion in the chapter that projecting into the future can aid in clarifying goals. Use it either individually or with a work group to help identify important goals and arrange them according to priorities.

Project yourself into the year _____ (five, ten years hence). Imagine that you are working in a school. If you had your fondest wish, what would your work there be like in _____? Please try to be as specific as possible in answering the following questions. In each case tell how you would like it to be in _____.

1. My age is now _____

2. My position in the school district is _____.

3. Some of the kinds of activities I engage in each day are _____

   _____

   _____

4. My responsibilities or functions are to _____

   _____

   _____

5. What is it you especially like about your work? _____

   _____

   _____

6. What results of your work make you especially proud? _____

   _____

   _____

Analysis and Reflection: Look back at your answers. Some of the things you foresee doing or results you foresee producing are different from the way they are now. Select the most important differences—not necessarily the biggest differences or those most difficult to achieve, but the differences you feel are the most valuable and satisfying.

7. What are the two or three things most worth accomplishing by _____?

   _____

   _____

8. What are the chief satisfactions you feel from these accomplishments? _____

_____

9. Looking back over your answers to the above questions, what do you seem to be saying about school goals for _____? Please write two or three goals that you believe contain the more important elements to your answers above.

To _____

_____

To _____

_____

CHECKING MY GROUP BEHAVIOR

PURPOSE: One way a beginning teacher can contribute to school improvement is to model good group behavior. The purpose of this tool is to help you uncover your strengths and weaknesses as a group member.

DIRECTIONS: After a meeting that you have participated in, rate the extent to which you performed each of the following group behaviors.

1. I offered facts, gave my opinions and ideas, and provided suggestions and relevant information to help the group discussion.

   Never   1   2   3   4   5   6   7   *Always*

2. I expressed my willingness to cooperate with other group members and my expectations that they would also be cooperative.

   Never   1   2   3   4   5   6   7   *Always*

3. I was open and candid in my dealings with the entire group.

   Never   1   2   3   4   5   6   7   *Always*

4. I gave support to group members who were on the spot and struggling to express themselves intellectually or emotionally.

   Never   1   2   3   4   5   6   7   *Always*

5. I took risks in expressing new ideas and current feelings during a group discussion.

   Never   1   2   3   4   5   6   7   *Always*

6. I communicated to other group members that I was aware of and appreciated their abilities, talents, capabilities, skills, and resources.

   Never   1   2   3   4   5   6   7   *Always*

7. I offered help and assistance to anyone in the group in order to bring up the performance of everyone.

   Never   1   2   3   4   5   6   7   *Always*

8. I accepted and supported the openness of other group members, supporting them for taking risks and encouraging individuality in group members.

   Never   1   2   3   4   5   6   7   *Always*

9. I shared any materials, books, sources of information, or other resources I had with the other group members in order to promote the success of all members and the group as a whole.

   Never   1   2   3   4   5   6   7   *Always*

10. I often paraphrased or summarized what other members said before I responded or commented.

    Never   1   2   3   4   5   6   7   *Always*

11. I leveled with other group members.

    Never   1   2   3   4   5   6   7   *Always*

12. I warmly encouraged all members to participate, gave recognition for their contributions, demonstrated acceptance of and openness to their ideas, and generally was friendly and responsive to them.

    Never   1   2   3   4   5   6   7   *Always*

Analysis and Reflection: What were your strengths and weaknesses as a group member? Pick 3 of the 12 behaviors described above and write two sample statements for each, indicating what you might say, were you to perform that behavior.

CHANGE PROCESS INTERVIEW

PURPOSE: School change is a very complex process involving individual change as well as organizational change. This aid will give you the opportunity to investigate change from the perspective of people who have experienced it. This in turn may help you cope with change in your own career.

DIRECTIONS: Use the questions below as a guide in interviewing teachers or principals about change projects with which they are familiar.

1. Have you ever been involved with a school change or improvement project?

2. Can you describe the nature of the change or improvement?

3. Where did the idea for the change come from? The central office? The principal? Teachers? Parents?

4. How did you react at first to the change? Were you all for it, or did you have reservations? What kinds of reservations did you have?

5. How did others react to the change at first? What were their reservations?

6. What was your role in implementing the change? How did you react?

7. How did the change project turn out? Successfully? Unsuccessfully?

Using Computers in Classrooms

Chapter 12 discussed the topic of educational innovation and change. The use of computers is definitely one of the major innovations that must be considered. Although it is still unclear how pervasive computers will become in classrooms of the future, their impact will certainly be important and their appropriate use is a matter educators must grapple with in the years to come.

This special topic section will provide information about how computers are currently being used in classrooms, the effects of computer-based instruction, and how beginning teachers can get started with using computers. The intent of this section is to provide a brief overview and to motivate further exploration. To begin with, consider two scenarios:

A kindergarten class is preparing to use LOGO, a computer programming environment. A large map with roads and houses is on the floor, and two of the houses have pictures on them—one of a lion, the other of a rabbit.

To begin the lesson, the teacher gives the children a toy car with a dog sitting in it. She tells the children that the dog's car can go right, left, forward, and backward. The teacher says that it is the dog's birthday, and his friend the lion has called him to come over to get a birthday present. She instructs the children to work in pairs and to practice getting the car to the lion's house. When the dog reaches the lion's house, the teacher tells the children that he needs to go back and get tickets, one from rabbit and one from lion, before he can get the birthday present.

Next the teacher introduces the children to a floor robot that can be instructed by their microcomputer to go in the same directions as the car—right, left, forward, and backward. Using the computer, the children instruct the robot which direction to move, again trying to visit the houses on the map.

In a high school science class a gifted student has been identified with an interest in nuclear energy. Ten years ago information on this topic available to the student would have been limited to that in the city or county library. She would have read about nuclear energy and written a report on the topic. If she had been a perfectionist, she would have hired someone to type her report before she handed it in.

Today this student is thoroughly computer literate. She has access to a microcomputer, software, a modem, and several computer networks, such as The

Source and BRS, a bibliographic search network. Instead to going to the library, she is able to conduct an extensive computerized bibliographic search on nuclear energy. She also searches current wire service reports for current events related to nuclear energy. She uses a computer simulation that examines nuclear energy and checks the accuracy of the simulation against data she has gathered. She even writes her own simulation. When it comes time to write her report, she does it herself with her word processor and publishes it on the school's electronic network.

These examples illustrate two different but equally powerful applications of the computer in the classroom. In the first, young children learn mapping, directions, and how to use a computer keyboard in an imaginative, playful setting. In the second, a high school student uses the computer to extend and challenge her knowledge of nuclear energy. Unlike the behaviorists' "teaching machines," which you may have experienced in school, today's microcomputers offer a multitude of applications and are becoming readily accessible to students. They provide challenging and provocative opportunities for teachers.

EDUCATIONAL APPLICATIONS OF MICROCOMPUTERS

Computers in the classroom can serve a variety of educational purposes.

First, the computer can be used as a tool to perform such functions as word processing, accessing information, calculating, or data analysis. The student is the user of the computer, like a writer using a word processor.

Second, computers can be used as tutors. Tutoring applications involve using the computer to "teach" students specific content. Commonly referred to as Computer Assisted Instruction (CAI), tutoring applications employ varying amounts of structure and student control. In all instances, however, the computer acts as a teacher to the student.

Third, the computer can become the learner. Learner applications involve students in programming the computer. LOGO, Pascal, and BASIC are examples of common programming languages students might learn and teach to the computer.

Fourth, the computer can be a subject for study. When students study about computers they learn new vocabulary and concepts; they learn how computers work and they consider the role of computers in an information society. The student acts as a learner with the computer as content.

Finally, computers can be used to manage classroom information. Management applications include using the computer to schedule, to keep records, or to test, grade, and plan. In this instance, the teacher or the student acts as the manager of the computer.

Categories of CAI

CAI constitutes one of the most frequent applications of computers in the classroom. CAI programs fall into three general categories: drill and practice, tutorials, and simulations.

DRILL AND PRACTICE

Drill and practice, as the name implies, provides students with opportunities to practice. Using individualized repetitions, students rehearse specific predetermined content or skills in question and answer format until mastery is achieved. The strengths of drill and practice include immediate feedback, ease of use, and efficiency in skill learning. Some programs record student responses or scores for future reference by students and teachers. The primary weakness of drill and practice is its narrow focus on skill acquisition, with no concern for concept development.

TUTORIALS

In some ways, tutorials are like sophisticated textbooks. They provide information as well as questions and answers. Tutorials involve the same type of presentation as drill and practice, but they are designed to branch into different areas according to student responses. Although still individualized and feedback oriented, tutorials involve the learner more actively than drill and practice. They are best suited for situations in which a set of concepts and information must be learned.

SIMULATIONS

Computer simulations promote critical and higher-level thinking. Usually, they provide a model of some aspect of reality that would be difficult to observe in the classroom, such as mixing chemicals, creating three-dimensional graphs, or flying an airplane. Simulations allow for exploration and discovery requiring more open-ended responses and are most appropriate for situations that may be too dangerous, abstract, inaccessible, expensive, or time-consuming to be done in the classroom.

HOW EFFECTIVE ARE MICROCOMPUTERS IN THE CLASSROOM? ▬▬▬▬

Microcomputers have been touted as revolutionary for teaching and learning, but how effective are they? Even though the microcomputer was introduced into the classroom on a large scale only a few years ago, research programs have already focused on their effectiveness, and this research should be considered by beginning teachers.

Instructional Effects

Roblyer (1985) reviewed the research on the instructional effects of computers and provided the following summary:

- ▪ The use of computers in elementary schools appears to produce higher achievement effects than does their use with older students.

- Computer-based instruction achieves consistently higher effects than other instructional treatments to which it is compared in experimental situations. The effects, however, are usually small or moderate.
- Computer-based instruction that supplements other forms of instruction seems to result in greater effects than when the computer is used by itself.
- Computer-based instruction results in significant reductions of instructional time. It also produces favorable attitudes toward computers by students.
- In reading, nondrill CAI used in small groups produces better results than does individual, drill-type use. In math, nondrill also achieves higher effects overall. Younger and lower-ability students, however, seem to learn comparatively better from drill, whereas higher-ability students appear to profit more from tutorial-type CAI.
- In general, mathematics students seems to profit more from computer-based instruction than reading or language arts students; but at the college level, results are just the opposite.
- At least two researchers have found that, although computer-based methods usually result in increased student achievement, the effects are often less than those obtained from noncomputer strategies, such as instructional television or improved reading and study skills programs.

Research on the effects of computers on thinking and problem-solving skills is somewhat mixed. Transfer of problem-solving skills learned on the computer to other areas has not been demonstrated. However, when students are instructed to transfer a particular skill they do so more readily than when they are expected to do so spontaneously. Problem-solving and thinking skills are difficult to measure and the continuing research programs on these topics should be watched.

Several questions have not yet been sufficiently answered by research. Feedback, motivation, screen design, graphics, and learner control are aspects of CAI that require further research.

Social Effects

The question of the effects of computers on social interaction has generated a sizable body of research with surprisingly consistent results. The computer appears to increase social interaction, and students often prefer working at computers in pairs. The once-expressed fear that students sitting in front of computers would become isolated and antisocial has been relieved somewhat by the observation of positive social interactions and cooperation occurring around the computer.

Studies of student attitudes have generally shown that students like using computers and are motivated by them. What elements of the computer are motivating—color, sound, game-like qualities, or newness—and whether motivation increases achievement are still open questions.

Concerns of social inequity regarding computers have also been widely discussed. Unequal access to computers by disadvantaged or minority students implies that the benefits of technology could accrue to already advantaged white, upper-class populations, creating a new form of discrimination. Unequal application and training for computer use by females implies that higher-level thinking and training could create a technological discrimination favoring males in knowledge and work opportunities. For example, boys may tend to take computer science while girls take data entry. Software could also reflect sex bias. For example, a hypothetical "GI Joe" program may encourage active solutions, while "Rainbow Bright" encourages passive solutions. Problems of inequity are not new to our society, but if uneven distribution and use of technology are allowed, computers may only serve to widen existing gaps.

A final social concern about computers is their effect on the way students may come to think about themselves. Sherry Turkle (1984) gives a fascinating, readable account of people's psychological responses to the computer. Until now, she says, the criteria for humanness have often been defined by comparing humans to animals. People reason, use language, and possess self-awareness, which animals do not. Turkle observed young children and adolescents approach the question of whether or not computers are alive and how machines and humans differ. She reported that young children tend to project issues of feelings, intentions, and psychology onto the computer, whereas adolescents focus on issues of control, mastery, and identity. Turkle hypothesizes that the similarities and distinctions between machines and humans, computers and brains, human intelligence and artificial intelligence may occupy more and more of our thinking and eventually change the criteria by which humanness is defined.

GETTING STARTED

First Steps

As you consider how you might want to use computers in your classroom, keep in mind the complex issues involved in implementing any new idea or approach in schools. Remember also, as described in Chapter 12, that as users of something new, individuals go through various stages of concern and that the nature of the school itself will influence what is possible.

Most schools and school districts today have microcomputers and have developed specific procedures for using them. In addition, many state departments of education have developed recommendations and curricular guidelines for teachers to follow. A good first step for the beginning teacher is to check with administrators, central office personnel, and state education agencies to see what exists. Other important earlier activities might include browsing through a computer store and reading magazines and journals that focus on computers in education and attending a workshop or taking a course on computers.

In many schools teachers will find existing plans for the management of computer resources and a ready supply of computers and instructional software.

If these plans and resources do not exist in your school, then more effort will be required to get started with computers.

If you are just beginning to use computers, start small and be relaxed. Watching students interact with the computer is one way of learning what to expect. The younger generation often approaches the computer with less "computer phobia" and fewer preconceptions than those of us who did not grow up with computers in our homes and schools.

Choosing Software

Existing software determines the outcome of any use of the computer. Unfortunately, high-quality educational software is not as plentiful as teachers might wish. However, teachers can influence the selection of software and, if careful procedures for choosing software are followed, selection decisions can increase the potential success of a computer curriculum.

Clements (1985) has proposed the following steps for choosing software:

1. Establish learning goals to determine just what the program should do.
2. Look into organizations, journals, and data bases that can help locate and evaluate software.
3. Ensure that service is available.
4. Obtain the program and documentation. If you cannot obtain the program for a preview, find out if you can get a demonstration; see if field testing was done; read reviews; check the company's reputation. If you can obtain the program for a preview, go through the program as a successful student and as a less successful student; observe students using the program; read through the documentation.
5. Complete an evaluation checklist.
6. Make a decision. Share evaluations with other teachers. If you decide not to purchase the software, return it promptly with the evaluation form.

In general, the evaluation and selection of software should attend to issues of appropriateness of content, instructional and design quality, social and emotional effects, adequacy of performance and operation, clarity of documentation, and the pedagogical and instructional relationship to your goals for students.

TEACHERS AND COMPUTERS

Will computers replace teachers? Some early predictions suggested that computers would decrease the need for teachers. That scenario seems unlikely to develop, given that supplemental CAI appears more effective than replacement CAI. The most effective computer learning takes place within a well-designed curriculum in which the computer is one of several instructional tools and approaches in the teacher's repertoire. It is likely that teachers will remain responsible for planning and organizing various learning activities into a meaningful whole. If the computer can reduce instructional time in skill areas, the teacher is then freed to pursue other, perhaps higher-order, teaching activities. At best, the computer can improve the teacher's options and capabilities in delivering effective instruction. As Clements (1985) has so clearly observed, "The goal is to design a complete and powerful educational environment for children, including good teachers, meaningful computer applications, and much more" (p. 115).

Books for the Professional

Culbertson, J. A., and Cunningham, L. L. (Eds.). (1986). *Microcomputers and education.* Chicago: National Society for the Study of Education. This is an overview including articles on networking, curriculum, classroom organization, literacy, higher-order thinking, vocational education, system-wide application models, and broad application issues such as citizenship.

Grady, M. T., and Gawronski, J. D. (Eds.). (1983). *Computers in curriculum and instruction.* Alexandria, Va.: ASCD. This is an overview for teachers of kindergarten through grade 12, including planning for computers, choosing hardware and software, implementation models, literacy for teachers, literacy for students, uses in subject areas, and future implications.

Papert, S. (1980). *Mindstorms: Children, computers, and powerful ideas.* New York: Basic Books. This classic book provides the theoretical foundations for discovery-oriented computer environments, particularly LOGO.

Turkle, S. (1984). *The second self: Computers and the human spirit.* New York: Simon and Schuster. Based on interviews with children, adolescents, and adults this book focuses on psychological attitudes and feelings toward the computer as it affects our development, thinking, and social life.

CHAPTER 13

MAIN IDEAS

- Entry into the world of work is an event that is experienced universally by people in all walks of life. Sometimes the process is easy; often it is difficult.

- Sociologists refer to the transition from the family and educational institutions to the work institution as organizational socialization.

- There is a well-established research base on the socialization of beginning teachers, including studies of what happens to beginning teachers, how successful beginning teachers start the first year, and how successful beginning teachers launch their careers.

- For most beginning teachers, the first year of teaching is characterized by "reality shock." The way beginning teachers are prepared to deal with this shock is an important ingredient of first-year success.

- Successful beginning teachers attend to several important aspects of their new jobs: getting off to a good start with students, finding school leadership projects, establishing professional networks, learning the evaluation procedures for permanent certification and tenure, and taking steps to stay alive and flourish.

The First Year
of Teaching

Starting any new endeavor, particularly one's first professional job, is as difficult and anxiety producing as it is stimulating. In some ways what beginning teachers face as they meet their first classes is not much different from what other professionals face in new jobs. After a long period of education, professionals are eager to meet challenges and rewards associated with their chosen careers. At the same time they are worried about how well they are going to do. Trial attorneys, for example, worry about their first cases; nurses experience anxiety as they work their first night shifts alone; and business school graduates feel nervous as they apply their newly acquired skills for the first time in large corporations. Regardless of how well individuals are prepared technically, anxiety and difficulties inevitably attend initial practice in real-life settings. As beginners pass from the status of novice to that of fully socialized member of a profession, these difficulties and anxieties gradually disappear.

Fortunately, a great deal is known about the problems faced by beginning teachers as well as about what successful beginners do to make their first teaching experience satisfying and growth producing. How to survive and flourish during your first year of teaching is the subject of this chapter.

PERSPECTIVE AND RATIONALE

Succeeding in one's first teaching job seems crucial to someone who has prepared long and hard for teaching. Although the first year is always difficult, it can also be rewarding, particularly for those who are prepared for the professional and technical demands of teaching and for the psychological stress of the induction period. No amount of preparation, however, will eliminate completely the problems faced by beginning teachers. An understanding of several important ideas associated with initial teaching and professional socialization can provide a needed perspective on what happens during the first year.

Concerns and Problems of Beginning Teachers

Studies such as those conducted by Tisher (1978) in Australia, by Lacey (1977) in Great Britain, and by Ryan (1980) and McDonald and Elias (1980) in the United States found that beginning teachers reported a common set of concerns. Those mentioned most often included: (1) classroom management and discipline, (2) inability to find needed materials, (3) evaluation of student work, (4) interacting with parents, and (5) feelings of isolation. Unfortunately these topics are sometimes neglected in preservice teacher education programs, perhaps because of the discrepancies between the preservice and in-service situations.

Organizational Socialization

Sociologists view entry into the world of work as a universal process involving the young adult's transition from the family and educational institutions to the work institution. Each society has social arrangements that facilitate or hinder this transition. In agricultural communities, for example, the transition process usually moves quite smoothly. Youths learn adult roles directly from their parents and other adults by performing work-related tasks from a very young age. Similarly, the apprenticeship system used in some occupations helps complete the transition to work through carefully supervised, on-the-job training over a long period of time. As societies become more complex, this transition process is less smooth and informal, particularly for complex jobs. Families cannot begin to provide the necessary training, and the natural alternative, formal schooling, gives only general and incomplete preparation, particularly for such complicated jobs as teaching.

In Chapter 11, the concepts role and role systems were introduced. You will remember that *role* was defined as a set of behavioral expectations associated with a particular position, such as teaching. *Role system* expresses the interconnections of various roles within a particular organizational setting. In schools the role system includes such major roles as teacher, student, administrator, various specialists, and parents. Sociologists (for example, Louis, 1980) use the term *socialization* to describe the process of learning a role and a role system. Through this process individuals come to appreciate the values, knowledge, and behavior associated with a particular profession and organization. For teachers, this process proceeds through the following stages:

ANTICIPATORY SOCIALIZATION

This is the period of formal training, including student teaching, where many aspects of the teacher's work are learned and where certain expectations are developed. During this period positive rather than negative aspects of the role are usually emphasized, and ideal rather than realistic teaching practices are generally taught.

INITIAL CONTACT

This is the contact usually made during the job interview or initial visit to a school system. Employers generally put their best face forward during the interview by emphasizing the positive characteristics of the teaching position.

REALITY SHOCK

When teachers actually begin their first jobs, many of them experience numerous surprises or what some have labeled "reality shock." Drawing on the work of Louis (1980), Isaacson (1981) described the following surprises typically experienced by first-job holders:

1. The first form of surprise occurs when *conscious expectations about the job* are not fulfilled in the newcomer's early job experience.
2. A second form of surprise arises when *expectations (both conscious and unconscious) about oneself* are not met. Choice of occupation and the new organization are often based on assumptions about one's own skills, values, etc. During the encounter phase, errors in assumptions sometimes emerge, and the newcomer must cope with the recognition that s/he is different from her/his previous perceptions.
3. A third form of surprise arises when *unconscious job expectations* are unmet or when features of the job are unanticipated. Job aspects not previously considered become significant because their presence or absence is undesirable once encountered.
4. A fourth form of surprise arises from difficulties in *accurately forecasting internal reactions* to a particular new experience. How new experiences feel, as opposed to how the person expected them to feel, is difficult to anticipate and often surprising.
5. A final form of surprise comes from *cultural assumptions* brought by the newcomer from previous settings as operating guides in the new setting, and they fail. (pp. 2.11–2.12)

The Socialization of Teachers

The socialization process is difficult in any profession, and novices always experience some degree of reality shock. Beginning teachers have special challenges not faced by new role occupants in other professions because of the way education and schools are organized. For example, beginning teachers are given the same leadership responsibilities as the more experienced teachers on the faculty. Full leadership responsibility is something other professionals do not have to worry about until they have learned their jobs more fully. Also, socialization and induction in other professions are the responsibility of experienced peers. Because of the ways schools are organized, beginning teachers are usually left alone with little direct help from colleagues. Even though this organizational neglect presents special problems for beginning teachers, there is a bright side. One, it gives beginning teachers considerable leeway to chart their own course; and two, the knowledge base regarding initial teaching is rather well developed and can provide valuable insights for making the first year successful. A sample of that research is described in the next section.

SAMPLING THE RESEARCH BASE

Many aspects of the experiences of teachers during their first year on the job have been studied. Three specific lines of inquiry have yielded information about what beginning teachers can do to make their first year successful: (1) studies about the nature of the first-year experience, (2) studies about how successful teachers start the school year, and (3) studies about how successful teachers continue to grow and learn during their early years of teaching.

The First Year and Reality Shock

For over three decades researchers have studied the experiences of beginning teachers. A common theme running through all of this research is that the "reality shock" for teachers is more severe than it is for novices in other professions. McDonald and Elias (1980), who conducted comprehensive research on the problems of beginning teachers, attribute much of the difficulty to the feeling of being a "stranger in a new land":

> The beginning teacher is a stranger in a new land, the territory of which and whose rules and customs and culture are unknown, but who has to assume a significant role in that society. If the problem is put in this manner, it is easy to see that we are studying a general problem in human experience as well as a particular problem in adaptation to a specific institution and to a specific social role. (p. 200)

Kevin Ryan (1980), who has studied beginning teachers for almost three decades, explained why the reality shock for new teachers is so overwhelming. He argued that the beginning teacher's familiarity (not strangeness) with the classroom environment leads to much of the problem.

> [The beginning teacher] thinks he knows what he's getting into. The daily life of a teacher holds few secrets for him; he is no stranger to the school. He has been there before. The shock comes when the beginner changes from audience to actor. The role which he had seen played out thousands of times is now his. The familiar scene of the classroom is reversed, and he encounters a startling new situation. (p. 171)

Nancy Isaacson (1981) was part of a team of researchers at the University of

Oregon who studied beginning teachers in that state for a number of years in the late 1970s. She expanded on the analyses of Ryan and of McDonald and Elias:

> The reasons for the reality/culture shock are many and varied. . . . Surprise about how difficult it is to reach secondary students, underestimation of the difficulties in motivating them; overestimation of their own skills as disciplinarians; failure to anticipate the amount of time and work necessary to keep up with daily paperwork; surprise at the volume of administrative tasks; emotional and physical drain which leaves little energy for anything else in their lives; pain from the unprovoked hostility from their students and the students' disdain for the subject the teacher cherishes. . . . [For] many new teachers, the role of teacher is not the only adjustment they are making in their lives. Many are first encountering adjustments from living alone, a new marriage, adjusting to a new community, financial independence, and the complexities of social interaction with members of the opposite sex. Perhaps the most surprising thing of all . . . is that the newcomer learns that the teacher's official role in the classroom does not permit her/him the luxury of being oneself. (p. 217)

Beginning the School Year

Some observer has written that "discipline problems seem to belong to the beginning teacher in the way that pimples belong to the teenager." Studies in classroom management, particularly as it is influenced by teacher behaviors during the opening of school, represent a second line of inquiry important for beginning teachers.

Common sense and personal experience suggest that what happens during the first few moments in any relationship shapes future interactions. This is certainly true in classrooms. As teachers meet their classes for the first time, they are sized up by their students. Initial lessons are perceived as potentially interesting or boring; management procedures are judged as tight or loose; and teachers themselves are judged as good, bad, nice, or cranky. Once relationships are fixed, they seem to stay that way. Particularly in the area of classroom management, patterns established at the beginning of the year are difficult to change later. If students get out of control early, it becomes difficult to get them back; if initial lessons are disjointed, it becomes difficult for later learning activities to proceed smoothly.

But what should beginning teachers do to start the school year successfully? During the late 1970s and early 1980s, a comprehensive research effort was launched at the University of Texas to find answers to this question. You are already familiar with some of this research. It was introduced in the chapter on classroom management and served as the basis for many of the recommendations made there. Research Summary 13.1 summarizes another study that focuses directly on effective classroom management at the beginning of the school year.

=========== **RESEARCH SUMMARY** ===========
13.1

Emmer, E. T., Evertson, C. M., and Anderson, L. M. (1980). Effective classroom management at the beginning of the school year. *The Elementary School Journal, 80,* 219–231.

PROBLEM: The researchers were interested in finding out how effective teachers begin the school year, specifically their use of basic principles of classroom organization and management.

SAMPLE The sample in this study was comprised of 27 third-grade teachers and their students in eight elementary schools. The schools served populations of students from upper-lower and lower–middle-class backgrounds. In one school most children were black, in two schools most were Mexican-American, and five schools had a mix of students. Six of the teachers were first-year teachers.

PROCEDURES: Trained observers gathered information about each teacher's organization and management practices by visiting classrooms. Twelve classrooms were visited during the first morning of school; all 27 classrooms were observed at least once during the first two days. Each teacher in the study was observed at least eight times during the first three weeks. Teachers were also observed later in the year and were interviewed twice. Data collected included:

- Organization and management practices using a Classroom Narrative Record
- Student on-task behavior using a Student Engagement Rating Form
- Ratings of teacher organization and management behaviors

Using a variety of ratings, and controlling for the achievement of students in the classrooms, the researchers were able to identify seven teachers who were very effective managers and seven who were clearly less effective based on student engagement compared to off-task behaviors.

POINTERS FOR READING RESEARCH: There are no new research concepts introduced in this study. The researchers did, however, include considerable information in their data tables, and readers wil have to study each very carefully. Also, the researchers' conclusions are based on their extensive observations, so the discussion and implications section includes statements in their own words.

RESULTS This is a two-part study. First the researchers studied the differences between more effective and less effective managers during the first three weeks of school. They found considerable and significant differences as can be observed in Table 1. Several of the variables included in the study have been excluded because they are similar to those you already studied in Chapter 6.

As can be observed in Table 1 there are considerable and significant differences between more and less effective managers. The important part of this study, however, is the researchers' finding that there is considerable stability between beginning of the year management effectiveness and later in the year behaviors. These relationships are shown in Table 2.

DISCUSSION AND IMPLICATIONS: As can be observed from Table 1, there were considerable and significant differences between the more effective managers and the

TABLE 1 Component Ratings and Student Engagement Rates for Seven More Effective and for Seven Less Effective Managers During the First Three Weeks of School

Variable	More Effective Managers Mean	Less Effective Managers Mean	$p<$
Behavior Management			
Variety of rewards	4.3	3.1	.05
Signals appropriate behavior	5.4	3.8	.01
Eye contact	6.1	4.9	.01
States desired attitude	5.5	3.9	.01
Reinforces inattentive behavior	2.7	3.6	.ns
Disruptive pupil behavior	3.0	4.8	.05
Meeting Students' Concerns			
Attention spans considered in lesson design	5.2	2.8	.01
High degree of student success	5.5	3.9	.01
Content related to student interest	5.2	3.6	.01
Reasonable work standards	5.8	4.6	.05
Student Engagement Rates			
On-task, all activities	.86	.75	.05
On-task, in content	.65	.59	.10
Off-task, unsanctioned	.07	.16	.05

SOURCE: Adapted from E. T. Emmer, C. M. Evertson, and L. M. Anderson (1980), p.224.

TABLE 2 Coefficients of Correlation Between Rating of Variables for Two Time Periods: Beginning of Year and Remainder of Year ($N = 27$)

Variable	Correlation
Student Engagement Ratings	
On-task, all activities	.51
On-task, all academic activities	.46
Off-task, unsanctioned	.54
Narrative Rating Variables	
Behavior control	.83
Instructional leadership	.74
Students' concerns	.68
Physical arrangements	.41

SOURCE: Adapted from E. T. Emmer, C. M. Evertson, L. M. Anderson (1980), p. 222.

less effective managers in two important areas: behavior management and meeting student concerns, and as shown in Table 2, initial behaviors were stable during the rest of the school year. The researchers reached the following conclusions about differences between more and less effective managers:

1. More effective managers had more contact with students during the first few days and spent considerable time explaining rules and procedures.

(cont'd)

━━━━━━━━━━━━━━━━━━━━ **RESEARCH SUMMARY** ━━━━━━━━━━━━━━━━━━━━
13.1 (continued)

2. More effective managers had better instructional procedures and made the "first" academic activities enjoyable.
3. More effective managers were sensitive to student needs and concerns during the first few days of school, specifically in gauging attention span, level of difficulty of lessons, and overall judgment about what to do.
4. More effective managers exhibited better listening and affective skills.

In the researchers' own words here are the implications they derived from the study: "Effective classroom organization and management during the year can be predicted from the first several weeks of the school year. The teaching characteristics and behaviors that appear to discriminate best among more effective and less effective managers include the quality of leadership exhibited by the teacher in managing behavior and instruction, in planning for student concerns, and in coping with constraints. The more effective managers had a workable system of rules and procedures which they taught to their students during the first several weeks. They monitored their students carefully and did not 'turn them loose' without careful directions. They did not appear to treat inappropriate behavior differently than the less effective managers, but they stopped it sooner. Consequences of appropriate and inappropriate behavior were clearer in their classrooms and were applied more consistently. Thus, these teachers established their credibility early and they were predictable" (p. 230).

"The present study provides additional evidence of the importance of the teacher's activities at the beginning of the year. In particular we would stress the necessity of an efficient system for organizing procedures, rules, and initial activities, and for treating the communication of this system to the pupils as a major teaching task at the beginning of the year. The present study suggests that such a system, augmented by the teacher's ability to monitor, to respond to pupil concerns, and to use basic communication skills (both instructional and affective) will facilitate classroom management throughout the year" (p. 231).

Career Development of Teachers

A third line of inquiry important for beginning teachers is the research that looks at the career and professional development of teachers. Just as what happens in the classroom during the first few days affects later events, so what happens in the teacher's professional life outside the classroom during the first year also sets the stage for future years.

Of particular importance is the way beginning teachers view themselves as learners and how they approach learning in their personal and professional lives. Socialization into teaching is a major "shaping event" in the professional lives of teachers. This experience "has a powerful influence on how teachers develop, what their concepts of effectiveness become, and their attitudes toward continuing professional development for the remainder of their careers." (Isaacson, 1981, p. 2.8)

Joyce, Hersh, and McKibbin (1983) interviewed 300 teachers and surveyed 3,000 more in California during the early 1980s. They found great variability in the degree to which teachers grew and remained reflective about their teaching. They reported:

> We uncovered some striking examples of persons who have developed intense growth-producing activities. We found a Spanish teacher who, at her own expense, spent two months in Mexico working on her language skills because she felt they were getting rusty. We found an English teacher who has created a beautiful and intense sex education course as a result of her concern about the ignorance of her students and of many of her community members. We found autoshop teachers who study new developments by the major domestic and foreign automotive manufacturers. We found teachers who are intensely reflective about their teaching and delighted in interchange with others, and teachers who appear to insulate themselves from interchange which might affect the way they view themselves and their children. (pp. 162–63)

Joyce, Hersh, and McKibbin (1983) developed categories to describe the various types of teachers they found in their sample.

1. *The Omnivore*   Omnivores are teachers who are constant and active learners. They use every aspect of the formal and informal system to enrich their professional and personal lives. They are avid readers, workshop attenders, and have broad interests in the performing arts, sports, and travel.
2. *The Active Consumer*   These teachers are active in their learning. They show less initiative than omnivores but nonetheless lead active lives and participate in a full range of personal and professional growth activities.
3. *The Passive Consumer*   These teachers take workshops and courses when offered, but they rarely seek out or initiate learning experiences. The number of personal and professional activities in which they become involved are, in fact, quite narrow.
4. *The Entrenched*   These teachers are, as the name implies, entrenched. They seldom take courses or workshops unless they are paid to do so. They are against efforts to improve their school and for the most part they teach and lead their personal lives as they have for many years.
5. *The Withdrawn*   These teachers have no regular outside interests and they are essentially withdrawn from all professional growth opportunities. They are difficult to involve and, as with entrenched teachers, their personal and professional lives follow patterns established many years earlier.

Joyce, Hersh, and McKibbin did not focus on the beginning teacher. However, during the late 1970s and early 1980s, researchers at the University of Oregon followed one group of beginning teachers for a three-year period. The researchers were trying to find out how beginning teachers attended to their own professional development and whether continued learning was related to performance and effectiveness. One study growing out of this research is found in Research Summary 13.2.

MAKING THE FIRST YEAR PRODUCTIVE

Previous sections of this chapter have emphasized the difficulties faced by beginning teachers and the problems they encounter as they begin their teaching careers. Beginning teachers should not leave this discussion with the feeling that these problems and difficulties are insurmountable. They are not. As Kevin Ryan and his colleagues (1980) observed, "Three million people have gone through the first year of teaching" (p. 3), and they have survived. In fact, many look back upon the first year of teaching and remember it as incredibly stimulating and growth producing. This section provides specific actions that will help beginning teachers as they get started with a new community, new students, and a new career.

Getting Off to a Good Start in the Community

Earlier it was noted that one of the reasons the first year is so difficult is because many life adjustments are forced upon a beginning teacher at one time: getting settled in a strange community, setting up housekeeping, getting married or choosing not to marry, learning how to cook, handling a budget, and so on. With appropriate planning, many of these nonteaching adjustments can be handled prior to the arrival of students. Here are several suggestions that can help:

- Plan to relocate in the community well before the first week of school to allow uninterrupted time for handling of relocation problems. This is a time to get a phone installed, to find a doctor, and to seek out favorite places to shop, to eat, and to entertain.
- Get to know the community, particularly if it is different from the one you grew up in. Walking through the neighborhoods that comprise the attendance boundaries of the school will provide insights into the backgrounds and the values of students. Reading a little about the history of the community also helps. A learning aid has been designed at the end of this chapter to assist with this task.
- Get to know the school. Several visits to the school prior to opening day will provide a working knowledge of important places in the school and make the place feel less strange and foreboding. Visiting the school at this time is also an excellent way to meet new colleagues before they are faced with their own day-to-day teaching demands.

Accomplishing these activities before the school year begins will permit you to concentrate your energy on students and instructional tasks.

RESEARCH SUMMARY
13.2

Arends, R. I. (1983). Beginning teachers as learners. *Journal of Educational Research, 76,* 235–242.

PROBLEM: Arends and his colleagues were interested in the nature and extent of learning experiences of beginning teachers, characteristics of beginners that might account for their learning, and whether or not active learners are judged more competent than less active learners.

SAMPLE AND SETTING: Forty-three beginning high school teachers in Oregon comprised the sample of the study. Beginning teachers were chosen at random from the total population of students who graduated from the University of Oregon in 1976 and 1977 and who found teaching positions in Oregon.

PROCEDURES: Beginning teachers were visited and interviewed twice—at the end of the first year of teaching and again at the end of the third year. Respondents were asked to recall all the learning experiences in which they had participated and the number of hours spent in each during the three-year period. In addition, the teacher's principal was asked to judge the competence of the beginning teacher using a rating scale. Learning activities were coded into 18 categories, such as workshops, clinics, community study, curriculum work, educational travel, faculty study groups, field testing materials, field trips, independent study, new teacher orientations, night classes, observations, presentations, private lessons, technical assistance, supervision, summer school.

RESULTS: Arends found that there was considerable variation in the amount of time beginning teachers devoted to their own learning during the first three years of teaching. For example, one beginning teacher spent a total of 951 hours on his learning as contrasted to another teacher who spent as little as 32 hours over a three-year period. Arends also found a significant relationship between the amount of time beginning teachers spend on learning and the rating given by their principals as to their effectiveness. Table 1 shows these data.

DISCUSSION AND IMPLICATIONS: The sheer amount of time devoted to deliberate, professionally related learning by beginning teachers was quite surprising. The data showed that beginning teachers, for the most part, continue as learners and in large ways.

Inspections of the individual learning profiles (not included here) showed great variability, however, among avid, average, and reluctant learners. These data tend to confirm the categories and variability in "growth states" reported by Joyce in his study of California teachers.

Finally, inspection of the individual learning profiles and the fact that those beginners rated most competent by their principals are also those that are the most avid learners confirms the notion that active learning should be encouraged.

Studies such as those conducted by Arends and by Joyce, Hersh, and McKibbin are starting to establish that there is great variability in the degree to which
(cont'd)

—————— **RESEARCH SUMMARY** ——————
13.2 (continued)

TABLE 1 **Total Hours of Learning Experiences for Beginning Teachers and Principals' Judgment of Effectiveness ($N = 24$)***

Subject	Hours of Learning	Principal's Rating
1	951	3.9
2	764	4.0
3	566	4.2
4	516	4.3
5	483	4.1
6	482	3.5
7	440	3.3
8	427	4.3
9	413	3.8
10	401	4.4
11	328	4.0
12	327	3.1
13	317	3.7
14	295	3.6
15	268	3.4
16	225	3.6
17	174	3.8
18	114	3.3
19	108	3.7
20	102	3.3
21	72	2.9
22	56	3.2
23	40	3.3
24	32	3.4

* Usable data was available on only 24 of the 43 subjects because several had left teaching during the three-year period. Correlation significant at .05 level of confidence.
SOURCE: R. Arends (1983), p. 241.

teachers continue to learn and grow. For beginning teachers this research has several implications:

1. Attitudes toward lifelong learning are normally established early in one's career. Beginning teachers should take steps to develop positive attitudes toward their own learning by making sure time is allocated for personal and professional growth.

2. Active learners take advantage of the environment for their personal and professional growth. Beginning teachers can learn how to use their environments in their preservice preparation and during their beginning years of teaching.

3. There are relationships between active learning and principals' judgments of effectiveness. That, however, does not mean that active learning makes one more effective. It could be that more effective teachers are also those who seek out more learning activities.

Getting Off to a Good Start With Students

Research Summary 13.1 provided information indicating how important the first few days of school can be in determining later success for teachers. The recommendations of the investigators who conducted that research are summarized here and organized into specific procedures beginning teachers can follow as they strive to get off to a good start with their students.

ESTABLISHING RAPPORT

Knowing that first impressions are important, a beginning teacher should be ready to make a good impression when students arrive the first morning. Students should be greeted at the door in a friendly and pleasant manner and encouraged to enter the room and find a seat. On the first day, most students will be on their good behavior because they also are trying to make good impressions. However, if inappropriate behavior is observed a beginning teacher must correct it immediately.

Remain Visible A beginning teacher should expect to be nervous during the first few minutes of student contact. Teachers with 25 years of teaching experience still get nervous as students enter the room for the first time. For some, a natural response to this anxiety is to hide in the crowd or to find something to do such as stacking books, sharpening pencils, or sorting papers. A beginning teacher must guard against such behavior and remain visible to students regardless of personal discomfort.

Extend a Warm Welcome As the bell rings, the teacher should be ready to start immediately. Introduce yourself to the class in a firm voice and extend a formal welcome to students. Again, this is likely to be a scary moment. If introductions and welcoming remarks do not come naturally to you, it would be a good idea to spend considerable time rehearsing them the night before.

Getting Acquainted In most classrooms, some students will know each other but others will be strangers. Teacher should start acquainting students with each other on the first day of school. One approach used by many experienced teachers is to have students write their names on five-by-eight cards that can be placed on their desks. This will also help the teacher learn the students' names. Some teachers also ask students who have not been in the school before to raise their hands and then extend a special welcome to them and spend a few minutes talking about where they went to school last year. Too much time should not be spent getting acquainted at this point because it is also important to teach a "real" lesson on the first day.

It is likely that beginning teachers will focus on their own discomfort and uncertainties during these first few minutes. Since many students will be experiencing these same feelings, teachers should be prepared to deal with students' anxieties along with their own.

THE FIRST LESSON

It is always difficult for teachers to decide whether course content or class rules and procedures should receive primary emphasis during their first class meeting. *Both must be done on the first day*. With older students, some teachers prefer to focus on the content of the course first, then follow with information about rules and procedures. With younger students, this order is often reversed. Regardless, the first learning activities should be selected to assure high motivation and a high degree of student success. This can be accomplished by selecting a very interesting topic and by planning the lesson based on information about students' prior knowledge. Experienced teachers in the school can be an invaluable resource for getting ideas for the first few lessons. They know about the interests of students in the school, and they also have a good understanding of students' prior knowledge.

Lessons during the first day and the first week should be uncomplicated, and they should focus on the whole class. A whole-class focus is recommended for two reasons. One, most students know how to behave in this learning setting, and two, a whole-group focus enables the teacher to be visible and in charge. Small-group work, cooperative learning, and many other approaches that require student movement should be avoided until the beginning teacher feels confident with the class and students have learned the rules and expectations needed to make such learning activities successful.

INTRODUCING RULES AND PROCEDURES

Chapter 6 described the importance of clear rules and procedures for effective classroom management. The first day and week of school are the times when these rules and procedures must be introduced and taught to students. Experienced teachers post important rules and procedures and go over these with students on the first day. They keep their list of rules short, they explain the logic behind the rules, and they teach them with the same care as any other skill.

Getting off to a good start with students is crucial because it influences the rest of the school year. Many aspects of the first week can be greatly enhanced by good planning and attention to detail. Table 13.1 shows some important tasks for the first week of school and provides the recommendations made by the University of Texas researchers on how to "plan for a good beginning."

Exhibiting Leadership and Establishing Professional Networks

It is natural for beginning teachers to spend most of their energy on planning and delivering instruction. There are, however, other important functions that need attention. Launching one's career is just as important as launching one's first class.

EXHIBITING LEADERSHIP

The previous sections emphasized the importance that first impressions have on students. First impressions also affect the way beginning teachers are received by professional colleagues both inside and outside school.

One way that beginning teachers can become known among colleagues and win their regard is to exhibit leadership potential within the school or school system. Below are some examples, reported by principals and colleagues, of what several successful beginning teachers did to exhibit leadership during their first year (see Arends, 1979).

- Elaine taught on a fifth-sixth grade teaching team that had a weak science curriculum. Elaine had majored in biology in college and had more science background than other more experienced teachers on the team. She volunteered to revise the science curriculum for the team and found suitable materials for teachers to use. This leadership was applauded by team members and made Elaine a highly valued and respected team member.

- George was hired as a social studies teacher in a middle school. In discussions with students and colleagues, he found that for the past three years no one had paid any attention to the school's drama program. George had been in numerous college plays and volunteered to head up the drama club and to sponsor a spring play. The play was a huge success and George won respect for his willingness to take on this school-wide job.

- Valerie, a high school English teacher, was upset about the hall behavior of the students in the building wing where she had been assigned. After getting things off to a good start in her own class, she began discussing the hall problem with other teachers in the wing. Under her leadership they established a set of rules for hall behavior and together agreed on ways to monitor student behavior between classes.

Obviously, beginning teachers should not overextend themselves by assuming too many leadership responsibilities. However, it is important to pick at least one project that has the potential for school-wide attention and devote energy toward getting successful results.

ATTENDING TO PROFESSIONAL GROWTH

Throughout this book the idea that learning to teach is a lifelong process has been emphasized. The learning process for teachers includes developing habits of reflection, finding ways to keep abreast of current research on teaching and learning, and keeping up-to-date in one's subject. It is easy for beginning teachers to fall into the trap of having their first class and their first school become all-consuming and to forget about their own needs as learners. From the very first week, time should be set aside for the teacher's own professional development

Table 13.1 Planning for a Good Start

TASK	RECOMMENDATION
Obtaining books and checking them out to students	Know school procedures for keeping track of books. Be prepared to record book numbers for each student on forms or in the grade book. Some teachers wait until the second day and check out textbooks during a seatwork assignment.
Required paperwork	Make sure all required forms, reports, etc. are on hand and organized for appropriate use. Required paperwork will vary from school to school.
Class rosters	Have class rosters organized (by period in high school) and pay attention to students with any special needs. Class rosters will change over the first days of school as new students arrive and as class sizes are leveled out across the school.
Seating assignments	Wait until class rosters have stabilized before assigning seats (normally the third or fourth day of school). Some teachers seat students alphabetically; others let students choose their own seat. Seating assignments, regardless of the method used, help the beginning teacher learn students' names and control student movement. Most teachers change the seating arrangement periodically.
First-week schedules	Know in detail the schedules for the first week. In secondary schools, classes are often shortened for one reason or another during this time. In elementary schools, planned assemblies are common.
Tardiness	Many students will be tardy during the first days of school. They, too, are struggling to find the right room and so on. Start enforcing tardiness policies during the third or fourth day. Warn students of this policy the previous day.

Table 13.1 Planning for a Good Start (Continued)

TASK	RECOMMENDATION
Administrative tasks	Be prepared to accomplish administrative tasks efficiently. These tasks will vary, but in most schools will include: attendance checking, hall procedures, use of school equipment, various signups for special school events, and reporting requirements.
Rules and procedures	Explain rules on the first day. Teach procedures during the first week. Come back to both as needed and try to remain consistent in their use.
Course requirements	Course or class requirements should be explained to students during the first week. For older students these requirements (tests, major papers, projects, etc.) should be given to students in writing. Teachers should emphasize that major requirements are not just tasks to be accomplished for a grade, but major challenges for students to enhance their education.
Beginning-class routine	Be prepared to start class smoothly. Whatever routine is chosen, it should be efficient and one where students remain in their seats without talking while waiting for instruction to begin.
Time fillers	Be prepared with special work sheets, puzzles, or special reading materials which can be used in case a lesson runs short or periods or the school day are extended.
Closing-class routine	Be prepared for closing class smoothly. Plans should include ways to collect student work and materials. In secondary schools, teachers must insist that dismissal is when they "say" and not the school's bell or buzzer system.

SOURCE: Emmer/Evertson/Sanford/Clements/Worsham, *Classroom management for secondary teachers*, © 1984, pp. 73–76. Adapted by permission of Prentice-Hall, Inc., Englewood Cliffs, NJ.

and for establishing professional networks beyond the environs of a particular school. This can be accomplished in a variety of ways.

Attend Beginning Teacher Workshops and Seminars Many school systems sponsor workshops and seminars for beginning teachers. Sometimes these are required; most often participation is voluntary. Beginning teachers should take advantage of these opportunities. Useful ideas about classroom management and teaching strategies can be found in these workshops and seminars. They also provide opportunities for the beginning teacher to meet other beginning teachers in the school system as well as more experienced teachers who often have been selected to lead these events.

Attend Regional and National Conferences One important way for beginning teachers to keep abreast of their subject fields and the latest instructional research is by attending regional and national conferences. In some school systems conference attendance will be encouraged through financial incentives. In other systems, beginning teachers will have to use their own funds. Either way, it is important for beginning teachers to set goals for themselves that will assure professional growth and professional networking through conference attendance. An Appendix at the end of this book lists the names and addresses of professional organizations that sponsor local and national meetings organized around research or topics of interest to classroom teachers.

Working Toward Permanent Certification and Tenure

Graduating from a teacher education program and securing a teaching position is obviously the first step in a teacher's career. Becoming a fully certified member of the profession and obtaining tenure in a school system is another. Certification and teacher evaluation procedures are under review in many states, and it is likely they will be changed rather dramatically during the next few years. Two trends can be predicted: (1) Initial certification in most states will be based on successful completion of an accredited teacher education program and receiving a passing score on the National Teacher's Exam. (2) Permanent certification and tenure will be based on evaluations of successful teaching performance during the first two or three years of teaching.

INITIAL CERTIFICATION AND THE NATIONAL TEACHER'S EXAM

Most professional workers are required to have a license before they are allowed to practice. In education, state governments have always had the legal authority for granting teachers their license to teach. Although this may change in the future, states currently grant two types of license: (1) an initial certificate, good for a few years, and (2) a permanent certificate, normally good for life. The general procedures in most states (except in emergency or shortage situations) are to require applicants for an initial certificate to graduate from an approved college-

or university-based teacher education program and to pass the National Teacher's Exam (NTE) or some other standarized test. Appendix D provides names and addresses for the government unit responsible for certification in each state. Information can be obtained for specific state certification requirements upon written request.

The NTE is a test prepared and administered nationally by the Educational Testing Service of Princeton, New Jersey. They publish a document called *Bulletin of Information*, which provides information about locally scheduled test dates and conditions. It is the applicants' responsibility to make appropriate arrangements for taking the NTE. Although the NTE is likely to undergo revision over the next several years, currently it has two major parts: the NTE Core Battery and the NTE Specialty Area Tests.

The Core Battery The core battery consists of three two-hour exams that are taken separately.

1. The *communication skills* section of the exam tests the prospective teacher's ability in the areas of writing, reading, and listening.
2. The *general knowledge* section of the exam tests the prospective teacher's knowledge of general information in the areas of literature and fine arts, mathematics, science, and social studies.

If beginning teachers have a good liberal arts background and have been successful in college, they can expect to do quite well on the communication skills and general knowledge sections of the NTE. These tests are not too much different from the Scholastic Aptitude Tests (SAT) taken by many students prior to entering college.

3. The *professional knowledge* section is the third exam in the core battery. This portion of the NTE tests the prospective teacher's knowledge regarding the processes and context of teaching. Many of the topics covered in this book are included on the professional knowledge exam. Below is a summary of the major topics of this exam as reported by the publishers of the NTE:

   Planning Identifying objectives, diagnosing student needs, and gathering resources
   Designing instructional activities Selecting strategies, grouping students, organizing resources, and evaluation
   Implementing instruction Establishing conditions to facilitate student learning, communicating expectations, and managing student behavior
   Instructional design Presenting information, giving directions, asking questions, guiding discussions, maintaining appropriate pacing, providing opportunities for practice, monitoring student progress, and providing feedback

Evaluating students Checking student progress, grading, reporting, using systematic observation, assessing instructional effectiveness, and evaluating program effectiveness

Other professional actions Encouraging students' self-worth, interacting with colleagues, working with parents, respecting human rights, and being knowledgeable about important educational issues

Context of teaching Recognizing the constitutional rights of students and recognizing the implications of state and federal laws regarding handicapped children, sex equity, racial justice, teaching in the child's language, and compulsory school attendance

Outside of classroom influences on teachers Knowing about school system policies, community and parent expectations, financial support for education, shifting societal patterns, and school governance

Outside of classroom influences on students Knowing developmental patterns and maturation, and recognizing the importance of the home and community environment

Specialty Area Tests The NTE currently has 26 specialty area tests (see Figure 13.1). These are two-hour tests on the prospective teacher's subject field.

At the present time, some states require the specialty tests but others do not. If the specialty test is required, the beginning teacher can obtain a study guide and information about each of the specialty tests from Educational Testing Services.

BEGINNING TEACHER EVALUATION SYSTEMS

In most states a passing score on the NTE after completing a teacher education program will give the beginning teacher a certificate to teach for two to five years.

Figure 13.1   NTE Specialty Area Tests

Agriculture
Art education
Audiology
Biology and general science
Business education
Chemistry, physics, and general science
Early childhood education
Education in the elementary school
Education of the mentally retarded
Educational administration and supervision
English language and literature
French
German

Guidance counselor
Home economics education
Industrial arts education
Teaching of reading
Mathematics
Media specialist
Music education
Physical education
Reading specialist
Social studies
Spanish
Speech communication
Speech-language pathology

A permanent certificate requires successful on-the-job performance. Tenure (permanent employment) in a school system is also tied to successful on-the-job performance in most instances. Today, many different procedures are being used by states and school systems to evaluate beginning teachers. A general pattern is emerging, however, that consists of variations of the following procedures:

- A school system or state agrees upon a set of teaching competencies on which the beginning teacher will be judged
- Procedures are developed for a team of people to observe the teacher on a number of occasions during the first or second year of teaching

Below is an example on how this process currently works in the state of Virginia.

Beginning Teacher Competencies Educators in the state of Virginia have created a list of teacher competencies for which beginning teachers must demonstrate mastery. Indicators (actions by teachers that can be observed) have also been written for each competency. Figure 13.2 displays the competencies and examples of indicators of each competency included in the Virginia system.

The Evaluation Process Although specific procedures vary, the evaluation process for beginning teachers normally consists of a series of classroom visits by the principal or an observation team consisting of the principal, an experienced teacher, and several specialists from the school district. In some instances, a college professor is included on the team. Observations occur several times (three to five) during the first and/or second year of teaching. Observers normally use an observation form like the sample that is shown in Figure 13.3, which is a composite of several existing forms.

Staying Alive and Flourishing the First Year

The final topic for this chapter is one that is extremely important for the beginning teacher: how to stay alive mentally and emotionally during the first year and how to flourish regardless of the circumstances.

KEEPING PERSPECTIVE

A description of role taking and organizational socialization was provided in the beginning section of this chapter. It is important for beginning teachers to understand this perspective. Regardless of a beginning teacher's readiness to perform the technical aspects of teaching, there will be difficulties to face because many of the problems of teacher induction are associated with the way schools are structured and the complexity of the teacher's role in our society. If this is kept in mind, beginning teachers will not assume total blame for difficulties they experience.

Figure 13.2   Virginia's Beginning Teacher Competencies and Indicators

Competency	Behavioral Indicator
1. Academic Learning Time: The competent teacher knows that learning is directly related to the amount of time learners are actively engaged in planned learning activities.	The beginning teacher should demonstrate knowledge of the importance of maximizing academic learning time by: ▪ Planning for efficient use of time ▪ Maintaining continuous focus on lesson topic
2. Accountability: The competent teacher knows the importance of holding learners responsible for completing assigned tasks.	The beginning teacher should demonstrate knowledge of the importance of learner accountability by: ▪ Planning just what tasks each learner is supposed to complete ▪ Clearly establishing consequences of not completing an assigned task
3. Clarity of Structure: The competent teacher knows that learning is facilitated if the lesson is presented in a clear systematic sequence consistent with the objectives of instruction.	The beginning teacher should demonstrate knowledge of the importance of clarity in the structure of a simple lesson or unit by: ▪ Preparing outlines, reviews, and summaries beforehand ▪ Beginning the lesson or unit with a statement of purpose
4. Individual Differences: The competent teacher knows that learners progress at different speeds, learn in different ways, and respond to different kinds of motivation.	The beginning teacher should demonstrate knowledge of the importance of adapting to individual differences by: ▪ Planning ways of dealing with individual differences in learners' abilities, cultural backgrounds, handicaps ▪ Providing alternate ways for different learners to achieve common objectives
5. Evaluation: The competent teacher knows that learner progress is facilitated by instructional objectives that are known to the learners and coincide with the objectives of evaluation.	The beginning teacher should demonstrate knowledge of the importance of formal/informal evaluation by: ▪ Planning evaluation (formal and informal) whenever he or she plans instruction ▪ Asking questions, observing learners' work, and checking learners' understanding regularly during instruction to evaluate progress
6. Consistent Rules: The competent teacher knows that rules for classroom behavior must be clear and consistent and that learners must understand and accept the rules and the consequences of violating them.	The beginning teacher should demonstrate knowledge of the importance of rules that are consistently enforced by: ▪ Setting rules that are known and understood by learners ▪ Reminding learners of a rule when they disobey by citing the rule

7. **Affective Climate**: The competent teacher knows that learning occurs more readily in a classroom environment that is nonpunitive and accepting.

The beginning teacher should demonstrate knowledge of the importance of the affective climate of the classroom by:
- Avoiding hostility and punitiveness
- Making the physical environment as pleasant and attractive as possible

8. **Learner Self-Concept**: The competent teacher knows that a learner's achievement may be enhanced by improving self-concept. Self-concept is enhanced if the teacher's expectations are high and if the teacher shows appreciation of the learner's personal worth.

The beginning teacher should demonstrate knowledge of the importance of enhancing learners' self-concepts by:
- Planning lessons that challenge learners
- Praising correct performance of difficult tasks or correct answers to a difficult question

9. **Meaningfulness**: The competent teacher knows that learning is facilitated when content is related to learner's interests, common experiences, or information with which they are familiar.

The beginning teacher should demonstrate knowledge of the importance of meaningful learning activities by:
- Planning ways of relating instruction to interests and previous knowledge of learners
- Pointing out relationships between lesson or unit content and things learners already know

10. **Planning**: The competent teacher knows the importance of deliberate and varied planning activities. Planning activities should include the teacher's knowledge of instructional objectives and activities, multiple instructional modes, the current professional literature, and the interpretation of test data.

The beginning teacher should demonstrate knowledge of the importance of planning by:
- Using relevant professional literature in defining objectives or choosing learning
- Planning for the use of more than one mode of instructional delivery

11. **Questioning Skill**: The competent teacher knows how to phrase convergent, divergent, and probing questions and use them to develop learners' academic knowledge.

The beginning teacher should demonstrate knowledge of the importance of skillful questioning by:
- Asking convergent questions that are relatively easy
- Giving feedback

12. **Reinforcement**: The competent teacher demonstrates awareness that the skillful use of reinforcement is an effective means of encouraging and discouraging particular behaviors.

The beginning teacher should demonstrate knowledge of reinforcement theory and its application to classroom teaching by:
- Giving positive rather than negative feedback
- Not using punishment to motivate learners

13. **Close Supervision**: The competent teacher knows that more is learned during individual, small, and whole group activities if the learners are monitored.

The beginning teacher should demonstrate knowledge of the importance of close supervision by:
- Monitoring activity of all learners
- Helping learners who have difficulties

SOURCE: From *Assisting the Beginning Teacher* by the Commonwealth of Virginia. Copyright © 1988 by the Commonwealth of Virginia. Reprinted by permission of the publisher Allyn and Bacon Inc.

Figure 13.3 A Sample Performance Evaluation for Beginning Teachers

Teacher's Name:_____Observer's Name:_____Date_____

Contextual Information

Number of Students	☐ 15-20	☐ 20-24 **Student Abilities**	☐ mostly average
	☐ 25-29	☐ 30-34	☐ mostly below average
	☐ 35-39	☐ 40+	☐ mostly above average
Resources Available	☐ few	**Physical Conditions**	☐ poor
	☐ adequate		☐ adequate
	☐ plentiful		☐ good

Grade level_____ Subject taught_____

Overall rating of level of difficulty of class being taught

☐ A very difficult class to teach

☐ An average class to teach

☐ A fairly easy class to teach

Teacher Planning. In planning for the observed lesson has the teacher:

	Yes	No	N/A*
•analyzed and interpreted student abilities and backgrounds?	☐	☐	☐
•chosen appropriate content?	☐	☐	☐
•clearly stated the goals of the lesson?	☐	☐	☐
•chosen activities (models or strategies) consistent with goals?	☐	☐	☐
•selected appropriate instructional materials?	☐	☐	☐
•devised means to evaluate the lesson?	☐	☐	☐

Classroom Activities and Participation.

What was the dominant activity (ies) for the lesson?

☐ Whole group
☐ Small group
☐ Seat work

What percentage of the students were on task?
(mark every 15 minutes)

☐ Time #1_____%
☐ Time #2_____%
☐ Time #3_____%

*Not applicable for this particular lesson

Conducting the Lesson. Did the teacher:

	Yes	No	N/A
•give purposes and objectives of the lesson?	☐	☐	☐
•establish set for students?	☐	☐	☐
•state expectations for student achievement and conduct?	☐	☐	☐
•use appropriate instructional strategies?	☐	☐	☐
•appropriately pace and sequence activities?	☐	☐	☐
•speak clearly?	☐	☐	☐
•encourage learners?	☐	☐	☐
•monitor learner activities?	☐	☐	☐
•check for learner understanding?	☐	☐	☐

Classroom Management. Did the teacher:

	Yes	No	N/A
•manage classroom time to focus on learning?	☐	☐	☐
•explain and monitor rules for student conduct?	☐	☐	☐
•deal with disruptions to keep smooth flow?	☐	☐	☐

Classroom Environment. Did the teacher:

	Yes	No	N/A
•organize physical setting for productive learning?	☐	☐	☐
•organize seating arrangement consistent with lesson?	☐	☐	☐

Ending the Lesson and Evaluation. Did the teacher:

	Yes	No	N/A
•review and check for learner understanding?	☐	☐	☐
•make appropriate assignments?	☐	☐	☐
•relate lesson goals to evaluation?	☐	☐	☐

Overall. Explain your overall judgement of the teacher's effectiveness._____

_____
_____
_____
_____
_____
_____

FINDING TIME

A common complaint of beginning teachers is that they simply cannot find the time to perform all the important tasks and functions associated with teaching. This is a common complaint of educators in general. Experienced teachers, principals, counselors, and the author of this book also express frustration in handling the multiple roles and task demands of their jobs. This lack of time is tightly connected with role overload and role complexity in education jobs. It also reflects many educators' inability to manage time effectively and to develop the determination and discipline to keep work demands realistic.

There are several approaches to time management that offer help to busy and overextended professionals. Richard Schmuck (1982) provided the following guidelines designed specifically for beginning teachers:

> 1. First analyze the tasks you actually do during a teaching day, week, or month. This "diagnosis" of time use should be carried out in writing, not just constructed mentally, through the use of a diary or log. Account for every 30 minutes during one work week, logging your time at the end of every half day. A formal diagnosis of this sort could also be a useful task for you during your student teaching when you might apply it not only to yourself but also to other teachers with whom you are working. Doing this will encourage you to talk with experienced teachers about how they make use of their time.
> 2. After you have this objective data about your use of time, assign priorities to the subtasks you are currently executing. What are the most important subtasks you must perform? Put those tasks into a list. Your values will determine, to a large extent, what subtasks you list as most important. This process of clarifying personal values is an ongoing task as you decide on priorities. If and when your values and priorities change, this list of important subtasks will inevitably need changing.
> 3. Next write out this list of priorities side-by-side with a comparable list of subtasks that have been ordered according to your previous diagnosis of actual time spent (see number 1 in this list). What does such a comparison reveal? Are there some subtasks that should receive more time and energy? Are there some subtasks that ought to be reduced in emphasis? Are there subtasks that ought to be dropped altogether? (pp. 114–115)

Schmuck also provides an example of how one beginning teacher used this approach. Her work is displayed in Figure 13.4.

SOME COMMON TIME TRAPS FOR BEGINNING TEACHERS

Planning for more effective use of time can also be enhanced by avoiding some common time traps. Following are examples reported by beginning teachers.

1. *Every piece of curriculum and all materials must be original.* Most college methods instructors place a premium on the creation of original materials. In many instances this practice is carried over into student teaching. It is important

Figure 13.4 Time Management Study of Middle School Beginning Teacher

Excerpt from Time Log: *Teaching Practicum, week of March 1, Redfield Middle School*
Carole Stoller

Morning

8:00–8:30	Arrived at school, picked up attendance forms, mimeographed quizzes, had coffee in teacher's room & discussed last night's PTA meeting with social studies teacher (5 mins.), went to class.
8:30–9:00	Home base activities (attendance, announcements, collected immunization forms, handled 2 tardy notices—took 15 mins.). Returned composition papers, introduced & administered promised quiz, disciplined classroom disruption.
9:00–9:30	Wrote reading assignment on board and answered students' questions on quiz. Completed attendance record. Collected quizzes, discussed two more questions.
9:30–9:50	Introduced assignment (5 mins.). Discussed item on last night's reading assignment questions. Disciplined classroom disruption—filled our detention slip.
9:50–10:00	Hall duty (talked to Mary about her math curriculum committee; glad I'm not on one yet).
10:00–10:30	Collected assignments, settled class (5 mins.). Read lesson's poem, led discussion (10 mins.), disciplined & sent Joseph to VP office again (must have taken 5 mins. to decide and fill out pass). Answered questions, only 2 or 3. Assigned poem commentary and new reading. Student journal report (5 mins., ran over a little).
10:30–10:50	Poetry Club meeting interrupted at least 5 times with questions or disruptions from other half of class doing reading assignment.
10:50–11:00	Hall duty and begin prep time.
11:00–11:30	Coffee in teacher's room. Surrendered prep time to informal meeting of classroom management committee so we wouldn't have to meet tonight to prepare for tomorrow's staff meeting.
11:30–12:15	Lunch duty (subbing for Don, out sick).

My priority list:

1 instructional time
2 lesson preparation
3 classroom discipline
4 interaction with fellow teachers, etc.
5 normal paperwork
6 promoting student socialization skills
7 professional activities

Matching

IDEAL &	ACTUAL
Instructional time	Instructional time
Lesson preparation	Discipline
Promoting student socialization	Paperwork
Paperwork	Interaction with fellow teachers
Discipline	Professional activities
Interaction with fellow teachers	Promoting student socialization
Professional activities	Lesson preparation

SOURCE: R. Schmuck (1982), Seeing how teachers fit in. In D. E. Orlosky (Ed.), Introduction to education. Columbus, Ohio: Charles E. Merrill, p. 115. Used with permission.

for teachers to be able to design materials for their students' use; consequently, the aim in methods courses and student teaching is to teach this skill. The time demands of full-time teaching, however, require beginning teachers (and experienced teachers for that matter) to use materials created by others. It is not plagiarism to use materials found in curriculum guides, workbooks, or materials given to you by other teachers in the school. In fact, one mark of a good teacher is knowing how to keep his or her eyes open for good ideas and how to borrow and to adapt freely for specific purposes.

2. *Every paper must be read and graded*. Several sections of this book have emphasized the importance of giving students good feedback about their work. The principle that good feedback promotes student growth is true. A beginning teacher, however, must guard against applying the principle in unrealistic ways. For example, a high school teacher who has 150 students might assign one paper a week and have students write one essay exam a week. If ten minutes were spent reading each paper and ten minutes correcting each exam, that would total 50 grading hours a week. Obviously, spending 50 hours beyond the school day would be unrealistic. Cutting it in half would be equally unrealistic, given all the other things teachers must do. The demands of the teacher's job require teachers to find ways to give feedback to students informally and to limit assignments that take a great deal of grading time. Beginning teachers should not feel guilty about this situation.

3. *The teacher should do it all*. Many beginning teachers, as a result of being in a leadership role for the first time, assume they must do everything themselves. However, they should not be reluctant to delegate responsibilities and tasks to others. Following are some tactics used by many experienced teachers:

- Delegate many classroom administrative and paper work tasks to students. Students see this as a privilege and it can save teachers time.
- Delegate grading of objective tests to students. If done appropriately, this approach can be a valuable learning experience.
- Delegate typing and duplication tasks to the school secretary and teacher aides. This requires some planning, but pays off in the long run.
- Delegate collecting materials for important units and lessons to the school librarian. They normally are delighted to provide assistance to beginning teachers.
- Delegate all of the above to parent helpers. Particularly in the elementary school, there are parents who want to help. This requires some planning and organization, but again it will be a timesaver in the long run.

4. *Every request must be responded to with* yes. The complexity of the school as a social organization means that many requests and demands are made on people's time. Most of these are legitimate and important in their own right. Beginning teachers, however, have to be careful that they do not become involved with too

many tasks and experience extreme role overload during the first year. Most colleagues will understand when a beginning teacher says, "I would love to work with you on that project, but right now I don't have a minute to spare." The principal and others in authority positions will also understand when a beginning teacher gives a polite but firm no to a request to take on a special assignment.

Alan Lakein, a well-known time management expert, provides additional helpful hints on how to get control of time. Twenty ways he saves time in his own life are listed in Figure 13.5.

FINDING A MENTOR

Several places in this book have described the loneliness and helplessness that sometimes characterize the teacher's role. These psychological conditions are experienced most acutely by beginning teachers. Trapped in their room all day with little adult interaction, beginning teachers may start to feel they are the only ones who care and may not know how to ask for assistance in a system poorly

---

Figure 13.5   Twenty Ways I Save Time

1. I don't waste time regretting my failures.
2. I don't waste my time feeling guilty about what I don't do.
3. I don't read newspapers or magazines (except occasionally).
4. I don't own a television set.
5. I've given up forever all "waiting time." If I have to "wait" I consider it a "gift of time" to relax, plan or do something I would not otherwise have done.
6. I carry blank 3 x 5 index cards in my pocket to jot down notes and ideas.
7. I always plan first thing in the morning and set priorities for the day.
8. I keep a list of specific items to be done each day, arrange them in priority order, and then do my best to get the important ones done as soon as possible.
9. I ask myself, "Would anything terrible happen If I didn't do this priority item?" If the answer is NO, I don't do it.
10. I always use the 80/20 rule (80 percent of the value comes from doing 20 percent of the items.)
11. I concentrate on one thing at a time.
12. I delegate everything I possibly can to others.
13. I generate as little paperwork as possible and throw away anything I possibly can.
14. I handle each piece of paper only once.
15. I keep my desk top cleared for action and put the most important thing in the center of my desk.
16. I have a place for everything (so I waste as little time as possible looking for things).
17. I save up all trivia for a three-hour session once a month.
18. I try not to think of work on the weekends.
19. I relax and "do nothing" rather frequently.
20. I recognize that inevitably some of my time will be spent on activities outside my control and don't fret about it.

SOURCE: From *How to Get Control of Your Time and Your Life* by Alan Lakein. Copyright © 1973 by Alan Lakein. Published by David McKay, a division of Random House, Inc.

organized for providing help. In teaching, as with most other adult roles, a mentor can be quite useful for learning complex roles.

In some schools, formal structures exist to help beginning teachers find and work with an experienced teacher who cares about how the beginner is doing and who is willing to take a special interest in his or her career development. In other schools, more informal means will have to be used to make this important connection. Regardless of whether the mentoring structure is formal or informal, the beginning teacher will need to make special efforts to make it work.

A mentor is not obtained by wearing a sign that says "I'm looking for a mentor." Instead, it comes by showing interest in a particular colleague's work, giving support to a colleague, and asking for help. The beginning teacher's initiation of this process with one or two likely candidates will in most instances bring results. From limited initial exchanges, the relationship may flourish until the beginning teacher can ask for daily feedback regarding ongoing teaching problems as well as larger professional and career development issues.

Summary

Beginning teachers find their first year of teaching difficult and perplexing as well as exhilarating. Regardless of initial preparation, many of the subtle aspects of teaching simply take time to learn, and this learning process can be both painful and rewarding. The socialization process is a major event shaping a beginning teacher's life and establishes long-term attitudes toward professional effectiveness and growth.

Successful beginning teachers are those who get settled into their communities well ahead of the opening of school and who prepare carefully to deal with the many new things happening to them at once. Doing the "right things" early in regard to classroom management and student motivation can get beginning teachers off to a good start with students and make the rest of the year productive. Similarly, finding time to build positive collegial relationships and professional networks will get beginning teachers off to a good start in their careers.

Youth in our society need well-prepared, thoughtful, and reflective teachers. Opportunities have never been better for teaching. To repeat the first sentence of this book, teaching offers a bright and rewarding career for those who can meet the intellectual and social challenges of the job.

Books for the Professional

Alschuler, A. S., et al. (1984). *Teacher burnout*. Washington, D.C.: National Education Association. This is an interesting little book that points out how teachers can recognize the signs of stress and how they can reduce stress through planning and time management.

Bluestein, J. (1982). *The beginning teacher's resource handbook*. Albuquerque, N.M.: Instructional Support Services, 260 Washington SE, Suite 64. This is an excellent collection of concrete work sheets and other resources to help beginning teachers plan for the many tasks they face during the first year.

Cooper, J. M., (Ed.). (1986). *Classroom teaching skills.* (Third edition). Lexington, Mass.: D.C. Heath. This book is a must for beginning teachers. It provides many concrete descriptions of important skills beginning teachers are asked to perform along with an adequate supply of study and activity work sheets.

Fuchs, E. (1969). *Teachers talk: View from inside city schools.* New York: Doubleday. This book gives an anthropologist's description of the experience of beginning teachers in inner-city schools during the sixties. It is still relevant today.

Ryan, K., et al. (1980). *Biting the apple: Accounts of first year teachers.* New York: Longman. This book contains detailed accounts of the personal and professional experiences of 13 first-year teachers.

CHAPTER 13
LEARNING AIDS FOR PLANNING, OBSERVATION, AND REFLECTION

- Assessing My Skills for Beginning to Teach
- Observing the Opening of School
- Charting the Characteristics of a School's Attendance Boundaries
- Interviewing Teachers About Their First Year
- Assessment for Professional Growth

ASSESSING MY SKILLS FOR BEGINNING TO TEACH

PURPOSE: Beginning to teach is difficult, but it is not impossible. The purpose of this aid is to help you take stock of your strengths and weaknesses. Armed with this knowledge, you can better plan how to improve your skills and thereby greatly increase your chances of success in managing the beginning of school.

DIRECTIONS: Check off the level of effectiveness or understanding you think you have for each of the skills associated with beginning school.

Skill or Competency	Level of Effectiveness		
	High	Medium	Low
A Good Start with the Community			
Getting to know the community	_____	_____	_____
Getting to know the school	_____	_____	_____
A Good Start with Students			
Establishing rapport	_____	_____	_____
Planning and conducting the first lesson	_____	_____	_____
Introducing rules and procedures	_____	_____	_____
Exhibiting Leadership in the School	_____	_____	_____
Establishing Professional Networks	_____	_____	_____
Working Toward Permanent Certification and Tenure	_____	_____	_____
Flourishing Mentally and Emotionally			
Keeping perspective	_____	_____	_____
Finding time	_____	_____	_____
Finding a mentor	_____	_____	_____

Analysis and Reflection: Write a short paragraph identifying the areas you plan to work on between now and your first teaching position.

OBSERVING THE OPENING OF SCHOOL

PURPOSE: There are many beginning-of-the-year tasks that need to be accomplished to ensure that the school year starts smoothly and continues smoothly. Observing an experienced teacher open school will help you understand how these tasks can be efficiently carried out.

DIRECTIONS: Observe a teacher in your subject area or grade level over the first few days of the school year. For each task listed, write under Comments what the teacher does or says that accomplishes that task.

Task	Comments
Obtaining books and checking them out to students	_____ _____ _____
Required paperwork on hand and organized	_____ _____ _____
Class roster organized	_____ _____ _____
Making seat assignments	_____ _____ _____
First week schedule known	_____ _____ _____
Enforcing tardy policy	_____ _____ _____
Doing administrative tasks efficiently	_____ _____ _____

Task	Comments
Explaining rules	_____
	_____
	_____
Teaching procedures	_____
	_____
	_____
Explaining course requirements	_____
	_____
	_____
Beginning class routine	_____
	_____
	_____
Time fillers on hand	_____
	_____
	_____
Closing class routine	_____
	_____
	_____
Other (specify)	_____
	_____
	_____

Analysis and Reflection: Did the teacher you observed accomplish all of the listed tasks? Did he or she accomplish other tasks that you think facilitated beginning school? Write a paragraph about how you might accomplish these tasks when you begin your first job.

CHARTING THE CHARACTERISTICS OF A SCHOOL'S
ATTENDANCE BOUNDARIES

PURPOSE: One very important beginning task is to get to know the community you will be teaching in. The purpose of this aid is to give a systematic means of doing so. Use it during student teaching to gain familarity with the process and with your students' community, and again before you begin teaching.

DIRECTIONS: Go to the central office of your school district and obtain an attendance boundary map for the school you will be charting. Spend an afternoon walking and/or driving around the area and make note of the characteristics listed below. Walking is best.

1. Make a rough sketch of the area, noting major streets and landmarks.

2. What is the predominant socioeconomic status (SES) of the neighborhood?

    _____

    _____

3. Is this neighborhood's SES (socioeconomic status) homogeneous, or are there pockets of differing SES? What are these? Where are they? _____

    _____

    _____

4. What conditions are homes in around the neighborhood? Are they mostly apartments, single family homes, or a mix? _____

    _____

    _____

5. What ethnic or racial groups are represented in the neighborhood? Which one is the majority group? _____

    _____

    _____

6. What age groups are represented in the neighborhood? Which is the majority?

_____

_____

_____

7. Count the number of churches. What religions do they represent? Where are they concentrated? _____

_____

_____

8. What is the economic base of the community? What industries are here? What commercial enterprises? What is the community's level of economic health?

_____

_____

_____

9. Does the community contain any centers for the arts or other cultural centers? What is their focus? Where are they located? _____

_____

_____

10. Where are the public libraries located? Stop in the library and skim the local newspaper. Find out if there is a local newspaper. Find out if there is a local history you might read. _____

_____

_____

11. What services does the community provide for children? _____

_____

_____

12. Describe the parks and other recreation facilities. _____

_____

_____

13. Where are the "hangouts"? _____

_____

_____

14. How would you characterize the "tone" of the community? Optimistic? Busy? Depressed? Orderly? Unruly? Quiet? _____

_____

_____

15. What other characteristics of this community stand out for you? _____

_____

_____

Analysis and Reflection: Write a paragraph about how you might incorporate the knowledge you've obtained about the community into your teaching. How will it help you establish rapport with students? How will it help you develop good working relationships with parents? How can you use the information in your lessons?

INTERVIEWING TEACHERS ABOUT THEIR FIRST YEAR

PURPOSE: When faced with difficulties, it's often helpful to find out how others have coped with similar difficulties. As discussed in the chapter, the first teaching year can be a stressful time, a time of reality shock. The purpose of this aid is to give you some ideas about how you might better deal with this stress by talking with other teachers about their first year experiences.

DIRECTIONS: Use the following questions as a guide in interviewing one to three teachers about their first teaching year.

1. What expectations did you hold about teaching prior to your first job?
2. What surprises occurred during your first year relative to those expectations?
3. What expectations did you have about your own skills for teaching prior to your first job?
4. What surprises occurred during your first year relative to those expectations?
5. During your first year of teaching what did you find most difficult?
   (a) About students
   (b) About colleagues
   (c) About the principal
   (d) About the school in general
6. What did you do to alleviate those difficulties?
7. During your first year what did you find most rewarding and stimulating?
8. What advice would you give to a beginning teacher about how to survive and flourish during the first year of teaching?

Analysis and Reflection: What expectations do you have about teaching? How have they been influenced by your talks with teachers about their first year? Write a few paragraphs about your expectations of teaching, and how you might cope if these expectations are not met.

ASSESSMENT FOR PROFESSIONAL GROWTH

PURPOSE: The end of this text is only the beginning of the next phase of your professional growth. The purpose of this aid is to help you gain perspective on your past and future professional development activities.

DIRECTIONS: Write a paragraph on each of the following questions.

1. What do you see as your major strengths as a teacher? _____

_____

_____

_____

2. What problems have you experienced in the past in developing these strengths?

_____

_____

_____

_____

3. Project yourself ahead seven years. Imagine you are in a helicopter, as it were, hovering over your life, seeing every aspect fully. Describe your life as a professional—What are you doing? How are you growing? How do colleagues relate to you? How do students relate to you? What have you accomplished? What do you wish to accomplish still? _____

_____

_____

_____

APPENDIX A

Research Centers and Laboratories Funded by the U.S. Department of Education

There are currently 12 research centers and 9 regional laboratories in the United States funded by the U.S. Department of Education. Research centers carry on programmatic research on particular educational topics. The center's name gives you a clue as to the type of research pursued at that site. Research centers produce research reports and summaries of research that can be obtained by teachers who write to the addresses listed here.

Laboratories are situated regionally around the United States. Each laboratory conducts research and also develops new programs and materials aimed specifically for use in public school classrooms. Many of the centers have newsletters that can be obtained by writing. Most conduct workshops and seminars within their regions on topics of interest to teachers.

Centers

Center for Bilingual Research and Second Language Education (CBRSLE)

University of California
1100 Glendon Avenue, Suite 1740
Los Angeles, CA 90024
(213) 825–8886

Center on Education and Employment

Teachers College
Columbia University
Box 174
New York, NY 10027
(212) 678–3091

Center for Effective Elementary and Middle Schools

Johns Hopkins University
3505 North Charles Street
Baltimore, MD 21218
(301) 338–7570

Center on Effective Secondary Schools

Wisconsin Center for Educational Research
School of Education
University of Wisconsin
1025 West Johnson Street
Madison, WI 53706
(608) 263–7575

Center for Postsecondary Governance and Finance

College of Education
4511 Knox Road
College Park, MD 20740
(301) 454–1568

Center for Improving Postsecondary Learning and Teaching

School of Education Building
University of Michigan
Ann Arbor, MI 48109–1259
(313) 764–9472

Center on State and Local Policy Development and Leadership

Eagleton Institute
Woodlawn Building, Neilson Campus
Rutgers University
New Brunswick, NJ 08901
(201) 828–2210

Center for Student Testing, Evaluation and Standards: Assessing and Improving Quality

Center for Study of Evaluation
UCLA Graduate School of Education
University of California at Los Angeles
Los Angeles, CA 90024
(213) 825–4711

Center on Teacher Education

College of Education
Erickson Hall
Michigan State University
East Lansing, MI 48824
(517) 353–1716

Center for the Study of Learning

LRDC Building
University of Pittsburgh
3939 O'Hara Street
Pittsburgh, PA 15260
(412) 624–4895

Center for the Study of Writing

School of Education
University of California, Berkeley
Berkeley, CA 94720
(415) 642–0746   (415) 642–0746

Educational Technology Center

Graduate School of Education Guthman Library
Harvard University
6 Apian Way
Cambridge, MA 02138
(617) 495–9373

Laboratories

Appalachia Educational Laboratory (AEL)

P.O. Box 1348
1031 Quarrier Street
Charleston, WV 25325
(304) 347–0400

Far West Laboratory for Educational Research and Development (FWL)

1855 Folsom Street
San Francisco, CA 94103
(415) 565–3000

Mid-Continent Regional Educational Laboratory (McREL)

Denver Office
Suite 201
1250 East ILLIF
Aurora, CO 80014
(303) 337–0990

North Central Region Educational Laboratory (NCREL)

290 South Main Street
Elmhurst, IL 60126
1 (800) 790–3741

Northwest Regional Educational Laboratory

Suite 500
101 SW Main Street
Portland, OR 97204
(503) 248–6800

Research for Better Schools (RBS)

444 North Third Street
Philadelphia, PA 19123
(215) 574–9300

Regional Laboratory for Education Improvement of the Northeast and Islands

290 South Main Street
Andover, MA 01810
(617) 470–0098

Southeastern Educational Improvement Laboratory (SEIL)

200 Park Avenue, Suite 204
Research Triangle Park, NC 27709

Southwest Educational Development Laboratory (SEDL)

211 East Seventh Street
Austin, TX 78701
(512) 476–6861

SOURCE: From the *Directory of Institutional Projects* (1986), Washington, DC: U.S. Department of Education.

APPENDIX B
Network of ERIC Clearinghouses

There are currently 16 ERIC clearinghouses in the United States, whose addresses are listed here. Each clearinghouse is responsible for a particular topic or field in education. Clearinghouses collect, abstract, and index research documents associated with education. They help disseminate this information by writing research summaries on important educational topics and by preparing annotated bibliographies.

Adult, Career and Vocational Education

Ohio State University
National Center for Research in Vocational
    Education
1960 Kenny Road
Columbus, OH 43210
(614) 486–3655

Counseling and Personnel Services

University of Michigan
School of Education, Room 2108
Ann Arbor, MI 48109
(313) 764–9492

Educational Management

University of Oregon
1787 Agate Street
Eugene, OR 97403
(503) 686–5043

Elementary and Early Childhood Education

University of Illinois
College of Education
805 W. Pennsylvania Avenue
Urbana, IL 61801
(217) 333–1386

Handicapped and Gifted Children

Council for Exceptional Children
1920 Association Drive
Reston, VA 22091
(703) 620–3660

Higher Education

George Washington University
One Dupont Circle NW
Suite 630
Washington, DC 20036
(202) 296–2597

Information Resources

Syracuse University
School of Education
Huntington Hall
Syracuse, NY 13210
(315) 423–3640

Junior Colleges

University of California at Los Angeles (UCLA)
Math Sciences Bldg., 8118
405 Hilgard Avenue
Los Angeles, CA 90024
(213) 825–3931

Languages and Linguistics

Center for Applied Linguistics (CAL)
1118 22nd Street NW
Washington, DC 20007
(202) 298–9292

Reading and Communication Skills

National Council of Teachers of English (NCTE)
1111 Kenyon Road
Urbana, IL 61801
(217) 328–3870

Rural Education and Small Schools

New Mexico State University
Box 3AP
Las Cruces, NM 88003
(505) 646–2623

Science, Mathematics and Environmental Education

Ohio State University
1200 Chambers Road, Room 310
Columbus, OH 43212
(614) 422–6717

Social Studies/Social Science Education

Social Studies Development Center
Indiana University
2805 E. 10th Street
Bloomington, IN 47405
(812) 335–3838

Teacher Education

American Assn. of Colleges for Teacher Education
    (AACTE)
One Dupont Circle NW
Suite 610
Washington, DC 20036
(202) 293–2450

Tests, Measurement and Evaluation

Educational Testing Service (ETS)
Rosedale Road
Princeton, NJ 08541
(609) 734–5181

Urban Education

Teachers College
Columbia University
Institute for Urban and Minority Education
Box 40
525 West 120th Street
New York, NY 10027
(212) 678–3433

SOURCE: From the *Directory of Institutional Projects* (1986), Washington, DC: U.S. Department of Education.

————————APPENDIX C————————
Professional Associations for Teachers

There are hundreds of associations whose purpose it is to help teachers and to improve education. This appendix lists the names and addresses of several major associations. Although most of these are supported by membership dues, students and nonmembers can obtain information upon request. Many have reduced membership fees for university students who are in the process of learning to teach.

American Council on the Teaching of Foreign Languages (ACTFL)

579 Broadway
Hastings-on-Hudson, NY 10706
(914) 478–2011

Teachers, program directors, and organizations involved in classical and modern foreign language instruction at all levels of education.

Association for Education Communications and Technology (AECT)

1126 16th Street NW
Washington, DC 20036
(202) 466–4780

Professional organization for persons interested in instructional technology; contains nine specific area divisions. Educational affiliates: Association for Special Education Technology, Community College Association for Instruction and Technology, Health Education Media Association, International Visual Literacy Association, Women in Instructional Technology, Minorities in Media, and Consortium of University Film Centers.

American Educational Research Association (AERA)

1230 17th Street NW
Washington, DC 20036
(202) 233–9485

Professional organization for education researchers; membership is divided among eleven divisions, each specific to a field of education research.

American Federation of Teachers (AFT)

555 New Jersey Avenue NW
Washington, DC 20001
(202) 879–4400

Professional union comprising teachers and nonsupervisory school personnel. AFT supports a wide variety of research and development projects on in-service teacher training for professional development and instructional improvement.

American Home Economics Association (AHEA)

2010 Massachusetts Avenue NW
Washington, DC 20036
(218) 726–7983

Professional organization for all persons involved in home economics and home economics education.

Association for Supervision and Curriculum Development (ASCD)

225 N. Washington Street
Alexandria, VA 22039
(703) 549–9110

Professional organization of school principals, curriculum directors, administrators, and teachers at the elementary, secondary, and university levels involved in curriculum development, supervision, and instruction, and interested in leadership development.

International Reading Association (IRA)

P.O. Box 8139
800 Barksdale Road
Newark, DE 19714–8139
(302) 731–1600

Professional organization for teachers and administrators of reading programs at all educational levels and for teacher educators.

Journalism Education Association (JEA)

Box 99
Blue Springs, MO 64015
(816) 229–1666

Professional organization for secondary school journalism teachers and publications directors and for educators of journalism teachers.

Music Teachers National Association (MTNA)

2113 Carew Tower
Cincinnati, OH 45202
(513) 421–1420

Professional society of music teachers in elementary, secondary, and university public and private schools and studios.

National Art Education Association (NAEA)

1916 Association Drive
Reston, VA 22091
(703) 860–8000

Professional organization for teachers of art at all school levels; also member institutions: museums, libraries, and colleges.

National Council for the Social Studies (NCSS)

3501 Newark Street NW
Washington, DC 20016
(202) 966–7840

Professional organization for teachers of social studies: anthropology, civics, economics, geography, history, political science, psychology, and sociology.

National Council of Teachers of English (NCTE)

1111 Kenyon Road
Urbana, IL 61801
(217) 328–3870

Professional organization for teachers of English at all educational levels and for professors of English education and administrators of language arts programs. Affiliated organizations: Conference on College Composition and Communication, Conference on Secondary School English Education, Conference for Secondary School English Department Chairs.

National Council of Teachers of Mathematics (NCTM)

1906 Association Drive
Reston, VA 22091
(703) 620–9840

Professional organization for teachers of mathematics K–12 and in two-year colleges and for educators of mathematics teachers.

National Education Association, Division of Instruction and Professional Development (NEA/IPD)

1201 16th Street NW
Washington, DC 20036
(202) 822–7370

NEA is a 1.7 million member teachers' union. Many special interest divisions conduct programs in teacher education, however the IPD division is most strongly dedicated to that area.

National Science Teachers Association (NSTA)

1742 Connecticut Avenue NW
Washington, DC 20009
(202) 328–5810

Professional organization for science educators at all educational levels.

National Vocational Agricultural Teachers' Association (NVATA)

P.O. Box 15051
Alexandria, VA 22309
(703) 780–1862

Professional organization for secondary, post-secondary and adult education teachers of vocational agriculture and teacher education personnel.

Phi Delta Kappa (PDK)

Eighth and Union
P.O. Box 789
Bloomington, IN 47402
(812) 339–1156

Professional organization expanded from an honorary fraternity for educators at all levels.

Teachers of English to Speakers of Other Languages (TESOL)

201 DC Transit Building
Georgetown University
Washington, DC 20057
(202) 625–4569

Professional organization for teachers of English as a second language at all levels. Organization has developed teacher certification standards adopted by state education agencies.

SOURCE: From the *Directory of Organizations Related to Teacher Education* (1986), Washington, DC: ERIC Clearinghouse on Teacher Education.

APPENDIX D
Stage and Territorial Agencies and Departments of Education Handling Matters of Certification and Professional Development

Currently certification in the United States is regulated by state governments. Here are addresses of the units in each state responsible for certification and professional development matters. Information about specific requirements can be obtained by writing to these units.

Alabama State Department of Education
State Office Building
Montgomery, AL 36130

Alaska Department of Education
Professional Teaching Practices Commission
650 W. International Airport Road
Anchorage, AK 99502

Arizona Department of Education
1535 West Jefferson
Phoenix, AZ 85007

Arkansas Department of Education
Teacher Education and Certification
State Education Building
4 Capitol Mall, Room 107B
Little Rock, AR 72201

California Commission on Teacher Credentialing
1020 O Street, Room 222
Sacramento, CA 95814

Colorado Commission on Teacher Education and
Certification
Colorado Department of Education
303 W. Colfax Avenue
Denver, CO 80204

Connecticut State Department of Education
P.O. Box 2219, Room 375
Hartford, CT 06145

State Department of Public Instruction
Certification and Personnel Division
P.O. Box 1402, Townsend Building
Dover, DE 19903

Office of Teacher Certification
415 12th Street NW
Washington, DC 20004

Florida State Department of Education
Office of Teacher Education, Certification and
Staff Development
G–20 Collins Building
Tallahassee, FL 32301

Georgia Department of Education
Division of Staff Development
1858 Twin Towers East
Atlanta, GA 30334

Hawaii Department of Education
Office of Personnel Services
P.O. Box 2360
Honolulu, HI 96804

Idaho State Department of Education
Jordan Office Building
Boise, ID 83720

Illinois Office of Education
100 N. First Street
Springfield, IL 62777

Indiana Department of Public Instruction
Teacher Education and Certification
State House, Room 229
Indianapolis, IN 46204

Iowa Department of Public Instruction
Grimes State Office Building
Des Moines, IA 50319

Kansas State Department of Education
Teacher Education and Certification
120 E. 10th Street
Topeka, KS 66612

Department of Education
Capitol Plaza Tower, 18th Floor
Frankfort, KY 40601

Louisiana Department of Education
Bureau of Higher Education and Teacher
  Certification
P.O. Box 94064
Baton Rouge, LA 70804–9064

Maine Department of Educational and Cultural
  Services
State House, Station 23
Augusta, ME 04333

Maryland State Department of Education
200 W. Baltimore Street
Baltimore, MD 21201

Massachusetts Department of Education
1385 Hancock Street
Quincy, MA 02169

Michigan Department of Education
P.O. Box 30008
Lansing, MI 48909

Minnesota Department of Education
Personnel Licensing and Placement
610 Capitol Square Building
550 Cedar
St. Paul, MN 55101

Mississippi Department of Education
P.O. Box 771
Jackson, MS 39205

Missouri Department of Elementary and
  Secondary Education
P.O. Box 480
Jefferson City, MO 65102

Office of Public Instruction
State Capitol
Helena, MT 59620

Nebraska Department of Education
301 Centennial Mall South
Lincoln, NE 68509

Nevada Department of Education
State Mail Room
Las Vegas, NV 89158

New Hampshire State Department of Education
Office of Teacher Education and Professional
  Standards
101 Pleasant Street
Concord, NH 03301

New Jersey Department of Education
225 West State Street
Trenton, NJ 08625

New Mexico State Department of Education
Education Building
Santa Fe, NM 87501–2786

New York State Department of Education
Cultural Education Center
Room 5A 11
Albany, NY 12230

North Carolina Department of Public
  Instruction
Raleigh, NC 27611

North Dakota Department of Public Instruction
Bismarck, ND 58505

Ohio Department of Education
65 S. Front Street, Room 1012
Columbus, OH 43215

State Department of Education
2500 North Lincoln Blvd.
Oklahoma City, OK 73105

Teacher Standards and Practices Commission
730 12th Street SE
Salem, OR 97310

Pennsylvania Department of Education
333 Market Street
Harrisburg, PA 17108

Department of Education
22 Hayes Street
Providence, RI 02908

South Carolina Department of Education
1004 Rutledge Building
1429 Senate Street
Columbia, SC 29201

South Dakota Department of Education and
    Cultural Affairs
Division of Education
700 N. Illinois
Pierre, SD 57501–2288

Tennessee State Department of Education
125 Cordell Hull Building
Nashville, TN 37219

Texas Education Agency
201 E. 11th Street
Austin, TX 78701

Utah State Office of Education
250 E. 500 South
Salt Lake City, UT 84111

Vermont State Department of Education
Educational Resources
120 State Street
Montpelier, VT 05602

Virginia Department of Education
P.O. Box 6–Q
Richmond, VA 23216–2060

Washington Department of Public Instruction
Old Capitol Complex
Olympia, WA 98504

Department of Education
B–304 Capitol Complex
Charleston, WV 25305

Wisconsin Department of Education
Bureau of Teacher Education, Certification and
    Placement
125 S. Webster Street
P.O. Box 7841
Madison, WI 53707

Wyoming State Department of Education
Certification and Accreditation Services Unit
Hathaway Building
Cheyenne, WY 82001

Department of Education
American Samoa 96799

Department of Education
P.O. Box DE
Agana, Guam 96910

Department of Education
Saipan, CM 96950

Commonwealth Department of Education
P.O. Box 759, Hato Rey
Puerto Rico 00919

SOURCE: From the *Directory of Organizations Related to Teacher Education* (1986), Washington, DC: ERIC Clearinghouse
on Teacher Education.

References for *Learning to Teach*

Adams, R. S., and Biddle, B. J. (1970). *Realities of teaching: Explorations with videotape*. New York: Holt, Rinehart and Winston.

Air force's B-1 bomber. *Washington Post*, August 18, 1985.

Allport, F. (1924). *Social psychology*, Boston: Houghton Mifflin.

Allport, G. (1954). *The nature of prejudice*. Cambridge, Mass.: Addison-Wesley.

Alschuler, A. S., et al. (1984). *Teacher burnout*. Washington, D.C.: National Education Association.

Alschuler, A. S., Tabor, D., and McIntyre, J. (1970). *Teaching achievement motivation: Theory and pratice in psychologial education*. Middletown, Conn.: Education Ventures.

A nation prepared: Teachers for the twenty-first century. (1986). New York: Carnegie Corporation.

Anderson, R. C., and Pearson, P. D. (1984). A schema-theoretic view of basic processes in reading. In P. D. Pearson (Ed.). *Handbook of reading research*. New York: Longman.

Andre, M. E. D., and Anderson, T. H. (1978–1979). The development and evaluation of a self-questioning study technique. *Reading Research Quarterly, 14*, 605–623.

Arends, R. I. (1979). *Evaluation of Secondary Teacher Education Graduates*. (Mimeographed). Eugene, Ore.: University of Oregon.

Arends, R. I. (1983). Beginning teachers as learners. *Journal of Educational Research, 76*, 235–242.

Arends, R. I., and Arends, J. (1977). *Systems change in educational settings*. New York: Human Sciences Press.

Arends, R. I., Schmuck, R. A., Milleman, M., Arends, J., and Wiseman, J. (1981). *School life and organizational psychology*. New York: Teachers College Press.

Arends, R. I., Schmuck, R. A., Milleman, M., Arends, J., and Wiseman, J. (1981). *Teacher handbook for school life and organizational psychology*. New York: Teachers College Press.

Argyris, C. (1970). *Intervention theory and method*. Reading, Mass.: Addison-Wesley.

Argyris, C., Putnam, R., and Smith, D. M. (1985). *Action science*. San Francisco: Jossey-Bass.

Aronson, E., Blaney, S. C., Sikes, J., and Snapp, M. (1978). *The jigsaw classroom*. Beverly Hills, Calif.: Sage Publications.

Atkinson, J. W. (Ed.). (1958). *Motives in fantasy, action and society*. New York: Van Nostrand.

Atkinson, J., and Feather, N. (1966). *A theory of achievement motivation*. New York: John Wiley.

Ausubel, D. P. (1960). The use of advance organizers in the learning and retention of meaningful verbal material. *Journal of Educational Psychology, 51,* 267–272.

Ausubel, D. P. (1963). *The psychology of meaningful verbal learning.* New York: Grune and Stratton.

Ausubel, D., Novak, J., and Hanesian, H. (1978). *Educational psychology: A cognitive view.* New York: Holt, Rinehart and Winston.

Bandura, A. (1977). *Social learning theory.* Englewood Cliffs, N.J.: Prentice–Hall.

Barker, R. G. (1968). *Ecological psychology.* Stanford, Calif.: Stanford University Press.

Beeson, G. W. (1981). Influence of knowledge context on the learning of intellectual skills. *American Educational Research Journal, 18,* 363–379.

Belcher, V. (1981). Mental imagery in basal manuals. (Mimeographed). College Park, Md.: Reading Center, University of Maryland.

Berliner, D. C. (1982a). Recognizing instructional variables. In D. E. Orlosky (Ed.), *Introduction to education.* Columbus: Charles E. Merrill.

Berliner, D. C. (1982b). *The executive functions of teaching.* Paper presented at Wingspread Conference on Relating Reading Research to Classroom Instruction, Racine, Wisc.

Berman, P., and McLaughlin, M. W. (1975). *Federal programs supporting education change, vol. IV: The findings in review.* Santa Monica, Calif.: Rand Corporation.

Bettencourt, E. M. (1979). *Effects of training teachers in enthusiasm on student achievement and attitudes.* (Doctoral dissertation). University of Oregon.

Biklen, D. (1985). *Achieving the complete school.* New York: Teachers College Press.

Block, J. H., and Anderson, L. W. (1975). *Mastery learning in classroom instruction.* New York: Macmillan.

Bloom, B. S., et al. (Eds.). (1956). *Taxonomy of educational objectives, handbook I: Cognitive domain.* New York: David McKay.

Bloom, B. S., Hastings, T. J., and Madaus, G. F. (1971). *Handbook on formative and summative evaluation of student learning.* New York: McGraw-Hill.

Bluestein, J. (1982). *The beginning teacher's resource handbook.* Albuquerque, N.M.: Instructional Support Services.

Bolton, N. (1977). *Concept formation.* Oxford: Pergamon Press.

Borg, W. R., and Gall, M. D. (1983). *Educational research: An introduction,* 4th ed. New York: Longman.

Borko, H., and Niles, J. A. (1987). Descriptions of teacher planning: Ideas for teachers and researchers. In V. Richardson-Koehler (Ed.), *Educators' Handbook: A Research Perspective.* New York: Longman.

Boyer, E. L. (1983). *High school: A report on secondary education in America.* New York: Harper and Row.

Bramson, R. M. (1981). *Coping with difficult people.* New York: Random House.

Brenton, Myron. (1970). *What's happened to teacher?* New York: Coward-McCann.

Brookover, W., Beady, C., Flood, P., Schweitzer, J., and Wisenbaker, J. (1979). *School social systems and student achievement: Schools can make a difference.* New York: Praeger.

Brophy, J. E. (1980). *Recent research on teaching.* East Lansing, Mich.: Institute for Research on Teaching, Michigan State University.

Brophy, J. E. (1981). Teacher praise: A functional analysis. *Review of Educational Research,* Spring, 5–32.

Brophy, J. E. (1982). Supplemental group management techniques. In D. Duke (Ed.), *Helping teachers manage classrooms.* Alexandria, Va.: Association for Supervision and Curriculum Development.

Brophy, J. E. (1983). Classroom organization and management. *The Elementary School Journal, 83,* 265–286.

Brophy, J. E., and Good, T. L. (1986). Teacher behavior and student achievement. In M. C. Wittrock (Ed.), *Handbook of research on teaching,* 3rd ed. New York: Macmillan.

Brophy, J. E., and Putnam, J. (1979). Classroom management in the early grades. In D. L. Duke (Ed.), *Classroom management.* Chicago, University of Chicago Press.

Brown, A. (1980). Metacognitive development and reading. In R. J. Sprio, B. Bruce, and W. F. Brewer, (Eds.), *Theoretical issues in reading comprehension.* Hillsdale, N.J.: Lawrence Erlbaum.

Bruner, J. (1960). *The process of education.* Cambridge: Harvard University Press.

Bruner, J. (1962). *On knowing: Essays for the left hand.* Cambridge: Harvard University Press.

Bruner, J. (1966). *Toward a theory of instruction.* Cambridge: Harvard University Press.

Bruner, J., Goodow, J., and Austin, G. (1956). *A study of thinking.* New York: John Wiley.

Bulletin of information. (1984). Princeton, N.J.: Educational Testing Service.

Calderhead, J. (1981). A psychological approach to research on teacher's classroom decision making. *British Educational Research Journal, 7,* 51–57.

Canter, L., and Canter, D. M. (1976). *Assertive discipline.* Los Angeles: Canter and Associates.

Carroll, J. B. (1963). A model of school learning. *Teachers College Record, 64,* 723–733.

Charters, W. W., Jr., and Gage, N. L. (1963). *Readings in the social psychology of education.* Boston: Allyn and Bacon.

Clark, C. M., and Lampert, M. (1986). The study of teacher thinking: Implications for teacher education. *Journal of Teacher Education, 37,* 27–31.

Clark, C. M., and Yinger, R. J. (1979). *Three studies of teacher planning.* East Lansing, Mich.: Institute for Research on Teaching, Michigan State University.

Clark, D. L., et al. (1980). *New perspectives on planning in educational organizations.* San Francisco: Far West Laboratory for Educational Research and Development.

Clark, D. L., McKibbin, S., and Malkas, M. (1981). *Alternative perspectives for viewing educational organizations.* San Francisco: Far West Laboratory for Educational Research and Development.

Clements, D. H. (1985). *Computers in early and primary education.* Englewood Cliffs, N.J.: Prentice-Hall.

Coats, E., and Smidchens, V. (1966). Audience recall as a function of speaker dynamisim. *Journal of Educational Psychology, 57,* 189–191.

Coleman, J. (1960). The adolescent subculture and academic achievement. *American Journal of Sociology, 65,* 337–347.

Coleman, J. (1961). *The adolescent society.* New York: Free Press.

Coleman, J. (1972). The children have outgrown the schools. *Psychology Today,* February, 72–82.

Coleman, J., et al. (1966). *Equality of educational opportunity.* Washington, D.C.: U.S. Government Printing Office.

Collins, A. M., and Quillian, M. R. (1969). Retrieval time from semantic memory. *Journal of Verbal Learning and Verbal Behavior, 8,* 240–247.

Collins, B. E., and Raven, E. E. (1954). Group structure: Attractions, coalitions, communication, and power. In G. Lindzey, and E. Aronson (Eds.), *The handbook of social psychology,* (2nd ed.), vol. 4. Reading, Mass.: Addison-Wesley.

Collins, M. L. (1978). Effects of enthusiasm training on preservice elementary teachers. *Journal of Teacher Education, 29,* 53–57.

Combs, A. W. (1965). *The professional education of teachers*. Boston: Allyn and Bacon.

Combs, A. W. (1982). *A personal approach to teaching: Beliefs that make a difference*. Boston: Allyn and Bacon.

Cooper, J. M. (Ed.). (1986). *Classroom teaching skills*, 3rd ed., Lexington, Mass.: D. C. Heath.

Copeland, W. D. (1980). Teaching-learning behaviors and the demands of the classroom environment. *Elementary School Journal, 80,* 163–177.

Culbertson, J. A., and Cunningham, L. L. (Eds.). (1986). *Microcomputers and education*. Chicago: University of Chicago Press.

Cypher, T., and Willower, D. J. (1984). The work behavior of secondary school teachers. *Journal of Research and Development, 18,* 17–24.

Dalin, Per. (1978). *Limits to educational change*. London: Macmillan.

Dashiell, F. F. (1935). Experimental studies of the influence of social situations on the behavior of individual adults. In C. Murchison (Ed.), *A handbook of social psychology*. Worcester, Mass.: Clark University Press.

Davey, B., and Porter, S. M. (1982). Comprehension-rating: A procedure to assist poor comprehenders. *Journal of Reading, 26,* 197–202.

Davidson, N. (Ed.). (in press). *Small group cooperative learning in mathematics: A handbook for teaching*. Reading, Mass.: Addison Wesley.

Denham, C., and Lieberman, A. (Eds.). (1980). *Time to learn*. Washington, D.C.: U.S. Department of Education.

Dewey, J. (1916). *Democracy and education*. New York: Macmillan.

Dewey, J. (1929). *The quest for certainty*. New York: Minton, Balch.

Dewey, J. (1933). *How we think*, rev. ed., Lexington, Mass.: D. C. Heath.

Dewey, J. (1938). *Experience and education*. New York: Macmillan.

Doyle, W. (1979). Classroom tasks and students' abilities. In P. L. Peterson and H. J. Walberg. (Eds.), *Research on teaching: Concepts, findings and implications*. Berkeley, Calif.: McCutchan.

Doyle, W. (1980). *Classroom management*. West Lafayette, Ind.: Kappa Delta Pi.

Doyle, W. (1986). Classroom organization and management. In M. C. Wittrock (Ed.), *Handbook of research on teaching*, 3rd ed. New York: Macmillan.

Doyle, W., and Carter, K. (1984). Academic tasks in classrooms. *Curriculum Inquiry, 14,* 129–149.

Doyle, W., and Good, T. L. (1982). *Focus on teaching: Readings from the Elementary School Journal*. Chicago: University of Chicago Press.

Dreher, M. J., and Gambrell, L. B. (1985). Teaching children to use a self-questioning strategy for studying expository prose. *Reading Improvement, 22,* 2–7.

Dreikurs, R. (1968). *Psychology in the classroom: A manual for teachers*, 2nd ed. New York: Harper and Row.

Dreikurs, R., and Grey, L. (1968). *A new approach to discipline: Logical consequences*. New York: Hawthorne Books.

Duchastel, P. C., and Brown, B. R. (1974). Incidental and relevant learning with instructional objectives. *Journal of Educational Psychology, 66,* 481–485.

Duke, D. (Ed.). (1979). *Classroom management*. Chicago: University of Chicago Press.

Duke, D. (Ed.). (1982). *Helping teachers manage classrooms*. Alexandria, Va.: Association for Supervision and Curriculum Development.

Duke, D., and Meckel, A. M. (1980). *Managing student behavior problems*. New York: Teachers College Press.

Dunkin, M. J., and Biddle, B. J. (1974). *The study of teaching*. New York: Holt, Rinehart and Winston.

Durkin, D. (1978–1979). What classroom observations reveal about reading comprehension instruction. *Reading Research Quarterly, 14,* 481–533.

Education that is multicultural: A curriculum infusion model. (1981). College Park, Md.: University of Maryland/Charles County Teacher Corps Project.

Egan, G. (1974). *The skilled helper: A model for systematic helping and interpersonal relationships.* Monterey, Calif.: Brooks/Cole.

Emmer, E. T., Evertson, C. M., and Anderson, L. M. (1980). Effective classroom management at the beginning of the school year. *The Elementary School Journal, 80,* 219–231.

Emmer, E. T., Evertson, C., Sanford, J., and Clements, B. S. (1982). *Improving classroom management: An experimental study in junior high school classrooms.* Austin, Tex.: Research and Development Center for Teacher Education, University of Texas.

Emmer, E. T., Evertson, C. M., Sanford, J. P., Clements, B. S., and Worsham, W. E. (1984). *Classroom management for secondary teachers.* Englewood Cliffs, N.J.: Prentice-Hall.

Evertson, C. M., and Emmer, E. T. (1982). Preventive classroom management. In Duke, D. (Ed.). *Helping teachers manage classrooms.* Alexandria, Va.: Association for Supervision and Curriculum Development.

Evertson, E., Emmer, E., Clements, B., Sanford, J., and Worsham, M. (1984). *Classroom management for elementary teachers.* Englewood Cliffs, N.J.: Prentice-Hall.

Evertson, C. M., Emmer, E. T., Sanford, J. P., and Clements, B. S. (1983). Improving classroom management: An experiment in elementary classrooms. *Elementary School Journal, 84,* 173–188.

Feiman-Nemser, S. (1983). Learning to teach. In L. S. Shulman and G. Sykes (Eds.), *Handbook of teaching and policy.* New York: Longman.

Feiman-Nemser, S., and Floden, R. E. (1986). In M. C. Wittrock (Ed.), *Handbook of research on teaching*, 3rd ed. New York: Macmillan.

Feitler, F., Weiner, W., and Blumberg, A. (1970). *The relationship between interpersonal relations orientations and preferred classroom physical settings.* Paper presented at the annual meeting of the American Educational Research Association, Minneapolis. (ERIC No. ED 039).

Fenstermacher, G. D., and Soltis, J. F. (1986). *Approaches to teaching.* New York: Teachers College Press.

Fisher, C. W., Berliner, D., Filby, N., Marliave, R., Cahen, L., Dishaw, M. (1980). Teaching behavior, academic learning time, and student achievement: An overview. In C. Denham and A. Lieberman (Eds.). *Time to learn.* Washington, D.C.: National Institute of Education, Department of Education, pp. 7–32.

Floyd, W. D. (1960). *An analysis of the oral questioning activity in selected Colorado primary classrooms.* (Doctoral dissertation). Colorado State College.

Ford, G. W., and Pugno, L. (Eds.). (1964). *The structure of knowledge and the curriculum.* Chicago: Rand McNally.

Fosmire, F., and Wallen, R. (1971). *STP problem solving.* (Mimeographed). Eugene, Ore.: University of Oregon.

Fox, R., Luszki, M., and Schmuck, R. (1966). *Diagnosing classroom learning environments.* Chicago: Science Research Associates.

Freeman, D., Kuhs, T., Porter, A., Knappen, L., Floden, R., Schmidt, W., Schwille, J.

(1980). *The fourth grade mathematics curriculum as inferred from textbooks and tests.* East Lansing, Mich.: Institute for Research on Teaching, Michigan State University. Research Series #82.

Freiberg, H. J., Cooper, J. M., and Ryan, K. (1980). *Those who can, teach: Learning guide.* Boston: Houghton Mifflin.

French, J. R. P., and Raven, B. H. (1959). The bases of social power. In D. Cartwright (Ed.), *Studies in social power.* Ann Arbor: University of Michigan Press.

Friedman, W. J. (1980). *The development of relational understanding of temporal and spatial terms.* (ERIC No. ED 178 176: Resources in Education).

Fuchs, E. (1969). *Teachers talk: View from inside city schools.* New York: Doubleday.

Fullan, M. (1982). *The meaning of educational change.* New York: Teachers College Press.

Fuller, F. (1969). Concerns of teachers: A developmental conceptualization. *American Educational Research Journal, 6,* 207–226.

Gage, N. L. (1978). *The scientific basis of the art of teaching.* New York: Teachers College Press.

Gage, N. L. (1984). *An update of the scientific basis of the art of teaching.* (Mimeographed). Palo Alto, Calif.: Stanford University.

Gagné, E. D. (1985). *The cognitive psychology of school learning.* Boston: Little, Brown.

Gagné, R. M. (1977). *The conditions of learning and theory of instruction.* (Third edition). New York: Holt, Rinehart and Winston.

Gagné, R. M. (1985). *The conditions of learning and theory of instruction,* 4th ed. New York: Holt, Rinehart and Winston.

Gagné, R. M., and Briggs, L. J. (1979). *Principles of instructional design.* New York: Holt, Rinehart and Winston.

Gagné, R. M., and White, R. (1978). Memory structures and learning outcomes. *Review of Educational Research, 48*(2), 187–222.

Gall, M. D. (1970). The use of questions in teaching. *Review of Educational Research, 40,* 707–721.

Gall, M. D., Dunning, B., and Weathersby, R. (1971). *Higher cognitive questioning: Teachers handbook.* Beverly Hills, Calif.: Macmillan Educational Services.

Gambrell, L. B., and Bales, R. J. (1986). Mental imagery and the comprehension monitoring performance of fourth and fifth grade poor readers. *Reading Research Quarterly, 21,* 454–464.

Garner, R. (1987). *Metacognition and reading comprehension.* Norwood, N.J.: Ablex.

Getzels, J. W., and Thelen, H. A. (1960). The classroom group as a unique social system. In N. Henry (Ed.), *The dynamics of instructional groups.* Chicago: National Society for the Study of Education, 59th Yearbook, Part 2.

Glass, G. (1981). *Effectiveness of special education.* Paper presented at Wingspread Conference, Racine, Wisc.

Glass, G., Cahen, L., Smith, M. L., and Filby, N. (1982). *School class size—Research and policy.* Beverly Hills, Calif.: Sage.

Glasser, W. (1969). *Schools without failure.* New York: Harper and Row.

Glasser, W. (1986). *Control theory in the classroom.* New York: Harper and Row.

Good, T. L., and Brophy, J. E. (1987). *Looking in classrooms,* 4th ed. New York: Harper and Row.

Good, T. L., and Grouws, D. A. (1979). The Missouri mathematics effectiveness project: An experimental study in fourth-grade classrooms. *Journal of Educational Psychology, 71,* 355–362.

Good, T. L., Grouws, D. A., and Ebmeier, H. (1983). *Active mathematics teaching*. New York: Longman.

Goodlad, J. (1975). *The dynamics of educational change*. New York: McGraw-Hill.

Goodlad, J. (1984). *A place called school: Prospects for the future*. New York: McGraw-Hill.

Goodlad, J., and Klein, M. (1970). *Behind the classroom door*. Worthington, Ohio: Charles A. Jones.

Gordon, T. (1974). *Teacher effectiveness training*. New York: Peter H. Wyden.

Grady, M. T., and Gawronski, J. D. (Eds.). (1983). *Computers in curriculum and instruction*. Alexandria, Va.: Association for Supervision and Curriculum Development.

Griffin, G. (1986). Clinical teacher education. In J. V. Hoffman and S. A. Edwards (Eds.), *Reality and reform in clinical teacher education*. New York: Random House.

Griffin, G. (Ed.). (1983). *Staff development*. Chicago: University of Chicago Press.

Gump, P. V. (1967). *The classroom behavior setting: Its nature and relation to student behavior*. Washington, D.C.: U.S. Office of Education.

Gump, P. V. (1982). School settings and their keeping. In D. L. Duke (Ed.), *Helping teachers manage classrooms*. Alexandria, Va.: Association for Supervision and Curriculum Development.

Hall, G. E., and Loucks, S. F. (1977). A developmental model for determining whether the treatment is actually implemented. *American Educational Research Journal, 14,* 263–276.

Hall, G. E., Wallace, A. C., and Dossett, W. A. (1973). *A developmental conceptualization of the adoption process within educational institutions*. Austin, Tex. Research and Development Center for Teacher Education, University of Texas.

Harnischseger, A., and Willey, D. (1978). Model of school learning. *Journal of Curriculum Studies, 10,* 214–220.

Hawk, P. (1986). Using graphic organizers to increase achievement in middle school life science. *Science Education, 70,* 81–87.

Hersh, R. (1982). *What makes some schools and teachers effective?* Eugene, Ore.: Center for Educational Policy and Management, University of Oregon.

Hiller, J. H., Gisher, G. A., and Kaess, W. (1969). A computer investigation of verbal characteristics of effective classroom lecturing. *American Educational Research Journal, 6,* 661–675.

Hodgkinson, H. L. (1983). Guess who's coming to college? *Higher Education, 17,* 281–287.

Horowitz, P., and Otto, D. (1973). *The teaching effectiveness of an alternative teaching facility*. Alberta, Canada. (ERIC No. ED 083 242).

Housner, L. D., and Griffey, D. C. (1985). Teacher cognition: Differences in planning and interactive decision making between experienced and inexperienced teachers. *Research Quarterly for Exercise and Sport, 56,* 45–53.

Hoy, Wayne, K. (1968). The influence of experience on the beginning teacher. *School Review, 76,* 312–323.

Hunt, D. (1970). A conceptual level matching model for coordinating learner characteristics with educational approaches. *Interchange: A Journal of Educational Studies, 1,*2–16.

Hunt, D. (1974). *Matching models in education*. Toronto: Ontario Institute for Studies in Education.

Hunter, M. C. (1976). *Improved instruction*. El Segundo, Calif.: TIP Publications.

Hunter, M. C. (1982). *Mastery teaching*. El Segundo, Calif.: TIP Publications.

Hunter, M. C. (1987). Beyond rereading Dewey: What's next? A response of Gibboney. *Educational Leadership, 44,* 51–53.

Isaacson, N. S. (1981). *Secondary teachers' perceptions of personal and organizational support during induction to teaching.* (Doctoral dissertation). University of Oregon.

Jackson, P. W. (1968). *Life in classrooms.* New York: Holt, Rinehart and Winston.

Jackson, P. W. (1986). *The practice of teaching.* New York: Teachers College Press.

Jantz, R., and Klawitter, K. (in press). The effectives of instruction on the learning of social studies concepts by fourth graders. *Journal of Instructional Psychology.*

Jencks, C., et al. (1972). *Inequality: A reassessment of the effect of family and schooling in America.* New York: Basic Books.

Johnson, D. W., and Johnson, F. P. (1975). *Joining together: Group theory and group skills.* Englewood Cliffs, N.J.: Prentice-Hall.

Johnson, D. W., and Johnson, R. T. (1975). *Learning together and alone: Cooperation, competition, and individualization.* Englewood Cliffs, N.J.: Prentice-Hall.

Johnson, R., Rynders, J., Johnson, D. W., Schmidt, B., and Haider, S. (1979). Interaction between handicapped and nonhandicapped teenagers as a function of situational goal structuring: Implications for mainstreaming. *American Educational Research Journal, 16,* 161–167.

Jones, B. F. (1985). *Student cognitive processing of text-based instruction: An interaction of the reader, the text and the teacher.* Paper presented at the annual meeting of the American Educational Research Association, Chicago.

Joyce, B., and Hartoonian, B. (1964). Teaching as problem solving. *Journal of Teacher Education, 15,* 420–427.

Joyce, B., Hersh, R., and McKibbin, M. (1983). *The structure of school improvement.* New York: Longman.

Joyce, B., and Weil, M. (1986). *Models of teaching,* 3rd ed. Englewood Cliffs, N.J.: Prentice-Hall.

Jung, C. (1972). Listening effectively. (Mimeographed). Portland, Ore.: Northwest Regional Educational Laboratory.

Kagen, S. (1985). *Cooperative learning: Resources for teachers.* Riverside, Calif.: University of California.

Kallen, H. M. (1924). *Culture and democracy in the United States.* New York: Boni and Liveright.

Katzer, J., Cook, K. H., and Crouch, W. W. (1982). *Evaluating information: A guide for users of social science research,* 2nd ed. Reading, Mass.: Addison-Wesley.

Kennedy, J. J., Bush, A. J., Cruickshank, D. R., and Haefele, D. (1978). *Additional investigations into the nature of teacher clarity.* Paper presented at annual meeting of American Educational Research Association, Toronto.

Kerlinger, F. N. (1964). *Foundations of Behavioral Research.* New York: Holt, Rinehart and Winston.

Klausmeier, H. (1980). *Learning and teaching concepts.* New York: Academic Press.

Kounin, J. S. (197?). *Discipline and group management in classrooms.* New York: Holt, Rinehart and Winston.

Krantz, P., and Risley, T. (1972). *The organization of group care environments: Behavioral ecology in the classroom.* Lawrence, Kan.: Kansas University. (ERIC No. ED 078 915).

Krug, M. (1976). *The melting of the ethnics.* Bloomington, Inc.: Phi Delta Kappa.

Kyzar, B. L. (1977). Noise pollution and schools: How much is too much? *CEFP Journal, 4,* 10–11.

Lacey, C. (1977). *The socialization of teachers.* London: Methuen.

Lakein, A. (1973). *How to get control of your time and your life.* New York: David McKay.

Lard, M., and Smith, L. (1979). *Low inference teacher clarity variables: Effects on student achievement*. Paper presented at the annual meeting of American Educational Research Association, San Francisco.

Lawton, J. T., and Wauska, S. K. (1979). The effects of different types of advance organizers on classification learning. *American Educational Research Journal, 16,* 223–239.

Leinhardt, G. (in press). Math lessons: A contrast of novice and expert competence. *Journal for Research in Mathematics Education.*

Leinhardt, G., and Greeno, J. (1986). The cognitive skill of teaching. *Journal of Educational Psychology, 78,* 75–95.

Lerup, Lars. (1977). *Building the unfinished: Architecture and human action.* Beverly Hills, Calif.: Sage Publications.

Lewin, K., Lippitt, R., and White, R. (1939). Patterns of aggressive behavior in experimentally created social climates. *Journal of Social Psychology, 10,* 271–299.

Lieberman, A., and Miller, L. (1984). *Teachers, their world, and their work.* Alexandria, Va.: Association of Supervision and Curriculum Development.

Lippitt, R., and White, R. (1963). An experimental study of leadership and group life. In W. W. Charters and N. L. Gage (Eds.), *Readings in the social psychology of education.* Boston: Allyn and Bacon.

Lortie, D. C. (1975). *School-teacher: A sociological study.* Chicago: University of Chicago Press.

Loucks-Horsley, S., and Hergert, L. F. (1985). *An action guide to school improvement.* Alexandria, Va.: The Network and Association for Supervision and Curriculum Development.

Louis, M. (1980). Surprise and sense-making: What newcomers experience in entering unfamiliar organizational settings. *Administrative Science Quarterly, 25,* 226–251.

Luft, J. (1970). *Group processes: An introduction to group dynamics.* Palo Alto, Calif.: National Press Books.

Luiten, J., Ames, W., and Aerson, G. (1980). A meta-analysis of advance organizers on learning and retention. *American Educational Research Journal, 17,* 211–218.

Lyman, F. (1983). *Journaling procedures.* (Mimeographed). College Park, Md.: University of Maryland.

Lyman, F. (1985). *Think-Pair-Share.* (Mimeographed). College Park, Md.: University of Maryland.

Lyman, F., Davie, A. R., and Eley, G. (1984). *Action research by student teachers and beginning teachers: An approach to developing problem solving in the classroom.* (Mimeographed). College Park, Md.: University of Maryland.

Lyon, M., and Gettinger, M. (1985). Differences in student performance on knowledge, comprehension, and application tasks: Implications for school learning. *Journal of Educational Psychology, 77,* 12–19.

Maccoby, E., T. Newcomb, and E. Hartley. (1958). *Readings in social psychology,* 3rd ed. New York: Holt, Rinehart and Winston.

Mager, R. F. (1962). *Preparing instructional objectives.* Palo Alto, Calif.: Fearon Publishers.

Mager, R. F. (1984). *Preparing instructional objectives,* 2nd rev. ed. D. S. Lake.

Mann, D. (1981). *Education policy analysis and the rent-a-troika business.* Paper presented at annual meeting of the American Educational Research Association, Los Angeles.

Markle, S. (1985). They teach concepts, don't they? *Educational Researcher, 4,* 3–9.

Martorella, P. H. (1982). Cognition research: Some implications for the design of social studies instructional materials. *Theory and Research in Social Education, 19,* 1–16.

Martorella, P. H. (1985). *Elementary social studies: Developing reflective, competent, and concerned citizens.* Boston: Little, Brown.

McClelland, D. C. (1958). Methods of measuring human motivation. In J. W. Atkinson (Ed.), *Motives in fantasy, action and society.* New York: Van Nostrand.

McClelland, D. C. (1961). *The achieving society.* New York: Van Nostrand.

McClelland, D. C. (1965). Toward a theory of motive acquisition. *American Psychologist, 20,* 321–333.

McDonald, F., and Elias, P. (1980). *Study of induction programs for beginning teachers.* Princeton, N.J.: Educational Testing Services.

McKinney, C., Burts, D., Ford, M., and Gilmore, A. (1985). The effects of the presentation order of examples and nonexamples on first-grade students' acquisition of coordinate concepts. *Journal of Educational Research, 78,* 310–314.

Merrill, M. D., and Tennyson, R. D. (1977). *Teaching concepts: An instructional design guide.* Englewood Cliffs, N.J.: Educational Technology.

Miles, M. B. (1964). (Ed.). *Innovations in education.* New York: Teachers College Press.

Miles, M. B. (1981). *Learning to work in groups,* 2nd ed. New York: Teachers College Press.

Mitzel, H. (1960). Teacher effectiveness. In C. W. Harris. (Ed.), *Encyclopedia of Educational Research,* 3rd ed. New York: Macmillan.

Mosenthal, P. B., Conley, M. W., Colella, A., and Davidson, R. (1985). The influence of prior knowledge and teacher lesson structure on children's production of narratives. *The Elementary School Journal, 85,* 621–633.

Motivation. (1983). *McRel Quality Education Folio.* Kansas City, Mo.: Mid-continent Regional Educational Laboratory.

Moyer, J. R. (1966). *An exploratory study of questioning in the instructional processes in selected elementary schools.* (Doctoral dissertation). Columbia University.

Muir, R. (1980). A teacher implements instructional changes using the BTES framework. In C. Denham and A. Lieberman (Eds.), *Time to learn.* Washington, D.C.: National Institute of Education, Department of Education, 197–209.

Naftulin, D. H., et al. (1973). The doctor fox lecture: A paradigm of educational seduction. *Journal of Medical Education, 48,* 630–635.

Newcomb, T. M. (1961). *The acquaintance process.* New York: Holt, Rinehart and Winston.

Norman, D. A. (1980). Cognitive engineering and education. In D. T. Tuma and F. Reif (Eds.), *Problem solving and education.* Hillsdale, N.J.: Lawrence Erlbaum.

Olshavsky, J. E. (1976–1977). Reading as problem solving: An investigation of strategies. *Reading Research Quarterly, 12,* 654–674.

Orlosky, D. E. (Ed.). (1982). *Introduction to education.* Columbus, Ohio: Charles E. Merrill.

Papert, S. (1980). *Mindstorms: Children, computers, and powerful ideas.* New York: Basic Books.

Paris, S. G. (1986). Teaching children to guide their reading and learning. In T. E. Raphael (Ed.), *The contexts of school-based literacy.* New York: Random House.

Park, Ok-Choon, and Tennyson, R. (1986). Computer-based response-sensitive design strategies for selecting presentation form and sequence of examples in learning of coordinate concepts. *Journal of Educational Psychology, 70,* 153–158.

Peddiwell, J. A. (1939). *The saber-tooth curriculum.* New York: McGraw-Hill.

Perry, W. (1969). *Forms of intellectual and ethical development during the college years.* New York: Holt, Rinehart and Winston.

Peterson, P. L., Marx, R. W., and Clark, C. (1978). Teacher planning, teacher behavior and student achievement. *American Educational Research Journal, 15,* 417–432.

Peterson, P. L., and Walberg, H. J. (Eds.). (1979). *Research on teaching*. Berkeley, Calif.: McCutchan.

Peterson, R. C., and Jacob, S. H. (1978). Evidence for the role of contexts in imagery and recall. *American Journal of Psychology, 91,* 305–311.

Piaget, J. (1963). *Psychology of intelligence*. Paterson, N.J.: Littlefield Adams.

Plisko, V. W., and Stern, J. D. (Eds.). (1985). *The conditions of education*. Washington, D.C.: National Center for Educational Statistics.

Popham, W. J., and Baker, E. I. (1970). *Systematic instruction*. Englewood Cliffs, N.J.: Prentice-Hall.

Posner, G. J., and Rudnitsky, A. N. (1986). *Course design: A guide to curriculum development for teachers,* 3rd ed. New York: Longman.

Preiser, W. (1972). Behavior of nursery school children under different spatial densities. *Man-Environment Systems, 2,* 247–250.

Prescott, E., Jones, E., and Kritchevsky, S. (1967). *Group day care as a child rearing environment: An observational study of day care programs*. (ERIC No. ED 024 453).

Pressley, M. (1976). Mental imagery helps eight-year-olds remember what they read. *Journal of Educational Psychology, 68,* 355–359.

Richardson-Koehler, V. (Ed.). (1987). *Educators' handbook: A research perspective*. New York: Longman.

Roblyer, J. D. (1985). *Measuring the impact of computers in instruction: A non-technical review of research for educators*. Washington, D.C.: AEDS.

Roehler, L. R., and Duffy, G. G. (1984). Direct explanation of comprehension processes. In G. G. Duffy, L. R. Roehler, and J. Mason (Eds.), *Comprehension instruction*. New York: Longman.

Rosenfield, P., Lambert, N., and Black, A. (1985). Desk arrangement effects on pupil classroom behavior. *Journal of Educational Psychology, 77,* 101–108.

Rosenshine, B. (1970). Enthusiastic teaching: A research review. *School Review, 78,* 499–514.

Rosenshine, B. (1971a). Objectively measured behavioral predictors of effectiveness in explaining. In I. D. Westbury and A. A. Bellack (Eds.), *Research into classroom processes*. New York: Teachers College Press.

Rosenshine, B. (1971b). *Teaching behaviors and student achievement*. London: National Foundation for Educational Research.

Rosenshine, B. (1979). Content, time and direct instruction. In P. L. Peterson and H. J. Walberg (Eds.), *Research on teaching*. Berkeley, Calif.: McCutchan.

Rosenshine, B. (1980). How time is spent in elementary classrooms. In C. Denham and A. Lieberman (Eds.). *Time to learn*. Washington, D.C.: U.S. Department of Education.

Rosenshine, B., and Furst, N. (1973). The use of direct observation to study teaching. In R. M. W. Travers (Ed.), *Second handbook of research on teaching*. Chicago: Rand McNally.

Rosenshine, B., and Stephens, R. (1986). Teaching functions. In M. C. Wittrock (Ed.), *Handbook of research on teaching,* 3rd ed. New York: Macmillan.

Rowe, M. B. (1974a). Wait-time and rewards as instructional variables, their influence on language, logic, and fate control: Part 1: Wait time. *Journal of Research in Science Teaching, 11,* 291–308.

Rowe, M. B. (1974b). Relation of wait-time and rewards to the development of language, logic, and fate control: Part 2: Rewards. *Journal of Research in Science Teaching, 11,* 291–308.

Rutter, M., Maughan, B., Mortimore, P., Ouston, J., and Smith, A. (1979). *Fifteen thousand hours: Secondary schools and their effects on children.* Cambridge: Harvard University Press.

Ryan, K. (Ed.). (1970). *Don't smile until Christmas: Accounts of the first year of teaching.* Chicago: University of Chicago Press.

Ryan, K., et al. (1980). *Biting the apple: Accounts of first year teachers.* New York: Longman.

Ryan, K., and Cooper, J. M. (1980). *Those who can, teach,* 3rd ed. Boston: Houghton Mifflin.

Ryle, G. (1949). The concept of mind. London: Hutchinson's University Library.

Sanford, J. P. (1984). Management and organization in science classrooms. *Journal of Research in Science Teaching, 21,* 575–587.

Santrock, J. W. (1976). Affect and facilitative self-control: Influence of ecological setting, cognition, and social agent. *Journal of Educational Psychology, 68,* (5), 529–535.

Sarason, S. (1971). *The culture of school and the problem of change.* Boston: Allyn and Bacon.

Sarason, S. (1982). *The culture of school and the problem of change,* 2nd ed. Boston: Allyn and Bacon.

Schmuck, R. A. (1963). Some relationships of peer liking patterns in the classroom to pupil attitudes and achievement. *School Review, 71,* 337–339.

Schmuck, R. A. (1982). Seeing how teachers fit in. In D. E. Orlosky (Ed.), *Introduction to education.* Columbus, Ohio: Charles E. Merrill.

Schmuck, R. A., and Runkel, P. (1986). *The handbook of organization development in schools,* 3rd ed. Palo Alto, Calif.: Mayfield.

Schmuck, R. A., Runkel, P., Arends, J., and Arends, R. (1977). *The second handbook of organization development in schools.* Palo Alto, Calif.: Mayfield.

Schmuck, R. A., and Schmuck, P. (1975). *A humanistic psychology of education: Making the school everybody's house.* Palo Alto, Calif.: Mayfield.

Schmuck, R. A., and Schmuck, P. (1983). *Group processes in the classroom,* 4th ed. Dubuque, Iowa: William C. Brown.

Schön, D. A. (1983). *The reflective practitioner.* San Francisco: Jossey-Bass.

Schön, D. A. (1986). *Educating the reflective practitioner.* San Francisco: Jossey-Bass.

Schreiber, J. E. (1967). *Teachers' question-asking techniques in social studies.* (Doctoral dissertation). University of Iowa.

Schuck, R. F. (1981). The impact of set induction on student achievement and retention. *Journal of Educational Research, 74,* 227–232.

Schwebel, A., and Cherlin, D. (1972). Physical and social distancing in teacher-pupil relationships. *Journal of Educational Psychology, 63,* 543–550.

Sharon, S., et al. (1984). *Cooperative learning in the classroom: Research in desegregated schools.* Hillsdale, N.J.: Lawrence Erlbaum.

Sharon, S., and Sharon, Y. (1976). *Small group teaching.* Englewood Cliffs, N.J.: Education Technology.

Shaefer, W., and Lissitz, R. (1987). Measurement training for school personnel: Recommendations and Reality. *Journal of Teacher Education, 38,* 57–63.

Shavelson, R. (1976). Teacher decision making. In N. L. Gage (Ed.), *The psychology of teaching method.* Chicago: University of Chicago Press.

Sieber, R. T. (1979). Classmates as workmates: Informal peer activity in the elementary school. *Anthropology and Educational Quarterly, 10,* 207–235.

Silberman, C. (1970). *Crisis in the classroom.* New York: Vintage Books.

Sirotnik, K. (1983). What you see is what you get—Consistency, persistency, and mediocrity in the classroom. *Harvard Educational Review, 53,* 16–31.

Sizer, T. (1984). *Horace's compromise: The dilemma of the American high school.* Boston: Houghton-Mifflin.

Slavin, R. (1980). Effects of individual learning expectations on student achievement. *Journal of Educational Psychology, 72,* 520–524.

Slavin, R. (1983). *Cooperative learning.* New York: Longman.

Slavin, R. (1984). Students motivating students to excell: Incentives, cooperative tasks and student achievement. *The Elementary School Journal, 85,* 53–62.

Slavin, R. (1986). *Using student team learning,* 3rd ed. Baltimore, Md.: Center for Research on Elementary and Middle Schools. Johns Hopkins University.

Slavin, R. E., and Karweit, N. L. (1984). Mastery learning and student teams: A factorial experiment in urban general mathematics classes. *American Educational Research Journal, 21,* 725–736.

Slavin, R., Sharon, S., Kagan, S., Hertz-Lazarowitz, R., Webb, C., and Schmuck, R. (Eds.). (1985). *Learning to cooperate, cooperating to learn.* New York: Plenum Press.

Sprinthall, N., and Thies-Sprinthall, L. (1983). The teacher as an adult learner: A cognitive-developmental view. In G. Griffin (Ed.), *Staff Development.* Chicago: University of Chicago Press.

Stallings, J., and Kaskowitz, D. (1974). *Follow Through classroom observation evaluation 1972–1974.* (SRI Project URU–7370). Stanford, Calif.: Stanford Research Institute.

Starkey, D. (1980). *The origins of concept formation: Object sorting and object preference in early infancy.* (ERIC No. ED 175555: Resources in Education).

Stevens, R. (1912). The question as a measure of efficiency in instruction: A critical study of classroom practice. *Teachers College Contributions to Education,* no. 48. New York: Teachers College, Columbia University.

Taba, H. (1967). *Teachers handbook for elementary social studies.* Palo Alto, Calif.: Addison-Wesley.

Taylor, B., Harris, L., and Pearson, P. D. (1988). *Reading difficulties: Instruction and diagnosis.* New York: Random House.

Taylor, B. L., Sullivan, E. W., and Dollar, B. (1978). *Mapping teacher corps projects: A planning resource book.* New York: Center for Policy Research.

Tenbrink, T. D. (1986). Evaluation. In J. M. Cooper (Ed.), *Classroom teaching skills,* 3rd ed. Lexington, Mass.: D. C. Heath.

Tennyson, R., and Cocchiarella, M. (1986). An empirically based instructional design theory for teaching concepts. *Review of Educational Research, 56,* 40–71.

Thelen, H. A. (1954). *Dynamics of groups at work.* Chicago: University of Chicago Press.

Thelen, H. A. (1960). *Education and the human quest.* New York: Harper and Row.

Time on task. (1982). Alexandria, Va.: American Association of School Administrators.

Timpson, W. M. and Tobin, D. N. (1982). *Teaching as performing.* Englewood Cliffs, N.J.: Prentice-Hall.

Tisher, R. P., et al. (1978). The induction of beginning teachers in Australia. (ERIC No. ED 151 325).

Turkle, S. (1984). *The second self: Computers and the human spirit.* New York: Simon and Schuster.

Tyler, R. W. (1950). *Basic principles of curriculum and instruction.* Chicago: University of Chicago Press.

Virginia Beginning Teacher Assistance Program. (1986). Richmond, Va.: Virginia State Department of Education. (Forthcoming by Allyn and Bacon.)

Walberg, H. J. (1986). Syntheses of research on teaching. In M. C. Wittrock (Ed.), *Handbook of research on teaching*, 3rd ed. New York: Macmillan.

Walberg, H. J., Schiller, D., and Haertel, G. D. (1979). The quiet revolution in educational research. *Phi Delta Kappan, 61,* 179–182.

Walcott, H. (1973). *The man in the principal's office: An ethnography.* New York: Holt, Rinehart and Winston.

Wallen, J. L. (1972). Effective interpersonal communications. In R. Pino, R. Emory, and C. Jung. *Interpersonal communications.* Portland, Ore.: Northwest Regional Educational Laboratory.

Waller, W. (1932). *The sociology of teaching.* New York: Russell and Russell.

Weick, K. E. (1976). Educational organizations as loosely coupled systems. *Administrative Science Quarterly, 21,* 1–19.

Weick, K. E. (1979). *The social psychology of organizing*, 2nd ed. Reading, Mass.: Addison-Wesley.

Weiner, B. (Ed.). (1974). *Achievement motivation and attribution theory.* Morristown, N.J.: General Learning Corporation.

Weiner, B. (1979). A theory of motivation for some classroom experiences. *Journal of Educational Psychology, 71,* 3–25.

Weinstein, C. F., and Mayer, R. E. (1986). The teaching of learning strategies. In M. C. Wittrock, (Ed.). *Handbook of research on teaching*, 3rd ed. New York: Macmillan.

Weinstein, C. S. (1977). Modifying student behavior in an open classroom through changes in the physical design. *American Educational Research Journal, 14,* 249–262.

Welch, L., and Long, L. (1940). The higher structural phases of concept formation. *Journal of Psychology, 9,* 59–95.

Wilkinson, L. C. (Ed.). (1982). *Communicating in the classroom.* New York: Academic Press.

Wilson, R. M., and Gambrell, L. B. (1987). *Teaching reading comprehension in the elementary school.* Boston: Allyn and Bacon.

Winne, P. H., and Marx, R. W. (1982). Students' and teachers' views of thinking processes for classroom learning. *Elementary School Journal, 82,* 499.

Wittrock, M. C. (Ed.). (1986). *Handbook of research on teaching*, 3rd ed. New York: Macmillan.

Yinger, R. (1980). A study of teacher planning. *The Elementary School Journal, 80,* 107–127.

Zahorik, J. (1970). The effects of planning on teaching. *The Elementary School Journal, 71,* 143–151.

Acknowledgments

Photos *Cover:* Jeff Lowenthall/Woodfin Camp & Associates. *Part 1:* Steve Takatsuno/The Picture Cube. *Part 2:* Rae Russel. *Part 3:* Michal Heron/Woodfin Camp & Associates. *Part 4:* Peter Vadnai.

Text *Page 12:* Summarizes a report prepared by the Carnegie Forum on Education and the Economy's Task Force on Teaching as a Profession. The Carnegie Forum is a program of the Carnegie Corporation of New York. *Pages 81–82:* Material from W. K. Hoy published 1986 by The University of Chicago Press. *Pages 92–93:* Material from P. C. Duchastel and B. R. Brown copyright 1974 by the American Psychological Association. Adapted by permission of the publisher and author. *Pages 96–97:* Material from P. Peterson, R. Marx, and C. Clark copyright 1978, AERA, Washington, DC. *Pages 136–137:* Material from C. S. Weinstein copyright 1977, AERA, Washington, DC. *Pages 138–139:* Material from P. Rosenfield, N. Lambert, and A. Black copyright 1985 by the American Psychological Association. Adapted by permission of the publisher and author. *Pages 163–164:* Quotation reprinted from W. Doyle, Classroom organization and management with permission of Macmillan Publishing Company from *Handbook of research on teaching*, Third Edition, M. C. Whitrock, Editor. Copyright © 1985 by the American Research Association. *Pages 170–171:* Material from J. W. Santrock copyright 1976 by the American Psychological Association. Adapted with permission of the publisher and author. *Pages 172–174:* Material from R. Lippitt and R. White from *Readings in social psychology* 3rd ed., E. E. Maccoby, T. M. Newcomb, and F. L. Hartley (1958) © Holt, Rinehart & Winston. Reprinted by permission of Holt, Rinehart & Winston Inc. *Pages 176–177:* Material from W. Copeland published 1980 by The University of Chicago Press. *Pages 216–217:* Material from J. S. Kounin (1970) © Holt, Rinehart & Winston. Reprinted by permission of Holt, Rinehart & Winston Inc. *Pages 218–220:* Material from J. P. Sanford published New York: Wiley, 1984. Used with permission. *Pages 270–271:* Material from R. F. Schuck reprinted with permission of the Helen Dwight Reid Educational Foundation. Published by Heldref Publications, 4000 Albermarle St., N.W., Washington, DC 20016. Copyright © 1981. *Pages 272–273:* Material from G. W. Beeson copyright 1981, AERA, Washington, DC. *Pages 274–275:* Material from J. H. Hiller, G. A. Gisher, and W. Kaess copyright 1969, AERA, Washington, DC. *Pages 328–329:* Material from C. McKinney, D. Burts, M. F. Ford, and A. Gilmore reprinted with permission of the Helen Dwight Reid Educational Foundation. Published by Heldref Publications, 4000 Albermarle St., N.W., Washington, DC. 20016. Copyright © 1985. *Pages 334–335:* Material from P. Hawk published New York: Wiley, 1986. Used with permission. *Pages 370–371:* Material from T. L. Good and D. A. Grouws copyright 1971 by the American Psychological Association. Adapted with permission of the publisher and author. *Pages 372–373:* Material from M. Lyon and M. Gettinger copyright 1985 by the American Psychological Association. Adapted with permission of the publisher and author. *Pages 415–416:* Material from R. Johnson et al. copyright 1979, AERA, Washington, DC. *Pages 417–418:* Material from R. E. Slavin and M. L. Karweit copyright 1984, AERA, Washington, DC. *Pages 463–465:* Quotations reprinted from J. Bluestein (1982) from *The beginning teacher's resource handbook*. Albuquerque, NM: Instructional Support Services. Used with permission of the publisher and author. *Pages 492–494:* Material from G. E. Hall and S. F. Loucks copyright 1977, AERA, Washington, DC. *Pages 496–498:* Quoted materials from S. Sarason (1971) *The culture of school and the problem of change* reprinted by permission of Allyn & Bacon. *Pages 502–503, 510–511:* Quotations reprinted by permission of the publisher from M. Fullan, *The meaning of educational change* (New York: Teachers College Press, © 1982, by Teachers College, Columbia University. All rights reserved.), pp. 91–92, 123–124. *Pages 534–536:* Material from E. T. Emmer, C. M. Evertson, and L. M. Anderson published 1980 by The University of Chicago Press. *Pages 539–540:* Material from R. I. Arends reprinted with permission of the Helen Dwight Reid Educational Foundation. Published by Heldref Publications, 4000 Albermarle St., N.W., Washington, DC 20016. Copyright © 1983.

Name Index

Adams, R. S., 132, 134–135
Aerson, G., 269
Allport, G., 404, 405, 407
Alschuler, A. S., 161, 558
Ames, W., 269
Anderson, L. M., 534–536
Anderson, R. C., 397
Anderson, T. H., 398
Andre, M., 398
Arends, J. H., 184, 188, 495, 503–509, 516
Arends, R. I., 161, 184, 188, 473, 476, 495, 503–509, 516, 539–540, 543
Argyris, C., 499, 500
Aronson, E., 409, 429
Atkinson, J., 161
Ausubel, D., 262, 263, 264, 269, 325

Baker, E., 89
Bales, R., 396, 397
Bandura, A., 368, 378
Banks, J., 209
Barker, R., 213
Beeson, G. W., 272–273
Beginning Teacher Evaluation Study in California, The, 129, 130–131, 137
Belcher, V., 396
Benjamin, H., 486
Berliner, D. C., 16, 17, 100, 110, 111
Bettencourt, E., 271
Biddle, B. J., 73, 74, 132, 134–135, 212, 259
Biklen, D., 209
Black, A., 138–139
Blaney, S. C., 429
Bloom, B. S., 278–279, 289, 294, 311, 313, 315, 316, 372, 412
Bluestein, J., 463–465, 558
Blumberg, A., 133

Bolton, N., 351
Borg, W. R., 80, 271, 276, 309
Borko, H., 46
Boyer, E. L., 466
Bozman, M., 229
Bramson, R. M., 242
Brenton, M., 7
Briggs, L. J., 89, 349, 364–365, 375, 385
Brookover, W., 452
Brophy, J. E., 56, 61, 66–67, 212, 235, 236, 286, 290, 306, 434
Brown, B. R., 91, 92–93, 94
Bruner, J., 260, 262, 277, 294, 324, 325, 326
Burts, D., 328–329
Bush, A., 286

Cahen, L., 136
Calderhead, J., 46
Canter, D., 213
Canter, L., 213
Carnegie Forum on Education and the Economy, The, 12
Carroll, J. B., 124, 127
Carter, K., 214–215, 223, 234, 249
Charters, W. W., 174
Cherlin, D., 132
Clark, C. M., 46, 88, 89, 95, 96–97
Clements, B., 221, 238, 242, 544–545
Clements, D., 525, 526
Coats, E., 276
Cocchiarella, M., 345
Coleman, J., 170–171, 407, 449, 454, 487
Collins, A. M., 264, 270, 271
Collins, M. L., 302–303
Combs, A. W., 61, 489, 490
Cook, K. H., 80
Cooper, J. M., 61, 64, 316, 559

Subject Index

About the Author

Richard I. Arends received his Ph.D. in education from the University of Oregon, where he taught from 1975 to 1983. He is currently professor of education and chairman of the curriculum and instruction department at the University of Maryland. A former elementary, junior high school, and high school teacher, his special interests are the social psychology of education, teaching, teacher education, organizational development and school improvement.